Supervisors
宣（国際基督教大学準教授） Masayoshi Hirose（ICU）
久子（ハワイ大学専任講師） Kakuko Shoji（Univ. of Hawaii）

Editorial Staff
由美子 Yumiko Kawamoto
久美子 Kumiko Osaki

編集協力／Contributing Editors
真美子 Mamiko Murakami ／高橋洋子 Yoko Takahashi
哲生 Tetsuo Kinoshita ／加藤由美子 Yumiko Kato
力 Tsutomu Ueno ／椎野久美子 Kumiko Shiino
時敏 Tokisato Yanagimachi ／渡邉久美 Kumi Watanabe
本容 Yo Iwamoto ／富山ますみ Masumi Tomiyama
田温子 Atsuko Sakata ／高橋由宇子 Yuuko Takahashi

文校閲／Translators
arrell S. Frentz ／Marie Bedell ／Grace S. Onaga

イラスト／Illustrators
木元ひわこ Hiwako Kimoto
松並良仁 Yoshihito Matsunami

装丁・レイアウト／Design
鈴木堯（タウハウス） Takashi Suzuki（Tauhaus）
瀧上アサ子（タウハウス） Asako Takigami（Tauhaus）

Published by Kodansha Ltd., 2-12-21, Otowa Bunkyo-ku, Tokyo 112
Distributed outside of Japan by Kodansha International Ltd.

ISBN 4-06-123282-7
ISBN 4-7700-1919-X (Outside of Japan)

しずか／おだや
■ *shizuka* ■ *odayaka*

しずか［静か］ ■ *shizuka* ■ quiet

①うるさい音がしないようすです（例1, 2）。
Shizuka indicates an absence of loud or annoying noise (ex.1, 2).
②落ち着いていて、おとなしいようすを表します（例3, 4, 5）。
It may also describe a calm and gentle state (ex.3, 4, 5).

1) 図書館は静かだから、よく勉強できる。
Toshokanwa shizukadakara, yoku benkyoodekiru.
It is quiet in the library, so (we) can study well.

2) 私のうちは、静かな住宅地にある。
Watashino uchiwa, shizukana juutakuchini aru.
My house is located in a very quiet residential area.

3) 病気の時は、静かに寝ているほうがいい。
Byookino tokiwa, shizukani neteiru hooga ii.
It's best to stay quiet in bed when (you) are sick.

4) 彼女はとても静かな人で、いるのかいないのか分からないくらいだ。
Kanojowa totemo shizukana hitode, irunoka inainoka wakaranai-kuraida.
She is a very quiet person. (We) don't even notice when she is around.

5) この入り江は波が静かで、釣りをするのに最高だ。
Kono iriewa namiga shizukade, tsurio surunoni saikooda.
The water in this inlet is very calm, so it's the best place to fish.

おだやか［穏やか］ ■ *odayaka* ■ calm

平和でもめごとがなく、落ち着いた雰囲気です。なごやかで温かく、心が安

…で,
…。
…説明
…索引を利用して，1語づつでも調べることができます。

14.漢字
同音で意味の近い語の場合の使い分けもできるようにとりあげ，説明してあります。ひらがなで書くことが多い場合は，用例文中では，ひらがなにしてあります。

15.ローマ字
イタリック体で書いてあります。項目の見出しや説明文中では，ひらがなどおりの表記です。

16.英訳
主なものだけをあげ，そのほかは，用例文で扱っています。

17.ことばの意味分類記号
それぞれの語を意味の要素で分類し，9つの記号で表してあります。

18.説明文
意味区分が2つ以上のとき，①②…と分けて説明してあります。英訳がついています。

19.日本文の中では隠れている主語などで，英文中にでてくるものを(I)のように( )つきで示しました。

- 心や頭で感じることを表すことば
- 体で感じることを表すことば
- 状態の変化を表すことば
- つなぎのことば
- ものの名前

EFFECTIV
JAPANES
USAGE GUI

A Concise Explanation of Frequently Confused Words and Phr

日本語学習 使い分け辞典

講談社

監修／S
広瀬正
庄司香
執筆／
河元
尾崎
執筆
村上
木下
上野
柳
岩
坂
英
D

まえがき

「美しい」と「きれい」は意味のよく似ていることばで、英語ではどちらも beautiful で表します。けれども、日本語では、それぞれに微妙な使い分けがあります。

このように意味の似ていることばには、「多少使い方を間違えても、まあ許される」というときと、「ちょっと間違えると、おかしなことになる」というときがあります。そこで、意味や使い方の似ていることばを正しく使い分けて、豊かな表現を身につけられるようにと、この「日本語学習使い分け辞典」を作りました。

この辞典は、日本語を学ぼうとする人を主な対象としていますが、日本語教育に携わる人や日本の学生・日本語をより深く理解したい人にも役立つものと思います。

見出し語は、日本語を学んでいる人々にとって使い分けがむずかしい語を中心に、302項目708語を選びました。意味と使い分けの説明は、わかりやすい日本語で、自習に便利なように、漢字にはふりがなをつけ、用例にはローマ字も示しました。また、紙などで隠して読み進めるように、ふりがなは漢字の下の部分につけました。漢字を読み書きする力を上げる助けとなるでしょう。そして、すべてに英訳をつけ、イラストもたくさん入れました。さらに、それぞれの語の意味分野が一目でわかるように、9種類の分類記号で示しました。

用例は、日常的な題材を選びました。使い分け辞典という性格から、文法用語は特に使わず、むしろ実際に文を作るときに役立つように、用例文の中で語をいろいろな品詞や形に変化させてあります。そして、文化的なことがらなどは、特に注をつけて説明しました。

項目解説とは別に、コラムを設け、短い読み物で語句についての知識の整理が、楽しみながらできるようにしました。

巻末にひらがな項目索引、見出し語のひらがな語索引とローマ字索引英語つき、ことばの意味分類索引をつけました。調べたい語がどこからでもすぐに引けると思います。動詞の活用表とともに、大いに活用してください。

また、この辞典を長く育てていくために、読者の皆様からのご指摘・ご意見を心より歓迎いたします。

この辞典は、日本と海外の日本語教育に携わる多くの方々および、講談社辞典局の星園子さんとフリーエディター村上真美子さんの創意工夫と献身的な努力と協力によってできました。改めて感謝の意を表します。

広瀬正宜／庄司香久子

Preface

In Japanese, there are many words which appear to mean the same thing but are actually quite different.

For example, although the words *utsukushii* and *kirei* are both translated as 'beautiful' in English, there are slight differences in usage between them. Depending on the circumstances, these differences may give rise to a situation in which although the usage is slightly incorrect, it is permissible, or if the usage is slightly incorrect, the meaning changes entirely. For this reason we have created this dictionary, which we hope will help students of Japanese to learn a variety of expressions and to use them correctly.

This dictionary was primarily created for persons who want to learn Japanese. We believe, however, that it will also be useful to anyone who wants to gain a deeper understanding of the language, including Japanese language educators and students who are Japanese natives.

302 entries containing 708 headwords were chosen from among those terms that students have shown to have had difficulty using correctly. Each entry contains an easy-to-understand definition and explanation in Japanese, with illustrations often complementing the entries. For convenience of self study, *furigana* is provided for all *kanji* characters, and each example sentence is accompanied by a romanized version. *Furigana* is printed below each *kanji* character so that the reader may be able to improve his or her *kanji* proficiency by masking the *furigana* with a piece of paper while reading. English translations are provided to aid in comparison between the two languages. Moreover, each entry is designated with one of nine symbols for quick recognition of its

definition classification.

The example sentences provided are of themes and subjects one might find in everyday conversation. Because this is a usage guide, grammatical terminology is generally not included. The example sentences instead contain many different parts of speech and sentence structure variations, so that they will be of practical use to the reader in creating natural sounding sentences. Special explanations of many words and phrases of cultural interest are also provided. In addition to the explanations of the entries, we have included several short stories, or columns, as an interesting way of presenting various words.

Indexes under the categories of entry, *hiragana*, *roomaji* with English translations, and definition have been provided toward the end of the book for quick reference. We would also like to invite those using this dictionary to make use of the verb charts provided in the back as well.

Finally, in the interest of improving this dictionary in future editions, we eagerly invite comments and ideas from all readers.

This dictionary is the result of the creativity and dedication of many Japanese educators in both Japan and overseas, and Ms. Mamiko Murakami, a freelance editor, and Ms. Sonoko Hoshi of the dictionary division of Kodansha Publishers. We would also like to express our sincere gratitude to all those who participated in this project.

Masayoshi Hirose／Kakuko Shoji

この辞典の使い方

1．見出し語の書き表し方

(a)各組ごとに、はじめにひらがなで示し、続けてローマ字で示した。

(b)それぞれの語は、はじめにひらがな、ついで［　］内に漢字を示し、ローマ字、英訳、意味記号の順であげた。

(c)他の語につくものは、それを「～」で示した。

2．表記について

(1)日本語

(a)常用漢字、現代かなづかい、送りがなの付け方（以上内閣告示）を基準とした。

(b)語の意味・用法の説明及び用例の漢字にはすべてふりがなをつけた。ただし、数字は、特別な読み方をする場合につけた。

(c)見出し語として漢字で表記してあっても、日常ひらがなで表すことが多いものは、説明や用例ではひらがな書きにした。

(d)数詞は、熟語以外は算用数字を使った。

(2)ローマ字

(a)発音の助けとなるようにローマ字をつけた。したがって、たとえば、「10分」は、かな書きでは「じっぷん」と表すことになっているが、ローマ字では実際に多く聞かれる発音を表すために「*juppun*」とした。

(b)基本的にヘボン式にしたがった。

(c)つまる音「っ」は、すぐ後の子音字を重ねて表すが、「ch」の場合は「 t 」を使って「tch」と表す。

すっかり　*sukkari*
絶対（ぜったい）　*zettai*
一致（いっち）　*itchi*

(d)外来語の「ティ、テュ、ディ、デュ、ファ、フィ、フェ、フォ」などを表すときには、「ti, tyu, di, dyu, fa, fi, fe, fo」とした。

(e)長くのばす母音は、例のように同じ文字を重ねて表した。

一般にひらがなの「え段」＋「い」で表されるものは「ei」、「お段」＋「う」で表されるものは「oo」と表した。ただし、動詞の活用語尾の

「う」は、「u」で表した。

おばあさん	*obaasan*
おじいさん	*ojiisan*
セーター	*seetaa*
衛生（えいせい）	*eisei*
相当（そうとう）	*sootoo*
問（と）う	*tou*

a	あ	*i*	い	*u*	う	*e*	え	*o*	お						
ka	か	*ki*	き	*ku*	く	*ke*	け	*ko*	こ	*kya*	きゃ	*kyu*	きゅ	*kyo*	きょ
sa	さ	*shi*	し	*su*	す	*se*	せ	*so*	そ	*sha*	しゃ	*shu*	しゅ	*sho*	しょ
ta	た	*chi*	ち	*tsu*	つ	*te*	て	*to*	と	*cha*	ちゃ	*chu*	ちゅ	*cho*	ちょ
na	な	*ni*	に	*nu*	ぬ	*ne*	ね	*no*	の	*nya*	にゃ	*nyu*	にゅ	*nyo*	にょ
ha	は	*hi*	ひ	*fu*	ふ	*he*	へ	*ho*	ほ	*hya*	ひゃ	*hyu*	ひゅ	*hyo*	ひょ
ma	ま	*mi*	み	*mu*	む	*me*	め	*mo*	も	*mya*	みゃ	*myu*	みゅ	*myo*	みょ
ya	や			*yu*	ゆ			*yo*	よ						
ra	ら	*ri*	り	*ru*	る	*re*	れ	*ro*	ろ	*rya*	りゃ	*ryu*	りゅ	*ryo*	りょ
wa	わ							*o*	を						
n	ん														
ga	が	*gi*	ぎ	*gu*	ぐ	*ge*	げ	*go*	ご	*gya*	ぎゃ	*gyu*	ぎゅ	*gyo*	ぎょ
za	ざ	*ji*	じ	*zu*	ず	*ze*	ぜ	*zo*	ぞ	*ja*	じゃ	*ju*	じゅ	*jo*	じょ
da	だ	*ji*	ぢ	*zu*	づ	*de*	で	*do*	ど						
ba	ば	*bi*	び	*bu*	ぶ	*be*	べ	*bo*	ぼ	*bya*	びゃ	*byu*	びゅ	*byo*	びょ
pa	ぱ	*pi*	ぴ	*pu*	ぷ	*pe*	ぺ	*po*	ぽ	*pya*	ぴゃ	*pyu*	ぴゅ	*pyo*	ぴょ

(f)見出し語と説明文は、他の辞書をひく場合のことを考えて、ひらがなのつづり通りに表した。しかし、コラムと活用表は発音通りに表した。スペースは、どちらの場合も語の単位がわかるように、語の区切りごとに入れた。

見出し語、説明文：　～そうだ　*～ sou da*

コラム、活用表：　見(み)ようとした　*miyoo to shita*

(g)用例文は発音に近い形で表し、発音の際の目安となるように、切れ目を原則として文節単位にしたが、ひとまとまりが長くなりすぎる場合には、15文字前後を目安に切り、ハイフン「-」を入れた。

おもしろそうだ　*omoshirosooda*

行（い）かないかもしれない　*ikanaikamo-shirenai*

(h)はねる音「ん」のすぐ後に母音や「y」が続くときは、間にハイフンを入れた。

千円（せんえん）　*sen-en*

婚約（こんやく）　*kon-yaku*

(i)助詞をそのままつけると、母音が3つ以上続いてわかりにくい場合には、ハイフンを入れた。

放送（ほうそう）を　*hoosoo-o*

3．意味・用法の説明について

(a)はじめに日本語で説明し、つぎに英語の訳文をつけた。

(b)意味・用法は、各組の語を使い分ける上で関係のあるものに限った。

(c)各組の意味・用法を分類した場合には、①、②…として分け、それぞれに説明をつけた。

(d)説明文の要点部分を太字（ゴチック体）で表した。

(e)対応する用例文の番号を説明文の中に（　）で示した。

4．用例について

(a)各文ごとに、ふりがな付き漢字かなまじり、ローマ字、英訳の順であげた。

(b)語を入れかえることによって、応用できるように、日常使える、わかりやすい文とした。

(c)項目語の語尾変化がわかるように、できるだけ多くの用例文を入れた。

5．英訳について

(a)自然な英語に訳してあるが、直訳の方が語句の意味がわかりやすい場合には、それを先にあげ、自然な表現は（　）に入れて示した。

(b)日本語にないが、英語に必要な語（たとえば主語の「I」など）は、（I）のように（　）に入れて示した。

(c)日本語文からは男女が不明な場合には、「he」あるいは「one」で表した。

(d)英文中で使われる日本語の語句はイタリック体で示したが、人名や地名など固有名詞は普通体のままとした。つづりは、英字新聞・雑誌のものを参考にした。

6．ことばの意味分類記号について

(a)各語を意味の要素によって分類し、記号で表した。

(b)意味要素の分類記号は、つぎの9種類である。

程度や量を表すことば

時間や場所、位置を表すことば

動きを表すことば

ようすを表すことば

心で感じることを表すことば

体で感じることを表すことば

状態の変化を表すことば

つなぎのことば

ものの名前

7．その他の記号

（　）かっこは、つぎの４つの場合に使ってある。

(a)説明文の中で、対応する用例の番号を表すとき。

(b)意味を言い替えるとき。

(c)英文中で語を補うとき。

(d)見出し語の頭に用法を示す語句をつけるとき。

（〜て）おく　　（〜た）きり

（〜に）よって　　（手に）もつ

＊星印（アステリスク）は、用例中、日本の生活や習慣などを表す語（日本文化の生活語）に注をつけて説明してあることを示す。p.732参照

8．索引について

検索に便利なように巻末につぎの４種類の索引をつけ、どこからでも目的の語が見つけられるようにした。

(a)ひらがな項目索引（目次）

２、３語で成り立っている１項目の最初の語をあいうえお順に並べた。

(b)ひらがな語索引

この辞典で取り上げた語をあいうえお順に並べた。

(c)ローマ字索引英語つき

ローマ字表記の語をＡＢＣ順に並べ、英語をつけた。

(d)ことばの意味分類索引

語を意味要素の分類記号でまとめた。

9．読み物学習コラムについて

日本での生活の中で、まちがいやすい日本語の、正しい使い方を、読み物ふうに、大きな活字で入れた。p.732参照

10．付録について

表紙の見返しや巻末に、使い方図解、日本地図、動詞の活用表をつけた。

How To Use This Dictionary

1. Listing of entries

(a) Each heading group is printed in *hiragana* followed by its romanized spelling.
(b) Each individual entry is printed in *hiragana* followed by its *kanji* character (inside the [ ]), romanized spelling, English translation, and definition classification symbol.
(c) When the headword is used together with another word, a '～' is used.

2. Notation

(1) Japanese

(a) All *kanji*, *kana* spellings, and *okurigana* are based on standards approved by the Japanese government.
(b) *Furigana* is provided for all *kanji* in the definitions, explanations, and example sentences. Numerals with special readings are also provided with *furigana*.
(c) In cases in which a term has been expressed both in *hiragana* and *kanji* in the heading, but the common usage is in *hiragana*, only *hiragana* is used in the explanation and example sentences.
(d) Numerals are printed in Arabic figures unless part of an idiomatic expression.

(2) Romanization

(a) Romanized spelling (*roomaji*) is provided to aid in pronunciation. For example, 10分 is written in *hiragana* as じっぷん, and as *juppun* in *roomaji* to indicate the most common pronunciation.
(b) As a rule, the Hepburn system of romanization is followed.
(c) A small つ in *hiragana* is indicated in *roomaji* by doubling the following consonant sound, except in the case of 'ch', which is written with a 't' to make a 'tch' sound.

すっかり	*sukkari*
絶対（ぜったい）	*zettai*
一致（いっち）	*itchi*

(d) Foreign loan words using the *katakana* spellings ティ，テュ，ディ，デュ，ファ，フィ，フェ and フォ are written *ti*, *tyu*, *di*, *dyu*, *fa*, *fi*, *fe* and *fo*.

(e) Extended vowel sounds are spelled by doubling the vowel as shown in the examples below. A *hiragana* combination of an え -root and い is written as '*ei*'. A combination of an お -root and う is written as '*oo*'. An exception to this is the verb ending of う, which is written as '*u*'.

おばあさん	*obaasan*
おじいさん	*ojiisan*
セーター	*seetaa*
衛生（えいせい）	*eisei*
相当（そうとう）	*sootoo*
問（と）う	*tou*

a	あ	*i*	い	*u*	う	*e*	え	*o*	お						
ka	か	*ki*	き	*ku*	く	*ke*	け	*ko*	こ	*kya*	きゃ	*kyu*	きゅ	*kyo*	きょ
sa	さ	*shi*	し	*su*	す	*se*	せ	*so*	そ	*sha*	しゃ	*shu*	しゅ	*sho*	しょ
ta	た	*chi*	ち	*tsu*	つ	*te*	て	*to*	と	*cha*	ちゃ	*chu*	ちゅ	*cho*	ちょ
na	な	*ni*	に	*nu*	ぬ	*ne*	ね	*no*	の	*nya*	にゃ	*nyu*	にゅ	*nyo*	にょ
ha	は	*hi*	ひ	*fu*	ふ	*he*	へ	*ho*	ほ	*hya*	ひゃ	*hyu*	ひゅ	*hyo*	ひょ
ma	ま	*mi*	み	*mu*	む	*me*	め	*mo*	も	*mya*	みゃ	*myu*	みゅ	*myo*	みょ
ya	や			*yu*	ゆ			*yo*	よ						
ra	ら	*ri*	り	*ru*	る	*re*	れ	*ro*	ろ	*rya*	りゃ	*ryu*	りゅ	*ryo*	りょ
wa	わ							*o*	を						
n	ん														
ga	が	*gi*	ぎ	*gu*	ぐ	*ge*	げ	*go*	ご	*gya*	ぎゃ	*gyu*	ぎゅ	*gyo*	ぎょ
za	ざ	*ji*	じ	*zu*	ず	*ze*	ぜ	*zo*	ぞ	*ja*	じゃ	*ju*	じゅ	*jo*	じょ
da	だ	*ji*	ぢ	*zu*	づ	*de*	で	*do*	ど						
ba	ば	*bi*	び	*bu*	ぶ	*be*	べ	*bo*	ぼ	*bya*	びゃ	*byu*	びゅ	*byo*	びょ
pa	ぱ	*pi*	ぴ	*pu*	ぷ	*pe*	ぺ	*po*	ぽ	*pya*	ぴゃ	*pyu*	ぴゅ	*pyo*	ぴょ

(f) Words that appear as a headword or in the explanatory text are spelled in *roomaji* in a manner that closely matches their *hiragana* spelling, that is, as is found in most other dictionaries. On the other hand, words that appear in the columns and usage charts are spelled in a manner that most closely approximates their pronunciation. In both cases spaces are placed between each word to aid in understanding the individual parts of the sentence.

Headword, explanatory text:

〜そうだ 〜 *sou da*

Column, usage charts:

見（み）ようとした *miyoo to shita*

(g) In the example sentences, spellings in *roomaji* are as per their pronunciation, and words are arranged into groups which best represent how they are said in spoken Japanese. In cases in which word groupings are longer than 15 letters, a hyphen (-) is placed at a suitable point.

おもしろそうだ *omoshirosooda*

行（い）かないかもしれない *ikanaikamo-shirenai*

(h) A hyphen is also inserted between 'ん' and vowel or 'y' sound.

千円（せんえん） *sen-en*

婚約（こんやく） *kon-yaku*

(i) If three or more vowel sounds are grouped together because a particle is attached to a noun, a hyphen is added for clarification.

放送を *hoosoo-o*

3. Explanations of definition and usage

(a) Each entry is first explained in Japanese and followed by an English translation.

(b) Explanations of meaning and usage are limited to those that help differentiate one word from the others in the group.

(c) When there is more than one meaning or usage for a word, each is explained in a separate section, e.g., section ①, section ②, etc.

(d) The essential points in each explanation are highlighted in boldface type.

(e) Corresponding example sentences are indicated by the numbers inside the parentheses '(　)'.

4. Example sentence

(a) Each example sentence is printed in Japanese (with *furigana*), *roomaji* and English.

(b) In order that the reader will be able to apply the entry word, easily understandable sentences that can be used in daily conversation have been inserted.

(c) As many example sentences as possible have been included so that the conjugation of the entry word can be understood.

5. English translations

(a) Natural English is used in most of the example sentences. However, in cases in which direct translation from Japanese more simply indicates the meaning of the headword, the direct translation is printed first with the natural English expression printed within the parentheses.

(b) In cases in which a word is not part of the Japanese text but is necessary in English (for example, 'I'), the word is placed within parentheses, e.g., (I).

(c) When the gender of a person mentioned in an example sentence is undetermined, 'he' or 'one' is used.

(d) Japanese words which appear in the English text are printed in italics. Japanese personal and place names, however, are printed in standard type. English language newspapers and magazines were used as a reference when determining appropriate spellings.

6. Definition classification symbols

(a) Each entry is assigned a classification symbol based on its essential meaning.

(b) The following symbols are used to indicate that the word describes:

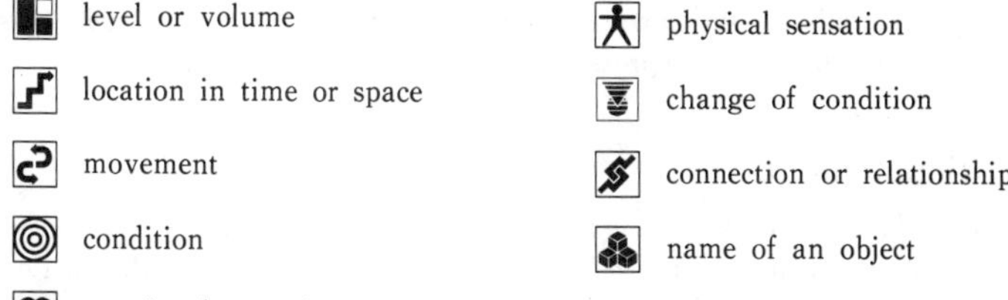

7. Other notation

( ) The following may appear within parentheses:

(a) Numbers of example sentences which correspond to an explanation in the text.

(b) Interchangeable meanings.

(c) Words that supplement the English text.

(d) Words or phrases which may be placed before the headword in a grammatical structure.

(～て) おく　　(～た) きり
(～に) よって　　(手に) もつ

＊ Asterisks are used in the example sentences to refer the reader to a supplemental explanation regarding daily life or customs in Japan (Japanese cultural vocabulary). See page 732.

8. The indexes

Four indexes are provided at the end of the dictionary to aid in finding any of the words listed.

(a) *Hiragana* heading index (contents)

The first word of each grouping is listed in *hiragana* (あいうえお) order.

(b) Word index (in *hiragana*)

All entry words within each grouping are listed in *hiragana* (あいうえお) order.

(c) *Roomaji* index with English translations.

All words found in this dictionary are listed in alphabetical order according to their romanized spelling, with their English translation provided.

(d) Definition index

Definitions are grouped according to their classification and listed here.

9. Readers' Column

Brief materials on the correct usage of commonly used but easily misunderstood Japanese expressions have been inserted in large print type. See page 732.

10. Supplements

An explanation of sample entries, a map of Japan and a verb usage chart are provided on the cover flyleaf and at the end of the dictionary.

あいだに／うちに

■*aida ni*　　■*uchi ni*

あいだに［間に］

■*aida ni*
■during ; between

①ある時点からある時点まで、というような**区切られた時間**に何かをする・何かが起こることを表すとき使います（例1, 2, 3, 4）。

This is used to indicate an interval of time, delimited by a beginning and ending point, during which one does something or something takes place (ex.1, 2, 3, 4).

②**ものとものにはさまれた部分**・場所・空間に何かがあることを表すとき使います（例5, 6, 7）。人と人との関係にも使います（例８）。

It is also used to indicate spatial location between two objects (ex.5, 6, 7). *Aida ni* may be used when speaking of relationships between people (ex.8).

1）あなたが出かけている間に山本さんから電話がありました。
Anataga dekaketeiru aidani Yamamotosankara denwaga arimashita.
There was a phone call from Ms. Yamamoto while you were out.

2）私は休みの間に車の運転免許をとった。
Watashiwa yasumino aidani kurumano untenmenkyoo totta.
I got my driver's license during my vacation.

3）1985年から1990年の間に、この地域の人口は倍に増えた。
Senkyuuhyaku-hachijuugo-nenkara senkyuuhyaku-kyuujuu-nenno aidani, kono chiikino jinkoowa baini fueta.
The population of this region doubled between 1985 and 1990.

4）私はいつも夜10時から11時の間に寝ます。
Watashiwa itsumo yoru juujikara juuichijino aidani nemasu.
I always go to bed between 10 and 11 o'clock.

5）イギリスとフランスの間にドーバー海峡がある。
Igirisuto Furansuno aidani Doobaa-kaikyooga aru.
The Straits of Dover is between England and France.

6）本棚と壁の間に、辞書が落ちてしまった。

Hondanato kabeno aidani, jishoga ochiteshimatta.
A dictionary fell between the bookcase and the wall.

7) 私の家から駅までの間に3つ信号があります。
Watashino iekara ekimadeno aidani mittsu shingooga arimasu.
There are three traffic lights between my house and the station.

8) 私たち親子の間に秘密はない。
Watashitachi oyakono aidani himitsuwa nai.
There are no secrets between parents and children in our family.

うちに
- *uchi ni*
- while ; before

---

①ある続いている状態や**ことがらが終わる前**に、**何かをする**・**何か**が**起こる**ことを表すとき使います（例9, 10, 11, 12, 13）。「明るいうちに帰って来なさい」は「明るい状態が過ぎると暗くなる」という意識を含みます。「暗くならないうちに〜」のような「〜ないうちに」も同じように使いますが、「暗くなってはいけない・良くない」という意識をより強く含みます。

This is used to express that something will take place or be done before some continuing situation or event ends (ex.9, 10, 11, 12, 13). *Akarui uchi ni kaette-kinasai* (come home while it's light) implies the notion that 'when the condition of being light has passed, it will get dark'. The expression ～*nai uchi ni,* as in *kuraku naranai uchi ni,* is used in the same way but more strongly includes the sense that 'becoming dark is not good / won't do'.

②ひとつのことがらや状態が進行していくのと**同時に**、自然に**別のことがらが発生**してくるときや、別の状態になっていくとき使います（例14, 15, 16）。

Uchi ni is also used when a new or different event or state develops at the same time that another event or state is in progress (ex.14, 15, 16).

---

9) 若いうちにたくさん勉強しておいたほうがいい。
Wakai uchini takusan benkyoo-shiteoita hooga ii.
You ought to study a lot while you're young.

10) 今日のうちにこの仕事を仕上げなくてはならない。
Kyoono uchini kono shigotoo shiagenakutewa-naranai.
(I) have to finish up this job before the day is out.

11) 料理が冷めないうちに召し上がってください。
Ryooriga samenai uchini meshiagatte kudasai.
Please eat it before it gets cold.

12) 虫歯は、ひどくならないうちに治したほうがいい。
Mushibawa, hidokunaranai uchini naoshita hooga ii.
Cavities ought to be taken care of before they get bad.

13) 雨が降らないうちに早く帰ろう。
Amega furanai uchini hayaku kaeroo.
Let's go home quickly before it rains.

14) 本を読んでいるうちに、眠くなってしまった。
Hon-o yondeiru uchini, nemukunatte-shimatta.
(I) became drowsy while I was reading.

15) 彼とつき合っているうちに、人柄が分かってきた。
Kareto tsukiatteiru uchini, hitogaraga wakattekita.
(I've) gotten to know what he's like while we've been going together.

16) どんなことでも、練習や失敗をくり返しているうちにじょうずになる。
Donna kotodemo, renshuuya shippaio kurikaeshiteiru uchini joozuni naru.
No matter what it is, you will get good at something through repeated practice and failure.

あがる／のぼる

■ *agaru* ■ *noboru*

あがる［上がる・挙がる・揚がる］ ■ *agaru* ■ to rise ; to go up

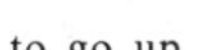

①**低い所から高い所へ移動する**ことです（例1, 2, 3, 4, 5, 6, 7）。移動した所、位置、程度など移動の結果に重点があります。
To move upward (ex.1, 2, 3, 4, 5, 6, 7) ; the focus is on the result of the movement, such as a destination, location, or degree (of temperature, quality, etc.).

②成績・評判・値段など、**ものごとの価値や程度が高くなる**ことです（例8, 9, 10）。また、「終わる、完了する」の意味で例11、「出る」の意味で例12、

「緊張してふだんの落ち着きがなくなる」の意味で例13のようにも使います。

It may also indicate that the degree or value of something, such as grades, reputation, or price, moves higher (ex.8, 9, 10). There are also cases when it means 'to finish or complete' (ex.11), or 'to appear' (ex.12), or 'to become nervous from tension or stress' (ex.13).

ほとんどの場合、漢字は「上がる」を使いますが、「花火・旗」などは「揚がる」と書き、「手・候補」などは「挙がる」と書きます。

In most cases the *kanji* 上がる is used for *agaru*, however 揚がる is used for shooting fireworks, hoisting flags, etc., and 挙がる for raising hands, nominating candidates, etc.

---

1) エレベーターで屋上に上がる。

Erebeetaade okujooni agaru.
We go up to the rooftop by elevator.

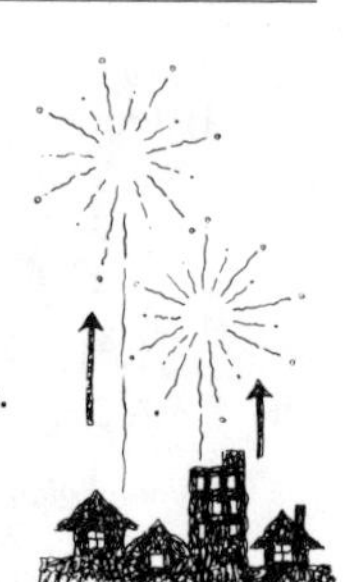

2) 階段を上がってすぐ右のドアが、私のうちです。

Kaidan-o agatte sugu migino doaga, watashino uchidesu.
Go up the stairs, and the door on the right is my place.

3) 彼はステージに上がって話し始めた。

Karewa suteejini agatte hanashi-hajimeta.
He got up on the stage and started talking.

4) 「質問はありませんか」と議長が聞くと、ぱっと数人の手が挙がった。

"*Shitsumonwa arimasenka?*" *to gichooga kikuto, patto suuninno tega agatta.*
When the chairman asked, "Do you have any questions?" several people's hands shot up.

5) 夜空に鮮やかな花火が、つぎつぎと揚がった。

Yozorani azayakana hanabiga, tsugitsugito agatta.
Brilliant fireworks shot up in to the night sky one after the other.

6) 大使館の庭に国旗が揚がっている。

Taishikanno niwani kokkiga agatteiru.
The national flag is flying in the embassy courtyard.

7) デパートの屋上に、アドバルーンが上がっている。

Depaatono okujooni, adobaruunga agatteiru.
An advertising balloon is flying over the department store.

8) 彼はこのごろ急に成績が上がった。

Karewa konogoro kyuuni seisekiga agatta.
His grades have suddenly gone up recently.

9) 物価は上がるのに給料は上がらないので生活が大変です。
Bukkawa agarunoni kyuuryoowa agaranainode seikatsuga taihendesu.
Although prices continue to rise, (my) salary doesn't increase, so it's hard making ends meet.

10) やせようと思って運動を始めたけれど、なかなか効果が上がらない。
Yaseyooto omotte undoo-o hajimetakeredo, nakanaka kookaga agaranai.
(I) started exercising intending to lose weight, but it is not as effective as I expected.

11) 雨が上がってきれいな虹がかかった。
Amega agatte kireina nijiga kakatta.
The rain stopped and a beautiful rainbow appeared.

12) おふろから上がったら冷たいビールが飲みたい。
Ofurokara agattara tsumetai biiruga nomitai.
(I) want to drink a cold beer after I get out of the bath.

13) 私は初めて舞台に立ったとき、あがってしまいセリフを忘れた。
Watashiwa hajimete butaini tatta toki, agatteshimai serifuo wasureta.
When I stepped onto the stage for the first time, I became so nervous that I forgot my lines.

のぼる［登る・上る・昇る］

■ *noboru*
■ to climb ; to go up 

低い所から高い所に移動することですが（例14, 15, 16, 17, 18）、高い所を目指して徐々に**移動していく過程に重点**があります。基本的には、「山に登る」「木に登る」などのように自分の力で移動するものについて使います。「あがっている」が例６、７のように動作の結果について使うのに対し、「のぼっている」は現在進行や、続いている動作、状態を表します（例19）。また、「話題になる」の意味で例20、「食事として出る」の意味で例21のようにも使います。

To move from a low position to a high position (ex.14, 15, 16, 17, 18). The high position is considered to be the objective and therefore the focus is on the process of moving toward it. Basically, it is used in examples such as *yama ni noboru* (to climb a mountain), or *ki ni noboru* (to climb a tree), to mean to move upward on one's own power without outside help. While *agatte iru* indicates the resultant state of a rising action, as shown in Examples 6 and 7, *nobotte iru* suggests a continuous rising condition (ex.19). Also, as in Example 20, it is used to mean 'to become a topic of conversation', and in Example 21, 'to be served as a meal'.

---

14) 今度(こんど)の休(やす)みに山(やま)に登(のぼ)るのが楽(たの)しみだ。
Kondono yasumini yamani noborunoga tanoshimida.
(I'm) looking forward to climbing the mountain on my next day off.

15) 子供(こども)のころ、よくこの木(き)に登(のぼ)った。
Kodomono koro, yoku kono kini nobotta.
(I) often climbed this tree when (I) was a child.

16) 私(わたし)は健康(けんこう)のために、エレベーターを使(つか)わずに階段(かいだん)を上(のぼ)ることにしている。
Watashiwa kenkoono tameni, erebeetaao tsukawazuni kaidan-o noboru kotoni shiteiru.
For the sake of my health, I've decided to climb the stairs instead of using the elevator.

17) 鮭(さけ)は産卵(さんらん)の時期(じき)になると、産(う)まれた川(かわ)を上(のぼ)ってくる。
Sakewa sanranno jikini naruto, umareta kawao nobottekuru.
During the spawning season, salmon swim up the river to where they were born to lay eggs.

18) 朝日(あさひ)が昇(のぼ)ると、一日(いちにち)が始(はじ)まる。
Asahiga noboruto, ichinichiga hajimaru.
When the sun rises, (my) day begins.

19) 煙突(えんとつ)の煙(けむり)がまっすぐ上(うえ)に上(のぼ)っている。
Entotsuno kemuriga massugu ueni nobotteiru.
The smoke from the chimney is going straight up.

20) このごろ彼(かれ)の離婚(りこん)がさかんに人々(ひとびと)の話題(わだい)に上(のぼ)っている。
Konogoro kareno rikonga sakanni hitobitono wadaini nobotteiru.
Lately, his divorce has become a favorite topic in people's conversations.

21) 最近(さいきん)、海外(かいがい)からの珍(めずら)しい食(た)べ物(もの)が食卓(しょくたく)に上(のぼ)るようになった。
Saikin, kaigaikarano mezurashii tabemonoga shokutakuni noboruyooni natta.
Recently, (we) have been having more exotic foreign foods on our dining table.

あき／から

■*aki*　■*kara*

あき［空き］　■*aki*　■empty ; vacant　◎

①「空き缶・空きびん・空き箱」のように「あき＋名詞」として使い、「中には何も入っていない・**中身がないいれもの**」の意味です。**本来入っていたものや、入っているはずのものが入っていない、**という意識を強く含みます。したがって、現在使っていない場所や空間についても「空き地・空き部屋・空き家」などと使います。「空き時間」は何もする予定がない時間のことです（例1, 2, 3, 4)。

Aki is used in the form *aki*＋noun, e.g., *akikan* (can), *akibin* (bottle), and *akibako* (box), to refer to a container which has nothing inside, or whose contents are gone. It strongly implies that the original contents, or what was expected to be inside, is not there. Thus, *aki* is also used with regard to location or space which is not presently in use, e.g., *akichi* (vacant lot), *akibeya* (vacant room), and *akiya* (vacant house). *Akijikan* refers to time for which nothing has been scheduled (ex.1, 2, 3, 4).

②例５のように「空きがある・ない」という使い方もします。

As in Example 5, the expression *aki ga aru / nai* is also used.

---

1) 観光地には、よく空き缶や空きびんがころがっている。
Kankoochiniwa, yoku akikan-ya akibinga korogatteiru.
There are often empty cans and bottles strewn about tourist resorts.

2) 子供の頃空き地で、かくれんぼや缶けりをして遊んだものだ。
Kodomono koro akichide, kakurenboya kankerio shite asonda monoda.
When (I) was a child, I used to play hide-and-seek and kick-the-can in vacant lots.

3) 私の家の隣は、空き家だ。
Watashino ieno tonariwa, akiyada.
The house next to mine is vacant.

4) A：英語がうまくなりましたね。

Ｂ：ええ、空き時間に英語のテープを聞いていたんですよ。

Ａ： *Eigoga umaku-narimashitane.*
(You've) gotten good at English, haven't you?

Ｂ： *Ee, akijikanni Eigono teepuo kiiteitandesuyo.*
Uh huh, (I've) been listening to English tapes in my spare time.

5）コンサートの予約をしたいのですが、座席の空きはありますか。

Konsaatono yoyakuo shitainodesuga, zasekino akiwa arimasuka?
(I'd) like to reserve some seats for the concert. Are there seats available?

から［空］ ■ *kara* ■ empty 

①中には何も入っていない・**中身がない**というようすを表します。この場合話しことばでは「からっぽ」とも言います（例6, 7, 8）。

Kara denotes that an object has nothing inside, or contains nothing. In this case, the colloquial expression *karappo* is also used (ex.6, 7, 8).

②**かたちだけで本当の中身がない**・効果がないという意味で使います（例9, 10, 11）。

It is used also to mean 'in form only', 'not the actual contents', or 'having no effect' (ex.9, 10, 11).

6）スーパーマーケットの横に、空の段ボール箱が積んである。

Suupaa-maakettono yokoni, karano danboorubakoga tsundearu.
Empty cardboard boxes are piled up next to the supermarket.

7）きのう食べてしまったので、クッキーの箱は空です。

Kinoo tabeteshimatta-node, kukkiino hakowa karadesu.
(We) ate all of the cookies yesterday, so the cookie box is empty.

8）私が帰ると、家の中は空っぽでだれもいなかった。

Watashiga kaeruto, ieno nakawa karappode daremo inakatta.
When I got home the house was empty (no one was there).

9）今年は空梅雨だった。

Kotoshiwa karatsuyudatta.
We had a dry rainy season this year.

10）思い切りバットを振ったが、空振りだった。

Omoikiri battoo futtaga, karaburidatta.
(I) swung the bat with all my might, but I missed.

11) 車が溝にはまって、車輪が空回りした。
くるま みぞ しゃりん からまわ
Kurumaga mizoni hamatte, sharinga karamawarishita.
My car got stuck in a ditch and its tires spun (in the mud).

あきらか／たしか
■ *akiraka* ■ *tashika*

あきらか［明らか］ ■ *akiraka* ■ obvious ; clear 
あき

だれが見ても**はっきりしている、疑いようがない**ようすを表すとき使います。自分の主観ではなく世の中**一般の客観的判断**です（例1,2,3）。また「明らかにする」はものごとを**表面に出す、公表する**という意味です（例4,5）。

Akiraka suggests that something is clear and without doubt from anyone's viewpoint. It is not used to refer to one's own subjective opinion, but instead to universal or commonly held judgments (ex.1, 2, 3). The expression *akiraka ni suru* means to expose something, or make something public (ex.4, 5).

1) こんなに証拠があるのだから、彼が犯人であることは明らかだ。
しょうこ かれ はんにん あき
Konnani shookoga aruno dakara, karega hanninde aru kotowa akirakada.
With this kind of evidence, it's obvious that he is the criminal.

2) 事故の原因は明らかにスピードの出しすぎです。
じこ げんいん あき だ
Jikono gen-inwa akirakani supiidono dashisugidesu.
It's clear that the cause of the accident was speeding.

3) 彼の考え方は、明らかにまちがっている。
かれ かんが かた あき
Kareno kangaekatawa, akirakani machigatteiru.
His way of thinking is clearly wrong.

4) 調査で公害の原因が明らかになった。
ちょうさ こうがい げんいん あき
Choosade koogaino gen-inga akirakani natta.
After the investigation, the cause of the pollution became evident.

5) 事件の真相は、いずれ明らかになるでしょう。
じけん しんそう あき

Jikenno shinsoowa, izure akirakani narudeshoo.
The truth behind this incident will probably become clear someday.

たしか［確か］

■ *tashika*
■ certain ; reliable 

---

①まちがいがない、信用できるというようすや自信を表すとき使います。事実や経験などによる自分の判断にも、世の中一般の判断にも使います（例6, 7, 8, 9, 10）。

Tashika is used when expressing confidence that something is reliable, trustworthy, or not wrong. It may be used when speaking of judgments made based on personal experience, or on commonly held fact (ex.6, 7, 8, 9, 10).

②「自分の記憶に間違いがなければ……」というように思い出しながら述べるとき使います（例11, 12）。

It is also used when one is speaking from memory, as in 'If I remember correctly, ...'(ex.11, 12).

6）そのことについては、本で調べたから確かだ。
Sono kotoni tsuitewa, honde shirabetakara tashikada.
(I'm) sure about this because I looked it up in a book.

7）彼のことなら、本人に直接聞くのが一番確かだ。
Kareno kotonara, honninni chokusetsu kikunoga ichiban tashikada.
If it concerns him, we would know for sure if we asked him directly.

8）確かな証拠もないのに人を疑ってはいけない。
Tashikana shookomo nainoni hitoo utagattewa ikenai.
You should not be suspicious of someone without any definite proof (against him).

9）彼女の料理の腕は、確かだ。
Kanojono ryoorino udewa, tashikada.
She is an expert cook.

10）ゆうべ見たのは、確かにＵＦＯだ。
Yuube mitanowa, tashikani yuufooda.
(I'm) sure that what I saw last night was a UFO.

11）あなたのお父さんは、確か京都の出身でしたよね。

Anatano otoosanwa, tashika Kyootono shusshindeshitayone.
If memory serves me right, your father is from Kyoto, isn't he?

12) 彼女の誕生日は、確か９月13日だったと思う。
Kanojono tanjoobiwa, tashika kugatsu juusannichi-dattato omou.
If (I) remember correctly, her birthday was September 13.

あける／ひらく

■ *akeru* ■ *hiraku*

あける［開ける・空ける・明ける］ ■ *akeru* ■ to open

①閉じているもの、ふさいでいるものの一部や全部をずらしたりとりのぞいて、すき間や出入り口を作ることです（例1, 2, 3, 4）。

To make an opening or space by moving or removing part or all of something that is closed (ex.1, 2, 3, 4).

②そこにあるものをどかして、何もない状態にすることで、時間や場所にも使います（例5, 6, 7）。

To make a vacant space by removing things from where they were. *Akeru* may also be used when speaking of time (ex.5, 6, 7).

③一定の時間・期間が過ぎて新しい時間が始まることです（例8, 9）。

Akeru may also indicate that after a certain time period, such as a vacation, a new time period begins (ex.8, 9).

①は「開ける」、②は「空ける」、③は「明ける」と書きます。

In definition ① *akeru* is written 開ける, in ② it is written 空ける, and in ③ it is written 明ける.

---

1) 駅前のパン屋は、朝９時に店を開ける。
Ekimaeno pan-yawa, asa kujini miseo akeru.
The bakery in front of the station opens at 9:00 am.

2) 窓を開けたらさわやかな風が部屋に入ってきた。
Madoo aketara sawayakana kazega heyani haittekita.

When I opened a window, a refreshing breeze came into the room.

3) 暑いですね。窓を開けましょうか。

Atsuidesune. Madoo akemashooka?

It's hot! Shall I open the window?

4) きりで壁に穴を開けた。

Kiride kabeni anao aketa.

He made a hole in the wall with a gimlet.

5) 救急車が通ります。道を空けてください。

Kyuu-kyuushaga toorimasu. Michio akete kudasai.

An ambulance is coming. Please clear the road.

6) 次の月曜は予定を空けておいてください。会議がありますので。

Tsugino getsuyoowa yoteio aketeoite kudasai. Kaigiga arimasunode.

Please keep next Monday open. We may have a meeting then.

7) ちょっと家を空けたすきに、どろぼうに入られた。

Chotto ieo aketa sukini, dorobooni hairareta.

A burglar broke into my house, although I was only out for a short while.

8) うっとうしい梅雨が明けると夏が来る。

Uttooshii tsuyuga akeruto natsuga kuru.

As soon as the depressing rainy season ends, summer will come.

9) 本を読むのに夢中になっていたら、いつの間にか夜が明けていた。

Hon-o yomunoni muchuuni natteitara, itsunomanika yoga aketeita.

I was reading a book so intently that I didn't even notice that dawn had broke.

ひらく［開く］

■ *hiraku*
■ to open ; to start 

①閉じているものを**広げる**こと。あるいは広がることです。本来は、傘、本、手、足、花など一つにまとまっているものを一点を中心に広げていく動作です（例10, 11, 12, 13）。戸や窓などの場合は左右の動きではなく、外に押して開ける動きです（例14）。「あけ放たれた状態にする・なる」という意味で例15のような使い方もします。

To open something that is closed; or to spread out something. Basically, *hiraku* means to open something that has parts, like an umbrella, book, hand, leg or flower, that open or spread out from a single point (ex. 10, 11, 12, 13). When referring to a door or window, the movement is not to the right or left, but outward (ex.14). It may also mean, as in Example 15, to cause something to become and remain open.

②事業(じぎょう)、会合(かいごう)、展覧会(てんらんかい)などのものごとを始(はじ)めることです（例(れい)16, 17)。

To open or start things such as a business, conference, or exhibition (ex.16, 17).

---

10) 人込(ひとご)みで、急(きゅう)に傘(かさ)を開(ひら)くと危(あぶ)ない。
Hitogomide, kyuuni kasao hirakuto abunai.
It's dangerous to open your umbrella suddenly in a crowd.

11) 桜(さくら)の花(はな)が去年(きょねん)より2週間(しゅうかん)早(はや)く開(ひら)いた。
Sakurano hanaga kyonenyori nishuukan hayaku hiraita.
The cherry blossoms bloomed two weeks earlier than last year.

12) 父(ちち)がくれた包(つつ)みを開(ひら)くと、すてきなオルゴールが出(で)てきた。
Chichiga kureta tsutsumio hirakuto, sutekina orugooruga detekita.
When I opened a package given to me by my father, there was a beautiful music box inside.

13) 教科書(きょうかしょ)の37ページを開(ひら)いてください。
Kyookashono sanjuunana-peejio hiraite kudasai.
Please open your textbook to page 37.

14) 美術館(びじゅつかん)の門(もん)は、毎朝(まいあさ)10時(じ)に開(ひら)く。
Bijutsukanno monwa, maiasa juujini hiraku.
The art museum gate opens at ten o'clock every morning.

15) 彼(かれ)はやっとこのごろ心(こころ)を開(ひら)いて話(はなし)をするようになった。
Karewa yatto konogoro kokoroo hiraite hanashio suruyooni natta.
He has finally started to open up to us.

16) あの銀行(ぎんこう)は、今度(こんど)神田(かんだ)に支店(してん)を開(ひら)くことになった。
Ano ginkoowa, kondo Kandani shiten-o hirakukotoni natta.
It has been decided that that bank will open a branch in Kanda.

17) 私(わたし)はこの秋(あき)に、写真展(しゃしんてん)を開(ひら)きます。
Watashiwa kono akini, shashinten-o hirakimasu.
I am going to put on a photo exhibition this fall.

～あげる／～きる／～おわる

■～*ageru* ■～*kiru* ■～*owaru*

～あげる ■～*ageru* ■to finish

動詞の後ろについてその行為の結果、ことがらが**完成する**意味を表します。「～あげる」と「～終わる」は入れかえても使える場合が多いのですが、「～あげる」の方が「完全・満足」という意味が強いです。ですから「～あげる」といっしょに使える動詞のほとんどは、「書く・縫う・作る・みがく……」など最後には完成するものです（例1, 2, 3)。

Ageru indicates that something is completed as a result of a particular action. ～*owaru* and ～*ageru* are in most cases interchangeable, but ～*ageru* implies more of a sense of satisfaction. A verb that takes the ～*ageru* ending indicates that the action will be completed in the end (ex.1, 2, 3).

1) 私は、徹夜してレポートを書きあげた。
Watashiwa, tetsuyashite repootoo kakiageta.
I stayed up all night to finish writing my report.

2) 彼女は、たった１日でスーツを縫いあげた。
Kanojowa, tattaichinichide suutsuo nuiageta.
She managed to finish the suit in one day.

3) 私のおばは、３人の息子を立派に育てあげた。
Watashino obawa, sanninno musukoo rippani sodateageta.
My aunt did a splendid job of raising her three sons.

～きる ■～*kiru* ■to use up ; run out of 

①動詞の後ろについて「終わりまで・**すっかり～する**・もう残りがない」というとき使います（例4, 5, 6)。

～*kiru* attached to the end of a verb indicates that the action continues until the end, it is completed, or there is nothing more remaining (ex.4, 5, 6).

②ものごとが**限界に達する**というようなとき（例7, 8）、「～きって（いる）」の形でよく使われます。

It also shows that something has reached its limit (ex.7, 8). The form ～*kitte* (*iru*) is often used.

---

4) ボールペンのインクを、全部使いきった。

Boorupenno inkuo, zenbu tsukaikitta.
(I've) used up all the ink in the pen.

5) 昨夜のパーティーでは食べきれない程のごちそうが出た。

Sakuyano paatiidewa tabekirenai hodono gochisooga deta.
There was more than enough food at the party last night.

6) 私は、1000ページもある本を、あまりおもしろかったので一晩で読みきった。

Watashiwa, senpeejimo aru hon-o, amari omoshirokattanode hitobande yomikitta.
I read a book 1,000 pages long in one night because it was so interesting.

7) 父は、毎日疲れきって会社から帰って来る。

Chichiwa, mainichi tsukarekitte kaishakara kaettekuru.
My father comes home from work dead tired every night.

8) 彼は、山の中で道に迷って10日間も水だけで過ごしたので、発見されたときはすっかり体が弱りきっていた。

Karewa, yamano nakade michini mayotte tookakanmo mizudakede sugoshitanode, hakkensareta tokiwa sukkari karadaga yowarikitteita.
He got lost in the mountains and lived ten full days on nothing but water, so when he was found he was extremely weak.

～おわる

■ ～*owaru*
■ to finish ; end

動作を表す動詞の後ろについて、その動作が**時間の経過とともに、おしまいになった**、というとき使います（例9, 10, 11）。

When attached to an action verb, ～*owaru* merely indicates that the action eventually comes an end (ex.9, 10, 11).

---

9) 読み終わった新聞は、もとの場所にもどしておいてください。

Yomiowatta shinbunwa, motono bashoni modoshiteoite kudasai.
When (you) have finished reading the newspaper, please put it back to where it was.

10) 食べ終わったら自分で食器を洗いなさい。
Tabeowattara jibunde shokkio arainasai.
When (you) finish eating, wash your own dishes.

11) 手紙を書き終わったら、すぐに出しに行くつもりです。
Tegamio kakiowattara, suguni dashini ikutsumoridesu.
(I'm) going to mail the letter as soon as I finish writing it.

あせる/さめる

■ *aseru* ■ *sameru*

あせる ■ *aseru* ■ to fade

物の色が、太陽や熱などに**さらされ**たり、時間がたつことによって、**薄くなる**とき使います（例1, 2, 3, 4）。なんとなく、きたない・みすぼらしいというような感じがします。花の色のように、後からつけた色ではなく本来の色が抜けていくときには、「あせる」しか使いません。

Aseru indicates that the color of something becomes lighter due to exposure to elements such as heat or the sun, or the passage of time (ex.1, 2, 3, 4). A feeling of dirtiness or shabbiness is implied. When one is describing the loss of an object's original color (i.e., not a color that has been added later, such as that of a flower) *aseru* is the only verb that may be used.

1) 1週間も咲いていると、花の色はだいぶあせる。
Isshuukanmo saiteiruto, hanano irowa daibu aseru.
The color of a flower fades considerably if it's been in bloom for a week.

2) 彼は、かなり色あせた服を着ている。
Karewa, kanari iroaseta fukuo kiteiru.
He is wearing rather faded clothes.

3) その部屋のカーテンは、かなり色があせて古ぼけている。
Sono heyano kaatenwa, kanari iroga asete furuboketeiru.
The curtains in that room are quite faded and worn.

4) 古い映画館に、色あせたポスターが張ってある。
Furui eigakanni, iroaseta posutaaga hattearu.
There are faded posters hanging in the old movie theater.

さめる［褪める・冷める・覚める］ ■*sameru* ■to fade ; to cool down 

①色が抜けていって**もとの生地の色に近づく**という意味で使います（例5, 6）。

Sameru is used to signify that the color of something returns to the original color of the material it is made of (ex.5, 6).

②熱いものが**気温に近い温度**になるとき使います（例7, 8）。

It also denotes that the temperature of something hot approaches the air temperature (ex.7, 8).

③熱心に思う**気持ち・関心・興味**などが**無くなる**とき使います（例9, 10）。

In some cases it may mean that feelings such as passion, admiration, or interest subside (ex.9, 10).

④眠っている・酔っている・麻酔がきいているというような**無意識の状態から意識をとりもどした**状態になるとき使います（例11, 12, 13）。

Sameru may also mean that one returns to a normal state of consciousness after sleep, drunkenness, being under anesthesia, etc. (ex.11, 12, 13).

①は「褪める」と書き、②と③は「冷める」、④は「覚める」と書きます。

In definition ① the *kanji* 褪める is written, in ② and ③ 冷める is used and in ④ 覚める is written.

---

5) 日焼けした肌も、秋の終わりには、ほとんどさめる。
Hiyakeshita hadamo, akino owariniwa, hotondo sameru.
(My) suntan will fade by the end of autumn.

6) 何度も洗ったので、ジーンズの色がさめてきた。
Nandomo arattanode, jiinzuno iroga sametekita.
The color of my jeans has faded because (I've) washed them so many times.

7) 話に夢中になっているうちに、紅茶が冷めてしまった。
Hanashini muchuuni natteiru uchini, koochaga sameteshimatta.
(I) was so absorbed in the conversation that my tea got cold.

8) 冷めたみそしるは、おいしくない。
Sameta misoshiruwa, oishikunai.
Lukewarm *miso* soup is not very tasty.

9) もう彼への愛は、冷めてしまった。
Moo kareeno aiwa, sameteshimatta.
(My) love for him has faded.

10) 彼のカメラに対する情熱は、当分冷めそうもない。
Kareno kamerani taisuru joonetsuwa, toobun samesoomonai.
It doesn't look like he'll lose his passion for cameras anytime soon.

11) 目ざまし時計のベルの音で目が覚めた。
Mezamashi-dokeino beruno otode mega sameta.
(I) awoke to the buzz of my alarm clock.

12) 熱いシャワーをあびて、やっと酔いが覚めた。
Atsui shawaao abite, yatto yoiga sameta.
(I) was finally able to sober up after taking a hot shower.

13) 医師は、彼の麻酔が覚めるまで、ずっとそばにいた。
Ishiwa, kareno masuiga samerumade, zutto sobani ita.
The doctor stayed by his side until the anesthesia wore off.

あそこ／あちら／むこう

■*asoko* ■*achira* ■*mukou*

あそこ ■*asoko* ■(over) there

①話し手からも聞き手からも**それほど離れてはいない**、ある**特定の場所**を指します。その場所は今いるところから見えたり、手で指し示すことができる範囲にあります（例1, 2, 3)。

Asoko designates a place removed, but not too distant, from both the speaker and the listener. The place referred to is within a range where it can be seen, or pointed out (ex.1, 2, 3).

②**現在話題になっている場所**を言うときにも使います（例4, 5）。

It is also used to refer to a place which has been previously mentioned in conversation (ex. 4, 5).

---

1) 地下鉄の入り口は、あそこです。
Chikatetsuno iriguchiwa, asokodesu.
The subway entrance is over there.

2) あそこにいるのが、私の妹です。
Asokoni irunoga, watashino imootodesu.
The person over there is my younger sister.

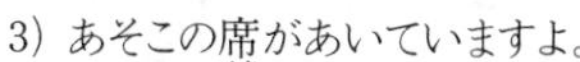

3) あそこの席があいていますよ。
Asokono sekiga aiteimasuyo.
That seat is open.

4) 駅前の喫茶店を知っていますか。あそこで4時に会いましょう。
Ekimaeno kissaten-o shitteimasuka? Asokode yojini aimashoo.
Do you know the coffee shop in front of the station? Let's meet there at four o'clock.

5) 来月から北海道ですね、あそこは寒いから、気をつけてください。
Raigetsukara Hokkaidoodesune, asokowa samuikara, kio tsukete kudasai.
You'll be in Hokkaido starting next month, right? It's cold there so please be careful.

あちら
■ *achira*
■ (over) there

---

①**「あそこ」のていねいな言い方**ですが、すこし遠い方向や場所も意味することがあります（例6, 7, 8）。

Achira is a more polite way of saying *asoko*, however it also may refer to a direction or place somewhat more distant (ex.6, 7, 8).

②**「あの人」のていねいな言いかた**です（例9, 10）。

It is also a polite way of saying *ano hito* (that person) (ex.9, 10).

---

6) ここが会議室です。先生のお席はあちらです。

Kokoga kaigishitsudesu. Senseino osekiwa achiradesu.
This is the conference room. Your seat is over there, professor.

7) あちらに居る方が、この会社の社長さんです。

Achirani iru kataga, kono kaishano shachoosandesu.
The gentleman over there is the president of our company.

8) 今から九州へ行きます。あちらに着いたら電話をします。

Imakara Kyuushuue ikimasu. Achirani tsuitara denwao shimasu.
I'm going to Kyushu now. I'll call when I get there.

9) ご紹介します。こちらは石川さんです。あちらは林さんです。

Goshookai shimasu. Kochirawa Ishikawasandesu. Achirawa Hayashisandesu.
Let me do the introductions. This is Mr. Ishikawa. That is Ms. Hayashi over there.

10) あちらはどなたですか。

Achirawa donatadesuka?
Who is that person over there?

むこう［向こう］

■ *mukou*
■ beyond ; (on) the other side

---

①見えるか見えないかぐらい**遠いところ**や**方向**、**自分と反対側**を指し、**へだてられている**という意味を強く含みます（例11, 12）。

Mukou refers to a distant place or direction which may or may not be visible, or to a location / position opposite to that of the speaker. It emphasizes strongly that there is a separation, either by an object or a spatial gap (ex. 11, 12).

②話題になっている**特定の場所・外国**など**遠い所**を指します（例13, 14）。

It may refer to a place which has been mentioned in conversation, or to a foreign country, etc., which is distant from one's present location (ex.13, 14).

③話し手とは**反対の立場・対立する立場**にいる**第三者**を指すときに使います（例15, 16）。

It is also used to refer to a third party who is in an opposite or confrontational position with respect to the speaker (ex.14, 15).

---

11) 線路の向こうに、ひまわりがたくさん咲いている。
Senrono mukooni, himawariga takusan saiteiru.
There are a lot of sunflowers blooming on the other side of the tracks.

12) 駅のむこう側に、大きいスーパーがあります。
Ekino mukoogawani, ookii suupaaga arimasu.
There is a big supermarket on the other side of the station.

13) このベルトはドイツ製です。向こうにいたとき買ったんですよ。
Kono berutowa Doitsuseidesu. Mukooni ita toki kattandesuyo.
This belt is German made. (I) bought it when I was there.

14) 長い間外国でのんびり暮らしていたので、向こうでの生活が忘れられない。
Nagaiaida gaikokude nonbiri kurashiteitanode, mukoodeno seikatsuga wasurerarenai.
We had such a relaxed life abroad for so long. (I'll) never forget our time there.

15) 向こうが先に手を出したのに、私が叱られてしまいました。
Mukooga sakini teo dashitanoni, watashiga shikararete-shimaimashita.
I ended up getting scolded when it was the other guy who hit first.

16) 彼女と結婚したいのに、向こうの両親が反対しているので、困っています。
Kanojoto kekkonshitainoni, mukoono ryooshinga hantai-shiteirunode, komatte-imasu.
(I) want to marry her, but I'm having problems because her parents are opposed.

あたかも／いかにも

■ *atakamo* ■ *ikanimo*

あたかも ■ *atakamo* ■ just as if

実際はちがうのに、**そうであるかのよう**に見える。～に似ている・そっくりだというようすを表すとき使います。「あたかも～のよう」と使うことが多く、「まるで～のよう」と同じように使いますが、「あたかも」は少し硬いことばです（例1, 2, 3, 4）。

This indicates that something looks as if it were the very thing, although it is not. It is also used to indicate that two things are similar or exactly alike. *Atakamo ～no yoo* is often used in the same way as *marude ～no yoo*, however it is a little more formal (ex.1, 2, 3, 4).

---

1) この人形(にんぎょう)は、あたかも生(い)きているようだ。
Kono ningyoowa, atakamo ikiteiruyooda.
This doll looks as if it were alive.

2) 彼(かれ)は、あたかもその事件(じけん)の全(すべ)てを知(し)っているかのように話(はな)した。
Karewa, atakamo sono jikenno subeteo shitteirukanoyooni hanashita.
He talked as if he knew every detail of the incident.

3) 大嵐(おおあらし)をくぐりぬけてきた船(ふね)は、あたかもゆうれい船(せん)のようだった。
Ooarashio kugurinuketekita funewa, atakamo yuurei-sennoyoodatta.
The ship that had passed through the typhoon looked just like a ghost ship.

4) 刑事(けいじ)は、あたかも私(わたし)が犯人(はんにん)であるかのようににらんだ。
Keijiwa, atakamo watashiga hanninde arukanoyooni niranda.
The detective glared at me as if I were the criminal.

いかにも

■ *ikanimo*
■ as if ; really

人(ひと)やもの・ことがらの特徴(とくちょう)がよく表(あらわ)れていて**ほんとうにそうだと納得(なっとく)する**とき使(つか)います。「いかにも～そう」「いかにも～らしい」「いかにも～よう」と使(つか)うことが多(おお)いです（例(れい)5, 6, 7, 8）。

Ikanimo is used when the characteristics or traits of something or someone are apparent, and the speaker feels they are a true representation (of the thing or person). *Ikanimo* is most often used in idiomatic clauses, such as *ikanimo ～soo, ikanimo ～rashii,* and *ikanimo ～yoo* (ex.5, 6, 7, 8).

---

5) このセーターは、いかにも暖(あたた)かそうだ。
Kono seetaawa, ikanimo atatakasooda.
This sweater looks really warm.

6) 彼(かれ)は、山(やま)の頂上(ちょうじょう)でいかにもおいしそうに水(みず)を飲(の)んだ。
Karewa, yamano choojoode ikanimo oishisooni mizuo nonda.

The way he drank the water on the mountain top made it look so delicious.

7) さとうと塩(しお)をまちがえるなんて、いかにも君(きみ)らしいよ。

Satooto shioo machigaerunante, ikanimo kimirashiiyo.
You mean you used sugar by mistake instead of salt? That sounds just like you.

8) これは、いかにも子供(こども)が喜(よろこ)びそうな映画(えいが)だ。

Korewa, ikanimo kodomoga yorokobisoona eigada.
That movie seems to be just the kind that children would like.

あたたかい／ぬるい

■ *atatakai* ■ *nurui*

あたたかい［暖(あたた)かい・温(あたた)かい］ ■ *atatakai* ■ warm [大]

①**寒(さむ)くない・冷(つめ)たくないここちよい温度(おんど)**を表(あらわ)します。気温(きおん)や気候(きこう)（暖房(だんぼう)などによるときにも）に使(つか)うときには「暖(あたた)かい」と書(か)き、そのほかは「温(あたた)かい」と書(か)きます（例(れい)1, 2, 3, 4, 5）。

Atatakai indicates a temperature which is comfortable and not cold. The *kanji* 暖かい is used when referring to air temperature (even when warmed by a heater) or climate ; in other instances 温かい is used (ex.1, 2, 3, 4, 5).

②**思(おも)いやりや愛情(あいじょう)がこもっている**という意味(いみ)で使(つか)います（例(れい)6, 7）。

It is also used to mean warmhearted, thoughtful, etc. (ex.6, 7).

---

1) 今年(ことし)の冬(ふゆ)は去年(きょねん)より暖(あたた)かい。

Kotoshino fuyuwa kyonenyori atatakai.
This year's winter is warmer than last year's.

2) 今(いま)ヒーターをつけたので、すぐに部屋(へや)が暖(あたた)かくなりますよ。

Ima hiitaao tsuketanode, suguni heyaga atatakaku narimasuyo.
(I've) just turned on the heater, so the room will soon warm up.

3) 母(はは)が編(あ)んでくれたセーターはとても暖(あたた)かい。

Hahaga andekureta seetaawa totemo atatakai.
The sweater that my mother knit me is very warm.

4) 寒(さむ)い日(ひ)は、何(なに)か温(あたた)かいものが食(た)べたい。
Samui hiwa, nanika atatakai monoga tabetai.
(I) want to eat something hot on cold days.

5) 北風(きたかぜ)が吹(ふ)いていたけれど、走(はし)って帰(かえ)ってきたら体(からだ)が温(あたた)かくなった。
Kitakazega fuiteitakeredo, hashitte kaettekitara karadaga atatakaku natta.
A (cold) north wind was blowing, but (I) warmed up by running home.

6) 私(わたし)は旅先(たびさき)で、いろいろな人(ひと)から温(あたた)かいもてなしを受(う)けた。
Watashiwa tabisakide, iroirona hitokara atatakai motenashio uketa.
(I) was warmly treated by many people while on my trip.

7) 彼(かれ)らは、子供(こども)たちの成長(せいちょう)を温(あたた)かく見守(みまも)っている。
Karerawa, kodomotachino seichoo-o atatakaku mimamotteiru.
They are keeping a kind eye on their children's growth.

ぬるい ■*nurui* ■lukewarm 大

もともと冷(つめ)たかったものが、時間(じかん)がたつうちに温度(おんど)が少(すこ)し上(あ)がったり、またその逆(ぎゃく)だったりというように、**期待(きたい)していた温度(おんど)とちがうという不快感(ふかいかん)**を表(あらわ)すとき使(つか)います（例(れい)8, 9, 10）。「もっと熱(あつ)い・もっと冷(つめ)たい」状態(じょうたい)であるべきだと思(おも)っていたのに、そうではなかったという不満(ふまん)の気持(きも)ちの表(あらわ)れです。例(れい)11, 12は、やり方(かた)にきびしさがない・不十分(ふじゅうぶん)だという意味(いみ)です。

This expresses an unpleasantly lukewarm temperature. At times it may mean 'not hot enough' (indicating the speaker expected something to be hotter), and at other times it implies 'not cold enough' (although something was cold before, it has become warm) (ex.8, 9, 10). It suggests a feeling of dissatisfaction, therefore the meaning may be extended to include situations described in Examples 11 and 12 in which something is not strict enough, not sufficient, etc.

---

8) ぬるいお風呂(ふろ)に入ると、かぜをひきますよ。
Nurui ofuroni hairuto, kazeo hikimasuyo.
You'll catch a cold if you take a bath in lukewarm water.

9) このビールは、ぬるくてまずい。

Kono biiruwa, nurukute mazui.
This beer is not good because it's lukewarm.

10) みそ汁がぬるかったら、あたため直してください。
Misoshiruga nurukattara, atatame naoshite kudasai.
If the *miso* soup is lukewarm, please reheat it.

11) 親達は暴力をふるった生徒に対する学校の処分が手ぬるいと批判した。
Oyatachiwa, booryokuo furutta seitoni taisuru gakkoono shobunga tenuruito hihanshita.
The parents criticized the school for being lenient with students who had perpetrated violence.

12) 警察の手ぬるい捜査で、犯人をのがした。
Keisatsuno tenurui soosade, hannin-o nogashita.
Because of their lax investigation, the police were unable to capture the suspect.

「〜で」と「〜に」

新井さんの13歳になる孫の大介は、アメリカで生まれて育ちました。そして先月、日本に帰って来ました。ですから、ときどき日本語の使い方をまちがえることがあります。ある日、新井さんは子犬をもらってきました。早速、大介が犬小屋を作ると言い出しました。「おじいさん、外は寒いので、ぼくの部屋で犬小屋を作ってもいいですか」と大介が聞いたので、「ああ、いいよ」と新井さんは答えました。ところが、でき上がった犬小屋を見て新井さんは、驚きました。大きくて、部屋の入り口から出せません。「子犬を外においたら、寒くてかわいそうだと思って…」と大介は言いました。

「〜で」は、動作が行われる場所を表し、「〜に」は、存在する場所や目的の場所を表します。大介は、正しくは、「ぼくの部屋に…」と言うべきでした。そうすれば新井さんは、「庭に作りなさい」と言ったでしょう。

To 'do' or 'be'

Mr. Arai's grandson, Daisuke, is a thirteen year old who was born and raised in the United States, so although he can speak Japanese, he is often prone to make mistakes. Last month he returned to Japan with his family.

One day, Mr. Arai was given a puppy, and Daisuke immediately said he wanted to build a doghouse for it, saying, "Grandfather, it's cold outside, so is that all right if I make a doghouse... *boku no heya de*[1]*?*" Mr. Arai gave his permission, but was later surprised to find that the completed doghouse was far too big to get through the door. Daisuke defended himself by saying, "I thought it would be cruel to leave the puppy outside in the cold."

The preposition ~*de* indicates the location at which an action is performed, while ~*ni* refers to the place in which something exists, or the place that something is planned for. Therefore, Daisuke should have said, "*Boku no heya ni...*," to which Mr. Arai would have probably replied, "*Niwa ni tsukurinasai.*[2]"

1 *in my room*
2 *Make it in the yard.*

あたり ■*atari*
■neighborhood ; around (here)

だいたいの場所・おおよその時間、そしてあの人だったらどうだろうか、などを表すとき使います。「あたり」だけで使うのは場所を表すときだけで（例1, 2）

ほとんどは、「あしたあたり・あのあたり・～さんあたり」のように具体的な時間・場所・人を表す語の後につけて使います（例3, 4）。

Atari is used to indicate an approximate location or time, or when giving a person's name as a possible candidate (to do something). When *atari* is used independently or with a demonstrative pronoun such as *kono* and *ano*, it refers to a specific place or location (ex.1, 2). *Atari* is generally used with specific words like *ashita atari* (date), *ano atari* (place), or *～san atari* (person) (ex.3, 4).

---

1) 目が覚めて、あたりを見渡すと、一面の銀世界だった。
Mega samete, atario miwatasuto, ichimenno ginsekaidatta.
When (I) woke up and looked around, I found that everything was covered with snow.

2) 私が住んでいるあたりは、工場が多い。
Watashiga sundeiru atariwa, koojooga ooi.
In the vicinity where I live there are many factories.

3) A：そろそろお花見の時期ですね。
B：そうですね。来週あたりが、ちょうど見ごろでしょう。
A： *Sorosoro ohanami*no jikidesune.* *p.450
It's almost the time for cherry blossom viewing, isn't it?
B： *Soodesune. Raishuuatariga, choodo migorodeshoo.*
Yes, it is. I guess next week will be the best time to see them.

4) カメラのことなら、原田さんあたりが詳しいのではないでしょうか。
Kamerano kotonara, Haradasan atariga kuwashiinodewa naideshooka.
If it has to do with cameras, I think if anyone, Mr. Harada will know best.

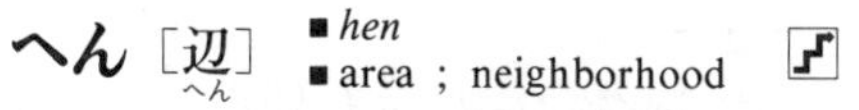

へん［辺］ ■*hen* ■area ; neighborhood

だいたいの場所や部分を表すことばです。「あたり」とちがって「へん」はその語だけでは使いません。「**この、その、あの**」などと**いっしょに使います**（例5, 6）。ふつう人や時間には使いませんが、とりあえずそこでものごとの区切りをつけるというときには、時間の意味にも使います（例7, 8）。

Hen indicates an approximate place or location. Unlike *atari*, it is not used independently. It is generally used with a demonstrative pronoun such as *kono*, *sono*, or *ano*, as in the expressions, *kono hen* and *sono hen* (ex.5, 6). Also unlike *atari*, *hen* is generally not used when speaking of people or time, but it can be used when the speaker wishes to bring something to an end (ex.7, 8).

5) A：この辺(へん)で私(わたし)のはさみ見(み)なかった？

B：さあ、この辺(へん)にはなかったよ。

A： *Konohende watashino hasami minakatta?*
Have you seen my scissors around here?

B： *Saa, konohenniwa nakattayo.*
Well, I haven't seen them here.

6) その辺(へん)が２人(ふたり)の意見(いけん)が、くい違(ちが)うところです。

Sonohenga futarino ikenga, kuichigau tokorodesu.
Their opinions differ at that point.

7) この辺(へん)で、今日(きょう)の仕事(しごと)は終(お)わりにしましょう。

Konohende, kyoono shigotowa owarini shimashoo.
Let's stop work here for the day.

8) その辺(へん)で、もうけんかはやめなさい。

Sonohende, moo kenkawa yamenasai!
That's enough! Stop fighting!

あたる／ぶつかる

■*ataru* ■*butsukaru*

あたる［当(あ)たる］

■*ataru*
■to hit ; to touch ; to win (a lottery)

①あるものが、ほかのものにふれる・接触(せっしょく)するときに使(つか)います（例(れい)1, 2, 3)。「的(まと)や目的(もくてき)のものに**命中(めいちゅう)する**」という意味(いみ)を含(ふく)みます。

Ataru means that something touches or makes contact with something else (ex.1, 2, 3). It may imply that the object hits a target or goal.

②光(ひかり)や風(かぜ)や、暖(あたた)かさなどにふれることです（例(れい)4, 5, 6)。

To be exposed to light, wind, warmth, etc. (ex.4, 5, 6).

③等(ひと)しい・相当(そうとう)するというとき使(つか)います（例(れい)7, 8, 9)。

To be equal or equivalent to something else (ex.7, 8, 9).

④予想したことや答えなどが正解であるときや、宝くじなどに当選するときに使います（例10, 11)。

It also indicates that one's prediction or answer is correct, or that one wins a prize in a public lottery, etc. (ex.10, 11).

---

1) 私の投げたボールが、子供に当たってしまった。
Watashino nageta booruga, kodomoni atatteshimatta.
The ball I threw unfortunately hit a child.

2) 木の実が落ちてきて、私の頭に当たった。
Kinomiga ochitekite, watashino atamani atatta.
A nut fell from the tree and hit me on the head.

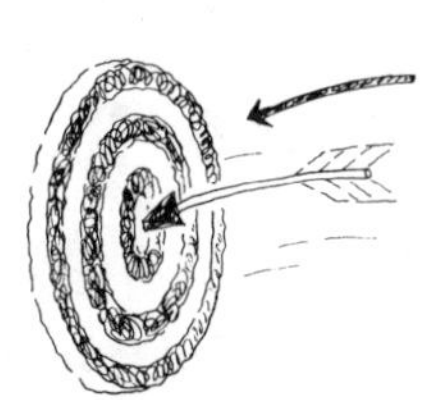

3) 彼の放った矢は、的のまん中に当たった。
Kareno hanatta yawa, matono mannakani atatta.
The arrow he shot hit the bulls-eye.

4) 気分が悪いので、少し外の風に当たってきます。
Kibunga waruinode, sukoshi sotono kazeni atattekimasu.
(I) don't feel good, so I will go out to get some fresh air.

5) この部屋は、よく日が当たるので暖かい。
Kono heyawa, yoku higa atarunode atatakai.
This room gets lots of sun, so it's very warm in here.

6) 外はひどい雪だったので、私は部屋に入るとまずストーブに当たった。
Sotowa hidoi yukidattanode, watashiwa heyani hairuto mazu sutoobuni atatta.
It was snowing so hard outside that, as soon as I entered the room, I stood by the heater.

7) Ａ：彼はあなたの何に当たりますか。
Ｂ：おじです。

Ａ： *Karewa anatano nanini atarimasuka?* What relation is he to you?
Ｂ： *Ojidesu.* He's my uncle.

8) 来月の15日は、この会社の創立記念日に当たります。
Raigetsuno juugonichiwa, kono kaishano sooritsukinenbini atarimasu.
The 15th of next month is the anniversary of the founding of this company.

9) 1ポンドは、約450グラムに当たります。
Ichipondowa, yaku yonhyaku-gojuu-guramuni atarimasu.
One pound is equal to about 450 grams.

10) やっぱり、彼女の予想が当たって、雨になったね。
Yappari, kanojono yosooga atatte, ameni nattane.
Her prediction was right after all — it's raining now.

11) 彼女の占いは、良く当たる。
Kanojono uranaiwa, yoku ataru.
Her fortune-telling often turns out to be true.

ぶつかる

■ *butsukaru*
■ to hit (against) ; to run (into) 

---

①ものとものが、比較的強く接触するとき使います（例12, 13）。スピードや、それにともなう**衝撃が感じられます**。したがって、意見の違いなどで人と争ったり（例14）、また困難なことに出会ったとき（例15）などにも使います。

Butsukaru is used to indicate that something hits something else relatively forcefully (ex.12, 13). There is a feeling of speed and shock. Accordingly, *butsukaru* may also be used to mean to argue with others who have a different opinion (ex.14), or to encounter hardship (ex.15).

②日時が重なるとき使います（例16）。

Butsukaru may also indicate that there is a conflict in time (ex.16).

③ある場所や建物などにつきあたることです（例17）。

To arrive at a place or building (ex.17).

12) この先の交差点で、トラックとバイクがぶつかった。
Kono sakino koosatende, torakkuto baikuga butsukatta.
At the intersection up ahead a truck and a motorcycle collided.

13) あわてていたので、ガラス戸に気がつかないで、ぶつかってしまった。
Awateteitanode, garasudoni kigatsukanaide, butsukatte-shimatta.
(I) was in a hurry so I didn't notice the glass door and banged into it.

14) 私の就職のことで父とぶつかってしまった。
Watashino shuushokuno kotode chichito butsukatte-shimatta.
I ended up arguing with my father about where I should work.

15) 思いがけない困難にぶつかって、私はすっかり落ち込んでしまった。
Omoigakenai konnanni butsukatte, watashiwa sukkari ochikonde-shimatta.
Up against unexpected hardship, I became very depressed.

16) 親友の結婚式と、私の司法試験がぶつかってしまった。
Shin-yuuno kekkonshikito, watashino shihoo-shikenga butsukatte-shimatta.
My close friend's wedding fell on the same day as my Bar exams.

17) この道をまっすぐ行って、大通りにぶつかったら右に曲がってください。
Kono michio massugu itte oodoorini butsukattara migini magatte kudasai.
If (you) go straight down this road, you'll hit a wide street. From there, turn right.

あっさり／さっぱり／からっと

■ *assari* ■ *sappari* ■ *karatto*

あっさり

■ *assari*
■ light ; easy

①性質・形状がしつこくない。また味つけが、**濃くなく快い**と感じるとき使います（例1, 2, 3）。

Assari expresses a pleasant and refreshing feeling in the quality, shape, or taste of something (ex.1, 2, 3).

②**かんたん**に、という意味で使います（例4, 5）。

It is also used to express that something is done easily (ex.4, 5).

1) 彼女は、いやな事はすぐに忘れる、あっさりした性格です。
Kanojowa, iyana kotowa suguni wasureru, assarishita seikakudesu.
She easily forgets about unpleasant things. She is a very down-to-earth person.

2) 朝は、脂っこいものよりあっさりした和食の方がいいです。
Asawa, aburakkoi monoyori assarishita washokuno hooga iidesu.
For breakfast, (I) prefer light Japanese food to oily food.

3) 彼女は、今日は何のかざりもないあっさりしたドレスを着ている。
Kanojowa, kyoowa nanno kazarimonai assarishita doresuo kiteiru.

She is wearing a very simply styled dress with no accessories.

4) 私達は、第1試合であっさり負けてしまった。
Watashitachiwa, daiichishiaide assari maketeshimatta.
We slid into defeat in our first match.

5) 彼は、とてもむずかしい数学の問題を、あっさり解いてしまった。
Karewa, totemo muzukashii suugakuno mondaio, assari toiteshimatta.
He quickly solved a difficult mathematics problem.

さっぱり

■ *sappari*
■ refreshing ; neat ; completely 

---

①いつまでもこだわったり、くり返し**考えこんだりしない性格**（例6）、**味つけが濃くない**・脂っこくないとき（例7）、また体や衣服などのよごれを落としたり、きれいで**気持ちのよいようす**などを表すとき（例8）使います。

Sappari is used to describe a carefree or easygoing personality (ex.6), a light, unoily taste in food (ex.7), or a clean, refreshing feeling in one's body or clothes (ex.8).

②完全に（例9）、まったく、まるで（例10）の意味で使います。

It may also be used to mean 'completely' (ex.9), 'entirely', or '(not) at all' (ex. 10).

---

6) 彼はさっぱりした性格なので、怒っても次の日はもう機嫌がなおっている。
Karewa sapparishita seikakunanode, okottemo tsugino hiwa moo kigenga naotteiru.
Since he is a very easygoing person, even if he gets mad, he gets over it by the next day.

7) 私はあまいココアよりも、さっぱりしたレモンジュースが飲みたい。
Watashiwa amai kokoayorimo, sapparishita remonjuusuga nomitai.
Rather than sweet cocoa, I'd prefer to drink some light lemon juice.

8) お風呂に入ってさっぱりした。
Ofuroni haitte sapparishita.
After taking a bath, (I) felt refreshed.

9) あんな男とは、きれいさっぱり別れました。
Anna otokotowa, kireisappari wakaremashita.

(I) broke up with that jerk.

10) 私は、外国語はさっぱりわからない。
Watashiwa, gaikokugowa sappari wakaranai.
I don't understand foreign languages at all.

からっと ■ *karatto* ■ clear ; crisp 

性格・料理（揚げもの）・天気などの湿りけがなく、明るくさわやかなようすを表すとき使います（例11, 12, 13)。「からりと」も同じ意味ですが、今は「からっと」の方がよく使われます。

Karatto expresses a pleasant and refreshing quality in things such as personality, crisp fried food, nice weather, etc. (ex.11, 12, 13). *Kararito* has the same meaning, but *karatto* is much more commonly used in modern Japanese.

11) 彼女は、からっとしていて、けんかをしてもすぐにまた仲直りできる。
Kanojowa, karattoshiteite, kenkao shitemo suguni mata nakanaoridekiru.
She never bears a grudge against others, so even if we have an arguement, we make up quickly.

12) この天ぷらは、からっと揚がっていておいしい。
Kono tenpurawa, karatto agatteite oishii.
This *tempura* is tasty because it's crispy and not oily.

13) 梅雨が終わって、空がからっと晴れ上がった。
Tsuyuga owatte, soraga karatto hareagatta.
The rainy season has ended, and the sky has cleared up completely.

あつまる／まとまる

■ *atsumaru* ■ *matomaru*

あつまる［集まる］ ■ *atsumaru* ■ to gather ; to assemble

3人以上の人や物などが、あちらこちらから同じところに寄って来るときや（例

1,2,3)、結果として同じ種類のものが同じところに多く存在するとき（例4,5）使います。

This is used when three or more people or things come together in one place (ex.1, 2, 3). It is also used to indicate that a large number of similar objects are concentrated in one place (ex.4, 5).

---

1) 会議を始めますので集まってください。
Kaigio hajimemasunode atsumatte-kudasai.
We're starting the meeting, so everybody come together, please.

2) あしたの朝９時、新宿駅南口に集まることになっています。
Ashitano asa kuji, Shinjukueki minamiguchini atsumarukotoni natteimasu.
(We're) supposed to meet at the south entrance of Shinjuku Station tomorrow morning at 9:00 am.

3) 原宿には、いつもたくさんの若者が集まってくる。
Harajukuniwa, itsumo takusanno wakamonoga atsumattekuru.
Lots of young people always come to hang out together in Harajuku.

4) フィリピンは、小さな島がたくさん集まってできています。
Firipinwa, chiisana shimaga takusan atsumatte dekiteimasu.
The Philippines are formed by many small islands grouped together.

5) 京都には、多くのお寺が集まっている。
Kyootoniwa, ookuno oteraga atsumatteiru.
A lot of temples are concentrated in Kyoto.

まとまる

■ *matomaru*
■ to be collected ; to be united

ばらばらの人や物が、一つの**グループや単位になる**とき（例6,7,8）や、対立していたことがらが**解決したり**、**考えが**うまく**一つになったり**したとき（例9,10,11）使います。

Matomaru is used when a number of separate people or objects form a single group or unit (ex.6, 7, 8). It may also be used when matters which have been in conflict are resolved, or when ideas or thoughts reach agreement (ex.9, 10, 11).

---

6) 団体旅行のときは、まとまって行動しなくてはならない。

Dantai-ryokoono tokiwa, matomatte koodoo-shinakutewa-naranai.
On group tours you have to do things with the others.

7) 手元(てもと)に、ある程度(ていど)まとまったお金(かね)がないと不安(ふあん)だ。
Temotoni, aruteido matomatta okanega naito fuanda.
If (I) don't have a certain amount of money on hand I feel insecure.

8) このたび、あの作家(さっか)の作品(さくひん)が１冊(さつ)の本(ほん)にまとまった。
Konotabi, ano sakkano sakuhinga issatsuno honni matomatta.
The works of that author were recently compiled into a single book.

9) 10か月(げつ)かかって、やっと交渉(こうしょう)がまとまった。
Jukkagetsu kakatte, yatto kooshooga matomatta.
It took ten months for the negotiations to finally be settled.

10) 旅行(りょこう)の相談(そうだん)が、なかなかまとまらない。
Ryokoono soodanga, nakanaka matomaranai.
Our travel arrangements just won't fall into place.

11) 来週(らいしゅう)までにレポートを書(か)かなければならないのに、考(かんが)えがまとまらないので困(こま)っています。
Raishuumadeni repootoo kakanakereba-naranainoni, kangaega matomaranai-node komatteimasu.
(I'm) really in a bind because I have to write up my report by next week, and I just can't get my ideas together.

あつめる／よせる

■*atsumeru* ■*yoseru*

あつめる［集(あつ)める］ ■*atsumeru* ■to collect ; to gather 

①**同種類(どうしゅるい)のもの**を、ある程度(ていど)**多(おお)く一(いっ)か所(しょ)に来(く)る**ようにすることです（例(れい)1, 2, 3)。多(おお)くの場合(ばあい)、はっきりした目的(もくてき)があります。

To bring together many of the same kind of things in one place (ex.1, 2, 3). In many cases the speaker has a definite purpose for the objects in mind.

②**同情(どうじょう)・注目(ちゅうもく)**など**関心(かんしん)をひきつける**ことです（例(れい)4, 5)。

To attract sympathy, attention or interest (ex.4, 5).

---

1) 私(わたし)の趣味(しゅみ)は切手(きって)を集(あつ)めることです。
Watashino shumiwa kitteo atsumeru kotodesu.
My hobby is collecting postage stamps.

2) 地震(じしん)で大(おお)きな被害(ひがい)を受(う)けた人々(ひとびと)のために、寄付(きふ)を集(あつ)めた。
Jishinde ookina higaio uketa hitobitono tameni, kifuo atsumeta.
(We) collected donations for the people who were severely affected by the earthquake.

3) みつばちは、花(はな)のみつを集(あつ)めてはちみつを作(つく)る。
Mitsubachiwa, hanano mitsuo atsumete hachimitsuo tsukuru.
Honey bees collect nectar from flowers to make honey.

4) 事故(じこ)にあった子供(こども)は、多(おお)くの人(ひと)の同情(どうじょう)を集(あつ)めた。
Jikoni atta kodomowa, ookuno hitono doojoo-o atsumeta.
The child who was involved in the accident received sympathy from many people.

5) この映画(えいが)は、実話(じつわ)だということで世(よ)の中(なか)の関心(かんしん)を集(あつ)めている。
Kono eigawa, jitsuwadato yuu kotode yononakano kanshin-o atsumete-iru.
This movie has been attracting attention because it's based on a true story.

よせる［寄(よ)せる］ ■*yoseru* ■to draw near ; to collect 

---

①ものをほかのものに**近(ちか)づける・近(ちか)づけて置(お)く**ことです（例(れい)6, 7, 8, 9, 10)。ちらばっているものを一か所(いっしょ)にもってくる・一か所(いっしょ)にまとめておく、という意味(いみ)も含(ふく)みます。

To place something closer or to come closer to something else (ex.6, 7, 8, 9, 10). It also means to gather scattered objects together in one place.

②あることがらに、**心(こころ)や関心(かんしん)を強(つよ)くむける**ことです（例(れい)11, 12)。

To pay special attention or to specially care for a certain thing (ex.11, 12).

---

6) 車(くるま)を、もう少(すこ)し左(ひだり)に寄(よ)せて止(と)めてくれませんか。
Kurumao, moosukoshi hidarini yosete tomete-kuremasenka?

Would (you) please park your car a little more to the left?

7) テーブルを壁ぎわに寄せれば、部屋が広く使えるでしょう。
Teeburuo kabegiwani yosereba, heyaga hiroku tsukaerudeshoo.
If (you) place the table closer to the wall, you can use this room more spaciously.

8) 船長は、船を岸壁に寄せた。
Senchoowa, funeo ganpekini yoseta.
The captain moved the ship closer to the pier.

9) ひだをたくさん寄せたカーテンを作った。
Hidao takusan yoseta kaaten-o tsukutta.
(I) made a curtain with a lot of pleats.

10) 庭の落ち葉を一か所に寄せて、たき火をした。
Niwano ochibao ikkashoni yosete, takibio shita.
(I) collected fallen leaves in the garden and made a bonfire.

11) 彼は彼女に心を寄せている。
Karewa kanojoni kokoroo yoseteiru.
He is falling in love with her.

12) この番組に対するご意見、ご感想をお寄せください。
Kono bangumini taisuru goiken, gokansoo-o oyosekudasai.
Please send in (your) opinions and impressions of this program.

あてる／ぶつける

■ *ateru* ■ *butsukeru*

あてる［当てる］ ■ *ateru* ■ to hit ; touch ; to expose to 

①ものをほかのものに**接触させる**ことです。衝撃を伴うとき（例1, 2）にも、ぴったりとくっつけるというとき（例3, 4, 5）にも使います。

To allow an object to make contact with another object. This action may carry with it shock or impact (ex.1, 2), or be intended to closely join or attach (ex.3, 4, 5).

②ねらいや目標をそれないように**命中させる**ことです。例6,7のような実際の動作にも、例8,9のように判断・予想・答えなどを的中させるときにも使います。また、例10のように答えさせるために指名するときにも使います。

To directly hit the target or goal one is aiming at. In Examples 6 and 7 it is used in a literal sense to show actual movement, and in Examples 8 and 9 it is used figuratively to suggest that one's judgment, prediction, or answer is right on the mark. Also, as in Example 10, it may be used when someone designates another person to answer a question.

③**風・光・雨などにさらす**ことです（例11, 12)。

To expose something to wind, light, rain, etc. (ex.11, 12).

1）角を曲がるときちょっと電柱に当てて、車のドアがへこんでしまった。

Kadoo magaru toki chotto denchuuni atete、kurumano doaga hekondeshimatta.

When (I) turned the corner I just barely touched the power pole, but the door of my car got dented.

2）あのピッチャーは、きょうの試合で２度もバッターにボールを当てた。

Ano pitchaawa, kyoono shiaide nidomo battaani booruo ateta.

That pitcher hit two batters in today's game.

3）母親は子供の額に手を当てて、熱があるかどうかをみた。

Hahaoyawa kodomono hitaini teo atete, netsuga aruka dookao mita.

The mother felt her child's forehead with her hand to see if there was a fever.

4）テニスで顔が日に焼けてしまったので、ぬらしたタオルを当てて冷やした。

Tenisude kaoga hini yakete-shimattanode, nurashita taoruo atete hiyashita.

My face got sunburned while playing tennis, so (I) applied a wet towel to cool it.

5）ほんとうに、やましいところはないかどうか胸に手を当ててよく考えてごらんなさい。

Hontooni, yamashii tokorowa naika dooka muneni teo atete yoku kangaete-gorannasai.

(You) should think hard, and (with your hand over your heart) ask yourself if you really have nothing to feel guilty about.

6）矢を的に当てるのは、むずかしい。

Yao matoni aterunowa, muzukashii.
It is difficult to hit a target with an arrow.

7) きょうのドッジボールで、ぼくは４人(にん)にボールを当(あ)てたよ。
Kyoono dojji-boorude, bokuwa yoninni booruo atetayo.
I hit four people with the ball in today's dodge-ball game!

8) 私(わたし)がゆうべ何(なに)を食(た)べたか、当(あ)ててごらん。
Watashiga yuube nanio tabetaka, ategoran.
Guess what I had for dinner last night.

9) 彼女(かのじょ)はテレビのクイズで、温泉旅行(おんせんりょこう)を当(あ)てました。
Kanojowa terebino kuizude, onsenryokoo-o atemashita.
She won a trip to a hot spring resort in a TV quiz show.

10) 授業中(じゅぎょうちゅう)ぼんやりしていたら、突然先生(とつぜんせんせい)に当(あ)てられた。
Jugyoochuu bon-yarishiteitara, totsuzen senseini aterareta.
When (I) was daydreaming in class, the teacher suddenly picked on me (to answer a question).

11) 部屋(へや)の鉢植(はちう)えは、たまに日(ひ)に当(あ)てないと枯(か)れてしまいます。
Heyano hachiuewa, tamani hini atenaito karete-shimaimasu.
If you don't move houseplants into the sun once in a while, they will die.

12) 写真(しゃしん)のフイルムに光(ひかり)を当(あ)てると、黒(くろ)くなる。
Shashinno fuirumuni hikario ateruto, kurokunaru.
If you expose photographic film to the light, it will turn black.

ぶつける

■ *butsukeru*
■ to hit (against...) ; to crash (into) 

ものをほかのものに接触(せっしょく)させることです。**勢(いきお)い**があり、**衝撃(しょうげき)を伴(ともな)い**ます（例(れい)13, 14, 15）。また、怒(いか)りや不満(ふまん)などの激(はげ)しい**感情(かんじょう)を人(ひと)に向(む)ける**ときにも使(つか)います（例(れい)16, 17）。

To cause something to make contact with something else. There is a sense of accompanying force or impact (ex.13, 14, 15). It is also used when strong emotions, such as anger or dissatisfaction, are directed at a person (ex.16, 17).

---

13) 車(くるま)を塀(へい)にぶつけて、修理(しゅうり)するのにお金(かね)がかかった。

Kurumao heini butsukete, shuurisurunoni okanega kakatta.
(I) crashed my car into a wall, and it cost a lot of money to repair it.

14) 屋根裏部屋は天井が低いから、頭をぶつけないように気をつけて。
Yaneurabeyawa tenjooga hikuikara, atamao butsukenaiyooni kiotsukete.
The attic ceiling is low so be careful not to bump your head.

15) この犬は、子供に石をぶつけられてけがをしたんです。
Kono inuwa, kodomoni ishio butsukerarete kegao shitandesu.
This dog was injured because it was hit by a stone thrown by a child.

16) 私は彼に日頃の不満をぶつけた。
Watashiwa kareni higorono fuman-o butsuketa.
I finally couldn't help letting him know of my dissatisfaction with him.

17) 私はこの怒りを、誰にぶつけたらいいのか分からない。
Watashiwa kono ikario, dareni butsuketara iinoka wakaranai.
I don't know who I should vent my anger on.

あと／もう

■*ato* ■*mou*

あと ■*ato* ■still ; remaining ; later

目標に達するまでの残りの数や量を表すとき使います。「あと＋数詞（人・本・時間……）」や「あと少し・あとちょっと」などの形で使います（例1, 2, 3, 4）。

Ato specifies the number or amount remaining until an objective is attained. It is used in structures such as *ato*＋numeral (*nin, hon, jikan*...), and *ato sukoshi* or *ato chotto* (ex.1, 2, 3, 4).

1) あと５分で昼休みです。
Ato gofunde hiruyasumidesu.
Five more minutes until lunchbreak.

2) この車は４人乗りだから、あと１人乗れますよ。

Kono kurumawa yoninnoridakara, ato hitori noremasuyo.
There is room for four in this car, so one more person can get in.

3) 今90万円あるから、あと10万円ためれば、ちょうど100万円になる。
Ima kyuujuuman-en arukara, ato juuman-en tamereba, choodo hyakuman-enni naru.
(I) have ¥900,000 now, so if I can save ¥100,000 more, I'll have ¥1,000,000.

4) あと少しで夏休みも終わりだ。
Ato sukoshide natsuyasumimo owarida.
Summer vacation will be over soon.

もう ■ *mou* ■ more ; already 

---

①「**さらに**」の意味で、今の**状態**に**加える数量・程度**を表すとき使います(例5, 6, 7)。「まもなく」の意味で使うこともあります(例8, 9)。
Mou is used when mentioning an amount or degree to be added to the present situation (ex.5, 6, 7). It may also be used to mean 'soon' (ex.8, 9).

②すでに**終わった状態**や、**限界に達している**ということを表します(例10, 11, 12)。
It also indicates that something is already finished, or has reached the limit (ex.10, 11, 12).

③**感情を強く表現**するとき使います(例13, 14, 15)。
It may also be used when strongly expressing emotions (ex.13, 14, 15).

---

5) A：コーヒー、もう1杯いかがですか。
B：はい、いただきます。

A: *Koohii, moo ippai ikagadesuka?* How about another cup of coffee?
B: *Hai, itadakimasu.* Yes, please. Thank you.

6) もう一度、言ってください。
Moo ichido, ittekudasai. Please say it again.

7) もう1軒、家がほしい。
Moo ikken, iega hoshii. (I) want to have one more house.

8) もう3時間もすると、日がくれる。
Moo san-jikanmo suruto, higa kureru.
In just three hours the sun will set.

9) もうすぐ朝です。
Moo sugu asadesu. It will be morning soon.

10) きのう買った牛乳は、もう飲んでしまった。
Kinoo katta gyuunyuuwa, moo nondeshimatta.
(I've) already drunk the milk I bought yesterday.

11) いやなことは、もう忘れよう。
Iyana kotowa, moo wasureyoo.
(It was an awful experience so) Let's forget about it.

12) この本箱には、もう1冊も本が入らない。
Kono honbakoniwa, moo issatsumo honga hairanai.
Not even one more book will fit into this bookcase.

13) もう、うれしくてうれしくて……。
Moo, ureshikute ureshikute...! (I) am so very happy!

14) もう痛くてしようがない。
Moo itakute shooganai. It hurts so much I can't stand it.

15) もう、いや。
Moo, iya! That's enough! I can't take anymore.

あとで/のちほど

■*ato de* ■*nochihodo*

あとで ■*ato de* ■later ; after 

①少し時間がたってから・近い将来、という意味です(例1, 2)。
Ato de means 'after a little while', or 'in the near future' (ex.1, 2).

②ある動作やものごとが終わり、次のことがひき続いて起こることを表します(例3, 4)。

It also indicates the occurence of another action or event right after a previous one has ceased (ex.3, 4).

1) まだおなかがすかないので、食事はもう少しあとでいただきます。
Mada onakaga sukanainode, shokujiwa moo sukoshi atode itadakimasu.
(I'm) not hungry yet, so I'll eat a little later.

2) 私の部屋は、あとで片付けますから、そのままにしておいてください。
Watashino heyawa atode katazukemasukara, sono mamani shiteoite kudasai.
I'll clean up my room later, so please leave everything as it is.

3) 電車をとびおりたあとで、かさをおき忘れたことに気がついた。
Denshao tobiorita atode, kasao okiwasureta kotoni kiga tsuita.
After getting off the train, (I) realized that I had left my umbrella behind.

4) 私は、彼にきついことを言ったあとで反省した。
Watashiwa, kareni kitsui kotoo itta atode hanseishita.
I felt bad after speaking to him so harshly.

のちほど ■*nochihodo* ■later

少し時間がたってから・近い将来、という意味で使います（例5, 6, 7）。「あとで」よりも**ていねいで改まった言い方**です。「〜たのちほど、〜ののちほど」のような使い方はしないで、その語だけで使います。

Nochihodo means 'after a little while' or 'in the near future' (ex.5, 6, 7). It is a more formal and polite expression than *ato de*. *Nochihodo* is only used by itself, therefore saying *~ta nochihodo* or *~no nochihodo* is incorrect.

5) 課長はただ今出かけておりますので、のちほどこちらから電話するよう、申し伝えます。
Kachoowa tadaima dekakete-orimasunode, nochihodo kochirakara denwasuruyoo, mooshi-tsutaemasu.
The manager is out now, so (I'll) ask him to call you back later.

6) この件につきましては、のちほど詳しくご説明いたします。
Kono kenni tsukimashitewa, nochihodo kuwashiku gosetsumei itashimasu.

(I'll) explain this in more detail later.

7) では、のちほどまたお目(め)にかかりましょう。

Dewa, nochihodo mata omeni kakarimashoo.
Well then, let's meet again later.

あふれる／こぼれる

■ *afureru* ■ *koboreru*

あふれる ■ *afureru* ■ to overflow

①**いっぱい**になって**入(はい)りきらずに**、一部(いちぶ)が外(そと)へ出(で)てしまうことです（例(れい)1, 2, 3, 4）。

Afureru means that something is filled to the rim and a part of the contents overflow (ex.1, 2, 3, 4).

②感情(かんじょう)やその場(ば)のようすにも使(つか)い、そのような気持(きも)ちや雰囲気(ふんいき)がいっぱいだ・満(み)ちているということです（例(れい)5, 6, 7）。

Afureru is also used to describe things such as emotions, feelings, or a mood as being strong or overwhelming (ex.5, 6, 7).

1) おふろにお湯(ゆ)を入(い)れ過(す)ぎてあふれた。

Ofuroni oyuo iresugite afureta.
(I) put too much water in the bathtub so it overflowed.

2) 大雨(おおあめ)で川(かわ)の水(みず)があふれて、家(いえ)が流(なが)された。

Ooamede kawano mizuga afurete, iega nagasareta.
The river overflowed its banks and washed away some houses.

3) 年末(ねんまつ)のデパートには、買(か)い物客(ものきゃく)があふれている。

Nenmatsuno depaatoniwa, kaimonokyakuga afureteiru.
Department stores are overcrowded with shoppers at the end of year.

4) 今(いま)の世(よ)の中(なか)、物(もの)があふれるほどある国(くに)と、そうでない国(くに)との差(さ)が激(はげ)しい。

Imano yononaka, monoga afureruhodo aru kunito, soodenai kunitono saga

hageshii.
In the present world, the gap between rich countries and poor countries is great.

5) 悲しい知らせに彼女の目には涙があふれてきた。
Kanashii shiraseni kanojono meniwa namidaga afuretekita.
Her eyes started to well up with tears when she heard the sad news.

6) 朝の市場は活気にあふれている。
Asano ichibawa kakkini afureteiru.
In the morning, the open markets are bustling with activity.

7) 入学試験の合格発表を待つ彼の顔は、自信にあふれていた。
Nyuugaku-shikenno gookakuhappyoo-o matsu kareno kaowa, jishinni afureteita.
His face looked full of confidence as he waited for the result of his college entrance exam.

こぼれる

■ *koboreru*
■ to spill ; to drop

---

①入れ物に入っていたものの一部や全部が外へ出ることです。「あふれる」が入りきらずに出てしまうのに対し、「こぼれる」はそれ以外に**入れ物が揺れたり倒れたり穴が開いたり**という、入れ物の状態の変化によることもあります（例8, 9, 10, 11）。また、こぼれて下に落ちるという意味も含みます。

Koboreru means that a part or all of the contents of something flows or spills out. *Afureru* suggests that something in a container overflows because there is not enough space, while in the case of *koboreru* shaking, falling or the opening of a hole in the container may also be the cause of the spillage. The word implies that the spilled objects fall or flow down (ex.8, 9, 10, 11).

②「笑い、涙」のように思わず現れる感情表現に使います（例12, 13）。「喜び、悲しみ、自信」などのように見てわからないものや、その場の雰囲気には使いません。

Koboreru also means that physical expressions of emotion or feeling, such as laughing or crying, are unexpectedly revealed (ex.12, 13).
However, *koboreru* is not used to describe the mood of a place or emotional states, such as pleasure, sorrow, or confidence, which are not visible to the eye.

---

8) 急いで運んだので、バケツの水がこぼれた。
Isoide hakondanode, baketsuno mizuga koboreta.
Water spilled from the bucket I was carrying because I walked too fast.

9) 受け皿にコーヒーがこぼれている。
Ukezarani koohiiga koboreteiru.
There is coffee spilled onto the saucer.

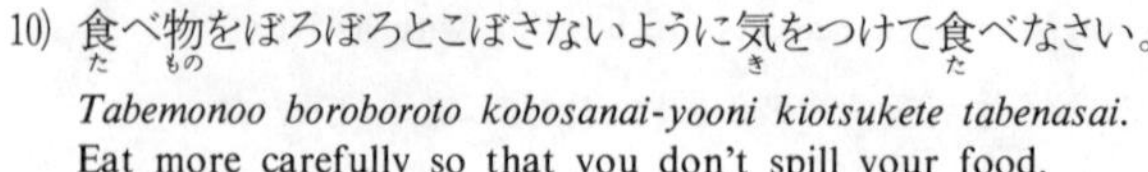

10) 食べ物をぼろぼろとこぼさないように気をつけて食べなさい。
Tabemonoo boroboroto kobosanai-yooni kiotsukete tabenasai.
Eat more carefully so that you don't spill your food.

11) 袋が破れて塩がこぼれてしまった。
Fukuroga yaburete shioga koborete-shimatta.
Unfortunately, the bag was torn and the salt spilled out.

12) サーカスの動物のゆかいなしぐさを見て、思わず笑みがこぼれた。
Saakasu no doobutsuno yukaina shigusao mite, omowazu emiga koboreta.
The acts of the circus animals were so delightful that I couldn't help smiling.

13) その映画はとても感動的だったので、私は涙がこぼれるのをとめることができなかった。
Sono eigawa totemo kandooteki-datta node, watashiwa namidaga koboreru-noo tomeru kotoga dekinakatta.
I was so moved by the movie that I couldn't stop crying.

あまり～ない／たいして～ない

■ *amari～nai* ■ *taishite～nai*

あまり～ない

■ *amari～nai*
■ not very... ; not so...

数量や回数・程度などが、**多くない**・**高くない**というようすを表すとき使います（例1, 2, 3, 4）。「あまりおもしろくない」は、どちらかというと「おもしろくない」とほとんど変わりはありません。「～ない」を少しやわらげて言うときに、「あまり～ない」を使うことが多いのです。

Amari ～nai indicates a condition in which an amount, level, or number of times is not high or great (ex.1, 2, 3, 4). There is almost no difference in meaning between *amari omoshiroku nai* (not very interesting) and *omoshiroku nai* (not interesting). *Amari* is often added to a *～nai* sentence to slightly soften the negative meaning.

---

1) このごろ仕事が忙しくて、あまりテレビを見る暇がない。
Konogoro shigotoga isogashikute, amari terebio miru himaga nai.
(I've) been so busy at work these days that I haven't been able to watch much television.

2) 今年の冬はあまり寒くない。
Kotoshino fuyuwa amari samukunai.
It isn't very cold this winter.

3) 私は、人前で話をするのはあまり好きではない。
Watashiwa, hitomaede hanashio surunowa amari sukidewanai.
I don't like speaking in front of people very much.

4) 彼は大学生なのに遊んでばかりいて、あまり大学へ行かない。
Karewa daigakuseinanoni asondebakariite, amari daigakue ikanai.
Although he is a university student, he just fools around and almost never goes to school.

たいして～ない

■ *taishite～nai*
■ not very... ; not much...

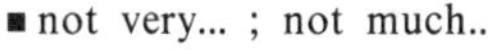

数量や程度が多くない・高くないというようすを表すとき使います（例5, 6, 7)。「数量がかなり多い・程度がかなり高い」と思っていたり、聞いていたりしたことがそれほどでもないという期待はずれや予想外の気持ちを含みます。

This indicates that the amount or level of something is not high or large (ex.5, 6, 7). It includes a sense that the quantity or degree of something has turned out to be not as great or high as one had thought or been led to expect.

---

5) バーゲンといっても、あの店はたいして安くしない。
Baagento ittemo, ano misewa taishite yasukushinai.

Even during bargain sales, that store isn't very cheap.

6) この問題はたいして難しくないから、５分もあれば解ける。

Kono mondaiwa taishite muzukashikunaikara, gofunmo areba tokeru.
This problem is not very difficult, so you should be able to solve it in about five minutes.

7) 彼はたいしてえらくもないのに、いつもいばっている。

Karewa taishite erakumo nainoni, itsumo ibatteiru.
Even though he isn't so special, he always acts arrogant.

お願いします

日本で過ごすときに、「お願いします」を知っているととても役に立ちます。たとえば、タクシーに乗ったら「秋葉原（行きたい所）、お願いします」と言えば、連れて行ってくれます。また小包を郵便局に持って行って「お願いします」と言えば、書いてある住所に送ってくれます。洗濯物も同じです。洗濯屋に持って行って「お願いします」と、置いて来ます。買いたいものを指して、あるいはレジに持って行って「(これ)お願いします」と言えば、ものの名前がわからなくても、「これをください」という言い方がわからなくても、だいじょうぶです。

私の友人のアランが電話をかけたときに「桜木さんをお願いします」というところを、「桜木さんを、ください」と言ってしまいました。ま、そんな失敗はないしょですが…。

とにかく、「お願いします」は「すみません」と同じくらい役に立つことばです。

Please

Onegaishimasu is an expression that will prove to be very useful to anyone spending time in Japan. For example, when you get into a taxi, if you say "*Akihabara* (destination), *onegaishimasu*[1]," the taxi will take you to Akihabara. Then, too, when you bring a package to the post office, if you say "*onegaishimasu*[2]," the package will be delivered to the designated address. You can take your laundry to the cleaners and leave it to be cleaned by saying "*onegaishimasu*[3]." When you point out to a store clerk an item you want to buy, or bring it to the register, if you say "(*kore*) *onegaishimasu*[4]," you'll be understood even if you don't know the object's name in Japanese or the expression *kore o kudasai*[5].

While making a phone call, a friend of mine named Allan once made the mistake of asking for a person by the name of Sakuragi by saying, "*Sakuragi-san o kudasai*[6]," instead of saying, "*Sakuragi-san o onegaishimasu*[7]." This isn't really such a terrible mistake, but it does sound a little odd.

Anyway, *onegaishimasu* is an expression that will be just as useful to you as *sumimasen.*

1 *Please take me to Akihabara.*
2 *I would like to send this package.*
3 *I would like to have this drycleaned, please.*
4 *I would like this one, please.*
5 *May I have this one, please.*
6 *May I have Mr. Sakuragi, please?*
7 *May I speak to Mr. Sakuragi, please?*

あまる／のこる

■*amaru* ■*nokoru*

あまる［余る］

■*amaru*
■to be left over ; to be too much 

①物・人・時間などが、**必要な量を使ってもまだある**ことです（例1, 2, 3, 4)。数学では、計算上で端数が出ることです（例５）。

Amaru indicates that after the required amount of something (objects, people, time, etc.) is used, a portion still remains (ex.1, 2, 3, 4). In mathematics, it is used to show that a fraction remains after a calculation (ex.5).

②ことがらや評価などが、自分の**能力以上**だ・**程度をこえる**という意味です(例6, 7, 8)。

It may be used to show that something (a responsibility, an honor, etc.) is beyond one's ability or capacity (ex.6, 7, 8).

---

1) 仕事が早く終わって時間が余ったので、デパートに行った。
Shigotoga hayaku owatte jikanga amattanode, depaatoni itta.
(I) finished my work earlier than expected and had time to spare, so I went to a department store.

2) 彼の会社は不景気で人が余っているそうです。
Kareno kaishawa fukeikide hitoga amatteirusoodesu.
(I) heard that business at his company is slow, so they laid off extra workers.

3) おすしをたくさん作ったら、食べきれずに余ってしまった。
Osushio takusan tsukuttara, tabekirezuni amatteshimatta.
(I) made too much *sushi*, so I have lots of leftovers.

4) 余ったお菓子は、持って帰ってもいいですよ。
Amatta okashiwa, mottekaettemo iidesuyo.
(You) may take the rest of the sweets home with you.

5) １０を３で割ると１余る。
Juuo sande waruto ichi amaru.
If you divide ten by three, you'll get a remainder of one.

6) こんなにすばらしい賞をいただくなんて、身に余る光栄です。
Konnani subarashii shoo-o itadakunante, mini amaru kooeidesu.
(I) feel very honored to receive such a wonderful award. It's really much more than I deserve.

7) 彼の行動は、自分勝手で目に余る。忠告したほうがいいよ。
Kareno koodoowa jibunkattede meni amaru. Chuukokushitahooga iiyo.
His behavior is selfish and unacceptable, so you should speak to him.

8) こんなに責任の重い仕事は、とても私の手に余りますので、お断りします。
Konnani sekininno omoi shigotowa, totemo watashino teni amarimasunode, okotowari-shimasu.

I'm sorry, but a job like this that carries so much responsibility is more than I can handle, so I (must) refuse.

のこる［残(のこ)る］ ■ *nokoru* ■ to remain 

物(もの)やことがら、人(ひと)などの一部(いちぶ)あるいは全部(ぜんぶ)が、ある程度(ていど)の時間(じかん)がたった後(あと)もまだそこに**存在(そんざい)する**ことです（例(れい)9, 10, 11, 12, 13, 14）。**消(き)えない**という意味(いみ)を含(ふく)みます。

Nokoru is used to mean that someone or a part or the whole of something still exists even after some time has passed (ex.9, 10, 11, 12, 13, 14). It implies that the thing or person in question does not disappear or die.

9) 彼(かれ)は大学(だいがく)を卒業(そつぎょう)して、研究室(けんきゅうしつ)に残(のこ)っている。
Karewa daigakuo sotsugyooshite, kenkyuushitsuni nokotteiru.
Even after graduating, he has remained at the university to continue his research.

10) 私(わたし)の夫(おっと)は、毎日(まいにち)遅(おそ)くまで会社(かいしゃ)に残(のこ)って仕事(しごと)をしている。
Watashino ottowa, mainichi osokumade kaishani nokotte shigotoo shiteiru.
My husband stays late working at the office everyday.

11) 弟(おとうと)はお年玉(としだま)でゲームを買(か)い、残(のこ)ったお金(かね)を貯金(ちょきん)した。
Otootowa otoshidamade geemuo kai, nokotta okaneo chokinshita.
My younger brother bought a game with some of the money he had been given as a New Year's present, and saved the rest.

12) 竜巻(たつまき)が通(とお)り過(す)ぎた後(あと)には、何(なに)も残(のこ)らなかった。
Tatsumakiga toorisugita-atoniwa, nanimo nokoranakatta.
Nothing was left after the tornado past.

13) 精一杯(せいいっぱい)努力(どりょく)したのだから、結果(けっか)はどうでも悔(く)いは残(のこ)らない。
Seiippai doryoku-shitanodakara, kekkawa doodemo kuiwa nokoranai.
(I) tried my best, so no matter what the result is, I'll have no regrets.

14) 彼(かれ)の顔(かお)には、事故(じこ)の傷跡(きずあと)が残(のこ)った。
Kareno kaoniwa, jikono kizuatoga nokotta.
He still has a scar on his face from the accident.

あらためる／かえる／なおす

■*aratameru* ■*kaeru* ■*naosu*

あらためる［改める］ ■*aratameru* ■to change ; to revise

①まちがっている・良くない・適切ではない、などのものごとを、**正しい適切な状態になるようにする**ことです（例1, 2, 3)。

To alter something that is incorrect, bad, or unsuitable so that it is suitable or correct (ex.1, 2, 3).

②**まちがっていないかどうか、**調べたり確かめたりするという意味で使います（例4, 5)。

To check and confirm whether or not something is not wrong (ex.4, 5).

1) 夜更かし朝寝坊の習慣は、これから改めます。
Yofukashi asaneboono shuukanwa, korekara aratamemasu.
(I'm) going to change my habit of staying up late and sleeping in morning.

2) 時代に合わない法律は改めたほうがいい、という意見がある。
Jidaini awanai hooritsuwa aratameta hooga ii, to yuu ikenga aru.
Some people think that we should change outdated laws.

3) 目上の人と話すときには、ことばを改めなさい。
Meueno hitoto hanasu tokiniwa, kotobao aratamenasai.
Make sure (you) use proper language when speaking to your superiors.

4) 役所に提出する書類がそろっているかどうか、もう一度改めた。
Yakushoni teishutsusuru shoruiga sorotteiruka dooka, mooichido aratameta.
(I) double-checked to see if the papers I'm going to submit to city hall were in order.

5) この封筒に50万円入っています。中を改めてください。
Kono fuutooni gojuuman-en haitteimasu. Nakao aratamete kudasai.
There should be ¥500,000 in this envelope. Please check to see that it's all there.

かえる［変える・換える・替える・代える］

■ *kaeru*
■ to change

①ものごとの形や状態を**前とちがうものにする**ことです（例6, 7, 8, 9, 10）。

To alter the shape or status of something so that it is different from its previous shape or status (ex.6, 7, 8, 9, 10).

②それまであったものと**同じ働きをする別のものと交換**することです（例11, 12, 13）。

To replace something that has existed with something else that performs the same function (ex.11, 12, 13).

③何かのかわりに、ほかのもので済ませたり間に合わせたりすることです（例14, 15）。①は「変える」と書き、②は「換える」、または「替える」（特にお金に関することや、予備があるようなものに使う）、そして③は「代える」と書きます。

To make do with or settle for something as a substitute for something else (ex.14, 15). In definition ① the *kanji* 変える is used, in ② 換える or, especially in cases which involve money or a spare part, 替える is used, and in ③ 代える is written.

---

6) 長い髪を切って、流行の髪型に変えました。
Nagai kamio kitte, ryuukoono kamigatani kaemashita.
(I've) cut my long hair and changed it to a more fashionable hairstyle.

7) 家具の並べ方を変えたら、部屋が広くなった感じがする。
Kaguno narabe-katao kaetara, heyaga hirokunatta kanjiga suru.
(I) changed the arrangement of the furniture, and now the room feels bigger.

8) 彼は病気をしてから、食生活を変えた。
Karewa byookio shitekara, shokuseikatsuo kaeta.
He changed his eating habits after his illness.

9) 彼女は、財布がなくなっていることに気づいて、顔色を変えた。
Kanojowa, saifuga nakunatteiru kotoni kizuite, kaoiroo kaeta.
Her face turned ashen when she realized her wallet was missing.

10) 都合が悪くなったので、待ち合わせの場所と時間を変えてもらえませんか。
Tsugooga warukunattanode, machiawaseno bashoto jikan-o kaete moraemasenka?

(I'm) afraid something has come up, so do (you) think you could possibly change the time and place we will meet?

11) このセーター、ちょっと大きすぎるので、もう少し小さいのに換えてください。
Kono seetaa, chotto ookisugirunode, moosukoshi chiisainoni kaete kudasai.
This sweater is a bit too big, so (I'd) like to exchange it for a little smaller one.

12) 窓を開けて、空気を換えましょう。
Madoo akete, kuukio kaemashoo.
Let's open up the window and get some fresh air in here.

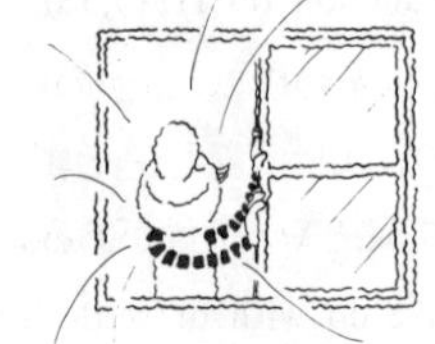

13) 銀行で、円をドルに替えた。
Ginkoode, en-o doruni kaeta.
(I) exchanged yen for dollars at the bank.

14) 人の命は、お金には代えられない。
Hitono inochiwa, okaneniwa kaerarenai.
Money can not replace human life.

15) 卒業式のあと、私たちは感謝の気持ちに代えて、先生に花束を贈った。
Sotsugyoo-shikino ato, watashitachiwa kanshano kimochini kaete, senseini hanatabao okutta.
After the graduation ceremony, we gave a bouquet of flowers to our teacher as a token of our appreciation.

なおす［直す・治す］ ■*naosu* ■to repair ; to cure

①こわれたり乱れたりしたものを、また**元の状態や良い状態にもどす**ことです（例16, 17, 18, 19）。また、誤りを正しくするという意味でも使います（例20, 21）。

To restore something that is broken or is in disorder to its original state or a better condition (ex.16, 17, 18, 19). It is also used to mean to correct a mistake (ex.20, 21).

②**翻訳する・換算する**などの意味で使います（例22, 23）。

To translate or convert something (ex.22, 23).

③病気やけがを**治療する**ことです（例24, 25）。
①と②は「直す」と書き、③は「治す」と書きます。

To heal or cure a disease or injury (ex.24, 25).

In definitions ① and ② the *kanji* 直す is written, and in ③ 治す is used.

---

16) 兄(あに)は、こわれたおもちゃを直(なお)すのがうまい。
Aniwa, kowareta omochao naosunoga umai.
My older brother is good at fixing broken toys.

17) 時計(とけい)が遅(おく)れていたので、直(なお)しておきました。
Tokeiga okureteitanode, naoshite okimashita.
The clock was running slow so (I) reset it.

18) 食事(しょくじ)が済(す)むと、彼女(かのじょ)は化粧(けしょう)を直(なお)すために席(せき)を立(た)った。
Shokujiga sumuto, kanojowa keshoo-o naosutameni sekio tatta.
After eating, she left her seat to touch up her make-up.

19) 記念写真(きねんしゃしん)を撮(と)る前(まえ)に、風(かぜ)で乱(みだ)れた髪(かみ)の毛(け)を直(なお)しました。
Kinen-shashin-o toru maeni, kazede midareta kaminokeo naoshimashita.
Before the commemorative photograph was taken, (I) fixed my hair that had been messed up by the wind.

20) 答案用紙(とうあんようし)を返(かえ)してもらったら、まちがえた所(ところ)を直(なお)しておこう。
Tooan-yooshio kaeshite-morattara, machigaeta tokoroo naoshiteokoo.
When (I) get the answer sheets back, I'll correct my mistakes.

21) 書(か)き損(そこ)なった字(じ)を修正液(しゅうせいえき)で消(け)して直(なお)しました。
Kakisokonatta jio shuuseiekide keshite naoshimashita.
(I) erased the words I had written wrong with retouching liquid, and rewrote them.

22) 次(つぎ)の英文(えいぶん)を読(よ)んで、下線(かせん)の部分(ぶぶん)を日本語(にほんご)に直(なお)しなさい。
Tsugino eibun-o yonde, kasenno bubun-o Nihongoni naoshinasai.
Please read the following English passage, and translate the underlined portions into Japanese.

23) 当時(とうじ)の100円(えん)は、今(いま)のお金(かね)に直(なお)すと1000円(えん)以上(いじょう)の価値(かち)があった。
Toojino hyakuenwa, imano okaneni naosuto sen-en ijoono kachiga atta.
¥100 in those days would be worth over ¥1,000 if converted into today's money.

24) むし歯(ば)は早(はや)く治(なお)したほうがいい。
Mushibawa hayaku naoshita hooga ii.
(You) should have your cavities taken care of at once.

25) 早(はや)くかぜを治(なお)したかったら、おとなしく寝(ね)ていなさい。

Hayaku kazeo naoshitakattara, otonashiku neteinasai.
If (you) want to get rid of your cold quickly, you should rest quietly.

ある／いる

■*aru* ■*iru*

ある

■*aru*
■to be ; to exist 

ものやことがらなどの存在や、権利・財産などの所有を表します（例1, 2, 3, 4, 5, 6, 7)。**具体的なものにも抽象的なことがらにも使います**。家族（夫・妻・子供……）の存在を表すとき使います（例８）。
This verb indicates the existence of things or events, or expresses possession or ownership of rights, property, etc. (ex.1, 2, 3, 4, 5, 6, 7). It is used for both tangible and intangible objects. It is also used to state that one has a family (husband, wife, children, etc.)(ex.8).

1) 私の会社は、銀座にある。
Watashino kaishawa, Ginzani aru.
My company is in Ginza.

2) 京都にはお寺がたくさんある。
Kyootoniwa oteraga tàkusan aru.
There are many temples in Kyoto.

3) わたしが子供のころ、うちには車が３台あった。
Watashiga kodomono koro, uchiniwa kurumaga sandai atta.
When I was a child my family had three cars.

4) きのう私の家の近くで火事がありました。
Kinoo watashino ieno chikakude kajiga arimashita.
There was a fire near my house yesterday.

5) 日本では二十歳以上の人には、選挙権がある。
Nihondewa hatachiijoono hitoniwa, senkyokenga aru.
In Japan, people who are 20 years of age or older have the right to vote.

6) 彼は文章を書く才能がある。

Karewa bunshoo-o kaku sainooga aru.
He has a gift for writing.

7) きょうはとても忙しいので、ゆっくりお茶を飲む暇もありません。

Kyoowa totemo isogashiinode, yukkuri ochao nomu himamo arimasen.
Today (I) am so busy that I don't even have time for a cup of tea.

8) 姉には子供が３人あるが、私には子供はない。

Aneniwa kodomoga sannin aruga, watashiniwa kodomowa nai.
My (elder) sister has three children, but I don't have any.

いる

■ *iru*
■ to be ; to exist ◎

---

①人や動物のように、**生きているものの存在**を表します（例9, 10, 11, 12, 13）。

Iru indicates the existence of human beings or animals (ex.9, 10, 11, 12, 13).

②タクシーやバスなどにも使います（例14, 15）。この場合は、運転者が乗ってその役割を果たしている状態のときです。したがって「展示場に新車が100台いる」とは使いません。

Iru may also be used when speaking of vehicles, such as taxis or buses, which have drivers operating them (ex.14, 15). However, *iru* cannot be used for new cars on display in a car show. In other words, it is incorrect to say '*Tenjijoo ni shinsha ga hyaku-dai iru.*'(There are 100 new cars in the car show.)

9) この池には魚がいる。

Kono ikeniwa sakanaga iru.
There are fish in this pond.

10) このクラスにはドイツ人はいますが、フランス人はいません。

Kono kurasuniwa Doitsujinwa imasuga, Furansujinwa imasen.
In this class there are German students, but no French students.

11) 私には弟がいます。

Watashiniwa otootoga imasu.
I have a younger brother.

12) 私は学生時代、広島にいました。

Watashiwa gakuseijidai, Hiroshimani imashita.
I lived in Hiroshima when I was a student.

13) 私(わたし)はあなたといつまでもいっしょにいたい。
Watashiwa anatato itsumademo isshoni itai.
I want to be with you forever.

14) 駅前(えきまえ)にはいつも、2〜3台(だい)タクシーがいる。
Ekimaeniwa itsumo, nisandai takushiiga iru.
There are always two or three taxis in front of the station.

15) 手(て)を上(あ)げても、止(と)まってくれるタクシーは1台(だい)もいなかった。
Teo agetemo, tomattekureru takushiiwa ichidaimo inakatta.
Even though (I) had my hand raised no taxis would stop for me.

あれる／すさむ

■ *areru* ■ *susamu*

あれる［荒(あ)れる］ ■ *areru* ■ to be rough 

①ものごとや人(ひと)の心(こころ)などが、**平和(へいわ)ではなくなったり、おだやかでなくなったりする**ことです（例(れい)1, 2）。人(ひと)の場合(ばあい)には、あばれたり乱暴(らんぼう)をするなど、暴力的(ぼうりょくてき)になったり、正常(せいじょう)な社会生活(しゃかいせいかつ)をしていないようすも表(あらわ)します。
Areru indicates that a situation or a person's mental state becomes unsettled or disturbed (ex.1, 2). Also, when a person is the subject, it suggests that he or she becomes violent or out of control, and does not act within the norms of society.

②表面(ひょうめん)が平(たい)らだったり、なめらかだったものが、**でこぼこになったり、がさがさになったり**、悪(わる)い状態(じょうたい)になることです（例(れい)3, 4）。
It also denotes that the surface of something which is normally flat or smooth becomes rough, bumpy, or otherwise deteriorates in condition (ex.3, 4).

---

1) 台風(たいふう)が近(ちか)づいてきたので、海(うみ)が荒(あ)れている。
Taifuuga chikazuite-kitanode, umiga areteiru.
A typhoon is approaching, so the sea has become rough.

2) あのころは、酒(さけ)を飲(の)んであばれたり、けんかをしたり、ずいぶん荒(あ)れた生活(せいかつ)をしていた。

Ano korowa, sakeo nonde abaretari, kenkao shitari, zuibun areta seikatsuo shiteita.
In those days (I) led a wild lifestyle, with a lot of drinking, fighting, and troublemaking.

3) 私(わたし)は冷(つめ)たい風(かぜ)にあたると、手(て)やくちびるがすぐ荒(あ)れる。

Watashiwa tsumetai kazeni ataruto, teya kuchibiruga sugu areru.
Whenever there is a cold wind, my hands and lips quickly become chapped.

4) 忙(いそが)しくてしばらく手入(てい)れをしなかったので、庭(にわ)が荒(あ)れてしまった。

Isogashikute shibaraku teireo shinakattanode, niwaga areteshimatta.
(I've) been too busy to care for my garden for some time now, so it has become overgrown.

すさむ ■ *susamu* ■ to become desolate 

不幸(ふこう)がたび重(かさ)なって、絶望的(ぜつぼうてき)になったり気力(きりょく)を失(うしな)ったりして、正常(せいじょう)な生活(せいかつ)ではなくなることです。**すねたりひがんだりして、社会(しゃかい)とのかかわりを断(た)ってしまう**というような感(かん)じです。心(こころ)が貧(まず)しくなるという意味(いみ)も含(ふく)みます（例(れい)5, 6, 7)。

To become full of dispair and be unable to lead a normal life because of repeated misfortune. There is a sense that one sulks and feels like withdrawing from society. *Susamu* implies a feeling of loneliness or desolation (ex.5, 6, 7).

---

5) 彼(かれ)は戦争(せんそう)で家(いえ)も家族(かぞく)も失(うしな)い、生(い)きる気力(きりょく)をなくして、すさんだ生活(せいかつ)をしていた。

Karewa sensoode iemo kazokumo ushinai, ikiru kiryokuo nakushite, susanda seikatsuo shiteita.
After losing his family and home in the war he led a desolate life, having lost all will to live.

6) 親友(しんゆう)の裏切(うらぎ)り、破産(はさん)と悪(わる)いことが重(かさ)なり、彼(かれ)の心(こころ)はすさんでいった。

Shin-yuuno uragiri, hasanto warui kotoga kasanari, kareno kokorowa susandeitta.

After a series of unfortunate events, including his close friend's betrayal and going bankrupt, he became desolate.

7) 物があふれ、生活は豊かなのに、心がすさんでいる人がふえている。
Monoga afure, seikatsuwa yutaka nanoni, kokoroga susandeiru hitoga fueteiru.
The number of people who have many material possesions and wealthy lifestyles, but poor hearts, is rising.

あんがい／いがい／おもったより

■ *angai* ■ *igai* ■ *omotta yori*

あんがい［案外］ ■ *angai* ■ unexpectedly

予想していたことと**実際とが違う**というようすを表すとき使います（例1, 2, 3, 4, 5)。

Angai indicates that the outcome of something is different from what one predicted or expected (ex.1, 2, 3, 4, 5).

1) 娘が初めて焼いたケーキは、案外上手にできていた。
Musumega hajimete yaita keekiwa, angai joozuni dekiteita.
My daughter did surprisingly well on her first attempt at baking a cake.

2) いい天気なので散歩に出たら、外は案外寒かった。
Ii tenkinanode sanponi detara, sotowa angai samukatta.
The weather was fine so (I) went out for a walk, but I found it unexpectedly cold outside.

3) 彼は気むずかしそうに見えるが、話してみると案外おもしろい人だ。
Karewa kimuzukashisooni mieruga, hanashitemiruto angai omoshiroi hitoda.
He looks like a difficult person, but once you speak to him you'll find he is a surprisingly interesting man.

4) 天気予報であしたは雨だといっているが、案外雪になるかもしれない。
Tenkiyohoode ashitawa amedato itteiruga, angai yukini narukamoshirenai.
The weather report says it will rain tomorrow, but maybe by some chance it will turn to snow.

5) 東京から仙台までは遠いと思っていたけれど、新幹線で行ったら案外早く着いた。

Tookyookara Sendaimadewa tooito omotteitakeredo, Shinkansende ittara angai hayaku tsuita.

(I) thought that Sendai was far away from Tokyo, but when I went there by *Shinkansen*, I arrived surprisingly quickly.

いがい［意外］

■ *igai*
■ unexpectedly 

考えていたことや**思っていたことと実際のこととが大きく違う**ようすを表すとき使います。「あんがい」よりも、**驚きの程度が強く**、「思ってもいなかった」という意味を含みます（例6, 7, 8, 9）。

Igai is used when expressing that something is actually much different from what was expected or anticipated. It implies a stronger feeling of surprise than *angai*, as if the speaker had not considered the actual situation at all (ex.6, 7, 8, 9).

---

6) 東京に住んでいても、東京生まれの人は意外に少ない。

Tookyooni sundeitemo, Tookyooumareno hitowa igaini sukunai.

Among people now living in Tokyo, the number of people actually born in the city is surprisingly small.

7) 彼は英語が上手なのに、一度も海外へ行ったことがないとは意外だ。

Karewa eigoga joozunanoni, ichidomo kaigaie itta kotoga naitowa igaida.

It is truly amazing that he speaks English so well, even though he has never been overseas.

8) あの映画の意外な結末に驚いたのは、私だけではないだろう。

Ano eigano igaina ketsumatsuni odoroitanowa, watashidakedewa naidaroo.

I'm sure I'm not the only one that was surprised by the unexpected ending of that movie.

9) 友人が胃の手術をしたというので、お見舞いに行ったら、意外に元気そうで安心した。

Yuujinga ino shujutsuo shitato yuunode, omimaini ittara, igaini genkisoode anshinshita.

When (I) went to the hospital to visit my friend who had had stomach surgery, I was relieved to find him looking better than I had expected.

おもったより［思ったより］

■ *omotta yori*
■ unexpectedly

自分が思っていたことと実際のことがらの程度が違う、ということを述べるとき使います。**人それぞれの基準や判断に基づいています**（例10, 11, 12）。後ろに否定形がくるときは、「思ったほど〜ない」となります（例13）。

Omotta yori is used when saying that something turns out to be different from what was expected; what is 'expected' is based on the speaker's individual standards or judgment (ex.10, 11, 12). When used in negative situations it takes the form *omotta hodo ~nai* (ex.13).

10) 車の修理代が思ったより高かった。
Kurumano shuuridaiga omottayori takakatta.
It cost more than (I) expected to fix my car.

11) 今日のテストは、思ったよりやさしかった。
Kyoono tesutowa, omottayori yasashikatta.
Today's test was easier than (I) thought it would be.

12) 初もうでに行ったら、今年は思ったより人が少なかった。
Hatsumoodeni ittara, kotoshiwa omottayori hitoga sukunakatta.
When (I) went to visit the shrine on New Year's Day, I found that there were a lot less people out than I had expected this year.

13) 今、話題になっている本を読んでみたが、思ったほどおもしろくなかった。
Ima, wadaini natteiru hon-o yondemitaga, omottahodo omoshirokunakatta.
Although I read the much talked-about book, it wasn't as interesting as I thought it would be.

いいかげん／てきとう

■ *iikagen* ■ *tekitou*

いいかげん

■ *iikagen*
■ irresponsible ; groundless ; limit

①ものごとのやり方が、**無責任**だ・まじめではない・**雑**だ、というようすを表します（例1, 2, 3）。したがって、結果は不完全だったり、**根拠のない**無責任なも

のだったりします。

This suggests that the manner in which one does something is irresponsible, insincere, or sloppy (ex.1, 2, 3), leading to incomplete, groundless or undependable results.

②「もうこの辺で、その程度で」という**限度**や**限界**の気持ちを表します（例4, 5)。

It is also used to express feelings of limitation (ex.4, 5).

---

1) あの人は約束を守らない、いいかげんな人だ。
Ano hitowa yakusokuo mamoranai, iikagenna hitoda.
He is an irresponsible person who never keeps his promises.

2) この時計はデザインはいいけれど、つくりがいいかげんだ。
Kono tokeiwa dezainwa iikeredo, tsukuriga iikagenda.
The design of this clock is nice, but it is poorly made.

3) 彼の言うことはいいかげんだから信用できない。
Kareno yuu kotowa iikagendakara shin-yoo dekinai.
He talks a lot of nonsense so you can't trust him.

4) いつまでも起きていないで、いいかげんに寝なさい。
Itsumademo okiteinaide, iikagenni nenasai.
How long are you going to stay up? Hurry up and go to bed.

5) 人のうわさ話は、もういいかげんにやめてください。
Hitono uwasabanashiwa, moo iikagenni yamete kudasai.
Please stop this silly gossip about other people!

てきとう［適当］

■ *tekitou*
■ suitable ; irresponsible 

---

①ものごとの程度・分量・状態などが、その目的や要求に**程よく合っている**ようすを表します。「ぴったりだ・適切だ」という意味から（例6, 7)、「比較的満足できる・多すぎも少なすぎもしない」という意味まで（例8, 9）広く使います。

Tekitou indicates that the quantity, level, or condition of something meets what is asked for or required. In Examples 6 and 7 it means 'just right' or 'perfect for', and in Examples 8 and 9 it means 'satisfactory' or 'not too much or too little'.

②することが、**無責任で手を抜いている**ようすを表し「いいかげん」とほぼ同じ意味で使います（例10, 11)。

It may also be used in nearly the same manner as *iikagen* to mean 'irresponsible' (ex.10, 11).

---

6) 上司のお葬式に行くのに適当な服がない。
Jooshino osooshikini ikunoni tekitoona fukuga nai.
I don't have the proper clothes to wear to my boss' funeral.

7) 彼女は子供の世話をしてくれる適当な人を探している。
Kanojowa kodomono sewao shitekureru tekitoona hitoo sagashiteiru.
She is looking for just the right person to take care of her child.

8) 疲れたら、適当に休憩をとってください。
Tsukaretara, tekitooni kyuukeio totte kudasai.
If you get tired, please rest as often as you like.

9) スープに入れる野菜は、適当な大きさに切っておいてください。
Suupuni ireru yasaiwa, tekitoona ookisani kitteoite kudasai.
Please cut the vegetables for the soup as large as you like.

10) 彼に何をきいても、適当な返事しか返ってきませんよ。
Kareni nanio kiitemo, tekitoona henjishika kaette kimasenyo.
No matter what you ask him, he only gives vague answers.

11) 試験の答えがわからないので、適当に○×をつけておいた。
Shikenno kotaega wakaranainode, tekitooni maru-batsuo tsuketeoita.
I didn't know the answers to the test questions so I just marked true or false at random.

いえ／うち

■*ie* ■*uchi*

いえ［家］ ■*ie* ■house ; family

---

①**人が住む**ための**建物**のことです（例1, 2, 3)。

A building built for the purpose of providing shelter for people (ex.1, 2, 3).

②**夫婦**や**親子**などの**人の集団**つまり**家庭**、または先祖から続いているつながりを表します（例4, 5）。

A group consisting of a married couple and children, i.e., a family, or the continuous connection between ancestors and descendants (ex.4, 5).

---

1) この家はもう古いので、あちこちいたんでいる。

Kono iewa moo furuinode, achikochi itandeiru.

This house is quite old, so there are many places in need of repair.

2) 彼は20代の若さで自分の家を建てた。

Karewa nijuudaino wakasade jibunno ieo tateta.

When he was a young man in his 20's, he built his own house.

3) 私は彼女を家まで送って行った。

Watashiwa kanojoo iemade okutteitta.

I accompanied her to her house.

4) 彼は貧しい家に生まれたが、努力して大統領になった。

Karewa mazushii ieni umaretaga, doryokushite daitooryooni natta.

Although he was born into a poor family, through great effort, he became president.

5) 私の家は、代々学者です。

Watashino iewa, daidai gakushadesu.

There have been scholars in my family for generations.

うち

■ *uchi*
■ house ; home

---

①「家」と同じように、人が住むための建物のことです。そこに**住んでいる人を含んだ言い方**です（例6, 7）。

As does *ie*, *uchi* refers to a building built as a dwelling for people, however the people who live in the building are also included in the meaning (ex.6, 7).

②自分の家や家族を表すときに使います。また、学校や会社など**自分が所属するグループ**について言うときにも使います（例8, 9, 10, 11）。「うち」のほうが「家」よりも広い意味を持ち、多く使われます。

It is also used to refer to one's own house or family. It may also refer to a group the speaker belongs to, for example a school or company (ex.8, 9, 10, 11). *Uchi* has a broader meaning than *ie*, and is more frequently used.

6) 彼女(かのじょ)は、赤(あか)い屋根(やね)の大(おお)きなうちに住(す)んでいる。
Kanojowa, akai yaneno ookina uchini sundeiru.
She lives in a big house with a red roof.

7) この辺(へん)のうちは、ほとんどが建(た)て売(う)りです。
Kono henno uchiwa, hotondoga tateuridesu.
Most of the houses in this area were ready-built.

8) 疲(つか)れたから、早(はや)くうちに帰(かえ)りたい。
Tsukaretakara, hayaku uchini kaeritai.
I'm tired, so I'd like to go home early.

9) うちは4人家族(にんかぞく)です。
Uchiwa yoninkazokudesu.
There are four people in my family.

10) あしたは一日中(いちにちじゆう)うちにいます。
Ashitawa ichinichijuu uchini imasu.
I'll be home all day tomorrow.

11) これが、うちの会社(かいしゃ)の新製品(しんせいひん)です。
Korega, uchino kaishano shinseihindesu.
This is my company's latest product.

いく／くる

■*iku* ■*kuru*

いく［行(い)く］ ■*iku* ■to go

現在(げんざい)いる所(ところ)から、**別(べつ)の所(ところ)に移動(いどう)**する、**進(すす)むこと**です（例(れい)1, 2, 3, 4, 5）。例(れい)6の「うまくいく」は、ものごとが望(のぞ)ましい方向(ほうこう)に進(すす)むという意味(いみ)です。「大学(だいがく)（学校(がっこう)）に行(い)く」には、例(れい)4のように通学(つうがく)するという意味(いみ)と、例(れい)5のように進学(しんがく)するの2(ふた)

つの意味があります。

To move or advance from a present position to another (ex.1, 2, 3, 4, 5). In Example 6 it is used to indicate that something goes according to plan. In the expression *daigaku* (*gakkoo*) *ni iku* 'go to university (school)', it can mean either 'commute' (ex.4), or 'attend' (ex.5).

---

1) これから私は、友だちを迎えに東京駅へ行きます。
Korekara watashiwa, tomodachio mukaeni Tookyooekie ikimasu.
I'm going to Tokyo station to meet my friend now.

2) きょうは天気がいいので、散歩に行こうと思います。
Kyoowa tenkiga iinode, sanponi ikooto omoimasu.
Since it's a nice day, I think I'll go for a walk.

3) たまには、私もコンサートに行きたい。
Tamaniwa, watashimo konsaatoni ikitai.
I'd like to go to a concert once in a while, too.

4) きょうは、2時までに大学へ行かなくてはならない。
Kyoowa nijimadeni daigakue ikanakutewa naranai.
(I) have to go to school by two o'clock today.

5) 私の娘は、東京の大学に行きたがっている。
Watashino musumewa, Tookyoono daigakuni ikitagatteiru.
My daughter wants to go to a university in Tokyo.

6) 兄はこのごろ、仕事がうまくいかなくてイライラしている。
Aniwa konogoro, shigotoga umaku ikanakute irairashiteiru.
My (elder) brother is irritable these days because his job isn't going so well.

くる［来る］ ■ *kuru* ■ to come

①人やものが移動するのを、迎える側（こちら）からとらえた言い方です。人が、ある場所に到着した場合には、「（ここに）来た」と、来た人自身も使います（例7, 8, 9）。

This is an expression used by someone receiving or meeting a person or object which is moving toward them. When someone has arrived someplace, the arriving person may use *kuru* with respect to himself, as in (*koko ni*) *kita*

('I'm here' or 'I came here') (ex.7, 8, 9).

②**季節がめぐってき**たり、**何かをする時期になる**ことです（例10, 11)。

It is also used to show the coming of a season or the appropriate time for doing something (ex.10, 11).

---

7) 来月、中国からペンフレンドが来ます。

Raigetsu, Chuugokukara penfurendoga kimasu.
My pen-pal from China is coming next month.

8) A：あした、私のうちに来ませんか。

B：はい、よろこんで。

A： *Ashita, watashino uchini kimasenka?*
Won't you come over to my house tomorrow?
B： *Hai, yorokonde.* Oh, I'd be happy to.

9) 明るいうちに来るつもりだったのに、遅くなってごめんなさい。

Akarui uchini kuru tsumoridattanoni, osokunatte gomennasai.
(I'm) sorry I'm late. I had planned to come while it was still light out.

10) 春が来た。

Haruga kita. Spring has come.

11) この研究は、いつかきっと認められる日が来るだろう。

Kono kenkyuuwa, itsuka kitto mitomerareru higa kurudaroo.
The day when this research is recognized will certainly come.

いくら~ても／どんなに~ても

■ *ikura~temo* ■ *donna ni~temo*

いくら~ても

■ *ikura~temo*
■ no matter how much (many...)

「~」部分のことがらが、「~ても」に続くことがらに何の影響も与えないというとき使います。この場合の「いくら」は「~」の度合いの高さを強調し、**数量や回数の多さに限界がないほどだ**という意味を表します（例1, 2, 3, 4, 5)。

This expression carries the connotation that the event or state named after *ikura* has no influence on the event or condition mentioned following *～te mo*. In this case, *ikura* is used for emphasis, and indicates that the amount, volume, or number of times referred to is seemingly infinite (ex.1, 2, 3, 4, 5).

1) いくら考えても、この問題は解けない。
Ikura kangaetemo, kono mondaiwa tokenai.
However much I think about this problem, I can't solve it.

2) 私がいくら言っても、彼はたばこをやめようとしない。
Watashiga ikura ittemo, karewa tabakoo yameyooto shinai.
He won't even try to stop smoking, no matter how much I ask him to.

3) 子供たちはテレビに夢中で、いくら呼んでも返事もしない。
Kodomo-tachiwa terebini muchuude, ikura yondemo henjimo shinai.
The children are so absorbed in watching TV that no matter how much I call them they don't answer.

4) 彼女は、いくら食べても太らない体質だ。
Kanojowa, ikura tabetemo futoranai taishitsuda.
She never gets fat, no matter how much she eats.

5) いくら若くても、３日も続けて徹夜をしたら体に毒です。
Ikura wakakutemo, mikkamo tsuzukete tetsuyao shitara karadani dokudesu.
No matter how young you are, going three days without sleep is bad for you.

どんなに～ても

■ *donna ni～temo*
■ no matter how

「いくら～ても」と同じように、「～」の度合いの高さを強調します。ほとんど、同じ意味で使いますが、「いくら」が量や数・回数の多さを表すのに対し、「どんなに」は、**方法や手段などの種類の多さを、より強く表します**。したがって、「いくら言っても聞かない」は何度も言ったのに、という意味で、「どんなに言っても……」は、強く言ったりやさしく言ったりいろいろな言い方で言ったのに、という意味を含んでいます（例6, 7, 8, 9）。

This expression is used in nearly the same way as *ikura ～temo*, i.e., to emphasize a high degree or amount. However, *donna ni* denotes that a great variety of different methods or means is used in attempting to do something, while *ikura* refers more to the large amount or high number of times. An example of this difference may be ; *ikura ittemo kikanai*, which indicates that the speaker has said the same thing many times without result, and *donna ni ittemo...* which suggests that the speaker has tried various ways of speaking (i.e., strongly, politely, etc.)(ex.6, 7, 8, 9).

---

6) どんなに捜(さが)しても、失(な)くしたかぎは出(で)てこなかった。

Donnani sagashitemo, nakushita kagiwa detekonakatta.
I couldn't find the key I lost, no matter where I looked.

7) 私(わたし)は、朝(あさ)どんなに忙(いそが)しくても、新聞(しんぶん)の見出(みだ)しには目(め)を通(とお)す。

Watashiwa, asa donnani isogashikutemo, shinbunno midashiniwa meo toosu.
No matter how busy I am in the morning, I always at least read the newspaper headlines.

8) 私(わたし)がどんなに説明(せつめい)しても、だれも分(わ)かってはくれなかった。

Watashiga donnani setsumeishitemo, daremo wakattewa kurenakatta.
No matter how I tried to explain it, nobody seemed to understand.

9) どんなになだめても、赤(あか)ん坊(ぼう)は泣(な)きやもうとしなかった。

Donnani nadametemo, akanboowa nakiyamooto shinakatta.
No matter how I tried to soothe the baby, he wouldn't stop crying.

いじめる／いびる／ぎゃくたいする

■ *ijimeru* ■ *ibiru* ■ *gyakutai suru*

いじめる

■ *ijimeru*
■ to tease ; to pick on

力(ちから)の強(つよ)いものが弱(よわ)いものに対(たい)して、**いやがることをわざとする**ことです。「いびる」「虐待(ぎゃくたい)する」より行(おこな)いが単純(たんじゅん)で、子供(こども)っぽいとき使(つか)います（例(れい)1, 2, 3, 4)。

To intentionally cause discomfort to a person in a weaker position. It has a more simplistic meaning than *ibiru* or *gyakutai suru*, and is therefore used to describe childish or mischievous actions (ex.1, 2, 3, 4).

---

1) 動物(どうぶつ)をいじめてはいけません。

Doobutsuo ijimetewa ikemasen.

(You) must not tease animals.

2) 親(おや)：どうしたの。どうして泣(な)いているの。

子(こ)：太郎兄(たろうにい)ちゃんがいじめたの。

Oya : *Dooshitano? Dooshite naiteiruno?*
Parent : What's wrong? Why are you crying?
Ko : *Taroo-niichanga ijimetano.*
Child : Taroo (older brother) was mean to me.

3) 子供(こども)のころ、君(きみ)には、よくいじめられたよ。

Kodomono koro, kiminiwa, yoku ijimeraretayo.
When we were children, you used to pick on me a lot, you know.

4) 私(わたし)は小(ちい)さいころ、弟(おとうと)をいじめてよく母(はは)にしかられた。

Watashiwa chiisaikoro, otooto-o ijimete yoku hahani shikarareta.
When I was a child, I was often scolded by my mother for teasing my little brother.

いびる

■ *ibiru*
■ to be mean to ; to be hard on 

悪意(あくい)**が強**(つよ)**く**こもっていて、「いじめる」より**陰湿**(いんしつ)**さが増**(ま)**し**、言葉(ことば)や行動(こうどう)で、意地悪(いじわる)なことをする場合(ばあい)に使(つか)います。往々(おうおう)にして1回限(かいかぎ)りではありません(例(れい)5, 6, 7)。

This expression implies a stronger feeling of ill-will than *ijimeru*, and is used when one uses words or actions of malice. It refers to frequent, recurring behavior, not to just a single instance (ex.5, 6, 7).

---

5) 古(ふる)い社員(しやいん)が新入社員(しんにゆうしやいん)をいびった。

Furui shainga shinnyuushain-o ibitta.
The older employee was being hard on the new employee.

6) むかしの嫁(よめ)は、よく姑(しゆうとめ)にいびられたそうだ。

Mukashino yomewa, yoku shuutomeni ibiraretasooda.
I've heard that, a long time ago, wives were often treated cruelly by their mothers-in-law.

7) A：新入社員(しんにゆうしやいん)をいびるのは、やめなさいよ。

B：あら、礼儀(れいぎ)を教(おし)えているだけよ。

A : *Shinnyuushain-o ibirunowa, yamenasaiyo.*
Stop being mean to the new employees.

B： *Ara, reigio oshieteirudakeyo.*
Huh? I'm only teaching them some manners.

ぎゃくたいする［虐待する］ ■ *gyakutai suru* ■ to mistreat

強い立場の人が弱い人に暴力をふるったり、精神的や肉体的に痛めつけ、苦しめる場合に使います。時間も短い時間でなく、長い時間にわたることが多いです。正当な扱いをしないという意味を含みます（例8, 9, 10）。

This verb indicates that a person in a position of power uses violence against, causes physical or psychological injuries, or in other ways causes suffering to a weaker person. It usually describes action that occurs over a long period of time, and implies improper or unconventional treatment (ex.8, 9, 10).

8) 幼児を虐待することは、重大な罪です。
Yoojio gyakutaisurukotowa, juudaina tsumidesu.
It is a serious crime to mistreat young children.

9) 戦後、彼は囚人を虐待した罪でさばかれた。
Sengo, karewa shuujin-o gyakutaishita tsumide sabakareta.
After the war, he was tried for torturing prisoners.

10) 幼いころ、虐待されたことは、いつまでも心の傷として残る。
Osanai koro, gyakutaisareta kotowa, itsumademo kokorono kizutoshite nokoru.
When one is abused as a child, the psychological injuries remain forever.

お兄ちゃんて誰？

ガードナー夫人の家の隣に、森さん一家が住んでいます。ご主人、奥さん、ご主人の父親、15歳の長男、そして10歳の次男の5人家族です。ガードナー夫人は森夫人とよくおし

ゃべりをしますが、ときどき森夫人が誰のことを言っているのか、わからなくなることがあります。森夫人はこんなふうに言ったのです。「うちのお父さん、仕事だ、つき合いだって毎晩遅いのよ。おじいちゃんはダンス教室に通っているの。お兄ちゃんはもうすぐ高校入試なのに、ちっとも勉強しなくて…」森家のお父さんは、森氏の父親です。でも彼はもう引退しているはずですが…。それに夫人のお兄さんが中学生？　夫人のおじいさんといえば何歳なのでしょう?!　ガードナー夫人は混乱してしまいました。

では説明しましょう。日本では、家族の中で一番年下の者から見た呼び方で、家族を呼ぶことが多いのです。ですから「お父さん」は夫である森氏を、また「おじいちゃん」は森氏の父親を、そして「お兄ちゃん」は次男のお兄ちゃんにあたる長男を指します。ほんとうはこのような呼び方を他人の前でするのはおかしいのですが、親しい人の前では使ってしまうことが多いのです。

Who is *oniichan*[1]?

The Mori family lives next to Mrs. Gardner's house. There are five people in the family: Mr. and Mrs. Mori, Mr. Mori's father, their eldest son who is 15 years old, and their younger son who is 10 years old. Mrs. Gardner often chats with Mrs. Mori, but sometimes she gets confused about whom Mrs. Mori is talking. For example, Mrs. Mori may say, "*Otoosan* comes back late everyday because work and work related socializing keeps him late. *Ojiichan* goes to dance class. *Oniichan* never studies although the high school entrance examination is coming up soon." The Mori family's *otoosan* is Mr. Mori's father, but supposedly he has already retired. Is Mrs. Mori's *oniisan* a junior high school student? How old could Mrs. Mori's *ojiisan* be ?! All of this leaves Mrs. Gardner completely confused.

In Japan, it is very common to address or refer to family members from the point of view of the youngest member. Therefore, *otoosan* refers to Mr. Mori, her husband. *Ojiichan* refers to Mr. Mori's father and *Oniichan* is their eldest son. Actually, it is a little awkward to use this form of address in front of those outside of the family, but it is often used when speaking to someone who is close to the speaker, like a close friend or neighbor.

[1] *older brother or son*

いそがしい／せわしい／あわただしい

■ *isogashii* ■ *sewashii* ■ *awatadashii*

いそがしい［忙しい］ ■ *isogashii* ■ busy ◎

しなければならないことがたくさんあって、**休む暇がない**ことです（例1, 2, 3, 4）。

Isogashii indicates that there are so many things one must do that there is no time to relax (ex.1, 2, 3, 4).

1）私の仕事は、月曜日が特に忙しい。
Watashino shigotowa, getsuyoobiga tokuni isogashii.
My job is especially busy on Mondays.

2）あしたの旅行の仕度で忙しい。
Ashitano ryokoono shitakude isogashii.
(I'm) busy preparing for tomorrow's trip.

3）彼はどんなに忙しくても疲れた顔は見せない。
Karewa donnani isogashikutemo tsukareta kaowa misenai.
No matter how busy he is, he never shows his exhaustion.

4）きょうは目が回るほど忙しかった。
Kyoowa mega mawaruhodo isogashikatta.
(I) was so busy today, I felt as if my head was spinning. (I was as busy as a bee today.)

せわしい 

■ *sewashii*
■ busy ; restless

次々にいろいろなことが起こったり、ものごとの動き、**変化が激しく落ち着かない**ことです（例5, 6, 7)。少し強めた言い方ですが、「せわしない」も同じように使います（例８）。

This expresses a condition of restlessness due to an occurrence of events one after another, or a sudden change in things (ex.5, 6, 7). *Sewashinai* may be used in the same way as *sewashii*, but is a slightly stronger expression (ex.8).

5) さっきから立ったり座ったり、あなたは全くせわしい人だ。
Sakkikara tattari suwattari, anatawa mattaku sewashii hitoda.
You've been standing up and sitting down constantly. You sure are a fidgety person.

6) 年の暮れは何かとせわしい。
Toshino kurewa nanikato sewashii.
The end of the year is very busy in many respects.

7) ぼくには都会の生活はせわしすぎる。
Bokuniwa tokaino seikatsuwa sewashisugiru.
Life in the city is too hectic for me.

8) そんなにせわしなく動き回らないで、少しじっとしていなさい。
Sonnani sewashinaku ugokimawaranaide, sukoshi jitto shiteinasai.
Stop fidgeting around and be still for a while!

あわただしい 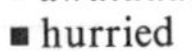 

■ *awatadashii*
■ hurried

さしせまった感じや追い立てられるような忙しさを表します（例9, 10)。また何か重大なことが起きて人の出入りが激しく**落ち着かないようす**も表し、緊張感があります（例11, 12)。

Awatadashii expresses a hurried state due to pressing circumstances or feelings of urgency (ex.9, 10). It may also indicate that, because a serious event has occured, there is an unsettled situation in which people are frantically rushing in and out (ex. 11, 12).

9) 閉店まぎわのデパートで、勤め帰りの人があわただしく買い物をしていく。

Heiten-magiwano depaatode, tsutomegaerino hitoga awatadashiku kaimonoo shiteiku.
Just before closing, the department store becomes full of people who have stopped on their way home from work to hurriedly shop.

10) 彼はうちに来て15分もすると、これからアルバイトがあるからといってあわただしく帰っていった。
Karewa uchini kite juugofunmo suruto, korekara arubaitoga arukarato itte awatadashiku kaetteitta.
He came over to visit me, but after just 15 minutes he rushed out, saying he had to do his part-time job.

11) 急病人が運びこまれたので、病院の中はあわただしい空気に包まれた。
Kyuubyooninga hakobikomareta-node, byooinno nakawa awatadashii kuukini tsutsumareta.
Because a seriously ill patient was brought in, the mood in the hospital suddenly became very hectic.

12) 一夜明けて、事故の現場はあわただしい朝をむかえた。
Ichiya akete, jikono genbawa awatadashii asao mukaeta.
When dawn broke, the scene of the accident became chaotic.

いそぐ／あわてる／あせる

■ *isogu* ■ *awateru* ■ *aseru*

いそぐ［急ぐ］ ■ *isogu* ■ to hurry

短い時間でものごとをしよう、早く終わらせようとするとき使います。「あわてる」「あせる」は、無意識的ですが「急ぐ」は**意識的**、つまり自分でそうしようと考えて行動するとき使います（例1, 2, 3）。
To try to finish something in a short period of time or quickly; *awateru* and *aseru* are unconsciously done, but *isogu* is intentional (ex.1, 2, 3).

1) 急げば、最終電車に間にあう。
Isogeba, saishuudenshani maniau.
If (you) hurry, you'll be able to catch the last train.

2) 7時から見たい番組があるので、急いで帰ろう。
じ　み　ばんぐみ　いそ　かえ
Shichijikara mitai bangumiga arunode, isoide kaeroo.
The TV program (I) want to see starts at seven, so I guess I'll hurry on home.

3) 横断歩道の途中で信号が黄色に変わったので、急いで渡った。
おうだんほどう　とちゅう　しんごう　きいろ　か　いそ　わた
Oodanhodoono tochuude shingooga kiironi kawattanode, isoide watatta.
The signal turned yellow while (I) was still in the crosswalk, so I hurried across.

あわてる

■ *awateru*
■ to panic ; to get flustered ; to rush 

思いもよらないことが起きてしまい、どうしようかとうろたえたり**冷静さを欠いて行動**するというとき使います。**気持ちが混乱**したとき使います（例4, 5, 6, 7)。
おも　お　れいせい　か　こうどう　つか　きも　こんらん　つか　れい

Awateru indicates that because something unexpected happened one is upset and acts in confusion, wondering what he should do (ex.4, 5, 6, 7).

4) 家にさいふを忘れて、あわてて取りにもどった。
いえ　わす　と
Ieni saifuo wasurete, awatete torini modotta.
(I) left my wallet at home, so I frantically hurried back to get it.

5) 地震のとき、あわてて外に飛び出すのは危険だ。
じしん　そと　と　だ　きけん
Jishinno toki, awatete sotoni tobidasunowa kikenda.
In an earthquake, it's dangerous to frantically rush outside.

6) パスポートを落としたときは、さすがにあわてた。
お
Pasupootoo otoshita tokiwa, sasugani awateta.
When (I) lost my passport, I of course started to panic.

7) 彼女は、どんなときにもあわてないで、落ち着いた行動がとれる人です。
かのじょ　お　つ　こうどう　ひと
Kanojowa, donna tokinimo awatenaide, ochitsuita koodooga toreru hitodesu.
She is a person who will act very calmly without panicking in any situation.

あせる

■ *aseru*
■ to hurry ; to fret 

思うようにものごとが進まないのに、**時間が足りなかったり、緊張したり**して
おも　すす　じかん　た　きんちょう

心理的な圧力を強く感じるとき使います。「できなかったらどうしよう……」「うまくいかなかったらどうしよう……」という不安も含んでいます（例8, 9, 10）。

To feel nervousness or pressure because things are not progressing as expected or there is not enough time. Anxieties such as 'What shall I do if I cannot do this?' and 'What shall I do if things do not go smoothly?' are included (ex.8, 9, 10).

8) テストの時、どんどん時間が過ぎていくのに、問題が解けなくてあせった。
Tesutono toki, dondon jikanga sugiteikunoni, mondaiga tokenakute asetta.
On the last test, (I) had to hurry because time was slipping by and there were still some questions I hadn't answered.

9) まだ若いんだから、あせらないで本当に進みたい道をみつけなさい。
Mada wakaindakara, aseranaide hontooni susumitai michio mitsukenasai.
(You) are still young, so don't rush. Find the course you really want to take in life.

10) 会議に遅れそうになってあせって家をとび出したら、大事な書類を忘れた。
Kaigini okuresooninatte asette ieo tobidashitara, daijina shoruio wasureta.
(I) rushed out of the house thinking that I might be late for the meeting, and left some important documents behind.

いたい／うずく

■ *itai* ■ *uzuku*

いたい［痛い］ ■ *itai* ■ painful ; sore 大

①けが・病気または何かの原因で、体に**痛みを感じるようす**を表すとき使います。感じたその瞬間に思わず叫んでしまうようなときにも、続けて痛いときにも使います（例1, 2, 3）。

Itai expresses physical pain due to injury, sickness, or other causes. It may be shouted involuntarily in moments of brief pain, or used to describe continuing pain (ex.1, 2, 3).

②**精神的に苦しさ**を感じたり、**困った**ということを表すとき使います（例4, 5）。

例6は、「何の影響もない」という意味です。

It is also used to express mental pain or feelings of difficulty (ex.4, 5). The expression in Example 6 means 'to have no influence or effect on'.

---

1) 痛い。ドアに指をはさんじゃった。
Itai! Doani yubio hasanjatta.
Ouch! My finger got caught in the door!

2) ゆうべお酒を飲みすぎて、今日は頭が痛い。
Yuube osakeo nomisugite, kyoowa atamaga itai.
(I) had too much to drink yesterday, and today I have a headache.

3) 歯が痛くなったら、すぐに歯医者に行ったほうがいい。
Haga itakunattara, suguni haishani itta hooga ii.
If (you) get a toothache you should go to the dentist right away.

4) 給料日前の１万円の出費は痛い。
Kyuuryoobi maeno ichiman-enno shuppiwa itai.
A 10,000 yen expense just before payday hurts.

5) 娘が一流大学に合格したのはうれしいけれど、高い入学金を払わなければならないと思うと、頭が痛い。
Musumega ichiryuu-daigakuni gookaku-shitanowa ureshiikeredo, takai nyuugakukin-o harawanakereba-naranaito omouto, atamaga itai.
I'm happy my daughter was accepted by a first-rate university, but it's painful to think of the expensive matriculation fee I'll have to pay.

6) そんなこと、痛くもかゆくもない。
Sonna koto, itakumo kayukumo nai.
I'm not the least bit concerned about that.

うずく ■*uzuku* ■to ache 大

①「痛さ」を、もっと**詳しく**どんなふうに「痛い」のか**説明する言い方**です。傷口などが脈を打つように続けてずきずき痛むようすを表すとき使います。瞬間的な痛さには使いません（例7, 8, 9）。

Uzuku is used to describe physical pain in a more detailed manner than *itai,* as in sensations of throbbing or aching. It is not used for momentary pain (ex.7, 8, 9).

②過去の心の傷（悪いことをしてしまった・悲しかった……など）を思い出して後悔したり、悲しみがもう一度もどってくる気持ちを表すとき使います（例10）。
It is also used when remembering feelings of regret over past actions, or when feelings of sadness come over one once again (ex.10).

7) 一晩中、歯がうずいてしかたがなかった。
Hitobanjuu, haga uzuite shikataga nakatta.
(My) tooth ached unbearably all night long.

8) 傷口が化膿したらしく、ずきずきとうずく。
Kizuguchiga kanooshitarashiku, zukizukito uzuku.
The wound aches terribly and appears to have festered.

9) 雨の日には、昔骨折した足がうずく。
Amenohiniwa, mukashi kossetsushita ashiga uzuku.
The leg that (I) broke long ago aches on rainy days.

10) あんなにいい人を裏切ってしまって、今も心がうずく。
Annani ii hitoo uragitteshimatte, imamo kokoroga uzuku.
Even now, my heart aches when (I) think of how I betrayed that kind person.

いちいち／ひとつひとつ

■ *ichiichi* ■ *hitotsu hitotsu*

いちいち

■ *ichiichi*
■ one by one ; in detail 

人のすることやことがらのそれぞれに、**もれなく対応したり、とりあげたりする**ようすを表すとき使います。面倒でわずらわしい・うるさくて迷惑だ、などの感じを含みます（例1, 2, 3, 4）。
Ichiichi is used to denote a manner of doing something in detail or paying attention to every individual thing or every single action that someone does. It expresses a feeling on the part of the speaker of trouble or annoyance, or of being inconvenienced or bothered (ex.1, 2, 3, 4).

1) お母さんたら、私のすることに、いちいちうるさいんだから。
Okaasantara, watashino suru kotoni, ichiichi urusaindakara!
Mother! You always find fault with everything I do!

2) 子供がすることに、いちいち注意してもはじまらない。
Kodomoga suru kotoni, ichiichi chuuishitemo hajimaranai.
Nagging children over everything they do is useless.

3) 手紙を出す度に、いちいち切手を買うのは面倒だからまとめて買っておこう。
Tegamio dasu tabini, ichiichi kitteo kaunowa mendoodakara matomete katteo-koo.
It's troublesome to buy a postage stamp each time (I) send a letter, so I'll buy a bunch now (and keep them on hand).

4) ハイジャック防止のため、空港では、乗客の荷物をいちいち検査した。
Haijakku booshino tame, kuukoodewa, jookyakuno nimotsuo ichiichi kensa-shita.
At the airport, each piece of the passengers' luggage was inspected for the purpose of preventing hijacking.

ひとつひとつ［一つ一つ］

■ *hitotsu hitotsu*
■ one by one ; each

もののや**ことがらのそれぞれについて、とりあげたり扱ったりする**ようすを表すときに使います(例5, 6, 7, 8)。**細かい・ていねいだ**という感じを含みます。
This expression denotes a manner of doing something in which one deals with or refers to every individual thing or detail (ex.5, 6, 7, 8). It includes a sense of polite and careful attention to detail.

---

5) 小さな工場では、できた人形を一つ一つ、人の手で紙に包んでいた。
Chiisana koobadewa, dekita ningyoo-o hitotsuhitotsu, hitono tede kamini tsu-tsundeita.
In the small factory, they were hand-wrapping the finished dolls individu-ally in paper.

6) 検事は、証拠を一つ一つあげて容疑者にせまった。
Kenjiwa, shookoo hitotsuhitotsu agete yoogishani sematta.
The prosecutor closed in on the suspect by presenting the evidence one by one.

7) 彼女は、発掘された土器のかけらを一つ一つ合わせて、もとどおりにした。
Kanojowa, hakkutsusareta dokino kakerao hitotsuhitotsu awasete, moto doorini shita.
She restored a broken piece of pottery found during the excavation by putting it back together piece by piece.

8) ロンドンで過ごした学生時代の一つ一つのことが、良い思い出だ。
Londonde sugoshita gakuseijidaino hitotsuhitotsuno kotoga, yoi omoideda.
Every little thing (I) experienced during my school days spent in London is a fond memory.

いちおう／とりあえず

■ *ichiou* ■ *toriaezu*

いちおう［一応］ ■ *ichiou* ■ just in case ; for the time being

---

①念のため、用心のためというとき使います（例１）。

Ichiou is used to indicate that one does something in case of an eventuality or to be cautious (ex.1).

②十分ではないけれど表面上の最低基準だけは満たす、つまり、**ひととおりなんとかする・なる**というとき使います（例2, 3, 4, 5, 6, 7）。

It also indicates that, although it may not be enough, at least basic requirements or expectations will be fulfilled (ex.2, 3, 4, 5, 6, 7).

---

1) 雨が降るかどうかわからないけれど、いちおう傘を持っていこう。
Amega furuka dooka wakaranaikeredo, ichioo kasao motteikoo.
(I) don't know whether it will rain or not, but I will take my umbrella just in case.

2) あなたの言い分もいちおうわかりました。
Anatano iibunmo ichioo wakarimashita.
(I) basically understand what you're saying.

3) 熱は、いちおう下がりました。
Netsuwa, ichioo sagarimashita.

(His) fever has come down for the time being.

4) いちおう手当(てあ)てはしておきましたが、まだ痛(いた)むようなら、あした また病院(びょういん)に来(き)てください。

Ichioo teatewa shiteokimashitaga, mada itamuyoonara, ashita mata byooinni kitekudasai.

(We've) given the wound temporary treatment, but if it continues to hurt, please come back to the hospital tomorrow.

5) こんどの旅行(りょこう)にいくらぐらいかかるか、いちおう計算(けいさん)してみました。

Kondono ryokooni ikuragurai kakaruka, ichioo keisan-shitemimashita.

(I've) figured out about how much I think we will need for this trip.

6) 新(あたら)しい家(いえ)も、いちおうの形(かたち)はできてきました。

Atarashii iemo, ichioono katachiwa dekitekimashita.

You can tell more or less how the new house will look.

7) 彼(かれ)には、あんなにお世話(せわ)になったのだから、いちおうのあいさつは、しておくべきです。

Kareniwa, annani osewani nattanodakara, ichioono aisatsuwa, shiteokubeki-desu.

Since he took care of you so well, you should at least express your appreciation to him.

とりあえず

■ *toriaezu*
■ for the time being 

不十分(ふじゅうぶん)ではあるけれど、時間(じかん)がないので**仮(かり)にそうしておく**・こまかいことにとらわれず**今必要(いまひつよう)なことだけを優先(ゆうせん)**しておくというとき、ほかにやることはあるのだけれど、今(いま)やれること・すぐできることを先(さき)にしておくという意味(いみ)のとき使(つか)います（例(れい)8, 9, 10)。

This is used to indicate that, because of a lack of time, the speaker will perform only the most important tasks at hand or provide only what resources are available at present, leaving the rest to be completed later (ex.8, 9, 10).

---

8) 窓(まど)ガラスに、ひびが入(はい)ってしまった。とりあえずテープではっておこう。

Madogarasuni, hibiga haitteshimatta. Toriaezu teepude hatteokoo.

The window pane has a crack. (I'll) tape it up for the time being.

9) 食事(しょくじ)のしたくができるまで、とりあえずビールでもいかがですか。

Shokujino shitakuga dekirumade, toriaezu biirudemo ikagadesuka?
Would (you) like to have some beer while you are waiting for the meal?

10) きょうはそんなにお金を持っていないけれど、とりあえず2万円なら貸してあげられます。

Kyoowa sonnani okaneo motteinaikeredo, toriaezu niman-ennara kashite-ageraremasu.
Although (I) don't have that much money with me today, I can lend you ¥20,000 for now.

いちじ／ひととき／いっこく

■ *ichiji* ■ *hitotoki* ■ *ikkoku*

いちじ［一時］

■ *ichiji*
■ a brief period ; once 

ほんの少しの時間、少しの間を表します。数分から、かつて一時期という意味の数年まで幅広く使います（例1, 2, 3, 4）。例5, 6は、「その場だけの」という意味です。

Ichiji represents a short period of time. The time referred to may range from a few minutes to several years when referring to the past (ex.1, 2, 3, 4). In Examples 5 and 6, it means 'at that time', or 'at that place'.

1) きょうの関東地方の天気は、くもり一時雨です。

Kyoono Kantoochihoono tenkiwa, kumori-ichiji-amedesu.
The weather today in the Kanto plain will be cloudy with periods of rain.

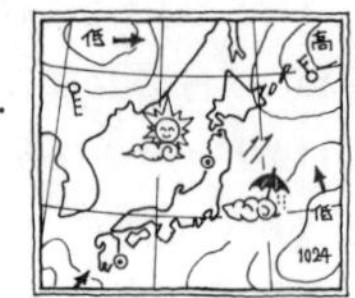

2) 映画館で火事があり、一時大変な騒ぎになった。

Eigakande kajiga ari, ichiji taihenna sawagini natta.
A fire broke out in the movie theater, and there was a brief moment of panic.

3) 一時はかなり心配したが、彼の病気は日に日によくなってきている。

Ichijiwa kanari shinpaishitaga, kareno byookiwa hinihini yokunattekiteiru.
We were briefly worried about his illness, but his condition is improving day by day.

4) 私は一時、サッカーに夢中だった。
Watashiwa ichiji, sakkaani muchuudatta.
I was once very enthusiastic about soccer.

5) 私は、あのとき一時の感情で会社を辞めてしまったことを、今でも後悔している。
Watashiwa, ano toki ichijino kanjoode kaishao yameteshimatta kotoo, imademo kookaishiteiru.
Even now I regret that I quit my job on an impulse.

6) 息子が司法試験を受けるというんだが、どうせ一時の気まぐれだろう。
Musukoga shihooshiken-o ukeruto yuundaga, doose ichijino kimaguredaroo.
My son says he wants to take the Bar exam, but I'm sure this will turn out to be another of his momentary whims.

ひととき ■*hitotoki* ■a brief time

ある**短い**時間を指します。ほとんどの場合「楽しい」などのことばと共に使い、**落ち着いた、おだやかな時間**です（例7, 8, 9）。

Hitotoki points out a certain short period of time. In most cases, it is used together with words like *tanoshii* to describe a relaxed or quiet period (ex.7, 8, 9).

---

7) 食後のひとときは、雑誌を見たり、レコードを聞いたりして過ごす。
Shokugono hitotokiwa, zasshio mitari, rekoodoo kiitarishite sugosu.
After eating, (I) spend time doing things like reading magazines or listening to music.

8) ゆうべ、学生時代の友人と食事をしながら、思い出話をした。本当に楽しいひとときだった。
Yuube, gakuseijidaino yuujinto shokujio shinagara, omoidebanashio shita. Hontooni tanoshii hitotokidatta.
Last night (I) had dinner with an old school friend and talked about old times. It was a really enjoyable time.

9) 都会の生活に疲れた人々が、ひとときの安らぎを求めて、この温泉場にやってくる。
Tokaino seikatsuni tsukareta hitobitoga, hitotokino yasuragio motomete, kono onsenbani yattekuru.

People who are tired of life in the city often come to this hot-spring resort to calm their nerves.

いっこく［一刻］ ■*ikkoku* ■a short time

過ぎていく時間の中の、**ほんのわずかの時**を表します。ほとんどが慣用句的に使い、**文語的**ないい方です（例10, 11, 12）。

This word refers to an extremely short period in time that is singled out from the flow of time. It is generally used in idiomatic expressions found in written language (ex.10, 11, 12).

10) このニュースを、一刻も早く家族に知らせたい。

Kono nyuusuo, ikkokumo hayaku kazokuni shirasetai.

(I) want to let my family know of this news as soon as possible.

11) 火事の消火活動は、一刻を争う。

Kajino shooka-katsudoowa, ikkokuo arasou.

Fighting fires is a race against time.

12) これ以上手当てが遅れたら、病人の命にかかわる。もう一刻の猶予もならない。

Kore ijoo teatega okuretara, byooninno inochini kakawaru. Moo ikkokuno yuuyomo naranai.

If we wait any longer the patient will die. We cannot delay even a second.

いちだんと／いっそう／ひときわ

■*ichidanto* ■*issou* ■*hitokiwa*

いちだんと［一段と］ ■*ichidanto* ■(a step) further ; greater

ものごとの**程度や状態が**徐々にではなく、階段を１段のぼるように**急に大きく変わって**、今までとはあきらかにちがうとき使います（例1, 2, 3, 4, 5）。

This expression is used to indicate that the degree or state of something undergoes a sudden and great change, which makes it as noticeably different from its preceding state as stepping up one step of a stairway. Thus, it is not used to refer to gradual change (ex.1, 2, 3, 4, 5).

1) 彼は、最近ピアノがいちだんとじょうずになった。
Karewa, saikin pianoga ichidanto joozuni natta.
Recently, his piano playing has improved a lot.

2) 新しいスーツを着た彼はいちだんと立派に見えた。
Atarashii suutsuo kita karewa ichidanto rippani mieta.
He looked all the more splendid in his new suit.

3) 大陸からの寒気団の影響で、いちだんと冷えこみがきびしくなる。
Tairikukarano kankidanno eikyoode, ichidanto hiekomiga kibishikunaru.
Due to the effects of the cold front (moving in) from the continent, it will become much colder.

4) 今度出たビールはいちだんと味がいい。
Kondo deta biiruwa ichidanto ajiga ii.
The new beer that has just come out (on the market) tastes much better (than the others).

5) 彼は演説の途中で、いちだんと声をはりあげた。
Karewa enzetsuno tochuude, ichidanto koeo hariageta.
In the middle of his speech he suddenly raised his voice a notch.

いっそう［一層］

■*issou*
■all the more

たとえば、「改良をして味が良くなる・日がたつにつれて暖かくなる」など、ある状態が加わったり、進んだりすることによって、**ものごとの程度が今まで以上になる**とき使います（例6, 7, 8）。「いちだんと」のように「急に・大きく変わる」という点ではなく、「ますます・もっと程度が上がる」ところに重点があります。「よりいっそう」は強調した使い方です（例9）。

Issou denotes that there is an increase or change in the degree of something above and beyond its current state, which is brought about by some additional circumstance or by (natural) progression, as for example, 'it will taste better (if you improve the recipe)', or 'it gets warmer (as the days pass)' (ex.6, 7, 8). The point is not that there is suddenly a great change, but instead that there is a gradual and continuing increase in degree. *Yori issou* is the emphatic form of *issou* (ex.9).

6) 雨は夜になって、いっそう激しさを増した。
Amewa yoruni natte, issoo hageshisao mashita.
After nightfall, the rain became even more violent.

7) すいかは、冷やすといっそうおいしくなる。
Suikawa, hiyasuto issoo oishiku naru.
Watermelon tastes that much better when it's chilled.

8) このひどい暑さで、水不足はいっそう深刻な問題となった。
Kono hidoi atsusade, mizubusokuwa issoo shinkokuna mondaito natta.
Because of this terrible heat, the water shortage has become an even more serious problem.

9) 一流の芸術家になるためには、よりいっそう努力しなければならない。
Ichiryuuno geijutsukani naru tameniwa, yoriissoo doryoku-shinakereba naranai.
If (you) want to be a first-class artist, you must work harder.

ひときわ

■ *hitokiwa*
■ especially ; remarkably 

同種類の集まりの中から、**特に目立つものをとりあげる**とき使います。「いちだんと」「いっそう」のように状態の変化する度合いを表すのではありません(例10, 11, 12, 13)。

Hitokiwa is used when singling out something or someone as being special from among a group of things or people of the same kind. It does not suggest any degree of change (ex.10, 11, 12, 13).

10) 学生のころから、彼はひときわ目立つ存在だった。
Gakuseino korokara, karewa hitokiwa medatsu sonzaidatta.
Ever since he was a student he has been the center of attention.

11) 彼の論文は、ひときわすぐれている。
Kareno ronbunwa, hitokiwa sugureteiru.
His paper is exceptionally good.

12) 鯨の中でも、シロナガスクジラはひときわ大きい。

Kujirano nakademo, shironagasu-kujirawa hitokiwa ookii.
Even among whales, the blue whale is exceptionally large.

13) 秋の山では、紅葉したもみじがひときわ美しい。
あき やま こうよう うつく
Akino yamadewa, kooyooshita momijiga hitokiwa utsukushii.
In autumn, the changing maple leaves in the mountains are exceptionally beautiful.

いちどに／いっぺんに

■*ichido ni* ■*ippen ni*

いちどに［一度に］ ■*ichido ni* ■at once
いちど

いろいろなことを、**まとめて1回でする**ようすを表します（例1,2,3,4)。回数が1回だということを強調しています。
かい あらわ れい かいすう かい きょうちょう

Ichido ni is used when indicating that one performs several actions at once (ex.1, 2, 3, 4). It emphasizes that the action occurs only once.

1) この洗濯機は、一度にワイシャツが20枚洗える。
せんたくき いちど まい あら
Kono sentakkiwa, ichidoni waishatsuga nijuumai araeru.
This washing machine can wash 20 dress shirts at once.

2) こんなにたくさんの荷物は、一度に運べないから、分けて運ぼう。
にもつ いちど はこ わ はこ
Konnani takusanno nimotsuwa, ichidoni hakobenaikara, wakete hakoboo.
(We) can't carry all of this stuff at once, so let's carry it a little at a time.

3) 一度に2つのことをしようとすると失敗する。
いちど ふた しっぱい
Ichidoni futatsunokotoo shiyooto suruto shippaisuru.
If (you) try to do two things at once, you'll fail.

4) 姉は、3人子供がいる人と再婚して、一度に3人の子供の母親になった。
あね にん こども ひと さいこん いちど にん こども ははおや
Anewa, san-nin kodomoga iru hitoto saikonshite, ichidoni san-ninno kodomono hahaoyani natta.
My (elder) sister got re-married to a man with three children, so she became a mother of three all at once.

いっぺんに ■*ippen ni* ■at once

「1回に」「一度に」の話しことばで、**くだけた言い方**です（例5, 6）。途中の段階や過程を飛びこえて**急に、ある状態になる**ようすを表します（例7, 8）。
Ippen ni is a more informal way of saying *ichido ni* and *ikkai ni* (ex.5, 6). It may also indicate that an intermediate stage or process is skipped and a new condition is suddenly created (ex.7, 8).

5) みんながいっぺんに言っても分からないから、1人ずつ言いなさい。
Minnaga ippenni ittemo wakaranaikara, hitorizutsu iinasai.
(I) can't understand you if you all talk at once, so speak one at a time.

6) 彼女は日曜日に、1週間分の料理をいっぺんにしてしまう。
Kanojowa nichiyoobini, isshuukan-bunno ryoorio ippenni shite shimau.
She does all of her cooking for the week on Sundays.

7) ずっと好きだった人と初めて食事に行ったら、食べ方が下品だったので、いっぺんに気持ちがさめてしまった。
Zutto sukidatta hitoto hajimete shokujini ittara, tabekataga gehindattanode, ippenni kimochiga sameteshimatta.
When (I) went out to eat for the first time with the boy I had liked for so long, I saw his awful eating habits, and my ardor suddenly cooled.

8) 彼は、初めて出した写真集で、いっぺんに有名になった。
Karewa, hajimete dashita shashinshuude, ippenni yuumeini natta.
With the first publication of a collection of his photos, he immediately became famous.

いちばん／もっとも

■*ichiban* ■*mottomo*

いちばん［一番］ ■*ichiban* ■number one ; the most ; best

①**順番・順位のあるものの、初めのもの**を指して使います（例1, 2, 3）。程

度についても、順番をつけたようにして、「いちばん寒い・いちばん大きい」などのように、「もうここから先はない・これ以上はない」という使い方をします(例4, 5)。「いちばん」は1つしかありません。

Ichiban is used when pointing out the first thing of an ordered collection of things (ex.1, 2, 3). Even when referring to degree an order is assumed, as in *ichiban samui* (the coldest), or *ichiban ookii* (the biggest), because it is implied that 'there is nothing more than or beyond this' (ex.4, 5). There is never more than one *ichiban*.

②例6, 7は、「なによりもいい」という意味です。

In Examples 6 and 7 it is used to mean 'better than anything else'.

---

1) うちでいちばん背が高いのは兄で、2番目が父です。
Uchide ichiban sega takainowa anide, nibanmega chichidesu.
The tallest member of my family is my (older) brother, and the next tallest is my father.

2) 彼は今回のテストで1番だった。
Karewa konkaino tesutode ichiban datta.
He had the best score on the last test.

3) この写真の、いちばん左に写っているのが妹です。
Kono shashinno, ichiban hidarini utsutteirunoga imootodesu.
In this picture, the person on the far left is my younger sister.

4) 琵琶湖は、日本でいちばん大きい湖です。
Biwakowa, Nihonde ichiban ookii mizuumidesu.
Lake Biwa is the largest lake in Japan.

5) うちでいちばん日当たりがいいのは、この部屋だ。
Uchide ichiban hiatariga iinowa, kono heyada.
The room that gets more sunlight than any other room in the house is this one.

6) 魚のことなら、彼に聞くのが一番だ。
Sakanano kotonara, kareni kikunoga ichibanda.
If (you) want to know about fish, the best thing you could do is ask him.

7) 星空の美しさは、何といっても冬が一番です。
Hoshizorano utsukushisawa, nanto ittemo fuyuga ichibandesu.

By far the best time to view the beauty of the night sky is in the winter.

もっとも［最も］

■ *mottomo*
■ most ; extremely 

いくつかのものごとを**比べたときに**、あることがらや状態の程度が、**それ以上のものがないほど上**だというとき使います（例8, 9, 10, 11）。「いちばん」よりも**改まった言い方**です。例12のように唯一のものを指すのではなく、かなり上の方の部類に属しているという意味で使うこともあります。

Mottomo is used when the degree or condition of something is unsurpassed when compared to several other things (ex.8, 9, 10, 11). As in Example 12, it may be used to refer to a number of things that belong to a rather high class or category, instead of a single 'best' or 'number one'. It is a more formal expression than *ichiban.*

8) きのうの台風で最も被害が大きかったのは、房総半島西岸です。
Kinoono taifuude mottomo higaiga ookikattanowa, Boosoohantoo-seigandesu.
The place most damaged in yesterday's typhoon was the west coast of the Boso Peninsula.

9) 裏切りは、人間として最も恥ずべき行為だ。
Uragiriwa, ningentoshite mottomo hazubeki kooida.
Betrayal is the most shameful act a human being can commit.

10) この製品の最もすぐれている点は、軽いことです。
Kono seihinno mottomo sugureteiru tenwa, karui kotodesu.
The best thing about this product is that it's light.

11) この作家は、今 最も注 目されている。
Kono sakkawa, ima mottomo chuumoku sareteiru.
This writer is attracting the most attention these days.

12) すし・てんぷら・すきやきは、外国人に最もよく知られている日本の食べ物です。
Sushi, tenpura, sukiyakiwa, gaikokujinni mottomo yoku shirareteiru Nihonno tabemonodesu.
Sushi, *tempura*, and *sukiyaki* are among the Japanese dishes most known to foreigners.

いっきに／ひといきに

■ *ikkini* ■ *hitoiki ni*

いっきに［一気(いっき)に］ ■ *ikkini* ■ at a breath 

ものごとを、途中(とちゅう)で**休(やす)んだり速度(そくど)や能率(のうりつ)を落(お)としたりしないで**、最初(さいしょ)から最後(さいご)まで集中(しゅうちゅう)して終(お)わらせてしまうようすを表(あらわ)します。**勢(いきお)いや集中力(しゅうちゅうりょく)**が感(かん)じられます（例(れい)1, 2, 3, 4）。

This indicates the state of having completed something without taking a break or slowing down ; it imparts a feeling of energy or concentration (ex. 1, 2, 3, 4).

1) ホームに電車(でんしゃ)が入(はい)ってきたので、駅(えき)の階段(かいだん)をいっきにかけおりた。
Hoomuni denshaga haittekitanode, ekino kaidan-o ikkini kakeorita.
The train had pulled up to the platform, so (I) dashed down the stairs.

2) この小説(しょうせつ)は筋(すじ)がおもしろかったので、いっきに読(よ)んでしまった。
Kono shoosetsuwa sujiga omoshirokatta-node, ikkini yondeshimatta.
The plot of this novel was very interesting, so (I) read it all in one sitting.

3) 私(わたし)たちは、「乾杯(かんぱい)」の音頭(おんど)でいっきにビールを飲(の)みほした。
Watashitachiwa, 'kanpai' no ondode ikkini biiruo nomihoshita.
After saying 'cheers!', we all downed our glasses of beer.

4) 地震(じしん)で建物(たてもの)がいっきにくずれ落(お)ちるのを見(み)た。
Jishinde tatemonoga ikkini kuzureochirunoo mita.
(We) saw the building crash down all at once in the earthquake.

ひといきに［一息(ひといき)に］ ■ *hitoiki ni* ■ at a breath ; at once 

ものごとを、途中(とちゅう)で休(やす)まないで、**ひじょうに短(みじか)い時間(じかん)**でやってしまうようすを表(あらわ)します（例(れい)5, 6, 7）。「いっきに」は、集中(しゅうちゅう)して全力(ぜんりょく)でものごとを終(お)わらせる勢(いきお)いのよさを表(あらわ)し、「ひといきに」は、ものごとをやってしまう時間(じかん)の短(みじか)さを表(あらわ)します。

Hitoiki ni is used when one finishes up something in a very short time without taking a break (ex.5, 6, 7). *Ikkini* focuses on the concentration involved, while the focus of *hitoiki ni* is on the shortness of time spent.

---

5) のどがかわいていたので、コップの水(みず)をひといきに飲(の)んでしまった。
Nodoga kawaiteitanode, koppuno mizuo hitoikini nondeshimatta.
(I) was very thirsty, so I drank the cup of water in one gulp.

6) 早口(はやくち)ことばは、言(い)いにくいことばをひといきに言(い)わなければならない。
Hayakuchi-kotobawa, iinikui kotobao hitoikini iwanakereba naranai.
(You) have to say something hard to say all at once to make a tongue twister.

7) 頂上(ちょうじょう)まであとひといきだ。
Choojoomade ato hitoikida.
There's just a bit more to go until (we) reach the summit.

すみません

日本語(にほんご)の「すみません」は、とても広(ひろ)い意味(いみ)で使(つか)われます。

「遅(おそ)くなってごめんなさい」「ごめいわくをおかけして申(もう)し訳(わけ)ありません」などと謝(あやま)るときや、人(ひと)の足(あし)を踏(ふ)んでしまったり、ちょっとぶつかってしまったとき、また、人(ひと)の横(よこ)をすりぬけたりするときに「失礼(しつれい)します」という意味(いみ)で使(つか)います。

そして、「ちょっと来(き)てください」「どなたか、いませんか」などと呼(よ)びかけたり、「ちょっとお聞(き)きしたいんですが」などというときも「すみません」と話(はな)しかけます。

それから、「どうもありがとうございます」などとお礼(れい)を言(い)うときにも「すみません」は使われます。いつでも使えるオールマイティーのことばです。けれども、何もかもを「すみません」で済ませてしまわずに、謝るときには「ごめんなさい」、感謝するときには「ありがとう」もきちんと使えるといいですね。

Sumimasen

The Japanese word *sumimasen* is used in a lot of different situations. For example, in instances when you apologize for being late, causing trouble, stepping on someone's foot, or lightly bumping into someone, *sumimasen* is used to mean 'I'm sorry'.

It may also be used to mean 'excuse me' when you ask another person to come, call out to see if anybody is at home, or when you want to ask a question.

Also, when expressing gratitude to someone it may be used to mean 'thank you'. As you can see, *sumimasen* is a very useful word. However, instead of relying on it in all situations, you should also learn how to use the more conventional words—*gomennasai* to apologize, and *arigatoo* to express gratitude.

いっけん／ひとめ／いちべつ

■ *ikken* ■ *hitome* ■ *ichibetsu*

いっけん［一見］

■ *ikken*
■ (at) a glance 

ざっと見る・一度見るというときや、ちょっと考えるというとき使います（例1, 2, 3, 4, 5)。「一見に値する（一見の価値がある）・一見して～とわかる・一見～のようだが……」などのように決まった形で使うことが多いです。

Ikken is used when one looks over something roughly, takes a brief look at something, or has a first impression (ex.1, 2, 3, 4, 5). Most of the time, *ikken* is used in fixed expressions like *ikken ni atai suru* (*～no kachi ga aru*) (worth taking a look at), *ikken shite ～to wakaru* (to be able to understand / recognize ～at a glance), and *ikken ～no youdaga* (it looks like ～at first glance).

1) あの展覧会は、一見の価値がある。
Ano tenrankaiwa, ikkenno kachiga aru.
That exhibition is worth taking a look at.

2) 「百聞は一見にしかず」と同じ意味のことわざは多くの国にある。
'Hyakubunwa ikkenni shikazu' to onaji imino kotowazawa ookuno kunini aru.
There are many countries which have proverbs similar to 'Seeing is believing'.

3) この絵は、一見してピカソの作品だとわかる。
Kono ewa, ikkenshite Pikasono sakuhindato wakaru.
At one glance, you can tell this painting is Picasso's work.

4) このゲームは一見やさしそうですが、やってみるとむずかしい。
Kono geemuwa ikken yasashisoodesuga, yattemiruto muzukashii.
This game at first looks easy, but if (you) try it, you'll find it's difficult.

5) 彼の意見は一見正しいようだが、よく考えるとまちがっている。
Kareno ikenwa ikken tadashiiyoodaga, yoku kangaeruto machigatteiru.
His opinion sounds right, but if you think about it carefully, it's really wrong.

ひとめ［一目］ ■ *hitome* ■ at a glance ; at first sight 

---

①**ちょっと見る**というとき（例6, 7, 8, 9, 10）「ひとめでわかる・ひとめ会いたい・ひとめ見たい」のように使います。

Hitome is used when one just glances at something; it is used in idiomatic expressions such as *hitome de wakaru* (to be clear at a glance), *hitome aitai* (want to see someone even just for a short time), and *hitome mitai* (want to take one look) (ex.6, 7, 8, 9, 10).

②**一度に見える範囲**を指すとき使います（例11）。

Hitome is also used when one is able to see an entire area at a glance (ex.11).

---

6) 彼らが兄弟だということは、ひとめでわかる。
Karerga kyoodaidato yuu kotowa, hitomede wakaru.
You can easily see that they are brothers.

7) 彼は、そのダイヤモンドがにせものだと、ひとめでわかった。

Karewa, sono daiyamondoga nisemonodato, hitomede wakatta.
He knew at one look that the diamond was fake.

8) 彼は年老いた両親にひとめ会いたくて、10年ぶりに日本に帰ってきた。
Karewa toshioita ryooshinni hitome aitakute, juunenburini Nihonni kaettekita.
He came back to Japan for the first time in ten years in order to see his aging parents.

9) 人気タレントをひとめ見ようと、テレビ局の前にファンが大勢つめかけた。
Ninkitarentoo hitome miyooto, terebikyokuno maeni fanga oozei tsumekaketa.
A large crowd gathered outside the TV studio, hoping to get a glimpse of the popular TV personality.

10) 私は彼に、ひとめぼれしてしまった。
Watashiwa kareni, hitomebore shiteshimatta.
I fell in love with him at first sight.

11) このビルの屋上から、町がひとめで見わたせる。
Kono biruno okujookara, machiga hitomede miwataseru.
You can see the entire town from the top of this building.

いちべつ

■ *ichibetsu*
■ (at) a glance 

「ひとめ」のように、**一瞬ちらっと見る**とき使いますが（例12, 13, 14)、とくに関心はひかれないという意味や、軽蔑の気持ちを含みます。書きことばでかたい言い方です。

Like *hitome*, *ichibetsu* means to take a quick look (ex.12, 13, 14), however it implies that the speaker is not interested in the matter very much, or that he feels contempt for it. It is not used in spoken language and is rather formal.

---

12) 待ちかまえた記者団にはいちべつもくれず、首相はさっさと車に乗りこんだ。
Machikamaeta kishadanniwa ichibetsumo kurezu, shushoowa sassato kurumani norikonda.
The Prime Minister quickly got into the car, without even a glance at the group of reporters that was waiting for him.

13) 彼女は、私が心をこめて贈った花をいちべつしただけで、「ありがとう」ともいわなかった。

Kanojowa, watashiga kokoroo komete okutta hanao ichibetsu-shitadakede, 'Arigatoo' tomo iwanakatta.
She just glanced at the flowers I had sent with all my heart, and didn't even say "thank you".

14) 彼は私の意見を聞こうともせずに、冷たい目でいちべつしただけだった。
Karewa watashino iken-o kikootomo sezuni, tsumetai mede ichibetsushita-dakedatta.
He didn't even try to listen to my opinion, and just gave me a cold look.

いっせいに／どうじに

■ *isseini* ■ *doujini*

いっせいに［一斉に］

■ *isseini*
■ at once ; all together

多数のものが、同じ時にそろって同じ行動を始めるようすを表します（例1, 2, 3, 4）。

Isseini indicates a situation in which many things begin performing the same action at the same time (ex.1, 2, 3, 4).

---

1) スタートの合図で、マラソンの選手たちはいっせいに走りだした。
Sutaatono aizude, marasonno senshutachiwa isseini hashiridashita.
When the start signal was given, all of the marathon runners began running together.

2) 大統領の演説が終わると、いっせいに拍手がわき起こった。
Daitooryoono enzetsuga owaruto, isseini hakushuga wakiokotta.
When the President's speech ended, the entire audience broke into applause.

3) 12月に入ると、商店街はいっせいに歳末大売り出しを始める。
Juunigatsuni hairuto, shootengaiwa isseini saimatsu-oouridashio hajimeru.
When December comes around, all the shops in the shopping center begin end-of-the-year sales at the same time.

4) あした、国立大学の入試が全国いっせいに行われる。
Ashita, kokuritsu-daigakuno nyuushiga zenkoku isseini okonawareru.

All of the national universities will hold their entrance examinations tomorrow.

どうじに［同時に］

■ *doujini*
■ at the same time

あることがらが起こったちょうどその時に、という意味で使います（例5, 6, 7）。また、２つ以上のことがらや状態が**並行して進行**していくようすを表すときにも使います（例8, 9, 10）。

Doujini denotes a time simultaneous to or concurrent with an action or event (ex.5, 6, 7). It may also indicate that two or more actions or conditions progress in a parallel manner (ex.8, 9, 10).

5) 銀行の正面入り口は午前９時の時報と同時に開けられる。
Ginkoono shoomen-iriguchiwa gozen kujino jihooto doojini akerareru.
The main doors of the bank are opened as soon as the nine o'clock chime sounds.

6) 彼の書いた本は発売と同時に売り切れた。
Kareno kaita honwa hatsubaito doojini urikireta.
His book sold out as soon as it was released.

7) 救急車はけが人を乗せると同時に病院へと向かった。
Kyuukyuushawa keganin-o noseruto doojini byooin-eto mukkata.
The ambulance headed for the hospital the minute the injured person was put inside.

8) 学生結婚したので、私は学生であると同時に主婦でもあった。
Gakuseikekkon-shitanode, watashiwa gakuseide aruto doojini shufudemo atta.
I married while still in school, so I was a housewife and a student at the same time.

9) この番組は日本とハワイで同時に放送されている。
Kono bangumiwa Nihonto Hawaide doojini hoosoo sareteiru.
This program is being simultaneously broadcast in Japan and Hawaii.

10) 彼女と私は同時にゴールのテープを切った。
Kanojoto watashiwa doojini gooruno teepuo kitta.
She and I broke the tape at the finish line at the same time.

いっそ／おもいきって

■*isso*　■*omoikitte*

いっそ

■*isso*
■(I) would rather

あまり良くない現在の状態から抜け出すために、「いっそ」の後に述べる状態を選ぶとき使います。たとえもっとひどいことになっても、まるでちがう状態を選んだほうがましだという、**投げやりで感情的**な「逃げたい」という気持ち（例1,2,3）、「いちかばちかやってみよう」と**強い決意で積極的**に解決しようとする気持ちも（例４）表します。

In this expression, what is said after *isso* indicates the choice the speaker would make in order to get away from undesirable circumstances. *Isso* implies two meanings ; a rash or emotional desire to escape a situation by choosing a completely different one, even if it is worse (ex.1, 2, 3), and a positive 'work things out' or 'give it a try' attitude (ex.4).

1) こんなにつらい人生を送るのなら、いっそ死んだほうがましだ。
Konnani tsurai jinseio okurunonara, isso shinda hooga mashida.
If (I) must live such a hard life as this, I'd rather die.

2) 心のこもらないプレゼントなら、いっそもらわないほうがいい。
Kokorono komoranai purezentonara, isso morawanai hooga ii.
If the heart isn't in the gift, (I'd) rather not receive it.

3) あんないやな社長の言うことを聞かなければならないのなら、いっそ会社を辞めてしまおうか。
Anna iyana shachoono yuukotoo kikanakereba-naranainonara, isso kaishao yameteshimaooka.
If (I) have to listen to such an annoying president, I wonder if I shouldn't quit working for this company.

4) このテレビは古くて、よく故障する。いっそ新しいのを買ったほうがいい。
Kono terebiwa furukute, yoku koshoosuru. Isso atarashiinoo kattahooga ii.
This TV is old and always breaking down, which is all the more reason to buy a new one.

おもいきって［思い切って］ ■ *omoikitte* ■ to finally decide to 

迷いやためらいを捨てて、**良い結果になることを期待して積極的に行動する**ときや、ある決断のもとに新しい行動にふみ切るとき使います（例5, 6, 7, 8)。「思い切って」の後にくることばは、希望や強い決意を含んでいます。

This expression is used when one decides to stop hesitating and act positively, hoping for a better outcome or to make a new start (ex.5, 6, 7, 8). *Omoikitte* is usually followed by words expressing a hope or firm decision.

5) こわかったけれど思い切って水に飛び込んだら体が浮いた。

Kowakattakeredo omoikitte mizuni tobikondara karadaga uita.
Although (I) was scared, I made up my mind and jumped into the water ; and I found that I floated.

6) 思い切って、いらない物を捨てたら部屋がすっきりした。

Omoikitte, iranai monoo sutetara heyaga sukkirishita.
(I) forced myself to throw away everything I didn't need, and now my room looks very neat.

7) 思い切って会社を辞めて、独立することにしました。

Omoikitte kaishao yamete, dokuritsusuru kotoni shimashita.
(I) decided to up and quit the company and become independent.

8) いろいろ考えたけれど思い切って家を買うことにした。

Iroiro kangaetakeredo omoikitte ieo kau kotoni shita.
After thinking everything over, (I) decided to go all the way and buy a house.

いったん／ひとまず

■ *ittan* ■ *hitomazu*

いったん ■ *ittan* ■ once

①続いている動作や状態を**一時的に中断**して、またすぐ次の動作や行動を始めるときに使います（例1, 2, 3)。

Ittan is used to indicate the temporary interruption of an action or state, which will begin again almost immediately (ex.1, 2, 3).

②ある状態になったら**なかなか変えられない**、というときに使います(例4, 5)。

It may also indicate that once a certain condition is reached there can be no further change (ex.4, 5).

---

1) 車は踏切の手前でいったん停止して、安全を確認しなければならない。

Kurumawa fumikirino temaede ittan teishishite, anzen-o kakunin shinakereba naranai.

You must briefly stop the car at railroad crossings to make sure it's safe to cross.

2) 約束の時間までだいぶあるので、いったんうちに帰って出直します。

Yakusokuno jikanmade daibu arunode, ittan uchini kaette denaoshimasu.

There is still some time before my appointment, so (I'll) return home for a bit and then go out again.

3) 図書館で借りた本は、読み終わっていなくても期限がきたらいったん返さなくてはならない。

Toshokande karita honwa, yomiowatte-inakutemo kigenga kitara ittan kaesanakutewa naranai.

(You) have to briefly return the books you've checked out of the library when they're due, even if you haven't finished reading them yet.

4) 私はいったん決めたことは、必ず実行する。

Watashiwa ittan kimeta kotowa, kanarazu jikkoosuru.

Once I've made up my mind to do something, I always follow it through.

5) 彼はがんこで、いったん言いだしたらきかない。

Karewa gankode, ittan iidashitara kikanai.

He's stubborn. Once he's said something, he doesn't listen to anyone else.

ひとまず

■*hitomazu*
■for the time being

続いている動作や状態を**適当な区切りで中断**するときに使います(例6, 7, 8)。しばらくして、また同じ動作や状態が起こるという意味を含んでいます。「今のところは」「とりあえず」のように、その場はそれでよしとする感じを含みます。

Hitomazu is used when a continuing action or condition is interrupted at a suitable point (ex.6, 7, 8). It is implied that the action or condition will resume after a short time. *Hitomazu* may also suggest that something is sufficient for the time being, in the same way as the expressions *ima no tokoro wa* and *toriaezu*.

6) 午前中の仕事は、ひとまずこの辺で終わりにして食事にしよう。
Gozenchuuno shigotowa, hitomazu konohende owarini shite shokujini shiyoo.
Let's take a break from the work (we've) been doing all morning and get something to eat.

7) 薬でひとまず熱は下がったけれど、まだ体がだるい。
Kusuride hitomazu netsuwa sagattakeredo, mada karadaga darui.
The medicine has brought my fever down for the moment, but (I) still feel weak.

8) むずかしい話はひとまずおいといて、お茶でも飲みませんか。
Muzukashii hanashiwa hitomazu oitoite, ochademo nomimasenka?
Why don't (we) set aside this serious talk for a moment and have some tea?

いっぽう／かたほう

■ *ippou* ■ *katahou*

いっぽう［一方］ ■ *ippou* ■ one side

①2つあるもののうちの1つを指すとき使います（例1, 2)。

Ippou is used when referring to one of two things (ex.1, 2).

②ある1つの方向や方面を指すとき使います。「〜する一方だ」は1つの方面に片寄っていることを表し（例3, 4)、「〜する一方，〜する一方で」は、何かをしながらまたほかに別なことをするというとき使います（例5, 6)。

It may also be used to point out a certain direction or area. *〜suru ippou da* means that something keeps happening with a certain tendency (ex.3, 4), while *〜suru ippou* or *〜suru ippou de* is used when doing two or more things at the same time (ex.5, 6).

1) 彼ら2人のうち、どちらか一方が先に謝らなければ、けんかは終わらない。
Karera futarino uchi, dochiraka ippooga sakini ayamaranakereba, kenkawa owaranai.
If one of those two doesn't apologize first, the argument will never end.

2) 学芸会で、子供たちは二組に分かれて、一方は歌を歌い、もう一方はダンスを踊った。
Gakugeikaide, kodomotachiwa futakumini wakarete, ippoowa utao utai, moo ippoowa dansuo odotta.
For the school drama, the children were divided into groups; one group sang and the other danced.

3) 雨が降り続き、川は水かさを増す一方だ。
Amega furitsuzuki, kawawa mizukasao masu ippooda.
It keeps on raining and raining and the rivers just get fuller and fuller.

4) だれも住んでいないので、この家は荒れる一方です。
Daremo sundeinainode, kono iewa areru ippoodesu.
Nobody lives in it, so this house is getting more and more run down.

5) 父は本屋を経営する一方で小説も書いている。
Chichiwa hon-yao keieisuru ippoode shoosetsumo kaiteiru.
At the same time as he's running the book store, my father is also writing a novel.

6) 私は看護婦として患者の世話をする一方、家では2人の子供の母親だ。
Watashiwa kangofutoshite kanjano sewao suru ippoo, iedewa futarino kodomono hahaoyada.
While I'm a nurse looking after patients, I'm also a mother of two.

かたほう［片方］

■ *katahou*
■ one side ; one of two

一対になっているものや、**一組になっているもののうちの1つ**を指すことばです（例7, 8, 9, 10)。話しことばで「かたいっぽう」「かたっぽ」などと言うこともあります。

Katahou is used when referring to one part of a pair or set (ex.7, 8, 9, 10). *Kataippou* and *katappo* are colloquial expressions of the same word.

7) 混んだ電車の中で、私はイヤリングを片方無くしてしまった。
Konda denshano nakade, watashiwa iyaringuo katahoo nakushiteshimatta.
I lost one of my earrings on a crowded train.

8) うちの猫の目は、片方が金色でもう片方が銀色です。
Uchino nekono mewa, katahooga kin-irode moo katahooga gin-irodesu.
One of my cat's eyes is gold, and the other is silver.

9) 犬が私の靴を、かたいっぽうくわえていってしまった。
Inuga watashino kutsuo, kataippoo kuwaete-itteshimatta.
(My) dog grabbed one of my shoes in his mouth and ran off with it.

10) 手袋が、かたっぽ見あたらない。
Tebukuroga, katappo miataranai.
(I) can't find one of my gloves.

いつも／いつでも／しょっちゅう

■ *itsumo* ■ *itsu demo* ■ *shotchuu*

いつも ■ *itsumo* ■ always 

①**行動**や**状態**などが、**日常の習慣のように**なっていて変わらないようすを表します（例1, 2, 3)。したがってものごとの回数の多さも表します。

This indicates that a behavior or condition is routine ; it also indicates frequent occurrence (ex.1, 2, 3).

②「ふつうの場合」のように、ある決まっているようすやことがらを表します（例4, 5, 6)。

Like the expression *futsuu no baai*, it expresses a certain established or regular action or state (ex.4, 5, 6).

1) 私は、いつもこの店で買い物をする。
Watashiwa, itsumo kono misede kaimonoo suru.
I always shop at this store.

2) この庭(にわ)は、いつもきれいに手入(てい)れがしてある。

Kono niwawa, itsumo kireini teirega shitearu.
This garden is always well maintained.

3) 彼(かれ)は、いつも人(ひと)の悪口(わるくち)ばかり言(い)うから嫌(きら)いだ。

Karewa, itsumo hitono warukuchibakari yuukara kiraida.
(I) can't stand him because he is constantly saying bad things about other people.

4) 今年(ことし)の桜(さくら)は、いつもの年(とし)より咲(さ)くのが遅(おそ)い。

Kotoshino sakurawa, itsumono toshiyori sakunoga osoi.
This year, the cherry blossoms are blooming later than they do in ordinary years.

5) この公園(こうえん)は、いつもは人(ひと)が少(すく)ないのに、きょうはずいぶん人(ひと)がいる。

Kono kooenwa, itsumowa hitoga sukunainoni, kyoowa zuibun hitoga iru.
We usually don't see many people in this park, but it's crowded today.

6) いつものところで待(ま)っています。

Itsumono tokorode matteimasu.
(I'll) wait for (you) at our usual meeting place.

いつでも

■ *itsu demo*
■ always ; at any time 

---

①行動(こうどう)や状況(じょうきょう)が、どんな時(とき)にもふだんと変(か)わらないようすを表(あらわ)します（例(れい)7, 8, 9, 10）。この場合(ばあい)は「いつも」を同(おな)じ意味(いみ)で使(つか)うことができますが、「いつも」よりも**少(すこ)し強(つよ)い言(い)い方(かた)**です。

Itsu demo indicates that a behavior or state always remains unchanged (ex.7, 8, 9, 10). In this case, *itsumo* and *itsu demo* can be used interchangeably, however *itsu demo* sounds a little stronger.

②時間(じかん)や状況(じょうきょう)にとらわれずにものごとができるようすを表(あらわ)すとき使(つか)います。「～できる・～していい・～かまわない」などの「可能(かのう)・許可(きょか)・許容(きょよう)」を表(あらわ)すことばといっしょに使(つか)うことが多(おお)いです（例(れい)11）。**どんな時(とき)でも・常(つね)に・例外(れいがい)なく**という意味(いみ)です。

It is also used when something occurs at any time, always, without exception, or without being controlled by time and circumstance. *Itsu demo* is often used with words or phrases such as ～*dekiru*, ～*shite ii*, and ～*kamawanai*, which express ability, approval, and permission respectively (ex.11).

---

7) 彼は、いつでも待ち合わせの時間に遅れて来る。
Karewa, itsudemo machiawaseno jikanni okuretekuru.
He always comes late to appointments.

8) 彼女はいつでもすぐに怒る。
Kanojowa itsudemo suguni okoru.
She gets mad very easily.

9) 私はいつでもビタミン剤を持ち歩いている。
Watashiwa itsudemo bitaminzaio mochiaruiteiru.
I always have my vitamin pills with me.

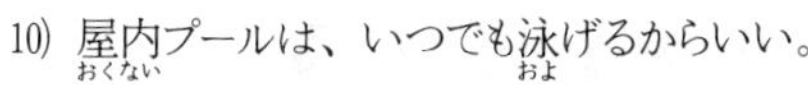

10) 屋内プールは、いつでも泳げるからいい。
Okunai-puuruwa, itsudemo oyogerukara ii.
Indoor pools are nice because you can swim anytime.

11) 困った時は、いつでも相談にいらっしゃい。
Komatta tokiwa, itsudemo soodanni irasshai.
You may come to talk to (me) anytime you're in trouble.

しょっちゅう ■ *shotchuu* ■ often 

「**何度も・ひんぱんに**」などのように、ことがらの**回数の多さ**を表します（例12, 13, 14, 15)。「いつも・いつでも」よりも、「回数の多さ・頻度」に重点があります。話しことばで、よく使われます。

This indicates frequent occurrence in the same way as *nando mo* and *hinpan ni* (ex.12, 13, 14, 15). Compared to *itsumo* and *itsu demo*, the focus of *shotchuu* is on frequency. It is often used in spoken language.

---

12) 兄は、仕事でしょっちゅう外国へ行く。
Aniwa, shigotode shotchuu gaikokue iku.
My (elder) brother goes abroad on business quite often.

13) 学生時代には、しょっちゅう友達と朝まで語り明かしたものだ。
Gakusei-jidainiwa, shotchuu tomodachito asamade katariakashita monoda.
When (I) was a student, I often stayed up until morning talking to my friends.

14) 息子は、小さい頃、しょっちゅう熱を出していた。

Musukowa, chiisai koro, shotchuu netsuo dashiteita.

My son often had fevers when he was little.

15) A：ゆうべ、本を読みながら寝てしまったよ。

B：ぼくなんか、そんなことしょっちゅうさ。

A： *Yuube, hon-o yominagara neteshimattayo.*
Last night, (I) fell asleep while reading a book.

B： *Bokunanka, sonna koto shotchuusa.*
That happens to me quite a lot.

いぶす／くすぶる／けむる

■ *ibusu* ■ *kusuburu* ■ *kemuru*

いぶす

■ *ibusu*
■ to smoke (something) 

煙を出して、**物にあてたり**、包んだりするとき使います。その煙で虫や動物を追い払ったり（例1, 2）、物質を変化させたりします（例3, 4, 5）。また、硫黄で、銀や銅を黒っぽく変化させるときも「いぶす」と使います（例6）。

To smoke something, or to envelope something in smoke in order to chase away insects or animals (ex.1, 2), or to change the quality of something with smoke (ex.3, 4, 5).
To darken metals such as silver and copper with sulfur (ex.6).

1) 昔は、蚊とり線香の煙でいぶして、蚊を追い払った。

Mukashiwa, katorisenkoono kemuride ibushite, kao oiharatta.

We used to keep mosquitoes away (by smoking them out) with smoke from a mosquito incense coil.

2) 巣に煙を入れて、きつねをいぶし出す。

Suni kemurio irete, kitsuneo ibushidasu.

We force a fox out by smoking its den.

3) 魚をいぶして、くんせいにする。

Sakanao ibushite, kunseini suru.

Fish is smoked by hanging it over a fire.

4) 桜のチップでいぶしたハムは、おいしい。
Sakurano chippude ibushita hamuwa, oishii.
Ham smoked with chips of cherry wood is delicious.

5) 丸太をいぶして作った柱は、私の家の自慢です。
Marutao ibushite tsukutta hashirawa, watashino ieno jimandesu.
A pillar made from a burnished log is our family's pride and joy.

6) 私は父の誕生日に、いぶし銀のネクタイピンをおくりました。
Watashiwa chichino tanjoobini, ibushiginno nekutaipin-o okurimashita.
I gave an oxidized silver tie pin to my father on his birthday.

くすぶる ■*kusuburu* ■to smolder 

---

①すぐに**火が起きなかったり**（例7）勢いよく燃えなかったり、**完全に燃えきってしまわなくて煙がでている**（例8）というとき使います。

Kusuburu indicates that a fire does not start right away (ex.7), is not burning vigorously, or is smoking without completely catching fire (ex.8).

②家の中にとじこもってばかりいて、楽しくないようす（例9）や、問題がいつまでも解決しないでこじれている状態にも使います（例10）。

It may be used to describe a person who always stays at home, having no enjoyment or activities (ex.9). It also describes a problematic situation which lingers on without being solved (ex.10).

---

7) まきが、なかなか燃えないでくすぶっている。
Makiga, nakanaka moenaide kusubutteiru.
The wood won't catch fire, and is just smoldering.

8) ゆうべの火事の現場は、まだくすぶっている。
Yuubeno kajino genbawa, mada kusubutteiru.
Things are still smoldering at the scene of last night's fire.

9) 家の中でくすぶっていないで、たまにはいっしょに、映画にでも行こうよ。
Ieno nakade kusubutte-inaide, tamaniwa isshoni, eiganidemo ikooyo.
Don't just stay cooped up in the house. Let's go do something like see a movie together once in a while.

10) この問題は、２国間でもう10年もくすぶっている。

Kono mondaiwa, nikokukande moo juunenmo kusubutteiru.
This issue has been smoldering between the two countries for ten years.

けむる［煙る］

■ *kemuru*
■ to smoke ; to be hazy 

①煙がたくさん出ているようすを表すとき（例11）や、ある空間が煙でいっぱいになるとき（例12）使います。

Kemuru indicates that a great amount of smoke is coming out from somewhere (ex.11), or that a certain area or space becomes full of smoke (ex.12).

②遠い景色が小雨や霧などでぼんやりかすんで見えるとき（例13）使います。

Also, *kemuru* is used to describe a distant view that looks smoky or clouded because of fog, mist, etc. (ex.13).

11) このまきは、湿っていて煙ってばかりいる。
Kono makiwa, shimetteite kemuttebakariiru.
This firewood is damp and just smokes.

12) えんとつがない山小屋では、火をたくと小屋の中が煙ってしまう。
Entotsuga nai yamagoyadewa, hio takuto koyano nakaga kemutteshimau.
If (you) make a fire in a mountain hut without a chimney, the hut will fill with smoke.

13) 朝霧に煙っている白樺の林が美しい。
Asagirini kemutteiru shirakabano hayashiga utsukushii.
The forest of white birch trees in the hazy morning mist is beautiful.

いま／げんざい／ただいま

■ *ima* ■ *genzai* ■ *tadaima*

いま［今］

■ *ima*
■ now

①時を表すことばで、過去でも未来でもない「**この一瞬**」から「**このごろ**」「**現代**」まで幅広く使います（例1, 2, 3, 4, 5)。

Ima is used to refer to the present moment or period in time. It refers to neither the future nor the past, but instead is used in different situations with various meanings from 'this moment', to 'nowadays', to 'the present age' (ex.1, 2, 3, 4, 5).

②ごく近い過去や未来を表します（例6, 7)。

It may be used to refer to the very recent past or near future (ex.6, 7).

---

1) Ａ：今何時ですか。

　Ｂ：４時10分です。

　A: *Ima nanjidesuka?* What time is it?

　B: *Yojijuppundesu.* It's 4:10.

2) 私は今、自分のセーターを編んでいる。

Watashiwa ima, jibunno seetaao andeiru.

I am now knitting my own sweater.

3) 部長は今、会議中です。

Buchoowa ima, kaigichuudesu.

The manager is in a meeting now.

4) 今住んでいる家は狭いので、もっと広いところに引っ越したい。

Ima sundeiru iewa semainode, motto hiroi tokoroni hikkoshitai.

The house I'm living in now is very small, so I'd like to move to a larger one.

5) 昔、この辺は野原だったのに、今はビルだらけだ。

Mukashi, konohenwa noharadattanoni, imawa birudarakeda.

This area was once all field, but now there is nothing but buildings.

6) 青木さんは、用があるといって今帰りましたよ。

Aokisanwa, yooga aruto itte ima kaerimashitayo.

Mr. Aoki has just left, saying he has something to do.

7) ちょっと待って、今行くから。

Chotto matte, ima ikukara.

Wait a minite, (I'll) be right there.

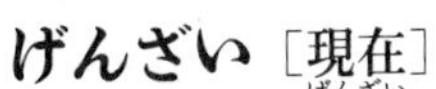

げんざい［現在］

■*genzai*
■the present time

時を表すことばです。過去のことでも未来のことでもありません（例8, 9, 10)。「今」ほど「この瞬間」という意味は強くなく、「**自分が存在しているこの時**」といった感じです。「現在」は「今」よりも改まった場合や、書きことばで多く使われます。また、例11，12のように、日時を表すことばを前につけて、ある特定の時点を述べるときに使います。

This word is used to indicate time, however it does not refer to either the past or future (ex.8, 9, 10). Unlike *ima*, it does not emphasize the present moment, but instead refers more to 'this time in which we exist'. It is more often used in formal situations and in writing than is *ima*. As in Examples 11 and 12, when a time or date occurs before it, *genzai* marks that specific point in time.

---

8) 現在、私は東京に住んでいる。
Genzai, watashiwa Tookyooni sundeiru.
I'm currently living in Tokyo.

9) 彼の乗った船は、現在フィリピン沖に向かっています。
Kareno notta funewa, genzai Firipin-okini mukatteimasu.
The ship he is on is presently headed for the seas off the Philippines.

10) この市の人口は、現在約12万人です。
Kono shino jinkoowa, genzai yaku juunimannin-desu.
The population of this city is currently around 120,000 people.

11) 台風は、今日正午現在、沖縄の南方海上を北に向かって進んでいます。
Taifuuwa, kyoo shoogo genzai, Okinawano nanpookaijoo-o kitani mukatte susundeimasu.
As of noon today, the typhoon was in the sea south of Okinawa, and moving north.

12) この学校の卒業生は、今年３月31日現在で、10万人を超えたそうです。
Kono gakkoono sotsugyooseiwa, kotoshi sangatsu sanjuuichinichi genzaide, juumannin-o koetasoodesu.
It appears that as of March 31 of this year, the number of graduates from this school has exceeded 100,000.

ただいま

■ *tadaima*
■ just now

---

①「今」の、**ていねいで改まった言い方**です（例13, 14, 15)。「今」とほとん

ど同じ意味ですが、「ただいま」のほうが「ちょうどいま」「たったいま」あるいは「すぐに・ただちに」のように、時間の短さを強調しています。「ただいまから」の場合、「ただいまから5年前」のように過去にさかのぼる使い方はしません。

Tadaima is a more formal way of saying *ima* (ex.13, 14, 15). Although it has nearly the same meaning as *ima*, it places more emphasis on the shortness of time, as in, 'this very instant' or 'immediately'. It may not be used in expressions such as *tadaima kara go-nen mae* to refer to past passage of time.

②外から帰ったときのあいさつのことばです（例16）。

It is also used as a greeting by one who is returning from outside (ex.16).

---

13) ただいまから、市民運動会を開催いたします。
Tadaimakara, shimin-undookaio kaisai-itashimasu.
The Citizens Athletic Meet will now begin.

14) 父は、ただいま出かけております。
Chichiwa, tadaima dekaketeorimasu.
My father is out right now.

15) ただいまお茶をお持ちします。
Tadaima ochao omochishimasu.
(I) will bring you some tea right away.

16) 子：おかあさん、ただいま。
母：あ、おかえりなさい。
Ko: *Okaasan, tadaima.* Child: Mom. I'm home!
Haha: *A, okaerinasai.* Mother: Ah! You're back (welcome back).

いまから／これから

■ *ima kara* ■ *korekara*

いまから［今から］ ■ *ima kara* ■ starting from now 

出発点は「今・現在」ですという意味に使います。未来に対しても（例1, 2, 3）、過去に対しても（例4, 5）使います。

Ima kara indicates that the present time is being used as a reference point when referring to events in the future (ex.1, 2, 3), or the past (ex.4, 5).

---

1) 今から買い物に行ってきます。

Imakara kaimononi ittekimasu.
(I'm) going out to do some shopping now.

2) 今から10分後に駅で会いましょう。

Imakara juppungoni ekide aimashoo.
Let's meet at the station ten minutes from now.

3) 来月の団体旅行の予約は、今からでも間に合いますか。

Raigetsuno dantai-ryokoono yoyakuwa, imakarademo maniaimasuka?
Can (I) still make a reservation for next month's group tour?

4) あれは今から３年前の事件です。

Arewa imakara sannenmaeno jikendesu.
That is an incident that occurred three years ago.

5) 彼がブラジルに移住したのは、今から20年前のことです。

Karega Burajiruni ijuushitanowa, imakara nijuunenmaeno kotodesu.
It was 20 years ago that he emigrated to Brazil.

これから ■ *korekara* ■ starting now ; from now (on) 

---

①「今から」と同じように「**現在**」を**出発点として、未来**のことを述べるとき使います（例6, 7）。

Korekara is used in the same way as *imakara* to express that the present time is being used as a starting point when speaking about the future (ex.6, 7).

②「将来は」というとき使います（例8, 9）。「これから〜年前」という過去を述べる使い方はしません。

It may also be used when speaking generally about the future (ex.8, 9). However, unlike *imakara*, it cannot be used in expressions like *korekara* ～*nen mae* to refer to past events.

---

6) これから工場を案内しますので、私のあとについて来てください。

Korekara koojoo-o annai-shimasunode, watashino atoni tsuitekite kudasai.

I will now show you around the factory, so please follow me.

7) これから会議を始めます。ご出席の方は会議室にお集まりください。
Korekara kaigio hajimemasu. Goshussekino katawa kaigi-shitsuni oatsumari kudasai.
The meeting will now begin. Those who are attending, please gather in the conference room.

8) 記者：これから注目される交通手段は何ですか。
学者：これからは、リニアモーターカーだと思います。
Kisya : *Korekara chuumokusareru kootsuu-shudanwa nandesuka?*
Reporter : What modes of transportation are being looked at for the future?
Gakusha : *Korekarawa, rinia-mootaakaadato omoimasu.*
Scholar : I think (one of them is) linear motor cars.

9) 父：もう二度とこんなことをしてはいけないよ。
息子：これから気をつけます。
Chichi : *Moo nidoto konna kotoo shitewa ikenaiyo.*
Father : (You) must never do this kind of thing again!
Musuko : *Korekara kio tsukemasu.*
Son : (I'll) be more careful from now on.

いる／かかる／ひつよう

■ *iru*　■ *kakaru*　■ *hitsuyou*

いる［要る］

■ *iru*
■ to need ; to require 

あることをするのに、**なくてはならないもの**や金などを表すときに使います。時間についてはあまり使いません（例1, 2, 3, 4, 5）。

Iru indicates that something, such as money, is required in order to do a certain task. It is generally not used when referring to time (ex.1, 2, 3, 4, 5).

1) 海外旅行をするときは、パスポートがいります。
Kaigai-ryokoo-o suru tokiwa, pasupootoga irimasu.
(You) must have a passport when you travel to foreign countries.

2) ビザをとるとき、手数料として5000円いります。

Bizao toru toki, tesuuryootoshite gosen-en irimasu.
(You) must pay a ¥5,000 handling charge when getting a visa.

3) 天気予報で晴れるといっていたから、傘はいらないと思います。

Tenkiyohoode hareruto itteitakara, kasawa iranaito omoimasu.
I don't think (we'll) need to have an umbrella because the weather forecast said that it would clear up later.

4) 何か新しいことをはじめるには、勇気がいる。

Nanika atarashii kotoo hajimeruniwa, yuukiga iru.
Whenever (you) start something new, you must have courage.

5) 手術は成功しました。もう心配はいりません。

Shujutsuwa seikoo-shimashita. Moo shinpaiwa irimasen.
The surgery was a success. There's no need to worry any longer.

かかる

■ *kakaru*
■ to take ; to require 

あることをするのに**使わなければならない時間・金・労力**などを表すとき使います。とくに時間に多く使いますが、ものには使いません（例6, 7, 8, 9, 10)。

Kakaru is used when referring to something (time, money, or labor, etc.) that is required to perform an action. *Kakaru* is primarily used when speaking of time, and not of things (ex.6, 7, 8, 9, 10).

---

6) 東京から大阪まで新幹線で３時間かかります。

Tookyookara Oosakamade Shinkansende sanjikan kakarimasu.
It takes three hours to go from Tokyo to Osaka on the *Shinkansen*.

7) 東京から北京まで航空便で10日かかります。

Tookyookara Pekinmade kookuubinde tooka kakarimasu.
It takes ten days for air mail to arrive in Beijing from Tokyo.

8) いまの世の中、何をするにも、お金がかかる。

Imano yononaka, nanio surunimo, okanega kakaru.
In today's world, everything costs money.

9) （税関で）ウイスキー３本以上だと、いくら税金がかかりますか。

(Zeikan de)Uisukii sanbon-ijoodato, ikura zeikinga kakarimasuka?

(At customs) How much is the tax if (I'm) bringing in more than three bottles of whisky?

10) 子供がまだ小さいので、手がかかります。

Kodomoga mada chiisainode, tega kakarimasu.
Our children are still young, so (I) must spend a lot of time taking care of them.

ひつよう［必要］

■ *hitsuyou*
■ to need ; to require 

「いる」の書きことばですが、「いる」より強く、「必ずいる」「欠かせない」「なければどうしようもない」という意味で使います（例11, 12, 13, 14）。「必要」を使うときは、社会的理由や、規則とか義務といった、自分以外の理由による、客観的な見方が加わったときです。

This is a more formal written equivalent of *iru*, however, it is stronger and suggests that 'something is absolutely needed', 'cannot be omitted' or 'cannot be done without' (ex.11, 12, 13, 14). *Hitsuyou* is often used when speaking of rules or responsibilities that are required by society.

---

11) カレーを作るには、いろいろな香辛料が必要です。

*Karee*o tsukuruniwa, iroirona kooshinryooga hitsuyoodesu.* * p.702
Various kinds of spices are needed to make curry.

12) パスポートをとるとき、写真と住民票が必要です。

Pasupootoo torutoki, shashinto juuminhyooga hitsuyoodesu.
It is necessary to have a photo and a certificate of resident registration in order to obtain a passport (in Japan).

13) A：お金が必要なら、銀行で借りますが……。

B：その必要はありません。

A： *Okanega hitsuyoonara, ginkoode karimasuga…*
If I need money, maybe I should borrow it from the bank.
B： *Sono hitsuyoowa arimasen.* There is no need to do that.

14) 車を運転するには運転免許証が必要です。

Kurumao untensuruniwa unten-menkyoshooga hitsuyoodesu.
You are required to have a driver's license in order to drive a car.

私の家族・親族 FAMILY TREE

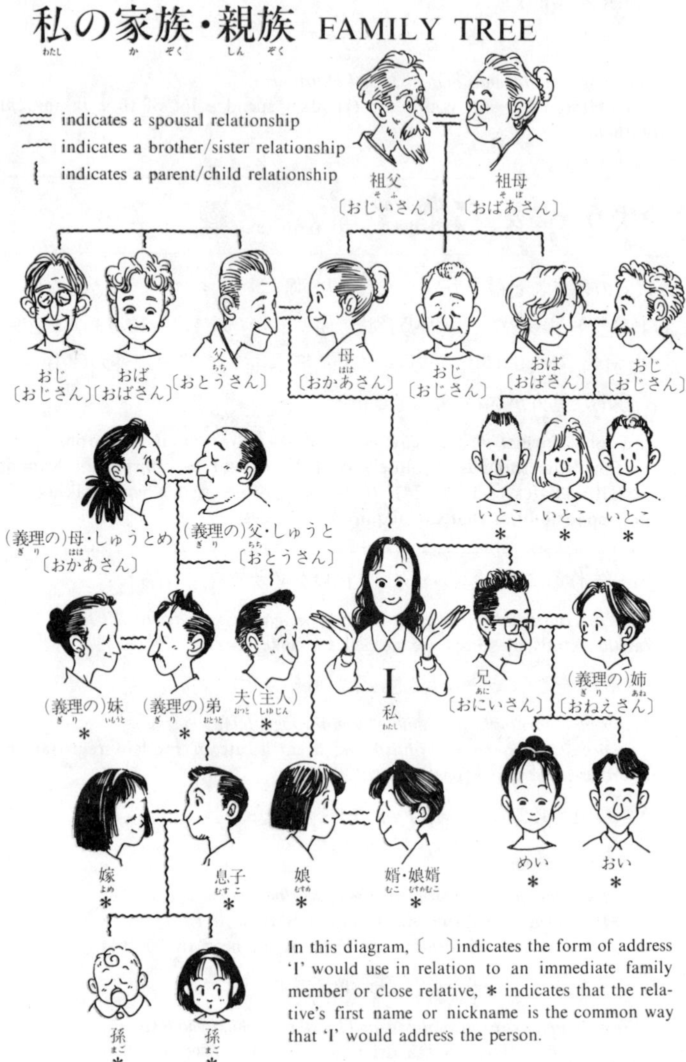

In this diagram, 〔 〕indicates the form of address 'I' would use in relation to an immediate family member or close relative, * indicates that the relative's first name or nickname is the common way that 'I' would address the person.

いれもの／うつわ／ようき

■ *iremono* ■ *utsuwa* ■ *youki*

いれもの［入れ物］ ■ *iremono* ■ container 

何かを**入れるもの**のことです。ビニール袋や紙袋のように、やわらかいものから、箱やびんなどの硬い材質のものまで、広く使われることばです（例1, 2, 3）。

Iremono is an object that is used to put things in. The word *iremono* refers to various kinds of container, from soft vinyl or paper bags to hard boxes or bottles (ex.1, 2, 3).

1) A：これ、君にあげるよ。
   B：何か入れ物ないかなあ。
   A： *Kore, kimini ageruyo.* This is for you. (I give this to you.)
   B： *Nanika iremono naikanaa?* Do you have something to put it in?

2) 子：お父さん、魚をつってきたんだけど……。
   父：この入れ物に入れなさい。
   Ko : *Otoosan, sakanao tsutte-kitandakedo...*
   Child : Dad, I caught a fish.
   Chichi : *Kono iremononi irenasai.*
   Father : Put it in this container.

3) A：きれいな入れ物ですね。
   B：ええ、化粧品が入っていたんですよ。
   A： *Kireina iremonodesune.* That's a pretty case, isn't it!
   B： *Ee, keshoohinga haitteitandesuyo.* Yes, it had cosmetics in it.

うつわ［器］ ■ *utsuwa* ■ container ; receptacle 

物を入れるものという意味では入れ物と同じですが、**材質が**ガラス・陶器・木などのように**硬いもの**のとき使います。多くの場合、食器を表します（例4, 5）。また、能力や人格などを総合した人間としての大きさや、責任のある立場に立つのに、ふさわしいかどうかなどを表(あらわ)すときにも使(つか)います（例(れい)6, 7）。

Utsuwa is similar to *iremono*, however the material the container is made of is hard, such as glass, china, or wood. In many cases, it refers to a container for food (ex.4, 5). In addition, *utsuwa* may be used to denote the overall stature, competence, character, etc., of a person, or the suitability of someone to occupy a position of responsibility (ex.6, 7).

---

4) セルフサービスのレストランでは、食(た)べた器(うつわ)は自分(じぶん)でかたづけます。
Serufu-saabisuno resutorandewa, tabeta utsuwawa jibunde katazukemasu.
At a self-service restaurant, you have to clear away your own dishes.

5) 果物(くだもの)をガラスの器(うつわ)に入(い)れると、見栄(みば)えがする。
Kudamonoo garasuno utsuwani ireruto, mibaega suru.
Fruit looks very attractive in a glass container.

6) 彼(かれ)は大臣(だいじん)の器(うつわ)ではない。
Karewa daijinno utsuwadewa nai.
He doesn't have the caliber to be a minister (of state).

7) あの人(ひと)は人間(にんげん)として器(うつわ)が小(ちい)さい。
Ano hitowa ningentoshite utsuwaga chiisai.
He is a man of low caliber.

ようき［容器(ようき)］ ■*youki* ■container 

何(なに)かを入(い)れるために作(つく)られたもので、使(つか)いみちが決(き)まっています。多(おお)くの場合(ばあい)、材質(ざいしつ)が硬(かた)く、ふたがしてあって、**中(なか)のものが外(そと)に出(で)ないようになっています。**少(すこ)し硬(かた)い表現(ひょうげん)です（例(れい)8, 9, 10）。

Youki is used when the purpose of the container is clear. In most cases the material of a *youki* is hard, and it has a lid or cover to seal things inside. *Youki* is more commonly used in formal language (ex.8, 9, 10).

---

8) 理科室(りかしつ)にガラスの容器(ようき)に入(はい)った標本(ひょうほん)が並(なら)んでいる。
Rikashitsuni garasuno yookini haitta hyoohonga narandeiru.
The specimens are lined up in glass containers in the science laboratory.

9) いらなくなったプラスチック容器(ようき)で、夏休(なつやす)みの工作(こうさく)を作(つく)った。
Iranakunatta purasuchikku-yookide, natsuyasumino koosakuo tsukutta.

I made my summer craft project out of plastic containers that no one wanted any more.

10) あの食品(しょくひん)メーカーの容器(ようき)はデザインがいい。

Ano shokuhin-meekaano yookiwa dezainga ii.
The designs of the containers of that food processing company are very good.

いろいろ／さまざま

■ *iroiro* ■ *samazama*

いろいろ ■ *iroiro* ■ various 

たくさんの種類(しゅるい)があるというようすを表(あらわ)します。「いろいろ」は「さまざま」よりも一般的(いっぱんてき)に広(ひろ)く使(つか)われ、ほとんどの場合(ばあい)「さまざま」の代(か)わりをすることができます。「いろいろな」を話(はな)しことばで「いろんな」とも言(い)います（例(れい)1, 2, 3, 4, 5）。

Iroiro expresses the existence of many kinds of things. Although it is interchangeable with *samazama* in most cases, *iroiro* is the more generally used expression. In daily conversation *iroiro na* may be shortened to *ironna* (ex.1, 2, 3, 4, 5).

1) きのうデパートで、いろいろなものを買(か)いました。

Kinoo depaatode, iroirona monoo kaimashita.
(I) bought many different things at the department store yesterday.

2) 日本(にほん)に来(き)て、いろいろな人(ひと)と友達(ともだち)になりました。

Nihonni kite, iroirona hitoto tomodachini narimashita.
Since I came to Japan, I've made friends with all kinds of people.

3) いろいろ考(かんが)えてみたけれど、結論(けつろん)が出(で)ない。

Iroiro kangaete-mitakeredo, ketsuronga denai.
(I've) tried thinking about it a lot of different ways, but I can't make a decision.

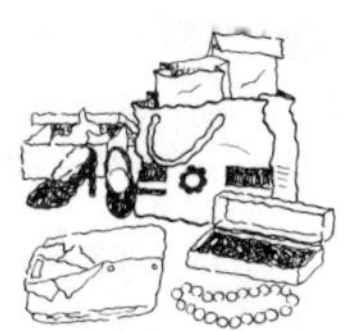

4) 水族館(すいぞくかん)には、いろんな魚(さかな)がいて楽(たの)しい。

Suizokukanniwa, ironna sakanaga ite tanoshii.
Aquariums are fun because they have so many kinds of fish.

5) いろいろとお世話になり、ありがとうございました。

Iroiroto osewani nari, arigatoo gozaimashita.
Thank you for doing so much for me.

さまざま

■ *samazama*
■ various ; diverse ; all kinds 

たくさんの種類があるようすを表しますが、「いろいろ」よりも**少しかたい言い方**です。単に「たくさん」というのではなく例６のように日本＝着物、ベトナム＝アオザイ、インド＝サリーなどといった、**それぞれに違いがある**という意味が強く含まれています。「さまざまお世話になりました・〜ありがとう・〜文句を言う」などのようには使いません（例6, 7, 8, 9）。

This expression also indicates the existence of many things, but is a more formal style of speaking than *iroiro*. It does not simply mean 'many', but attempts to point out the individual differences of each thing involved, as for example in Example 6, a Japanese *kimono*, a Vietnamese ao dai, an Indian sari, etc. It may not be used in expressions such as *samazama osewa ni narimashita* (I'm indebted to you), *samazama arigatou* (thank you for everything), or *samazama monku o iu* (complain a lot). In these cases *iroiro* must be used (ex.6, 7, 8, 9).

---

6) 選手たちはさまざまな民族衣装で、閉会式に参加した。

Senshutachiwa samazamana minzoku-ishoode, heikaishikini sankashita.
The athletes each wore the native costumes of their various countries at the closing ceremony.

7) 瀬戸内海には大小さまざまな島が浮かんでいる。

Setonaikainiwa daishoo samazamana shimaga ukandeiru.
There are all kinds of islands, large and small, in the Seto Inland Sea.

8) 今回の事件についての人々の反応は、さまざまだった。

Konkaino jikenni tsuiteno hitobitono hannoowa, samazamadatta.
People's reactions to this incident were varied.

9) 話し合いでは、さまざまな意見が出された。

Hanashiaidewa, samazamana ikenga dašareta.
All kinds of opinions were expressed at the discussion.

うく／うかぶ

■*uku*　■*ukabu*

うく［浮く］ ■*uku* ■to float

①物が水など液体の**表面に行く**ことです。また、底を離れて液体の中にとどまったり、地面を離れて空中にとどまることです（例1, 2, 3, 4）。
To float on the surface of a liquid (such as water) or to be suspended in a liquid or the air (ex.1, 2, 3, 4).

②**位置が定まらない**不安定なようすを表します（例５）。
Uku also expresses an unstable condition where the location of an object is not fixed (ex.5).

1) 油は水に浮く。
Aburawa mizuni uku.
Oil floats on water.

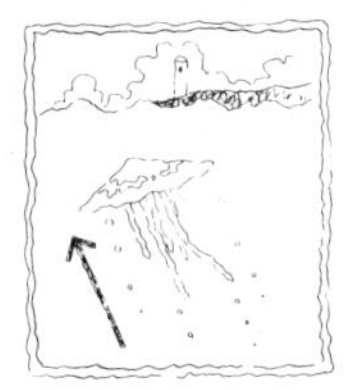

2) 無重力状態では、体は宙に浮く。
Mujuuryoku-jootaidewa, karadawa chuuni uku.
In zero-gravity, the body will float in the air.

3) ひげ鯨は、海の中に浮いているプランクトンなどを食べる。
Higekujirawa, umino nakani uiteiru purankuton-nadoo taberu.
Whalebone whales eat plankton and other organisms which live in the sea.

4) 小さい箱が浮いたり沈んだりしながら川を流れていく。
Chiisai hakoga uitari shizundari shinagara kawao nagareteiku.
A small box is bobbing up and down as it drifts down the river.

5) 彼女はいつも自分の意見だけが正しいと主張するので、クラスの中で浮いている。

Kanojowa itsumo jibunno ikendakega tadashiito shuchoosurunode, kurasuno nakade uiteiru.
She doesn't get along well with the other students because she always insists that she is right.

うかぶ［浮かぶ］ ■ *ukabu* ■ to float

---

①物体が液体の表面や空中に在ることです（例6, 7, 8, 9)。

Ukabu indicates that something exists on the surface of a liquid, in the air, etc. (ex.6, 7, 8, 9).

②ものごとが表面に現れることです（例10)。思いつく・考えつくあるいは心に描きだされるというときも、また感情が表情となって表れるときも使います（例11, 12, 13)。

It may also signify that something appears on or rises to the surface (ex.10). *Ukabu* is also used to express that something (such as an idea) comes to mind, a feeling 'arises within one', or an emotion is expressed on one's face (ex.11, 12, 13).

---

6) 空に白い雲が浮かんでいる。

Sorani shiroi kumoga ukandeiru.
A white cloud is drifting across the sky.

7) 青空に熱気球がぽっかりと浮かんでいる。

Aozorani netsukikyuuga pokkarito ukandeiru.
A hot-air balloon is floating across the blue sky.

8) 夜空に大きな月が、ぽっかりと浮かんでいる。

Yozorani ookina tsukiga, pokkarito ukandeiru.
The big moon is 'rising' in the evening sky.

9) 小豆島は、瀬戸内海に浮かぶ島です。

Shoodo-shimawa, Setonaikaini ukabu shimadesu.
Shoodo-shima is an island in the Seto Inland Sea.

10) 目撃者の証言から、彼が容疑者として浮かんできた。
Mokugekishano shoogenkara, karega yoogishatoshite ukandekita.
Because of the testimony of the witness, he became a suspect.

11) 疲れているときは、なかなか良い考えが浮かばない。
Tsukareteiru tokiwa, nakanaka yoi kangaega ukabanai.
When one is tired, it is difficult to come up with good ideas.

12) その知らせを聞いたときの彼女の喜ぶ顔が目に浮かぶようだ。
Sono shiraseo kiita tokino kanojono yorokobu kaoga meni ukabuyooda.
I can imagine how happy she will be when she hears the news (the image of her happy face is floating in front of my eyes).

13) 眠っている子供を見つめる母親の顔に、ほほえみが浮かんだ。
Nemutteiru kodomoo mitsumeru hahaoyano kaoni, hohoemiga ukanda.
As the mother looked at her sleeping child, a smile appeared on her face.

うつ／たたく

■ *utsu* ■ *tataku*

うつ［打つ］ ■ *utsu* ■ to hit ; to strike

手や**物**などを**何か**に**強く当てる**ことです。そして、音を出す・物を飛ばすなどの**目的が比較的はっきり**しています。また、「打つ」は「たたく」よりも**瞬間的な勢い・衝撃**があります（例1, 2, 3）。例4は、ぶつけたなどのように結果的に「打つ」ときの使い方です。また、人の心に強く感動をあたえるときにも使います（例5, 6）。

To strike something forcefully with a hand or instrument. A relatively clear objective to the action, for example to make a sound or to send something flying, is implied. *Utsu* suggests more of a momentary force or impact than does *tataku* (ex.1, 2, 3). As in Example 4, *utsu* may be used to refer to a resultant blow or hit.
In addition, it may be used to indicate that one is deeply impressed by something (ex.5, 6).

1) 彼のボールは、速くてなかなか打てない。
Kareno booruwa, hayakute nakanaka utenai.
His pitches are so fast that (I) can't hit them.

2) 私は、かなづちでくぎを打っていて、けがをした。
Watashiwa, kanazuchide kugio utteite, kegao shita.
I hurt myself when I was driving in a nail with a hammer.

3) 彼は、今日２本ホームランを打った。
Karewa, kyoo nihon hoomuran-o utta.
He hit two homeruns today.

4) 太郎は、スケート場で転んで頭を打った。
Taroowa, sukeetojoode koronde atamao utta.
Taro fell and hit his head at the skating rink.

5) 病気に負けずに明るく生きている少年の姿に人々は心を打たれた。
Byookini makezuni akaruku ikiteiru shoonenno sugatani hitobitowa kokoroo utareta.
People's hearts were touched by the sight of the boy, who was cheerfully getting on with his life without giving in to his illness.

6) 彼女の熱演は私の胸を強く打った。
Kanojono netsuenwa watashino muneo tsuyoku utta.
Her stirring performance moved me.

たたく

■ *tataku*
■ to hit ; to knock ; to beat 

手や物などを何かに**ぶつけるように当てる**ことです。その動作を**繰り返している**感じがあります。また、その衝撃や音を利用して注意を促したり、何かを探ったりするという意味を含みます（例7, 8, 9, 10, 11）。

To strike something with a hand or instrument. There is a feeling that the action is repeated, and it may be implied that one uses the impact or sound created to raise attention, search for something, etc. (ex.7, 8, 9, 10, 11).

7) 悪口を言われて、メアリーはジョンを思い切りたたいた。
Warukuchio iwarete, Meariiwa Jon-o omoikiri tataita.
Mary hit John as hard as she could for saying bad things about her.

8) だれかがドアをたたく音で、目が覚めた。

Darekaga doao tataku otode, mega sameta.
I awoke to the sound of someone knocking at the door.

9) 何でも欲しいものを買ってやると言うと、子供は手をたたいて喜んだ。

Nandemo hoshii monoo katteyaruto yuuto, kodomowa teo tataite yorokonda.
My child clapped his hands with joy when (I) told him I'd buy him anything he wants.

10) 祖父は年に1回、祭りで太鼓をたたくのを楽しみにしている。

Sofuwa nenni ikkai, matsuride taikoo tatakunoo tanoshimini shiteiru.
My grandfather looks forward to playing the *taiko* (Japanese drum) at the festival each year.

11) 私は肉を焼くまえに、棒でたたいて軟らかくした。

Watashiwa nikuo yaku maeni, boode tataite yawarakakushita.
I pounded the meat with a cudgel to tenderize it before cooking.

うっかり／つい

▪ *ukkari* ▪ *tsui*

うっかり ▪ *ukkari* ▪ careless 

ぼんやりしていたり、**不注意**で何かをしてしまうとき使います。習慣ではない失敗に使います（例1, 2, 3, 4）。

Ukkari is used when one does something absent-mindedly or carelessly. It is often used when an unexpected or uncharacteristic mistake is made (ex.1, 2, 3, 4).

1) きのう、うっかりして家のかぎをかけるのを忘れた。

Kinoo, ukkarishite ieno kagio kakerunoo wasureta.
Yesterday, (I) carelessly forgot to lock the door to my home.

2) うっかりストーブにさわって、やけどをした。

Ukkari sutoobuni sawatte, yakedoo shita.
(I) carelessly touched the heater and burned myself.

3) たいせつな秘密(ひみつ)をうっかりしゃべってしまった。

Taisetsuna himitsuo ukkari shabette-shimatta.
(I) carelessly blurted out an important secret.

4) うっかりしていて運転免許証(うんてんめんきょしょう)の期限(きげん)がきれているのを忘(わす)れていた。

Ukkarishiteite unten-menkyoshoono kigenga kireteirunoo wasureteita.
(I) carelessly forgot that my driver's license had expired.

つい

■ *tsui*
■ by habit ; without thinking 

ほんとうはしないほうがいいことを、がまんできずにしてしまったり、また習慣(しゅうかん)やくせになっていることがでてしまう・「〜しがちだ」というようすを表(あらわ)すとき使(つか)います(例(れい)5, 6, 7, 8)。

Tsui is used when one is unable to prevent himself from doing something which should not be done, or to express doing something that has become a habit or tendency (ex.5, 6, 7, 8).

---

5) セールスマンに勧(すす)められて、つい高(たか)い香水(こうすい)を買(か)ってしまった。

Seerusumanni susumerarete, tsui takai koosuio katteshimatta.
Pressured by the salesman, (I) ended up buying the expensive perfume.

6) つい、かっとなって弟(おとうと)をなぐってしまった。

Tsui, kattonatte otootoo nagutteshimatta.
(I) just blew up and hit my brother.

7) いつも早(はや)く寝(ね)ようと思(おも)っているのに、
本(ほん)を読(よ)みだすとつい夜(よ)ふかしをしてしまう。

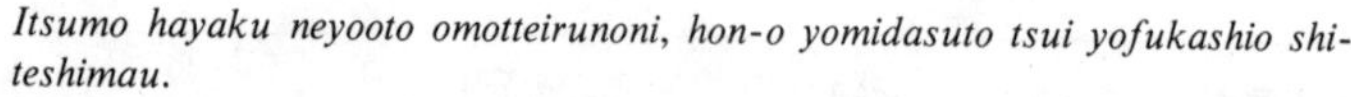

Itsumo hayaku neyooto omotteirunoni, hon-o yomidasuto tsui yofukashio shiteshimau.
(I) always intend to go to bed early, but once I start reading I end up staying up late.

8) 彼がうそつきなのはわかっていても、話を聞いているとつい同情しちゃう。
Karega usotsukinanowa wakatteitemo, hanashio kiiteiruto tsui doojooshichau.
Although (I) know all along that he's a liar, when I listen to him I end up sympathizing with him.

うまい／おいしい

■ *umai* ■ *oishii*

うまい ■ *umai* ■ good ; skilled 大

①**味がいい**という意味で、多くは男性が使います（例1, 2）。
Umai means that a food is tasty, and is used predominately in male speech (ex.1, 2).

②**上手だ**という意味で使います（例3, 4）。
It may also mean that one is skillful or good at doing something (ex.3, 4).

③自分にとって**つごうがよい**とか**利益がある**という意味があります（例5）。
Umai may also describe something as convenient or profitable (ex.5).

1) 厚：このラーメン、うまいね。
勝：うん、うまい。
Atsushi : *Kono raamen**, *umaine.* This *ramen* is delicious, isn't it?
Masaru : *Un, umai.* Yeah, good!
—— * *Raamen* is a popular meal in Japan, consisting of Chinese style noodles served in a soup broth and topped with meat and vegetables.

2) この喫茶店のコーヒーはすごくうまいよ。
Kono kissatenno koohiiwa sugoku umaiyo.
The coffee at this shop is extremely good, you know.

3) 田中先生は日本語の教え方がうまい。
Tanakasenseiwa Nihongono oshiekataga umai.
Mr. Tanaka is very good at teaching Japanese.

4) A：次は高橋君のサーブだよ。

B：うまい。さすがは高橋君(たかはしくん)だ。

A： *Tsugiwa Takahashikun*∗*no saabudayo.* ∗p.411
It's Takahashi's turn to serve next.

B： *Umai. Sasugawa Takahashikunda.*
Great serve! But what else would you expect from Takahashi?

5) 1万円(まんえん)が10日(とおか)で100万円(まんえん)になるなんて、そんなうまい話(はなし)があるわけがない。
Ichiman-enga tookade hyakuman-enni narunante, sonna umai hanashiga aru wakega nai.
How can you make ¥1,000,000 out of ¥10,000 in ten days? That's too good to be true.

おいしい ■*oishii* ■delicious [大]

味(あじ)がいいという意味(いみ)です（例(れい)6, 7, 8)。「うまい」の例(れい)3, 4のように「教(おし)え方(かた)がおいしい」とか「絵(え)がおいしい」など、「上手(じょうず)だ」の意味(いみ)には使(つか)えません。

Oishii means that a food is tasty and delicious (ex.6, 7, 8). *Oishii* cannot be used in such cases as those in Examples 3 and 4 to refer to skillfulness.

---

6) まり子(こ)：このケーキおいしいわね。

なおみ：そうね、おいしいわね。

Mariko : *Kono keeki oishiiwane.* This cake is very tasty!
Naomi : *Soone, oishiiwane.* Yes, it is, isn't it?

7) この地方(ちほう)の水(みず)はおいしい。
Kono chihoono mizuwa oishii.
The water in this area is delicious.

8) 山(やま)の頂上(ちょうじょう)で、おいしい空気(くうき)を胸(むね)いっぱい吸(す)いました。
Yamano choojoode, oishii kuukio muneippai suimashita.
We breathed fresh clean air on the mountain top.

うらむ／にくむ

■*uramu* ■*nikumu*

うらむ［恨む］ ■*uramu* ■to hold a grudge (against) 

相手が自分にしたことを、ひどいと感じたり、また「自分が今、こんなにいやな思いをしているのは**相手のせいだ**」と、いつまでも**相手を悪く思う**ことです（例1, 2, 3, 4, 5, 6）。

To hold a permanent grudge or feelings of ill-will against someone who has done something terrible to oneself, or is responsible for a bad experience one is now undergoing (ex.1, 2, 3, 4, 5, 6).

1) 彼は、子供のころ自分をいじめていた同級生のことを今でもうらんでいる。
Karewa, kodomono koro jibun-o ijimeteita dookyuuseino kotoo imademo urandeiru.
Even to this day, he still thinks ill of that kid in his class that used to bully him as a child.

2) 彼女はいつも貧しかったけれど、自分の運命をうらんだことはなかった。
Kanojowa itsumo mazushikatta-keredo, jibunno unmeio uranda kotowa nakatta.
She has always been poor, but she has never felt bitter about her fate.

3) バレーボール部の厳しい特訓で、ずいぶんコーチをうらんだけれど、今では感謝している。
Bareeboorubuno kibishii tokkunde, zuibun koochio urandakeredo, imadewa kanshashiteiru.
(I) used to resent my coach for her strict training regimen in the volleyball club, but now I appreciate her.

4) 親切だと思ってしたのに、よろこばれないでうらまれてしまった。
Shinsetsudato omotte shitanoni, yorokobarenaide uramarete-shimatta.
(I) did it out of kindness, but they weren't pleased at all; I ended up being resented.

5) 日本には「四谷怪談」、「番町皿屋敷」など、死んだあとも人をうらんでお化けになるという話がある。
Nihonniwa 'Yotsuya Kaidan','Banchoo Sarayashiki' nado, shinda atomo hitoo urande obakeni naruto yuu hanashiga aru.
In Japan there are tales such as *Yotsuya Kaidan* and *Bancho Sarayashiki* in which a dead person returns as a ghost to haunt someone.

6) うらまれるのもいやだが、人をうらむのはもっといやだ。
Uramarerunomo iyadaga, hitoo uramunowa motto iyada.
(I) don't like having someone hold a grudge against me, but I dislike even more holding a grudge against someone else.

にくむ［憎む］ ■***nikumu*** ■to hate 

「**嫌いだ**」という気持ちを**激しく感じる**ことです。相手がなにかしたときも、また、とくに理由がなくても、「いやだ・嫌いだ」と憎むこともあります（例7, 8, 9, 10）。

To feel a violent dislike toward someone, whether that person has done something, or for no particular reason (ex.7, 8, 9, 10).

---

7) 彼女は、家族を捨てて家出をした母より、そうさせた男を憎んでいた。
Kanojowa, kazokuo sutete iedeo shita hahayori, soosaseta otokoo nikundeita.
She hated, not her mother, who had abandoned her family and left home, but the man who made her do it.

8) 人に憎まれてでも出世したいとは思わない。
Hitoni nikumaretedemo shusseshitai-towa omowanai.
(I) don't want to get ahead in the world if it means being hated by others.

9) 彼は子供の時から、不正を憎む気持ちが強かった。
Karewa kodomono tokikara, fuseio nikumu kimochiga tsuyokatta.
Ever since he was a child he has had strong feelings of hatred against injustice.

10) 彼女は、大切な家族を奪った戦争を憎んでいる。
Kanojowa, taisetsuna kazokuo ubatta sensoo-o nikundeiru.
She hates the war that robbed her of her precious family.

うる／ばいきゃくする／うりはらう

■***uru*** ■***baikyaku suru*** ■***uriharau***

うる［売る］ ■*uru* ■to sell

物を渡して、お金をもらうことです。個人的な場合も（例1, 2）、店の人のようにそれを仕事としている場合もあります（例3, 4, 5）。

To give something to somebody in exchange for money. *Uru* may be used for sales made on a personal basis (ex.1, 2), or by someone working in a shop (ex.3, 4, 5).

1) 私は、乗らなくなった自転車を、友達に1000円で売った。
Watashiwa, noranakunatta jitenshao, tomodachini sen-ende utta.
I sold the bicycle I don't ride anymore to my friend for ¥1,000.

2) 彼は今乗っている車を売りたがっている。
Karewa ima notteiru kurumao uritagatteiru.
He wants to sell the car he's driving now.

3) 野菜を売る店を八百屋という。
Yasaio urumiseo yaoyato yuu.
A shop that sells vegetables is called a *yaoya* (green-grocer).

4) あの画家は、気に入った人にしか自分の作品を売らない。
Ano gakawa, kiniitta hitonishika jibunno sakuhin-o uranai.
That artist only sells his works to people he likes.

5) デパートでは、何でも売っている。
Depaatodewa, nandemo utteiru.
They sell everything at a department store.

ばいきゃくする［売却する］ ■*baikyaku suru* ■to sell

「売る」と同じように物を渡して、お金をもらうことです。「土地・株・会社」など**比較的値段の高いもの**について使う少しかたい表現です（例6, 7, 8）。

As does *uru*, this means to transfer ownership of an object to another person in exchange for money. However, *baikyaku suru* is a slightly more formal expression, and refers to the sale of relatively high priced items, i.e., property, stock, or a company (ex.6, 7, 8).

6) 不動産を売却すると税金がかかる。
ふどうさん　ばいきゃく　ぜいきん

Fudoosan-o baikyakusuruto zeikinga kakaru.
When (you) sell a piece of real estate, you must pay taxes.

7) 彼は莫大な借金を返すために、農場を売却した。
かれ　ばくだい　しゃっきん　かえ　のうじょう　ばいきゃく

Karewa bakudaina shakkin-o kaesu tameni, noojoo-o baikyakushita.
He sold his farm to pay back his enormous debt.

8) 彼女は、亡くなった父親が集めた数枚の名画を、画商に売却した。
かのじょ　な　ちちおや　あつ　すうまい　めいが　がしょう　ばいきゃく

Kanojowa, nakunatta chichioyaga atsumeta suumaino meigao, gashooni baikyakushita.
After her father died, she sold several of the famous paintings he had collected to an art dealer.

うりはらう［売り払う］
う　はら

■ *uriharau*
■ to sell off ; to dispose of 

自分の持っていたもののすべてを売るという意味で使います（例 9, 10, 11）。
じぶん　も　う　いみ　つか　れい

To entirely sell off all of something one owns (ex.9, 10, 11).

---

9) 私の友人は、家財道具を売り払って、一家で海外に移住した。
わたし　ゆうじん　かざいどうぐ　う　はら　いっか　かいがい　いじゅう

Watashino yuujinwa, kazaidooguo uriharatte, ikkade kaigaini ijuushita.
My friend sold off all of the household goods he had, and emigrated overseas with his family.

10) 彼女は女優だったころの服をすべて売り払って、そのお金を慈善団体に寄付した。
かのじょ　じょゆう　ふく　う　はら　かね　じぜんだんたい　き　ふ

Kanojowa joyuudatta korono fukuo subete uriharatte, sono okaneo jizendantaini kifushita.
She sold all of the clothes she had accumulated during her days as an actress, and donated the money to a charitable organization.

11) 宝石どろぼうの一味がつかまったが、宝石はすでに売り払われた後だった。
ほうせき　いちみ　ほうせき　う　はら　あと

Hoosekidoroboono ichimiga tsukamattaga, hoosekiwa sudeni uriharawareta atodatta.
They caught the gang of jewel thieves, but not before all of the jewels they had stolen had been disposed of.

うるさい／さわがしい／にぎやか

■ *urusai* ■ *sawagashii* ■ *nigiyaka*

うるさい

■ *urusai*
■ noisy ; bothersome 

①音(おと)が耳(みみ)にじゃまに感(かん)じるときの**不快(ふかい)なようす**を表(あらわ)します（例(れい)1, 2, 3）。

This word is used when expressing displeasure or discomfort when a sound is annoying to one's ears (ex.1, 2, 3).

②いやなことがくり返(かえ)し行(おこな)われたり、しつこくされたりしたときに感(かん)じるようすです。動作(どうさ)だけでなく、同(おな)じようなことを何度(なんど)も言(い)われたりするときや、**余計(よけい)でわずらわしいもの**についても同(おな)じです（例(れい)4, 5）。

Urusai also expresses annoyance when an unpleasant event occurs persistently and repeatedly. It is used not only with reference to actions, but also when one is repeatedly told something that is unnecessary and annoying (ex.4, 5).

③何(なに)か一(ひと)つのことがらの、細(こま)かいところまでその人(ひと)なりのはっきりとした考(かんが)えをもっていることです（例(れい)6）。

It may also be used to indicate that one has his own definite ideas about small matters or details, i.e., picky, fussy, or particular (ex.6).

---

1) 私(わたし)の家(いえ)は飛行場(ひこうじょう)に近(ちか)いので、音(おと)がうるさい。
Watashino iewa hikoojooni chikainode, otoga urusai.
My house is near an airport so the noise is loud (it is noisy).

2) 暴走族(ぼうそうぞく)のバイクの音(おと)がうるさくて眠(ねむ)れない。
*Boosoozoku** *no baikuno otoga urusakute nemurenai.*
The noise of the bikers is so loud (I) can't sleep.
—— * *Boosoozoku* are bands of young people that drive cars and motorcycles recklessly and loudly late at night without regard for traffic laws.

3) まわりがうるさいので、電話(でんわ)の声(こえ)が聞(き)こえない。
Mawariga urusainode, denwano koega kikoenai.
There is so much noise (I) can't hear the voice on the telephone.

4) 両親(りょうしん)は、早(はや)く結婚(けっこん)しろとうるさく言(い)う。

Ryooshinwa, hayaku kekkonshiroto urusaku yuu.
My parents are pestering me to get married.

5) 子供(こども)たちにうるさくせがまれて、猫(ねこ)をかうことにした。
Kodomotachini urusaku segamarete, nekoo kau kotoni shita.
(I) was bugged so much by my kids that I decided to get them a cat.

6) 彼(かれ)は、味(あじ)にうるさい。
Karewa, ajini urusai.
He's particular about flavor.

さわがしい［騒(さわ)がしい］

■ *sawagashii*
■ noisy ; boisterous

---

①静(しず)かな雰囲気(ふんいき)をこわすような**雑然(ざつぜん)とした音(おと)**や**声(こえ)**が聞(き)こえてくるようすを表(あらわ)します（例(れい)7, 8, 9)。

This word refers to random sounds or voices which disturb a peaceful atmosphere (ex.7, 8, 9).

②また、人(ひと)の心(こころ)を乱(みだ)すような事件(じけん)やことがらのために、**世(よ)の中(なか)が落(お)ち着(つ)かないようす**にも使(つか)います（例(れい)10)。

It is used also to refer to an unsettled state in the world arising from mind-troubling events (ex.10).

---

7) 外(そと)が騒(さわ)がしいけれど、近(ちか)くで火事(かじ)でもあったのだろうか。
Sotoga sawagashiikeredo, chikakude kajidemo attanodarooka.
It's noisy outside—I wonder if there's been a fire or something nearby.

8) 騒(さわ)がしい都会(とかい)をさけて、静(しず)かなホテルに泊(と)まりに来(き)た。
Sawagashii tokaio sakete, shizukana hoteruni tomarinikita.
I came to get away from the noisy city and stay at a quiet hotel.

9) 人(ひと)だかりがして騒(さわ)がしいので行(い)ってみたら、交通事故(こうつうじこ)だった。
Hitodakariga shite sawagashiinode ittemitara, kootsuujikodatta.
There were crowds and a hullabaloo, so I went to look and found there had been a traffic accident.

10) ハイジャックだ、誘拐(ゆうかい)だと騒(さわ)がしい世(よ)の中(なか)だ。
Haijakkuda, yuukaidato sawagashii yononakada.
Hijacks and kidnappings—what a troubled world!

にぎやか ■ *nigiyaka* ■ bustling

人が多く集まっていて、**活気がある**ようすを表します。陽気だ・盛況だという感じがあり、不快な感じはそれほど強くありません（例11, 12, 13）。「にぎやかな人」は、よくしゃべったり笑ったりして、その場で**目立つ存在**の人のことです（例14）。

Nigiyaka expresses the liveliness created by a large number of people. It includes a sense of cheer and activity, and does not imply unpleasant feelings (ex.11, 12, 13).
Nigiyaka na hito is a person who laughs and is talkative, and stands out in a crowd (ex.14).

11) このあたりは、昼間は人通りが多くてにぎやかだが、夜になるとさびしい。
Kono atariwa, hirumawa hitodooriga ookute nigiyakadaga, yoruni naruto sabishii.
This area is bustling with many people passing through in the daytime, but at night it's rather deserted.

12) 父：２階はずいぶんにぎやかだね。
母：裕二のお友だちが来ているんですよ。
Chichi : *Nikaiwa zuibun nigiyakadane.*
Father : They're a bit boisterous upstairs, aren't they?
Haha : *Yuujino otomodachiga kiteirundesuyo.*
Mother : That's because Yuji's friends are here.

13) ふたごが産まれて、うちは急ににぎやかになった。
Futagoga umarete, uchiwa kyuuni nigiyakani natta.
When the twins were born, it suddenly got lively around our house.

14) 山田さん、いつもはあんなににぎやかなのに、きょうはずいぶんおとなしいですね。どうしたんでしょう。
Yamadasan, itsumowa annani nigiyakananoni, kyoowa zuibun otonashiidesune. Dooshitandeshoo?
Ms. Yamada is usually so cheery, but today she's really subdued. I wonder what is the matter.

うれしい／たのしい／ゆかい

■ *ureshii* ■ *tanoshii* ■ *yukai*

うれしい

■ *ureshii*
■ happy ; glad ♥

望んでいたことや期待していたことが思い通りになったときや、好ましいことがあったとき、**喜びや感激を表して使います**。明るく晴れやかなとても快い気持ちです（例1, 2, 3, 4, 5）。

Ureshii is used to express the pleasure of being moved or excited when something good happens, or when things go as the speaker wished them to. It implies a cheerful and happy feeling (ex.1, 2, 3, 4, 5).

1) お目にかかれて、とてもうれしい。

Omeni kakarete, totemo ureshii.
(I'm) so glad to see you!

2) A：はい、誕生日のプレゼント。

B：わあ、うれしい。ありがとう。

A : *Hai, tanjoobino purezento.*
Here is a birthday present for you.

B : *Waa, ureshii. Arigatoo.*
Wow, I'm so happy! Thank you!

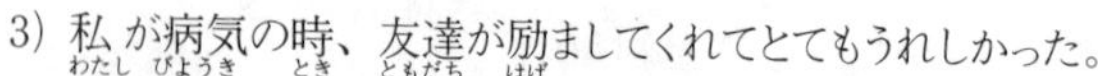

3) 私が病気の時、友達が励ましてくれてとてもうれしかった。

Watashiga byookino toki, tomodachiga hagemashite-kurete totemo ureshikatta.
My friend gave me moral support while I was sick, and it made me very happy.

4) 初めて自転車を買ってもらった日、うれしくて眠れなかった。

Hajimete jitenshao kattemoratta hi, ureshikute nemurenakatta.
On the day (I) received my first bicycle I was so happy I couldn't sleep.

5) その時、孫が産まれたという、うれしい知らせが届いた。

Sono toki, magoga umaretato yuu, ureshii shirasega todoita.
At that moment, (we) heard the good news that our grandchild had been born.

たのしい［楽しい］

■ *tanoshii*
■ fun ; cheerful 

いやなことやつまらないことがなく、**明るいいい雰囲気**を表します（例6, 7, 8, 9）。「うれしい」は「入学試験に受かってうれしい」のように、具体的な一つ一つの出来事に対応して使いますが、「楽しい」は、その**瞬間ではなく、全体の雰囲気が充実しているようす**を表します。「楽しむ」は動詞です（例10）。

Tanoshii expresses a casual and light mood, void of unpleasantness or boredom (ex.6, 7, 8, 9). Unlike *ureshii*, which suggests a reaction to a specific event, as in the example *Nyuugakushiken ni ukatte ureshii* (I'm so happy that I passed the school entrance examination), *tanoshii* describes the overall atmosphere. *Tanoshimu* is the verb form (ex.10).

6) 夏休みのキャンプは、料理を作ったり魚をつったりしてとても楽しかった。
Natsuyasumino kyanpuwa, ryoorio tsukuttari sakanao tsuttarishite totemo tanoshikatta.
Summer camp was a lot of fun because (we) did things such as cooking and fishing.

7) 私は家族と話をしているときが一番楽しい。
Watashiwa kazokuto hanashio shiteiru tokiga ichiban tanoshii.
To me, the time I spend talking with my family is the most enjoyable.

8) 私の息子は、今度の日曜日に遊園地に行くのを楽しみにしている。
Watashino musukowa, kondono nichiyoobini yuuenchini ikunoo tanoshimini shiteiru.
My son is looking forward to going to the amusement park this Sunday.

9) 私はときどき、楽しかった子供のころを思い出す。
Watashiwa tokidoki, tanoshikatta kodomono koroo omoidasu.
Sometimes, I recall the happy days of my childhood.

10) 弟は、スポーツをしたり旅行をしたり、学生生活を楽しんでいる。
Otootowa, supootsuo shitari ryokoo-o shitari, gakusei-seikatsuo tanoshindeiru.
My (younger) brother is enjoying his school life, because he is able to do things such as travel and play sports.

ゆかい

■ *yukai*
■ amusing ; fun ; cheerful 

明るくておもしろい、おかしいというようすを表します。**思わず笑ってしまうような陽気な気分**です。「楽しい人」よりも「ゆかいな人」の方が、もっと冗談を言ったりふざけたりして人を笑わせる雰囲気を持っています（例11, 12, 13, 14）。

Yukai expresses a cheerful, interesting, or funny state. The mood is so lively that one may unintentionally burst out laughing. A person described as a *yukaina hito* has an even more cheerful personality than a *tanoshii hito*; he jokes around and makes people laugh more (ex.11, 12, 13, 14).

---

11) サーカスのピエロのしぐさはいつ見てもゆかいだ。

Saakasuno pierono shigusawa itsumitemo yukaida.
It's always fun to watch the clown acts at the circus.

12) 彼はものまねがじょうずで、みんなを笑わせるゆかいな男の子だ。

Karewa monomanega joozude, minnao warawaseru yukaina otokonokoda.
He is a funny boy who is good at mimicry and making people laugh.

13) きのうの映画はとてもゆかいだった。笑いすぎておなかが痛くなっちゃった。

Kinoono eigawa totemo yukaidatta. Waraisugite onakaga itaku natchatta.
The movie (I) saw yesterday was very funny. I laughed so much that my stomach hurt.

14) いやなことがあったときでも、陽気な彼と話をしているとだんだんゆかいになってくる。

Iyana kotoga atta tokidemo, yookina kareto hanashio shiteiruto dandan yukaini nattekuru.
Even when something bad happens, if (I) talk to him, his sunny personality has a way of making me gradually begin to feel cheery.

おう／おいかける

■ *ou*　■ *oikakeru*

おう［追う］ ■ *ou* ■ to follow ; to chase 

前にいるものや、**先に行ったものに近づこう・ついて行こう**とすることです（例1, 2, 3）。抽象的な目的を求めるときにも使います。また、例4, 5は追いた

てて向こうへ行かせるという意味です。

To move closer to or behind something that is in front or has gone ahead (ex.1, 2, 3). It may also be used when one looks for something abstract. In Examples 4 and 5 it means to drive away or repulse.

---

1) 猫がねずみを追って走っていった。
Nekoga nezumio otte hashitteitta.
The cat ran after the mouse.

2) 忘れ物を届けようと父を追ったけれど、追いつくことはできなかった。
Wasuremonoo todokeyooto chichio ottakeredo, oitsuku kotowa dekinakatta.
(I) chased after my father to give him something he had forgotten, but I couldn't catch up with him.

3) 警察は、銀行強盗の行方を追っている。
Keisatsuwa, ginkoo-gootoono yukueo otteiru.
The police are on the trail of the bank robber.

4) 遊牧民は、羊を追って移動する。
Yuuboku-minwa, hitsujio otte idoosuru.
Nomads migrate, driving their sheep ahead of them.

5) 牛がしっぽで、はえを追っている。
Ushiga shippode, haeo otteiru.
The cows are driving away flies with their tails.

おいかける［追いかける］

■ *oikakeru*
■ to chase (in order to catch) 

逃げていくものや遠ざかっていくもの・先に行くものを**つかまえるために**、急いで近づいていくことです（例6, 7, 8）。

To move quickly after something that is escaping, or moving away or ahead, in order to catch it (ex.6, 7, 8).

---

6) パトカーはサイレンを鳴らしながら、犯人の車を追いかけた。
Patokaawa sairen-o narashinagara, hanninno kurumao oikaketa.
The police car chased after the suspect's car with its siren wailing.

7) 私の財布をすった男を追いかけたけれど、見失ってしまった。
Watashino saifuo sutta otokoo oikaketakeredo, miushinatte-shimatta.

(I) chased after the man that stole my wallet, but I lost sight of him.

8) 犬に追いかけられて、必死で逃げた。
Inuni oikakerarete, hisshide nigeta.
(I) ran like crazy to get away from the dog that was chasing me.

お忘れ物ですよ

エディがアルバイトをしているレストランで、お客さんが手袋を忘れて帰りました。エディが気づいて、すぐに追いかけました。そして大声で言いました。「あなたは手袋を忘れましたよ」お客さんは、お礼を言って受け取りましたが、ほんの少し不愉快そうでした。

ではどう言えば良かったのでしょうか。この場合は、「お忘れ物ですよ」や「手袋をお忘れですよ」などのように、状態や状況について言う方が、より優しくていねいです。「手袋を忘れましたよ」もひどく悪いというのではありませんが、エディの言い方では、失敗をとがめているような感じがします。「あなたは〜した」というのは、良くない結果について言うときには、特に強く感じられるのです。お客さんが不愉快そうだったのは、そのためです。

このことを知ったエディは、次の日、道で前を歩いていた人が手帳を落として気づかなかったとき、「落とし物ですよ」と言って拾ってあげました。

Owasure mono desu yo

A customer left her gloves behind when she was leaving the restaurant that Eddie works at. Eddie noticed the gloves and quickly went out after her, shouting, "*Anata wa tebukuro o wasure mashita yo.*[1]" The customer took the gloves and thanked Eddie, but she seemed to be somewhat displeased.

So, how should Eddie have called out to the customer? In this case he should have said something like "*Owasure mono desu yo*[2]" or "*Tebukuro o owasure desu yo,*[3]" which are ways of speaking that are more appropriate for the situation because they come across as softer and more polite. It is not really all that bad to say, "*Tebukuro o wasure mashita yo*[4]" ; but the way Eddie said it with the words *anata wa...* connotes that he is reproaching the customer for her mistake.

When someone says "*Anata wa ～shita*[5]," it is often interpreted by the listener in a negative way, and this was the reason for the customer's displeasure.

The next day, after Eddie had become aware of this fact, a person walking ahead of him dropped his address book. Eddie saw this, said, "*Otoshi mono desu yo,*[6]" and handed it over to him.

1 *You forgot your gloves.*
2 *(This) is something forgotten (by you).*
3 *You forgot your gloves (polite expression).*
4 *(You) forgot your gloves.*
5 *You did...*
6 *(This) is something dropped (by you).*

おおい／たくさん／いっぱい

■ *ooi* ■ *takusan* ■ *ippai*

おおい［多い］ ■ *ooi* ■ many ; much ; a lot of 

量・回数など、数量が大きいことです。ほかのものと比べたときの数量の大きさを表します（例1, 2, 3, 4）。「少ない」に対応します。

Ooi expresses that the amount of something is large, or the frequency of events is high. The amount of something described as *ooi* is considered to be large when compared to something else (ex.1, 2, 3, 4). The opposite of *ooi* is *sukunai*, which means 'few'.

1) 東京は、人口が多い。
Tookyoowa, jinkooga ooi.
The population of Tokyo is very large.

2) レモンには、ビタミンCが多い。
Remonniwa, bitaminsiiga ooi.
There is a lot of vitamin C in lemons.

3) 日本は、地震が多い国だ。
Nihonwa, jishinga ooi kunida.
Japan has a lot of earthquakes.

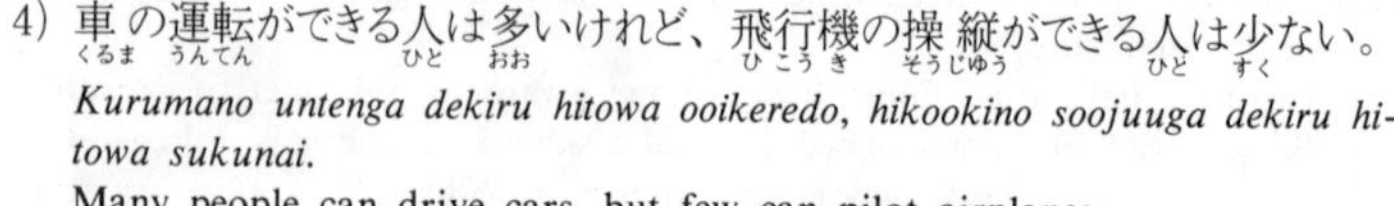

4) 車の運転ができる人は多いけれど、飛行機の操縦ができる人は少ない。
Kurumano untenga dekiru hitowa ooikeredo, hikookino soojuuga dekiru hitowa sukunai.
Many people can drive cars, but few can pilot airplanes.

たくさん

■ *takusan*
■ many ; much ; a lot of

①**数量が多い**ようすを表します（例5, 6, 7）。
This denotes a large quantity or volume (ex.5, 6, 7).

②今の**量や程度で十分だ、これ以上は必要ない**というとき使います（例8, 9)。また、例10のように、そんなことはもういやだ、という拒絶の意味にも使います。

It also denotes that the present amount or degree is considered to be enough, and no more is needed (ex.8, 9). It may also be used, as in Example 10, to indicate refusal because one is 'unable to withstand anymore'.

---

5) うちの庭で、いちごがたくさんとれました。
Uchino niwade, ichigoga takusan toremashita.
We were able to get a lot of strawberries from our garden.

6) 日光には、いつもたくさんの観光客が訪れる。
Nikkooniwa, itsumo takusanno kankookyakuga otozureru.
There are always many tourists visiting Nikko.

7) 私には友だちがたくさんいる。
Watashiniwa tomodachiga takusan iru.

I have many friends.

8) キャンプに行くのに、わざわざ新しい服を買わなくても、ふだん着でたくさんだ。

Kyanpuni ikunoni, wazawaza atarashii fukuo kawanakutemo, fudangide takusanda.
You don't have to buy new clothes just to go camping—ordinary clothes will be sufficient.

9) A：ご飯、もう1膳いかがですか。
B：いいえ、もうたくさんです。

A： *Gohan, moo ichizen ikagadesuka?*
How about another bowl of rice?
B： *Iie, moo takusandesu.*
No, thank you. I've had more than enough.

10) もう君のぐちを聞かされるのは、たくさんだ。

Moo kimino guchio kikasarerunowa, takusanda.
I've had enough of listening to your complaints.

いっぱい ■*ippai* ■a lot of ; full

数量が多いようすを表します（例11, 12, 13）。「たくさん」とほぼ同じ使い方をしますが、「いっぱい」は、**会話で使うことが多く、くだけた感じ**です。ですから時には子供っぽく感じられることもあります。また、「容量を十分に満たしている」あるいは「もうそれ以上余裕がない」という意味も表します（例14, 15）。

Ippai has nearly the same meaning as *takusan*, indicating a large amount or volume (ex.11, 12, 13). However, *ippai* is more commonly used in conversation and has a more casual feel, so it may occasionally sound childish. It may also indicate that something is full, or that there is no room for more (ex.14, 15).

---

11) 新宿には、いつもいっぱい人がいる。

Shinjukuniwa, itsumo ippai hitoga iru.
Shinjuku is always full of people.

12) 箱の中に、お菓子がいっぱい入っている。

Hakono nakani, okashiga ippai haitteiru.

This box is full of sweets.

13) 世の中には、いやな事がいっぱいある。

Yononakaniwa, iyana kotoga ippai aru.

There are many terrible things in the world.

14) うれしさで胸がいっぱいになり、何も言えなかった。

Ureshisade munega ippaini nari, nanimo ienakatta.

(I) was so full of happiness that I couldn't say anything. (I was too happy for words.)

15) おなかがいっぱいになると、眠くなる。

Onakaga ippaini naruto, nemuku naru.

I get sleepy when I have a full stomach.

おかげ／せい／ため

■ *okage*　■ *sei*　■ *tame*

おかげ

■ *okage*
■ thanks to ; owe〜 (to〜) 

ものごとが良い結果になったときに、その原因となった**ことがら**や**人**などに**感謝の気持ちを表す**とき使います（例1, 2, 3）。また、逆に悪い結果になったときにも、その原因に批難の気持ちをこめて使います（例4, 5）。「**おかげさまで**」は、実際に世話になった人に**感謝の気持ち**を述べるときに使います。また、例6のように、実際に世話になったわけではないけれど、気にかけてくれたことに対する感謝や、良い結果になったことの喜びを謙虚に述べるとき使います。

Okage is used when expressing gratitude to someone or something that has helped bring about a positive result (ex.1, 2, 3). It may also be used in the opposite situation; that is, to lay blame on someone or something for a bad result (ex.4, 5). The expression *okagesama de* is used to show gratitude to someone who has performed a service for or taken care of the speaker in some way. However, as in Example 6, it may be used when the person has not actually done anything, but the speaker wishes to thank him for his concern, or to modestly express happiness that something has turned out well.

---

1) 電気製品が発達したおかげで、昔と比べると家事はずいぶん楽になった。
Denkiseihinga hattatsushita okagede, mukashito kuraberuto kajiwa zuibun rakuni natta.
Thanks to the development of electrical appliances, housework is much easier now than it was in the old days.

2) 私が無事に大学を卒業できたのも、両親のおかげだと思っています。
Watashiga bujini daigakuo sotsugyoo dekitanomo, ryooshinno okagedato omotteimasu.
I think I owe it to my parents that I was able to successfully graduate from college.

3) 私が成功したのは、いろいろな人が助けてくれたおかげだ。
Watashiga seikooshitanowa, iroirona hitoga tasuketekureta okageda.
It was due to the help of many people that I was able to succeed.

4) 子供が病気になったおかげで、家族旅行に行かれなくなった。
Kodomoga byookini natta okagede, kazoku-ryokooni ikarenaku natta.
My child became ill, so we weren't able to take our family trip.

5) 夜中のまちがい電話のおかげで、寝不足になってしまった。
Yonakano machigaidenwano okagede, nebusokuni natteshimatta.
Somebody misdialed my number in the middle of the night, so I didn't get enough sleep.

6) A：このごろ、お母さんの具合はいかがですか。

B：ええ、おかげさまで、だいぶよくなりました。

A： *Konogoro, okaasanno guaiwa ikagadesuka?*
How is your mother doing these days?
B： *Ee, okagesamade, daibu yokunarimashita.*
She's become much better, thank you (for asking).

せい ■ *sei* ■ blame

結果が悪かったとき、その**原因**となった**ことがら**や**人**を**指す**とき使います。**批難**や不平・不満**の気持ち**を強く含んでいて、会話でよく使います（例7,8）。また「～のせいにする」は、責任を本当の原因ではないものに押しつけることです（例9,10）。

Sei is used when pointing out the person or thing that is the cause of an unsatisfactory result. Feelings of dissatisfaction are included and it is often used in spoken Japanese when criticizing or complaining about something (ex.7, 8). *~no sei ni suru* is an expression that is used when someone transfers the blame from the true cause to another person or thing (ex.9, 10).

---

7) 台風が続いて来たせいで、野菜が値上がりしている。
Taifuuga tsuzuitekita seide, yasaiga neagarishiteiru.
Because a series of typhoons have passed through, the price of vegetables has been going up.

8) ゆうべ飲みすぎたせいで、頭が痛い。
Yuube nomisugita seide, atamaga itai.
My head hurts because (I) drank too much last night.

9) あの人は自分の失敗でも、人のせいにする。
Ano hitowa jibunno shippaidemo, hitono seinisuru.
Even when something is his own fault, he blames other people.

10) 子：どうして起こしてくれなかったの。遅刻しちゃうよ。
母：人のせいにしないで、自分で起きなさい。
Ko: *Dooshite okoshite kurenakattano? Chikokushichauyo.*
Child: Why didn't you wake me? I'm going to be late.
Haha: *Hitono seini shinaide, jibunde okinasai.*
Mother: Don't blame me. Get yourself out of bed.

ため

■ *tame*
■ reason ; cause 

---

①ものごとが起きた時の、**原因や理由**を述べるとき使います。良い結果にも悪い結果にも使います（例11, 12, 13, 14）。少し改まったいい方です。
Tame is used when referring to the reason or cause of an event. It may be used when speaking about both good and bad outcomes (ex.11, 12, 13, 14). It is a slightly formal expression.

②**目的を述べる**ときにも使います（例15, 16）。
It is also used when one is explaining an objective or purpose (ex.15, 16).

---

11) 父が北海道に転勤になったために、引っ越すことになった。

Chichiga Hokkaidooni tenkinni natta tameni, hikkosu kotoni natta.
Because my father is being transferred to Hokkaido, my family is going to move.

12) 今年は暖冬のために、いつもの年より早く梅の花が咲いた。
Kotoshiwa dantoono tameni, itsumono toshiyori hayaku umeno hanaga saita.
It was a warm winter this year, so the plum trees blossomed earlier than usual.

13) ストーブを消し忘れたために、火事になった。
Sutoobuo keshiwasureta tameni, kajini natta.
The fire started because (I) forgot to turn off the heater.

14) 大雪のために、電車が遅れた。
Ooyukino tameni, denshaga okureta.
The trains were delayed because of the heavy snowfall.

15) 彼らは子供の将来のために、毎月貯金している。
Karerawa kodomono shooraino tameni, maitsuki chokinshiteiru.
They are saving some money each month for their child's future.

16) 私は朝起きると、新鮮な空気を入れるために窓を開けます。
Watashiwa asa okiruto, shinsenna kuukio ireru tameni madoo akemasu.
When I wake up in the morning I open the window to let in fresh air.

おきに／ごとに

■*oki ni* ■*goto ni*

おきに ■*oki ni* ■every (other)

「数量表現＋おきに」の形で、同じことがらや状態がくり返し起こるときの、**間隔を表す**とき使います。したがって「１日おきに」というと「１日間をおいて次の日、また１日間をおいて……」そして「２日おきに」は「３日に１度」というようになります（例1, 2, 3, 4）。

Oki ni is used after numbers or counters to indicate the interval between a repetition of events, actions, or conditions. For instance, *ichinichi oki ni* means 'with an interval of one day' (namely, every other day) and *futsuka oki ni* means 'once every three days' (ex.1, 2, 3, 4).

1) 5分おきにバスが出る。
ふん　で
Gofun-okini basuga deru.
A bus leaves every five minutes.

2) 私は、1日おきに洗濯します。
わたし　にち　せんたく
Watashiwa, ichinichiokini sentakushimasu.
I do laundry every other day.

3) この薬は、6時間おきに飲まなければならない。
くすり　じかん　の
Kono kusuriwa, rokujikan-okini nomanakereba-naranai.
You must take this medicine every six hours.

4) 道路には、50メートルおきに街灯が立っている。
どうろ　がいとう　た
Dooroniwa, gojuumeetoruokini gaitooga tatteiru.
On the street, there are street lights (standing) every 50 meters.

ごとに ■*goto ni* ■every ; each

多くの場合「数量表現＋ごとに」の形で使います（例5, 6, 7, 8)。この場合の数量を一つのまとまりと考え、**そのまとまり一つ一つについて、もれなくものごとや状態がくり返す**とき使います。したがって「1日ごとに」というと「毎日」になり「2日ごとに」は「2日に1度」という意味になります。
おお　ばあい　すうりょうひょうげん　かたち　つか　れい　ばあい　すうりょう　ひと　かんが　ひと　ひと　じょうたい　かえ　つか　にち　まい　にち　ふつか　ふつか　ど　いみ

In most cases, this is used after numbers and counters as seen in the examples (ex.5, 6, 7, 8). The number designated by *goto ni* is treated as one group, which is then used when referring to repetitive things and conditions. Accordingly, *ichinichi goto ni* means 'everyday' and *futsuka goto ni* means 'every two days'.

5) 日本の会社では、ふつう半年ごとにボーナスが出る。
にほん　かいしゃ　はんとし　で
Nihonno kaishadewa, futsuu hantoshigotoni boonasuga deru.
Japanese companies usually pay bonuses every six months.

6) オリンピックは4年ごとに開かれる。
よねん　ひら
Orinpikkuwa yonengotoni hirakareru.
The Olympics are held every four years.

7) このレストランのメニューは、1週間ごとに変わる。
しゅうかん　か

Kono resutoranno menyuuwa, isshuukangotoni kawaru.
The menu at this restaurant changes every week.

8) このはかりは5グラムごとに目盛りがついている。

Kono hakariwa goguramugotoni memoriga tsuiteiru.
This scale is marked in units of five grams.

(〜て) おく/(〜て) ある

■(*〜te*) *oku* ■(*〜te*) *aru*

(〜て) おく ■(*〜te*) *oku* ■to leave ; to keep

①ある目的や準備のために、**前もって何かをしたり用意する**とき、「他動詞(て形) +おく」の形で使います(例1, 2, 3, 4)。

(〜*te*) *oku* is used in the form 'transitive verb-*te oku*' to indicate that the action of the verb is done beforehand, as preparation or for some special purpose (ex.1, 2, 3, 4).

②**そのままにする**というとき使います(例5, 6, 7)。

友達や親しい人の間では「買っとく・言っとく・聞いとく」などのように「〜 *te oku*」の「 *e* 」を言わないことが多いです。

It is also used to mean 'leave something as is' (ex.5, 6, 7). In casual speech among friends the sound /*e*/ in (〜*te*) *oku* is dropped, resulting in the frequently used forms *kattoku*, *ittoku*, *kiitoku*, etc.

---

1) 友達が来るので、部屋をそうじしておきます。

Tomodachiga kurunode, heyao soojishite-okimasu.
Friends are coming so (I'm) going to clean up the room.

2) 旅行に行く前に、ホテルを予約しておく。

Ryokooni ikumaeni, hoteruo yoyakushiteoku.
(I'm) going to get hotel reservations before I leave for my trip.

3) 明日は忙しいから、今夜はゆっくり寝ておいたほうがいい。

Ashitawa isogashiikara, konyawa yukkuri neteoita hooga ii.
Tommorrow will be a busy day, so (you'd) better get a good night's

sleep tonight.

4) あさってまでに、会議の書類を作っておいてください。

Asattemadeni, kaigino shoruio tsukutteoite kudasai.
Please get the documents for the conference made up by the day after tomorrow.

5) 暑いから、窓を開けておいてください。

Atsuikara, madoo aketeoite kudasai.
It's hot, so please leave the windows open.

6) 言いたい人には言わせておけばいい。

Iitai hitoniwa iwaseteokeba ii.
We should just let whoever wants to say something speak.

7) よく眠っているから、このまま寝かせておこう。

Yoku nemutteirukara, konomama nekaseteokoo.
Let's just let her sleep, since (she's) sleeping so soundly.

（～て）ある

■ (*~te*) *aru*
■ to remain ; to keep 

前もってしたことが、今もそのままの状態であるとき、「他動詞（て形）＋ある」の形で使います。つまり「～した・～ておいた」こと（結果）が継続している状態です（例8, 9, 10, 11, 12, 13）。

This expression is used in the form 'transitive verb *~te aru*' to indicate that the action of the verb has been done in advance and that the resultant state is still continuing (ex.8, 9, 10, 11, 12, 13).

8) 私の部屋は、そうじしてあります。

Watashino heyawa, soojishitearimasu.
My room has been cleaned up.

9) 冷蔵庫に、くだものが冷やしてあります。

Reizookoni, kudamonoga hiyashitearimasu.
There is some fruit chilling in the refrigerator.

10) そのことは、もう彼に言ってあります。

Sono kotowa, moo kareni ittearimasu.
(I) have already told him about that.

11) 歩道には、花が植えてある。
Hodooniwa, hanaga uetearu.
Some flowers have been planted along the sidewalk.

12) こんなところに空き缶が捨ててあるよ。
Konna tokoroni akikanga sutetearuyo.
Someone has thrown empty cans even here!

13) 図書館には、本がたくさん置いてある。
Toshokanniwa, honga takusan oitearu.
There are lots of books in the library.

おく／のせる／つむ／かさねる

■ *oku* ■ *noseru* ■ *tsumu* ■ *kasaneru*

おく［置く］ ■ *oku* ■ to put ; to set (down)

①ものをある程度平らなところに位置させるとき使います（例1, 2）。
To place something on a relatively flat surface (ex.1, 2).

②人を雇ったり、または決まった役割の場所にいるようにすることです（例3）。
To hire someone or place them in position for an assigned role (ex.3).

③時間や距離などをあけることです（例4, 5）。
To leave an interval of time or distance (ex.4, 5).

---

1) テーブルの上に花瓶を置く。
Teeburuno ueni kabin-o oku.
(I'll) put the flower vase on the table.

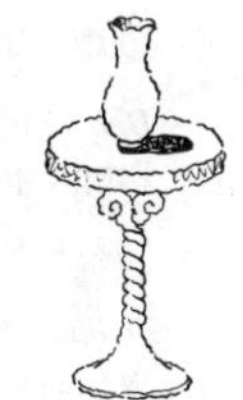

2) 父は、庭に大きな石や灯籠を置いて日本庭園を造った。
Chichiwa, niwani ookina ishiya tooroo-o oite nihonteien-o tsukutta.
My father created a Japanese garden by placing things such as large rocks and stone lanterns in our yard.

3) 来月から、店にパートの店員を置くことにした。

Raigetsukara, miseni paatono ten-in-o oku kotonishita.

(We) decided to hire a part-time clerk for the store, starting next month.

4) 商談は、あまり間を置くとまとまらないことがある。

Shoodanwa, amari aidao okuto matomaranai kotoga aru.

There are times business negotiations fail because there is too much time between meetings.

5) パン屋は、交番の１軒置いたとなりにあります。

Pan-yawa, koobanno ikken oita tonarini arimasu.

The bakery is located two doors down from the police box.

のせる［載せる・乗せる］ ■ *noseru* ■ to put (load) on

①ものを何かの**上に位置させる**ことです（例6, 7, 8）。

To place an object on top of something (ex.6, 7, 8).

②新聞・雑誌・本に**文などを出す**ことです（例９）。

To publish an article, etc., in a newspaper, magazine, or book (ex.9).

③人やものなどを乗り物の**中に入れる**ことです（例10, 11）。

To carry people or things in a vehicle (ex.10, 11).

①②は「載せる」と書き、③は「乗せる」と書きます。

For definitions ①, ② the *kanji* 載せる is used, while 乗せる is used for ③.

---

6) 電車の網棚に、荷物をのせる。

Denshano amidanani, nimotsuo noseru.

People put their baggage on the luggage rack of the train.

7) お茶をお盆にのせて出す。

Ochao obonni nosete dasu.

We serve tea on a tray.

8) 彼は、靴をみがいてもらうために、足を台の上にのせた。

Karewa, kutsuo migaitemorau tameni, ashio daino ueni noseta.

He put his foot up on the stand in order to get his shoes polished.

9) 私(わたし)の会社(かいしゃ)で出(だ)している雑誌(ざっし)に、あなたの小説(しょうせつ)を載(の)せたいのですが……。
Watashino kaishade dashiteiru zasshini, anatano shoosetsuo nosetainodesuga...
I would like to print your novel in the magazine which my company publishes.

10) ベビーカーに赤(あか)ちゃんを乗(の)せて、公園(こうえん)に行(い)きました。
Bebiikaani akachan-o nosete, kooenni ikimashita.
(We) put the baby in the baby carriage and went to the park.

11) 新(あたら)しい車(くるま)を買(か)ったんですって。今度(こんど)、乗(の)せてください。
Atarashii kurumao kattandesutte? Kondo, nosete kudasai.
Did (you) say you bought a new car? Give me a ride in it sometime, please.

つむ［積(つ)む］

■ *tsumu*
■ to pile up ; to load

---

①ものの上(うえ)に**ものを置(お)いて**いくことです（例(れい)12, 13）。その結果(けっか)、どんどん**高(たか)く**なっていきます。

To place something on another thing, and as a result, a pile is formed (ex. 12, 13).

②**荷物(にもつ)**など、ものを乗(の)り物(もの)の**中(なか)に入(い)れる**ことです（例(れい)14）。

To place something in a vehicle like a pickup truck (ex.14).

③経験(けいけん)や練習(れんしゅう)などをくり返(かえ)している内(うち)に**程度(ていど)が高(たか)く**なっていく、というとき使(つか)います（例(れい)15）。

Tsumu also denotes that the level of something (skill, knowledge, etc.) becomes higher through repetitive practice or experience (ex.15).

---

12) 倉庫(そうこ)の中(なか)には、大(おお)きな箱(はこ)がいくつも積(つ)んである。
Sookono nakaniwa, ookina hakoga ikutsumo tsundearu.
Many big boxes are piled up in the warehouse.

13) 彼(かれ)の机(つくえ)の上(うえ)には、本(ほん)が山(やま)のように積(つ)んである。
Kareno tsukueno ueniwa, honga yamanoyooni tsundearu.
There's a mountain of books piled on his desk.

14) トラックに、引(ひ)っ越(こ)しの荷物(にもつ)を積(つ)む。

Torakkuni, hikkoshino nimotsuo tsumu.
(We) are going to load the things we are moving onto the van.

15) 彼女は、経験を積んだ医師なので、信頼できます。
Kanojowa, keiken-o tsunda ishinanode, shinrai dekimasu.
She is a very experienced doctor, so you can trust her.

かさねる［重ねる］

- *kasaneru*
- to pile on ; to layer

---

①同じ大きさや種類のものを、上に置くことです（例16, 17）。

To pile up things of the same size or kind (ex.16, 17).

②失敗・苦労・注意・経験・練習など同じことを何度もくり返していくことです（例18, 19, 20）。

It also denotes repetition or re-occurrence of one thing, e.g., failure, hardship, warning, experience, or practice (ex.18, 19, 20).

---

16) 同じ大きさのお皿は、重ねて食器棚にしまってください。
Onaji ookisano osarawa, kasanete shokkidanani shimatte kudasai.
Please stack the plates in piles of the same size and put them in the cupboard.

17) 寒いので、靴下を２枚重ねてはいて出かけました。
Samuinode, kutsushitao nimai kasanete haite dekakemashita.
(I) went out wearing double a layer of socks because it was cold.

18) エジソンは、何回も失敗を重ねてやっと電球を発明することに成功した。
Ejisonwa, nankaimo shippaio kasanete yatto denkyuuo hatsumeisuru kotoni seikooshita.
Thomas Edison finally succeeded in inventing the electric light bulb after a succession of failures.

19) 彼は、歳を重ねるごとに、やさしい性格になっていった。
Karewa, toshio kasanerugotoni, yasashii seikakuni natteitta.
He became kinder as he got older.

20) 彼は、苦労に苦労を重ねた末に、体をこわして入院してしまった。
Karewa, kurooni kuroo-o kasaneta sueni, karadao kowashite nyuuin-shite-shimatta.

Because he went through so many hardships, he ended up getting sick and being hospitalized.

おこる／しかる

■ *okoru* ■ *shikaru*

おこる［怒る］ ■ *okoru* ■ to be angry ; to scold 

①不愉快だ、気に入らない、不満だ、**腹が立つ**などの感情をがまんできずに表面に出すことです（例1, 2, 3, 4, 5, 6）。

To show such feelings as displeasure, dissatisfaction, or anger because of inability to tolerate something (ex.1, 2, 3, 4, 5, 6).

②目上の人が目下の人の良くない態度や行いに腹を立て、強く**感情的**に注意することです（例7, 8）。

To reprimand or rebuke someone in anger. *Okoru* may not be used to denote censure of someone who is older or of superior social standing (ex.7, 8).

1) 彼は、自分の思い通りにならないとすぐに怒る。
Karewa, jibunno omoidoorini naranaito suguni okoru.
He gets mad very easily if things don't go his way.

2) 妹は、母に誕生日を忘れられたと怒っている。
Imootowa, hahani tanjoobio wasureraretato okotteiru.
My younger sister is angry because our mother forgot about her birthday.

3) 彼はこのごろ機嫌が悪くて、怒ってばかりいる。
Karewa konogoro kigenga warukute, okottebakariiru.
He has been in a bad mood recently and is always angry.

4) この町の住民は、税金が高すぎると怒っている。
Kono machino juuminwa, zeikinga takasugiruto okotteiru.
The people of this town are angry because taxes are too high.

5) こんなに謝っているのだから、もう怒らなくてもいいでしょう。

Konnani ayamatte-irunodakara, moo okoranakutemo iideshoo.
I have already apologized this much. Why do you have to be so angry?

6) 天気(てんき)が悪(わる)いなんて怒(おこ)っても、仕方(しかた)がない。
Tenkiga waruinante okottemo, shikataganai.
It's no use getting angry about bad weather. (You) can't do anything about it.

7) 私(わたし)は、父(ちち)の大切(たいせつ)な本(ほん)に落書(らくが)きをして怒(おこ)られた。
Watashiwa, chichino taisetsuna honni rakugakio shite okorareta.
I was scolded by my father because I scribbled in his valuable book.

8) お母(かあ)さんに口答(くちごた)えをして怒(おこ)られた。
Okaasanni kuchigotaeo shite okorareta.
(I) talked back to my mother, so she got angry with me.

しかる［叱(しか)る］ ■ *shikaru* ■ to scold 

目上(めうえ)の人(ひと)が目下(めした)の人(ひと)の良(よ)くない態度(たいど)や行(おこな)いに対(たい)し、よい方向(ほうこう)に導(みちび)こう、直(なお)させようと強(つよ)く**注意(ちゅうい)する**ことです。「怒(おこ)る」よりも理性的(りせいてき)な感(かん)じで、必(かなら)ず特定(とくてい)の相手(あいて)があります（例(れい)9, 10, 11, 12）。

Shikaru is similar to definition ② of *okoru*, however it is more intentional and rational, as in scolding a person with the intention of correcting wrong behavior, while *okoru* is more emotional and spontaneous. Use of *shikaru* necessitates the existence of another person who is the object of the speaker's concern (ex.9, 10, 11, 12).

---

9) 先生(せんせい)は、勉強(べんきょう)をしない学生(がくせい)をしかった。
Senseiwa, benkyoo-o shinai gakuseio shikatta.
The teacher scolded the student who didn't study.

10) 私(わたし)は、弟(おとうと)をいじめて母(はは)にしかられた。
Watashiwa, otootoo ijimete hahani shikarareta.
My mother scolded me because I harassed my younger brother.

11) 兄(あに)は、この間(あいだ)父(ちち)にしかられてから、家(いえ)の手伝(てつだ)いをするようになった。
Aniwa, konoaida chichini shikararetekara, ieno tetsudaio suruyooni natta.
After my older brother had been scolded by my dad, he started to help with household chores.

12) あの子は、どんなにしかられてもいたずらを止めない。
Ano kowa, donnani shikararetemo itazurao yamenai.
The child never stops getting into mischief, no matter how much he is scolded.

おしえる／しらせる

■ *oshieru* ■ *shiraseru*

おしえる［教える］

■ *oshieru*
■ to teach ; to tell

相手のまだ知らないこと・わからないこと・身についていないことなどを、**わかるようにする**とき使います。教える方は人以外にも、自然だったり社会だったりもします。その場合は「～から学びとる」という意味です（例1,2,3,4)。

To make another person understand something, or to explain unknown or unfamiliar things to him. *Oshieru* may also be used when speaking of inanimate or abstract things, such as society or nature. In such cases, the verb means 'to learn from' (ex.1, 2, 3, 4).

---

1) 先生、この問題がわからないんです。教えてください。
Sensei, kono mondaiga wakaranaindesu. Oshiete kudasai.
Teacher, (I) don't understand this problem. Please explain it to me.

2) 鈴木さんは、高校で日本史を教えている。
Suzukisanwa, kookoode Nihonshio oshieteiru.
Mr. Suzuki is teaching Japanese history at a high school.

3) 私は先週の日曜日、子供に自転車の乗り方を教えました。
Watashiwa senshuuno nichiyoobi, kodomoni jitenshano norikatao oshiemashita.
I taught my child how to ride a bicycle last Sunday.

4) 冬山は、しばしば自然のおそろしさを教える。
Fuyuyamawa, shibashiba shizenno osoroshisao oshieru.
A mountain in winter often teaches us how terrifying Mother Nature can be.

しらせる［知らせる］

■ *shiraseru*
■ to let ～know ; to tell

手紙・電話・何かの合図または口頭などで、必要なときに**相手に情報を伝える**ことです（例5, 6, 7, 8）。テレビ、新聞など公共のもので広く人々に伝えるときも同じように使います。

Shiraseru means to convey information to somebody orally or by letter, telephone, or other means at a time that it is required (ex.5, 6, 7, 8). It can also be used in situations in which the general public is informed of something by public media, such as television and newspapers.

5) 私は会議室にいますので、山田さんが来たら知らせてください。
Watashiwa kaigishitsuni imasunode, Yamadasanga kitara shirasete kudasai.
I'll be in the conference room, so please let me know when Mr. Yamada arrives.

6) あなたの家へ行くときは、電話で知らせます。
Anatano iee ikutokiwa, denwade shirasemasu.
I'll call you to let you know when I'm coming over.

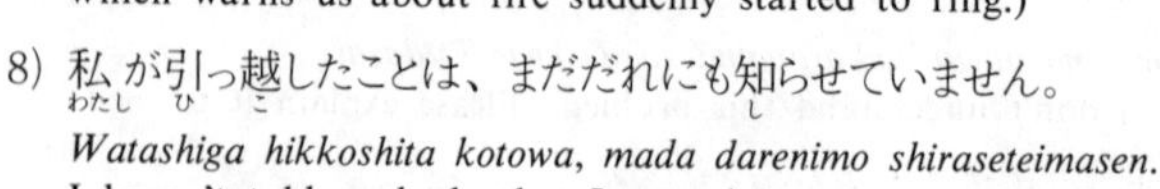

7) 火事を知らせる警報器のベルが、突然鳴りだした。
Kajio shiraseru keihookino beruga, totsuzen naridashita.
The fire alarm suddenly started to ring. (The alarm bell which warns us about fire suddenly started to ring.)

8) 私が引っ越したことは、まだだれにも知らせていません。
Watashiga hikkoshita kotowa, mada darenimo shiraseteimasen.
I haven't told anybody that I moved yet.

おす／おさえる

■ *osu* ■ *osaeru*

おす［押す］

■ *osu*
■ to push

ものに一方から**力や圧力を加える**ことです（例1, 2, 3, 4）。結果的に、ものを動かすこともあります。

To apply pressure or force to one side of an object. As a result, the object may be moved (ex.1, 2, 3, 4).

---

1) 非常ボタンを押すと、エレベーターは止まります。
Hijoobotan-o osuto, erebeetaawa tomarimasu.
If (you) push the emergency button, the elevator will stop.

2) 彼女は天気のいい日は、うば車を押して公園へ行く。
Kanojowa tenkino ii hiwa, ubagurumao oshite kooen-e iku.
On nice days she pushes the baby carriage to the park.

3) 電車に乗るとき、ひとに押されてころびそうになった。
Denshani norutoki, hitoni osarete korobisooninatta.
When (I) was getting on the train, I got pushed by someone and just about fell.

4) この扉は、押しても引いてもあかない。
Kono tobirawa, oshitemo hiitemo akanai.
This door won't open, whether (I) push it or pull it.

おさえる[押さえる・抑える]

■ *osaeru*
■ to hold down ; to suppress

---

①力を加えて、**ものの動きを止めよう**とすることです（例5, 6, 7, 8, 9）。

To attempt to stop the movement of something by applying force to it (ex.5, 6, 7, 8, 9).

②**感情**やものごとが、それ以上大きくなったり広がったりしないように、**こらえたり、くいとめたり**することです（例10, 11, 12）。

To suppress things such as emotions so they do not become any greater or worse (ex.10, 11, 12).

①は「押さえる」と書き、②は「抑える」と書きます。

In definition ①, *osaeru* is written 押さえる, and in ② 抑える is used.

---

5) 急に強い風がふいたので、彼女はあわててぼうしを押さえた。
Kyuuni tsuyoi kazega fuitanode, kanojowa awatete booshio osaeta.
A strong wind came up suddenly so she quickly grabbed on to her hat.

6) ゆうべの地震のとき、私は本棚が倒れないように押さえていた。
Yuubeno jishinno toki, watashiwa hondanaga taorenaiyooni osaeteita.
During last night's earthquake, I held on to the bookcase so it wouldn't topple over.

7) ドアが閉まらないように、ちょっと押さえていてくれませんか。
Doaga shimaranaiyooni, chotto osaeteite kuremasenka?
Could (you) hold on to this door so it doesn't close?

8) 彼女は、涙をハンカチでそっと押さえた。
Kanojowa, namidao hankachide sotto osaeta.
She quietly kept her tears in check with her handkerchief.

9) 彼は、傷口をタオルで押さえて、病院に行った。
Karewa, kizuguchio taorude osaete, byooinni itta.
He pressed a towel against the wound and went to the hospital.

10) 彼女は、薬で足の痛みを抑えて、試合に出場した。
Kanojowa, kusuride ashino itamio osaete, shiaini shutsujooshita.
She controlled the pain in her leg with medication and played in the match.

11) 彼は怒りを抑えて、冷静に話し合おうとした。
Karewa ikario osaete, reiseini hanashiaooto shita.
He suppressed his anger and tried to talk with them calmly.

12) この薬品には、金属の酸化を抑える働きがある。
Kono yakuhinniwa, kinzokuno sankao osaeru hatarakiga aru.
This chemical has a quality that suppresses oxidation in metal.

おそい／のろい

■ *osoi* ■ *noroi*

おそい［遅い］

■ *osoi*
■ slow ; late ◎

①何かをするのに**時間がかかる**、あるいはその**動きが速くない**ことです（例1,2,3,4）。

Osoi indicates that something or someone takes a long time to do something, or is slow in movement (ex.1, 2, 3, 4).

②時刻が**早くない**ときや、何かをするのにちょうど良い**時刻**や**時期が過ぎてしまった**、というとき使います（例5, 6, 7）。

Osoi also indicates that the time is late, or that something is late in terms of timing (ex.5, 6, 7).

---

1) 自転車は自動車より遅い。
Jitenshawa jidooshayori osoi.
The bicycle is slower than the automobile.

2) あの仕立て屋は、仕事は遅いがていねいだ。
Ano shitateyawa, shigotowa osoiga teineida.
That tailor is slow, but he does a good job.

3) 私はフランス語を習っているけれど上達が遅いので恥ずかしい。
Watashiwa Furansugoo naratte-irukeredo jootatsuga osoinode hazukashii.
I am learning French, but my progress is embarrassingly slow.

4) 姉は出かけるしたくが遅かったので、電車に乗りおくれました。
Anewa dekakeru shitakuga osokattanode, denshani nori-okuremashita.
My sister was so slow in getting ready that she missed the train.

5) 私の父は、いつも夜帰りが遅い。
Watashino chichiwa, itsumo yoru kaeriga osoi.
My father always comes home late.

6) こんなに夜遅く、よその家を訪ねるのは非常識だ。
Konnani yoru osoku, yosono ieo tazunerunowa hijooshikida.
Visiting someone's house this late at night is very thoughtless.

7) 今さら謝っても、もう遅い。
Imasara ayamattemo, moo osoi.
It's too late now to apologize.

のろい ■*noroi* ■slow ◎

何かをするのに**時間がかかる**、**動きが鈍い**というとき使います（例8, 9, 10, 11）。速くない・鈍いことを非難したりばかにしたりする気持ちを含んでいます。

Noroi is used when something or someone is slow in doing something or moving (ex.8, 9, 10, 11). It is usually used in a negative sense, i.e., when making fun of or criticizing slowness.

8) 彼は計算がのろい。
Karewa keisanga noroi.
He is slow at calculating.

9) 私は足がのろいから運動会はきらいだ。
Watashiwa ashiga noroikara undookaiwa kiraida.
I hate (school) athletic meets because I am a slow runner.

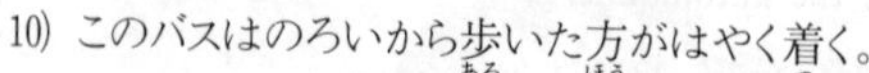

10) このバスはのろいから歩いた方がはやく着く。
Kono basuwa noroikara aruita hooga hayaku tsuku.
This bus is going so slowly that (we) could get there faster by walking.

11) きみがのろいから、ぼくたちのチームは負けたんだ。
Kimiga noroikara, bokutachino chiimuwa maketanda.
It's because you're such a slow-poke that our team lost the game.

「お待ちどおさま」と「お待たせしました」

教授と待ち合わせていたジェフは、約束の時間に５分遅れてしまいました。教授の顔を見るなり彼は「お待ちどおさま」と言いました。

その時教授は、「お待たせしました」と遅刻して教室に入って来たカールのことを思い出しました。「お待ちどおさま」は何かができあがるのを期待して待っているようなとき、たとえばおかあさんが子供に「お待ちどおさま、したくができたわ、さあでかけましょう」というときのように、目上の人が目下の人に使います。あるいはすしなどの出前のとき「はいどうぞ」に近い意味で「お待ちどおさま」を使うのです。

また「お待たせしました」は、待っていてくださいと頼んだことに対して、「待たせて悪かった」「待っていただいてありがとうございます」という気持ちを含んで使います。ですからジェフもカールも遅れたことを謝るには、「遅くなって申し訳ありません」と言うべきです。

Omachidoosama and *omatase shimashita*

Jeff was five minutes late for his appointment with his professor, so as soon as he saw the professor's face, he said, "*Omachidoosama*[1]."

This caused the professor to recall the time when, coming into the classroom late, another student named Carl said, "*Omatase shimashita*[2]." *Omachidoosama* is used when someone has been waiting for you in order to do something. For instance, a mother may say to a child who has been waiting for her to get ready to go out, "*Omachidoosama*, I'm ready; let's go." As in this example, *omachidoosama* is used when speaking to a person who is lower in rank or position, or who is younger. It is also used by a person who delivers something like food, in which case *omachidoosama* is similar in meaning to *hai, doozo* (here you are).

On the other hand, *omatase shimashita* is said to show your appreciation to someone when you have returned after having asked them to wait for you.

Both Jeff and Carl should have said, "*Osokunatte, mooshiwakearimasen*[3]" to apologize for being late.

1 *I am (something is) ready. Thank you for waiting.*
2 *I am sorry to have kept you waiting.*
3 *I am really sorry for being late.*

おそろしい／こわい

■ *osoroshii* ■ *kowai*

おそろしい［恐ろしい］ ■ *osoroshii* ■ frightening ; terrible 

ふつうでは考えられないほど**異常なことがら**や、**不気味なもの**・気持ちの悪いものを見たり接したりしたときに感じるようすです。「何が起こるか分からない」という未知なものへの不安も表します。また残酷・無情・凄惨なことがらに使います（例1, 2, 3, 4, 5）。

Osoroshii expresses fear arising from something so out of the ordinary as to be unthinkable, or from seeing or coming in contact with something eerie or unpleasant. It also expresses apprehension toward a future, unknown event when one doesn't know what is going to happen. It is also used to mean cruel, heartless, or tragic (ex.1, 2, 3, 4, 5).

1) 人と人が殺し合う戦争ほど恐ろしいものはない。
Hitoto hitoga koroshiau sensoohodo osoroshii monowa nai.
There is nothing so terrible as people killing each other in war.

2) これは、ほんの少しでたくさんの人の命を奪う恐ろしい薬です。
Korewa, honno sukoshide takusanno hitono inochio ubau osoroshii kusuridesu.
This is a fearful drug, of which only a small amount would take the lives of many people.

3) ここから先は、うっかり迷いこんだら二度と出てこられないという恐ろしい密林だ。
Kokokara sakiwa, ukkari mayoikondara nidoto dete korarenaito yuu osoroshii mitsurinda.
From here on is a frighteningly dense jungle, from which if (you) make the least mistake and get lost, you will never be able to get out.

4) 小さななだれが、恐ろしい災害をひきおこした。
Chiisana nadarega, osoroshii saigaio hikiokoshita.
A small snowslide brought about a terrible disaster.

5) 少女たちを誘拐した恐ろしい犯人が、やっとつかまった。

Shoojotachio yuukaishita osoroshii hanninga, yatto tsukamatta.
The terrible criminal who was kidnapping young girls was finally caught.

こわい［怖い］ ■ *kowai* ■ scary ; fearful 

危険なことや困ることが起こるのではないか、そして自分に危害が及ぶかもしれないという不安や恐怖を表します（例6, 7, 8, 9）。「こわい先生」は、生徒にきびしい・厳格だ・すぐに叱るなどの雰囲気がありますが、本当は良い先生なのかもしれません。しかし「おそろしい人」というと、人間的な道からはずれたことが平気でできる、残酷で非情な人という感じです。

Kowai expresses fear or anxiety that some dangerous or troublesome event will take place, or that some harm is going to befall oneself (ex.6, 7, 8, 9). An example of usage may be: a *kowai* teacher is one who may really be a good teacher, but who is known to be strict or stern and quick to reprimand, while an *osoroshii* person is someone who can readily depart from the ways of humanity, i.e., cruel and heartless.

6) 私は犬がこわい。
Watashiwa inuga kowai.
I'm afraid of dogs.

7) 彼女はこわい映画を見るのが好きだ。
Kanojowa kowai eigao mirunoga sukida.
She likes to see scary movies.

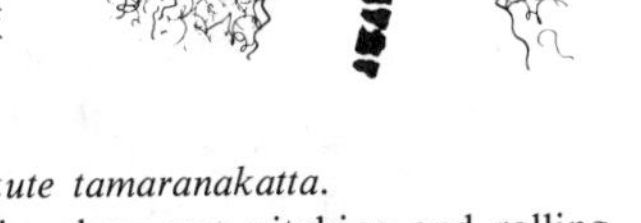

8) 飛行機がゆれたので、私はこわくてたまらなかった。
Hikookiga yuretanode, watashiwa kowakute tamaranakatta.
I was scared out of my wits because the plane was pitching and rolling.

9) 私の担任の先生は、ふだんはやさしいけれど、本気で怒るととてもこわい。
Watashino tanninno senseiwa, fudanwa yasashiikeredo, honkide okoruto totemo kowai.
My homeroom teacher is usually nice, but when he gets truly angry, he's quite terrifying.

おそわる／ならう／まなぶ／べんきょうする

■*osowaru* ■*narau* ■*manabu* ■*benkyou suru*

おそわる［教わる］ ■*osowaru* ■to learn (from)

知らないことやわからないことの**知識**や**情報**を、だれかから**得る**ことです。その場だけのことでも、ある程度の期間でもかまいません（例1, 2, 3, 4)。

To receive knowledge or information one did not previously know from someone. *Osowaru* may refer to knowledge gained on the spot, or over a long period of time (ex.1, 2, 3, 4).

1）来週から青木さんの家で、お花を教わることになりました。
Raishuukara Aokisanno iede, ohana o osowaru kotoni narimashita.
(I've) decided that I'm going to learn flower arrangement at the Aokis' house starting next week.

2）私は父に教わったとおりのやり方で、魚をつかまえた。
Watashiwa chichini osowatta toorino yarikatade, sakanao tsukamaeta.
I was able to catch a fish by fishing the way my father taught me.

3）私は高校生のとき、吉田先生に数学を教わった。
Watashiwa kookooseino toki, Yoshidasenseini suugakuo osowatta.
When I was a high school student, I learned mathematics from Mr. Yoshida.

4）先月私たちは、佐々木さんに教わった温泉に行って来ました。
Sengetsu watashitachiwa, Sasakisanni osowatta onsenni itte kimashita.
Last month, we went to the hot-spring (resort) about which we had learned from Mr. Sasaki.

ならう［習う］ ■*narau* ■to learn ; to study ; to take lessons

ものごとの**技術**や**やり方**を、**先生**や**専門の人**あるいは、そのことをよく知っている人に**教えてもらう**ことです。ある程度の期間をかけるという感じがあります（例5, 6, 7, 8）。

To learn a skill, technique, or method of doing something from a teacher or expert. It is implied that a certain amount of time is required (ex.5, 6, 7, 8).

---

5) 私は子供のころバレエを習っていました。
Watashiwa kodomono koro bareeo naratteimashita.
I took classical ballet lessons when I was a child.

6) 私は習ったことはないけれど、ギターが弾ける。
Watashiwa naratta kotowa naikeredo, gitaaga hikeru.
Although I've never taken lessons, I can play the guitar.

7) 私は最近スペイン語を習い始めました。
Watashiwa saikin Supeingoo narai hajimemashita.
I've recently begun learning (studying) Spanish.

8) 料理なんて習わなくても、慣れればじょうずになりますよ。
Ryoorinante narawanakutemo, narereba joozuni narimasuyo.
Even if you don't take cooking lessons you'll become good if you do it enough (get used to it).

まなぶ［学ぶ］

■ *manabu*
■ to learn ; to study 

人に教えてもらったり、また、教えてもらわなくても、体験したり見たりして、学問や**知識・技術など**役立つことを**身につけていく**ことです（例9, 10, 11, 12）。

To acquire useful learning, knowledge, technique, etc., through experiencing or watching, with or without a teacher (ex.9, 10, 11, 12).

---

9) 加藤さんと私は、同じ大学で学びました。
Katoosanto watashiwa, onaji daigakude manabimashita.
Mr. Kato and I studied at the same university.

10) 彼は大学で学んだことを生かして、製薬会社で研究をしている。
Karewa daigakude mananda kotoo ikashite, seiyakugaishade kenkyuuo shiteiru.
He's putting to work what he learned at the university by doing research at a pharmaceutical company.

11) 子供たちはキャンプ生活から、多くのことを学んだ。
Kodomotachiwa kyanpu-seikatsukara, ookuno kotoo mananda.
The children learned a lot from their time at (summer) camp.

12) 今回の経験から私は、友情の尊さを学んだ。
Konkaino keikenkara watashiwa, yuujoono tootosao mananda.
I learned the true value of friendship from this experience.

べんきょうする［勉強する］

■ *benkyou suru*
■ to study

学問や**知識**などを**身につけるために努力する**ことです。どちらかというと技術よりも**学問的なこと**に多く使います（例13, 14, 15, 16）。例17は、ためになる経験をした、という意味です。

To strive to acquire learning, knowledge, etc. It is generally used to refer to scholarly matters and not technique or skill (ex.13, 14, 15, 16). In Example 17 it is used to indicate that the speaker feels that an experience proved to be a useful one.

13) 私は1日に3時間勉強する。
Watashiwa ichinichini sanjikan benkyoosuru.
I study three hours every day.

14) 私の弟は勉強するのが大嫌いです。
Watashino otootowa benkyoo-surunoga daikiraidesu.
My (little) brother hates studying.

15) 試験が近いんだから、もっと勉強しなさい。
Shikenga chikaindakara, motto benkyoo-shinasai.
The test is coming up soon, so study harder.

16) 兄は今、大学で医学を勉強している。
Aniwa ima, daigakude igakuo benkyoo-shiteiru.
My (elder) brother is studying medicine at the university.

17) その失敗は、彼女にとっていい勉強になった。
Sono shippaiwa, kanojoni totte ii benkyooni natta.
That failure was a good lesson for her.

おだてる／ちやほやする

■ *odateru* ■ *chiyahoya suru*

おだてる

■ *odateru*
■ to flatter (someone into)

相手に何かをやらせようという目的や気に入られたいという下心で、**おせじやいい気分にさせるようなこと**を言って、さかんに**ほめること**です（例1, 2, 3)。

To eagerly praise a person in order to make him happy, to get him to do something, or to curry his favor (ex.1, 2, 3).

1) A：きみって頭が良くて、親切で、友達思いでほんとうにいい人だね。
B：いくらおだてたって、お金は貸さないよ。
A：*Kimitte atamaga yokute, shinsetsude, tomodachiomoide hontooni iihitodane.*
You are truly a fine person; you're smart, kind, and caring toward your friends.
B：*Ikura odatetatte, okanewa kasanaiyo.*
I don't care how much you flatter me, I won't lend you money.

2) あんまりおだてられたので、ついその気になって彼の分まで宿題をひき受けてしまった。
Anmari odateraretanode, tsui sonokini natte kareno bunmade shukudaio hikiukete shimatta.
He flattered me so much that (I) ended up doing his homework.

3) 彼はおだてられると調子に乗って何でもする。
Karewa odaterareruto chooshini notte nandemo suru.
He'll do anything, if you flatter him.

ちやほやする

■ *chiyahoya suru*
■ to pamper

かわいいから、好きだから、自分の利益になる立場の人だからなどの理由で、相手を**必要以上に大切にあつかったり世話をする**ことです。甘やかすという

意味を強く含み、ちやほやされることによってわがままになったり、いい気になったりします（例4, 5, 6)。

To pay too much attention to or care for someone more than is necessary because the person is cute, lovable, or useful to one. It implies pampering; therefore by being *chiyahoya sareru* (flattered and spoiled) one may become selfish or conceited (ex.4, 5, 6).

4) 彼女は、小さい頃からちやほやされて育ったので、わがままになった。
Kanojowa, chiisai korokara chiyahoyasarete sodattanode, wagamamani natta.
She has become selfish because she has been spoiled ever since she was a child.

5) あの社長の奥さんは、みんなにちやほやされるのが好きだ。
Ano shachoono okusanwa, minnani chiyahoyasarerunoga sukida.
That president's wife loves having everyone make a fuss over her.

6) えらい人の子供だからって、ちやほやすることはない。
Eraihitono kodomodakaratte, chiyahoyasuru kotowa nai.
Just because the child is that of a high-ranking person, you don't have to fuss over him.

おとす／すてる

■ *otosu* ■ *suteru*

おとす［落とす］

■ *otosu*
■ to drop ; to lose

①ものを**上から下に**行かせることです。意図的（例1, 2)、無意識・不注意（例3, 4）のどちらの場合にも使います。

To move an object from a higher position to a lower one. The action may be intentional (ex.1, 2), or unintentional (ex.3, 4).

②信用・評判・単位など、保っていたものや**必要なものをなくしたり、ぬかしていたりする**ことです。持ち物を外でなくすという意味もあります（例5, 6, 7, 8)。

To lose or omit something important, such as a college credit, reputation, or a person's trust. Also, to lose an object outside (ex.5, 6, 7, 8).

③ものごとの程度・品質・段階・力などを低くしたり、下げたりすることです(例9, 10, 11, 12, 13)。しみ・ほこり・泥など汚れをとり除くときにも使います。

To reduce or lower the power, quality, degree, rank, etc. of something (ex.9, 10, 11, 12, 13). Also, to remove dirt, stains, mud, etc.

---

1) 彼は、古井戸に石を落として、水があるかどうかを確かめた。
Karewa, furuidoni ishio otoshite, mizuga aruka dookao tashikameta.
He checked to see if there was water in the old well by dropping a stone in it.

2) 子供たちが、棒で柿の実を落とそうとしていた。
Kodomotachiga, boode kakinomio otosooto shiteita.
The children were attempting to knock down the persimmons from the tree with a stick.

3) 突然猫が飛び出して来たので、びっくりして持っていたバッグを落としてしまった。
Totsuzen nekoga tobidashite kitanode, bikkurishite motteita bagguo otoshite shimatta.
Because the cat suddenly jumped out, I dropped the bag I was carrying in surprise.

4) 時計は、落としたりぶつけたりしないように気をつけなさい。
Tokeiwa, otoshitari butsuketari shinaiyooni kio tsukenasai.
Be careful in handling the clock so that you don't drop it or bang it around.

5) あの会社は、今回のできごとですっかり信用を落とした。
Ano kaishawa, konkaino dekigotode sukkari shin-yoo-o otoshita.
That company has lost a lot of credibility because of its recent actions.

6) 彼は山で命を落とした。
Karewa yamade inochio otoshita.
He lost his life in the mountains.

7) 試験の点数が悪かったので、単位を落とした。
Shikenno tensuuga warukattanode, tan-io otoshita.
My exam score was low, so I flunked the course (I lost the credits).

8) さいふをどこかで落としてしまった。

Saifuo dokokade otoshite-shimatta.
(I) lost my wallet somewhere.

9) 列車は、駅に近づくとスピードを落とした。
Resshawa, ekini chikazukuto supiidoo otoshita.
The train slowed down as it neared the station.

10) 私は体重を落とすために、毎朝ジョギングをしています。
Watashiwa taijuuo otosu tameni, maiasa joginguo shiteimasu.
I am jogging every morning in order to lose weight.

11) あの会社はもうけが少なくても、製品の質は落とさない。
Ano kaishawa mookega sukunakutemo, seihinno shitsuwa otosanai.
Even if that company is not making much money, it has not lowered the quality of its products.

12) くつの泥をよく落としてから入ってください。
Kutsuno doroo yoku otoshitekara haitte kudasai.
Please clean the mud off your shoes well before you come in.

13) 姉は家に帰るとすぐに化粧を落とす。
Anewa ieni kaeruto suguni keshoo-o otosu.
My elder sister removes her make-up as soon as she comes home.

すてる［捨てる］

■ *suteru*
■ to discard ; to throw away 

---

①**いらなくなったもの**を手放す・**処分する**ことです。単にものだけ（例14, 15, 16）でなく、「地位・家庭・財産」など**抽象的なことがら**（例17, 18）にも広く使います。

To dispose of something which is no longer needed (ex.14, 15, 16). It may also be used for abstract concepts such as 'position', 'family', 'fortune', etc. (ex.17, 18).

②**あきらめる・やめる**という意味で使います（例19, 20, 21）。

It is used also to mean 'to give up' (ex.19, 20, 21).

---

14) 私は毎週月曜日に、ゴミを捨てます。
Watashiwa maishuu getsuyoobini, gomio sutemasu.
I put out my trash every Monday.

15) ゴミは、決められた場所に捨ててください。
Gomiwa, kimerareta bashoni sutetekudasai.
Please put your garbage in the designated area.

16) 私は、着なくなった服を捨てないで、人にあげることにしている。
Watashiwa, kinakunatta fukuo sutenaide, hitoni ageru kotoni shiteiru.
I've decided to give away clothes I don't wear anymore instead of throwing them away.

17) 彼は、ふるさとを捨て、都会で暮らし始めた。
Karewa, furusatoo sute, tokaide kurashi-hajimeta.
He left his hometown and started a new life in the city.

18) 王子は、地位も名誉も捨てて彼女との恋にかけた。
Oojiwa, chiimo meiyomo sutete kanojotono koini kaketa.
The prince gave up his social status and fame for his love for her.

19) 彼女は、途中でその試合を捨ててしまった。
Kanojowa, tochuude sono shiaio suteteshimatta.
She gave up in the middle of the match.

20) どんなに苦しいときにも、彼女は希望を捨てなかった。
Donnani kurushii tokinimo, kanojowa kiboo-o sutenakatta.
No matter how hard her life got, she never gave up hope.

21) そんな甘い考えは捨てなさい。
Sonna amai kangaewa sutenasai.
Forget such Pollyanna notions.

おなじ/ひとしい

■ *onaji* ■ *hitoshii*

おなじ [同じ] ■ *onaji* ■ same 

① 2つあるいは、それ以上のものや、ことがらのあいだに、**ちがいがないこと、かわりのないこと**に使います(例1, 2, 3, 4)。

Onaji means that there is no difference or change between two or more items (ex.1, 2, 3, 4).

②何らかの部分で多少のちがいはあっても、本質としての**種類にちがいがない・共通である・仲間である**というとき使います（例５）。

It is also used to indicate that, although there may be some differences in their essential nature, two or more items do not differ in type, share a common feature, or belong together in some way (ex.5).

③そのもの、それ自身をさすとき使います（例6, 7）。

Onaji may also be used to mean 'the very same thing or person' (ex.6, 7).

1）いつも同じものを食べるのは、からだによくない。

Itsumo onaji monoo taberunowa, karadani yokunai.
It's not good for one's health to eat the same thing all the time.

2）これと同じものを作ってください。

Koreto onaji monoo tsukutte kudasai.
Please make one just like this.

3）自動車で行っても、電車で行っても、かかる時間は同じです。

Jidooshade ittemo, denshade ittemo, kakaru jikanwa onajidesu.
It takes the same amount of time whether you go by car or by train.

4）使いやすい辞書があったのですが、なくしてしまって、それと同じものを買いました。

Tsukaiyasui jishoga attanodesuga, nakushite-shimatte, soreto onaji monoo kaimashita.
(I) had a dictionary that was very easy to use, but I lost it, so I bought another one just like it.

5）同じ兄弟でも性格が違う。

Onaji kyoodaidemo seikakuga chigau.
Even though they are brothers, they have different personalities.

6）きょうは同じ患者が３回も病院に来た。

Kyoowa onaji kanjaga sankaimo byooinni kita.
The same patient came to the hospital three times today!

7）私は、首相と同じ大学を卒業しました。

Watashiwa, shushooto onaji daigakuo sotsugyoo-shimashita.

I graduated from the same university as the Prime Minister.

ひとしい［等しい］ ■ *hitoshii* ■ equivalent 

2つ以上のもののあいだの、**数量や程度に百パーセント違わない価値**があるというとき使います。ほとんどの場合、数字で表すことができます。場所・時間には使いません。人の行いについては「〜に等しい……」という文型で使います（例8, 9, 10, 11, 12, 13）。

This expression is used when the quantity or quality of two or more things are 100% equal. In most cases, the equality can be indicated by numerals. It is not used for time and place when referring to human behavior, the pattern ～*ni hitoshii* is used (ex.8, 9, 10, 11, 12, 13).

8) 二等辺三角形は、2辺の長さが等しい三角形です。
Nitoohen-sankakkeiwa, nihenno nagasaga hitoshii sankakkeidesu.
An isosceles triangle is a triangle with two equal sides.

9) 5×4と2×10の答えは等しい。
Go kakeru yonto ni kakeru juuno kotaewa hitoshii.
The totals of 5×4 and 2×10 are the same.

10) 等しいときの記号は＝で表します。
Hitoshii tokino kigoowa ＝de arawashimasu.
The sign for equivalency is '＝'.

11) カリフォルニアと日本の面積はほぼ等しい。
Kariforuniato Nihonno mensekiwa hobo hitoshii.
The land area of California and that of Japan are roughly the same.

12) 真冬に海に飛び込むなんて、自殺行為に等しい。
Mafuyuni umini tobikomunante, jisatsukooini hitoshii.
Jumping into the sea in the middle of winter is tantamount to committing suicide.

13) 彼の言っていることはほとんど脅迫に等しい。
Kareno itteiru kotowa hotondo kyoohakuni hitoshii.
What he is saying is virtually the same as a threat.

おもいだす／おぼえる

■ *omoidasu*　　■ *oboeru*

おもいだす［思い出す］

■ *omoidasu*
■ to recall ; to remember

忘れていたことや過去の経験が、再び心によみがえることです（例1, 2, 3, 4）。

To remember or recall something that had been previously forgotten, or that was experienced in the past (ex.1, 2, 3, 4).

1）きのう母に買い物を頼まれたのを、今思い出した。
Kinoo hahani kaimonoo tanomaretanoo, ima omoidashita.
(I) just remembered that I was asked by my mother to do some shopping for her yesterday.

2）子供の頃の失敗を思い出すと、今でも恥ずかしくなる。
Kodomono korono shippaio omoidasuto, imademo hazukashikunaru.
Even now, whenever (I) recall the mistakes I made when I was a child, I feel ashamed of myself.

3）この曲は聞いたことはあるけれど、曲名が思い出せない。
Kono kyokuwa kiitakotowa arukeredo, kyokumeiga omoidasenai.
(I) know I've heard this song before, but I can't recall the title.

4）遠く離れて暮らしても、私のことをときどき思い出してください。
Tooku hanarete kurashitemo, watashino kotoo tokidoki omoidashite kudasai.
Even when we are living far apart, please think of me sometimes.

おぼえる［覚える］

■ *oboeru*
■ to memorize ; to remember

①ものごとを記憶して忘れないでいることです（例5, 6, 7, 8）。

To fix something in one's memory and try not to forget it (ex.5, 6, 7, 8).

②知識や技術、技能などをしっかりと身につけることです（例9, 10）。

To fully acquire knowledge, a technique, or a skill (ex.9, 10).

③例11は、「感じた」という意味で、「痛み・胸さわぎ」などにも使います。

In Example 11, it means 'felt', and may also be used to mean 'to feel pain or uneasiness'.

5) 私は、小さい頃に住んでいた町のことをまだ覚えている。
Watashiwa, chiisai koroni sundeita machino kotoo mada oboeteiru.
I still remember the town where I lived as a child.

6) 私のことを覚えていますか。
Watashino kotoo oboeteimasuka?
Do you remember me?

7) 彼は、歴史の年号を覚えるのが得意だ。
Karewa, rekishino nengoo-o oboerunoga tokuida.
He is good at remembering the names of the eras in history.

8) 彼の家の電話番号は、覚えやすい。
Kareno ieno denwabangoowa, oboeyasui.
His home telephone number is easy to remember.

9) 私は小学生のとき、泳ぎを覚えた。
Watashiwa shoogakuseino toki, oyogio oboeta.
I learned how to swim when I was an elementary school student.

10) 私はこの機械の使い方が、なかなか覚えられない。
Watashiwa kono kikaino tsukaikataga, nakanaka oboerarenai.
I'm having a hard time learning how to use this machine.

11) 私は、彼の話に怒りを覚えた。
Watashiwa, kareno hanashini ikario oboeta.
I was very angry when I heard his story.

おもう／かんがえる

■ *omou* ■ *kangaeru*

おもう［思う］ ■ *omou* ■ to think 

頭や心に浮かぶ・感じることです。「考える」よりも**直観的で情緒的**です。

omou・kangaeru/おもう・かんがえる

感情(かんじょう)や意志(いし)を表現(ひょうげん)したり、想像(そうぞう)・希望(きぼう)・感想(かんそう)・意見(いけん)など、いろいろなことを述(の)べるとき使(つか)います。意見(いけん)・主張(しゅちょう)のおわりにつけて、**やわらげた表現(ひょうげん)**として使(つか)うことが多(おお)いです(例(れい)1, 2, 3, 4, 5, 6)。

To mentally or emotionally sense something. *Omou* is much more intuitive and emotional than *kangaeru*. It is used to express one's emotion, will, etc., or to state an opinion. *Omou* is often used at the end of a sentence expressing conjecture, hope, opinion, or argument in order to make one's statement softer (ex.1, 2, 3, 4, 5, 6).

---

1) 初(はじ)めて東京(とうきょう)に来(き)たとき、なんて人(ひと)が多(おお)いのだろうと思(おも)った。

Hajimete Tookyooni kita toki, nante hitoga ooinodarooto omotta.

When (I) came to Tokyo for the first time, I was amazed by the large number of people.

2) いつも不思議(ふしぎ)だと思(おも)うんだけれど、超能力(ちょうのうりょく)というのはほんとうにあるのだろうか。

Itsumo fushigidato omoundakeredo, choonooryokuto yuunowa hontooni arunodarooka.

(I) always think it's incredible... I wonder if there's really such a thing as superhuman power.

3) 連休(れんきゅう)にいなかへ帰(かえ)ろうと思(おも)う。

Renkyuuni inakae kaerooto omou.

(I) think I'll go to my hometown for the long holiday.

4) 品川(しながわ)の水族館(すいぞくかん)は思(おも)ったほど広(ひろ)くなかった。

Shinagawano suizokukanwa omottahodo hirokunakatta.

The aquarium in Shinagawa wasn't as big as I had thought.

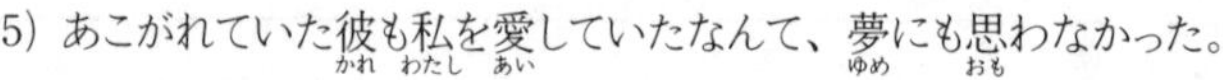

5) あこがれていた彼(かれ)も私(わたし)を愛(あい)していたなんて、夢(ゆめ)にも思(おも)わなかった。

Akogareteita karemo watashio aishiteitanante, yumenimo omowanakatta.

(I) didn't even dream that the guy I've been in love with loved me too.

6) 現在(げんざい)の進行状態(しんこうじょうたい)から見(み)て、このビルの3月完成(がつかんせい)は無理(むり)だと思(おも)います。

Genzaino shinkoo-jootaikara mite, kono biruno sangatsu kanseiwa muridato omoimasu.

Looking at the current state of progress, (I) think it will be impossible to finish this building by March.

かんがえる［考える］ ■*kangaeru* ■to think about ; to consider 

①知識や感覚などをもとに、ものごとのすじみちをたてたり判断する**知的な頭の働き**で、結論を出そうとする**目的意識がはっきりして**います。したがって計算問題を解くなど勉強については、「思う」ではなく「考える」を使います（例7, 8, 9, 10）。

Kangaeru refers to the intellectual mental process of making judgments or forming logical ideas based on reason or sense. There is a clear sense of attempting to reach a conclusion. Thus, when referring to academic matters such as mathematical calculations, *kangaeru* is used rather than *omou* (ex.7, 8, 9, 10).

②理論や学説などを打ち立てたり、発明や工夫をするとき使います（例11,12）。

To construct a hypothesis or theory, or to invent or devise something (ex.11, 12).

---

7) 試験勉強をしなかったので、この問題はいくら考えてもわからない。

Shikenbenkyoo-o shinakattanode, kono mondaiwa ikura kangaetemo wakaranai.
(I) didn't study for the exam, so I can't figure out this question no matter how much I think about it.

8) 成人式を迎えたのだから、これからはよく考えて行動しなさい。

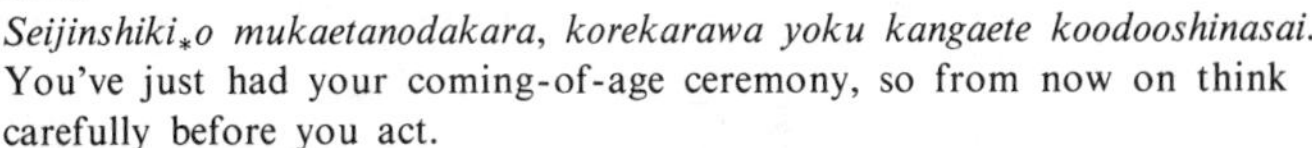

*Seijinshiki***o mukaetanodakara, korekarawa yoku kangaete koodooshinasai.*
You've just had your coming-of-age ceremony, so from now on think carefully before you act.
—— * *Seijinshiki* (coming-of-age ceremony)
The *seijinshiki* is a ceremony that is held on January 15th of each year, in which 20 year-olds throughout the nation are recognized as adults.

9) きのう、「環境問題を考える会」に出席した。

Kinoo, 'Kankyoo-mondaio kangaeru kai' ni shussekishita.
Yesterday (I) attended a meeting for the 'Consideration of the Environmental Problems'.

10) お考えが変わったら、ご連絡ください。

Okangaega kawattara, gorenrakukudasai.

If (you) change your mind, please contact (me).

11) アルキメデスが入浴中に「アルキメデスの原理」を考えついた話は有名だ。
にゅうよくちゅう げんり かんが はなし ゆうめい

Arukimedesuga nyuuyoku-chuuni 'Arukimedesuno genri' o kangaetsuita hanashiwa yuumeida.
The story that Archimedes thought up the "Archimedes' Principle" while bathing is famous.

12) あんパンは日本人が考えたものです。
にほんじん かんが

Anpanwa Nihonjinga kangaeta monodesu.
Sweetbean-filled rolls were invented by the Japanese.

おもしろい／おかしい／へん／かわっている

■ *omoshiroi* ■ *okashii* ■ *hen* ■ *kawatte iru*

おもしろい

■ *omoshiroi*
■ interesting ; amusing 

興味を持ったり**心をひかれ**たりするものや、**楽しい**というようすを表します。また、**愉快で**、**笑いだしたい**ような感じも含みます（例1, 2, 3, 4, 5）。例6は、思い通りの結果にならない不満や不快な気持ちを表しています。
きょうみ も こころ たの あらわ ゆかい わら かん ふく れい れい おも どお けっか ふまん ふかい きも あらわ

Omoshiroi is used in situations in which one is interested in or amused by something. It may suggest a pleasant feeling in which one wants to burst out laughing (ex.1, 2, 3, 4, 5). In Example 6, it indicates feelings of dissatisfaction or unpleasantness because something didn't turn out the way one wished.

---

1) この推理小説は、とてもおもしろい。
すいりしょうせつ

Kono suirishoosetsuwa, totemo omoshiroi.
This detective story is very interesting.

2) 彼の研究テーマは、なかなかおもしろい。
かれ けんきゅう

Kareno kenkyuuteemawa, nakanaka omoshiroi.
His research topic is quite interesting.

3) 木に登るなんて、おもしろい魚ですね。
き のぼ さかな

Kini noborunante, omoshiroi sakanadesune.
A fish that can climb trees is truly interesting.

4) きのう見た映画は、あまりおもしろくなかった。

Kinoo mita eigawa, amari omoshiroku-nakatta.
The movie (I) saw yesterday wasn't much fun.

5) 彼女はいつも、おもしろい話をして人を笑わせる。

Kanojowa itsumo, omoshiroi hanashio shite hitoo warawaseru.
She always makes people laugh by telling funny stories.

6) 彼は、上司に注意されたのがおもしろくなくて、会社を辞めてしまった。

Karewa, jooshini chuuisaretanoga omoshirokunakute, kaishao yamete shimatta.
He disliked being reprimanded by his boss, so he quit the company.

おかしい

■ *okashii*
■ amusing ; strange ; odd 

---

①愉快だったり**こっけいだったり**して**笑いたく**なるような感じを表します(例7,8)。

Okashii expresses a feeling in which one wants to laugh because a situation is pleasurable or amusing (ex.7, 8).

②正常ではない・ふつうとはちがう、正しくない・まちがっている、または、不思議だという意味で使います(例9, 10, 11)。

It may also mean that something is not normal, is incorrect or mistaken, or is a mystery (ex.9, 10, 11).

---

7) 彼のものまねがおかしくて、大笑いした。

Kareno monomanega okashikute, oowaraishita.
His impersonations were so funny that (I) roared with laughter.

8) 彼女は身ぶりが大げさで、見ているとおかしくてたまらない。

Kanojowa miburiga oogesade, miteiruto okashikute tamaranai.
Her gestures are so exaggerated that, watching her, (I) can't help laughing.

9) エンジンの調子がおかしいので、車を修理に出した。

Enjinno chooshiga okashiinode, kurumao shuurini dashita.
There was something wrong with my car's engine, so (I) took it in to be repaired.

10) 1週間も前に出した手紙がまだ着かないなんて、おかしい。

Isshuukanmo maeni dashita tegamiga mada tsukanainante, okashii.
It's odd that the letter (I) sent a week ago hasn't reached yet.

11) 食べすぎたので、胃がおかしい。

Tabesugitanode, iga okashii.
(I) ate too much, so now I have an upset stomach.

へん［変］

■ *hen*
■ strange ; odd 

ふつうとはちがう**異常なようす**を表すとき使います。そして、そのようなものごとに対する**不審な気持ち**や、**不快感**などを含んでいます（例12, 13, 14, 15）。

This is used to express that something is not normal or is different from what is usual, and therefore the speaker feels suspicious, uneasy, or dissatisfied with it (ex.12, 13, 14, 15).

---

12) かぜをひいて、声が変になった。

Kazeo hiite, koega henni natta.
My voice sounds strange because (I) have a cold.

13) この牛乳、変な味がするよ。くさっているんじゃない。

Kono gyuunyuu, henna ajiga suruyo. Kusatteirunjanai?
This milk tastes funny. Are you sure it hasn't gone bad?

14) 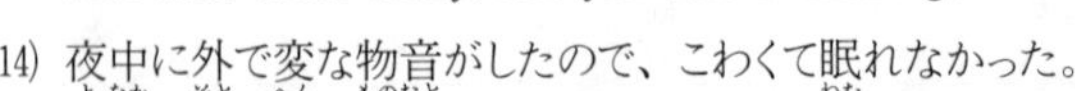
夜中に外で変な物音がしたので、こわくて眠れなかった。

Yonakani sotode henna monootoga shitanode, kowakute nemurenakatta.
During the night (I) heard some strange noises outside, and I was so scared that I couldn't sleep.

15) きょうの彼女は、ちょっとようすが変です。何か困ったことがあるのかもしれません。

Kyoono kanojowa, chotto yoosuga hendesu. Nanika komatta kotoga arunokamo shiremasen.
She seems a bit strange today. (I) wonder if something is bothering her.

かわっている［変わっている］

■ *kawatte iru*
■ unusual ; different 

ふつうとはちょっと**ちがっているようす**を表します（例16, 17, 18, 19)。珍しい・個性的だといった良い意味にも、また悪い意味にも使います。名詞の前につくときは「変わった」となることもあります。

This describes something as being slightly unusual (ex.16, 17, 18, 19). It is used when referring to a rare or peculiar characteristic of something, and may be good or bad in meaning. When placed in front of a noun, *kawatte iru* may change in form to *kawatta.*

16) 彼の名前は変わっているから、みんなにすぐ覚えてもらえる。
Kareno namaewa kawatteirukara, minnani sugu oboetemoraeru.
His name is a bit unusual, so everybody remembers it right away.

17) このブラウスはデザインが変わっている。
Kono burausuwa dezainga kawatteiru.
The design of this blouse sure is different.

18) うちには、泳ぐのが好きな変わった猫がいます。
Uchiniwa, oyogunoga sukina kawatta nekoga imasu.
(We) have an unusual cat that likes swimming.

19) 彼は変わっているから、近所の人にあいさつもしない。
Karewa kawatteirukara, kinjono hitoni aisatsumo shinai.
He is a strange man. He never even says ‘hello’ to his neighbors.

おもわず／おもいがけない

■ *omowazu* ■ *omoigakenai*

おもわず［思わず］ ■ *omowazu* ■ unconsciously 

自分ではそうするつもりではないのに、何かのきっかけで**無意識に、反射的に**何か**をしてしまう**ようすを表します（例1, 2, 3, 4)。

Omowazu indicates that one does something unintentionally or reflexively and without prior thought or planning (ex.1, 2, 3, 4).

1) 彼の話があまりにおかしかったので、思わず吹き出してしまった。

Kareno hanashiga amarini okashikattanode, omowazu fukidashite-shimatta.
His story was so funny that (I) suddenly burst out laughing.

2) 豪華な宝石のショーを見ていたら、思わずため息が出てしまった。
Gookana hoosekino shoo-o miteitara, omowazu tameikiga deteshimatta.
(I) couldn't help but gasp when I saw the fabulous gem show.

3) 暗がりから猫がとび出して来たので、思わず大声を上げてしまった。
Kuragarikara nekoga tobidashite-kitanode, omowazu oogoeo ageteshimatta.
(I) instinctively screamed because a cat suddenly jumped out from the dark.

4) 彼女の悲しい身の上話を聞いて、思わずもらい泣きした。
Kanojono kanashii minouebanashio kiite, omowazu morainakishita.
While listening to her sad life's story, (I) couldn't help but to cry.

おもいがけない［思いがけない］ ■*omoigakenai* ■unexpected 

まったく考えてもみなかったことや**予期していなかった**ことを言うとき使います。**意外だ**という意味です（例5, 6, 7, 8）。多くの場合、「おもいがけない話、できごと、ところ」などのように名詞について使います。

This is used when speaking of something unexpected, i.e., without prior thought or anticipation (ex.5, 6, 7, 8). In most cases, *omoigakenai* is used together with a noun, as in *omoigakenai hanashi* (a surprising story), *omoigakenai dekigoto* (an unexpected incident), or *omoigakenai tokoro* (an unexpected place).

---

5) 初めて書いた小説が、思いがけなく雑誌に載ることになった。
Hajimete kaita shoosetsuga, omoigakenaku zasshini noru kotoni natta.
Amazingly, (my) first novel was printed in a magazine.

6) きょう地下鉄の中で思いがけない人に会ったよ。だれだと思う。幼稚園の時の和田先生。
Kyoo chikatetsuno nakade omoigakenai hitoni attayo. Daredato omou? Yoochienno tokino Wada-sensei.
Guess who (I) met on the subway today! Ms. Wada, our old kindergarten teacher.

7) 彼が入院したという思いがけない知らせを聞いて、私はあわててお見舞いに行った。

Karega nyuuinshitato yuu omoigakenai shiraseo kiite, watashiwa awatete omimaini itta.
When I heard the surprising news about his hospitalization, I rushed over to visit him.

8) 思いがけないおくりもの、どうもありがとう。
Omoigakenai okurimono, doomoarigatoo.
Thank you for this unexpected gift.

おりる／くだる

■ *oriru* ■ *kudaru*

おりる［下りる・降りる］ ■ *oriru* ■ to descend ; to go down

①人や物が**高いところから低いところへ移動**して、ある場所・位置に到達するときに使います。どこを移動しているかよりも、どこかに着くということに重点があります（例1, 2, 3, 4）。

(Of a person or thing) To move from a higher to a lower place and reach a certain location or position. Emphasis is on arriving somewhere rather than on the place where motion takes place (ex.1, 2, 3, 4).

②**乗り物**から**外に出る**こと、あるいは乗り物に乗っていない状態になることです（例5, 6, 7）。

To get out or off of a vehicle (ex.5, 6, 7).

③申し込みに対して官庁などの**公的機関**や**権限**のあるところから、許可・予算・決定などが**与えられる**ことです（例8, 9）。

To be granted permission, a budget, a decision, etc., in response to an application to a public agency or authority (ex.8, 9).

④役目・仕事・計画・勝負などを自分から途中で止めるときに使います（例10, 11）。

To quit or drop out of a role, job, plan, match, etc. of one's own volition (ex.10, 11).

①、②、④は「降りる」と書き、③は「下りる」と書きます。①の中でも例４のように、そのもの自体が下へ行くものや、例３のように目的地へ行く（下がる）というときには、「下りる」と書きます。

In definitions ①, ②, and ④ the *kanji* 降りる is written, while in ③ 下りる is used. However, under definition ① there are cases in which 下りる is written, including sentences like those in Example 4, to show that an object itself moves downward, and Example 3, to indicate that something goes (down) toward its destination.

---

1) 階段を降りるとき、足を踏みはずしてけがをしてしまった。
Kaidan-o oriru toki, ashio fumihazushite kegao shiteshimatta.
(I) missed a step when I was going down the stairs and hurt myself.

2) 歌手は客席に降りて観客と握手をした。
Kashuwa kyakusekini orite kankyakuto akushuo shita.
The singer came down from the stage and shook hands with the audience.

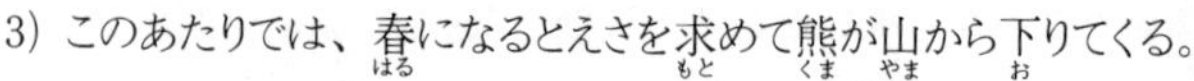

3) このあたりでは、春になるとえさを求めて熊が山から下りてくる。
Kono ataridewa, haruni naruto esao motomete kumaga yamakara oritekuru.
Around these parts, bears come down from the mountains looking for food when spring comes.

4) あまりのすばらしい演奏に幕が下りても拍手が鳴りやまなかった。
Amarino subarashii ensooni makuga oritemo hakushuga nariyamanakatta.
Even after the curtain descended, applause for the splendid performance didn't come to an end.

5) 気分が悪くなったので、途中で電車を降りた。
Kibunga warukunattanode, tochuude denshao orita.
I got off the train midway because (I) started feeling ill.

6) 客：東京ドームに行きたいんですが……。
駅員：あの電車に乗って水道橋駅で降りてください。
Kyaku : *Tokyo Doomuni ikitaindesuga...*
Passenger : (I'd) like to go to Tokyo Dome.
Ekiin : *Ano denshani notte Suidoobashiekide orite kudasai.*
Station employee : Take that train and get off at Suidobashi station.

7) 自転車の２人乗りは危ないから、はやく降りなさい。
Jitenshano futarinoriwa abunaikara, hayaku orinasai.
It's dangerous to ride double on a bicycle—get off now.

8) 申請をしてから保険金が下りるまで１年もかかった。
Shinseio shitekara hokenkinga orirumade ichinenmo kakatta.
After submitting the claim it took a whole year for the insurance money to come.

9) 抗ガン剤を開発したが、厚生省の認可がまだ下りていないので、実際の治療には使えない。
Kooganzaio kaihatsushitaga, Kooseishoono ninkaga mada oriteinainode, jissaino chiryooniwa tsukaenai.
(They've) developed an anti-cancer drug, but it still can't be used for actual treatment because approval has not yet been granted by the Ministry of Health and Welfare.

10) 彼は監督と意見が合わず、主役を降りてしまった。
Karewa kantokuto ikenga awazu, shuyakuo oriteshimatta.
He dropped out of the leading role because he and the director had a difference of opinion.

11) 彼は、次の選挙に立候補するために、テレビの番組を降りた。
Karewa, tsugino senkyoni rikkoohosuru tameni, terebino bangumio orita.
He resigned from the TV program to run as a candidate in the next election.

くだる［下る］

■ *kudaru*
■ to descend ; to issue 

---

①山道・坂・川など**傾斜のあるところ**を、高いところから低いところへ**移動する**とき使います。比較的時間がかかったり、距離が長いときに使い、**移動の過程に重点**があります（例12, 13, 14）。
This expression is used when there is movement down an incline such as a mountain road, slope or river (i.e., from a high place to a low place). It is used in situations in which the speaker wishes to emphasize the movement process, and when a relatively long period of time is required or the distance is long (ex.12, 13, 14).

②官庁などの公的機関や**権威・権力のあるところ**から、**命令・判決・決定**

などが出されるときに使います。一方的に出される、さからえないという意味が強く、許可・予算などには使いません（例15, 16)。

It is also used when a command, judgment, decision, etc., is issued or handed down by a public agency or someone, such as a government official, in a position of authority or power. A sense that the decision is unilaterally imposed and unopposable is strong ; thus it is not used in cases in which one grants permission, authorizes a budget, etc. (ex.15, 16).

例17のように「～（数量）を下らない」というのは、見積もった数量よりも絶対多い（多くなる）ということを強調するときの使い方です。

The expression ～ (quantity) *o kudaranai* (ex.17) emphasizes that a quantity is undeniably greater than estimated.

---

12) 夏休みにコロラド川をカヌーで下る計画を立てています。
Natsuyasumini Kororadogawao kanuude kudaru keikakuo tateteimasu.
(We're) making plans to go down the Colorado River by canoe during our summer vacation.

13) この道を５キロぐらい下ったところに山小屋がある。
Kono michio gokirogurai kudatta tokoroni yamagoyaga aru.
There's a mountain hut about five kilometers down this road.

14) この川をずっと下っていくと太平洋に出る。
Kono kawao zutto kudatteikuto Taiheiyooni deru.
If (you) keep going down this river you'll reach the Pacific Ocean.

15) 昨日の裁判で被告に有罪判決が下った。
Kinoono saibande hikokuni yuuzai-hanketsuga kudatta.
A judgment of 'guilty' was passed on the accused at yesterday's trial.

16) 労使交渉は決裂し、ストライキ実行の指令が下った。
Rooshi-kooshoowa ketsuretsushi, sutoraikijikkoono shireiga kudatta.
Labor-management negotiations broke down, and the order was given to go ahead with the strike.

17) 優勝戦に来た観客は、４万人を下らないだろう。
Yuushoosenni kita kankyakuwa, yonmannin-o kudaranaidaroo.
There must have been no less than 40,000 spectators who came to see the championship tournament.

下がる

「下りる・下る」と似たことばに「下がる」があります。もちろん上から下へという垂直の動きを表しますが、それ以外にも「(人が) 後退する・退く・ひっこむ・裏に行く」という意味があります。舞台の場合、「下りる」は「役をやめる・もう出演しない」ということですが「下がる」は、その場から裏へ引っこむことです。

駅のアナウンスで、「電車が来ます。(白線の内側に) 下がってお待ちください」というのを聞いたことがあるでしょう。これがもし「(ホームから) 下りてお待ちください」ならば、こわいことになりますね。

Sagaru

A word similar in meaning to the words *oriru* and *kudaru* is *sagaru*. All three indicate vertical movement from a high to a low position, however *sagaru* may also be used to mean ‘to move back’ or ‘to withdraw’. For instance, when speaking of an actor on a stage, saying *oriru* would mean that the person goes down from the stage (that is retires from acting) , while *sagaru* would simply mean that the person moves from the stage to the backstage area.
When at a train station you may have heard the announcement “The train is approaching, *sagatte omachikudasai*[1] (inside the white safety line) .” Imagine what would happen if the announcement said “*orite omachikudasai* (from the platform) [2].”

1 *Please step back.*
2 *Please step down.*

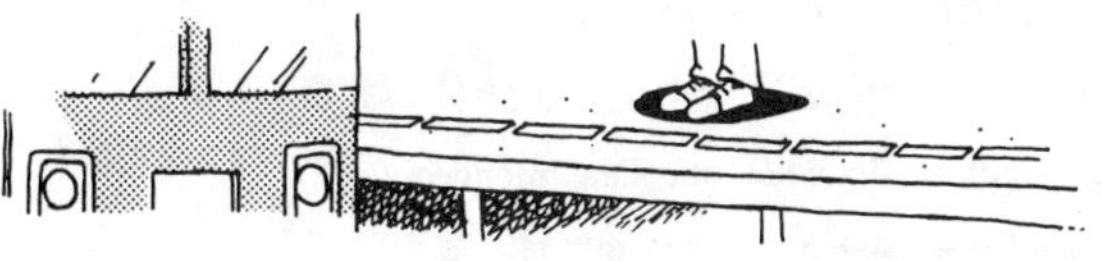

おわる／やめる／すむ

■*owaru*　■*yameru*　■*sumu*

おわる［終(お)わる］ ■*owaru* ■to end ; to finish

ある程度(ていど)の時間(じかん)がたって、ものごとが終点(しゅうてん)に達(たっ)したとき使(つか)います(例(れい)1, 2, 3, 4)。

Owaru indicates that something reaches the final stage or objective after a certain period of time (ex.1, 2, 3, 4).

1) 会議(かいぎ)は4時(よじ)に終(お)わる。
Kaigiwa yojini owaru.
The meeting will end at four o'clock.

2) やっと仕事(しごと)が終(お)わった。
Yatto shigotoga owatta.
Finally, (I've) finished my work.

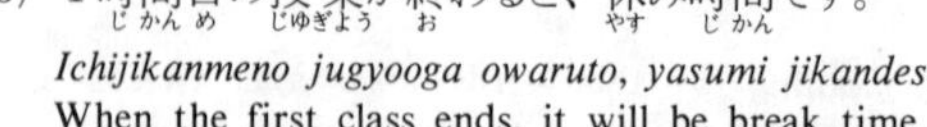

3) 1時間目(じかんめ)の授業(じゅぎょう)が終(お)わると、休(やす)み時間(じかん)です。
Ichijikanmeno jugyooga owaruto, yasumi jikandesu.
When the first class ends, it will be break time.

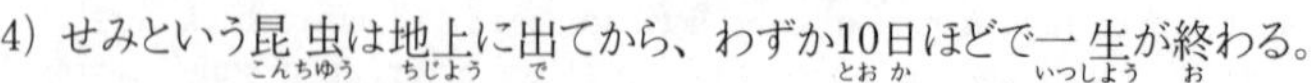

4) せみという昆虫(こんちゅう)は地上(ちじょう)に出(で)てから、わずか10日(とおか)ほどで一生(いっしょう)が終(お)わる。
Semito yuu konchuuwa chijooni detekara, wazuka tookahodode isshooga owaru.
The cicada's life ends within about ten short days after it comes out of the ground.

やめる［止(や)める・辞(や)める］ ■*yameru* ■to quit ; to stop

①続(つづ)けてきたことを、中止(ちゅうし)するとき使(つか)います（例(れい)5, 6, 7）。

To stop what one is doing (ex.5, 6, 7).

②これからやろうとすることを中止(ちゅうし)するとき使(つか)います（例(れい)8）。

To decide not to do what one had intended (ex.8).

③職(しょく)や地位(ちい)を引退(いんたい)するとき（例(れい)9）使(つか)います。

To retire or resign (ex.9).

①と②は「止める」と書き、③は「辞める」と書きます。

The *kanji* for definitions ① and ② is 止める while in ③ 辞める is used.

---

5) ぼくは今日から、たばこを止める。

Bokuwa kyookara, tabakoo yameru.
I'm quitting smoking as of today.

6) もう泣くのは止めなさい。

Moo nakunowa yamenasai.
Stop crying! (That's enough!)

7) ゲームはやめて、外で遊ぼうよ。

Geemuwa yamete, sotode asobooyo.
Let's quit this game and play outside.

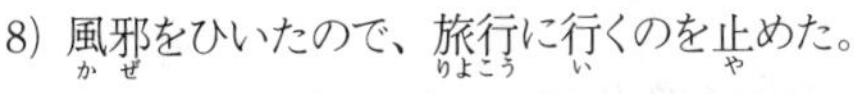

8) 風邪をひいたので、旅行に行くのを止めた。

Kazeo hiitanode, ryokooni ikunoo yameta.
(I) decided not to go on the trip because I caught a cold.

9) 彼は、20年間勤めた会社を辞めて、故郷に帰った。

Karewa, nijuunenkan tsutometa kaishao yamete, kokyooni kaetta.
He quit the company where he had worked for twenty years and returned to his hometown.

すむ［済む］

■ *sumu*
■ to end ; to finish ; to be over 

---

①「**終わる**」と同じ意味のとき使います（例10, 11）。

Sumu is used like *owaru* to indicate that something reaches the final stage and finishes (ex.10, 11).

②なんとか、その場を**切りぬける**というとき（例12, 13, 14）使います。「気が済む」というのは、「不愉快・不満」などの気持ちが時間の経過や、何らかの事により解決することです（例15）。

It is also used when one is somehow able to find his way out of a troubling situation (ex.12, 13, 14). The expression *ki ga sumu* means feelings of discomfort or dissatisfaction are dispelled due to the passage of time or settlement of a problem (ex.15).

---

10) 勉強がすんだら、遊びに行こう。
Benkyooga sundara, asobini ikoo.
Let's go out and have some fun when (we) finish studying.

11) 私は食事がすむと、いつもすぐ食器を洗います。
Watashiwa shokujiga sumuto, itsumo sugu shokkio araimasu.
I always wash my dishes as soon as I finish eating.

12) 金ですむのなら話は簡単ですが……。
Kanede sumunonara hanashiwa kantandesuga...
It would be easy if money could solve the problem, but...

13) 傘を持って行ったので、突然雨にふられてもぬれないですんだ。
Kasao motte ittanode, totsuzen ameni furaretemo nurenaide sunda.
Even though (I) was caught in a sudden downpour, I didn't get wet because I had my umbrella.

14) 電話でことが足りれば、行かなくてもすむ。
Denwade kotoga tarireba, ikanakutemo sumu.
If a telephone call resolves the matter, (I) won't have to go.

15) これだけ泣いたら気がすんだでしょう。
Koredake naitara kiga sundadeshoo.
I'll bet you feel much better now that you've cried it all out.

かえって／むしろ

■ *kaette* ■ *mushiro*

かえって

■ *kaette*
■ contrary (to one's expectation)

予想と反対の結果になったとき使います。現在の悪い状態を良くしようと行った結果が、前より悪くなったとき（例1, 2, 3)、また逆に、悪い状態が結果として良い状態になったとき（例４）にも使います。

This suggests that the outcome of something was contrary to one's expectation. It is also used when a favorable situation turns bad (ex.1, 2, 3), or a bad situation ends up well (ex.4).

1) ズボンについたペンキを落とそうとこすったら、かえって広がってしまった。
Zubonni tsuita penkio otosooto kosuttara, kaette hirogatte-shimatta.
(I) tried to rub out the paint stain on my pants, and it got worse instead.

2) 暑い東京を離れて山に来たが、今年はかえってこちらの方が暑い。
Atsui Tookyoo-o hanarete yamani kitaga, kotoshiwa kaette kochirano hooga atsui.
(I) left the heat of Tokyo and came to the mountains, but this year it's hotter here (than there).

3) スキャンダルをもみ消そうとした政治家は、かえって前より不利な立場になった。
Sukyandaruo momikesootoshita seijikawa, kaette maeyori furina tachibani natta.
The politician, who tried to hush up his scandal, just ended up getting into more trouble.

4) 失敗がかえって良い結果を生むこともある。
Shippaiga kaette yoi kekkao umu kotomo aru.
There are times when failure turns out for the better.

むしろ
■ *mushiro*
■ rather (than...)

「**A**（より）**むしろ B**」の形で、ＡＢ２つのことがらを比べると、**B の方が良いと思う**、というとき使います。Ａには現在の状態や常識的な考え方がくることが多く、Ｂには、話し手の考えがきます（例5, 6, 7, 8）。

When used in the pattern 'A (*yori*) *mushiro* B' it means that, after comparison, one thinks, 'B is better than A'. A usually refers to the present state or a conventional idea, while B is the speaker's own idea (ex.5, 6, 7, 8).

---

5) 彼は、学生というよりむしろ実業家だ。
Karewa, gakuseito yuuyori mushiro jitsugyookada.
He's not just a student; if anything, you'd have to call him a businessman.

6) 車が渋滞しているときは、歩いた方がむしろ早い。
Kurumaga juutaishiteiru tokiwa, aruita hooga mushiro hayai.

When there's a traffic jam, it's actually faster if you walk.

7) 少しぐらいの風邪は、薬を飲むよりむしろ早く寝た方がいい。
Sukoshiguraino kazewa, kusurio nomuyori mushiro hayaku neta hooga ii.
If it's not a severe cold, just going to bed early is better than taking medicine.

8) 夜遅く疲れた頭で考えるより、むしろ朝早く起きて考えた方がいい。
Yoru osoku tsukareta atamade kangaeruyori, mushiro asa hayaku okite kangaeta hooga ii.
Rather than thinking late at night when your brain is tired, it is better to get up early and do your thinking then.

かえる／もどる

■*kaeru* ■*modoru*

かえる［返る・帰る］ ■*kaeru* ■to return ; to go home

①ものやことがらが、**再び元のところ・本来あるべき場所に移動する**ことです（例1, 2, 3）。「初心にかえる・我にかえる」などのような抽象的なことにも使います。

This verb indicates that a thing or matter moves back to its original or proper position (ex.1, 2, 3). *Kaeru* may be used in abstract situations, for example *shoshin ni kaeru* (return to one's original intention) and *ware ni kaeru* (come back to oneself, get one's thoughts back in order).

②こちらのしたことに**相手が反応する**ことです（例4, 5）。

It may indicate that something one does causes a reply or reaction from one's partner (ex.4, 5).

③人間や動物が、**元のところ・本来あるべき場所に移動する**ことです。バスや電車などの乗り物にも使います（例6, 7, 8）。

Kaeru is also used when a person or animal moves back to its original place, or the place it belongs. In this sense it may also be used with buses, trains, or other similar vehicles (ex.6, 7, 8).

①と②は「返る」と書き、③は「帰る」と書きます。

In definitions ① and ②, the *kanji* 返る is written, and in definition ③ 帰る is used.

1) 定期預金(ていきよきん)は、満期(まんき)になると利息(りそく)がついて返(かえ)ってくる。
Teikiyokinwa, mankini naruto risokuga tsuite kaettekuru.
When (your) time deposit account reaches maturity, you will receive interest.

2) 修理(しゅうり)に出(だ)していたカメラが、きょう返(かえ)ってきた。
Shuurini dashiteita kameraga, kyoo kaettekita.
The camera that (I) sent in to be repaired came back today.

3) あの人(ひと)に貸(か)した本(ほん)が、まだ返(かえ)ってこない。
Ano hitoni kashita honga, mada kaettekonai.
That person hasn't returned the book (I) lent him. (The book I lent him hasn't come back yet.)

4) たいていのことは彼(かれ)にきけば、的確(てきかく)な答(こた)えが返(かえ)ってくる。
Taiteino kotowa kareni kikeba, tekikakuna kotaega kaettekuru.
He'll give you a precise answer for almost anything you ask him.

5) 「おはよう」と声(こえ)をかけたら、生徒(せいと)たちから明(あか)るい声(こえ)で返事(へんじ)が返(かえ)ってきた。
"Ohayoo" to koeo kaketara, seitotachikara akarui koede henjiga kaettekita.
When (I) said "Good morning!", my students responded with cheerful voices.

6) 疲(つか)れているようだから、もう帰(かえ)った方(ほう)がいいよ。
Tsukareteiru-yoodakara, moo kaetta hooga iiyo.
(You) look tired so maybe you should go home.

7) 先月(せんげつ)から行方(ゆくえ)のわからなかった犬(いぬ)が、きのう帰(かえ)ってきた。
Sengetsukara yukueno wakaranakatta inuga, kinoo kaettekita.
The dog (we) lost last month came home yesterday.

8) 父(ちち)の乗(の)った船(ふね)は、あした長(なが)い航海(こうかい)を終(お)えて帰(かえ)ってくる。
Chichino notta funewa, ashita nagai kookaio oete kaettekuru.
The ship my father is on will return from its long voyage tomorrow.

もどる [戻(もど)る] ■ *modoru* ■ to return

①**一度移動**(いちどいどう)**したものや変化**(へんか)**したもの**が、元(もと)の所(ところ)に来(き)たり、**元**(もと)**の状態**(じょうたい)**になる**ことです(例(れい)9, 10, 11, 12, 13)。

Modoru indicates that something that has moved or undergone change returns to its original location or condition (ex.9, 10, 11, 12, 13).

②一度通った所を、**もと来た方向に進む**ことです（例14, 15）。引き返す所は、途中のある一点でもかまいません。

To move back to a place one has already passed (ex.14, 15). The point of turning back may be anywhere along the original path of movement.

---

9) おととい出した手紙が、宛先不明で戻ってきた。

Ototoi dashita tegamiga, atesakifumeide modottekita.

The letter (I) sent two days ago came back because the forwarding address was unclear.

10) 盗まれた名画は、無事美術館に戻った。

Nusumareta meigawa, buji bijutsukanni modotta.

The stolen painting was safely returned to the art museum.

11) 悲しみを乗りこえた彼女に、笑顔が戻った。

Kanashimio norikoeta kanojoni, egaoga modotta.

She has gotten over her sadness, and a smile has returned to her face.

12) 夏が終わって、この海岸に静けさが戻ってきた。

Natsuga owatte, kono kaiganni shizukesaga modottekita.

Summer is over, and peace and quiet has even returned to this beach.

13) 今度の山火事で失われた緑が戻るまでに、長い年月がかかるだろう。

Kondono yamakajide ushinawareta midoriga modorumadeni, nagai nengetsuga kakarudaroo.

After this last forest fire, (I'm) sure it will take years for the greenery to return.

14) 満員電車を降りそこなって、次の駅から戻ってきた。

Man-indenshao orisokonatte, tsugino ekikara modottekita.

(I) was unable to get off the crowded train (at my station), so I had to come back from the next station.

15) 落とした定期券をさがしながら、駅まで戻った。

*Otoshita teikiken*o sagashinagara, ekimade modotta.*

(I) came back to the station, looking for the commuter pass I had dropped.

——* Japanese commuters often use a pre-paid pass (定期券 *teikiken*) when riding on trains or buses to and from work. The passes are popular because they are sold at a slightly discounted rate compared to the regular fare.

～かかる／～かける／～そうだ

■ ～*kakaru* ■ ～*kakeru* ■ ～*sou da*

～かかる

■ *kakaru*
■ to be about to ～ ; almost 

動作や**ことがら**が始まって、**途中**である**状**態を表します。そのことがらが進行していってもう少しでそうなってしまう、という意味を含みます（例1, 2, 3, 4）。例4の「乗りかかった船」は、ものごとを始めてしまったので、途中でやめるわけにはいかないという意味です。

～*kakaru* expresses a condition in which an action has started and is now in progress. It suggests that the action will reach completion shortly (ex.1, 2, 3, 4). In Example 4, the expression *norikakatta fune* refers to the idea that since one has started something, it would not be proper to stop midway.

1）夫の上着のボタンがとれかかっている。
Ottono uwagino botanga torekakatteiru.
The button on my husband's jacket is about to come off.

2）私は子供のころ、池で溺れかかったことがある。
Watashiwa kodomono koro, ikede oborekakatta kotoga aru.
There was a time when I was a child that I almost drowned in a pond.

3）私の靴ひもが古くなってきれかかっている。
Watashino kutsuhimoga furukunatte kirekakatteiru.
My shoestrings have become old and are about to break.

4）乗りかかった船だから、最後まで手伝います。
Norikakatta funedakara, saigomade tetsudaimasu.
I've helped you this far, so I'll help you until the end.

～かける

■ *kakeru*
■ to start to ～ ; to be about to ～ 

ある動作やことがらをし始めて、その**途中である**ということや、**今にもするところだ**、ということを表します。「~かかる」はほとんど「~かける」で代用されます。「~かける」には「~かかる」よりも、やや進んだ状態であるという感じがあります（例5, 6, 7, 8）。

~kakeru indicates that one has begun an action and is currently involved with it. In almost all cases *~kakeru* may be used in place of *~kakaru*, although it expresses a slightly more advanced state (ex.5, 6, 7, 8).

---

5) 彼女は何か言いかけて途中でやめた。
Kanojowa nanika iikakete tochuude yameta.
She started to say something but stopped.

6) 父は新聞を読みかけたままにして、どこかへ行ってしまった。
Chichiwa shinbun-o yomikaketa-mamanishite, dokokae itteshimatta.
My father went somewhere, leaving the newspaper open at the place he was reading.

7) やっと風邪が治りかけたと思ったら、こんどは歯が痛くなってきた。
Yatto kazega naorikaketato omottara, kondowa haga itakunattekita.
Just when I thought I was finally over my cold, my tooth began to hurt.

8) 彼は帰りかけたが、用事を思い出したらしく、すぐまた戻ってきた。
Karewa kaerikaketaga, yoojio omoidashita-rashiku, sugu mata modottekita.
He had just left, but soon came back, as if he had remembered something he had to do.

~そうだ

- *~sou da*
- almost ; appear as if 

ある動作や状態がもうすぐ**そうなってしまうようだ**、ということを表します。**本当はそうではないかもしれないけれど**、そのように見える・感じるという意味を強く含みます（例9, 10, 11, 12, 13）。

~sou da is used to express that an action or condition is about to reach fruition. It strongly suggests that, although an event may not actually occur, it looks or feels to the speaker as if it will (ex.9, 10, 11, 12, 13).

---

9) 風でろうそくの火が、今にも消えそうです。
Kazede roosokuno higa, imanimo kiesoodesu.

The candle's flame looks as if it will be blown out by the wind any moment.

10) かれらは、100年以上前に建てられた崩れそうな家に住んでいた。

Karerawa, hyakunen-ijoo maeni taterareta kuzuresoona ieni sundeita.
They were living in a house built over 100 years earlier that looked like it would fall down any minute.

11) 私は階段でつまずいて、ころびそうになった。

Watashiwa kaidande tsumazuite, korobisooni natta.
I stumbled on the stairs and almost fell.

12) おなかがすいて、死にそうだ。

Onakaga suite, shinisooda.
I'm so hungry I feel as if I'm going to die.

13) 彼女は泣きそうな顔で、私に謝った。

Kanojowa nakisoona kaode, watashini ayamatta.
She looked like she was going to cry when she apologized to me.

かける／はしる

■ *kakeru* ■ *hashiru*

かける［駆ける］ ■ *kakeru* ■ to run 

人や馬などが、**足を勢いよく動かして速く進む**とき使います。両足が同時に地面からはなれる瞬間があり、「駆け回る・駆け巡る・駆け抜ける……」などのように複合動詞として多く使います（例1, 2, 3, 4, 5）。

To move forward quickly by moving the legs rapidly — used for humans or animals such as horses. There are moments when both feet leave the ground at the same time. *Kakeru* is often used in compound verbs, e.g., *kakemawaru* (to run around), *kakemeguru* (to run about), and *kakenukeru* (to run through) (ex.1, 2, 3, 4, 5).

1) 子供たちは楽しそうに海の方へかけていった。

Kodomotachiwa tanoshisooni umino hooe kaketeitta.
The children merrily ran to the beach.

2) 馬が牧場をかけまわっている。

Umaga bokujoo-o kakemawatteiru.
Horses are galloping around in the pasture.

3) 彼は、100段もの階段を一気にかけのぼった。

Karewa, hyakudanmono kaidan-o ikkini kakenobotta.
He ran up a stairway of 100 or more steps without resting.

4) 彼女は風のように人ごみをかけぬけて行った。

Kanojowa kazenoyooni hitogomio kakenuketeitta.
She ran like the wind through the crowd.

5) 彼女はころんだ子供のそばにかけ寄り、起こしてやった。

Kanojowa koronda kodomono sobani kakeyori, okoshiteyatta.
She ran up to the child who had fallen down and helped him to his feet.

はしる［走る］ ■*hashiru* ■to run

---

①「駆ける」と同じように速く進むとき使いますが、人や動物だけではなく、電車や車などにも使います（例6, 7, 8)。

Hashiru, like *kakeru*, means to move forward quickly, but is used not only for animals and people, but also for trains, cars, etc. (ex.6, 7, 8).

②感情的になったり、よくないことと考えられている方向に行くとき使います（例9, 10)。

To become emotional or go in a direction considered to be undesirable (ex.9, 10).

③道が通っている、という意味に使います（例11)。

It is also used to indicate that a street runs through something (such as a town) (ex.11).

---

6) 彼女は健康のために、毎朝10キロ走ることにしています。

Kanojowa kenkoono tameni, maiasa jukkiro hashirukotoni shiteimasu.
She makes it her daily routine to run ten kilometers every morning for the sake of her health.

7) 上越新幹線「スーパーあさひ」は最高時速275キロで走ります。

Jooetsu-Shinkansen 'Suupaa-Asahi' wa saikoojisoku nihyaku-nanajuugoki-rode hashirimasu.
The *Jooetsu Shinkansen 'Super-Asahi'* runs at a top speed of 275kilometers per hour.

8) 信号が青に変わったとたん、車はいっせいに走り出した。
Shingooga aoni kawattatotan, kurumawa isseini hashiridashita.
The moment the traffic light changed to green, all the cars started moving at once.

9) すぐに感情に走って自分を見失うのは、きみの悪いところです。
Suguni kanjooni hashitte jibun-o miushinaunowa, kimino warui tokorodesu.
Your failing is you readily let your emotions run and you lose hold of yourself.

10) 彼は、悪い仲間にさそわれて、悪の道に走ってしまった。
Karewa, warui nakamani sasowarete, akuno michini hashitteshimatta.
He was enticed by his corrupt friends and ended up on the road to crime.

11) その町には東西に１本大きな道が走っている。
Sonomachiniwa toozaini ippon ookina michiga hashitteiru.
There is one large boulevard that runs through the town from east to west.

かこむ／とりまく

■ *kakomu* ■ *torimaku*

かこむ［囲む］

■ *kakomu*
■ to surround ; to encircle 

なにかを中心にして、その**まわりにぐるりと**ほかのものが**存在する**ことです（例1, 2, 3, 4）。結果的に、内と外を隔てるという意味も含みます。人に対して使うときは、多くの場合、だれかを中心になごやかな時を過ごすという意味を持ちます（例５）。

Kakomu indicates the existence of something completely around an object, making it the center (ex.1, 2, 3, 4). As a result, it is implied that the inside and outside are separated. When referring to people, it is often used to mean to spend a pleasant time with one person as the center of conversation (ex.5).

1) 討論会の出席者は、テーブルを囲んですわった。
Tooronkaino shussekishawa, teeburuo kakonde suwatta.
The participants in the debate sat around the table.

2) AかBのうち、正しいものを○で囲みなさい。
Eeka biino uchi, tadashii monoo marude kakominasai.
Please circle A or B, depending on which is correct.

3) 彼は木立ちに囲まれた家に住んでいる。
Karewa kodachini kakomareta ieni sundeiru.
He lives in a house surrounded by a grove of trees.

4) 日本は四方を海に囲まれている。
Nihonwa shihoo-o umini kakomareteiru.
Japan is surrounded on all sides by the ocean.

5) 私たちはおばあちゃんを囲んで、楽しいひとときを過ごした。
Watashitachiwa obaachan-o kakonde, tanoshii hitotokio sugoshita.
We gathered around grandma and had a pleasant time together.

とりまく

■ *torimaku*
■ to surround ; to gather around 

①なにかを中心にして、そのまわりにぐるりとほかのものが存在することです。「囲む」よりも中心となるものに対しての注目度が高く、「逃がさない」という感じがあります（例6, 7, 8）。

Torimaku indicates the existence of something around an object, making it the center. The level of attention paid to the central object is higher with *torimaku* than with *kakomu*, and there is a sense that the central object is not allowed to escape (ex.6, 7, 8).

②自分よりお金や権力などのある人のそばにいて、きげんをとったりして、利益を得ようとすることです（例9, 10）。また、そういう人のことを「とりまき」と言います。

To associate with and make efforts to please someone with more money or authority than oneself in order to get personal gain (ex.9, 10). A person who does such things is referred to with the noun *torimaki*.

6) 国会解散についての考えを聞こうと、記者たちは首相をとりまいた。
Kokkai-kaisannitsuiteno kangaeo kikooto, kishatachiwa shushoo-o torimaita.
The reporters encircled the Prime Minister in order to ask about his thoughts on the dissolution of Parliament.

7) その村を山々がとりまいている。
Sono murao yamayamaga torimaiteiru.
That town is surrounded by mountains.
(Mountains surround that town.)

8) 私たちをとりまく社会について考えよう。
Watashitachio torimaku shakainitsuite kangaeyoo.
Let's think about the society of which we are a part.

9) あの歌手は、いつも若い女の子たちにとりまかれている。
Ano kashuwa, itsumo wakai onnanokotachini torimakareteiru.
That singer is always surrounded by young girls.

10) 立派な政治家には、悪いとりまきはついていない。
Rippana seijikaniwa, warui torimakiwa tsuiteinai.
An admirable politician is not associated with sycophants.

かじる/かむ

■ *kajiru* ■ *kamu*

かじる ■ *kajiru* ■ to bite ; to gnaw 

①固いものを、少しずつ**食いちぎる**、かみ取ることです(例1, 2, 3)。
To bite on something hard little by little and from the edge (ex.1, 2, 3).

②学問や語学などを、少しだけ勉強してみる・やってみるというとき使います(例4)。
When referring to studying, learning a language, etc., it means to do so on a trial basis and for a short while (ex.4).

1) あそこでりんごをかじっているのは、私の弟です。
Asokode ringoo kajitteirunowa, watashino otootodesu.

The one who is munching on an apple over there is my younger brother.

2) 私(わたし)たちはお茶(ちゃ)を飲(の)みながら、バリバリと音(おと)をたてて、おせんべいをかじった。

*Watashitachiwa ochao nominagara, baribarito otoo tatete, osenbei*o kajitta.*

We noisily munched on hard *senbei* while drinking tea.

—— * *Osenbei* is cracker made of rice that is toasted over an open flame and seasoned with soy sauce, salt, etc.

3) ねずみに、壁(かべ)をかじられた。

Nezumini, kabeo kajirareta.

We had our wall chewed up by rats (and it upset me).

4) 私(わたし)は、スペイン語(ご)をちょっとかじったことがある。

Watashiwa, Supeingoo chotto kajitta kotoga aru.

I studied Spanish only for a short while.

かむ

■ *kamu*
■ to bite ; to chew 

上(うえ)の歯(は)と下(した)の歯(は)を強(つよ)く合(あ)わせることです。そのことで食(た)べ物(もの)をこまかくしたり、また食(く)いついたりします（例(れい)5, 6, 7, 8）。

To forcefully bring the upper teeth and lower teeth together. *Kamu* may mean to chew in order to break food down into smaller pieces or to bite hard (ex.5, 6, 7, 8).

---

5) 彼女(かのじょ)は、いつもガムをかんでいる。

Kanojowa, itsumo gamuo kandeiru.

She is always chewing gum.

6) この肉(にく)は、固(かた)くてかめない。

Kono nikuwa, katakute kamenai.

This meat is too tough to chew.

7) つめをかむのは悪(わる)いくせだ。

Tsumeo kamunowa warui kuseda.

Biting your nails is a bad habit.

8) 子犬(こいぬ)を抱(だ)こうとしたら、親犬(おやいぬ)にかまれた。

Koinuo dakootoshitara, oyainuni kamareta.
(I) tried to pick up a puppy, but I was bitten by its mother.

がっかり／しつぼうする／きをおとす

■ *gakkari* ■ *shitsubou suru* ■ *ki o otosu*

がっかり

■ *gakkari*
■ to be disappointed ♥

ものごとが、期待通りにならなかったり、思っていたような良い結果にならなかったときに、「**残念だ・つまらない**」と**感じる気持ち**です（例1, 2, 3, 4）。そのために精神的に落ち込んだり、気が弱くなったりすることもあります。

To feel disappointed or disillusioned because something did not turn out well or as one had expected (ex.1, 2, 3, 4). As a result, one may feel depressed or withdrawn.

1) ぼくが電話で「正月には帰らない」と言ったら、田舎の両親はがっかりしていた。

Bokuga denwade "Shoogatsuniwa kaeranai" to ittara, inakano ryooshinwa gakkarishiteita.
When I called my parents to tell them that I wasn't going home for the New Year's holidays, they were disappointed.

2) 買ったばかりの財布をすられてしまい、彼はがっかりしている。

Kattabakarino saifuo surareteshimai, karewa gakkarishiteiru.
He's depressed because the wallet he'd just bought was stolen.

3) いくら不景気とはいえ、ボーナスが去年よりずっと少なくてがっかりだ。

Ikura fukeikitowa ie, boonasuga kyonenyori zutto sukunakute gakkarida.
I don't care how bad business is—I'm disappointed that this year's bonus is so much less than last year's.

4) 楽しみにしていたコンサートが中止になって、妹はがっかりしている。

Tanoshimini shiteita konsaatoga chuushininatte, imootowa gakkarishiteiru.
My (younger) sister is disappointed that the concert she was looking forward to was cancelled.

しつぼうする［失望する］

■*shitsubou suru*
■to despair ; to lose hope

ものごとに対する自分の思いや**期待・希望**などが**実際とは違った**とき、それまで持っていた思いや期待・希望などがなくなってしまうことです（例5, 6, 7）。「がっかり」より度合いが強く、ものごとが信じられない・信頼できないなどと感じることもあります。

To be disappointed because something is actually different than the way one had thought or expected. It is implied that one's wish or hope has been dashed (ex.5, 6, 7). *Shitsubou suru* is a stronger expression than *gakkari*, and suggests a sense that something is unbelievable or unreliable.

5) 審査員は誰一人、私の絵をわかってくれない。私は失望した。
Shinsainwa darehitori, watashino eo wakattekurenai. Watashiwa shitsubooshita.
Not even one of the judges understood my painting. I was so disappointed.

6) 父は、私が父の病院をつぐ意志のないことを知って、失望したらしい。
Chichiwa, watashiga chichino byooin-o tsugu ishino nai kotoo shitte, shitsu-boo-shitarashii.
My father seemed disappointed when he found out that I have no intention of succeeding him in his clinic (hospital).

7) あなたを信じてこの仕事をまかせるんだから、私を失望させないでください。
Anatao shinjite kono shigotoo makaserundakara, watashio shitsuboo sasenaidekudasai.
I'm counting on you for this job, so don't let me down (disappoint me).

きをおとす［気を落とす］

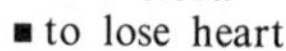

■*ki o otosu*
■to lose heart

思いもよらない**不幸にあったり、望ましくない状況に直面した**ときに、**気持ちが沈んだり悲しく**思ったりすることです（例8, 9, 10）。「がっかり」よりも、しばらくの間、立ち直れないという感じがあります。また、**客観的なことば**なので「私は気を落とした」のように、自分について使うことはありません。

Ki o otosu denotes sadness or despair due to unforeseen bad luck or being faced with an undesirable situation (ex.8, 9, 10). Compared to *gakkari*, *ki o otosu* suggests more of a sense that one will not recover for a while. Because it is an objective expression, it may not be used in sentences such as *watashi wa ki o otoshita* to refer to oneself.

---

8) 単位(たんい)がたりなくて進級(しんきゅう)できないとわかり、彼(かれ)はすっかり気(き)を落(お)としている。
Tan-iga tarinakute shinkyuu-dekinaito wakari, karewa sukkari kio otoshiteiru.
He's thoroughly discouraged because knows he doesn't have enough credits to move up (to the next class).

9) 火事(かじ)で家(いえ)は焼(や)けてしまったけれど、家族全員(かぞくぜんいん)が無事(ぶじ)だったんだから、そんなに気(き)を落(お)とさないでください。
Kajide iewa yaketeshimatta-keredo, kazoku zen-inga bujidattandakara, sonnani kio otosanaide kudasai.
Please don't be so depressed. Although (you) lost your house in the fire, your family is safe.

10) 彼女(かのじょ)は子供(こども)を事故(じこ)で亡(な)くし、すっかり気(き)を落(お)としてしまった。
Kanojowa kodomoo jikode nakushi, sukkari kio otoshiteshimatta.
She just completely lost heart when she lost her child in the accident.

「来(こ)なくていい」は「来(き)てはいけない」？

典子(のりこ)はこのごろ仕事(しごと)が忙(いそが)しくて大変(たいへん)です。今度(こんど)の日曜日(にちようび)に、仲(なか)の良(よ)いマリアが引(ひ)っ越(こ)すことになりました。典子(のりこ)はどんなに忙(いそが)しくても友達(ともだち)の引(ひ)っ越(こ)しは手伝(てつだ)うつもりでした。すると、もう1人(ひとり)の仲良(なかよ)し、セーラが言(い)いました。「典子(のりこ)、私(わたし)が手伝(てつだ)いに行(い)くから、あなたは来(こ)なくていい」それを聞(き)いて典子(のりこ)はムッとしました。セーラは、典子(のりこ)が忙(いそが)しいのを知(し)っていて「あなたはとても忙(いそが)しいのでしょう。私(わたし)が2人分(ふたりぶん)手伝(てつだ)うから、来(こ)なくてもいいんですよ」と親切(しんせつ)に言(い)ったつもりだったのです。

「来なくてもいい」は「来ても来なくてもどちらでもいい」ということですが、「来なくていい」は、どちらかというと「来るな・来てはいけない」という意味です。ですからこのようなときは、「忙しいでしょうから、無理しないでくださいね」と言うのがいいでしょう。

Does *konakute ii*[1] mean 'you must not come' ?

Noriko has been extremely busy at work lately. This coming Sunday, her friend Maria is going to be moving, and Noriko had been planning to help no matter how busy she is. However, another friend of hers named Sara said, "Noriko, I'll go and help, so *anata wa konakute ii*[2]." Noriko was offended when she heard this. Sara knew that Noriko was busy, so with kind intentions she meant to say, "You're busy, aren't you? I'll help her for the both of us, so it's all right if you don't come." In this type of situation we need to pay attention to the fact that while *konakute mo ii* means 'It doesn't matter whether you come or not' (We'll be fine even if you can't make it), *konakute ii* comes very close to meaning 'don't come' or 'you must not come'. In this situation it would be better to say, "I know you are busy, so *muri shinai de kudasai ne*[3]." By saying it this way you can avoid a big misunderstanding.

1 *It's OK for you not to come.*
2 *You should not come.*
3 *Don't go through too much trouble, OK?*

かど／すみ

■ *kado* ■ *sumi*

かど［角］ ■ *kado* ■ corner

①線や面が交じわってできた**とがったところ**、ものの角ばってつき出した部分を指して使います（例1, 2, 3)。道の曲がるところ（例4, 5)。

Kado refers to the outside of a corner, such as a corner of a desk, box or street (ex.1, 2, 3, 4, 5).

②ことば・性格(せいかく)・態度(たいど)がおだやかでなく、とげとげしいときやその場(ば)の雰囲気(ふんいき)が、とげとげしくなるとき（例(れい)6, 7, 8）使(つか)います。

It also expresses harshness or rigidness of personality or language, or an unfriendly atmosphere (ex.6, 7, 8).

---

1) 机(つくえ)の角(かど)にひじをぶつけて、あざができた。

Tsukueno kadoni hijio butsukete, azaga dekita.
I hit my elbow against a corner of the desk and got a bruise.

2) あんまりまちがいが多(おお)いので、消(け)しゴムの角(かど)が丸(まる)くなってしまった。

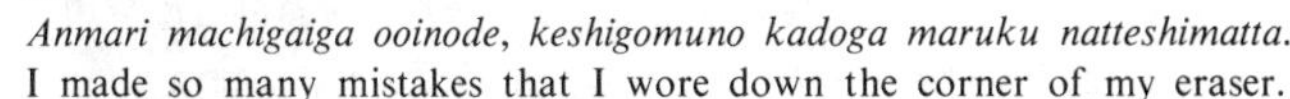

Anmari machigaiga ooinode, keshigomuno kadoga maruku natteshimatta.
I made so many mistakes that I wore down the corner of my eraser.

3) 落(お)として箱(はこ)の角(かど)がつぶれてしまった。

Otoshite hakono kadoga tsuburete-shimatta.
A corner of the box was smashed because I dropped it.

4) 私(わたし)の家(いえ)は、２つ目(ふため)の角(かど)を左(ひだり)に曲(ま)がったところです。

Watashino iewa, futatsumeno kadoo hidarini magatta tokorodesu.
You'll see my house right after you turn left at the second corner.

5) 曲(ま)がり角(かど)に標識(ひょうしき)が立(た)っている。

Magarikadoni hyooshikiga tatteiru.
There is a sign at the street corner.

6) そんな角(かど)のある言(い)い方(かた)は、相手(あいて)の心(こころ)を傷(きず)つけるよ。

Sonna kadono aru iikatawa, aiteno kokoroo kizutsukeruyo.
If you speak in such a harsh way, you'll hurt other people's feelings, you know.

7) 彼(かれ)は年(とし)とともに角(かど)がとれて、性格(せいかく)がまるくなった。

Karewa toshito tomoni kadoga torete, seikakuga maruku natta.
He has become more relaxed and kinder as he has gotten older.

8) ものも言(い)いようで角(かど)が立(た)つ。

Monomo iiyoode kadoga tatsu.
Whether or not you sound harsh depends on the way you speak.

すみ［隅］ ■*sumi* ■corner 

①折れ曲がった線や面に囲まれた空間の端のところ。つまり「角」を内側から見た部分を指して使います(例9, 10)。はがきの「隅」に書くことはできても、「角」に書くことはできませんし、部屋の中に入ってしまえば、「部屋の隅」はあっても、「部屋の角」はありません。

Sumi refers to the inside of a corner, such as a corner of a drawer, box or room. There is no *kado* inside a room, box or drawer (ex.9, 10). Accordingly, it is possible to write in a *sumi* of a postcard, but not possible to write in a *kado* of it.

②さらに「角」とは対応しないで、場所・**ものの部分の端の方**という意味で使います（例11, 12)。この場合、中心部ではない・めだたないところという感じです。そのようなところから、思いのほかばかにできない・意外な面を知って見なおすという意味で、「隅におけない」という使い方もします（例13, 14)。

Sometimes, *sumi* is used figuratively to refer to a section 'that is not in the central part' (ex.11,12). With this meaning it is used in expression *sumi ni okenai* to mean 'cannot be overlooked' or 'not unimportant' (ex.13, 14).

---

9) 招待状の隅に番号が書いてある。
Shootaijoono sumini bangooga kaitearu.
A number is written in the corner of the invitation card.

10) 部屋の隅に小さいごみ箱がある。
Heyano sumini chiisai gomibakoga aru.
There is a small trash can in the corner of the room.

11) 楽しそうに遊んでいる子供たちを、私は公園の隅でながめていた。
Tanoshisooni asondeiru kodomotachio, watashiwa kooenno sumide nagameteita.
I was watching children playing joyfully from a corner of the park.

12) 遠くはなれていても、私のことは心の隅にとめておいてください。
Tooku hanareteitemo, watashino kotowa kokorono sumini tometeoite kudasai.
Even though we are far apart, please save a place in your heart for me.

13) 初めて会った女性に、いきなりデートを申し込むなんて、君も隅におけないね。

Hajimete atta joseini, ikinari deetoo mooshikomu-nante, kimimo sumini okenaine.
Abruptly asking for a date with a woman whom you've just met for the first time—boy, you sure are something.

14) あの若さで会社の社長だなんて、彼もなかなか隅におけない。

Ano wakasade kaishano shachoodanante, karemo nakanaka sumini okenai.
He is the president of a company?! At his age?! Wow, he is quite a guy!

かなしい／さびしい

■ *kanashii* ■ *sabishii*

かなしい［悲しい］

■ *kanashii*
■ sad ; sorrowful

泣きたくなるくらいに、**心が痛んだり、沈んだ気持ちになったり**するようすを表すとき（例1, 2, 3, 4, 5）や、**残念だと嘆いたり**するようすを表すとき（例6, 7）使います。

Kanashii is used to indicate feelings of depression or heartbreak (ex.1, 2, 3, 4, 5). It may also be used to show sadness or sorrow due to a disappointing or regrettable situation (ex.6, 7).

1) かわいがっていた犬が死んだので、とても悲しい。

Kawaigatteita inuga shindanode, totemo kanashii.
(I'm) so sad because the dog I love has died.

2) 別れはいつも悲しいものだ。

Wakarewa itsumo kanashii monoda.
It's always sad to part with someone.

3) 悲しい映画を見たら、涙がとまらなかった。

Kanashii eigao mitara, namidaga tomaranakatta.
(I) couldn't stop crying after seeing that sad movie.

4) A：どうしたの、悲しそうな顔をして……。

B：去年亡くなった母を思い出したんです。

A： *Dooshitano? Kanashisoona kaoo shite…*
What's the matter? You look sad.

B： *Kyonen nakunatta hahao omoidashitandesu.*
I was just thinking about my mother who died last year.

5) そんなに泣かないで、私まで悲しくなるから……。

Sonnani nakanaide, watashimade kanashiku narukara…
Please don't cry so much—you'll make me sad, too.

6) 親友があんなに困っているのに、何もしてあげられない自分が悲しい。

Shin-yuuga annani komatteirunoni, nanimo shiteagerarenai jibunga kanashii.
I feel bad that I can't help my best friend, even though he is in so much trouble.

7) 人を信じられないなんて悲しいね。

Hitoo shinjirarenai-nante kanashiine.
It's a sad thing not to be able to believe in anybody.

さびしい［寂しい］ ■ *sabishii* ■ lonely 

---

①**孤独で心が満たされない、不安で心細い**気持ちを表します（例8, 9, 10）。

This is used when speaking of emotions of solitude or loneliness, as well as helplessness due to uncertainty (ex.8, 9, 10).

②**何かものたりない・にぎやかでない・あるべきものがない**ようすを表すとき使います（例11, 12, 13, 14）。

It may also be used to show that something is missing, lacking in liveliness or is unsatisfactory in some way (ex.11, 12, 13, 14).

---

8) 仲良しの友達が引っ越したので寂しい。

Nakayoshino tomodachiga hikkoshitanode sabishii.
(I'm) feeling lonely because my good friend moved away.

9) ひとりで暮らしていると、ときどき寂しくなる。

Hitoride kurashiteiruto, tokidoki sabishiku naru.
Since (I) have been living alone, I occasionally feel lonely.

10) あの子はいつもひとりぼっちで遊んでいて、寂しそうだね。

Ano kowa itsumo hitoribotchide asondeite, sabishisoodane.
That girl is always playing by herself, and sure seems lonely.

11) この部屋(へや)はなんだか寂(さび)しいね。絵(え)でも飾(かざ)ったら。
Kono heyawa nandaka sabishiine. Edemo kazattara?
This room seems a bit drab. Maybe you should hang a painting or something.

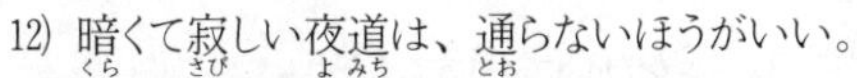

12) 暗(くら)くて寂(さび)しい夜道(よみち)は、通(とお)らないほうがいい。
Kurakute sabishii yomichiwa, tooranai hooga ii.
You shouldn't walk on dark and empty streets at night.

13) 多(おお)くの人(ひと)が都会(とかい)へ行(い)ってしまい、この村(むら)も寂(さび)しくなった。
Ookuno hitoga tokaie itteshimai, kono muramo sabishikunatta.
Since so many people have moved to the city, this village has become a lonely place.

14) 給料日前(きゅうりょうびまえ)は、いつもふところが寂(さび)しい。
Kyuuryoobimaewa, itsumo futokoroga sabishii.
My pockets are always empty just before payday.

かならず／きっと／きまって／ぜったい

■ *kanarazu* ■ *kitto* ■ *kimatte* ■ *zettai*

かならず［必(かなら)ず］

■ *kanarazu*
■ certainly ; without fail

①**例外(れいがい)なく・確(たし)かに・**百(ひゃく)パーセントそうなる（する）ということを表(あらわ)すとき使(つか)います（例(れい)1, 2, 3)。

Kanarazu is used when expressing that someone or something will become (do) something with 100% certainty and without exception (ex.1, 2, 3).

②**まちがいなくそうする、**という**強(つよ)い決意(けつい)・確信(かくしん)**を表(あらわ)すとき使(つか)います(例(れい)4, 5)。

It is also used when expressing strong conviction that one will do something without fail (ex.4, 5).

1) 酸素(さんそ)がなくなると必(かなら)ず火(ひ)は消(き)える。
Sansoga nakunaruto kanarazu hiwa kieru.
When the oxygen is gone, the fire will certainly go out.

2) あした、とても大切(たいせつ)な会議(かいぎ)があるので、必(かなら)ず10時(じ)までに来(き)てください。
Ashita, totemo taisetsuna kaigiga arunode, kanarazu juujimadeni kitekudasai.
There is an important meeting tomorrow, so please be absolutely sure you are here by ten o'clock.

3) 駐車(ちゅうしゃ)するときは、必(かなら)ずサイドブレーキをひいておいてください。
Chuushasuru tokiwa, kanarazu saidobureekio hiiteoitekudasai.
When parking your car, be sure to set the hand brake.

4) 私(わたし)は、寝(ね)る前(まえ)には必(かなら)ず歯(は)をみがきます。
Watashiwa, neru maeniwa kanarazu hao migakimasu.
I always make sure to brush my teeth before going to bed.

5) 私(わたし)は必(かなら)ず宇宙飛行士(うちゅうひこうし)になってみせます。
Watashiwa kanarazu uchuuhikooshini nattemisemasu.
I will definitely become an astronaut someday—you'll see.

きっと

- *kitto*
- (almost) certainly 

予想(よそう)したことや判断(はんだん)などが、まちがいなく**そうなるだろうというようす**を表(あらわ)すとき使(つか)います（例(れい)6, 7, 8)。「必(かなら)ず」ほど強(つよ)い意味(いみ)でないときにも使(つか)います。

Kitto is used when expressing confidence that something will turn out the way one predicts. It is used in situations requiring an expression not quite as strong as *kanarazu* (ex.6, 7, 8).

---

6) あの少年(しょうねん)なら、きっとオリンピック選手(せんしゅ)になれるだろう。
Ano shoonennara, kitto orinpikku-senshuni narerudaroo.
Knowing him, that boy will almost certainly be an Olympic athlete someday.

7) 彼(かれ)があれほどほめていたのだから、あのミュージカルは、きっとおもしろいにちがいない。
Karega arehodo homete-itanodakara, ano myuujikaruwa, kitto omoshiroini

chigainai.
He said all those good things about that musical, so it must be good.

8) 西(にし)の空(そら)が夕焼(ゆうや)けだ。あしたもきっと晴(は)れるよ。
Nishino soraga yuuyakeda. Ashitamo kitto hareruyo.
There is a glowing sunset in the western sky, so tomorrow is sure to be a nice day too.

きまって ■ *kimatte* ■ invariably ; without fail 

ある条件(じょうけん)のときには、**例外(れいがい)なくいつも**そのことが起(お)こるというとき使(つか)います（例(れい)9,10,11,12）。

This is used to indicate that, under a certain condition, a specific action will definitely occur (ex.9, 10, 11, 12).

---

9) 家(いえ)の近(ちか)くの湖(みずうみ)には、冬(ふゆ)になるときまって白鳥(はくちょう)がやってくる。
Ieno chikakuno mizuuminiwa, fuyuni naruto kimatte hakuchooga yattekuru.
Swans always come to the lake near my home when winter arrives.

10) あの2人(ふたり)は、顔(かお)を合(あ)わせるときまってけんかを始(はじ)める。
Ano futariwa, kaoo awaseruto kimatte kenkao hajimeru.
Those two invariably start fighting whenever they meet.

11) 私(わたし)の父(ちち)は、朝食(ちょうしょく)に、きまってたまごを食(た)べます。
Watashino chichiwa, chooshokuni, kimatte tamagoo tabemasu.
My father always has eggs for breakfast.

12) 私(わたし)は牛乳(ぎゅうにゅう)を飲(の)むと、きまっておなかが痛(いた)くなる。
Watashiwa gyuunyuuo nomuto, kimatte onakaga itakunaru.
I get a stomachache whenever I drink milk.

ぜったい［絶対(ぜったい)］ ■ *zettai* ■ absolute(ly) 

---

①他(ほか)に比(くら)べるものがなく、**それだけがすべて**だという意味(いみ)です（例(れい)13, 14）。

Zettai means that a specific something is all there is, and without comparison (ex.13, 14).

②「どうしても」「まちがいなく」「無条件(むじょうけん)に」「**百(ひゃく)パーセント**」というとき使(つか)いま

す（例15, 16, 17）。否定形のときは「けっして〜ない」という意味です（例18, 19, 20）。「絶対に」と使うこともあります。強い確信や意志を表しますが、それほど強くない調子で日常会話でもよく使われます。

Zettai is also used when saying that something will occur without fail or condition (ex.15, 16, 17). When used in a negative sentence, it has a meaning similar to *kesshite〜nai* (never) (ex.18, 19, 20). The expression *zettai ni* may be used both to strongly emphasize one's will or intention, or in a weaker conversational style.

---

13) 私の家では父の意見は絶対で、だれもさからえません。
Watashino iedewa chichino ikenwa zettaide, daremo sakaraemasen.
In my family, my father's word is law, so nobody can disobey him.

14) 私にとって神は絶対です。
Watashini totte kamiwa zettaidesu.
To me, God is absolute.

15) 私は戦争には、絶対反対です。
Watashiwa sensooniwa, zettai hantaidesu.
I am totally opposed to war.

16) 彼は、絶対に無実だ。
Karewa, zettaini mujitsuda.
He is completely innocent.

17) 彼女は病気が重く、絶対安静です。
Kanojowa byookiga omoku, zettai anseidesu.
Her illness is serious, so she needs absolute rest.

18) 私は一度会った人の名前は、絶対忘れない。
Watashiwa ichido atta hitono namaewa, zettai wasurenai.
I never forget the names of people I meet.

19) 彼は、絶対約束を破らない。
Karewa, zettai yakusokuo yaburanai.
He never breaks his promises.

20) ガソリンと灯油は、絶対にまちがえないようにしてください。
Gasorinto tooyuwa, zettaini machigaenai-yooni shite kudasai.
Be sure to never mistake gasoline for kerosene.

かなり／だいぶ

■ *kanari*　　■ *daibu*

かなり

■ *kanari*
■ quite ; extremely ; very

ものごとの量や質、程度などの大きさや高さを強調するとき使います（例1, 2, 3, 4, 5, 6）。「病気がだいぶよくなった」は、前と比べると良い状態になってきたことを表し、「病気がかなりよくなった」は、全快に近づいていることを表します。

Kanari is used to stress the greatness of a degree, level, quantity, quality, etc. (ex.1, 2, 3, 4, 5, 6). To say of an illness that it has *daibu yoku natta* implies that it has become better than it was previously, while *kanari yoku natta* implies that one is close to complete recovery.

1）荷物がかなり多いので、駅からタクシーで行きます。
Nimotsuga kanari ooinode, ekikara takushiide ikimasu.
(I've) got quite a lot of luggage, so I'm going to take a taxi from the station.

2）この問題は、簡単そうで、実際はかなりむずかしい。
Kono mondaiwa, kantansoode, jissaiwa kanari muzukashii.
This question seems simple, but actually it's quite difficult.

3）写真で見ると、彼はかなりハンサムだ。
Shashinde miruto, karewa kanari hansamuda.
Looking at his photograph, he's quite handsome.

4）彼の考えは、かなり偏っている。
Kareno kangaewa, kanari katayotteiru.
His ideas are very biased.

5）この店の板前は、若いけれども腕前はかなりのものです。
Kono miseno itamaewa, wakaikeredomo udemaewa kanarino monodesu.
The chef at this restaurant is young, but his skill is quite something.

6）今年の花火大会はかなりの人出が予想されている。
Kotoshino hanabitaikaiwa kanarino hitodega yosoosareteiru.

They're expecting a considerable crowd for this year's fireworks display.

だいぶ［大分］

■ *daibu*
■ much ; very

ものごとを、ほかのものやそれ以前の状態と比較して、量や質、程度などの変化の度合いが大きいことを表すときに使います（例7, 8, 9, 10, 11）。

Daibu is used to indicate that the rate or extent of change in degree, quality, quantity, etc., of something is great compared to a prior state or with another object (ex.7, 8, 9, 10, 11).

---

7) 息子は夏休みの間に、だいぶ背が伸びた。
Musukowa natsuyasumino aidani, daibu sega nobita.
My son grew considerably taller over the summer vacation.

8) 彼女は、だいぶ日本語がわかるようになりました。
Kanojowa, daibu Nihongoga wakaruyooni narimashita.
She has come to understand Japanese quite a bit.

9) きょうは、きのうよりだいぶ暖かい。
Kyoowa, kinooyori daibu atatakai.
Today is considerably warmer than yesterday.

10) この靴は、だいぶいたんでいる。
Kono kutsuwa, daibu itandeiru.
These shoes are very worn.

11) 交通事故の件数が、去年よりだいぶ減った。
Kootsuujikono kensuuga, kyonenyori daibu hetta.
The number of traffic accidents (this year) is much less than last year.

かぶせる／おおう

■ *kabuseru*　　■ *oou*

かぶせる

■ *kabuseru*
■ to cover 

---

①物に、それより大きい物を**上から載せて**、一部や全体を**かくす**とき使います（例1, 2, 3）。

To cover an object with something bigger in order to hide it completely or partially (ex.1, 2, 3).

②**上からかけてしまう**とき使います（例4）。

To hang or lay something on top of something else (ex.4).

③**責任**や**罪**などを**他人のせいにする**とき使います（例5, 6）。

To place blame or responsibility on someone else (ex.5, 6).

---

1) 日ざしが強い日には、子供にぼうしをかぶせます。
Hizashiga tsuyoi hiniwa, kodomoni booshio kabusemasu.
(I) put a hat on my child on days when the sun's rays are strong.

2) 農家では、りんごがなると虫がつかないように、ひとつひとつ紙のふくろをかぶせます。
Nookadewa, ringoga naruto mushiga tsukanaiyooni, hitotsuhitotsu kamino fukuroo kabusemasu.
As soon as fruit forms on the apple trees, farmers cover each apple with a paper bag so that insects won't get to it.

3) 料理が残ったら、ナプキンをかぶせておいてください。
Ryooriga nokottara, napukin-o kabuseteoite kudasai.
If there is any food left over, please cover it with a napkin.

4) チューリップの球根を植えて、上から土をかぶせました。
Chuurippuno kyuukon-o uete, uekara tsuchio kabusemashita.
(I) planted tulip bulbs and covered them with soil.

5) みんなでやったことなのに、私１人に責任をかぶせるなんてあんまりです。
Minnade yatta kotonanoni, watashihitorini sekinin-o kabuserunante anmaridesu.
We all did it, but they placed all the responsibility for it on me alone. That's not fair!

6) 彼はいつも自分の失敗を他人にかぶせるので、きらわれている。
Karewa itsumo jibunno shippaio taninni kabuserunode, kirawareteiru.
He always puts the blame for his own mistakes on others, so no one likes him.

おおう［覆う］ ■*oou* ■to wrap ; to cover

物の全体を**かくして、完全に見えないようにする**とき使い、中のものを光・空気・熱などからさえぎるという意味を強く含みます（例7, 8, 9, 10, 11）。その状態を表して、「おおわれる・おおわれている」の形で使うことが多く、助詞は「で」をとり「AをBでおおう」「Aは（が）Bでおおわれる」と使います。また例８のように受動態では、「に」を使うこともあります。

To hide all of something or to make it invisible; includes a strong sense of protecting the object from light, air or heat (ex.7, 8, 9, 10, 11). It is often used in the passive forms : *oowareru* (to be covered) and *oowarete iru* (to have been covered). In this case the particle *de* is used, e.g., *A o B de oou* (to cover A with B) or *A wa (ga) B de oowareru* (A is covered with B). However, as in Example 8, *ni* may also be used in passive sentences.

---

7) 寒い地方では、雪で作物がいたまないように畑をビニールシートでおおう。
Samui chihoodewa, yukide sakumotsuga itamanaiyooni hatakeo biniirushiitode oou.
In places where it's cold, they cover the ground with vinyl tarps so the crops in the fields aren't ruined by snow.

8) 町は一晩で雪におおわれた。
Machiwa hitobande yukini oowareta.
In one night the whole town was blanketed in snow.

9) でき上がった像は、発表の日まで布ですっぽりとおおわれていた。
Dekiagatta zoowa, happyoono himade nunode supporito oowareteita.
The finished statue was completely covered with a cloth until the day of its presentation.

10) 哺乳動物は一般に、体を毛でおおわれている。
Honyuu-doobutsuwa ippanni, karadao kede oowareteiru.
Most mammals are covered completely with fur.

11) 飛行機事故の現場は、目をおおいたくなるようなひどい状態だ。
Hikookijikono genbawa, meo ooitakunaruyoona hidoi jootaida.
The site of the plane crash is so terrible that (you'll) want to cover your eyes.

かり／いちじてき／りんじ

■ *kari* ■ *ichijiteki* ■ *rinji*

かり［仮］ ■ *kari* ■ temporary

①本物の代わりに他のものを短期間使うとき使います（例1, 2, 3）。**間に合わせ**という意味を含みます。「仮住まい・仮払い・仮免許・仮処分・仮契約……」のように、熟語として使うことが多いです。

Kari is used when one temporarily substitutes something for the real thing. That the something is makeshift is included in the meaning. It is used most often in compounds, as in *kari-zumai* (temporary residence), *kari-barai* (provisional payment), *kari-menkyo* (temporary permit), *kari-shobun* (provisional disposition), and *kari-keiyaku* (provisional agreement) (ex.1, 2, 3).

②本当のことではないけれど、もしそうだったら、**たとえば**……というとき使います（例4）。

It is also used to introduce a hypothetical or subjunctive idea, and is often used with a subjunctive or conditional clause (ex.4).

1) あの会社は、建て替えているところなので今は、仮の建物です。
Ano kaishawa, tatekaeteiru tokoronanode imawa, karino tatemonodesu.
The company is in a temporary building because they're rebuilding.

2) 本名が出せないので、仮にX氏としましょう。
Honmyooga dasenainode, karini Ekkusushito shimashoo.
Since (I) cannot reveal his real name, let's call him Mr. X for the time being.

3) ここは仮の住まいだから、家具が少ない。
Kokowa karino sumaidakara, kaguga sukunai.
Since this is my temporary residence, (I) don't have much furniture.

4) もし仮に宝くじで１億円が当たったらどうしますか。
Moshi karini takarakujide ichiokuenga atattara dooshimasuka?
If (you) won ¥100,000,000 in the lottery, what would you do?

いちじてき［一時的］ ■*ichijiteki* ■temporary

その時だけ・その場限りの意味で長続きしないというとき使います（例5, 6, 7, 8)。「仮」のように他のものを代わりに使うのではなく、**短期間に限って**というところに重点があります。

This expression is used to indicate that something is 'for the moment' or 'this time only' and will not continue for very long (ex.5, 6, 7, 8). It is not used in the same way as *kari* to denote using something as a substitute; the emphasis is on the short duration of time.

5) 荷物がじゃまなので、一時的にコインロッカーに預けた。
Nimotsuga jamananode, ichijitekini koinrokkaani azuketa.
My luggage is cumbersome, so (I) stored it in a coin-operated locker for a while.

6) きのうは、台風の影響で一時的に強い雨が降った。
Kinoowa, taifuuno eikyoode ichijitekini tsuyoi amega futta.
Yesterday, heavy rain fell for a short time because of a nearby typhoon.

7) 流行は一時的なもので、長続きしない。
Ryuukoowa ichijitekina monode, nagatsuzuki shinai.
Fashions are only temporary; they do not last long.

8) この痛みは、一時的なものだから心配いらない。
Kono itamiwa, ichijitekina monodakara shinpaiiranai.
It's only temporary pain so (you) don't have to worry.

りんじ［臨時］ ■*rinji* ■special ; extra ; temporary 

前から決まっているいつも通りのこと以外に、その場その時の**必要に応じて決めて行う特別なものごと**を表します（例9, 10, 11, 12, 13)。ずっと続くものではありません。「～ニュース・～休業・～便（飛行機）・～国会……」などのように熟語で使うことが多いです。

Rinji refers to a temporary decision or action which is made according to the necessity of a given moment, regardless of plans which were made in advance (ex.9, 10, 11, 12, 13). It is not used for matters that continue for a long time.

It is often used in compounds such as : *rinji-nyuusu* (special news bulletin), *rinji-kyuugyoo* (special holiday), *rinji-bin* (special flight), and *rinji-kokkai* (special session of the National Diet).

9) 夏休みの間、駅から海に行く臨時のバスが出る。
Natsuyasumino aida, ekikara umini iku rinjino basuga deru.
During summer vacation, special shuttles run between the station and the beach.

10) きょうは電車のストがあったので臨時休校だった。
Kyoowa denshano sutoga attanode rinji-kyuukoodatta.
There was a train strike today, so classes were temporarily suspended.

11) テレビの臨時ニュースが選挙速報を伝えている。
Terebino rinjinyuusuga senkyosokuhoo-o tsutaeteiru.
A special news broadcast has been covering the election returns.

12) アルバイトで臨時収入があったので、春のブラウスを買った。
Arubaitode rinjishuunyuuga attanode, haruno burausuo katta.
Since (I) got some extra money from my part-time job, I bought a blouse for spring.

13) きょう、隣の床屋さんは、臨時休業です。
Kyoo, tonarino tokoyasanwa, rinji-kyuugyoodesu.
The barbershop next door is temporarily closed today.

〜がる／〜ぶる／ふりをする

■〜*garu* ■〜*buru* ■*furi o suru*

〜がる

■〜*garu*
■to want ; to seem 

「〜したい」と強く思っているようすや、「欲しい・悲しい・うれしい・寒い」など感情や感覚がことばや態度に表れているとき使います（例1, 2, 3, 4, 5）。話に加わっていない第三者のようすに使い、「私は〜がる（〜がっている）」や「あなたは〜がる」とは使いません。

〜*garu* is used to describe a third person's wants, desires, emotions, or physical sensations, which have been expressed either verbally or by his behavior (ex.1, 2, 3, 4, 5). It is not used in first or second person situations.

1) 妹は、私の持っているものを何でも欲しがる。
Imootowa, watashino motteiru monoo nandemo hoshigaru.
My (younger) sister wants (to have) everything I have.

2) 人のいやがることをしてはいけない。
Hitono iyagaru kotoo shitewa ikenai.
(You) shouldn't do things that people dislike.

3) 子供は雨でも外で遊びたがる。
Kodomowa amedemo sotode asobitagaru.
Children want to play outside, even on rainy days.

4) 彼は北海道に行きたがっている。
Karewa Hokkaidooni ikitagatteiru.
He wants to go to Hokkaido.

5) 弟は犬を飼いたがっている。
Otootowa inuo kaitagatteiru.
My (younger) brother wants to have a dog.

~ぶる

- ~*buru*
- to pretend ; to pose as 

他人に良く思われたくて、**自分の人間性や身分などを実際よりも高く見せかける**ような態度をすることです（例6, 7, 8, 9, 10）。そのような人を他人が見て使うことばです。「本当はちがうのに……」と、批判する意味を含んでいます。自分に対しては使いません。動詞にはつきません。

This is used to describe the behavior of someone who is trying to give a false impression of himself, as if he were much better or more sophisticated than he actually is (ex.6, 7, 8, 9, 10). It suggests a feeling of criticism on the part of the speaker. It is not used when speaking of oneself or with verbs.

6) あの子はふだんいたずらばかりしているのに、先生の前ではいい子ぶる。
Ano kowa fudan itazurabakari shiteirunoni, senseino maedewa iikoburu.
That child is always doing naughty things, but he pretends to be good in front of his teachers.

7) 彼女は金持ちぶっているけれど、生活は大変らしい。

Kanojowa kanemochibutte-irukeredo, seikatsuwa taihenrashii.

She acts like a rich woman, but it seems that her life is hard.

8) 彼女は私と１つしか年が違わないのに、いつもお姉さんぶる。

Kanojowa watashito hitotsushika toshiga chigawanainoni, itsumo oneesan-buru.

She is only one year older than I am, but she always acts like a big sister.

9) いくら上品ぶっていても、育ちはすぐに分かる。

Ikura joohinbutteitemo, sodachiwa suguni wakaru.

No matter how much one tries to act elegantly, (you) can always tell the person's upbringing.

10) 隣のおじさんは、親切ぶって世話を焼くので少しわずらわしい。

Tonarino ojisanwa, shinsetsubutte sewao yakunode sukoshi wazurawashii.

The man next door is always doing things for me under the guise of kindness—he's a bit of a pain-in-the-neck.

ふりをする

■ *furi o suru*
■ to pretend

自分の立場を有利にするためや、らくにその場をきりぬけたいなどの理由で、**実際の自分とは違うようすや態度をする**ことです（例11, 12, 13, 14）。例15, 16のように、前に名詞が来るときには「〜のふりをする」という言い方をします。「〜ぶる」が自分を実際よりも良く見せかけるのに対し、「ふりをする」は、そうした方が得だと考えて、「大学生が高校生のふりをする」「勉強ができるのにできないふりをする」などと、自分の程度を低く見せるときにも使います。

This expression means to behave in such a way as to make one's own position more advantageous by pretending to be or do something different (ex. 11, 12, 13, 14). As seen in Examples 15 and 16, 〜*no furi o suru* is attached to the end of nouns. While 〜*buru* means that one tries to show oneself as better than what he actually is, *furi o suru* may be used when one tries to present himself as lower in status because he feels it is to his advantage. Examples might be a university student that pretends to be a high school student, or one who is smart that pretends not to be.

11) 私はお酒が飲めないので、乾杯のときは飲むふりをする。

Watashiwa osakega nomenainode, kanpaino tokiwa nomu furio suru.
I can't drink alcohol, so I only pretend to drink when there is a toast.

12) 子供に「勉強しなさい」と言ったのに、聞こえないふりをして遊びに行ってしまった。

Kodomoni "Benkyooshinasai" to ittanoni, kikoenai furio shite asobini itteshimatta.
Although (I) told my child to study, he pretended that he didn't hear me, and went out to play.

13) 電車の中で、私の前におじいさんが立ったけれど、疲れていて席を譲りたくないので寝たふりをした。

Denshano nakade, watashino maeni ojiisanga tattakeredo, tsukareteite sekio yuzuritakunainode neta furio shita.
Although there was an old man standing in front of me on the train, I was tired and didn't want to give up my seat, so (I) pretended to be asleep.

14) 新宿で知らない人に呼びとめられたけれど、こわいので、日本語が分からないふりをしました。

Shinjukude shiranai hitoni yobi-tomeraretakeredo, kowainode, Nihongoga wakaranai furio shimashita.
(I) was stopped by a stranger in Shinjuku, but being afraid of him, I pretended I didn't understand Japanese.

15) きのうは学校に行きたくなかったので、病気のふりをして休んだ。

Kinoowa gakkooni ikitakunakattanode, byookino furio shite yasunda.
Yesterday, (I) didn't want to go to school, so I acted like I was sick and stayed home.

16) 弟は中学生なのに、小学生のふりをして子供料金で電車に乗ったらしい。

Otootowa chuugakusei-nanoni, shoogakuseino furio shite kodomoryookinde denshani nottarashii.
Although my (younger) brother is a junior high school student, it seems he pretended to be an elementary school student and paid the children's fare to ride the train.

かわす／よける／さける

■ *kawasu* ■ *yokeru* ■ *sakeru*

かわす

■ *kawasu*
■ to evade ; to dodge

すばやく、とっさに体(からだ)を動(うご)かして、向(む)かってくる**災難(さいなん)から逃(のが)れる**とき使(つか)います(例(れい)1, 2, 3, 4)。批判(ひはん)や追及(ついきゅう)など、抽象的(ちゅうしょうてき)なことがらにも使(つか)います。

To quickly and instinctively move one's body away from oncoming harm (ex. 1, 2, 3, 4). *Kawasu* may also be used when speaking of evading abstract matters such as criticism or pursuit.

1) 彼(かれ)は飛(と)んで来(き)たボールを、うまくかわした。
Karewa tondekita booruo, umaku kawashita.
He skillfully dodged the ball thrown at him.

2) チャンピオンは挑戦者(ちょうせんしゃ)のパンチを、左(ひだり)にかわした。
Chanpionwa choosenshano panchio, hidarini kawashita.
The champion dodged to the left to avoid the challenger's punch.

3) 犯人(はんにん)は、パトカーの追跡(ついせき)をかわして逃(に)げた。
Hanninwa, patokaano tsuisekio kawashite nigeta.
The suspect escaped by shaking off the patrol cars that were chasing him.

4) 首相(しゅしょう)は、記者団(きしゃだん)の質問(しつもん)をうまくかわした。
Shushoowa, kishadanno shitsumon-o umaku kawashita.
The Prime Minister skillfully evaded questions from the team of reporters.

よける

■ *yokeru*
■ to avoid ; to evade

好(この)ましくないこと・困(こま)ること・災難(さいなん)などから**離(はな)れること**です(例(れい)5, 6, 7, 8)。「かわす」のように体(からだ)を動(うご)かして難(なん)をのがれるということだけでなく、あらかじめ防(ふせ)ぐ・離(はな)れる、あるいは、じゃまなものを移動(いどう)させてしまうという意味(いみ)も含(ふく)みます。

To move away from something undesirable, troublesome, or harmful (ex.5, 6, 7, 8). Not only does it have the same meaning as *kawasu*, i.e., to move one's body away from harm, but it also means to defend against, to move away from anticipated harm, or to remove an obstacle.

---

5) まがり角(かど)から急(きゅう)に、自転車(じてんしゃ)が出(で)て来(き)たので、あわててよけた。

Magarikadokara kyuuni, jitenshaga detekitanode, awatete yoketa.
A bicycle suddenly came around the corner, and (I) jumped aside to avoid it.

6) 少年(しょうねん)は、じょうずに水(みず)たまりをよけながら、自転車(じてんしゃ)を走(はし)らせて行(い)った。

Shoonenwa, joozuni mizutamario yokenagara, jitenshao hashiraseteitta.
The boy rode along on his bicycle, skillfully avoiding the puddles.

7) 強(つよ)い日差(ひざ)しをよけるために、日(ひ)がさをさします。

Tsuyoi hizashio yokerutameni, higasao sashimasu.
(One) can use a sunshade to ward off the strong sunlight.

8) 彼(かれ)はピーマンが嫌(きら)いなので、いつもよけて食(た)べます。

Karewa piimanga kirainanode, itsumo yokete tabemasu.
He hates green peppers so he always pushes them to the side when he eats.

さける［避(さ)ける］ ■ *sakeru* ■ to avoid

不都合(ふつごう)なこと・好(この)ましくないことに近寄(ちかよ)らないようにすることです（例(れい)9, 10, 11, 12, 13）。

To maintain a distance from something bothersome or undesirable (ex.9, 10, 11, 12, 13).

---

9) 駅(えき)での待(ま)ち合(あ)わせは、ラッシュアワーは避(さ)けたほうがいい。

Ekideno machiawasewa, rasshuawaawa saketa hooga ii.
(You) should avoid meeting people at the station during rush hour.

10) 事故(じこ)があった道路(どうろ)は渋滞(じゅうたい)するので、避(さ)けて違(ちが)う道(みち)を行(い)った。

Jikoga atta doorowa juutaisurunode, sakete chigau michio itta.
(I) took a different road to avoid the one jammed due to an accident.

11) 引退した女優は、人目を避けて静かに暮らしている。
Intaishita joyuuwa, hitomeo sakete shizukani kurashiteiru.
The retired actress is living a quiet life away from the public.

12) 彼は新しい恋人ができたらしく、このごろ私を避けている。
Karewa atarashii koibitoga dekitarashiku, konogoro watashio saketeiru.
He seems to have gotten a new girlfriend, because he has been avoiding me recently.

13) 彼の前で政治の話は避けたほうがいい。
Kareno maede seijino hanashiwa saketa hooga ii.
You should avoid talking about politics in front of him.

かんしん／かんどう

■ *kanshin* ■ *kandou*

かんしん［感心］ ■ *kanshin* ■ admiration

他人の行いやものごとについて、**ほめられるべきこと**だ・**良いことだと認めること**です（例1, 2, 3, 4, 5）。えらい・大したものだ・立派だ、などという評価です。目上の人に向かって「あなたは感心ですね」と言うのは失礼です。

To recognize as excellent or laudable the actions or behavior of another (ex.1, 2, 3, 4, 5). *Kanshin* expresses an evaluative judgment such as 'great', 'wonderful', 'outstanding', etc. It should not be used when speaking to someone in a superior position, e.g., *anata wa kanshin desu ne* (You're amazing!), because it is considered to be rude.

1) あの子はよく親の手伝いをする感心な子です。
Ano kowa yoku oyano tetsudaio suru kanshinna kodesu.
He is a good child who always helps his parents.

2) 彼の努力にはみんなが感心した。
Kareno doryokuniwa minnaga kanshinshita.
Everyone was impressed by his efforts.

3) だれにでも優しい彼女の態度には、いつも感心する。

Darenidemo yasashii kanojono taidoniwa, itsumo kanshinsuru.
(I've) always admired her kind attitude towards others, regardless of who they are.

4) 少年のピアノがあまりにも上手だったので、人びとは感心して聞いていた。
Shoonenno pianoga amarinimo joozudattanode, hitobitowa kanshinshite kiiteita.
The boy's piano playing was so good that everyone listened with admiration.

5) 人を疑うような態度は感心しない。
Hitoo utagauyoona taidowa kanshinshinai.
(I) don't care for that kind of suspicious attitude.

かんどう［感動］

■ *kandou*
■ impression ; to be impressed 

見たり聞いたりしたことに**強く心を打たれ、共感する**ことです。いつまでも心に残るような小説、映画その他芸術や、美しく心あたたまるできごとなどに接したときに**わき上がる感情**です（例6, 7, 8, 9, 10）。

To be moved emotionally by something heard or seen, or to have a strong feeling of sympathy. *Kandou* expresses the feeling or emotion that arises when one encounters a heart-warming or memorable incident, novel, movie, or work of art (ex.6, 7, 8, 9, 10).

---

6) 人びとは、困難を乗り越えて明るく生きる少女の姿に感動した。
Hitobitowa, konnan-o norikoete akaruku ikiru shoojono sugatani kandooshita.
Many people were touched when they saw the girl, who had overcome so many difficulties, living happily.

7) 山の頂上から見た雄大な景色には、だれもが感動した。
Yamano choojookara mita yuudaina keshikiniwa, daremoga kandooshita.
Everybody was moved by the majestic view from the top of the mountain.

8) あの映画の感動的なラストシーンでは、涙がとまらなかった。
Ano eigano kandootekina rasutoshiindewa, namidaga tomaranakatta.
(I) couldn't stop crying during the very moving final scene of that movie.

9) 美しいものにふれて感動する気持ちは、いつまでも失いたくない。
Utsukushii mononi furete kandoosuru kimochiwa, itsumademo ushinaitakunai.
(I) hope that I never lose the ability to be moved by things of beauty.

10) オーケストラの演奏が終わると感動の拍手がわき起こった。
Ookesutorano ensooga owaruto kandoono hakushuga wakiokotta.
As soon as the orchestra ended its performance, the audience broke into emotional applause.

すごい!!

リサは自分で焼いたケーキを持って、洋子の家に遊びに行きました。「わあ、すごい。これリサが作ったの…すごくおいしい」このあたりから洋子は「すごい」をマシンガンのように連発していったのです。「あさってすごい台風が来るんだって」「きのう見た映画、すごく怖かった」「日曜日に原宿に行ったら、すごい人だった」「となりの子猫、すごくかわいいの…」リサは、「すごい」ということばは、いいことにも悪いことにも使えて「すごく便利だ」と思いました。でも要注意！ 「すごい」をあまり多く使うと子供っぽいということは覚えておきましょう。

Wow, terrific!!

Lisa brought a cake she had baked over to her friend Yoko's house. Yoko said, "*Waa sugoi*[1]*!* Did you bake it yourself, Lisa? *Sugoku oishii.*[2]" After that, Yoko started to repeat *sugoi* in many of her sentences, including "*Asatte sugoi taifuu ga kurundatte*[3]," "*Kinoo mita eiga sugoku kowakatta*[4]," "*Nichiyoobi ni Harajuku ni ittara sugoi hito datta*[5]," and, "*Tonari no koneko sugoku kawaii no.*[6]" Lisa realized that *sugoi* is a very useful word that can be used in both good and bad situations. However, overuse of *sugoi* should be avoided as it may make the speaker's speech sound childish.

1 *Wow, terrific!*
2 *It tastes so good.*

3 *They say a terrible typhoon is coming the day after tomorrow.*
4 *The movie I saw yesterday was really frightening.*
5 *On Sunday, I went to Harajuku, but there were too many people.*
6 *My neighbor's kitten is very, very cute.*

がんばる／いっしょうけんめい／ひっし

■ *ganbaru* ■ *isshoukenmei* ■ *hisshi*

がんばる［頑張る］ ■ *ganbaru* ■ to persist 

①苦労や困難に負けないで、自分にとって**良い結果になるように努力する**ときや、元気を出して**しっかり何かをする**とき使います（例1, 2）。

Ganbaru is used when someone does his best or makes an effort to get the best result, without being defeated by hardship or difficulties (ex.1, 2).

②ある**場所を動かない**とき使います（例3, 4）。

It is also used when one does not move from a certain place (ex.3, 4).

③**自分の考えを通す**とき使います（例５）。また、「がんばって・がんばれ」のように励ましや応援にも使います。

In addition, it may mean 'to be determined in one's opinion' (ex.5). It is also used when cheering or encouraging others, as in, *ganbatte!* or *ganbare!* ('Good Luck!' or 'Do your best!').

1）あしたはテストだ。今夜は徹夜でがんばるぞ。
Ashitawa tesutoda. Kon-yawa tetsuyade ganbaruzo!
(I) have an examination tomorrow. I'll stay up the whole night and study hard!

2）私にとって初めてのマラソンだったが、最後までがんばって走った。
Watashini totte hajimeteno marasondattaga, saigomade ganbatte hashitta.
Although it was my very first marathon, I did my best and ran the race to the finish.

3）入り口でガードマンががんばっているので、関係者以外は中に入れない。

Iriguchide gaadomanga ganbatteirunode, kankeishaigaiwa nakani hairenai.
A security officer is standing guard at the entrance, so no one but the concerned parties can enter.

4) 少年は「サインをもらうまで帰らない」と、投手の家の前でがんばった。
Shoonenwa "sain-o moraumade kaeranai" to, tooshuno ieno maede ganbatta.
The boy stayed in front of the pitcher's house saying, "I'm not leaving until I get his autograph."

5) 彼は、反対意見が多い中で、自分の考えが正しいと最後までがんばった。
Karewa, hantaiikenga ooinakade, jibunno kangaega tadashiito saigomade ganbatta.
He insisted to the very end that he was right, although many of the people there had opposite opinions.

いっしょうけんめい［一生懸命］

■ *isshoukenmei*
■ (work / play) hard

働く・走る・勉強する……など動作を表す語の前にきて、「**力のかぎり〜する・熱心に〜する・夢中で〜する**」ようすや程度の高さを表すとき使います。したがって「いっしょうけんめいがんばる」という使い方もします（例6, 7, 8, 9, 10, 11)。「〜するのに（〜に）いっしょうけんめいだ」の形でも使います。

Isshoukenmei is used preceding action verbs such as *hataraku* (to work), *hashiru* (to run) and *benkyoo suru* (to study), and means 'as hard as possible', 'eagerly', or 'enthusiastically' (ex.6, 7, 8, 9, 10, 11). Therefore, it is possible to say *isshookenmei ganbaru* (to do one's best). It is also used in a patterns such as *~suru noni* (*~ni*) *isshoukenmei da* (to try one's best in order to do something).

---

6) 彼は、朝から晩までいっしょうけんめい働きます。
Karewa, asakara banmade isshookenmei hatarakimasu.
He works very hard from morning till night.

7) 運動会で、いっしょうけんめい走ったけれど、1番にはなれなかった。
Undookaide, isshookenmei hashittakeredo, ichibanniwa narenakatta.
(I) ran as fast as I could at the sports competition, but I was unable to come in first.

8) 彼女は、いっしょうけんめい法律を勉強して、弁護士になった。
Kanojowa, isshookenmei hooritsuo benkyooshite, bengoshini natta.

She studied law very hard and became an attorney.

9) 私の息子は、勉強よりも遊ぶことにいっしょうけんめいです。
Watashino musukowa, benkyooyorimo asobukotoni isshookenmeidesu.
My son is more eager to play around than to study.

10) 仕事にいっしょうけんめいになるのもいいけれど、たまには休んだほうがいい。
Shigotoni isshookenmeini narunomo iikeredo, tamaniwa yasunda hooga ii.
It's all right to work hard, but (you) should also take time off once in a while.

11) 彼は、彼女に好かれようといっしょうけんめいだ。
Karewa, kanojoni sukareyooto isshookenmeida.
He is trying his hardest to get her to like him.

ひっし［必死］

■ *hisshi*
■ desperate(ly) 

たとえ死んでもかまわないと思うくらいの強い気持ちで、**全力をつくすようす**を表すとき使います（例12, 13, 14, 15）。「一生懸命」よりも、**さしせまった感じ**です。

Hisshi suggests that the speaker is so determined to do something that he is willing to die if necessary. It indicates that the speaker is doing his best and has a very strong resolve. *Hisshi* has more of a feeling of urgency than does *isshoukenmei* (ex.12, 13, 14, 15).

---

12) ボートがひっくり返ったので、必死で岸まで泳いだ。
Bootoga hikkurikaettanode, hisshide kishimade oyoida.
The boat capsized, so (I) swam desperately to shore.

13) エレベーターの故障で中に閉じこめられたので、必死に助けを呼んだ。
Erebeetaano koshoode nakani tojikomeraretanode, hisshini tasukeo yonda.
(I) desperately called out for help when the elevator broke down and I got stuck inside.

14) 彼は、今日中に仕事を終わらせようと必死になっている。
Karewa, kyoojuuni shigotoo owaraseyooto hisshini natteiru.
He is hurrying to finish his work by today.

15) 母親の必死の祈りが通じたのか、子供の病気は急によくなってきた。
Hahaoyano hisshino inoriga tsuujitanoka, kodomono byookiwa kyuuni yokunattekita.
The child's sickness quickly improved, perhaps because his mother's desperate prayers were heard.

きく／こたえる

■*kiku* ■*kotaeru*

きく［効く・利く］ ■*kiku* ■to be effective ; to work

①ものごとの**ききめ**（効果）**が現れること**です（例1, 2）。

To have or produce an effect (ex.1, 2).

②機能が十分に**生かされる・～することができる・可能だ**という意味で使います（例3, 4, 5, 6, 7）。①は効く、②は利くと書きます。

To function well or to be able to do something (ex.3, 4, 5, 6, 7). For definition ①, the *kanji* 効く is used, and for ② 利く is used.

---

1) この痛み止めの薬は、よく効きます。
Kono itamidomeno kusuriwa, yoku kikimasu.
This pain-killer is very effective.

2) きのうの注意が効いたらしい。いつもあんなに乱暴な子が、きょうは友達と仲良く遊んでいる。
Kinoono chuuiga kiitarashii. Itsumo annani ranboona koga, kyoowa tomodachito nakayoku asondeiru.
It seems yesterday's warning was very effective. Today, that boy who is always wild is playing very nicely with his friends.

3) 私の自転車は、ブレーキが利かなくなったので修理に出してあります。
Watashino jitenshawa, bureekiga kikanaku-nattanode shuurini dashitearimasu.
The brakes on my bicycle were not working, so it is being repaired.

4) A：この花は、なんていい香りなんでしょう。

B：そう、今、風邪をひいて鼻が利かないからわからない。

A： *Kono hanawa, nante ii kaorinandeshoo!*
This flower has such a nice fragrance.

B： *Soo? Ima, kazeo hiite hanaga kikanaikara wakaranai.*
Is that so? I can't tell because I have a cold and my nose is stuffed up.

5) 最近、疲れやすくなって無理が利かなくなってきた。
Saikin, tsukareyasuku natte muriga kikanaku nattekita.
Lately, (I) get tired easily and I can't work so productively.

6) このシャツは絹だけれど、家で洗濯が利くそうです。
Kono shatsuwa kinudakeredo, iede sentakuga kikusoodesu.
Although this shirt is made from silk, they said (I) can wash it at home.

7) まだ子供が小さいので、自由が利かないんです。思うように外出もできません。
Mada kodomoga chiisainode, jiyuuga kikanaindesu. Omouyooni gaishutsumo dekimasen.
Since my child is still young, (I) am not free to do many things. I can't go out whenever I please.

こたえる

■ *kotaeru*
■ to have an effect on ; to be hard on 

---

①**精神的・肉体的な痛み**や**疲れ・衝撃**などを**強く感じる**とき使います（例8, 9, 10）。

To feel the effects of mental or physical pain, exhaustion, or strong shock (ex.8, 9, 10).

②「こたえられない」という形で、これは最高だという意味に使います（例11, 12）。

The negative *kotaerarenai* expresses that something is of the best or highest quality (ex.11, 12).

---

8) 彼は、きのう上司にどなられたのが、よほどこたえたらしい。きょうは、まじめに仕事をしているよ。

Karewa, kinoo jooshini donararetanoga, yohodo kotaetarashii. Kyoowa, majimeni shigotoo shiteiruyo.
It seems being yelled at by the boss yesterday really got to him. Today he is working very diligently.

9) 夜(よ)ふかしは、体(からだ)にこたえる。
Yofukashiwa, karadani kotaeru.
Staying up late is hard on one's body.

10) 私(わたし)は寒(さむ)がりなので、北国(きたぐに)の冬(ふゆ)は身(み)にこたえる。
Watashiwa samugarinanode, kitagunino fuyuwa mini kotaeru.
(I) get cold easily, so winter in the north is hard on me.

11) ふろ上(あ)がりのビールは、こたえられない。
Furoagarino biiruwa, kotaerarenai.
Cold beer after a hot bath is irresistibly good.

12) 恋人(こいびと)が作(つく)ってくれた料理(りょうり)は、こたえられないおいしさです。
Koibitoga tsukuttekureta ryooriwa, kotaerarenai oishisadesu.
The food my sweetheart prepared for me was irresistibly good.

きこえる／きかれる
■ *kikoeru* ■ *kikareru*

きこえる［聞(き)こえる］
■ *kikoeru*
■ (can) hear ; to sound (like)

①**音(おと)が自然(しぜん)に耳(みみ)に入(はい)ってくること**です（例(れい)1, 2, 3, 4, 5)。
This verb is used to indicate that sound naturally enters one's ear (ex.1, 2, 3, 4, 5).

②そのように受(う)けとれるという意味(いみ)で使(つか)います（例(れい)6, 7)。
It is also used to express that a certain meaning can be taken by the listener (ex.6, 7).

1) 隣(となり)のうちから毎日(まいにち)ピアノの音(おと)が聞(き)こえる。
Tonarino uchikara mainichi pianono otoga kikoeru.
(I) can hear piano sounds coming from the next house everyday.

2) 海辺のホテルでは、波の音が聞こえる部屋がいい。
Umibeno hoterudewa, namino otoga kikoeru heyaga ii.
At a seaside hotel, a room in which (you) can hear the waves is best.

3) そんなに大きな声を出さなくても聞こえます。
Sonnani ookina koeo dasanakutemo kikoemasu.
(You) don't have to speak so loudly. (I) can hear you (just fine).

4) 壁が薄いので、隣の部屋の話し声が聞こえてしまう。
Kabega usuinode, tonarino heyano hanashigoega kikoeteshimau.
The walls are thin so (I) can hear voices in the next room.

5) 外の工事がうるさくて、テレビの音がよく聞こえない。
Sotono koojiga urusakute, terebino otoga yoku kikoenai.
(I) can't hear the TV well because the construction work outside is so noisy.

6) 冗談に聞こえるかもしれないけれど、彼は宝くじで１億円当てたんですよ。
Joodanni kikoerukamo shirenaikeredo, karewa takarakujide ichiokuen atetandesuyo.
(I) know it sounds like a joke, but he won ¥100,000,000 in the lottery.

7) 彼の話を聞いていると、一方的に私が悪いように聞こえる。
Kareno hanashio kiiteiruto, ippootekini watashiga waruiyooni kikoeru.
If (you) listen to the way he tells it, it sounds like I'm the one who is wrong.

きかれる［聞かれる］

■ *kikareru*
■ to hear ; to be heard 

ある**意見や説**などが**耳に入ってくる**ことです。実際に音として入ってくるのではなく、**世の中で言われている**という意味です（例8, 9, 10）。

Kikareru is used when expressing that an opinion or rumor enters one's ear. It does not refer to the actual hearing of sound, but instead implies that things are being said in the world around (ex.8, 9, 10).

---

8) 最近、若い人たちの敬語の使い方が変だという声が聞かれる。
Saikin, wakai hitotachino keigono tsukaikataga hendato yuu koega kikareru.
Recently, (I've) heard people say that young people can't use polite expressions correctly.

9) この駅のまわりには駐車場が少ないので、立体的にしてたくさん置けるようにしては、という意見が聞かれるようになった。

Kono ekino mawariniwa chuushajooga sukunainode, rittaitekini shite takusan okeruyooni shitewa, to yuu ikenga kikareruyooni natta.
There are few places to park around the station, so (I've) heard people say that multi-storied parking is desirable.

10) あの歌手は２～３年前まで大変な人気だったのに、近ごろはめったに名前も聞かれなくなってしまった。

Ano kashuwa nisannen maemade taihenna ninkidattanoni, chikagorowa mettani namaemo kikarenaku natteshimatta.
He was a very popular singer two or three years ago, but these days you almost never hear his name.

きたない／きたならしい

■ *kitanai* ■ *kitanarashii*

きたない［汚い］

■ *kitanai*
■ dirty ; filthy 

汚れている・清潔ではない・きちんとしていない・不正だというとき使います(例1, 2, 3, 4, 5)。例６の「金にきたない」は、けちだという意味です。

This is used to indicate that something is unclean, untidy, immoral, or unjust (ex.1, 2, 3, 4, 5). In Example 6 means 'stingy' (with money).

---

1) きたない手で、ものを食べると病気になりますよ。

Kitanai tede, monoo taberuto byookini narimasuyo.
If (you) eat without washing your hands, you'll get sick.

2) １週間も掃除をしていないので、部屋がきたない。

Isshuukanmo soojio shiteinainode, heyaga kitanai.
Because (I) haven't cleaned up my room for a week, it's a mess.

3) 彼(かれ)の字(じ)はとてもきたないので、読(よ)むのに苦労(くろう)します。

Kareno jiwa totemo kitanainode, yomunoni kurooshimasu.
(I'm) having a hard time reading this because his handwriting is too messy.

4) 彼(かれ)は、きたないやり方(かた)で試合(しあい)に勝(か)った。

Karewa, kitanai yarikatade shiaini katta.
He won the game in an underhanded way.

5) きたない商売(しょうばい)でもうけたお金(かね)なんて、少(すこ)しもありがたいものではない。

Kitanai shoobaide mooketa okanenante, sukoshimo arigataimonodewa nai.
The money you earned from that immoral business is not welcome.

6) 彼(かれ)は金(かね)にきたないので、嫌(きら)われている。

Karewa kaneni kitanainode, kirawareteiru.
Because he is so stingy, nobody likes him.

きたならしい［汚(きたな)らしい］ ■*kitanarashii* ■dirty 

いかにも**不潔(ふけつ)に見(み)える・感(かん)じる**というときや、よごれているように見(み)える・感(かん)じるというとき**不快感(ふかいかん)を表(あらわ)して**使(つか)います。しかし実際(じっさい)に不潔(ふけつ)であるとは限(かぎ)りません(例(れい)7, 8, 9)。

Kitanarashii indicates that something appears dirty, filthy or unsanitary. This is more subjective than *kitanai*; in other words, when a speaker says *kitanarashii*, the thing itself may not actually be dirty, however the speaker feels dissatisfaction with it (ex.7, 8, 9).

---

7) きたならしいかっこうをしていると、だれにも相手(あいて)にされなくなりますよ。

Kitanarashii kakkoo-o shiteiruto, darenimo aiteni sarenakunarimasuyo.
If (you) wear such dirty clothes, nobody will associate with you.

8) この台所(だいどころ)は、古(ふる)くてきたならしく見(み)えますが、毎日(まいにち)ちゃんと掃除(そうじ)をしているんです。

Kono daidokorowa, furukute kitanarashiku miemasuga, mainichi chanto soojio shiteirundesu.
This kitchen may look old and dirty, but (I) clean it everyday.

9) 父(ちち)：そんなぼろぼろのジーンズなんかはいて、きたならしい。
息子(むすこ)：今(いま)はやっているんだよ。
Chichi : Sonna boroborono jiinzunanka haite, kitanarashii.
Father : You look unkempt wearing those ragged jeans.
Musuko : Ima hayatteirundayo.
Son : But this is what's in fashion!

きちんと／ちゃんと／しっかり

■ *kichinto* ■ *chanto* ■ *shikkari*

きちんと

■ *kichinto*
■ properly ; exactly 

ものごとやことがらが、**整然(せいぜん)と順序(じゅんじょ)よく整(ととの)っている**ことや、本来(ほんらい)あるべき**正(ただ)しい姿(すがた)や状態(じょうたい)を保(たも)っている**ようすを表(あらわ)します（例(れい)1, 2, 3）。例(れい)4のように人(ひと)に使(つか)うときは、その人(ひと)のことばづかいや態度(たいど)が「礼儀正(れいぎただ)しい・まじめだ・常識的(じょうしきてき)だ」ということを表(あらわ)します。服装(ふくそう)についても同(おな)じように使(つか)います（例(れい)5）。

Kichinto expresses an orderly and systematically arranged condition, or one that preserves the original and proper form (ex.1, 2, 3). When used when speaking of people, as in Example 4, it indicates that the person's manner of speech or behavior is courteous, sincere, or sensible.
It may be used in the same way with respect to clothing (ex.5).

1) 靴(くつ)は、きちんとそろえてぬぎなさい。
Kutsuwa, kichinto soroete nuginasai.
Take off (your) shoes and line them up neatly.

2) 姉(あね)の部屋(へや)は、いつもきちんとかたづいている。
Aneno heyawa, itsumo kichinto katazuiteiru.
My sister's room is always neat and tidy.

3) 目上(めうえ)の人(ひと)には、きちんとあいさつをしなさい。
Meueno hitoniwa, kichinto aisatsuo shinasai.
Greet your elders properly.

4) 彼(かれ)は、きちんとした人(ひと)だから、約束(やくそく)は必(かなら)ず守(まも)ります。

Karewa, kichintoshita hitodakara, yakusokuwa kanarazu mamorimasu.
He's a very conscientious person, so he would be certain to keep a promise.

5) 初めて訪問するお宅なんだから、きちんとした服装で行くべきだ。
Hajimete hoomonsuru otakunandakara, kichintoshita fukusoode ikubekida.
This will be your first visit to their home, so (you) ought to go dressed neatly and properly.

ちゃんと

■ *chanto*
■ neatly ; correctly 

ものごとやことがらが、**正しくて間違いがない**ようすや、本来あるべき姿や状態を保っているようすを表します（例6, 7, 8, 9, 10）。ほとんどの場合、「きちんと」と同じように使われますが、**話しことば**で多く使われます。そして「ちゃんと」には、「後で困らないように・間違わないで・完全に」などの意味が強く含まれます。例10の「ちゃんとした（会社）」というのは、信頼できる・確かな、あるいは社会的に認められているという意味です。

Chanto expresses the state of being correct and free of error, or of preserving the original and proper form or condition (ex.6, 7, 8, 9, 10). It is used like *kichinto* in most cases, but is a more colloquial expression. Also, *chanto* implies a strong sense of 'completely, without error, so that there will be no problems afterward'. In Example 10, *chanto shita kaisha* means that the company is reliable and proper, i.e., recognized by the community.

---

6) 私にも分かるようにちゃんと説明してください。
Watashinimo wakaruyooni chanto setsumeishite-kudasai.
Please explain it clearly so that even I can understand.

7) ちゃんと宿題をやっていけば、教室で困らなかったのに。
Chanto shukudaio yatteikeba, kyooshitsude komaranakatta-noni.
If only (I) had done my homework as I should have, I wouldn't have had trouble in class.

8) 頼まれた本、ちゃんと買っておきましたよ。
Tanomareta hon, chanto katte-okimashitayo.
(I) went right out and bought that book (you) asked me to get.

9) あなたの誕生日は５月11日でしょう、ちゃんと覚えているんだから。

Anatano tanjoobiwa gogatsu-juuichinichi-deshoo? Chanto oboete irundakara.
Your birthday is May 11, right? See, (I) remember it perfectly well.

10) 彼は、ちゃんとした会社に勤めている。
Karewa, chantoshita kaishani tsutometeiru.
He is working at a reputable company.

しっかり

■ *shikkari*
■ firm ; reliable 

こわれにくい・堅固だ・ぐらぐらしないという意味です。ものやことがら、また人に対しても使います（例11, 12, 13, 14）。「しっかりした人」は自分の意志がはっきりしていて強く正しく生きて行ける人という感じがします。「きちんと・ちゃんと」が「本来あるべき姿や状態を保つ・道理にかなう」というところに重点があるのに対し、「しっかり」は、**強さ**に重点があります。

Shikkari describes an object as solid, and not easily broken or wobbly. It is used of people, things and events (ex.11, 12, 13, 14). *Shikkari shita hito* is a person whose will is clearly defined, and who can get through life without difficulty. While *kichinto* and *chanto* focus on 'preserving the proper form or condition and being rational' *shikkari* focuses on strength or durability.

---

11) この家具は古いけれど、作りがしっかりしているので、まだまだ使える。
Kono kaguwa furuikeredo, tsukuriga shikkari-shiteirunode, madamada tsukaeru.
This piece of furniture is old, but it's very sturdily made so it'll still be usable for some time.

12) ジョギングの前に、靴のひもはしっかり結んでおいたほうがいい。
Joginguno maeni, kutsuno himowa shikkari musundeoita hooga ii.
(You'd) better tie those shoestrings tightly before you go jogging.

13) 台風の時は、傘をしっかり持っていないと風で飛ばされてしまう。
Taifuuno tokiwa, kasao shikkari motteinaito kazede tobasarete shimau.
If (you) don't hold on tightly to your umbrella during a typhoon it will get blown away.

14) 彼女は若いけれども、考え方がしっかりしている。
Kanojowa wakaikeredomo, kangaekataga shikkarishiteiru.
She's young, but she's very level-headed.

きつい／かたい

■ *kitsui* ■ *katai*

きつい

■ *kitsui*
■ tight ; hard 

①物と物の間に**ゆとりがなかったり、大きさが合わなかったり**して、**きゅうくつだ・しめつけられる**というようすを表すとき使います（例1, 2)。そして例3, 4のように離れにくいようすも表します。

Kitsui expresses a condition of constraint or tightness due to a lack of space between objects or a mismatch in size (ex.1, 2). In Examples 3 and 4 it indicates that it is difficult to detach or separate something from something else.

②ものごとが普通の程度以上で、**きびしくて大変だ・耐えられない**というようすや、感情的・時間的・金銭的にゆとりがないようすを表すとき使います（例5, 6, 7, 8, 9)。「きつい人」は性格がするどく自我が強いので、接した相手に良く思われませんが、「かたい人」は礼儀正しくまじめなので信用されます。

It may suggests that a situation is severe and difficult to bear, that one has no emotional or financial leeway, or that time is scarce (ex.5, 6, 7, 8, 9). A *kitsui hito* is a person with a caustic, arrogant nature, who thus is not well thought of by others, while a *katai hito* is considered to be courteous and sincere, and is therefore trusted.

---

1) 最近太ったので、ズボンがきつい。
Saikin futottanode, zubonga kitsui.
(I've) gained weight recently, so my trousers are tight.

2) 娘の靴は、私にはきつくてはけない。
Musumeno kutsuwa, watashiniwa kitsukute hakenai.
My daughter's shoes are too tight for me to wear.

3) びんのふたがきつくて開かない。
Binno futaga kitsukute akanai.
The lid on this jar is so tight it won't come off.

4) 靴ひもは、ほどけないようにきつく結びなさい。
Kutsuhimowa, hodokenaiyooni kitsuku musubinasai.

Tie your shoe strings tightly so they don't come undone.

5) あの人は優しそうな顔をしているけれど、性格はきつい。

Ano hitowa yasashisoona kaoo shiteirukeredo, seikakuwa kitsui.
He has a pleasant face but a stern personality.

6) 彼女は、言い方がきついから誤解される。

Kanojowa, iikataga kitsuikara gokaisareru.
She has a harsh way of speaking, so she is (often) misunderstood.

7) 私は息子が二度とあんなことをしないように、きつく注意した。

Watashiwa musukoga nidoto annakotoo shinaiyooni, kitsuku chuuishita.
I strongly warned my son to never do that again.

8) 仕事がきついので、この会社を辞めたい。

Shigotoga kitsuinode, kono kaishao yametai.
(I) want to quit this company because the work is too hard.

9) 10万円で1か月暮らすのは、ちょっときつい。

Juuman-ende ikkagetsu kurasunowa, chotto kitsui.
It's a bit difficult to live on ¥100,000 a month.

かたい［固い・堅い・硬い］

■ *katai*
■ hard ; strong ; tight

---

①ものの材質が**丈夫・しっかりしている・外からの力に変形しにくい**ことです（例10, 11, 12）。

Katai indicates that something is strong of material or firm in construction, and is resistant to external pressure (ex.10, 11, 12).

②強い力で**しっかりと結びついたり、組み合わさったりするようす**を表します。したがって、一度決めたことを**強く守り通す**ようすや、簡単には**変わらない態度**も表します（例13, 14, 15, 16, 17, 18, 19, 20）。例21は、「確実だ・まちがいない」という意味です。

It also describes something as firmly bound or combined. Therefore, it may describe a person who sticks firmly to a decision or who does not easily change his opinions (ex.13, 14, 15, 16, 17, 18, 19, 20). In Example 21 it means that something is certain and without error.

③緊張感や不快感などで、表情に穏やかさやゆとりが見られないようすです

（例22）。例23は、まじめできちんとしているけれど、おもしろみに欠けるという意味です。

It may also suggest that one's facial expression lacks a look of calmness or tranquility due to nervousness or displeasure (ex.22). In Example 23, it refers to something that is serious and orderly, but dry and uninteresting.

④「かたい」の漢字には「固い・硬い・堅い」の３つがありますが、ひらがなで書いてもかまいません。ふつう「固い」がよく使われ、「硬い」は石・金属などものの材質・性質に使い、「堅い」は性格などについて使うことが多いです。

Katai may be written using the *kanji* characters 固い, 硬い and 堅い, however as there are no clear rules on which *kanji* is used in which situation, *katai* may be written in *hiragana*. In general, however, 固い is used in most common situations, 硬い is used when referring to objects made of stone or metal, and 堅い is used when speaking of a person's personality.

---

10) ダイヤモンドは宝石の中で、いちばん硬い。
Daiyamondowa hoosekino nakade, ichiban katai.
Of all the jewels, diamonds are the hardest.

11) このパンは古くなったので少し固い。
Kono panwa furukunattanode sukoshi katai.
This bread is a little hard because it has gone stale.

12) 肉を焼きすぎると固くなる。
Nikuo yakisugiruto katakunaru.
Meat becomes tough if you overcook it.

13) ワインの栓が固くて抜けない。
Wainno senga katakute nukenai.
The cork on this wine bottle is so tight that (I) can't pull it out.

14) 靴ひもの結び目が固くてほどけない。
Kutsuhimono musubimega katakute hodokenai.
(I) can't untie my shoestrings because the knot is too tight.

15) 洗濯物は、固くしぼって干してください。
Sentakumonowa, kataku shibotte hoshitekudasai.
Wring the laundry tightly and hang them out to dry, please.

16) 両国の首相は、固い握手を交わした。
Ryookokuno shushoowa, katai akushuo kawashita.

The two Prime Ministers exchanged firm handshakes.

17) 彼(かれ)は年(とし)をとって、すっかり頭(あたま)が堅(かた)くなった。
Karewa toshio totte, sukkari atamaga katakunatta.
He has become quite stubborn in his old age.

18) 信用(しんよう)してください。私(わたし)は口(くち)が固(かた)いんです。絶対(ぜったい)に秘密(ひみつ)は守(まも)ります。
Shin-yooshite kudasai. Watashiwa kuchiga kataindesu. Zettaini himitsuwa mamorimasu.
Please trust me. I'm very tight-lipped so I'll keep your secret.

19) 父(ちち)は息子(むすこ)の無実(むじつ)を固(かた)く信(しん)じている。
Chichiwa musukono mujitsuo kataku shinjiteiru.
He firmly believes his son is innocent.

20) 飲酒運転(いんしゅうんてん)は固(かた)く禁(きん)じられている。
Inshuuntenwa kataku kinjirareteiru.
Driving while intoxicated is strictly prohibited.

21) この調子(ちょうし)でいけば、我(わ)が校(こう)の優勝(ゆうしょう)はかたい。
Kono chooshide ikeba, wagakoono yuushoowa katai.
If we keep playing like this, I'm sure that our school will win the championship.

22) あの俳優(はいゆう)は新人(しんじん)なのでまだ表情(ひょうじょう)が硬(かた)い。
Ano haiyuuwa shinjinnanode mada hyoojooga katai.
He's a new actor so he still has a tense expression.

23) 堅(かた)い話(はなし)は止(や)めて、楽(たの)しく飲(の)もうよ。
Katai hanashiwa yamete, tanoshiku nomooyo.
Let's knock off this serious talk and get to some drinking.

きにする／きになる

■ *ki ni suru* ■ *ki ni naru*

きにする［気(き)にする］ ■ *ki ni suru* ■ to worry 

ものごとに対(たい)して、**神経質**(しんけいしつ)になったり**心配**(しんぱい)になったりすることです（例(れい)1, 2, 3, 4）。

また、「心が傷つく・悩む」という意味も含み、「気にしていること」は、自分がいやでたまらないと思っている欠点などを指します（例5, 6)。

To become nervous or worried about something (ex.1, 2, 3, 4). It may also imply 'to be hurt by' or 'to be bothered by something' ; a characteristic that one does not like about oneself is referred to as *ki ni shite iru koto* (ex.5, 6).

---

1) 人の言うことなんか気にしないで、自分の思うとおりにやりなさい。
Hitono yuu kotonanka kini shinaide, jibunno omou toorini yarinasai.
Don't worry about what others say—just do as you like.

2) 彼は自分の失敗をいつまでも気にする性格だ。
Karewa jibunno shippaio itsumademo kinisuru seikakuda.
He's the type of person who always worries about his failures.

3) きのうのことなんか気にしてもしょうがない。
Kinoono kotonanka kini shitemo shooganai.
It's no use worrying about what happened yesterday.

4) A：ごめんなさい。

B：気にしないでください。

A： *Gomennasai.* I'm sorry.
B： *Kini shinaidekudasai.* Don't worry about it.

5) 彼女は太っているのを気にしている。
Kanojowa futotteirunoo kinishiteiru.
She's sensitive about her weight. (She's bothered by the fact that she's fat.)

6) 人が気にしていることは、言わないほうがいい。
Hitoga kini shiteiru kotowa, iwanai hooga ii.
(You) shouldn't talk about things other people are sensitive about.

きになる［気になる］

■ *ki ni naru*
■ to bother ; to worry ; to feel anxious

---

①「どうなるのだろう」というように、**何か問題があって心配**させられたり**不安**にさせられる、**心が落ちつかない**ようすを表します（例7, 8, 9, 10)。

To feel anxiety, worry, or restlessness due to a problem or uncertainty (ex.7, 8, 9, 10).

②ちょっと心がひかれる、興味がある、ほうってはおけないという気持ちになることです（例11, 12)。

To be unable to ignore something because of feelings of interest or fondness (ex.11, 12).

7) あしたの試験のことが気になって、なかなか眠れない。
Ashitano shikenno kotoga kini natte, nakanaka nemurenai.
(I'm) so worried about tomorrow's test that I can't sleep.

8) 私は、少しぐらい部屋がちらかっていても、全然気にならない。
Watashiwa, sukoshigurai heyaga chirakatteitemo, zenzen kini naranai.
I don't care at all if the room is a little messy.

9) あした、山に登るので天気が気になる。
Ashita, yamani noborunode tenkiga kini naru.
(I'm) going mountain climbing tomorrow, so I'm concerned about the weather.

10) 彼について、ちょっと気になるうわさを聞いた。
Kareni tsuite, chotto kini naru uwasao kiita.
(I've) heard a slightly disturbing rumor about him.

11) 彼女のことが気になるのは、きっと好きだからだよ。
Kanojono kotoga kini narunowa, kitto sukidakaradayo.
The fact that (you're) so concerned about her means that you must like her.

12) 彼女は、隣に越して来たのがどんな人だか気になるようだ。
Kanojowa, tonarini koshitekitanoga donna hitodaka kini naruyooda.
She seems anxious about what kind of person has moved in next door.

きのどく／かわいそう

■ *kinodoku* ■ *kawaisou*

きのどく［気の毒］

■ *kinodoku*
■ unfortunate ; pitiable 

①他人の不幸に同情して心が痛んだり、哀れんだりする気持ちです（例1, 2,

3, 4)。人間に対して使います。自分と同等か、あるいはそれ以上の立場の人や、それほど身近ではない人の不幸や良くない状態について「本来なら、もっと良い状態であってもいいはずなのに……」という同情の気持ちです。

This expresses a feeling of sympathy or compassion toward another person who has experienced misfortune (ex.1, 2, 3, 4). *Kinodoku* is used only toward a person who is of equal or higher status than, or who is not very close to, the speaker. When one says *kinodoku*, he feels sympathetically that 'this situation could have been much better if it had gone properly.'

②**迷惑をかけて申し訳ない**と思う気持ちの使い方です（例５）。

It also indicates that the speaker feels sorry for causing trouble for others (ex.5).

---

1) あんなに努力したのに報われないなんて、彼が気の毒です。
Annani doryokushitanoni mukuwarenainante, karega kinodokudesu.
Although he worked very hard, he never received any recognition. I feel sorry for him.

2) 気の毒に、彼女は事故で息子さんを失くしたそうです。
Kinodokuni, kanojowa jikode musukosan-o nakushitasoodesu.
What a shame! (I) hear she lost her son in an accident.

3) あんなに幸せだった彼女が、今は貧しい気の毒な生活をしている。
Annani shiawasedatta kanojoga, imawa mazushii kinodokuna seikatsuo shiteiru.
Although she was once very happy, she now lives a miserable life of poverty.

4) お気の毒に。何と申し上げて良いのかわかりません。
Okinodokuni. Nanto mooshiagete-yoinoka wakarimasen.
I'm sorry. (I) don't know what to say.

5) こんなに面倒なことをお願いしてしまって、気の毒なことをしました。
Konnani mendoona kotoo onegaishiteshimatte, kinodokuna kotoo shimashita.
(I) am very sorry that (I've) asked you to handle such a troublesome matter.

かわいそう

■ *kawaisou*
■ pitiful

子供など自分よりも弱い立場の人あるいは身近な関係にある人の、不幸・苦し

み・悲しみなどに深く同情したり、**あわれんだりする気持ち**です（例6, 7, 8, 9, 10）。動物や植物に対しても使います。「きのどく」よりも、思わず**救いの手を差しのべたくなるような愛情やいつくしみ**を含んでいます。

This indicates that the speaker deeply feels sorrow or pity for the misfortune, hardship, or sorrow of someone who is close to him or is in a weaker position (ex.6, 7, 8, 9, 10). *Kawaisou* may also be used when speaking of animals or plants. It expresses more of a sense of strong affection or concern for the person, as well as a desire to help, than does *kinodoku*.

6) あんなに小さい子が両親に一度に死なれるなんてかわいそうだ。
Annani chiisai koga ryooshinni ichidoni shinarerunante kawaisooda.
It's a pity that one so young should lose both parents at the same time.

7) かわいそうに、あの子は病気なんだって。
Kawaisooni, ano kowa byookinandatte.
I'm sorry to hear that child is sick.

8) かわいそうな物語を読んだら、涙が止まらなかった。
Kawaisoona monogatario yondara, namidaga tomaranakatta.
When (I) read that sad story, I could not stop crying.

9) かわいそうに、この子犬はけがをしているよ。
Kawaisooni, kono koinuwa kegao shiteiruyo.
Oh, no! This puppy is injured.

10) 猫に石をぶつけるなんてかわいそうだ。
Nekoni ishio butsukerunante kawaisooda.
Throwing rocks at a cat! Poor thing!

■ 〜gimi　■ 〜gachi

〜ぎみ ■ 〜gimi ■ tendency 

まだ程度はたいしたことはないけれど、「風邪をひいたようだ」とか「体重が増えすぎた」などのように、**現在**なんらかの**傾向や気配が感じられる**ことです（例

1, 2, 3, 4)。

This expresses a feeling that, although not serious at the moment, there seems to be a sign of or a tendency toward a particular condition, as in, feeling a cold coming on or sensing that one is a little overweight (ex.1, 2, 3, 4).

---

1) 私は近頃仕事が忙しくて疲れぎみです。
Watashiwa chikagoro shigotoga isogashikute tsukaregimi-desu.
My work has been busy as of late, so I've been feeling a bit tired.

2) 少しかぜぎみなので今夜は早く寝ます。
Sukoshi kazegimi-nanode kon-yawa hayaku nemasu.
(I) feel like I've got a cold coming on, so I think I'll go to bed early tonight.

3) 私の時計はおくれぎみなので修理に出した。
Watashino tokeiwa okuregimi-nanode shuurini dashita.
My watch seemed to be running slow, so I took it in to be repaired.

4) 私は最近太りぎみなのでジョギングを始めました。
Watashiwa saikin futorigimi-nanode joginguo hajimemashita.
I've taken up jogging because I feel I've gotten a bit heavy recently.

～がち

■ *~gachi*
■ tendency ; inclination

「よく欠席する」「病気になりやすい」などのように、**ある状態になることが多い、なりやすい**ということです（例5, 6, 7, 8, 9, 10)。「～ぎみ」も「～がち」も、どちらかというと良くない意味の語につく場合がほとんどです。

This suggests that a situation tends to occur often or easily, as in, 'to be absent often' or 'to become ill easily' (ex.5, 6, 7, 8, 9, 10). Both *~gimi* and *~gachi* are almost always used in a negative sense.

---

5) 彼は体が弱いので学校を休みがちです。
Karewa karadaga yowainode gakkoo-o yasumigachi-desu.
He is of frail build so he tends to miss school a lot.

6) 彼女は病気がちで青白い顔をしている。
Kanojowa byookigachide aojiroi kaoo shiteiru.
She is in poor health so she looks pale.

7) 兄(あに)は失恋(しつれん)してから沈(しず)みがちだ。
Aniwa shitsuren-shitekara shizumigachida.
My (elder) brother has been depressed a lot since splitting up with his girlfriend.

8) 弟(おとうと)はテレビに夢中(むちゅう)で、勉強(べんきょう)がおろそかになりがちです。
Otootowa terebini muchuude, benkyooga orosokani narigachidesu.
My (younger) brother gets so absorbed in watching TV that he tends to neglect doing his homework.

9) 彼(かれ)は欠席(けっせき)が多(おお)いので勉強(べんきょう)がおくれがちだ。
Karewa kessekiga ooinode benkyooga okuregachida.
He is often absent from class so he is apt to be behind the others.

10) 冬(ふゆ)になってからくもりがちの毎日(まいにち)です。
Fuyuni nattekara kumorigachino mainichidesu.
The skies are mostly cloudy everyday now that winter has come.

きめる／けっていする

■ *kimeru* ■ *kettei suru*

きめる［決(き)める］ ■ *kimeru* ■ to decide 

ものごとの**最終的**(さいしゅうてき)**な結論**(けつろん)**や結果**(けっか)**を出**(だ)**す**ことです（例(れい)1, 2, 3, 4）。
To make a final conclusion or to come up with a result (ex.1, 2, 3, 4).

1) 私(わたし)は父(ちち)の会社(かいしゃ)を継(つ)ぐことに決(き)めました。
Watashiwa chichino kaishao tsugukotoni kimemashita.
I've decided to succeed my father in his company.

2) 私(わたし)は、毎朝(まいあさ)9時(じ)の電車(でんしゃ)に乗(の)ることに決(き)めている。
Watashiwa, maiasa kujino denshani norukotoni kimeteiru.
I make it a rule to take the nine o'clock train every morning.

3) だれを委員長(いいんちょう)にするか、投票(とうひょう)で決(き)めよう。
Dareo iinchooni suruka, toohyoode kimeyoo.

Let's vote to decide who is going to be our committee chairman.

4) 私のうちでは、大切なことは家族みんなで話し合って決める。
Watashino uchidewa, taisetsuna kotowa kazoku minnade hanashiatte kimeru.
In my family, important issues are discussed and decided on by all.

けっていする［決定する］ ■*kettei suru* ■to decide 

「決める」と同様の意味です。ほとんどの場合、「決める」で言いかえられますが、**公の場面で、話し合った結果**というように公のものごとに使います（例5,6,7)。「私は～に決めた」のような個人的な結論には「決定する」は、ほとんど使いません。

In most cases *kettei suru* may be used interchangeably with *kimeru*. However, it most often refers to official or public decisions (ex.5, 6, 7). It is not used when speaking of personal decisions, as in *watashi wa ～ni kimeta* (I've decided to～).

5) 今日の試合で、彼の優勝が決定した。
Kyoono shiaide, kareno yuushooga ketteishita.
His victory was decided in today's match.

6) 次の会議で、理事が決定する。
Tsugino kaigide, rijiga ketteisuru.
(We) will decide on who will be the director at the next meeting.

7) 今年の株主総会の日時は、まだ決定していない。
Kotoshino kabunushi-sookaino nichijiwa, mada ketteishiteinai.
The date of this year's general shareholders' meeting has not been set yet.

けっこうです

ケイトは日本に来てからお花を習っています。今日も作品を先生に見ていただきました。「とてもじょうずです。けっこうですよ」と先生が

言いました。お茶の時間に先生が鈴木さんに「もう１杯いかがですか」と聞くと彼女は「もうけっこうです。ごちそうさまでした」と言いました。またしばらくお花のおけいこをしたあとで先生が「はい、今日はおしまいです。お帰りになってけっこうです」と言いました。ケイトが玄関でくつをはいていると、セールスマンが来て何かをしつこく売ろうとしました。すると先生は強い調子で「けっこうです」と断りました。「けっこうです」は、「じょうずだ」とほめたり、「～してもいい」と許可したり、「いらない」と断ったり、その場の状況で、いろいろな意味に使われることばだと、ケイトは知りました。

Kekkoo desu

Kate has been taking flower arrangement lessons since she came to Japan. Today she asked her teacher to comment on her work. Her teacher said, "It's very well done. *Kekkoo desu yo*[1]."

Later, at tea time, when the teacher asked another student, "Mrs. Suzuki, how about another cup of tea?" Mrs. Suzuki said, "*Moo kekkoo desu*[2]. It was delicious."

After the lesson was over, the teacher said, "We are done for today. *Okaeri ni natte kekkoo desu*[3]."

When Kate was putting on her shoes on at the front door, a salesman came and persistently tried to sell something to the teacher. The teacher refused and said in a very strong tone, "*Kekkoo desu!!*[4]" Kate found out that *kekkoo desu* is an expression having various meanings depending on the situation, as it may be used to praise, to allow, or to refuse.

1 *Fine job.*
2 *I'm fine (I don't want anymore).*
3 *It's OK for you to go home.*
4 *No, thank you!!*

きもち／きぶん

■ *kimochi* ■ *kibun*

きもち［気持ち］ ■ *kimochi* ■ feeling 

①思っていることや考え・感想・意志のことです（例1, 2, 3, 4, 5）。性格や心など、本来生まれ持っているものも含みます。

Kimochi refers to a person's thoughts, ideas, impressions and intentions (ex.1, 2, 3, 4, 5). The fact that the person has a personality or individual characteristics is implied.

②見たりふれたりしたものに対する、快・不快の表現に使い、「いい・悪い」で表す感覚です。「気持ちがいい」はさわやかさ・安心感・ここちよさなど快い感じを表すとき使います。「気持ちが悪い」は嫌悪感をもよおさせるものに対して使い、吐き気がするような体調の悪さも表します（例6, 7, 8, 9, 10, 11, 12）。

Kimochi is also used to describe sensations experienced through touch or sight. The expression *kimochi ga ii* indicates that something feels refreshing, secure, or comfortable, while *kimochi ga warui* describes something that instills feelings of hatred or disgust that causes the speaker to feel nauseous (ex.6, 7, 8, 9, 10, 11, 12).

1) 世界中どこへ行っても、子を思う母親の気持ちに変わりはない。
Sekaijuu dokoe ittemo, koo omou hahaoyano kimochini kawariwa nai.
The feeling of love that mothers have for their children is the same all over the world.

2) 彼女のことばは、私の気持ちを傷つけた。
Kanojono kotobawa, watashino kimochio kizutsuketa.
Her words hurt my feelings.

3) 彼女は、とても気持ちのやさしい人です。
Kanojowa, totemo kimochino yasashii hitodesu.
She is a very kind person.

4) 私は、あなたへの感謝の気持ちでいっぱいです。
Watashiwa, anataeno kanshano kimochide ippaidesu.
I am full of gratitude to you.

5) この仕事に参加したい、というあなたの気持ちはよくわかりました。
Kono shigotoni sankashitai, to yuu anatano kimochiwa yoku wakarimashita.
(I) fully understand your desire to work on this project.

6) 運動をした後のシャワーは、気持ちがいい。
Undoo-o shita atono shawaawa, kimochiga ii.
A shower after exercising feels good.

7) 窓を開けると、さわやかで気持ちのいい風が入ってきた。
Madoo akeruto, sawayakade kimochino ii kazega haittekita.
A refreshing breeze blew in when (I) opened the window.

8) 温泉にゆっくりつかったら、とてもいい気持ちだった。
Onsenni yukkuri tsukattara, totemo ii kimochidatta.
(I) felt refreshed after a long soak in the hot spring.

9) 彼は私の頼みを気持ちよく引き受けてくれた。
Karewa watashino tanomio kimochiyoku hikiuketekureta.
He handled my request willingly.

10) 私は、へびやとかげは気持ちが悪くて、見るのもいやです。
Watashiwa, hebiya tokagewa kimochiga warukute, mirunomo iyadesu.
I think snakes and lizards are disgusting. I hate even looking at them.

11) いくらホラー映画が好きでも、あまり気持ちの悪いのは見たくない。
Ikura horaaeigaga sukidemo, amari kimochino waruinowa mitakunai.
Although (I) really like horror films, I don't like seeing scenes that are too revolting.

12) バスに酔って、気持ちが悪くなってしまった。
Basuni yotte, kimochiga waruku natteshimatta.
(I) became carsick on the bus.

きぶん［気分］ ■ *kibun* ■ mood ; feeling 

①周囲の雰囲気や、置かれた状況によって変わる**そのときどきの**自分の心の状態・**感情**です（例13, 14, 15, 16, 17, 18）。また、ある状況におけるその場の雰囲気も表します（例19, 20）。

Kibun refers to emotions or temporary states of mind brought about by the atmosphere of a place or existing conditions (ex.13, 14, 15, 16, 17, 18). It may also be used when describing the mood of a place (ex.19, 20).

②**体調を表す**とき「気分がいい・悪い」のように使います（例21, 22, 23)。「気分がいい」はどちらかと言えば、病気の人の体調について使います。

Kibun may also be used to refer to physical sensations, i.e., 'to feel good / bad' (ex.21, 22, 23). The expression *kibun ga ii* is most often used to describe the condition of a sick person.

---

13) 家族といっしょに食事をしていると、とても幸せな気分になる。
Kazokuto isshoni shokujio shiteiruto, totemo shiawasena kibunni naru.
(I) feel very happy when I have a meal together with my family.

14) 勉強に疲れたので、気分転換に散歩に行ってこよう。
Benkyooni tsukaretanode, kibuntenkanni sanponi ittekoyoo.
(I'm) tired out from studying, so I think I'll take a walk for a change (to clear my head).

15) きょうは何をやってもうまくいかなくて、泣きたい気分だ。
Kyoowa nanio yattemo umaku ikanakute, nakitai kibunda.
Today (I) feel like crying because nothing I do is going right.

16) なんだか疲れてしまって、人と話をする気分にもなれない。
Nandaka tsukareteshimatte, hitoto hanashio suru kibunnimo narenai.
(I'm) a bit tired out and don't feel like talking to anybody.

17) 人にちやほやされるのは、悪い気分ではない。
Hitoni chiyahoya-sarerunowa, warui kibundewa nai.
(I) don't feel bad being pampered.

18) 彼はいつも、人の気分を害するようなことを言う。
Karewa itsumo, hitono kibun-o gaisuruyoona kotoo yuu.
He always says things that hurt other people's feelings.

19) 壁の絵を変えただけで、部屋の気分が変わった。
Kabeno eo kaetadakede, heyano kibunga kawatta.
The room felt different after (I) replaced the picture on the wall.

20) 高校野球で地元の高校が優勝したので、町中お祭り気分になっている。
Kookoo-yakyuude jimotono kookooga yuushooshitanode, machijuu omatsuri-kibunni natteiru.
The whole town is in a festive mood because the local high school won the national baseball championship.

21) 満員電車に乗っていたら、気分が悪くなってしまいました。
Man-indenshani notteitara, kibunga warukunatte-shimaimashita.
(I) felt sick after riding on a packed train.

22) 熱が下がって、だいぶ気分がよくなりました。
Netsuga sagatte, daibu kibunga yokunarimashita.
(My) fever has gone down and I'm feeling much better.

23) 妻は気分がすぐれないからと、早く寝てしまった。
Tsumawa kibunga sugurenaikarato, hayaku neteshimatta.
My wife went to bed early, saying that she wasn't feeling well.

きゅうに／とつぜん／いきなり

■ *kyuuni* ■ *totsuzen* ■ *ikinari*

きゅうに［急に］ ■ *kyuuni* ■ suddenly 

予想もしなかったのに**状態が激しく変化**するとき（例1, 2, 3）や、ものごとの**進み具合が驚くほど速い**とき（例４）使います。「突然・いきなり」は、主に目の前のできごとやその場のことがらに使い、例４のような場合には使いません。

Kyuuni is used to indicate that an unexpected and drastic change of state occurs abruptly (ex.1, 2, 3), or that something progresses surprisingly fast (ex.4). *Totsuzen* and *ikinari* are used when speaking of sudden action that occurs in front of a person, or at a particular place; therefore, they may not be used in sentences like the one in Example 4.

1) 前の車が急にブレーキをかけたので、もう少しでぶつかるところだった。
Maeno kurumaga kyuuni bureekio kaketanode, moosukoshide butsukaru tokorodatta.
(I) almost hit the car in front of me because its driver suddenly put on his brakes.

2) 夜中に、急におなかが痛くなったので病院へ行った。
Yonakani, kyuuni onakaga itakunattanode byooin-e itta.
(I) suddenly got a stomachache in the middle of the night, so I went

to the hospital.

3) 急(きゅう)に空(そら)が暗(くら)くなり、激(はげ)しい雨(あめ)が降(ふ)り出(だ)した。
Kyuuni soraga kurakunari, hageshii amega furidashita.
The sky suddenly became dark, and a heavy rain started to fall.

4) 私(わたし)の子供(こども)は、このごろ急(きゅう)に背(せ)が伸(の)びた。
Watashino kodomowa, konogoro kyuuni sega nobita.
My child has grown quite a lot all of a sudden.

とつぜん［突然(とつぜん)］

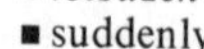

■ *totsuzen*
■ suddenly

全(まった)く予想(よそう)していなかったことや、それまでなかったことが、何(なん)の前触(まえぶ)れもなく**瞬間的(しゅんかんてき)に起(お)こる**ようすを表(あらわ)します（例(れい)5, 6, 7）。
Totsuzen indicates that something entirely unexpected occurs instantaneously (ex.5, 6, 7).

5) 突然(とつぜん)電気(でんき)が消(き)えた。
Totsuzen denkiga kieta.
The electricity suddenly went off.

6) 夜中(よなか)に突然(とつぜん)、電話(でんわ)のベルが鳴(な)ったので、飛(と)び起(お)きてしまった。
Yonakani totsuzen, denwano beruga nattanode, tobiokite-shimatta.
The telephone suddenly rang in a middle of night, making (me) jump out of bed.

7) 突然(とつぜん)大地震(おおじしん)が起(お)こって、町(まち)は大(おお)きな被害(ひがい)を受(う)けた。
Totsuzen oojishinga okotte, machiwa ookina higaio uketa.
Suddenly, a huge earthquake occurred, and the town suffered heavy damage.

いきなり

■ *ikinari*
■ suddenly

全(まった)く予期(よき)していないときや油断(ゆだん)しているときに、何(なに)かが起(お)こるようすや、「ふつうだったら踏(ふ)むはずの、順序(じゅんじょ)や手続(てつづ)きなどを踏(ふ)まないで、じかに」というようすを表(あらわ)すとき使(つか)います（例(れい)8, 9, 10, 11）。「**乱暴(らんぼう)だ・むちゃだ**」**という感(かん)じ**を含(ふく)ん

でいます。また、「いきなり」は、人間や動物がすることに使い、「いきなり雨が降ってきた」などのような、自然現象には使いません。

Ikinari is used to indicate that something occurs without warning, or catches the speaker off guard. It may also mean that a usual process or order is bypassed (ex.8, 9, 10, 11). *Ikinari* suggests a feeling of roughness or recklessness. Also, while it may be used when speaking of human or animal actions, it is not used in sentences like *ikinari ame ga futte kita* to describe natural phenomena.

---

8) 曲がり角で、いきなり子供が飛び出して来たので、あわてて急ブレーキを踏んだ。

Magarikadode, ikinari kodomoga tobidashite-kitanode, awatete kyuubureekio funda.
(I) had to hit the brakes because a child suddenly jumped into the street at a corner.

9) 議論の最中に、彼はいきなり私をなぐった。

Gironno saichuuni, karewa ikinari watashio nagutta.
In the middle of the argument he suddenly punched me.

10) ノックもしないで、いきなり人の部屋に入るのは失礼だ。

Nokkumo shinaide, ikinari hitono heyani hairunowa shitsureida.
It's rude to burst into someone's room without knocking.

11) 私たちの野球チームは、初出場でいきなり優勝してしまった。

Watashitachino yakyuu-chiimuwa, hatsu-shutsujoode ikinari yuushoo-shite-shimatta.
Our baseball team unexpectedly took the championship at our first appearance in the tournament.

きらい/いや

■ *kirai* ■ *iya*

きらい［嫌い］

■ *kirai*
■ to dislike ; to hate 

自分の好みにあわないことです。不快感で拒絶したいという気持ちを表すとき

使います（例1, 2, 3, 4）。

Kirai is used to describe something as not fitting the speaker's taste, and implies feelings of refusal due to displeasure or disagreement (ex.1, 2, 3, 4).

1）私は、子供のころにんじんが嫌いでした。
Watashiwa, kodomono koro ninjinga kiraideshita.
When I was a child I hated carrots.

2）母は、虫が大嫌いです。
Hahawa, mushiga daikiraidesu.
My mother hates insects.

3）私の嫌いな科目は数学です。
Watashino kiraina kamokuwa suugakudesu.
The subject I dislike the most is mathematics.

4）彼は、あんなに好きだったたばこが、最近嫌いになったそうです。
Karewa, annani sukidatta tabakoga, saikin kiraini nattasoodesu.
(I) hear he now dislikes the cigarettes he used to like so much.

いや［嫌］ ■*iya* ■to dislike 

---

①**不快だ、好きではない**ということです（例5, 6）。

Iya expresses displeasure or dislike (ex.5, 6).

②〜したくない・ものごとを受け入れる気にならない、などの**否定や拒絶の気持ち**を表すとき使います（例7, 8）。「嫌い」が長い間ずっと持っている気持ちであるのに対して、「いや」はその場や、今は……の否定・拒絶に使われることが多いです。

It may also be used to express not wanting to or refusal to do something (ex.7, 8). While *kirai* is used in cases of long term feelings of dislike, *iya* is often used for momentary refusal or denial.

5）腐った魚は、いやな臭いがする。
Kusatta sakanawa, iyana nioiga suru.
Rotten fish smells terrible.

6）いくら好きな食べ物でも、毎日食べ続ければいやになる。

Ikura sukina tabemonodemo, mainichi tabetsuzukereba iyani naru.
No matter how much (you) like a particular food, if you eat it everyday you'll get sick of it.

7) 母親(ははおや)：おつかいに行(い)って来(き)て。
子供(こども)：今(いま)、おもしろいテレビを見(み)てるんだからいや。
Hahaoya : *Otsukaini itte kite.*
Mother : Go and run this errand for (me).
Kodomo : *Ima, omoshiroi terebio miterundakara iya!*
Child : (I) don't want to! I'm watching an interesting TV show.

8) 私(わたし)は、時間(じかん)を守(まも)らない人(ひと)と仕事(しごと)をするのはいやです。
Watashiwa, jikan-o mamoranai hitoto shigotoo surunowa iyadesu.
I can't stand working with people who aren't punctual.

(〜た) きり／(〜た) まま
■ (〜*ta*) *kiri* ■ (〜*ta*) *mama*

(〜た)きり ■(〜*ta*) *kiri* ■since ◎

ものごとが、**ある状態(じょうたい)になって変(か)わらない・もどらない**というようすを表(あらわ)すとき使(つか)います（例(れい)1, 2, 3)。例(れい)4は、元気(げんき)で起(お)きられた人(ひと)が、ある時(とき)から起(お)き上(あ)がれない状態(じょうたい)になってしまったということです。

(〜*ta*) *kiri* is used to indicate that once something takes a certain state, it does not change or return to its original state (ex.1, 2, 3). In Example 4, it suggests that people who once were able to get out of bed are no longer able to do so.

---

1) 彼(かれ)とは、3年前(ねんまえ)に会(あ)ったきり一度(いちど)も会(あ)っていない。
Karetowa, sannenmaeni attakiri ichidomo atteinai.
(I) have not seen him since I met him three years ago.

2) 彼女(かのじょ)は、去年(きょねん)フランスに行(い)ったきり連絡(れんらく)がない。
Kanojowa, kyonen Furansuni ittakiri renrakuga nai.
Since she went to France last year, there has been no word from her.

3）父は朝早く出かけたきりまだ帰って来ません。
Chichiwa asa hayaku dekaketakiri mada kaettekimasen.
My father left early in the morning and has not come back yet.

4）最近日本では「寝たきり老人」が社会問題になっている。
Saikin Nihondewa 'netakiri roojin' ga shakai-mondaini natteiru.
Lately, bedridden elderly people have become a social problem in Japan.

（～た）まま

■(~*ta*) *mama*
■as (something) is

それまでの**状態を変えない**で・**改めない**で・**手を加えない**で、というとき使います。ある状態やようすが続いていることを表します（例5, 6, 7, 8)。「（～た）きり」は、「ある時点での突然の終了」を表しますが、「（～た）まま」は「続いていることや放置」を表します。「（～ない）まま」は、否定の形です。

~*mama* means that something is kept in the same state; i.e., a continuous state or condition is not changed, revised, or modified (ex.5, 6, 7, 8). While (~*ta*) *kiri* denotes that something suddenly ends at a certain point, (~*ta*) *mama* indicates that something is continued or is left as it was before. (~*nai*)*mama* is the negative form.

5）クーラーをつけたまま寝るのは体に良くない。
Kuuraao tsuketamama nerunowa karadani yokunai.
Sleeping with the air-conditioner left on is not good for one's health.

6）口にものを入れたまましゃべるのは、お行儀が悪いですよ。
Kuchini monoo iretamama shaberunowa, ogyoogiga waruidesuyo.
It's bad manners to talk with your mouth full.

7）きょうの話し合いは、結論が出ないまま終わりになった。
Kyoono hanashiaiwa, ketsuronga denaimama owarini natta.
Today's discussion ended without any conclusions being reached.

8）日本では、靴をはいたまま家に入る習慣はありません。
Nihondewa, kutsuo haitamama ieni hairu shuukanwa arimasen.
In Japan, it is not the custom to enter a house with your shoes on.

きる／さく／たつ

■ *kiru* ■ *saku* ■ *tatsu*

きる［切(き)る］ ■ *kiru* ■ to cut

①**ナイフやはさみなどで**、物(もの)を2(ふた)つ以上(いじょう)に**分(わ)けたり**、また**傷(きず)をつけたりする**とき使(つか)います（例(れい)1, 2, 3）。

To cut something into two or more pieces with a cutting instrument such as a knife or scissors, or to cut the surface of something (ex.1, 2, 3).

②自分(じぶん)の意志(いし)でものごとや人(ひと)との**つながり・関係(かんけい)をなくす**ときにも使(つか)います（例(れい)4, 5, 6）。例(れい)7は、スピードを出(だ)して進(すす)むようすを表(あらわ)します。

To purposely end a relationship with someone or something (ex.4, 5, 6). Example 7 means 'to move at high speed'.

1) のこぎりで木(き)を切(き)る。
Nokogiride kio kiru.
(I) cut a tree with a saw.

2) 私(わたし)は、先週(せんしゅう)髪(かみ)を切(き)りました。
Watashiwa, senshuu kamio kirimashita.
I cut my hair last week.

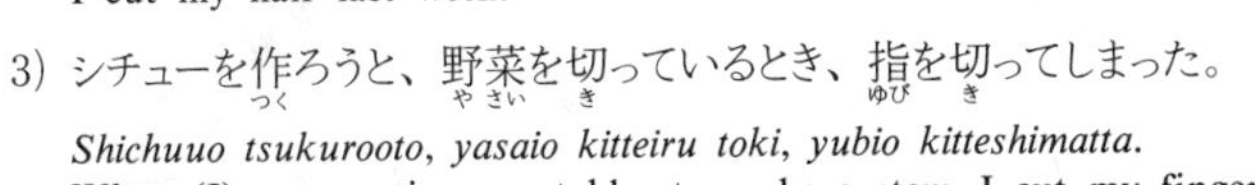

3) シチューを作(つく)ろうと、野菜(やさい)を切(き)っているとき、指(ゆび)を切(き)ってしまった。
Shichuuo tsukurooto, yasaio kitteiru toki, yubio kitteshimatta.
When (I) was cutting vegetables to make a stew, I cut my finger.

4) 寝(ね)る時(とき)は、電気(でんき)のスイッチを切(き)ってください。
Neru tokiwa, denkino suitchio kitte kudasai.
When (you) go to bed, please turn off the lights.

5) 彼(かれ)は、「おやすみなさい」と言(い)って電話(でんわ)を切(き)りました。
Karewa, "Oyasuminasai" to itte denwao kirimashita.
He said "good night" and hung up the phone.

6) あんな変(へん)な人(ひと)とは、さっさと手(て)を切(き)った方(ほう)がいい。
Anna henna hitotowa, sassato teo kitta hooga ii.
(You) should end your relationship with that strange man at once.

7) 初夏(しょか)に自転車(じてんしゃ)で、風(かぜ)を切(き)って走(はし)るのはとても気持(きも)ちがいい。
Shokani jitenshade, kazeo kitte hashirunowa totemo kimochiga ii.
In early summer, riding against the wind on a bicycle feels good.

さく［裂(さ)く・割(さ)く］

■ *saku*
■ to rip ; to tear apart

---

①布(ぬの)や紙(かみ)など、物(もの)を**無理(むり)に引(ひ)っぱって**2つ(ふた)以上(いじょう)に**分(わ)ける**とき使(つか)います（例(れい)8, 9, 10）。

To tear something like cloth or paper into two or more pieces by pulling hard on it (ex.8, 9, 10).

②自分(じぶん)以外(いがい)の2人(ふたり)の人(ひと)の関係(かんけい)を、**無理(むり)に引(ひ)きはなす**とき使(つか)います（例(れい)11）。
To force two people to separate or break up (ex.11).

③自分(じぶん)の時間(じかん)・お金(かね)などの一部(いちぶ)を無理(むり)をして相手(あいて)のために使(つか)うとき（例(れい)12）使(つか)います。

To spare a part of one's time or money for someone else (ex.12).

①と②は「裂(さ)く」と書(か)き、③は「割(さ)く」と書(か)きます。

For definitions ① and ② *saku* is written 裂く, for ③ it is written 割く.

---

8) 布(ぬの)をたてに裂(さ)く。
Nunoo tateni saku.
Tear the cloth along the warp.

9) くぎにひっかけて、ズボンを裂(さ)いてしまった。
Kugini hikkakete, zubon-o saiteshimatta.
I tore my pants on a nail.

10) 「さきいか」という食(た)べものは、干(ほ)したいかを裂(さ)いて作(つく)ります。
'*Sakiika*'*to yuu tabemonowa, hoshita ikao saite tsukurimasu.*
The food called *sakiika* is made by tearing dried squid into strips.

11) そう簡単(かんたん)に、私(わたし)たちの仲(なか)を裂(さ)くことはできない。
Soo kantanni, watashitachino nakao saku kotowa dekinai.
(They) can't break up our friendship so easily.

12) ちょっと相談(そうだん)したいことがあるのですが、お時間(じかん)を割(さ)いていただけませんか。
Chotto soodanshitai kotoga arunodesuga, ojikan-o saite itadakemasenka?
I'd like to discuss something with you. Do you have anytime?

たつ［裁(た)つ・断(た)つ・絶(た)つ］ ■*tatsu* ■to cut

①紙(かみ)や布(ぬの)などの、平面的(へいめんてき)な薄(うす)いものの必要(ひつよう)な部分(ぶぶん)だけを、切(き)って残(のこ)すとき使(つか)います（例(れい)13, 14）。

To cut out a needed portion from some flat and thin material such as paper or cloth (ex.13, 14).

②今(いま)まで続(つづ)いていたことをやめたり、なくしたりするとき（例(れい)15）使(つか)います。

To discontinue something that had been ongoing (ex.15).

③つながりをなくすことです（例(れい)16, 17, 18）。

To lose or eliminate a relationship or connection (ex.16, 17, 18).

①は「裁(た)つ」と書(か)き、②は「断(た)つ」，③は「絶(た)つ」と書(か)きます。

For definition ① the *kanji* character 裁つ is used, and for ② 断つ is used, and ③ 絶つ is used.

13) 服(ふく)を作(つく)る時(とき)には、まず布(ぬの)を裁(た)ちます。
Fukuo tsukuru tokiniwa, mazu nunoo tachimasu.
When making a dress, (you) first cut the cloth.

14) 紙(かみ)を裁(た)って大(おお)きさをそろえて、本(ほん)を作(つく)ります。
Kamio tatte ookisao soroete, hon-o tsukurimasu.
A book is made by cutting and sizing paper.

15) 彼(かれ)は飲酒運転(いんしゅうんてん)でつかまって以来(いらい)、酒(さけ)を断(た)った。
Karewa inshuuntende tsukamatte irai, sakeo tatta.
He has given up drinking ever since he was arrested for drunk-driving.

16) 新政府(しんせいふ)は、麻薬(まやく)の根(ね)を絶(た)とうと努力(どりょく)している。
Shinseifuwa, mayakuno neo tatooto doryokushiteiru.
The new government is making efforts to wipe out the very root of illegal drugs.

17) 駅前(えきまえ)の自転車(じてんしゃ)の放置(ほうち)は、あとを絶(た)たない。
Ekimaeno jitenshano hoochiwa, atoo tatanai.
The leaving of bicycles in front of stations never stops.

18) 有名(ゆうめい)な冒険家(ぼうけんか)の植村氏(うえむらし)は、マッキンリーで消息(しょうそく)を絶(た)った。

Yuumeina bookenkano Uemurashiwa, Makkinriide shoosokuo tatta.
Naomi Uemura, the famous adventurer, disappeared on Mt. McKinley.

きれい／うつくしい

■ *kirei* ■ *utsukushii*

きれい

■ *kirei*
■ beautiful ; clean 

---

①ものの形や色などが**整っている**、**鮮やか**だ、など**良い状態にあるようす**を表します（例1, 2, 3)。

Kirei indicates that the shape or color of something is arranged in a clear and pleasing fashion (ex.1, 2, 3).

②汚れていない**清潔な状態**を表します。さらに、悪い心や不道徳なものがない**純粋な心**を表します（例4, 5, 6, 7)。

It also expresses a clean or neat state, or implies innocence or lack of ill-will (ex.4, 5, 6, 7).

③「きれいに」の形で、「ひとつ残らず・全部・すっかり」の意味で使います（例8, 9)。

It may be used as an adverb meaning 'completely' or 'entirely' in the form *kirei ni* (ex. 8, 9).

---

1) 彼女の部屋に、きれいな花の絵が飾ってある。
Kanojono heyani, kireina hanano ega kazattearu.
Her room is decorated with a beautiful picture of flowers.

2) 真っ白なウエディングドレスを着た彼女は、とてもきれいだ。
Masshirona uedingudoresuo kita kanojowa, totemo kireida.
She looks very beautiful in her pure white wedding dress.

3) うちのカナリアは、きれいな声で鳴く。
Uchino kanariawa, kireina koede naku.
My canary sings with a beautiful voice.

4) 食事の前に、手をきれいに洗いなさい。

Shokujino maeni, teo kireini arainasai.
Wash your hands well before you eat.

5) 彼の部屋はいつもきれいにそうじしてある。
Kareno heyawa itsumo kireini soojishitearu.
His room is always nicely cleaned up.

6) このタオルは古いけれど、洗濯してあるからきれいです。
Kono taoruwa furuikeredo, sentaku-shitearukara kireidesu.
Although this towel is old, it has been washed so it's clean.

7) 正しい政治を行うために、きれいな選挙をするべきだ。
Tadashii seijio okonau tameni, kireina senkyoo surubekida.
In order to have honest government, (we) must have clean elections.

8) 出されたものは、残さずきれいに食べなさい。
Dasareta monowa, nokosazu kireini tabenasai.
Make sure (you) eat everything on your plate.

9) きのう覚えたフランス語の単語を、一晩寝たらきれいに忘れてしまった。
Kinoo oboeta Furansugono tangoo, hitoban netara kireini wasureteshimatta.
(I've) completely forgotten all of the French words I learned yesterday.

うつくしい［美しい］ ■ *utsukushii* ■ beautiful 

---

①**人の姿やものの色**、あるいは**音色**などが、華やかだ・鮮やかだ・すばらしいなどと**感動させるとき**に使います（例10, 11, 12, 13)。

Utsukushii indicates the speaker is impressed with the beauty, splendor, or magnificence of something. Examples may include a person's figure, or the color or sound of something (ex.10, 11, 12, 13).

②精神的や道徳的に価値があって、**感心だ・立派だ**というとき使います(例14)。

It may also be used to express that something has qualities of spiritual or moral value (ex.14).

①の場合、ふつう話しことばでは「きれい」を多く使い、「美しい」は書きことばです。「きれいな字」は、読みやすく、整っていてじょうずだという意味で、「美しい字」はより**芸術的に価値**がある、という意味を含みます。どちらかというと、「きれい」は個人的な評価で、「美しい」は世の中一般の評価です。

Utsukushii is more commonly used in written language and *kirei* in spoken language. In comparing usage, *kirei na ji* refers to neat, easy-to-read writing, while *utsukushii ji* implies more evaluation of its artistic value. In other words, things described as *utsukushii* are more conventionally and popularly accepted as beautiful, while *kirei* suggests a more personal and casual assessment of beauty.

---

10) 日本(にほん)では、5月(がつ)は木々(きぎ)の新緑(しんりょく)が美(うつく)しい季節(きせつ)だ。
Nihondewa, gogatsuwa kigino shinryokuga utsukushii kisetsuda.
In Japan, May is the month of beautiful new green leaves.

11) 津和野(つわの)は古(ふる)い家並(いえな)みが美(うつく)しく、小京都(しょうきょうと)と呼(よ)ばれている。
Tsuwanowa furui ienamiga utsukushiku, ShooKyoototo yobareteiru.
Tsuwano with its beautiful rows of old houses is called 'Little Kyoto'.

12) 雨(あめ)あがりに、空(そら)に美(うつく)しい虹(にじ)がかかった。
Ameagarini, sorani utsukushii nijiga kakatta.
After the rain stopped, there was a beautiful rainbow in the sky.

13) 教会(きょうかい)の前(まえ)を通(とお)ると、美(うつく)しい歌声(うたごえ)が聞(き)こえてきた。
Kyookaino maeo tooruto, utsukushii utagoega kikoetekita.
When (I) passed in front of the church, I heard beautiful voices singing.

14) 彼(かれ)らの美(うつく)しい友情(ゆうじょう)の話(はなし)は、人々(ひとびと)の心(こころ)を打(う)った。
Karerano utsukushii yuujoono hanashiwa, hitobitono kokoroo utta.
The story of their beautiful friendship touched people's hearts.

ぐうぜん／たまたま／まぐれ

■*guuzen* ■*tamatama* ■*magure*

ぐうぜん［偶然(ぐうぜん)］

■*guuzen*
■by chance ; by coincidence 

意図的(いとてき)なものでもなく、原因(げんいん)もないのに、**思(おも)いがけないことや予想(よそう)もしていなかったことが起(お)こる**ようすを表(あらわ)します（例(れい)1, 2, 3, 4, 5）。

Guuzen refers to a situation in which, without intention or cause, something unimagined or unforeseen occurs (ex.1, 2, 3, 4, 5).

1) こんなところで会うなんて、偶然ですね。
Konna tokorode aunante, guuzendesune.
What a coincidence that (we) should meet here.

2) あなたと生年月日が同じだなんて、そんな偶然があるんですね。
Anatato seinengappiga onajidanante, sonna guuzenga arundesune.
It's amazing that our birthdays happen to be on the same day.

3) 電車の中で偶然となりに座ったのは、小学校のときの先生だった。
Denshano nakade guuzen tonarini suwattanowa, shoogakkoono tokino sense-idatta.
By chance, the person who sat next to me on the train was a former elementary school teacher of mine.

4) 多くの発明が偶然から生まれている。
Ookuno hatsumeiga guuzenkara umareteiru.
Most inventions are a product of chance.

5) 偶然にも、娘の担任は私の幼なじみだった。
Guuzennimo, musumeno tanninwa watashino osananajimi-datta.
As luck would have it, my daughter's homeroom teacher turned out to be my childhood friend.

たまたま ▪ *tamatama* ▪ by chance 

いつもはそうではないのに、**その時に限って起こった**ことがらや状況を表します（例6, 7, 8, 9)。「**めったにあることではない**」という意味を強く含みます。

Tamatama expresses that, at a certain point in time a situation out of the ordinary occurs (ex.6, 7, 8, 9). The rarity of the situation is emphasized.

---

6) 喫茶店にバスが飛びこんだが、たまたま客がいなかったので、けが人はなかった。
Kissatenni basuga tobikondaga, tamatama kyakuga inakattanode, keganinwa nakatta.
A bus crashed into a coffee shop, but no one was injured because it just so happened that there weren't any customers there at the time.

7) いつもとは違う道をたまたま通ったら、すてきな花屋を見つけた。

Itsumotowa chigau michio tamatama toottara, sutekina hanayao mitsuketa.
(I) took a different road than I usually do, and by chance found a wonderful flower shop.

8) 山道で車が故障して困っていたら、たまたま通りかかった車の人が助けてくれた。
Yamamichide kurumaga koshooshite komatteitara, tamatama toorikakatta kurumano hitoga tasuketekureta.
(I) didn't know what to do when my car broke down on a mountain road, but a passing driver was kind enough to help me.

9) たまたま、会社を休んでうちにいたら、学生時代の友達から10年ぶりに電話がかかってきた。
Tamatama, kaishao yasunde uchini itara, gakuseijidaino tomodachikara juunenburini denwaga kakattekita.
(I) took the day off and just happened to be at home when an old school friend from whom I hadn't heard in ten years called me.

まぐれ
■ *magure*
■ by chance ; a fluke 

自分のしたことが、**運よく**考えてもみなかったほどの**良い結果になった**とき使います（例10, 11, 12, 13）。「宝くじ・ゲーム・クイズ・テスト」など運に左右されるものに、多く使われます。

Magure is used when something one does turns out much better than expected (ex.10, 11, 12, 13). It is often used when referring to success in things like a lottery, game, quiz, or test, in which there is an element of luck involved.

---

10) 初めて会った人を「鈴木さん」と呼んでみたら、まぐれで当たった。
Hajimete atta hitoo 'Suzukisan' to yondemitara, magurede atatta.
The first time (I) met him I took a chance and called him 'Mr. Suzuki,' and I was right!

11) 野球は苦手だけど、バットを振ったら、まぐれでヒットになった。
Yakyuuwa nigatedakedo, battoo futtara, magurede hittoni natta.
I'm very poor at baseball, but (I) swung the bat and was lucky enough to get a hit.

12) 絶対受からないと思っていた大学に受かったのは全くのまぐれだ。
Zettai ukaranaito omotteita daigakuni ukattanowa mattakuno magureda.
(I) sure was lucky to be accepted by that university, because I was sure I didn't have a chance.

13) 初めてのアーチェリーで的の中心に当てるなんてまぐれにちがいない。
Hajimeteno aacheriide matono chuushinni aterunante magureni chigainai.
It was pure luck that (I) was able to hit the bull's-eye the first time I tried archery.

くぎる／しきる

■ *kugiru* ■ *shikiru*

くぎる［区切る］ ■ *kugiru* ■ to divide

文章・時間・仕事などものごとを、**いくつかの部分やまとまりごとに分けること**です。部屋などの空間に使うときは、「しきる」のような「へだてる」という意味は強くなく、単に区分がわかれば良いのです（例1, 2, 3, 4）。

Kugiru means to divide something, such as a sentence, composition, time, or a job, into several parts or groups. When referring to a space, for example a room, *kugiru* simply means to divide into sections. This is unlike *shikiru*, which means to partition off (ex.1, 2, 3, 4).

1) 短く区切ってゆっくり読みますから、書き取ってください。
Mijikaku kugitte yukkuri yomimasukara, kakitotte kudasai.
(I'll) divide this into short segments and read it slowly, so please write it down.

2) この文章は、段落ごとに区切れば分かりやすい。
Kono bunshoowa, danrakugotoni kugireba wakariyasui.
This composition would be easier to comprehend if (you) read each paragraph separately.

3) 土地を4つに区切って貸すことにした。
Tochio yottsuni kugitte kasu kotoni shita.
(We) decided to divide this land into four lots to lease.

4) 私と弟は、時間を区切って交代でテレビゲームをします。
Watashito otootowa, jikan-o kugitte kootaide terebigeemuo shimasu.
My (younger) brother and I take turns playing video games.

しきる［仕切る］

■ *shikiru*
■ to divide ; to partition

部屋などの空間を、**何かでへだてて境界をはっきりさせる**ことです。外部から他のものが入ってくるのを防ぐ意味を含みます（例5, 6, 7, 8)。

Shikiru means to partition a space, like a room, with something in order to create clear divisions. It entails a sense of preventing entry (ex.5, 6, 7, 8).

5) 私と姉は、１つの部屋を本棚で仕切って使っている。
Watashito anewa, hitotsuno heyao hondanade shikitte tsukatteiru.
My (elder) sister and I are using one room partitioned with a bookcase.

6) 隣の部屋とは、うすい板１枚で仕切ってあるだけなので、話し声が聞こえてしまう。
Tonarino heyatowa, usui ita ichimaide shikittearu dakenanode, hanashigoega kikoeteshimau.
This room and the next are separated by only a thin board, so (I) can hear people there talking.

7) 彼の病室は二人部屋で、隣のベッドとはカーテンで仕切られている。
Kareno byooshitsuwa futaribeyade, tonarino beddotowa kaatende shikirare-teiru.
His hospital room is for two people ; he's separated from the other bed by a curtain.

8) 箱の中を細かく仕切って、小物入れにしている。
Hakono nakao komakaku shikitte, komonoireni shiteiru.
(I) divided up the inside of the box into little sections and use it to store small things.

くさる／いたむ

■*kusaru*　■*itamu*

くさる［腐る］

■*kusaru*
■to go bad ; to decay 

食べ物などが**古くなったり変質したり**して、**悪くなって**しまうことです（例1, 2, 3, 4, 5)。多くの場合、**いやなにおい**がしたり、**形がくずれたり**します。木や金属などが変質してくずれたりするときにも使います。

Kusaru indicates that food, etc., gets old and goes bad (ex.1, 2, 3, 4, 5). In many cases the object has a bad smell and changes shape. This word can also be used to describe the deterioration of wood or metal.

1) 夏は食べ物がすぐ腐る。
Natsuwa tabemonoga sugu kusaru.
Food soon goes bad during the summer.

2) 腐ったものを食べると、おなかをこわすよ。
Kusatta monoo taberuto, onakao kowasuyo.
If you eat something rotten, you'll get a stomachache, you know.

3) 海辺を歩いていたら、腐った魚のにおいがした。
Umibeo aruiteitara, kusatta sakanano nioiga shita.
When I was walking along the shore, it smelled like rotten fish.

4) 肉や魚は、冷蔵庫に入れておいたほうが腐りにくい。
Nikuya sakanawa, reizookoni ireteoitahooga kusarinikui.
Meat and fish are less likely to go bad if they are stored in the refrigerator.

5) この木の橋は腐っているので、渡るのは危険だ。
Kono kino hashiwa kusatteirunode, wataruno wa kikenda.
This wooden bridge has decayed, so it's dangerous to cross.

いたむ［傷む・痛む］

■*itamu*
■to be damaged ; to ache 

①食べ物の**一部分**に**傷**がついたり、**変質**したりすることです（例6, 7）。ものが使い古されたりして、**部分的にこわれたりきたなくなったり**するときにも使います（例8）。

This is used when a part of a food gets bruised and deteriorates (ex.6, 7). It can also be used in situations in which something becomes worn out, or partially breaks down or becomes dirty (ex.8).

②からだのある部分が、**病気やけが**などのために**痛みを感じる**ときに使います（例9, 10）。また、心が**悲しみやあわれみ・苦しみ**などを感じるときにも使います（例11）。

It may also be used when a part of the body hurts because of sickness or injury (ex.9, 10), or when one feels sad or sympathetic, or is in emotional pain (ex.11).

---

6) このりんごは少し傷んでいるけれど、とても甘い。

Kono ringowa sukoshi itandeirukeredo, totemo amai.
This apple is a little bruised but it's very sweet.

7) このお菓子は傷みやすいので、今日中に食べてください。

Kono okashiwa itamiyasuinode, kyoojuuni tabetekudasai.
These pastries are perishable so please eat them today.

8) 夫：この椅子も、だいぶ傷んでいるね。
妻：そうね。おじいちゃんが若い頃から使っているんですものね。

Otto : *Kono isumo, daibu itandeirune.*
Husband : This chair is also quite worn, isn't it?
Tsuma : *Soone. Ojiichanga wakai korokara tsukatteirun-desumonone.*
Wife : Yes, it is. It's been used continuously ever since grandpa was young, that's why.

9) ゆうべから歯が痛んでしかたがない。

Yuubekara haga itande shikataganai.
I've had a terrible toothache since last night.

10) 雨が降ると、昔骨折した足が痛む。

Amega furuto, mukashi kossetsushita ashiga itamu.
Whenever it rains the leg that I broke long ago hurts.

11) そのことを思うと、今でも胸が痛む。

Sono kotoo omouto, imademo munega itamu.
Even now, whenever I think about that, I feel bad.

くすくす／げらげら

■*kusukusu* ■*geragera*

くすくす ■*kusukusu* ■giggle ; chuckle 

笑っていることをほかの人に気付かれないようにおかしさをこらえているのに、**ついもれてしまう小さな笑い声**のようすを表します（例1, 2)。

Kusukusu suggests laughter that sneaks out in spite of one's efforts to contain it, often when trying to prevent other people from realizing how amused one is (ex.1, 2).

1) 彼女はくすくす笑いながらマンガを読んでいる。
Kanojowa kusukusu warainagara mangao yondeiru.
She's reading a comic book, giggling all the while.

2) 先生が計算をまちがえると、後ろの方でくすくす笑う声がした。
Senseiga keisan-o machigaeruto, ushirono hoode kusukusu warau koegashita.
Sounds of snickering rose from the back when the teacher made an error in calculation.

げらげら ■*geragera* ■laugh (out loud) 

大きな声で、遠慮なく**笑う**ようすや声を表します（例3, 4, 5)。

This is used when one laughs out loud and without reserve (ex.3, 4, 5).

3) 子供のころ私が大失敗した話を聞いて、みんなはげらげら笑った。
Kodomono koro watashiga daishippaishita hanashio kiite, minnawa geragera waratta.
Everybody howled with laughter when they heard the story about one of my childhood screw ups.

4) 観客は彼の物真似を見て、おなかを抱えてげらげら笑った。
Kankyakuwa kareno monomaneo mite, onakao kakaete geragera waratta.
The members of the audience clutched their stomachs in laughter when they saw his impersonations.

5) 人前で大きな口を開けてげらげら笑うのは、行儀が悪いと父に言われた。
Hitomaede ookina kuchio akete geragera waraunowa, gyoogiga waruito chichini iwareta.
(I) was told by my father that it is bad manners to laugh with one's mouth wide open in front of others.

くるくる／ぐるぐる／ころころ

■ *kurukuru* ■ *guruguru* ■ *korokoro*

くるくる

■ *kurukuru*
■ (go / turn) round and round 

---

①人やものなどが、軽そうに**何回も回ったり、回したりするようす**を表します（例1, 2, 3）。

Kurukuru expresses a gentle whirling or spinning motion of a person or thing which is turning in circles (ex.1, 2, 3).

②糸や紙などを**巻いたり、くるんだりするようす**を表します（例4, 5）。

It also expresses a coiled or wrapped state of an object such as thread or paper (ex.4, 5).

---

1) バレリーナは、くるくるとこまのように回った。
Bareriinawa, kurukuruto komanoyooni mawatta.
The ballerina spun around like a top.

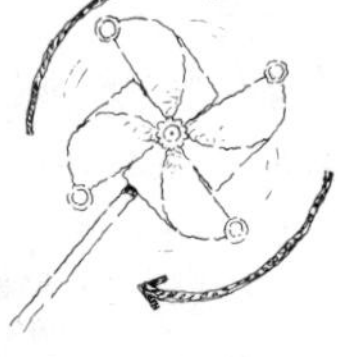

2) かざぐるまが、風でくるくると回っている。
Kazagurumaga, kazede kurukuruto mawatteiru.
The pinwheel is turning round and round in the wind.

3) 彼は、りんごをくるくると回しながら、皮をむいていった。
Karewa, ringoo kurukuruto mawashinagara, kawao muiteitta.
He peeled the apple by turning it round and round in his hands.

4) 彼女(かのじょ)は、はがしたポスターをくるくると巻(ま)いて片付(かたづ)けた。
Kanojowa, hagashita posutaao kurukuruto maite katazuketa.
She rolled up the poster she had taken down and put it away.

5) 母(はは)は、セーターをほどいた毛糸(けいと)をくるくると巻(ま)いて、毛糸玉(けいとだま)にした。
Hahawa, seetaao hodoita keitoo kurukuruto maite, keitodamani shita.
My mother took the yarn she had unravelled from a sweater and rolled it into a ball.

ぐるぐる

■ *guruguru*
■ (turn / go) round and round

---

①人(ひと)やものなどが、何回(なんかい)も回(まわ)ったり、回(まわ)したりするようすを表(あらわ)します（例(れい)6, 7, 8）。「**くるくる**」は、**軽(かる)くて速(はや)い動(うご)き**を表(あらわ)しますが、「ぐるぐる」は「くるくる」よりも**重(おも)くて大(おお)きい動(うご)き**です。

This expresses the revolving motion of a person or object turning around in circles (ex.6, 7, 8). *Kurukuru* suggests a light, quick movement, while *guruguru* expresses a heavier motion of greater scope.

②人(ひと)やものなどに、何(なに)かを何回(なんかい)も巻(ま)きつけるようすを表(あらわ)します（例(れい)9, 10）。

It may also express that something is wound or wrapped around an object or person many times (ex.9, 10).

---

6) 洗濯機(せんたくき)の中(なか)で、洗濯物(せんたくもの)がぐるぐる回(まわ)っている。
Sentakkino nakade, sentakumonoga guruguru mawatteiru.
The clothes are spinning around in the washing machine.

7) 遭難者(そうなんしゃ)は手(て)を大(おお)きくぐるぐると回(まわ)して、救助(きゅうじょ)のヘリコプターに合図(あいず)をした。
Soonanshawa teo ookiku guruguruto mawashite, kyuujono herikoputaani aizuo shita.
The survivor signalled the rescue helicopter by waving his hands in huge circles.

8) 道(みち)に迷(まよ)って、同(おな)じところをぐるぐる回(まわ)ってしまった。
Michini mayotte, onaji tokoroo guruguru mawatteshimatta.
(I) got lost, and ended up going around and around the same place in circles.

9) 姉(あね)は、牛肉(ぎゅうにく)に香辛料(こうしんりょう)をまぶし、たこ糸(いと)でぐるぐる巻(ま)いてオーブンに入(い)れた。
Anewa, gyuunikuni kooshinryoo-o mabushi, takoitode guruguru maite

oobun-ni ireta.
My (elder) sister sprinkled seasoning on the beef, wrapped it several times with cord and placed it in the oven.

10) 強盗は人質をロープでぐるぐるとしばった。
Gootoowa hitojichio roopude guruguruto shibatta.
The robber wound ropes around his hostages to tie them up.

ころころ ■*korokoro* ■roll over and over 

---

①ものが**軽く転がっていくようす**を表します（例11, 12, 13）。あまり大きくない比較的軽いものに使います。

Korokoro indicates that something rolls along gently (ex.11, 12, 13). It is used when referring to comparatively light objects.

②**子供**や**動物の子供**が、**太っていてかわいらしいようす**を表します（例14, 15）。

It also expresses the chubby cuteness of a child or baby animal (ex.14, 15).

③**考え方**や**態度**などが、何度も**よく変わるようす**を表します（例16）。

Korokoro may also express frequent change of mind or attitude (ex.16).

---

11) 私の足もとに、ボールがころころ転がってきた。
Watashino ashimotoni, booruga korokoro korogattekita.
A ball rolled up to my feet.

12) ネックレスの糸が切れて、真珠がころころと転がってしまった。
Nekkuresuno itoga kirete, shinjuga korokoroto korogatte-shimatta.
The string of my necklace broke and the pearls went tumbling about.

13) えんぴつが、ころころ転がって床に落ちてしまった。
Enpitsuga, korokoro korogatte yukani ochiteshimatta.
The pencil rolled and rolled and fell to the floor.

14) あの赤ちゃんは、ころころとよく太っていてかわいい。
Ano akachanwa, korokoroto yoku futotteite kawaii.
That baby is cute and chubby.

15) この間生まれた子犬たちは、どれもころころして元気がいい。
Kono aida umareta koinutachiwa, doremo korokoroshite genkiga ii.

The puppies born a while back are all so plump and playful.

16) 彼(かれ)の言(い)うことはころころと変(か)わるので、信用(しんよう)できない。
Kareno yuu kotowa korokoroto kawarunode, shin-yoodekinai.
What he says changes from one minute to the next, so (you) can't trust him.

良(よ)かったじゃない

きょう学校(がっこう)で、フランクは元気(げんき)がありませんでした。パスポートの入(はい)ったかばんを、なくしてしまったからです。その夜(よる)、フランクから仲良(なかよ)しの純(じゅん)に電話(でんわ)がかかってきました。

「純(じゅん)、かばんが見(み)つかりました。電車(でんしゃ)の中(なか)に忘(わす)れたのを、親切(しんせつ)な人(ひと)が駅(えき)に届(とど)けてくれたのです」うれしそうなフランクに純(じゅん)は言(い)いました。「良(よ)かったじゃない」するとフランクは腹(はら)を立(た)てたように言(い)いました。「友(とも)だちなのに、『良(よ)かったじゃない』なんてひどいよ」

たしかに「～じゃない」は「病気(びょうき)じゃない、親切(しんせつ)じゃない」などのように「～ではない」の話(はな)しことばとして、否定(ひてい)するとき使(つか)います。だからフランクは「良(よ)かった…ではない」、つまり「良(よ)くない」の意味(いみ)にとったのです。

でも純(じゅん)が言(い)った「良(よ)かったじゃない」は、「良(よ)かったね」という意味(いみ)で、「良(よ)かったではありませんか、ねえそうでしょう」と相手(あいて)の同意(どうい)を求(もと)める意味(いみ)なのです。

Yokatta ja nai

Today in school, Frank was depressed because he had lost his bag with his passport in it. That evening, Frank's good friend Jun received a call from him.

"Jun, the bag has been found. I left it on the train, and a kind person took it to the station office," Frank said. Jun said to an obviously jubilant Frank, "*Yokatta ja nai.*"

As soon as he said so, Frank replied angrily, "You're my friend, aren't you? How cruel of you to say *yokatta ja nai.*"

Certainly *～ja nai* is used in a number of instances to make a negative statement, including *byooki ja nai*[1] and *shinsetsu ja nai*[2]. That is the reason why Frank understood Jun to say 'that was not good'. However, Jun's *yokatta ja nai*[3] really meant 'that was good' or 'that was great'. It was a shortened version of 'That was great, wasn't it? Don't you think so?' and included a solicitation for agreement from the listener.

1 *'It's not a sickness' or 'I'm not sick'.*
2 *He (she) is not nice.*
3 *That was good, wasn't it?*

くわえる／たす

■ *kuwaeru* ■ *tasu*

くわえる［加(くわ)える］ ■ *kuwaeru* ■ to add (to)

①**数**(かず)の計算(けいさん)で、単(たん)に**合**(あ)**わせる**の意味(いみ)に使(つか)います（例(れい)１）。

To add numbers in calculation (ex.1).

②**いまあるものに**、また**他**(た)**のものを合**(あ)**わせ**て行(い)くとき使(つか)います。この場合(ばあい)は、同質(どうしつ)のものでも異質(いしつ)のものでもかまいません（例(れい)2, 3）。

To add something to something else that already exists. It is used both when speaking of combining like things or different things (ex.2, 3).

③**熱**(ねつ)**・力**(ちから)**・刺激**(しげき)**・危害**(きがい)などを**与**(あた)**える**というとき使(つか)います（例(れい)4, 5）。

To provide (heat, power, stimulus), or to inflict (injury)(ex.4, 5).

1) 1に3を加えると4になる。

Ichini san-o kuwaeruto yonni naru.
If you add three to one, you get four.

2) 二酸化マンガンに炭酸ナトリウムを加えると、酸素ができる。

Nisanka-manganni tansan-natoriumuo kuwaeruto, sansoga dekiru.
If sodium carbonate is added to manganese dioxide, oxygen will be produced.

3) 旅行に彼女を加えてもいいでしょうか。

Ryokooni kanojoo kuwaetemo iideshooka?
Is it all right if we include her on our trip?

4) 人に危害を加えるおそれのある犬は、つないでおかなければならない。

Hitoni kigaio kuwaeru osoreno aru inuwa, tsunaide okanakereba naranai.
Dogs that might inflict harm on people must be firmly chained.

5) アイロンは、熱と圧力を布に加えて、しわをのばします。

Aironwa, netsuto atsuryokuo nunoni kuwaete, shiwao nobashimasu.
An iron smooths out wrinkles by applying heat and pressure on the cloth.

たす［足す］ ■ *tasu* ■ to add

①「加える」と同様に**数の計算**で、単に**合わせる**の意味に使います。例6のような計算を足し算といいます。

As with *kuwaeru*, *tasu* may be used in calculation, and means simple addition. A calculation like that in Example 6 is called *tashizan* (addition).

②足りない分を**目的に合うように増す**ときに使います（例7, 8, 9）。

To increase an insufficient amount to meet requirements (ex.7, 8, 9).

6) 4 + 5 = 9は「4足す5は9」と読みます。

4+5=9 wa 'yontasu gowa kyuu' to yomimasu.
4+5=9 is read as 'four plus five equals nine'.

7) 兄の貯金とぼくの貯金を足して、車を買います。

Anino chokinto bokuno chokin-o tashite, kurumao kaimasu.
My brother and I will put our savings together and buy a car.

8) お風呂のお湯が足りなかったら、足してください。
Ofurono oyuga tarinakattara, tashite kudasai.
If there isn't enough hot water in the bathtub, please add more.

9) あずかったお金は500円不足でしたから、私が足して払っておきました。
Azukatta okanewa gohyakuen fusokudeshita-kara, watashiga tashite hara-tte-okimashita.
The money (you) gave me was ¥500 short, so (I) made up the difference with my own money.

くわしい／こまかい

■ *kuwashii* ■ *komakai*

くわしい［詳しい］ ■ *kuwashii* ■ detailed 

①初めてそのことがらに接した人にもわかるように、すみずみまでていねいに説明するようすや**情報が多い**ようすを表して使います（例1, 2, 3, 4, 5)。
This indicates that something is explained very carefully and in detail, or that a lot of information about something is provided so that it is clear even to people who have never encountered it before (ex.1, 2, 3, 4, 5).

②あることがらについて、よく知っている・**知識が豊富だ**というとき使います（例６）。
Kuwashii can describe a person as being very knowledgeable about something (ex.6).

---

1) 渋谷の詳しい地図がほしい。
Shibuyano kuwashii chizuga hoshii.
(I) want a detailed map of Shibuya.

2) この辞書は、とても詳しいのでわかりやすい。
Kono jishowa, totemo kuwashiinode wakariyasui.
This dictionary is easy to use because it explains things in detail.

3) A：彼、どうして会社を辞めたんですか。
B：詳しいことは知らないけれど、上司とけんかしたらしいよ。

A： *Kare, dooshite kaishao yametandesuka?*
Why did he quit his company?
B： *Kuwashii kotowa shiranaikeredo, jooshito kenka-shitarashiiyo.*
(I) don't know the details, but it seems that he had a quarrel with his boss.

4) 日本の伝統芸能について詳しく知りたい。
Nihonno dentoogeenooni tsuite kuwashiku shiritai.
(I) want to know all about Japan's traditional perfoming arts.

5) 今度の旅行について、詳しくは手紙で知らせます。
Kondono ryokooni tsuite, kuwashikuwa tegamide shirasemasu.
(We'll) let (you) know the details about the trip by mail.

6) 彼女は現代文学に詳しい。
Kanojowa gendaibungakuni kuwashii.
She is extremely knowledgeable about modern literature.

こまかい［細かい］

■ *komakai*
■ detailed ; minute

---

①ものの一つ一つが**とても小さい**ようすを表します。粉・砂・雨・文字・網の目……などのように同じものが数多くあるときにだけ使います（例7, 8）。

Komakai denotes that each part or section of something, e.g., powder, sand, rain, lettering, or netting, is very fine, small or dense. *Komakai* is used only when there are many of the same kind thing of present (ex.7, 8).

②ことがらの小さい部分の一つ一つをとりあげて、ていねいに説明するようすを表すとき使います。「**詳しい**」**が情報量の多さや内容を表す**のに対して、「**細かい**」**は、ことがらの一つ一つの小さい部分を表します**（例9, 10, 11, 12）。「細かいお金」というのは普通は、100円玉・50円玉というようなコインのことですし、お金をくずすことを「細かくする」と使います。また「詳しい」は、良い意味で使いますが、「細かい」は時には「必要以上に」や「わずらわしい」といった良くない意味で使うこともあります。

Komakai is also used when one explains something very carefully, covering each minute detail. *Kuwashii* refers to the richness of information, while *komakai* refers to each small, minute detail (ex.9, 10, 11, 12). *Komakai okane* normally means coins of small denomination, such as ¥100 and ¥50 coins. To change a large bill into small money is *komakaku suru* in Japanese.

Kuwashii is normally used in a positive sense, while *komakai* sometimes carries a negative connotation, such as 'more than is necessary' or 'being overly complicated'.

---

7) 霧のような細かい雨が降っている。
Kirino yoona komakai amega futteiru.
A misty rain is falling.

8) 父は、新聞のような細かい字を読むときは、めがねをかけます。
Chichiwa, shinbunnoyoona komakai jio yomu tokiwa, meganeo kakemasu.
When my father reads very small print, like that in the newspaper, he wears glasses.

9) きょうはもう遅いので、細かい打ち合わせはあしたにしよう。
Kyoowa moo osoinode, komakai uchiawasewa ashitani shiyoo.
It's already late, so let's discuss the matter in detail tomorrow.

10) あの事件について一つ一つ細かく説明してください。
Ano jikenni tsuite hitotsuhitotsu komakaku setsumeishite-kudasai.
Please explain that incident step by step and in detail.

11) 彼の秘書は、細かい事によく気がつく。
Kareno hishowa, komakai kotoni yoku kigatsuku.
His secretary always pays attention to details.

12) 彼はお金に細かいからきらわれている。
Karewa okaneni komakaikara kirawareteiru.
People dislike him because he is too fussy about money.

けいけん／たいけん

■ *keiken* ■ *taiken*

けいけん［経験］ ■ *keiken* ■ experience 

実際に自分で**見たり聞いたり行動してきたこと**を指します（例1, 2, 3, 4）。一度あるいは数度のことにも、または**長年の積み重ね**についても使います。それによって知識や技術を身につけるなど、その人のためになるという意味を含

みます。また、「～をしたことがある」という程度の軽い意味でも使います（例5, 6）。

Keiken is used when referring to an experience one has actually had oneself (ex.1, 2, 3, 4). The experience may have occurred only once, many times, or over many years. It is usually used in a positive sense, i.e., acquiring knowledge or technique through actual experience. On a casual level it is sometimes interchangeable with *～o shita koto ga aru* (I have done...) (ex.5, 6).

1）彼は経験が豊かな医師なので、信頼できる。
Karewa keikenga yutakana ishinanode, shinraidekiru.
He is a doctor with a great amount of experience so you can trust him.

2）彼女は10年間中国で暮らした経験を生かして、今は日本で中国料理を教えている。
Kanojowa juunenkan Chuugokude kurashita keiken-o ikashite, imawa Nihonde Chuugoku-ryoorio oshieteiru.
She is teaching Chinese cooking in Japan now, making use of her experience of having lived ten years in China.

3）私の経験から言うと、風邪をひいたら温かいものを食べて早く寝るに限る。
Watashino keikenkara yuuto, kazeo hiitara atatakai monoo tabete hayaku neruni kagiru.
It's been my experience that the best thing to do when you have a cold is to eat something warm and go to bed early.

4）あの会社では、経理の経験がある人を募集している。
Ano kaishadewa, keirino keikenga aru hitoo boshuushiteiru.
That company is looking for someone who has experience in accounting.

5）子供のころ友だちとけんかをして、泣かせたり泣かされたりした経験はだれにでもある。
Kodomono koro tomodachito kenkao shite, nakasetari nakasaretarishita keikenwa darenidemo aru.
Everybody has had the experience as a child of getting in a fight with a friend, and making him cry or being made to cry oneself.

6）私は、カナダに行った経験がある。
Watashiwa, Kanadani itta keikenga aru.
I have been to Canada.

たいけん［体験］ ■*taiken* ■experience 

実際に自分で見たり聞いたり行動した具体的なことを指します。**日常的なことではなく特別のこと**だという意味があり、「〜したことがある」という程度のことには使いません（例7, 8, 9, 10）。

Taiken is used to refer to a particular thing that someone has actually seen, heard, or done oneself. It usually refers to an out of the ordinary experience, and therefore cannot be used in ordinary situations (ex.7, 8, 9, 10).

7) 彼は戦争を体験しているので、人一倍平和のありがたみを知っている。
Karewa sensoo-o taikenshiteiru-node, hitoichibai heiwano arigatamio shitte-iru.
He has actually experienced war himself so he knows more than anyone the blessing of peace.

8) この小学校には、子供たちに農業を体験させるための畑がある。
Kono shoogakkooniwa, kodomotachini noogyoo-o taikensaseru tameno hatake-ga aru.
This elementary school has a field, which is used to expose the children to farming.

9) 彼は3か月で10キロやせた体験談を話してくれた。
Karewa sankagetsude jukkiro yaseta taikendan-o hanashitekureta.
He told us about his experience of losing ten kilograms in three months.

10) 私は無重力状態を一度体験してみたい。
Watashiwa mujuuryoku-jootaio ichido taikenshitemitai.
Just once, I would like to experience weightlessness.

けっきょく／とにかく

■*kekkyoku* ■*tonikaku*

けっきょく［結局］ ■*kekkyoku* ■eventually ; in the end

いろいろなことがあったけれど**最後には**、ということを表します。**最終的な結**

論を述べることばです（例1, 2, 3, 4, 5）。

Kekkyoku indicates that, although there were several possibilities, a conclusion is eventually reached. It is used when speaking of a final decision (ex.1, 2, 3, 4, 5).

---

1) いろいろ考えて、結局この青いセーターを買いました。
Iroiro kangaete, kekkyoku kono aoi seetaao kaimashita.
After a lot of thought, (I) ended up buying this blue sweater.

2) 何度も話し合ったが、結局意見はまとまらなかった。
Nandomo hanashiattaga, kekkyoku ikenwa matomaranakatta.
(We) discussed the matter repeatedly, but in the end we couldn't reach an agreement.

3) えらそうなことを言っても、結局人の助けがなければ何もできないじゃない。
Erasoona kotoo ittemo, kekkyoku hitono tasukega nakereba nanimo dekinaijanai.
(You) always talk big, but in the end you can't do anything without help.

4) 自分で時計を修理しようとしたけれど、結局うまくいかなかった。
Jibunde tokeio shuurishiyooto shitakeredo, kekkyoku umaku ikanakatta.
(I) tried to fix the clock by myself, but I didn't do a very good job.

5) 子供が大好きだった彼女は、結局幼稚園の先生になった。
Kodomoga daisukidatta kanojowa, kekkyoku yoochienno senseini natta.
She really liked children, so she became a kindergarten teacher.

とにかく ■ *tonikaku* ■ anyway 

---

①最終的な結論ではないけれど、**今できることや、するべきこと**を、まず**先にする**というとき使います（例6, 7, 8）。

Tonikaku indicates that, although a final decision has not been reached, one does what is possible or is required at the moment (ex.6, 7, 8).

②ものごとを強めて述べるとき使います（例9, 10）。

It is also used to emphasize a statement (ex.9, 10).

③そのことは良いとしても、さておき、という意味で使います（例11, 12）。「ともかく」とも使います。

Tonikaku may be used when one sets aside or disregards something, even though it may be good or interesting (ex.11, 12). *Tomokaku* may also be used with the same meaning.

6) 食事(しょくじ)はあとにして、とにかくこの用事(ようじ)を済(す)ませてしまおう。
Shokujiwa atonishite, tonikaku kono yoojio sumaseteshimaoo.
Anyway, let's finish this business up and then get something to eat.

7) 玄関先(げんかんさき)で立(た)ち話(ばなし)をしていてもしかたがありませんから、とにかく中(なか)へおはいりください。
Genkansakide tachibanashio shiteitemo shikataga arimasenkara, tonikaku nakae ohairikudasai.
We could stand in the doorway and talk all day, so why don't you come inside?

8) 疲(つか)れているときは、とにかく早(はや)く寝(ね)たほうがいい。
Tsukareteiru tokiwa, tonikaku hayaku neta hooga ii.
At any rate, when you're tired you should go to bed early.

9) 彼女(かのじょ)は、とにかく料理(りょうり)が上手(じょうず)です。
Kanojowa, tonikaku ryooriga joozudesu.
She is an especially good cook.

10) この店(みせ)の品物(しなもの)は、とにかく安(やす)いので評判(ひょうばん)だ。
Kono miseno shinamonowa, tonikaku yasuinode hyoobanda.
The stuff in that store is well-known to be cheap, if nothing else.

11) 彼(かれ)は見(み)た目(め)はとにかく、心(こころ)のやさしいいい人(ひと)だ。
Karewa mitamewa tonikaku, kokorono yasashii ii hitoda.
Appearances aside, he's a nice guy at heart.

12) プールならともかく、海(うみ)で泳(およ)ぐのは少(すこ)しこわい。
Puurunara tomokaku, umide oyogunowa sukoshi kowai.
(I) don't mind swimming in pools, but I'm a little afraid of the sea.

けなげ／いじらしい

■ *kenage* ■ *ijirashii*

けなげ ■ *kenage* ■ admirable ; brave 

弱いものや年少者、小さくてかれんなものが、困難に立ち向かって一生懸命努力しているようすを、ほめたり感心したりするとき使います(例1, 2, 3, 4)。

Kenage is used when praising or expressing admiration for someone or something weak, young, small or pretty that is striving against difficulty (ex.1, 2, 3, 4).

1) 彼女はまだ8歳なのに、両親が働いているので、けなげに弟の面倒を見ている。
Kanojowa mada hassainanoni, ryooshinga hataraite-irunode, kenageni otootono mendoo-o miteiru.
Even though she is only eight years old, she is bravely looking after her younger brother while her parents work.

2) 彼は家計を助けるため、小学生のころからずっと新聞配達をしているけなげな少年です。
Karewa kakeio tasukerutame, shoogakuseino korokara zutto shinbunhaitatsuo shiteiru kenagena shoonendesu.
He is a terrific boy. He has worked as a paperboy ever since he was an elementary school student in order to contribute to his family's finances.

3) 日の当たらないやせた土地でも、この花は一生懸命咲いて、けなげだ。
Hino ataranai yaseta tochidemo, kono hanawa isshookenmei saite, kenageda.
This flower has bloomed splendidly, in spite of the lack of sunlight and poor soil.

4) あの盲導犬は、けなげにも自分を犠牲にして、主人を事故から守った。
Ano moodookenwa, kenagenimo jibun-o giseinishite, shujin-o jikokara mamotta.
That Seeing Eye dog heroically sacrificed itself in order to protect its master from thc accident.

いじらしい ■ *ijirashii* ■ touching ; pathetic ; lovable 

幼い者・弱い者が、一生懸命に何かをしたり困難に耐えているようすが、痛々しくてあわれに感じるとき使います(例5, 6, 7)。

Ijirashii is used when the speaker feels pity for or is deeply touched by someone young or weak that is trying his or her best to overcome difficulty (ex.5, 6, 7).

---

5) 病気の母親を心配して、遊びにも行かずに看病している子供の姿がいじらしい。

Byookino hahaoyao shinpaishite, asobinimo ikazuni kanbyooshiteiru kodomono sugataga ijirashii.
It is moving to see the children so worried about their ailing mother that they stay home to care for her instead of going out to play.

6) 生まれたばかりの子馬が、よろめきながら自分で立ち上がろうとするようすは、とてもいじらしい。

Umareta bakarino koumaga, yoromekinagara jibunde tachiagarooto suru yoosuwa, totemo ijirashii.
It was heartwarming to see the newborn pony tottering about, struggling to stand on its own.

7) 試験に落ちてつらい思いをしているはずなのに、明るくふるまう娘がいじらしかった。

Shikenni ochite tsurai omoio shiteiru hazunanoni, akaruku furumau musumega ijirashikatta.
It was pitiful to see my daughter behaving so cheerfully when she should have been depressed over failing the exam.

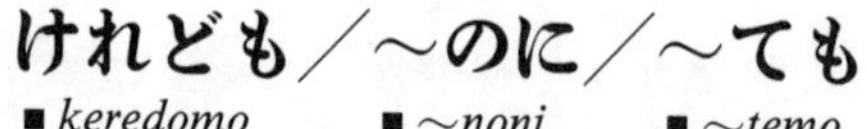

けれども

■ *keredomo*
■ but ; however 

---

①逆の関係にある2つのことがらを、つないで述べるとき使います（例1, 2, 3, 4, 5, 6）。

Keredomo is used when connecting two opposing or contrasting statements (ex.1, 2, 3, 4, 5, 6).

②前置きを述べたり話を展開させたりするとき使います。また、文の終わりにつけて、ものごとをはっきりと言わずに、やわらげる・遠慮がちに言うなどの使い方もします（例7, 8）。

It is also used when making prefatory remarks or when developing a story. When *keredomo* appears at the end of a sentence, one of its usages is to soften, rather than make clearer the speaker's remarks, and it expresses the speaker's inclination to be modest (ex.7, 8).

---

1) 歴史小説は、むずかしいけれどもおもしろい。
Rekishi-shoosetsuwa, muzukashii-keredomo omoshiroi.
Historical novels are difficult but interesting.

2) フランス語は話せるけれども読めない。
Furansugowa hanaseru-keredomo yomenai.
(I) can speak French, but can't read it.

3) 朝、熱があったけれども学校へ行った。
Asa, netsuga attakeredomo gakkooe itta.
Although (I) had a fever in the morning, I went to school.

4) 兄は背が高いけれどもぼくは背が低い。
Aniwa sega takaikeredomo bokuwa sega hikui.
My older brother is tall, but I am short.

5) ビールもいいけれどもワインも飲みたい。
Biirumo iikeredomo wainmo nomitai.
Beer is OK, but (I) want to have some wine, too.

6) 私は犬が好きだ。けれども猫はきらいだ。
Watashiwa inuga sukida. Keredomo nekowa kiraida.
I like dogs. However, I don't like cats.

7) もしもし……林ですけれども、みどりさんいらっしゃいますか。
Moshimoshi... Hayashidesukeredomo, Midorisan irasshaimasuka?
Hello. This is Mr.Hayashi. Is Midori there?

8) ちょっとお話ししたいことがあるんですけれども……。
Chotto ohanashishitai kotoga arundesukeredomo...
There's something (I'd) like to talk with you about.

～のに

■ ～*noni*
■ ～although ; but

「～のに」でつないだ、前のことがらと後のことがらに、矛盾やくいちがいがあるようすを述べるとき使います。不満や非難・驚きなど、話し手の強い感情を含みます（例9, 10, 11, 12, 13）。「風邪をひいたのに、学校へ行こう」のような、意思表示には使いません。

When ～*noni* is used to connect two statements, the speaker is saying that there is an apparent inconsistency or contradiction between the statements. The speaker's strong feelings of dissatisfaction, criticism, surprise, etc., may be implied (ex.9, 10, 11, 12, 13). It is incorrect to use *noni* in sentences such as *kaze o hiita noni gakkoo e ikoo* (even though I've got a cold, I think I'll go to school) because *noni* is not used when expressing one's own will.

9）10時に駅で待ち合わせたのに彼は来なかった。
Juujini ekide machiawasetanoni karewa konakatta.
Although (we) promised to meet at the station at ten, he didn't come.

10）一生懸命勉強したのに試験に落ちてしまった。
Isshookenmei benkyooshitanoni shikenni ochiteshimatta.
Although (I) studied as hard as I could, I failed the exam.

11）彼は若いのによく気がつく。
Karewa wakainoni yoku kigatsuku.
In spite of the fact that he is young, he is very attentive.

12）あれほど注意をしたのにまた同じ間違いをするなんて……。
Arehodo chuuio shitanoni mata onaji machigaio surunante...
Even though (I) warned him so many times; that (he) would make the same mistake again (is unbelievable).

13）買ったばかりの時計なのにもうこわれてしまった。
Katta bakarino tokeinanoni moo kowareteshimatta.
Although it's a brand new clock, it's already broken.

～ても

■ ～*temo*
■ even (though / if) ; but

①「たとえば～だとしたら」という、仮のことがらや、実際に起こったことがらをあ

げて、そのことがらとはふさわしくない・あわないということがらをつないで述べるとき使います（例14, 15, 16, 17）。

This expression is used when discussing matters in a hypothetical form, as in saying 'if〜 is the case', or, when raising matters that have actually occurred, this term expresses the idea that these matters are inappropriate or do not properly fit together (ex.14, 15, 16, 17).

②「〜てもいいですか」の形で**許可を求める**とき使います（例18, 19）。

It is also used in the form 〜 *temo iidesu ka* to ask for permission (ex.18, 19).

---

14) なぜ彼女があんなに怒ったのか、いくら考えてもわからない。

Naze kanojoga annani okottanoka, ikura kangaetemo wakaranai.
No matter how hard (I) try, I don't understand why she got so angry.

15) ダイヤモンドは小さくても高い。

Daiyamondowa chiisakutemo takai.
Diamonds are expensive, regardless of how small they may be.

16) この部屋は、1人で泊まっても2人で泊まっても料金は同じだ。

Kono heyawa, hitoride tomattemo futaride tomattemo ryookinwa onajida.
The room charge is the same, whether only one person stays or two people stay.

17) 彼はどんな仕事をやらせてもきちんとこなす。

Karewa donna shigotoo yarasetemo kichinto konasu.
No matter what kind of job he is assigned, he does it well.

18) もう帰ってもいいですか。

Moo kaettemo iidesuka?
May (I) leave now?

19) A：ここでたばこを吸ってもいいですか。

B：いいえ、映画館では、たばこを吸ってはいけません。

A： *Kokode tabakoo suttemo iidesuka?* May (I) smoke here?
B： *Iie, eigakandewa, tabakoo suttewa ikemasen.*
No, (you) mustn't smoke in a movie theater.

こえる／こす／すぎる

■*koeru* ■*kosu* ■*sugiru*

こえる［超える・越える］ ■*koeru* ■to go over ; to exceed

①ものごとの**数量**や**程度**が、**ある基準を上回る**ことです（例1, 2, 3, 4, 5, 6, 7)。

To go over or beyond a certain quantity, degree, level, etc. (ex.1, 2, 3, 4, 5, 6, 7).

②進行方向にある**障害となるものの上を通って、向こう側・先へ行くこと**です。大変な時期や状態を終えるという意味で、抽象的なことにも使います（例8, 9, 10)。「障害や困難を克服する・制限や枠などの外へ出る」という意味を強く含みます。

多くの場合、①は「超える」と書き、②は「越える」と書きます。

To go, pass, or reach across or beyond an obstacle in the path of progression. It is also used in an abstract sense meaning to come to the end of a serious or difficult period or condition (ex.8, 9, 10). It includes a strong sense of overcoming an obstacle or difficulty, or of exceeding a limit or boundary. In many instances definition ① is written 超える, and ② is written 越える.

---

1) 熱が39度を超えたら、この薬を飲んでください。
Netsuga sanjuukudoo koetara, kono kusurio nonde kudasai.
Take this medicine if (your) fever goes over 39℃.

2) 家計は今月も予算を大きく超えてしまいました。
Kakeiwa kongetsumo yosan-o ookiku koete-shimaimashita.
(Our) household expenses have far exceeded our budget this month, too.

3) この雨で川の水が増して危険水位を超えてしまった。
Kono amede kawano mizuga mashite kikensuiio koeteshimatta.
On account of all this rain, the river has swollen and risen above the danger level.

4) 社会の近代化は私達の想像をはるかに超えている。
Shakaino kindaikawa watashitachino soozoo-o harukani koeteiru.
The modernization of society has far and away exceeded our imagination.

5) 今日の入場者は10万人を超えた。

Kyoono nyuujooshawa juumannin-o koeta.
Today's attendance exceeded 100,000.

6) 私は標準体重を10キロも超えてしまった。
Watashiwa hyoojuntaijuuo jukkiromo koeteshimatta.
I'm more than 10 kilograms over my normal weight.

7) この車は時速100キロを超えると、警報がなる。
Kono kurumawa jisoku hyakkiroo koeruto, keihooga naru.
This car will sound an alarm if you go over 100 kph.

8) 彼の病状はどうやら峠を越えたらしい。
Kareno byoojoowa dooyara toogeo koetarashii.
He seems to have passed the point of crisis in his illness.

9) 旅券なしで国境を越えることはできない。
Ryokennashide kokkyoo-o koeru kotowa dekinai.
(You) can't cross the border without a passport.

10) 渡り鳥はいくつもの海や山を越えて旅をする。
Wataridoriwa ikutsumono umiya yamao koete tabio suru.
Migratory birds travel across many oceans and mountains.

こす［超す・越す］

■ *kosu*
■ to be more than ; to pass 

---

①ものごとの数量や程度が、ある基準を**上回ること**です（例11, 12, 13, 14）。

To exceed, or go over or beyond a certain quantity, degree, level, etc. (ex.11, 12, 13, 14).

②ある**時期を経過する**ことです（例15, 16）。

To pass through and beyond a certain period of time (ex.15, 16).

③**住む場所を変える・移る**というとき（例17）や向こう側へ行く・**通って行く**というとき使います（例18）。

It is used also to mean 'to change one's residence' (ex.17), as well as 'to go to the other side' or 'to pass through' (ex.18).

---

11) 日本の人口は、ずっと前に1億2千万人を超した。
Nihonno jinkoowa, zutto maeni ichioku-nisenmannin-o koshita.
The population of Japan went above 120,000,000 quite some time ago.

12) 彼(かれ)は結婚式(けっこんしき)に200人(にん)を超(こ)す人(ひと)を呼(よ)んだ。
Karewa kekkonshikini nihyakunin-o kosu hitoo yonda.
He invited over 200 people to his wedding.

13) 新薬(しんやく)の開発(かいはつ)で、よその会社(かいしゃ)に先(さき)を越(こ)されてしまった。
Shin-yakuno kaihatsude, yosono kaishani sakio kosarete-shimatta.
(Our) company was about to develop a new drug when another company beat us to it.

14) きのうは台風(たいふう)のせいで、１時間(じかん)に50ミリを超(こ)す大雨(おおあめ)が降(ふ)りました。
Kinoowa taifuuno seide, ichijikanni gojuumirio kosu ooamega furimashita.
During yesterday's typhoon, rain was falling at a rate of more than 50 ml per hour.

15) 北国(きたぐに)の熊(くま)は巣穴(すあな)の中(なか)で冬(ふゆ)を越(こ)す。
Kitagunino kumawa suanano nakade fuyuo kosu.
Bears in the north pass the winter inside their dens.

16) ９月(がつ)になると暑(あつ)さもようやく峠(とうげ)を越(こ)して涼(すず)しい風(かぜ)が吹(ふ)いてくる。
Kugatsuni naruto atsusamo yooyaku toogeo koshite suzushii kazega fuite-kuru.
Once September comes, we pass the peak of the hot season, and cool winds start to blow.

17) 新(あたら)しい家(いえ)に越(こ)したので一度(いちど)遊(あそ)びに来(き)てください。
Atarashii ieni koshitanode ichido asobini kite kudasai.
(We've) moved to our new house, so please come to visit sometime.

18) 通(とお)りをいくつも越(こ)していって、やっと探(さが)していた家(いえ)を見(み)つけた。
Toorio ikutsumo koshiteitte, yatto sagashiteita ieo mitsuketa.
After passing through many streets (I) finally found the house that I was seeking.

すぎる［過(す)ぎる］ ■*sugiru* ■to go beyond ; to pass 

①進(すす)んで行(い)くものが、ある**場所(ばしょ)や地点(ちてん)などを通(とお)って**止(と)まってしまわずに**進(すす)む**ことです（例(れい)19）。

To proceed beyond a certain place or point without stopping (ex.19).

②また、**時間(じかん)がたっていく**ことや「何(なん)らかの基準(きじゅん)を上回(うわまわ)る・～以上(いじょう)だ」という

意味で使います（例20, 21, 22, 23）。例24のように、「もったいない・不つりあいなくらい良い」という意味にも使います。

Sugiru is also used when speaking of the passage of time, or when saying that something is above / beyond some standard or criterion (ex.20, 21, 22, 23). It is also used; as in Example 24, with the meaning 'too good (for)' or 'good to the point of being an ill-match'.

19) 電車は中野駅を過ぎた。
Denshawa Nakanoekio sugita.
The train has passed Nakano station.

20) 私たちがこの町に来てから、10年が過ぎた。
Watashitachiga kono machini kitekara, juunenga sugita.
Ten years have passed since we came to this town.

21) 梅雨が過ぎると、本格的な夏がやってくる。
Tsuyuga sugiruto, honkakutekina natsuga yattekuru.
Once the rainy season is over, the real summer sets in.

22) 9時を過ぎたのに、まだ妹は起きてこない。
Kujio sugitanoni, mada imootowa okitekonai.
Though it's past nine, my (younger) sister hasn't gotten up yet.

23) 彼は二十歳を過ぎている。
Karewa hatachio sugiteiru.
He is over 20 years old.

24) 彼女は私には過ぎた妻です。
Kanojowa watashiniwa sugita tsumadesu.
She's too good a wife for me.

このごろ／ちかごろ／さいきん

■ *konogoro* ■ *chikagoro* ■ *saikin*

このごろ

■ *konogoro*
■ nowadays ; these days 

現在を含む、少し前からの期間を指します。今も続いている状態を述べるときに多く使います（例1, 2, 3, 4）。

Konogoro refers to the period of time beginning shortly before and continuing up to and including the present. It is commonly used when speaking of a currently continuing condition (ex.1, 2, 3, 4).

1）このごろ、どうも疲れやすい。

Konogoro, doomo tsukareyasui.
(I) find myself feeling easily fatigued these days.

2）このごろ、彼女は元気がない。

Konogoro, kanojowa genkiga nai.
She has seemed depressed lately.

3）このごろ、彼からさっぱり連絡がない。

Konogoro, karekara sappari renrakuga nai.
(I) haven't heard a word from him for a while.

4）台風のせいか、このごろ野菜が高くなった。

Taifuuno seika, konogoro yasaiga takaku natta.
(I) don't know if it's because of the typhoon, but the price of vegetables has gone up recently.

ちかごろ［近ごろ］

■ *chikagoro*
■ recently ; these days

少し前から現在までの期間を指します。**過去の時期と比較**して、現在のことを言っているという感じがあります（例5, 6, 7, 8）。また、「このごろ・最近」と比べると時間的な幅が、かなりあります。

Chikagoro refers to the period of time beginning a short time before and continuing to the present. There is a feeling that the speaker is comparing the present with the past (ex.5, 6, 7, 8). *Chikagoro* implies a broader period of time than do *konogoro* and *saikin*.

5）彼は近ごろ、白髪がふえた。

Karewa chikagoro, shiragaga fueta.
His hair has been graying recently.

6）昔は銭湯がたくさんあったのに、近ごろはあまり見かけなくなった。

Mukashiwa sentooga takusan attanoni, chikagorowa amari mikakenakunatta.

Although there used to be a lot of public baths around, nowadays they are hard to find.

7) 「近(ちか)ごろの若(わか)い者(もの)は礼儀(れいぎ)を知(し)らない」というのが、おじの口(くち)ぐせです。
'Chikagorono wakai monowa reigio shiranai' to yuunoga, ojino kuchiguse-desu.
My uncle has a habit of saying 'Young people these days have no manners'.

8) 近(ちか)ごろニューヨークで話題(わだい)になっているミュージカルが、秋(あき)に日本(にほん)でも上演(じょうえん)される。
Chikagoro Nyuuyookude wadaini natteiru myuujikaruga, akini Nihondemo jooensareru.
The musical that has been a hit in New York recently will be coming to Japan in the fall.

さいきん［最近(さいきん)］ ■ *saikin* ■ recently

---

①少(すこ)し前(まえ)から現在(げんざい)までの**ごく短(みじか)い期間(きかん)**のことを指(さ)します（例(れい)9, 10, 11, 12）。
Saikin refers to the very brief period of time beginning a short time before and continuing to the present (ex.9, 10, 11, 12).

②はっきりした日(ひ)にちは言(い)わないけれど、過去(かこ)の、ある一時点(いちじてん)を指(さ)して使(つか)います（例(れい)13, 14, 15）。「このごろ・近(ちか)ごろ」には、過去(かこ)の一点(いってん)だけをとらえる使(つか)い方(かた)はありません。

It may be used when speaking of a certain point of time in the past, without mentioning its specific date (ex.13, 14, 15). *Konogoro* and *chikagoro* may not be used to refer to a specific point of time in the past.

---

9) あなたは最近(さいきん)、どんな本(ほん)を読(よ)みましたか。
Anatawa saikin, donna hon-o yomimashitaka?
What kind of books have you read recently?

10) 最近(さいきん)私(わたし)たちの間(あいだ)で、歌舞伎(かぶき)を見(み)に行(い)くのがはやっている。
*Saikin watashitachino aidade, Kabuki*o mini ikunoga hayatteiru.*
Recently, we have gotten into seeing *Kabuki.*
—— * *Kabuki* is one of Japan's classical performing arts.
Kabuki plays, in which all roles are performed by men, feature exaggerated movements and extravagant make-up and costumes, which create a

very unique atmosphere.

11) 花屋でアルバイトをしたので、最近花の名前がわかるようになった。
Hanayade arubaitoo shitanode, saikin hanano namaega wakaruyooni natta.
Recently, (I've) gotten to know the names of flowers because I've been working part-time at a flower shop.

12) 前はよく音楽を聞きに行ったけれど、最近は全然行かなくなってしまった。
Maewa yoku ongakuo kikini ittakeredo, saikinwa zenzen ikanaku natteshimatta.
(I) used to go to concerts a lot, but nowadays I never go.

13) 彼が結婚したことを最近知りました。
Karega kekkonshita kotoo saikin shirimashita.
(I) recently heard that he's gotten married.

14) 最近、この宝石店で盗難事件があったそうだ。
Saikin, kono hoosekitende toonanjikenga attasooda.
I heard that there was a robbery at this jewelry store a short time ago.

15) 私は、つい最近香港に行ってきたばかりです。
Watashiwa, tsui saikin Honkonni ittekita bakaridesu.
I went to Hong Kong just the other day.

こむ／こんざつする

■*komu* ■*konzatsu suru*

こむ［込む］

■*komu*
■to be crowded ; to be congested 

店・建物・電車などある公の場所が、**自由に動けないほどいっぱいになる**ことです（例1, 2, 3, 4, 5, 6)。「道（道路）が込む」のように車に乗っているときにも使います。

Komu is used when public places such as stores, buildings or trains are packed with people. There is a sense that there are so many people that it's hard to move around (ex.1, 2, 3, 4, 5, 6). The subject of *komu* may be inanimate, as in the sentence *michi* (*dooro*) *ga komu* (the road is congested with cars).

---

1) 休み明けの銀行は込む。
Yasumiakeno ginkoowa komu.
Banks get crowded after holidays.

2) 昼間の電車は、ほとんど込まない。
Hirumano denshawa, hotondo komanai.
Trains rarely get crowded during the daytime.

3) 映画館は込んでいて、座れなかった。
Eigakanwa kondeite, suwarenakatta.
The movie theater was so crowded that (I) couldn't sit down.

4) 朝の通勤時間の電車は、とても込んでいる。
Asano tsuukinjikanno denshawa, totemo kondeiru.
The morning commuter trains are very crowded.

5) 六本木の交差点は、いつも車が込んでいる。
Roppongino koosatenwa, itsumo kurumaga kondeiru.
The Roppongi intersection is always congested with automobiles.

6) あの道は込むから、ちがう道を行こう。
Ano michiwa komukara, chigau michio ikoo.
That street gets congested, so let's take a different one.

こんざつする［混雑する］

■ *konzatsu suru*
■ to be crowded ; to be congested

ある公の場所に、自由に動けないほどたくさん人が集まっているようすを表します（例7, 8, 9, 10, 11)。「こむ」よりも、**整然としていない・統制や秩序がとれない状態**です。「こむ」と同様に車にも使います。

Konzatsu suru is used to indicate that there are so many people gathered at a public place that it is impossible to move around freely (ex.7, 8, 9, 10, 11). It is similar in meaning to *komu*, but the situation is considered to be worse, i.e., disordered or out of control. Like *komu*, *konzatsu suru* may be used when speaking of cars.

---

7) 駅の改札口は混雑するから、待ち合わせには向かない。
Eki no kaisatsu-guchiwa konzatsu-surukara, machiawaseniwa mukanai.
The station wicket area will be crowded, so it's not an ideal place to meet with someone.

8) 混雑した電車の中で、大声で話すのは迷惑だ。
Konzatsushita denshano nakade, oogoede hanasunowa meiwakuda.
Talking in a loud voice on a crowded train is an annoyance to others.

9) 霧で飛行機が飛ばなかったので、空港は乗客で混雑した。
Kiride hikookiga tobanakattanode, kuukoowa jookyakude konzatsushita.
All flights were cancelled due to fog, so the airport was crowded with passengers.

10) デパートのおもちゃ売り場の混雑の中で、子供とはぐれて大変だった。
Depaatono omochauribano konzatsuno nakade, kodomoto hagurete taihendatta.
It was terrible; (I) was separated from my child in the middle of a crowd in the toy section of the department store.

11) 来週の連休は天気がいいそうなので、行楽地はどこも混雑が予想される。
Raishuuno renkyuuwa tenkiga iisoonanode, koorakuchiwa dokomo konzatsuga yosoosareru.
The weather looks like it will be good during the consecutive holidays next week, so it is predicted that all the resort areas will be congested.

どこで食べますか？

リーとビルは映画館に来ました。きのう日本語のクラスのあとでリーが、「あした、映画を見て何か食べませんか」と誘ったのです。

映画が始まり、リーはだんだん物語にひきこまれていきました。するとそのとき、となりのビルが何か袋を手渡しました。「何これ？」リーは小声で聞きました。するとビルは「サンドイッチを持ってきたんだ。見ながらいっしょに食べようと思って…」と言いました。リーは「映画を見たあとで、食事をしましょう」と言ったつもりだったのですが、ビルは「映画を見ながら…」ととってしまったのです。

もしもリーが「見たあとで」をはっきりと表すように、「映画を見てから何か食べませんか」と言えば、ビルもサンドイッチを持って来なかったでしょう。

Where shall we eat?

Li and Bill went to a movie today because yesterday, after Japanese class, Li asked Bill, "*Ashita, eiga o mite nani ka tabemasen ka*[1]*?*"

After the movie had started, Bill suddenly handed a bag to Li just as she was getting into the story. "What's this?" she whispered. "I brought along some sandwiches to eat while we're watching the movie," he replied. What Li had meant to say yesterday was, "Let's eat after the movie," but Bill interpreted her to mean, "While we're watching the movie..."

If Li had originally indicated clearly that she wanted to eat after the movie by saying, "*Eiga o mite kara nani ka tabemasen ka*[2]*?*" Bill might not have brought sandwiches to the movie.

1 *Would you like to go to the movies and have something to eat?*
2 *Shall we get something to eat after watching a movie?*

こらえる／がまんする

■ *koraeru* ■ *gaman suru*

こらえる ■ *koraeru* ■ to endure

怒り・涙・笑いなどの**感情**をおさえたり、寒さや**痛みなど**の**感覚**に耐えて、**外に表さない**ことです（例1, 2, 3, 4, 5）。外からの強い力に負けないで持ちこたえるという意味を含みます。「がまんする」よりも「その場のこと」という感じが強く、また、ほとんどの場合は「がまんする」で言い換えられます。

To resist showing expressions of emotion, such as anger, tears, or laughter, or to endure feelings of cold, pain, etc. (ex.1, 2, 3, 4, 5). It is implied that one does not bend to pressure being applied externally. Although *koraeru* suggests endurance of a more momentary condition than does *gaman suru*, they are interchangeable in most cases.

---

1) 彼は手当てをしてもらっている間、じっと痛みをこらえた。
Karewa teateo shitemoratteiru aida, jitto itamio koraeta.
He quietly endured the pain while the doctor treated him (his injuries).

2) ヒーターがこわれたので、私たちは一晩寒さをこらえていた。
Hiitaaga kowaretanode, watashitachiwa hitoban samusao koraeteita.
We had to endure the cold night because our heater broke.

3) 少年は、くやしさをこらえきれずに大声で泣きだした。
Shoonenwa, kuyashisao koraekirezuni oogoede nakidashita.
The boy was unable to control his frustration and burst out crying.

4) 彼は怒りをこらえて、冷静に話をした。
Karewa ikario koraete, reiseini hanashio shita.
He kept his anger in check, and talked in a calm, collected manner.

5) 彼女の発表がつまらなかったので、あくびをこらえるのに苦労した。
Kanojono happyooga tsumaranakatta-node, akubio koraerunoni kurooshita.
Her presentation was so boring that (I) couldn't help yawn.

がまんする

■ *gaman suru*
■ to withstand ; to make do 

---

①いやなことに耐えたり、感情をかくしたりするとき、また**欲望や欲求をじっとおさえて今の状態のままでいる**とき使います（例6, 7, 8, 9)。

To maintain one's present state of mind or condition by enduring unpleasantness, suppressing emotion, or resisting temptation or desire (ex.6, 7, 8, 9).

②「～でがまんする」は「～で良いことにする」「～で代わりにする」という意味です（例10, 11)。

～de gaman suru means 'to make do with something' or 'to substitute something for something else, (ex.10, 11).

---

6) 狭くて汚い部屋ですが、ここでがまんしてください。

Semakute kitanai heyadesuga, kokode gamanshite-kudasai.
(I) know it's a small and dirty room, but please make do with it.

7) 頭が痛いのなら、がまんしないで薬を飲んだほうがいいですよ。
Atamaga itainonara, gamanshinaide kusurio nonda hooga iidesuyo.
If (you) have a headache, you should take some medicine instead of trying to endure it.

8) 私は、水が飲みたいのをがまんして、ゴールまで走り続けた。
Watashiwa, mizuga nomitainoo gamanshite, goorumade hashiritsuzuketa.
Although I was dying for a drink of water, I kept running all the way to the finish line.

9) ストーブがないと、寒くてがまんできません。
Sutoobuga naito, samukute gamandekimasen.
(I) won't be able to put up with the cold if I don't have a heater.

10) 赤いバラがほしかったけれど、なかったので、ピンクのでがまんした。
Akai baraga hoshikattakeredo, nakattanode, pinkunode gamanshita.
(I) wanted red roses, but there weren't any so I had to make do with pink.

11) 今コーヒーがないので、紅茶でがまんしてください。
Ima koohiiga nainode, koochade gamanshite kudasai.
(I) don't have any coffee, so would you mind a cup of tea instead?

～ごろ／～ぐらい（くらい）

■ *～goro* ■ *～gurai* (*kurai*)

～ごろ ■ *～goro* ■ around～

だいたいの**時刻や時期を表す**とき使います（例1, 2, 3, 4）。「２時間ごろ」などのような、時間や期間には使いません。

～goro is used when referring to an approximate point in time (ex.1, 2, 3, 4). It is not used when speaking of a period of time, therefore saying *ni-jikan goro* would be incorrect.

---

1) ゆうべ10時半ごろ、地震があった。
Yuube juujihangoro, jishinga atta.
There was an earthquake around 10:30 last night.

2) A：いつごろお引っ越しですか。
B：来月の予定です。
A： *Itsugoro ohikkoshidesuka?* About when will (you) move?
B： *Raigetsuno yoteidesu.* (I'm) planning to move next month.

3) 15世紀の中ごろ、火薬が発明された。
Juugoseikino nakagoro, kayakuga hatsumeisareta.
Gunpowder was invented around the middle of the 15th century.

4) あす昼ごろに東京駅に着く予定です。
Asu hirugoroni Tookyoo-ekini tsuku yoteidesu.
(I'm) planning to arrive at Tokyo Station around noon tomorrow.

～ぐらい（くらい）

■ *～gurai* (*kurai*)
■ around～ ; about

---

①**だいたいの数量や程度・基準**を表すとき使います（例5, 6, 7, 8）。「～ごろ」は時刻・時期についてだけ使いますが、「～ぐらい（くらい）」は、時間・期間にも使います。

～gurai (*kurai*) is used when making an approximation of something such as an amount, degree, or standard (ex.5, 6, 7, 8). When speaking of time, *～goro* is used only when referring to specific points in time, but *～gurai* (*kurai*) may be used with both points and periods of time.

②「**～と同じ程度・等しい**」ということを述べるとき使います（例9, 10, 11）。

～gurai (*kurai*) may also be used when saying that something is equivalent or similar to something else (ex.9, 10, 11).

③**最低の基準・限界・許容範囲**を述べるとき使います（例12, 13）。

It may also express the lowest standard or limit acceptable (ex.12, 13).

---

5) ゆうべは、４時間ぐらいしか寝ていない。
Yuubewa, yojikanguraishika neteinai.
(I) only slept about four hours last night.

6) けさは２時ぐらいに、一度目がさめた。

Kesawa nijiguraini, ichido mega sameta.
(I) woke up briefly at about two o'clock this morning.

7) 注文の品は、1週間ぐらいで届きます。
ちゅうもん しな しゅうかん とど
Chuumonno shinawa, isshuukanguraide todokimasu.
The products ordered will be delivered in about a week.

8) 彼の身長は180センチぐらいです。
かれ しんちょう
Kareno shinchoowa hyaku-hachijussenchi-guraidesu.
He is about 180 centimeters tall.

9) この犬は、成長すると子牛ぐらいの大きさになる。
いぬ せいちょう こうし おお
Kono inuwa, seichoosuruto koushiguraino ookisani naru.
When this dog is fully grown, it will be about the size of a calf.

10) 私にもあなたくらいの年の娘がいます。
わたし とし むすめ
Watashinimo anatakuraino toshino musumega imasu.
I also have a daughter about your age.

11) 私は彼女の心づかいが、涙が出るくらいうれしかった。
わたし かのじょ こころ なみだ で
Watashiwa kanojono kokorozukaiga, namidaga derukurai ureshikatta.
Her concern made me so happy I wanted to cry.

12) いくら忙しくても、電話ぐらいかけられるでしょう。
いそが でんわ
Ikura isogashikutemo, denwagurai kakerarerudeshoo?
No matter how busy you are, couldn't you at least phone?

13) 休みの日ぐらい、家でのんびりしたい。
やす ひ いえ
Yasumino higurai, iede nonbirishitai.
(I'd) like to take it easy at home, at least on my days off.

ころぶ／ころがる

■ *korobu* ■ *korogaru*

ころぶ［転ぶ］ ■ *korobu* ■ to fall down ; to tumble over
ころ

歩いたり走ったりしているときに、つまずく・すべるなど、バランスをくずして倒れることです（例1, 2, 3, 4）。例5, 6は慣用表現です。
ある はし たお れい れい かんようひょうげん

To stumble, slip, or lose one's balance while walking or running (ex.1, 2, 3, 4). Examples 5 and 6 are idiomatic expressions.

---

1) 歩(ある)き始(はじ)めたばかりの子供(こども)は、よく転(ころ)ぶ。
Arukihajimeta-bakarino kodomowa, yoku korobu.
A child who has just started to walk often falls.

2) スキーで転(ころ)んで、足(あし)の骨(ほね)を折(お)った。
Sukiide koronde, ashino honeo otta.
(I) fell down while skiing and broke a leg.

3) 道(みち)が悪(わる)いから、転(ころ)ばないように気(き)をつけて。
Michiga waruikara, korobanaiyooni kiotsukete.
The road is bad; be careful not to fall.

4) あの子(こ)は小(ち)さいのに、転(ころ)んでも泣(な)かなかった。
Ano kowa chiisainoni, korondemo nakanakatta.
Although that child is very young, she did not cry when she fell.

5) どっちに転(ころ)んでも損(そん)はしない。
Dotchini korondemo sonwa shinai.
Either way, (I) can't lose.

6) 彼(かれ)は、転(ころ)んでもただでは起(お)きない。
Karewa, korondemo tadadewa okinai.
Even when he suffers failure, he turns it into success.

ころがる［転(ころ)がる］ ■ *korogaru* ■ to roll 

---

①ものが、水平面(すいへいめん)や斜面(しゃめん)を**回転(かいてん)しながら進(すす)む**ことです（例(れい)7, 8)。

To roll on an even surface or down a slope (ex.7, 8).

②「転(ころ)がっている」という形(かたち)で、ものがその辺(へん)に無造作(むぞうさ)にある・**身近(みぢか)にいくらでもある**というとき使(つか)います（例(れい)9, 10)。

Korogatte iru describes a situation in which something is scattered about or easily found all over (ex.9, 10).

---

7) 坂道(さかみち)をボールが転(ころ)がる。
Sakamichio booruga korogaru.

A ball is rolling down the slope.

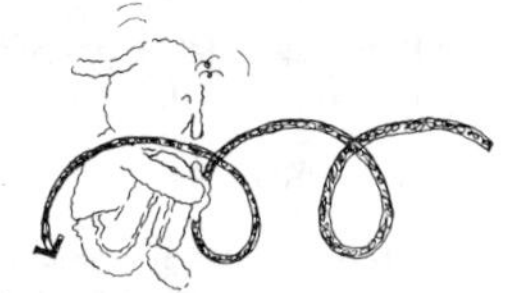

8) 空き缶が風に吹かれて転がっていく。
Akikanga kazeni fukarete korogatteiku.
An empty can is rolling about in the wind.

9) きみの部屋はちらかっているね。そこら中に物が転がっているよ。
Kimino heyawa chirakatteirune. Sokorajuuni monoga korogatteiruyo.
Your room is so messy. Things are scattered everywhere.

10) チャンスなんてどこに転がっているか、わからない。
Chansunante dokoni korogatteiruka, wakaranai.
Opportunities are everywhere; (you) just don't notice them.

さいごまで／あくまで

■ *saigomade* ■ *akumade*

さいごまで［最後まで］ ■ *saigomade* ■ until the end 

続いていたことが終わりになるときまで、という意味です。**時間の限界点・到達点に重点があります**（例1, 2, 3, 4, 5）。
Saigomade indicates that an action continues until its conclusion. Emphasis is placed on a time limit or point of conclusion (ex.1, 2, 3, 4, 5).

---

1) 私は、源氏物語を最後まで読んだことはない。
*Watashiwa, Genji-monogatari*o saigomade yonda kotowa nai.*
I've never read *Genji-Monogatari* to its conclusion.
——* A famous novel written by Murasaki Shikibu in the mid-Heian period (early 11th century)

2) 昨日のボクシングの試合は、最後まで結果がわからなかった。
Kinoono bokushinguno shiaiwa, saigomade kekkaga wakaranakatta.
All the way through yesterday's boxing match (I) couldn't tell who would win.

3) 一度引き受けた仕事は、つらくても最後までやらなければならない。
Ichido hikiuketa shigotowa, tsurakutemo saigomade yaranakereba-naranai.

Once you start a project you must see it through to the end, no matter how difficult it becomes.

4) 彼は、昨日最後まで教室に残っていた。

Karewa, kinoo saigomade kyooshitsuni nokotteita.

He stayed in the classroom to the very end yesterday.

5) 彼女は、いつも人の話を最後まで聞かないで、自分の意見を言う。

Kanojowa, itsumo hitono hanashio saigomade kikanaide, jibunno iken-o yuu.

She always throws in her own opinions, without letting people finish what they have to say.

あくまで ■*akumade* ■to the last 

①自分の**意見**や**考え**を、反対や障害があっても**変えないで保ち続ける**ようすを述べるとき使います(例6, 7, 8)。「最後まで」は単に終わりの時点までということを表し、「あくまで」は決して変えない**強い意志や決心**を表します。

Akumade is used when one expresses that he will maintain his opinion or way of thinking despite opposition or obstacle (ex.6, 7, 8). While *saigo made* simply means 'until the end point', *akumade* expresses unchanging will or determination.

②例9, 10のように、ことがらを「〜であることに変わりはない」と強調するとき使います。「あくまでも」と使うこともあります。

In Examples 9 and 10 it is used to emphasize that something will not change, and is sometimes said as *akumade mo.*

---

6) 私はあくまで暴力には反対だ。

Watashiwa akumade booryokuniwa hantaida.

I'm firmly against the use of violence.

7) 彼はあくまで自分が正しいと主張した。

Karewa akumade jibunga tadashiito shuchooshita.

He insisted he was right until the end.

8) 私はあくまでも彼女の無実を信じている。

Watashiwa akumademo kanojono mujitsuo shinjiteiru.

I firmly believe in her innocence.

9) 高原(こうげん)の風(かぜ)は涼(すず)しく、湖(みずうみ)はあくまでも青(あお)く澄(す)んでいた。

Koogenno kazewa suzushiku, mizuumiwa akumademo aoku sundeita.
The wind on the plateau is cool, and the lake water is always a clear blue.

10) これはあくまで私個人(わたしこじん)の意見(いけん)ですが、今回(こんかい)の契約(けいやく)は、もう少(すこ)し調(しら)べてからのほうがいいのでは……。

Korewa akumade watashi kojinno ikendesuga, konkaino keiyakuwa, moosukoshi shirabetekarano hooga iinodewa...
This is just my opinion, but don't (you) think we should check into this contract a bit further?

～さえ／～だって

■ ～*sae*　　■ ～*datte*

～さえ ■ ～*sae* ■ even

①ことがらの限度(げんど)・限界(げんかい)を表(あらわ)し、続(つづ)けて述(の)べる語(ご)（ことがら）を強調(きょうちょう)するとき使(つか)います（例(れい)1, 2, 3, 4）。非難(ひなん)や驚(おどろ)きを含(ふく)むこともあります。

The word ～*sae* defines the limits of something, and is used to emphasize the statement made following it. It may imply a feeling of surprise or blame (ex.1, 2, 3, 4).

②「～さえ～ば」という形(かたち)で、**最低限満(さいていげんみ)たされればよい条件(じょうけん)**を表(あらわ)します（例(れい)5, 6, 7, 8）。

The expression ～*sae*～*ba* is used when indicating the minimum standard that must be met for a favorable condition to result (ex.5, 6, 7, 8).

1) こんな漢字(かんじ)は小学生(しょうがくせい)でさえ書(か)けるのに、おとなのあなたが書(か)けないなんて恥(は)ずかしいですよ。

Konna kanjiwa shoogakuseidesae kakerunoni, otonano anataga kakenainante hazukashiidesuyo.
Any elementary school student can write this *kanji* character. You should be ashamed that you, an adult, can't write it yourself.

2) 今(いま)でさえ忙(いそが)しいのにもう１人(ひとり)家族(かぞく)が増(ふ)えたらどうしよう。
Imadesae isogashiinoni moohitori kazokuga fuetara dooshiyoo.
(I'm) busy enough as I am, so I don't know what I'll do if there is one more addition to my family.

3) 東京(とうきょう)まで電車(でんしゃ)でさえ１時間(じかん)かかるのに、歩(ある)いてなんか行(い)けない。
Tookyoomade denshadesae ichijikan kakarunoni, aruitenanka ikenai.
It takes an hour to get to Tokyo even by train, so there is no way (I) can walk there.

4) けさは東京(とうきょう)でさえこんなに寒(さむ)いんだから、北海道(ほっかいどう)はどんなだろう。
Kesawa Tookyoodesae konnani samuindakara, Hokkaidoowa donnadaroo.
If it's this cold even in Tokyo this morning, (I) wonder what Hokkaido is like.

5) あなたさえよければ、すぐ出(で)かけられます。
Anatasae yokereba, sugu dekakeraremasu.
If you are ready, we can leave right away.

6) 人間(にんげん)は水(みず)さえあれば３～４日(よっか)は生(い)きられるそうです。
Ningenwa mizusae areba san-yokkawa ikirarerusoodesu.
It is said that, if he has water, a human being can live (without eating) for three or four days.

7) あと歴史(れきし)の勉強(べんきょう)さえ終(お)われば試験勉強(しけんべんきょう)は完全(かんぜん)だ。
Ato rekishino benkyoosae owareba shiken-benkyoowa kanzenda!
If (I) just finish up my history studies, I'll be completely done studying for the test!

8) あなたの愛(あい)さえあれば何(なに)もいらない。
Anatano aisaeareba nanimo iranai.
If (I) have your love, I need nothing more.

～だって

■ *~datte*
■ too ; either

「～だって」の前(まえ)のものごとも**例外(れいがい)ではない**ということを表(あらわ)します。また「～さえ」と同(おな)じように、極端(きょくたん)な例(れい)を示(しめ)して、強調(きょうちょう)することもあります（例(れい)9, 10, 11, 12)。
This indicates that what is said before *datte* is not considered to be unusual or exceptional. It may be used like *sae* when giving an extreme example regarding the nature or makeup of something (ex.9, 10, 11, 12).

9) あの人にできたんだから、私にだってできないはずはない。
Ano hitoni dekitandakara, watashinidatte dekinai hazuwa nai.
He could do it, so I'm sure I can do it, too.

10) ビデオの使い方なんて、子供だって知っている。
Bideono tsukaikatanante, kodomodatte shitteiru.
Even a child knows how to use a VCR.

11) 赤ちゃんだって泳ぐんだから、あなただって泳げるはずです。
Akachandatte oyogundakara, anatadatte oyogeru-hazudesu.
If a baby can swim, you should be able to swim as well.

12) この頃彼女は料理に夢中で、パンだって自分で焼いているそうだ。
Konogoro kanojowa ryoorini muchuude, pandatte jibunde yaiteirusooda.
Recently, she has become very interested in cooking. I hear she even cooks her own bread.

さがす／さぐる／あさる

■ *sagasu* ■ *saguru* ■ *asaru*

さがす［捜す・探す］ ■ *sagasu* ■ to look for

なくしたものや**見失ったもの**、**欲しいもの**あるいは**人**を**見つけようとする**ことです。なくしたもの・見えなくなったものは「捜す」と書き（例1, 2, 3）、欲しいものには「探す」を使います（例4, 5）。

To look for someone or something that is missing, out of sight, or desired. When looking for something that is missing, the *kanji* 捜す is used (ex.1, 2, 3); when looking for something one desires, 探す is used (ex.4, 5).

1) 警察は、きのうの事故の目撃者を捜している。
Keesatsuwa, kinoono jikono mokugekishao sagashiteiru.
The police are looking for witnesses to yesterday's accident.

2) 私の大切な手帳が、いくら捜しても見つからない。
Watashino taisetsuna techooga, ikura sagashitemo mitsukaranai.
No matter where I look, I can't find my important notebook.

3) コンタクトレンズを落とすと、捜すのが大変だ。
Kontakuto-renzuo otosuto, sagasunoga taihenda.
When (you) drop a contact lens, it's a real pain to look for it.

4) 私はこの服に合う靴を探して、靴屋を何軒も見て歩いた。
Watashiwa kono fukuni au kutsuo sagashite, kutsuyao nangenmo mitearuita.
I went from shoe store to shoe store, looking for shoes that would match this outfit.

5) 彼は失業したので、今新しい仕事を探している。
Karewa shitsugyoo-shitanode, ima atarashii shigotoo sagashiteiru.
He lost his job and is looking for a new one now.

さぐる［探る］

■ *saguru*
■ to search for ; to feel for ; to explore 

---

①暗がりやポケットの中など**見えないところ**のものを、**手**や**足**でさわりながら**見つけようとする**ことです（例6, 7, 8)。

To search for something which cannot be seen by feeling around for it with one's hand or foot (in the darkness, in a pocket, etc.)(ex.6, 7, 8).

②相手に気づかれないように、相手のようすや事情、あるいは**情報**などを**こっそりと調べる**ことです（例9, 10)。

To secretly examine or investigate someone else (ex.9, 10).

---

6) 暗いところでかぎを落としたので、手で探って見つけた。
Kurai tokorode kagio otoshitanode, tede sagutte mitsuketa.
(I) dropped my key in a dark place, and I found it by feeling around with my hand.

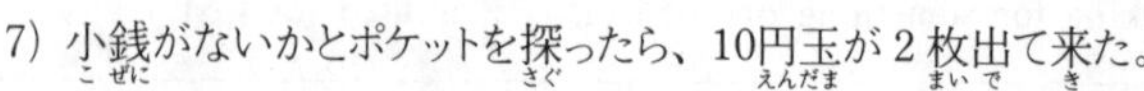

7) 小銭がないかとポケットを探ったら、10円玉が２枚出て来た。
Kozeniga naikato pokettoo saguttara, juuendamaga nimai detekita.
(I) checked my pocket to see if I had any change and I came up with two ten yen coins.

8) 彼は、急に深くなっているところはないかと、足で探りながら川を渡った。
Karewa, kyuuni fukaku natteiru tokorowa naikato, ashideségurinagara kawao watatta.

He kept checking the depth of the river with his feet while crossing in case there was a sudden drop.

9) 彼女はすぐに他人の秘密を探ろうとする。
Kanojowa suguni taninno himitsuo sagurooto suru.
She is always trying to find out other people's secrets.

10) 私は彼の本心を探ろうとしたけれど、結局わからなかった。
Watashiwa kareno honshin-o sagurooto shitakeredo, kekkyoku wakaranakatta.
I tried to find out what he was really thinking, but in the end, I couldn't.

あさる

■ *asaru*
■ to hunt for ; to scrounge

欲しいものを手に入れようと、**あちらこちら探しまわる**ことです。「えさをあさる」というのが本来の使い方です。ですから、人の行動に使うと「いやしい・下品だ」または「本能のまま」というような感じがします（例11, 12, 13)。

To search all over for something one wants. The original usage came from the phrase *esa o asaru*, which means 'to search for food' (as of animals, birds, etc.); therefore, when used to describe a person, it gives the impression that the person is vulgar, mean or is almost obsessed with finding the object, as if guided by animal instinct (ex.11, 12, 13).

---

11) のら猫がゴミ置き場でえさをあさっている。
Noranekoga gomiokibade esao asatteiru.
Stray cats are scavenging for food in the trash dump.

12) おなかがすいて眠れないので、夜中に台所へ行き、冷蔵庫をあさった。
Onakaga suite nemurenainode, yonakani daidokoroe iki, reizookoo asatta.
In the middle of the night (I) was so hungry that I couldn't sleep, so I went to the kitchen and scrounged around in the refrigerator.

13) どろぼうが、うちじゅうをあさって、お金や宝石を全部とっていってしまった。
Dorobooga, uchijuuo asatte, okaneya hoosekio zenbu totteitteshimatta.
The thief ransacked the entire house, making off with all the money and jewelry.

さかんに／しきりに

■ *sakan ni* ■ *shikirini*

さかんに ［盛んに］ ■ *sakan ni* ■ greatly ; vigorously

ものごとの程度が強い・大きい・激しいというようすを表します。「熱心だ・とても・大いに」などのように、そのものごと自体の**勢いや盛り上がり**を表します（例1, 2, 3, 4, 5）。

Sakan ni indicates that the degree of something is strong, great, or severe. Like *nesshin da*, *totemo*, *ooini* etc., it expresses a feeling of force or upsurge in something (ex.1, 2, 3, 4, 5).

1) 資源の再利用ということが、このごろさかんに言われている。
Shigenno sairiyooto yuu kotoga, konogoro sakanni iwareteiru.
There has been more and more talk about recycling lately.

2) 近頃あの会社では、新製品の宣伝をさかんにしている。
Chikagoro ano kaishadewa, shinseihinno senden-o sakanni shiteiru.
Recently, that company has been doing extensive advertising about their new product.

3) 彼はお気に入りの選手に、さかんに声援を送った。
Karewa okiniirino senshuni, sakanni seien-o okutta.
He vigorously cheered on his favorite athlete.

4) 彼女は、先日のコンサートがすばらしかったと、さかんにほめていた。
Kanojowa, senjitsuno konsaatoga subarashikattato, sakanni hometeita.
She kept raving about that concert she went to the other day.

5) 子供たちはさかんに水しぶきを上げて泳いでいる。
Kodomotachiwa sakanni mizushibukio agete oyoideiru.
The children are splashing vigorously while swimming.

しきりに ■ *shikirini* ■ frequently ; repeatedly

同じことを、**何度も何度もくり返す**ようすや、**切れ間がないようす**を表します

(例6, 7, 8, 9, 10)。それが、熱心さや程度の強さを表すこともあります。けれどもふつう「さかんに」は、ことがらに対する熱心さや、ものごとの盛り上がりを表し、「しきりに」は行われる回数の多さを表します。

Shikirini indicates that something is done repeatedly or unceasingly (ex.6, 7, 8, 9, 10). There are times when it may indicate eagerness or strength, but usually *sakan ni* expresses degree, while *shikirini* expresses the great number of times something is done.

---

6) デートに1時間遅れて来た彼は、しきりに謝った。
Deetoni ichijikan okuretekita karewa, shikirini ayamatta.
He kept apologizing for being an hour late for the date.

7) 初めてめがねをかけた息子は、気にしてしきりに手をやっている。
Hajimete meganeo kaketa musukowa, kinishite shikirini teo yatteiru.
My son, who has his first pair of glasses, is very conscious about them and keeps fiddling with them.

8) 朝から雨がしきりに降っている。
Asakara amega shikirini futteiru.
It's been raining non-stop since morning.

9) 兄はしきりに留学したがっています。
Aniwa shikirini ryuugaku-shitagatteimasu.
My (elder) brother keeps saying how much he wants to go abroad to study.

10) 子供がしきりに欲しがるので、きのうスケート靴を買ってやりました。
Kodomoga shikirini hoshigarunode, kinoo sukeetogutsuo katteyarimashita.
My child keeps saying he wants to have skates, so (I) decided to buy them yesterday.

さけぶ/どなる

■ *sakebu*　■ *donaru*

さけぶ [叫ぶ]

■ *sakebu*
■ to shout ; to scream 

---

①大きな声を出すことです(例1, 2, 3)。特定の相手がいなくても、**驚いたり・**

怖かったり、または**うれしかったり**など、**感情を思いきり表すときに大きな声を出して**しまうことも「さけぶ」と使います。

To shout or cry out in a loud voice (ex.1, 2, 3). It is used when giving vent to strong emotions in a loud voice, i.e., expressing surprise, fear, joy, etc. A listener need not be present.

②**世の中に対して、**何かを**強く主張する・訴える**とき使います（例4, 5)。

To advocate, plead, or make a strong public appeal (ex.4, 5).

---

1) 彼は「火事だ」と叫びながら、家の外へ飛び出した。
Karewa "Kajida!" to sakebinagara, ieno sotoe tobidashita.
He dashed out of the house screaming "Fire!"

2) 山道で大きなへびを見て、思わず「キャー」と叫んでしまった。
Yamamichide ookina hebio mite, omowazu "Kyaa!" to sakendeshimatta.
(I) couldn't help screaming "Eek!" when I saw a big snake on the mountain trail.

3) どんなに叫んでも、だれも助けに来てくれなかった。
Donnani sakendemo, daremo tasukeni kite kurenakatta.
No matter how much (I) shouted, nobody came to help me.

4) 私たちは戦争反対を叫び続けている。
Watashitachiwa sensoohantaio sakebi-tsuzuketeiru.
We continue to cry out against war.

5) 近頃、環境問題について、さかんに叫ばれている。
Chikagoro, kankyoomondaini tsuite, sakanni sakebareteiru.
These days everyone is raising a clamor about environmental problems.

どなる

■ *donaru*
■ to yell (at) ; to scold

大きな声で、相手を**叱りつける**ことです(例 6, 7, 8)。また、怒ったように大きな声で話すときにも使います（例９)。

To rebuke or scold someone severely in a loud voice (ex.6, 7, 8). Also, to speak angrily in a loud voice (ex.9).

---

6) あの先生は、気に入らないことがあるとすぐ生徒をどなる。

Ano senseiwa, kiniiranai kotoga aruto sugu seitoo donaru.
That teacher yells at his students whenever something doesn't suit him.

7) 夜中に大声で歌をうたったら、隣の人に「うるさい」とどなられた。
Yonakani oogoede utao utattara, tonarino hitoni "Urusai!"to donarareta.
When (I) sang too loudly in the middle of the night, my neighbor yelled at me to shut up.

8) 兄は、父の車を勝手に動かしてぶつけてしまい、父にどなられた。
Aniwa, chichino kurumao katteni ugokashite butsuketeshimai, chichini donarareta.
My (elder) brother got yelled at by my dad when he drove his car without permission and ran into something.

9) そんなに大声でどならなくても、ちゃんと聞こえますよ。
Sonnani oogoede donaranakutemo, chanto kikoemasuyo.
(You) don't have to shout so loud—(I) can hear you just fine.

さげる／かける／つる／つるす

■*sageru* ■*kakeru* ■*tsuru* ■*tsurusu*

さげる［下げる］ ■*sageru* ■to hang

ものの上の部分を固定して、上から下へたらすことです。また、かばんなどのように、ものの上の一部分を手に持つ場合にも使い、「提げる」と書きます（例1, 2, 3, 4, 5）。

To fix an object at the top so that the remaining part hangs freely. *Sageru* is also used to describe holding the upper part of an object, such as a bag or suitcase, in one's hand; in this case, it is written 提げる (ex.1, 2, 3, 4, 5).

1) この教室では、天井からスクリーンを下げて、スライドを映せる。
Kono kyooshitsudewa, tenjookara sukuriin-o sagete, suraidoo utsuseru.
They've set this classroom up so they can show slides by hanging a screen from the ceiling.

2) 彼女(かのじょ)は胸(むね)にペンダントを下(さ)げている。
Kanojowa muneni pendantoo sageteiru.
She is wearing a pendant on her chest.

3) 肩(かた)からカメラを下(さ)げているのが、私(わたし)のおじです。
Katakara kamerao sageteirunoga, watashino ojidesu.
The person with a camera hanging from his shoulder is my uncle.

4) おつかいに行(い)っていた母(はは)が、両手(りょうて)に重(おも)い買(か)い物袋(ものぶくろ)を提(さ)げて帰(かえ)ってきた。
Otsukaini itteita hahaga, ryooteni omoi kaimono-bukuroo sagete kaette kita.
My mother, who had been shopping, came home carrying a heavy shopping bag in each hand.

5) 父(ちち)は、会社(かいしゃ)に行(い)く時(とき)は、いつもかばんを提(さ)げて行(い)く。
Chichiwa, kaishani iku tokiwa, itsumo kaban-o sageteiku.
My dad always carries a briefcase when he goes to the office.

かける［掛(か)ける］

■ *kakeru*
■ to hang ; to hook (on) 

ものをある**ものの上(うえ)にかぶせる(載(の)せる)ようにして固定(こてい)する**ことです。たれ下(さ)がるようにするのが目的(もくてき)ではなく、**落(お)ちないように・はずれないように組(く)み合(あ)わせてとめる**、という感(かん)じを含(ふく)んでいます（例(れい)6, 7, 8, 9, 10, 11）。

To secure an object by hanging or hooking a portion of it over the top of something else. The objective is not to allow it to dangle, but to prevent it from falling or coming off (ex.6, 7, 8, 9, 10, 11).

---

6) 花(はな)の絵(え)を掛(か)けたら、部屋(へや)が明(あか)るくなった。
Hananoeo kaketara, heyaga akaruku natta.
The room became brighter when (I) hung a picture of flowers on the wall.

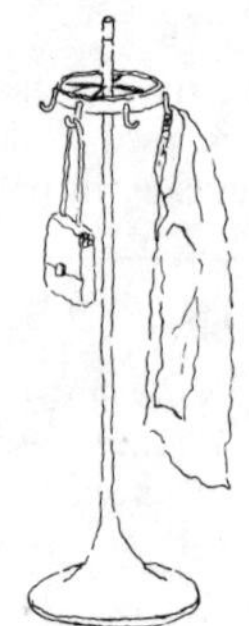

7) ぬいだ上着(うわぎ)はハンガーに掛(か)けておいてください。
Nuida uwagiwa hangaani kaketeoite kudasai.
Please hang the coat (you) took off on a hanger.

8) 窓(まど)にレースのカーテンを掛(か)けました。
Madoni reesuno kaaten-o kakemashita.
(I) hung a lace curtain on the window.

9) 私(わたし)の父(ちち)はめがねを掛(か)けている。
Watashino chichiwa meganeo kaketeiru.
My father is wearing glasses.

10) 新(あたら)しい家(いえ)の玄関(げんかん)に、「村上(むらかみ)」という表札(ひょうさつ)が掛(か)けてあった。
Atarashii ieno genkanni, 'Murakami' to yuu hyoosatsuga kaketeatta.
A nameplate reading 'Murakami' was on the front door of the newly completed house.

11) 祖母(そぼ)はいつも肩(かた)にショールを掛(か)けていた。
Sobowa itsumo katani shooruo kaketeita.
My grandmother always wears a shawl around her shoulders.

つる［吊(つ)る］

■ *tsuru*
■ to hang ; to suspend ; to sling 

ものが落(お)ちないように、あるいはその位置(いち)を保(たも)つように**上(うえ)から引(ひ)き上(あ)げるように固定(こてい)する**ことです（例(れい)12, 13, 14, 15）。

To raise and fix something so that it stays in place or doesn't fall (ex.12, 13, 14, 15).

---

12) 夏(なつ)、木(こ)かげにハンモックをつって昼寝(ひるね)をするのは気持(きも)ちがいい。
Natsu, kokageni hanmokkuo tsutte hiruneo surunowa kimochiga ii.
In the summer it feels good to nap in a hammock hung in the shade of the trees.

13) 博物館(はくぶつかん)に、恐竜(きょうりゅう)の模型(もけい)がピアノ線(せん)でつって展示(てんじ)してあった。
Hakubutsukanni, kyooryuuno mokeiga pianosende tsutte tenjishiteatta.
There was a model of a dinosaur suspended by piano strings in the museum.

14) 有名(ゆうめい)な俳優(はいゆう)がゆうべ、近(ちか)くのマンションで首(くび)をつって、死体(したい)で見(み)つかったことは今朝(けさ)のニュースで知(し)った。
Yuumeina haiyuuga yuube, chikakuno manshonde kubio tsutte, shitaide mitsukatta kotowa kesano nyuusude shitta.
(I) learned on this morning's news that a famous actor hung himself last night and was found dead in a condominium nearby.

15) 彼(かれ)は右腕(みぎうで)を骨折(こっせつ)したので、三角巾(さんかくきん)で腕(うで)をつっている。

Karewa migiudeo kossetsushitanode, sankakukinde udeo tsutteiru.
He broke his right arm, so he's got it in a sling.

つるす［吊す］

■ *tsurusu*
■ to hang ; to suspend

もののうえ上のほう方をとめて、うえ上から した下にたれ さ下がるようにすることです。おお多くの ばあい場合、ものがゆれ うご動くような じょうたい状態になります（れい例16, 17, 18, 19）。

To pin or fasten an object at its top so that it hangs vertically. In most cases the object sways or dangles (ex.16, 17, 18, 19).

16) うちでは、あめ雨の ひ日は せんたくもの洗濯物をロープにつるして へや部屋の なか中に ほ干します。

Uchidewa, ameno hiwa sentakumonoo roopuni tsurushite heyano nakani hoshimasu.
In my house, we hang our laundry to dry on a rope inside on rainy days.

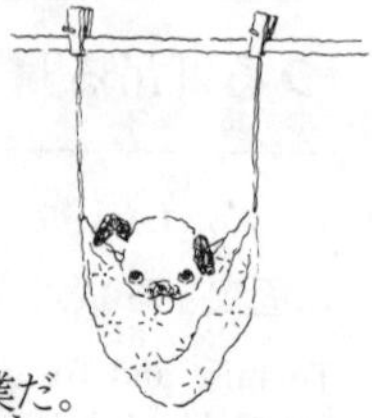

17) ビルにゴンドラをつるして まど窓をふくのは、とても きけん危険な さぎょう作業だ。

Biruni gondorao tsurushite madoo fukunowa, totemo kikenna sagyooda.
Cleaning the windows on a scaffold hanging from the side of a building is very dangerous work.

18) むかし昔、いなか田舎の じっか実家の のきした軒下に かき柿をつるして ほ干してあった ふゆ冬の ふうけい風景を、いま今でも なつ懐かしく おも思い だ出します。

Mukashi, inakano jikkano nokishitani kakio tsurushite hoshiteatta fuyuno fuukeio, imademo natsukashiku omoidashimasu.
Even today, (I) fondly remember the way my childhood home in the country looked in the winter, with persimmons drying under the eaves.

19) クリスマスツリーに、かざりをたくさんつるしました。

Kurisumasu-tsuriini, kazario takusan tsurushimashita.
(We) hung many ornaments on the Christmas tree.

さぞ／よほど

■ *sazo* ■ *yohodo*

さぞ
■ *sazo*
■ surely ; must

自分がまだ経験していないことや、相手のようす、気持ちなどに「**きっと・とても〜だろう**」などと**共感したり**推量することです（例1, 2, 3, 4, 5）。推量なので「〜だろう・〜でしょう・〜にちがいない」などといっしょに使います。

Sazo is used when speculating about something which one has not experienced or about someone else's feelings or appearance (ex.1, 2, 3, 4, 5). Since it is speculation, it is often used with such expressions as *〜daroo*, *〜deshoo* and *〜ni chigainai.*

1) 彼は息子が産まれて、さぞ喜んでいるでしょう。
Karewa musukoga umarete, sazo yorokonde-irudeshoo.
With the birth of a son, he must be quite happy.

2) 火事で家が焼けたんですって、さぞお困りでしょう。
Kajide iega yaketandesutte? Sazo okomarideshoo.
(I) heard (your) house burned down; you must really be in a bind.

3) 宇宙から地球を見たら、さぞきれいだろう。
Uchuukara chikyuuo mitara, sazo kireidaroo.
The earth must be very beautiful when viewed from space.

4) 川で釣ったばかりの魚を焼いて食べるなんて、さぞおいしいにちがいない。
Kawade tsuttabakarino sakanao yaite taberunante, sazo oishiini chigainai.
It must certainly be delicious to eat a grilled fish freshly caught from a river.

5) 彼女は、御主人を亡くしてさぞ悲しいことでしょう。
Kanojowa, goshujin-o nakushite sazo kanashiikotodeshoo.
She must be so grieved at having lost her husband.

よほど
■ *yohodo*
■ greatly , much

①ふつう考えられることや**予想より**もずっと**程度が上だ・範囲を超えている**というとき使います（例6, 7, 8, 9, 10）。

Yohodo denotes that something is of a much higher degree or greater extent than was expected or is usually considered possible (ex.6, 7, 8, 9, 10).

②もう少しで何かをしようと強く思ったけれど、実行しなかったとき使います（例11, 12)。「よっぽど」は話しことばで多く使われ、少し強調した言い方です。

It is also used when one had been on the very verge of doing something but did not carry it out (ex.11, 12). Colloquially, the slightly stronger *yoppodo* is often used.

---

6) よほどのことがない限り、あしたの同窓会には出席します。

Yohodono kotoga naikagiri, ashitano doosookainiwa shussekishimasu.
If there's nothing out of the ordinary tomorrow, (I'm) going to attend my class reunion.

7) 彼と仕事をするのなら、よほどの忍耐力がなければ無理だ。

Kareto shigotoo surunonara, yohodono nintairyokuga nakereba murida.
If (you're) going to be working with him you have to be extra patient, or things won't go well at all.

8) あの子が泣くなんて、よほどくやしかったにちがいない。

Ano koga nakunante, yohodo kuyashikattani chigainai.
For her to cry, she must have been really frustrated, you can be sure.

9) おぼれている人を助けるのは、よほど泳ぎが上手でなければ難しい。

Oboreteiru hitoo tasukerunowa, yohodo oyogiga joozudenakereba muzukashii.
Saving a drowning person is difficult if (you're) not extremely good at swimming.

10) あんな歌手よりも、私のほうがよっぽど歌がうまい。

Anna kashuyorimo, watashinohooga yoppodo utaga umai.
I'm a lot better at singing than that singer is.

11) よほど真実を打ちあけようかと思ったけれど、今はやめておいた。

Yohodo shinjitsuo uchiakeyookato omottakeredo, imawa yameteoita.
(I) really intended to tell (him) the truth, but now I've thought better of it.

12) あんなやつ、よっぽどなぐってやろうかと思ったよ。

Anna yatsu, yoppodo nagutteyarookato omottayo.
That jerk! (I) really wanted to punch (him) out.

さっそく／すぐ

■*sassoku*　■*sugu*

さっそく ■*sassoku* ■at once

あることがらに対して、**時間をおかずに何かをする**ようすを表すとき使います。人の意識的な行動に使います（例1, 2, 3, 4）。

Sassoku expresses a condition in which one does something without delay. It is used when speaking of the deliberate actions of people (ex.1, 2, 3, 4).

1) 彼女に頼んでおいた本が届いたので、昨日さっそくお礼の電話をしました。
Kanojoni tanondeoita honga todoitanode, kinoo sassoku oreino denwao shimashita.
The book (I) asked her for arrived, and I called to thank her at once yesterday.

2) 皆さんそろったので、さっそくですが会議を始めます。
Minasan sorottanode, sassokudesuga kaigio hajimemasu.
Since everybody is together (we'll) start the meeting now.

3) 彼は事務所へ来ると、さっそく仕事に取りかかった。
Karewa jimushoe kuruto, sassoku shigotoni torikakatta.
He began to work the moment he arrived in the office.

4) テレビで見た料理を、さっそく今夜作ってみます。
Terebide mita ryoorio, sassoku kon-ya tsukuttemimasu.
Tonight, (I'll) get right to making the dish I saw on the TV.

すぐ ■*sugu* ■immediately ; at once

あることがらと次のことがらの間の**時間が短い**ようすを表すとき使います。**簡単に・らくに・安易に**という意味も含みます（例5, 6, 7, 8, 9, 10）。また、距離の近さを表して使うこともあります（例11, 12）。

Sugu is used to express that there is little time between one action and the next. It may take the same meaning as *kantan ni*, *raku ni* and *an-i ni* (easily)(ex.5, 6, 7, 8, 9, 10). It may also express shortness in distance (ex.11, 12).

5) 連絡(れんらく)があったらすぐ出(で)かけられるように、準備(じゅんび)しておいてください。
Renrakuga attara sugu dekakerareru-yooni, junbishiteoite kudasai.
Please get ready so that (you) are able to leave as soon as you get word.

6) これはインスタント食品(しょくひん)ですから、温(あたた)めればすぐ食(た)べられます。
Korewa insutanto-shokuhindesukara, atatamereba sugu taberaremasu.
This is instant food so (you) can eat it immediately after heating it.

7) 子供(こども)は、ベッドに入(はい)るとすぐ寝(ね)てしまった。
Kodomowa, beddoni hairuto sugu neteshimatta.
The child fell asleep as soon as he got into bed.

8) もうすぐ終(お)わりますから、ちょっと待(ま)ってください。
Moosugu owarimasukara, chotto mattekudasai.
(I'll) be done soon so please wait a minute.

9) 地図(ちず)があったので、彼(かれ)のうちはすぐにみつかった。
Chizuga attanode, kareno uchiwa suguni mitsukatta.
(I) had a map so I easily found his house.

10) あの人(ひと)は何(なに)か問題(もんだい)がおきると、すぐにひとのせいにしたがる。
Ano hitowa nanika mondaiga okiruto, suguni hitono seini shitagaru.
That guy wants to blame others as soon as there is a problem.

11) あなたが探(さが)している本(ほん)は、すぐ目(め)の前(まえ)の棚(たな)にありますよ。
Anataga sagashiteiru honwa, sugu meno maeno tanani arimasuyo.
The book you are looking for is on the shelf right in front of you.

12) 私(わたし)が通(かよ)った小学校(しょうがっこう)は、公園(こうえん)のすぐそばにあります。
Watashiga kayotta shoogakkoowa, kooenno sugu sobani arimasu.
The elementary school I used to go to is right next to the park.

さむい／つめたい／すずしい

■ *samui* ■ *tsumetai* ■ *suzushii*

さむい［寒(さむ)い］ ■ *samui* ■ cold 大

①**気温が低い**と**体に感じる**ことです（例1, 2, 3, 4）。不快感を表します。

Samui indicates that one feels unpleasantly cold because the air temperature is low (ex.1, 2, 3, 4).

②寒いと感じるぐらいに「**恐ろしい・空しい**」などの意味で使います（例５）。

It is also used when one feels 'cold' due to emotions of fear or emptiness (ex.5).

---

1) 北国の冬はとても寒い。
Kitagunino fuyuwa totemo samui.
Winter in the northern countries is very cold.

2) 外は寒いから、コートを着て行ったほうがいいよ。
Sotowa samuikara, kootoo kiteitta hooga iiyo.
It's cold outside, so (you) should go wearing a coat.

3) 寒くてもスポーツをすれば体が温まる。
Samukutemo supootsuo sureba karadaga atatamaru.
Even if it's cold, your body will warm up if you play sports.

4) 寒い朝は、起きるのがつらい。
Samui asawa, okirunoga tsurai.
It's hard to get up on cold mornings.

5) 事故のようすを聞いて、背すじが寒くなった。
Jikono yoosuo kiite, sesujiga samuku natta.
When (I) heard about the accident, a chill ran up my spine.

つめたい ［冷たい］ ■*tsumetai* ■cold 大

---

①**ものの温度**がとても**低い**ことです。その「冷たさ」が気持ち良いとき（例6, 7）も、そうでないとき（例8, 9）も、両方使います。

Tsumetai expresses that the temperature of an object is cold. The sensation of coldness may be either pleasant (ex.6, 7) or unpleasant (ex.8, 9) to the speaker.

②相手に対する**思いやり**や、人間としての**優しさがない心**や**態度**に使います（例10, 11）。

「寒い」は気温なので体全体で感じますが、「冷たい」は、「冷たいもの」に触れた手・指・足など体の一部で瞬間的に感じます。

Additionally, it indicates that someone is uncaring or without kindness toward others (ex.10, 11).
Since *samui* is used when referring to the temperature of the air, the coldness is felt with the whole body. On the other hand, *tsumetai* is a partial or momentary feeling, which concerns only a part of the body, such as hands, fingers, or toes.

---

6) 何か冷たいものが飲みたい。
Nanika tsumetaimonoga nomitai.
(I) want to drink something cold.

7) 熱があったので、冷たいタオルを額にあてたら気持ちが良かった。
Netsuga attanode, tsumetai taoruo hitaini atetara kimochiga yokatta.
(I) had a fever, so when I put a cold towel on my forehead it felt good.

8) 雪どけ水は冷たくて、手をつけていると痛くなる。
Yukidokemizuwa tsumetakute, teo tsuketeiruto itaku naru.
Water from melted snow is cold, so if (you) put your hands in it, it hurts.

9) 外は冷たい雨が降っている。
Sotowa tsumetai amega futteiru.
A cold rain is falling outside.

10) 彼はこのごろ冷たくなった。私が嫌いになったのだろうか。
Karewa konogoro tsumetaku natta. Watashiga kiraini nattano darooka.
He has become cold lately. I wonder if he doesn't love me anymore.

11) 友達を裏切るなんて、心の冷たい人だ。
Tomodachio uragirunante, kokorono tsumetai hitoda.
What a cold-hearted person (he) is to betray a friend.

すずしい［涼しい］ ■*suzushii* ■cool 大

高い気温が少し下がって体に気持ち良く感じられることです（例12, 13, 14, 15）。さわやかさを表します。「涼しい顔」というのは、自分には関係がないというような顔や、平気な顔をすることです（例16）。

Suzushii expresses the comfortable and relaxed feeling one has when hot temperature cools off a little (ex.12, 13, 14, 15). The expression *suzushii kao* means that one has an unconcerned look or a calm expression on his face (ex.16).

12) 森(もり)の中(なか)は、夏(なつ)でも涼(すず)しい。
Morino nakawa, natsudemo suzushii.
Even in the summer, it's nice and cool in the forest.

13) 風(かぜ)が涼(すず)しくて気持(きも)ちがいい。
Kazega suzushikute kimochiga ii.
The cool wind feels good.

14) 彼女(かのじょ)の水色(みずいろ)のシャツは涼(すず)しそうだ。
Kanojono mizu-irono shatsuwa suzushisooda.
Her pale blue shirt looks cool and comfortable.

15) 秋(あき)が近(ちか)づき、だんだん涼(すず)しくなってきた。
Akiga chikazuki, dandan suzushiku nattekita.
As autumn approached, it gradually became cooler.

16) 彼(かれ)は自分(じぶん)が悪(わる)いのに涼(すず)しい顔(かお)をしている。
Karewa jibunga waruinoni suzushii kaoo shiteiru.
Although he is the one that is at fault, he looks unconcerned.

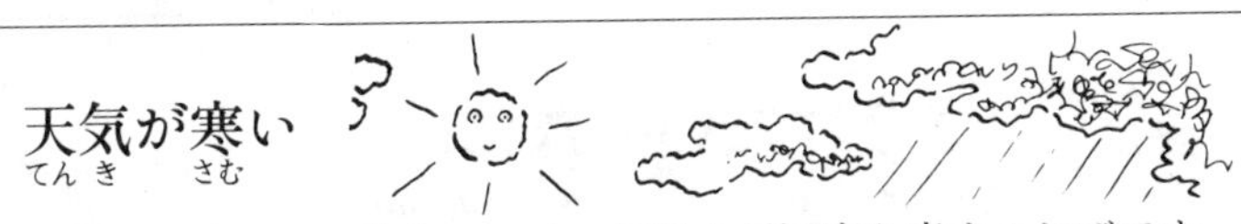

天気(てんき)が寒(さむ)い

「寒(さむ)い・涼(すず)しい・冷(つめ)たい」は、気温(きおん)など温度(おんど)を表(あらわ)すことばです。時々(ときどき)、気温(きおん)を天気(てんき)の一部(いちぶ)だと考(かんが)えて、「天気(てんき)が寒(さむ)い・天気(てんき)が涼(すず)しい・天気(てんき)が冷(つめ)たい」などと使(つか)う人(ひと)がいます。でもそれはまちがいです。天気(てんき)は「晴(は)れ・雨(あめ)・くもり」などの状態(じょうたい)で、「天気(てんき)がいい」のように「いい・悪(わる)い」で表(あらわ)します。けれども気温(きおん)について言(い)うときは、「きょうは寒(さむ)いですね」「南極(なんきょく)は1年中(ねんじゅう)寒(さむ)い」「涼(すず)しくて気持(きも)ちがいい」「風(かぜ)が冷(つめ)たい」のように、具体的(ぐたいてき)なものを指(さ)して表(あらわ)します。

Tenki ga samui[1]

Words such as *samui*, *suzushii*[2] and *tsumetai*[3] describe air temperature. You may sometimes hear someone say, *tenki ga samui*, *tenki ga suzushii*, or *tenki ga tsumetai* to describe the weather, however, these expressions are actually incorrect. *Tenki* refers to the weather being sunny, rainy or cloudy, which is expressed in terms of good or bad (*ii* or *warui*), i.e., *tenki ga ii*[4] or *tenki ga warui*[5]. On the other hand, when speaking about specific conditions such as the air temperature, sentences like '*Kyoo wa samui desu ne*[6],' '*Nankyoku wa ichinenjuu samui*[7],' '*Suzushikute kimochi ga ii*[8],' and '*Kaze ga tsumetai*[9]' are possible.

1 *This literally means 'The weather is cold'. However, this is incorrect Japanese. Samui means 'cold' in terms of climate, not weather.*
2 *'Cool' in terms of climate.*
3 *'Cold' to the touch, like a cold drink.*
4 *The weather is good (not rainy).*
5 *The weather is bad (rainy, stormy, windy, etc.).*
6 *It's cold today, isn't it?*
7 *It is cold all year long at the South Pole.*
8 *It is cool and feels good.*
9 *The wind is cold.*

さりげない／なにげない

■ *sarigenai* ■ *nanigenai*

さりげない

■ *sarigenai*
■ casual ; unconcerned 

自分の意図したことや行動を、まわりの人にはっきりと気づかせない**ひかえめなようす**を表します（例1, 2, 3, 4）。

Sarigenai indicates that one acts in an outwardly reserved manner, without letting his true intentions be known to others (ex.1, 2, 3, 4).

1) 彼女は、私が割ったコップをさりげなくかたづけてくれた。
Kanojowa, watashiga watta koppuo sarigenaku katazuketekureta.
She casually cleaned up the cup that I broke.

2) 彼は老人がエスカレーターにのるとき、さりげなく手をかした。
Karewa roojinga esukareetaani norutoki, sarigenaku teo kashita.
He casually helped the old man get on the escalator.

3) 「岸さんが来た」と、兄はさりげなく私に目で知らせてくれた。
'*Kishisanga kita*' *to, aniwa sarigenaku watashini mede shirasetekureta.*
My brother let me know with a nonchalant look that Mr. Kishi had arrived.

4) 林さんは、とても高価な食器をさりげなくふだんに使っている。
Hayashisanwa, totemo kookana shokkio sarigenaku fudanni tsukatteiru.
Mrs. Hayashi uses high priced china for everyday meals without thinking anything of it.

なにげない

■ *nanigenai*
■ casual

特に意識しないで行っているようすや、どうということのないようすを表します（例5, 6, 7, 8)。

Nanigenai indicates that one behaves in an unconcerned or unaware manner (ex.5, 6, 7, 8).

---

5) なにげなく買った雑誌に、友人の談話と写真があったのでびっくりした。
Nanigenaku katta zasshini, yuujinno danwato shashinga attanode bikkurishita.
(I) was surprised to see the interview and picture of my good friend in a magazine that I just happened to buy.

6) 仕事中になにげなく時計を見ると、もう12時だった。
Shigotochuuni nanigenaku tokeio miruto, moo juunijidatta.
(I) casually looked at the clock while working and found that it was already 12 o'clock.

7) なにげなく言ったことばが、人をきずつけることもある。
Nanigenaku itta kotobaga, hitoo kizutsukeru kotomo aru.
Even a casual remark might at times hurt somebody.

8) 私は、子供のなにげないことばに力づけられた。
Watashiwa, kodomono nanigenai kotobani chikarazukerareta.
I was cheered by the little things my child said.

さわる／ふれる

■*sawaru* ■*fureru*

さわる［触る・障る］ ■*sawaru* ■to touch ; to feel

①**何かに**、手あるいは体の一部が**接すること**、またはその逆のとき使います（例1, 2, 3, 4）。人が「さわる」ときは多くの場合、意識的な行動です。空気（気体）・電流のような形のないものには使いません。

To make contact with something with a hand or other part of the body, or the reverse (ex.1, 2, 3, 4). In most cases in which people are involved, the action is intentional. It may not be used when referring to contact made with shapeless things such as air, gases, or electrical current.

②**気分を害すること**です（例5, 6）。

To displease someone or hurt someone's feelings (ex.5, 6).

③ものごとの**じゃまや害になること**で（例7, 8）、「障る」と書きます。

To interfere with or harm something (ex.7, 8). The *kanji* 障る is used in this case.

1) アイロンが熱くなっているから、さわるとやけどをするよ。
Aironga atsuku natteirukara, sawaruto yakedoo suruyo.
The iron is hot, so if you touch it you'll get burned.

2) 私の人形にさわらないで。
Watashino ningyooni sawaranaide.
Don't touch my dolls.

3) 子供というのは、何でもさわりたがる。
Kodomoto yuunowa, nandemo sawaritagaru.
Children seem to like to touch things.

4) 桃はいたみやすいから、あまりさわってはいけません。
Momowa itamiyasuikara, amari sawattewa ikemasen.
Peaches are easily bruised, so (you) mustn't touch them too much.

5) あなたのためを思って忠告しますが、気にさわったらごめんなさい。

Anatano tameo omotte chuukoku shimasuga, kini sawattara gomennasai.
I'm giving you this warning for your own good; I'm sorry if I hurt you.

6) みんなが弟ばかりほめるものだから、ぼくはしゃくにさわった。

Minnaga ootootobakari homeru monodakara, bokuwa shakuni sawatta.
I was irritated because everybody was praising my brother.

7) あんまり興奮すると、体にさわりますよ。

Anmari koofunsuruto, karadani sawarimasuyo.
Too much excitement is bad for (you).

8) あしたの仕事にさわらないように、早く寝よう。

Ashitano shigotoni sawaranaiyooni, hayaku neyoo.
(I) think I'll go to bed early tonight so that I'm ready to work tomorrow.

ふれる［触れる］ ■*fureru* ■to touch

①何かに、手あるいは体の一部が接すること、またその逆のことです。ものとものが接するときにも使います。「さわる」よりも、「**軽く瞬間的に接する・意志的ではない**」という感じを含み、少し改まったことばです。空気（気体）や電流などを感じるときにも使います（例9, 10, 11）。

To make contact with something with a hand or other part of the body, or the reverse. It may also be used when two objects make contact. It is a slightly more formal expression than *sawaru*, and implies a lighter, more momentary and unintentional touch. It may be used when one feels things such as air, gases, or electrical current (ex.9, 10, 11).

②ものごとに何かの**かかわりをもつ**ことです（例12, 13, 14, 15）。

To have some kind of connection or relationship with something (ex.12, 13, 14, 15).

9) ネムノキの葉は、軽く手をふれただけで閉じてしまう。

Nemunokino hawa, karuku teo furetadakede tojiteshimau.
If (you) just lightly touch the leaves of a silk tree, they will close.

10) この美術館に展示してあるものに、手をふれないでください。

Kono bijutsukanni tenjishitearu mononi, teo furenaide kudasai.
Please don't touch the works on display in the art museum.

11) しばらく、外の空気にふれてこよう。
Shibaraku, sotono kuukini furetekoyoo.
Let's go out into the fresh air for a while.

12) 彼の温かい人柄にふれて、私は元気をとりもどした。
Kareno atatakai hitogarani furete, watashiwa genkio torimodoshita.
His warm personality cheered me up.

13) 海辺の家ですごした２週間、私は思う存分自然にふれることができた。
Umibeno iede sugoshita nishuukan, watashiwa omouzonbun shizenni fureru kotoga dekita.
During the two weeks that I stayed in the sea-side house, I was able to enjoy nature to my heart's content.

14) 彼には、人にふれられたくない過去がある。
Kareniwa, hitoni fureraretakunai kakoga aru.
He has a past that he would rather not have pried into.

15) 王の怒りにふれて、王女は城を追い出された。
Oono ikarini furete, oojowa shiroo oidasareta.
The princess was banished from the castle because she angered the king.

ざんねん／おしい

■ *zannen* ■ *oshii*

ざんねん［残念］ ■ *zannen* ■ regrettable

満足な結果にならなかったり、期待通りにならなかったりしたときの不満や、くやしさ・もの足りなさを表す気持ちです（例1, 2, 3, 4, 5）。相手の気持ちにこたえられなくて「申し訳ない」という意味も含みます。

This expresses a feeling of frustration or disappointment because something did not turn out satisfactorily, or as expected (ex.1, 2, 3, 4, 5). There may be an implied sense of apology on the part of the speaker for being unable to meet a counterpart's expectations.

1) 楽しみにしていた花火大会が、雨で中止になって残念だ。
Tanoshimini shiteita hanabitaikaiga, amede chuushini natte zannenda.
(I) was looking forward to the fireworks display very much, but it was unfortunately called off due to rain.

2) 風邪をひいて旅行に参加できなくなったのは残念だけれど、しかたがない。
Kazeo hiite ryokooni sankadekinaku-nattanowa zannendakeredo, shikataga nai.
It's too bad that (I) can't go on the trip because of my cold, but it just can't be helped.

3) 残念なことに、入学試験に落ちてしまいました。
Zannenna kotoni, nyuugaku-shikenni ochite-shimaimashita.
To (my) regret, I've failed the university entrance exam.

4) せっかく結婚式にご招待いただいたのに、伺えなくて残念です。
Sekkaku kekkonshikini goshootai-itadaitanoni, ukagaenakute zannendesu.
(I'm) honored that you have invited me to your wedding, but I'm afraid I can't come.

5) ご期待にそえなくて残念です。
Gokitaini soenakute zannendesu.
(I'm) sorry that I was unable to live up to your expectations.

おしい［惜しい］ ■*oshii* ■regrettable 

---

①もう少しで良い結果になるところだったのに、ならなかったことを、不満に思ったり、くやしく思ったりする気持ちです。「惜しくも・惜しいところで・惜しいことに」などの形で使うことが多いです（例6, 7, 8）。

Oshii is used when expressing feelings of frustration or disappointment because something that was very close to working out well does not in the end.
It is often used in the forms *oshikumo*, *oshii tokoro de*, and *oshii koto ni* (ex.6, 7, 8).

②大切なものを失ったり**無駄にしたくない**ということを表します。貴重だ、という意味を含みます（例9, 10, 11）。

It also is used when expressing that one does not want to lose or waste something important. It is implied that the speaker feels the object is valuable (ex.9, 10, 11).

---

6) 惜(お)しかったね、転(ころ)ばなければ君(きみ)が1着(ちゃく)だったのに。
Oshikattane! korobanakereba kimiga itchakudattanoni.
What a shame! If you wouldn't have fallen down you would have come in first.

7) めったにないチャンスを逃(の)がしてしまい、惜(お)しいことをしました。
Mettani nai chansuo nogashite-shimai, oshii kotoo shimashita.
Unfortunately, (I've) let a rare opportunity slip away.

8) せっかく作(つく)ったクッキーを、惜(お)しいことに焦(こ)がしてしまった。
Sekkaku tsukutta kukkiio, oshii kotoni kogashiteshimatta.
(I've) unfortunately burned the cookies I took so much trouble to make.

9) こんなくだらないことに私(わたし)の貴重(きちょう)な時間(じかん)を使(つか)うのは惜(お)しい。
Konna kudaranai kotoni watashino kichoona jikan-o tsukaunowa oshii.
It's a waste of my valuable time to do such trivial things.

10) この洗濯機(せんたくき)は型(かた)は古(ふる)いけれど、まだ使(つか)えるから捨(す)てるには惜(お)しい。
Kono sentakkiwa katawa furuikeredo, mada tsukaerukara suteruniwa oshii.
Although this washing machine is old, it still works, so it would be a waste to throw it away.

11) 住(す)みなれた家(いえ)を手放(てばな)すのは惜(お)しい。
Suminareta ieo tebanasunowa oshii.
It will be a shame to part with this dear old house.

しずか／おだやか

■ *shizuka* ■ *odayaka*

しずか［静(しず)か］ ■ *shizuka* ■ quiet 

---

①**うるさい音(おと)がしない**ようすです（例(れい)1, 2）。
Shizuka indicates an absence of loud or annoying noise (ex.1, 2).

②落(お)ち着(つ)いていて、おとなしいようすを表(あらわ)します（例(れい)3, 4, 5）。

It may also describe a calm and gentle state (ex.3, 4, 5).

1) 図書館は静かだから、よく勉強できる。
Toshokanwa shizukadakara, yoku benkyoodekiru.
It is quiet in the library, so (we) can study well.

2) 私のうちは、静かな住宅地にある。
Watashino uchiwa, shizukana juutakuchini aru.
My house is located in a very quiet residential area.

3) 病気の時は、静かに寝ているほうがいい。
Byookino tokiwa, shizukani neteiru hooga ii.
It's best to stay quiet in bed when (you) are sick.

4) 彼女はとても静かな人で、いるのかいないのか分からないくらいだ。
Kanojowa totemo shizukana hitode, irunoka inainoka wakaranai-kuraida.
She is a very quiet person. (We) don't even notice when she is around.

5) この入り江は波が静かで、釣りをするのに最高だ。
Kono iriewa namiga shizukade, tsurio surunoni saikooda.
The water in this inlet is very calm, so it's the best place to fish.

おだやか［穏やか］ ■*odayaka* ■calm 

平和で**もめごとがなく、落ち着いた雰囲気**です。なごやかで温かく、心が安まる感じです（例6, 7, 8, 9）。人の態度や性質にも使い「穏やかな人」は争いやもめごとを好まない温厚な人のことです。また、気候が温暖で気持ちがよいときにも使います。

Odayaka refers to an atmosphere or mood that is peaceful, problem-free and calm (ex.6, 7, 8, 9). *Odayaka na hito* refers to a gentle person who does not like to argue or cause disputes. Also, *odayaka na* may refer to a mild and pleasant climate.

6) きょうの海は波が穏やかだ。
Kyoono umiwa namiga odayakada.
The sea is very calm and tranquil today.

7) 彼は性格が穏やかなので、みんなに好かれている。

Karewa seikakuga odayakananode, minnani sukareteiru.
He is a very gentle person, so everybody likes him.

8) そんなにけんか腰(ごし)にならないで、穏(おだ)やかに話(はなし)をしなさい。
Sonnani kenkagoshini naranaide, odayakani hanashio shinasai.
Don't be so argumentative. Please speak more calmly.

9) きょうは一日(いちにち)、穏(おだ)やかな陽気(ようき)だった。
Kyoowa ichinichi, odayakana yookidatta.
It was very nice and warm all day today.

しつもん／ぎもん

■ *shitsumon* ■ *gimon*

しつもん［質問(しつもん)］ ■ *shitsumon* ■ question 

分(わ)からないことや知(し)りたいこと、あるいは試験問題(しけんもんだい)などのように相手(あいて)に答(こた)え**てもらいたいことを聞(き)く**とき使(つか)います（例(れい)1, 2, 3, 4）。

Shitsumon is a question asked in order to clarify a matter, to gain information about something, or to get the answer to something like a test question (ex.1, 2, 3, 4).

1) 先生(せんせい)は、「分(わ)からないことは何(なん)でも質問(しつもん)しなさい。」と言(い)いました。
Senseiwa, "Wakaranai kotowa nandemo shitsumonshinasai." to iimashita.
My teacher said, "Ask me about anything you don't understand."

2) テスト用紙(ようし)には、「問題(もんだい)をよく読(よ)んで、次(つぎ)の質問(しつもん)に答(こた)えなさい。」と書(か)いてある。
Tesutoyooshiniwa, 'Mondaio yoku yonde, tsugino shitsumonni kotaenasai.' to kaitearu.
On the test paper it says, 'Read the problem carefully, and answer the following questions.'

3) 入社試験(にゅうしゃしけん)の面接(めんせつ)でいろいろ質問(しつもん)されたが、緊張(きんちょう)していたのでうまく答(こた)えられなかった。
Nyuusha-shikenno mensetsude iroiro shitsumonsaretaga, kinchoo-shiteitanode

umaku kotaerarenakatta.
(I) was asked all kinds of questions at the job interview, but because I was so nervous I could not answer them well.

4) 大統領は、記者の質問にひとつひとつ答えた。
Daitooryoowa, kishano shitsumonni hitotsuhitotsu kotaeta.
The President responded to each of the reporters' questions.

ぎもん［疑問］

■ *gimon*
■ doubt ; question 

はっきり**分からない**、納得できない、**本当だろうか**、何か変だなどという思いです（例5, 6, 7, 8）。

Gimon refers to doubts in one's mind due to a lack of understanding, or because one is unconvinced that something is true (ex.5, 6, 7, 8).

---

5) 彼が言ったことは本当かどうか疑問だ。
Karega itta kotowa hontooka dooka gimonda.
(I) doubt whether what he said is true or not.

6) 私は疑問に思ったことはすぐ調べることにしている。
Watashiwa gimonni omotta kotowa sugu shiraberu kotoni shiteiru.
I make it a rule to investigate anything I find questionable right away.

7) 彼が横綱になることに、もはや疑問の余地はない。
Karega yokozuna＊*ni naru kotoni, mohaya gimonno yochiwa nai.*
There is no longer room to doubt that he'll become a *yokozuna* (a grand *sumo* champion). ＊ p.698

8) 彼女の説明で、長年の疑問が解けた。
Kanojono setsumeide, naganenno gimonga toketa.
Many years of doubt were cleared up by her explanation.

しばらく／とうぶん

■ *shibaraku* ■ *toubun*

しばらく

■ *shibaraku*
■ for a (little) while

ある程度の時間のことです。はっきりとした長さではなく「**少しの間・ちょっと**」を表すことも（例1, 2, 3)、それ以上を表すこともあります（例4, 5, 6, 7)。話の内容によって、だいたいどのくらいかを判断します。これから先のことだけではなく過去のできごとについても使います。

Shibaraku represents a specific period of time. It may be used to refer to short or momentary periods of time (ex.1, 2, 3), as well as long periods (ex.4, 5, 6, 7), depending on the topic of conversation. It may also be used when referring to events in either the future or the past.

1) すぐに戻って来ますので、ここでしばらくお待ちください。
Suguni modotte kimasunode, kokode shibaraku omachikudasai.
(I'll) be right back, so please wait here for a while.

2) にわか雨だから、しばらくすれば止むだろう。
Niwakaame-dakara, shibaraku sureba yamudaroo.
It's a sudden shower, so it will probably pass in a little while.

3) 散歩の途中で、気分が悪くなったので、公園のベンチでしばらく休んだ。
Sanpono tochuude, kibunga waruku nattanode, kooenno benchide shibaraku yasunda.
(I) suddenly felt ill while taking a walk, so I took a brief rest on a park bench.

4) 私は、しばらく東京を離れるつもりです。
Watashiwa, shibaraku Tookyoo-o hanareru tsumoridesu.
I plan to leave Tokyo for a while.

5) 私は大学を卒業してしばらくの間、証券会社に勤めていた。
Watashiwa daigakuo sotsugyooshite shibarakuno aida, shookengaishani tsutometeita.
After graduating from university I worked at a securities company for a while.

6) しばらくですね。お変わりありませんか。

Shibarakudesune. Okawari arimasenka?
(I) haven't seen you for a while. What's new?

7) 彼はしばらくぶりに故郷を訪れた。

Karewa shibarakuburini kokyoo-o otozureta.
He visited his hometown after being away for a long time.

とうぶん［当分］

■ *toubun*
■ for a while 

これから先必要な、ある程度の**時間の長さ**を表します（例8, 9, 10, 11)。これから（今から）先のことに使い、**過去のことには使いません**。「しばらく」のように「少しの間・短い時間」は表しません。時間が長くかかることを表します。したがって、「当分お待ちください」という使い方はしません。

Toubun is used when referring to a length of time that will be required (ex.8, 9, 10, 11), and is only used when speaking of the future. In addition, *toubun* is unlike *shibaraku* in that it may only be used when speaking of something that will take a long time. Therefore, the expression *toubun omachi kudasai* is not used.

---

8) 天気予報によると、当分雨は降らないそうです。

Tenkiyohooni yoruto, toobun amewa furanaisoodesu.
According to the weather report, (we) won't be having any rain for some time.

9) 足の骨を折ってしまったので、当分学校に行けそうもない。

Ashino honeo otte-shimattanode, toobun gakkooni ikesoomo nai.
(I) broke my leg, so it appears I won't be able to go to school for a while.

10) 彼女が遠くへ引っ越してしまったので、当分会えそうもない。

Kanojoga tookue hikkoshite-shimattanode, toobun aesoomo nai.
She's moved far away, so it doesn't look like I'll be able to see her for a long time.

11) 彼はこの町が気に入って、当分ここで暮らすことにしたそうだ。

Karewa kono machiga kiniitte, toobun kokode kurasu kotoni shitasooda.

He seems to like this town, and it appears that he's decided to live here for a while.

しまう／かたづける

■*shimau* ■*katazukeru*

しまう ■*shimau* ■to store ; to keep

①外(そと)に出(で)ているものを**中(なか)に入(い)れる**こと、あるいは使(つか)っていたもの、ちらかっているものを**元(もと)の場所(ばしょ)**や**決(き)められた場所(ばしょ)に収(おさ)める**ことです（例(れい)1, 2, 3, 4）。

To put something that has been taken out back into its place of storage, or to keep something in its place (ex.1, 2, 3, 4).

②動作(どうさ)が完了(かんりょう)することや、その結果(けっか)の状態(じょうたい)を強調(きょうちょう)するとき使(つか)います。とりかえしがつかないという気持(きも)ちを含(ふく)んで、余(あま)り好(この)ましくない結果(けっか)になるとき使(つか)うことが多(おお)いです。②は「動詞(どうし)＋てしまう」の形(かたち)で使(つか)い、話(はな)しことばでは「〜ちゃう・〜ちゃった」のようにも言(い)います（例(れい)5, 6, 7, 8）。

Shimau is also used to emphasize the completion of an action, or its resultant state. It suggests that the result is irreversible, and is often used when expressing regret about an unfavorable outcome. The contracted forms ~*chau* and ~*chatta* are the informal forms of ~*te shimau* and ~*te shimatta* (ex.5, 6, 7, 8).

1) 彼女(かのじょ)はセーターを引(ひ)き出(だ)しにしまった。
Kanojowa seetaao hikidashini shimatta.
She put her sweater away in the drawer.

2) 大切(たいせつ)なものは、金庫(きんこ)にしまっておきなさい。
Taisetsuna monowa, kinkoni shimatteokinasai.
Keep (your) valuables in the safe.

3) 戸棚(とだな)にケーキをしまって忘(わす)れていたら、かびが生(は)えていた。
Todanani keekio shimatte wasureteitara, kabiga haeteita.
(I) put the cake in the cupboard and forgot about it, so it became moldy.

4) 銀の食器は、やわらかい布でくるんで、しまったほうがいい。
Ginno shokkiwa, yawarakai nunode kurunde, shimatta hooga ii.
(You) should wrap silver tableware with a soft cloth before you put it away.

5) 私は大切な花びんを、落として割ってしまった。
Watashiwa taisetsuna kabin-o, otoshite watteshimatta.
I dropped and broke the valuable vase (to my regret).

6) 彼は働きすぎて、病気になってしまった。
Karewa hatarakisugite, byookini natteshimatta.
He worked too hard, and ended up getting sick.

7) うちの猫がいなくなっちゃった。
Uchino nekoga inakunatchatta.
My cat has disappeared.

8) 大変、さいふを落としちゃった。
Taihen! Saifuo otoshichatta.
Oh, no! (I) lost my purse.

かたづける［片付ける］
■ *katazukeru*
■ to clean up ; to straighten up

---

①**邪魔なもの**をどかして、**きれいにする**ことです。ものを整理したり、ちらかっているものや使ったものを元の場所に戻すときにも使います（例9, 10, 11)。

To make a place neat or clean by putting away things that are in the way; or to put things that are in disorder or used back to their proper place (ex.9, 10, 11).

②やらなければならないものごとを解決することです（例12, 13)。

To solve or finish up unfinished matters (ex.12, 13).

9) 遊んだおもちゃは、自分でかたづけなさい。
Asonda omochawa, jibunde katazukenasai.
Put away (your) toys when you're finished playing.

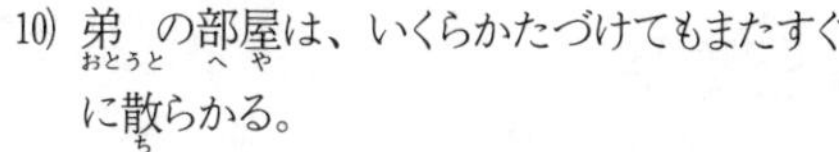

10) 弟の部屋は、いくらかたづけてもまたすぐに散らかる。

Otootono heyawa, ikura katazuketemo mata suguni chirakaru.
No matter how many times my (younger) brother straightens up his room, it immediately becomes messy again.

11) テーブルの上(うえ)をかたづけてから、お茶(ちゃ)にしましょう。
Teeburuno ueo katazuketekara, ochani shimashoo.
Let's have some tea after (we) clean up the table.

12) 私(わたし)はこの仕事(しごと)を、あしたまでにかたづけなければならない。
Watashiwa kono shigotoo, ashitamadeni katazukenakereba-naranai.
I must finish up this work by tomorrow.

13) 宿題(しゅくだい)がなかなかかたづかない。
Shukudaiga nakanaka katazukanai.
(I) just can't seem to get this homework done.

じめじめ／むしむし

■*jimejime* ■*mushimushi*

じめじめ ■*jimejime* ■moist ; damp 大

湿気(しっけ)が多(おお)いようすを表(あらわ)します（例(れい)1, 2, 3)。**不快(ふかい)だ**、という感(かん)じを含(ふく)みます。また、気分(きぶん)が晴(は)れやかでなく、**陰気(いんき)なようす**にも使(つか)います（例(れい)4, 5)。

Jimejime indicates high humidity (ex.1, 2, 3). A degree of unpleasantness is implied. *Jimejime* may also be used to describe a person's mood as not cheerful or depressed (ex.4, 5).

1) こけは、日(ひ)の当(あ)たらないじめじめした所(ところ)に生(は)えている。
Kokewa, hino ataranai jimejimeshita tokoroni haeteiru.
Moss grows in dark, damp places.

2) 梅雨時(つゆどき)は、じめじめしていてかびが生(は)えやすい。
Tsuyudokiwa, jimejimeshiteite kabiga haeyasui.
During the rainy season it's humid and mold grows quickly.

3) 洞窟(どうくつ)の中(なか)は、じめじめしていて気味(きみ)が悪(わる)い。

Dookutsuno nakawa, jimejimeshiteite kimiga warui.
Inside the cave it's damp and feels weird.

4) 彼は性格が暗く、じめじめしているので友人が少ない。
Karewa seikakuga kuraku, jimejime-shiteirunode yuujinga sukunai.
He has a dark, melancholy personality so he has few friends.

5) 他人の不幸や家庭のぐち、といったじめじめした話は聞きたくない。
Taninno fukooya kateino guchi, to itta jimejimeshita hanashiwa kikitakunai.
(I) really don't want to hear (your) complaining about your misfortune or your family.

むしむし ■*mushimushi* ■humid ; muggy 

湿度が高くてむし暑い気候を表します（例6, 7, 8）。
Mushimushi describes a climate as having a high percentage of humidity (ex.6, 7, 8).

6) 雨の日の満員電車の中は、むしむしする。
Ameno hino man-in-denshano nakawa, mushimushisuru.
On rainy days the interior of crowded trains becomes hot and sticky.

7) 部屋の中が、むしむしする。窓を開けてもいいですか。
Heyano nakaga, mushimushisuru. Madoo aketemo iidesuka?
This room feels humid. Is it all right if I open the window?

8) ゆうべは、むしむしして寝苦しかった。
Yuubewa, mushimushishite negurushikatta.
(I) had trouble sleeping last night becausc it was so muggy.

しめる／とじる／ふさぐ

■*shimeru* ■*tojiru* ■*fusagu*

しめる［閉める］ ■*shimeru* ■to close

窓や戸、引き出し、箱などの**開いている部分を小さくしてすきまをなくす**ことです。「閉じる」とちがい、「半分閉める」「少し閉める」こともできます（例1, 2, 3, 4）。

To reduce or eliminate an opening in objects such as a door, window, drawer, or box. Unlike *tojiru*, expressions such as *hanbun shimeru* (close halfway) and *sukoshi shimeru* (close partway) are possible (ex.1, 2, 3, 4).

1) 寒いから窓を閉めよう。
Samuikara madoo shimeyoo.
It's cold, so let's close the window.

2) 引き出しがあいていたので閉めた。
Hikidashiga aiteitanode shimeta.
The drawer was open so (I) closed it.

3) コーヒーの缶のふたはしっかり閉めておかないと、中身がしけてしまう。
Koohiino kanno futawa shikkari shimete okanaito, nakamiga shiketeshimau.
If (you) don't close the lid of the coffee can tightly, the contents will get damp.

4) 寮の門限に間に合わないと、入り口を閉められてしまう。
Ryoono mongenni maniawanaito, iriguchio shimerarete-shimau.
If (you) don't make it back before the dormitory curfew, the front door will be closed (and locked).

とじる［閉じる］ ■*tojiru* ■to close

①門、扉、本、目、口、花など、開いているものを、元の**開いていない状態にもどす**ことです。そのものにそなわっている、内と外をへだてるもの（戸、本の表紙、まぶた、唇、花びらなど）を使って、外との**つながりを断ち**ます

（例5, 6, 7, 8）。

To return an object, such as a gate, door, book, eye, mouth, or flower, to an unopened state. There is a sense that the object is used to separate the inside from the outside (ex.5, 6, 7, 8).

②「終わりになる」という意味で使います（例9, 10）。

It is also used to mean 'to bring to a conclusion' (ex.9, 10).

---

5) ポピーは夜になると花びらを閉じる。
Popiiwa yoruni naruto hanabirao tojiru.
Poppies close their pedals when night falls.

6) 目を閉じて音楽を聞くと、いろいろな情景が浮かんでくる。
Meo tojite ongakuo kikuto, iroirona jookeiga ukandekuru.
When (I) close my eyes and listen to music, I can imagine many different scenes.

7) 彼は読み終わると、そっと本を閉じた。
Karewa yomiowaruto, sotto hon-o tojita.
He closed the book softly when he finished reading.

8) ちょうが、羽を閉じて花にとまっている。
Chooga, haneo tojite hanani tomatteiru.
The butterfly is on the flower with its wings closed.

9) 彼は90歳で一生を閉じた。
Karewa kyuujussaide isshoo-o tojita.
His life came to an end at the age of 90.

10) 彼女は不況のため、親の代から続いていた店を閉じた。
Kanojowa fukyoono tame, oyano daikara tsuzuiteita miseo tojita.
Because of the bad economy, she closed the shop that had been in business since her parent's time.

ふさぐ

■*fusagu*
■ to close (up) ; to plug (up)

穴やすき間・出入り口などの**あいているところを、うめたり、おおったりしてものが出入りしないようにする**ことです（例11, 12, 13, 14, 15）。

To fill or cover an opening such as a hole, space, or entrance so that nothing may enter it (ex.11, 12, 13, 14, 15).

11) 壁(かべ)に穴(あな)があいてしまったから、板(いた)でふさいでおこう。
Kabeni anaga aiteshimattakara, itade fusaideokoo.
There is a hole in the wall so (I) guess I'll cover it with a board.

12) 洞窟(どうくつ)に人(ひと)が入(はい)らないように入(い)り口(ぐち)をふさいだ。
Dookutsuni hitoga hairanaiyooni iriguchio fusaida.
(I) closed the entrance of the cave so that no one can enter it.

13) 違法駐車(いほうちゅうしゃ)の車(くるま)が道(みち)をふさいでいて通(とお)れなかった。
Ihoochuushano kurumaga michio fusaideite toorenakatta.
The illegally parked car blocked up the road so (I) couldn't pass.

14) そんなところに物(もの)を置(お)いては場所(ばしょ)をふさいでしまうから片づけよう。
Sonna tokoroni monoo oitewa bashoo fusaide-shimaukara katazukeyoo.
If (we) leave things there they'll get in the way, so let's put them away.

15) 兄(あに)がドラムの練習(れんしゅう)を始(はじ)めたので、耳(みみ)をふさぎたくなった。
Aniga doramuno renshuuo hajimetanode, mimio fusagitaku natta.
My (elder) brother suddenly began practicing his drum, so (I) plugged my ears.

さようなら

オスカーは、日本(にほん)に来(き)てまだ間(ま)がないのですが、自分(じぶん)の国(くに)で2年間(ねんかん)日本語(にほんご)を勉強(べんきょう)してきたので、少(すこ)し自信(じしん)があります。

ある日、友(とも)だちの三島(みしま)さんの会社(かいしゃ)にアルバイトに行(い)きました。頼(たの)まれた仕事(しごと)が終(お)わり、オスカーは先(さき)に帰(かえ)ることにしました。職場(しょくば)では、先(さき)に帰(かえ)るあいさつに「さようなら」はあまり使(つか)わないと聞(き)いたことがあるオスカーは、大(おお)きな声(こえ)で「お先(さき)にお帰(かえ)りします」と言(い)いました。「お～する」は敬語表現(けいごひょうげん)だと考(かんが)えたのです。しかし、まわりの人(ひと)たちは笑(わら)いたいのをこらえています。

もちろん「お伺いする・お送りする」のような敬語表現はあるのですが、「お帰りします」という言い方はありません。この場合は「ほかの人たちがまだ働いているのに、先に帰ってすみません」の意味を含んだ「お先に失礼します」と言うのが

一般的です。そうすれば、ほかの人たちは「お疲れさまでした」と答えてくれるでしょう。どうしてもわからなくなったら、もちろん「さようなら」だっていいのです。

Sayoonara

Although Oscar has just arrived in Japan, he studied Japanese for two years in his own country, so he has some confidence in speaking. One day he went to a part-time job at a company where his friend Mr. Mishima worked. When he finished the job he was asked to do, he decided to go home ahead of time. Since he had heard that *sayoonara* is not usually used as a farewell at the workplace, he said loudly, "*Osakini okaerishimasu*,[1]" thinking that *o*(verb)～*suru*[2] is a humble, polite expression; however, the other people who heard this had to keep from laughing.

Of course, there are humble expressions such as *oukagai suru*[3] and *ookuri suru,*[4] but there is no such expression as *okaeri shimasu*. In this kind of situation, it is more appropriate to say "*Osakini shitsureishimasu*[5]" which implies, "I'm sorry to go home ahead of you when you are still working." When you say this, the listener will respond "*Otsukaresamadeshita.*[6]" But if you really don't know what to say, it is perfectly all right to say "*Sayoonara.*[7]"

1 *An incorrect expression for 'I am humbly going home ahead of you.'*
2 *A humble expression used when saying, 'I'll do (verb) for you.'*
3 *'I will humbly visit you' or 'I humbly ask you a question'.*
4 *I will humbly see you off.*
5 *Excuse me, I will go (home) ahead of you.*
6 *'You must be tired' or 'You've worked hard'.*
7 *Good-bye (but literally means, 'If we must depart, then good-bye').*

じゅんばんに/こうたいで/かわるがわる

■*junban ni*　■*koutai de*　■*kawarugawaru*

じゅんばんに［順番に］ ■*junban ni* ■in order 

並んでいるもの・続いているもの・何らかの法則があるものについて、それぞれの**配列や順序をくずさずに一つ一つとり上げていく**とき使います（例1, 2, 3)。

Junban ni is used when things that are lined up, continuous, or have a set arrangement are taken one at a time, without breaking the arrangement or order (ex.1, 2, 3).

1) 名前を呼ばれたら、１人ずつ順番に診察室にお入りください。
Namaeo yobaretara, hitorizutsu junbanni shinsatsushitsuni ohairi kudasai.
Please enter the examining room one at a time as (your) names are called.

2) ピカソの絵は、古いものから順番に「青の時代」「バラ色の時代」「キュビスムの時代」と分けられる。
Pikasono ewa, furui monokara junbanni 'aono jidai' 'barairono jidai' 'kyubisumuno jidai' to wakerareru.
Picasso's works are classified in order as 'the Blue Period', 'the Rose Period' and 'the Cubism Period'.

3) 彼は、たくさんある仕事を簡単なものから順番にかたづけていく。
Karewa, takusan aru shigotoo kantanna monokara junbanni katazuketeiku.
When he has a lot of work to do, he starts with the easiest task and works from there.

こうたいで［交代で］ ■*koutai de* ■in turns 

一つのことがらに対して時間や人数を決めて、**代わりあって行う**ようすを表すとき使います（例4, 5, 6)。

This is used when something is done on an alternating basis according to a determined amount of time, people, etc. (ex.4, 5, 6).

4) 東京から大阪まで、彼と私が交代で運転した。
Tookyookara Oosakamade, kareto watashiga kootaide untenshita.
We took turns driving from Tokyo to Osaka.

5) うちでは、私と弟が毎日交代で犬を散歩に連れて行きます。
Uchidewa, watashito otootoga mainichi kootaide inuo sanponi tsureteikimasu.
My (younger) brother and I take turns walking our dog every day.

6) この工場では、警備員が２人ずつ、２時間交代で見回っている。
Kono koojoodewa, keibiinga futarizutsu, nijikan kootaide mimawatteiru.
At this plant, security guards patrol in groups of two that relieve each other every two hours.

かわるがわる

■ *kawarugawaru*
■ in turns

何人かが、**うけわたすように切れ目なく同じ動作を引きつぐ**とき使います（例7, 8）。２人で代わりながら何かをするという意味もあります（例9, 10）。
Kawarugawaru is used when a number of people perform the same action one after another without a break (ex.7, 8). It may also mean that two people take turns doing something (ex.9, 10).

7) 同窓会に集まった昔の教え子たちが、私のところにかわるがわる挨拶にきてくれた。
Doosookaini atsumatta mukashino oshiegotachiga, watashino tokoroni kawarugawaru aisatsuni kitekureta.
At the class reunion my old students came up to greet me in turn.

8) 結婚式に招かれた人たちは、かわるがわるお祝いを述べた。
Kekkonshikini manekareta hitotachiwa, kawarugawaru oiwaio nobeta.
The guests at the wedding offered their congratulations one at a time.

9) 母が入院している間、私と姉でかわるがわる見舞いに行った。
Hahaga nyuuin shiteiruaida, watashito anede kawarugawaru mimaini itta.
My (elder) sister and I took turns visiting my mother while she was in the hospital.

10) 私と父は、岸までかわるがわるボートをこいで行った。
Watashito chichiwa, kishimade kawarugawaru bootoo koideitta.
My father and I took turns rowing until we reached the shore.

じょうず／とくい

■*jouzu* ■*tokui*

じょうず ［上手］ ■*jouzu* ■skill ; proficiency 

何かをする**技術が優れている、うまい**という評価です（例1, 2, 3, 4, 5)。ほめることばなので、自分には使いません。

Jouzu denotes superior skill at doing something (ex.1, 2, 3, 4, 5). Since this is used as a word of praise, it cannot be used to describe oneself.

1) 彼女は歌が上手です。
Kanojowa utaga joozudesu.
She is good at singing.

2) あなたはほんとうに絵が上手ですね。
Anatawa hontooni ega joozudesune.
You are really an excellent artist!

3) A：あなたと彼女とどちらがピアノが上手ですか。
B：2人ともへたです。
A： *Anatato kanojoto dochiraga pianoga joozudesuka?*
Which of you is better at the piano -- you or she?
B： *Futaritomo hetadesu.* Both of us are bad.

4) 私は、いくら練習してもさか立ちが上手にできない。
Watashiwa, ikura renshuushitemo sakadachiga joozuni dekinai.
No matter how much I practice, I can't stand on my head well.

5) 彼はこのごろ運転が上手になった。
Karewa konogoro untenga joozuni natta.
He has become very good at driving lately.

とくい［得意］

■ *tokui*
■ specialty ; forte ; pride 

①ものごとに対しての経験が深く、能力や技術が優れていて自信があることです（例6, 7, 8, 9, 10）。自分にも他人にも使います。

Tokui is used to describe someone who is very experienced at something, has superior abilities or skills, and is very self-confident (ex.6, 7, 8, 9, 10). This may be used in describing oneself or another person.

②満足のいく結果や他人に自慢できるような結果になって、うれしそうで誇らしげな他人のようすに使います（例11, 12）。

It is also used in describing someone besides oneself as being proud of or satisfied with the outcome of something, which he may boast about to others (ex.11, 12).

---

6) 彼は、フランス語が得意です。
Karewa, Furansugoga tokuidesu.
He is very good at French.

7) A：あなたの得意なスポーツは何ですか。
B：私はスポーツは苦手です。
A： *Anatano tokuina supootsuwa nandesuka?*
What sport are you best at?
B： *Watashiwa supootsuwa nigatedesu.*
I am not at all good at sports.

8) 私は小学生のころ算数が得意でした。
Watashiwa shoogakuseino koro sansuuga tokuideshita.
Math was my best subject in elementary school.

9) 彼の不得意な科目は、理科です。
Kareno futokuina kamokuwa, rikadesu.
His worst subject is science.

10) 私は水泳はあまり得意ではない。
Watashiwa suieiwa amari tokuidewa nai.
I'm not very good at swimming.

11) 兄は、野球の試合で３本もホームランを打ったと、得意になっている。
Aniwa, yakyuuno shiaide sanbonmo hoomuran-o uttato, tokuini natteiru.

My (elder) brother is proud of the three homeruns that he hit in the baseball game.

12) 彼は得意そうに、買ったばかりのスポーツカーを見せた。

Karewa tokuisooni, kattabakarino supootsukaao miseta.

He looked very proud showing off his brand-new sports car.

じょじょに／じわじわ

■*jojoni* ■*jiwajiwa*

じょじょに［徐徐に］ ■*jojoni* ■gradually 

ものごとの進み具合や変化が、速くはないようすを表します（例1, 2, 3, 4）。ゆっくりではあるけれど、「確実に進んでいる・いずれ結果が出る・結論に達する」という意味を含みます。

This indicates that something progresses or changes slowly (ex.1, 2, 3, 4). There is a feeling that, although slow, progress is steady and sooner or later a conclusion or result will be reached.

1) 天気は、じょじょに下り坂です。

Tenkiwa, jojoni kudarizakadesu.

The weather is gradually worsening.

2) つりをしていると、潮がじょじょに満ちてくるのが分かる。

Tsurio shiteiruto, shioga jojoni michitekurunoga wakaru.

While fishing, (I) can see the tide gradually rising.

3) 新しい仕事にも、じょじょに慣れてきた。

Atarashii shigotonimo, jojoni naretekita.

(I've) slowly but surely gotten used to my new job.

4) やっと病気がよくなったばかりなのだから、無理をしないで、じょじょに動いたほうがいいよ。

Yatto byookiga yokunatta bakari-nanodakara, murio shinaide, jojoni ugoita hooga iiyo.

(You've) just gotten over your illness, so you should start moving around little by little, and not overdo it.

じわじわ ■*jiwajiwa* ■gradually ; steadily 

ものごとが、**少しずつ増えていったり、変化していくようす**を表します（例5, 6, 7, 8)。速度よりも、増していく程度や量に重点があります。「喜び・うれしさ・悲しみ・不安」などの感情が、わき上がってくるようすを表すときによく使われます。

Jiwajiwa is used to express that something increases or changes at a gradual rate (ex.5, 6, 7, 8). It emphasizes an increase in degree or volume, rather than speed, and is often used when speaking of rising emotions such as joy, sadness, or anxiety.

5) 怖い映画を見ていたら、じわじわと冷や汗が出てきた。
Kowai eigao miteitara, jiwajiwato hiyaasega detekita.
While watching the horror film, (I) slowly began to break out into a cold sweat.

6) 優勝の喜びが、じわじわとわき上がってきた。
Yuushoono yorokobiga, jiwajiwato wakiagattekita.
Happiness over winning the championship mounted steadily.

7) 漢方薬は急には効かないが、時間をかけてじわじわと効いてくる。
Kanpooyakuwa kyuuniwa kikanaiga, jikan-o kakete jiwajiwato kiitekuru.
Chinese medicines aren't immediately effective, but over time they gradually begin to work.

8) 物価がじわじわと上がり、私たちの生活にも影響が出てきた。
Bukkaga jiwajiwato agari, watashitachino seikatsunimo eikyooga detekita.
Prices have been gradually rising and they've started having an effect on our lives.

しる／わかる

■ *shiru*　■ *wakaru*

しる［知る］ ■ *shiru* ■ to know 

経験や外からの情報により、ことがらや人などについての**知識を得ることです**（例1, 2, 3, 4, 5）。ほとんどの場合「知っている・知らない」のように、すでに知識や面識があるかどうか、記憶しているかどうかを表す使い方をします。例6は、「かかわりがない」という意味です。

To gain knowledge about something or someone through means such as experience or outside information (ex.1, 2, 3, 4, 5). In most cases it is used in the forms *shitteiru* (I know) or *shiranai* (I don't know) to indicate that one has or lacks knowledge, acquaintance, or memory of something. In Example 6 it is used to mean that the speaker has no connection with the subject.

1) 私は植物のことならなんでも知っている。
Watashiwa shokubutsuno kotonara nandemo shitteiru.
I know everything there is about plants.

2) A：彼女の電話番号を知っていますか。
B：いいえ、知りません。
A： *Kanojono denwa-bangoo-o shitteimasuka?*
Do (you) know her telephone number?
B： *Iie, shirimasen.* No, (I) don't.

3) 彼が作家だなんて知らなかった。
Karega sakkadanante shiranakatta.
(I) had no idea he is a writer.

4) 私はその金庫の開け方を知っている。
Watashiwa sono kinkono akekatao shitteiru.
I know how to open the safe.

5) 彼は礼儀を知らない。
Karewa reigio shiranai.
He has no manners at all.

6) いくら言っても聞かないんだから……、もう知らないよ。

Ikura ittemo kikanaindakara…, moo shiranaiyo.
No matter how many times (I) tell (you), you won't listen. I'll have nothing more to do with it.

わかる［分かる］ ■ *wakaru* ■ to understand ; to know 

ものごとの**意味や内容を理解すること**です（例7, 8, 9, 10, 11）。また、ものごとの結果などが、明らかになることも表します（例12, 13）。考えれば「わかる」ことはあっても、考えたから「知る」ということはありません。「話がわかる」「芸術がわかる」は、「理解がある・詳しい」という意味です（例14, 15）。「道がわかる」は、迷わないで目的地へ行けることを表します（例16）。

To comprehend the meaning, contents, etc. of something (ex.7, 8, 9, 10, 11). Also, to know the outcome of something (ex.12, 13). When referring to knowledge or understanding gained from thought alone *wakaru* may be used, but *shiru* may not. Expressions such as *hanashi ga wakaru* or *geijutsu ga wakaru* indicate a good understanding or detailed knowledge of something (ex.14, 15). *Michi ga wakaru* means that one can get to a destination without any confusion (ex.16).

7) この機械の使い方は、説明書を読めばわかる。

Kono kikaino tsukaikatawa, setsumeishoo yomeba wakaru.
If (you) read the instruction manual, you'll know how to operate this machine.

8) 彼女に電話をかけたいけれど、電話番号がわからない。

Kanojoni denwao kaketai keredo, denwabangooga wakaranai.
(I) want to give her a phone call, but I don't know her number.

9) 難しい数学の問題も、よく考えればわかる。

Muzukashii suugakuno mondaimo, yoku kangaereba wakaru.
(You'll) be able to figure out even difficult math problems if you think them through carefully.

10) 日本語がわかりますか。

Nihongoga wakarimasuka?
Do you understand Japanese? (Do you speak Japanese?)

11) A：あしたまでに、この仕事を終わらせてください。

Ｂ：わかりました。

Ａ： *Ashita madeni, kono shigotoo owarasete kudasai.*
Please complete this job by tomorrow.
Ｂ： *Wakarimashita.* All right.

12) 未来のことは、誰にもわからない。
Miraino kotowa, darenimo wakaranai.
Nobody knows what will happen in the future.

13) 試験の結果は１週間後にわかる。
Shikenno kekkawa isshuukangoni wakaru.
(He) will know the test results in a week.

14) あの先生は話がわかる。
Ano senseiwa hanashiga wakaru.
That teacher is very understanding.

15) 彼は、芸術がわかる。
Karewa, geijutsuga wakaru.
He is quite knowledgeable about art.

16) 図書館に行く道がわかりません。
Toshokanni iku michiga wakarimasen.
I don't know the way to the library.

すいすい／すらすら／すんなり

■ *suisui* ■ *surasura* ■ *sunnari*

すいすい

■ *suisui*
■ smoothly ; easily 

ものごとが**抵抗なく、らくに進む**ときや、軽く気持ちよく動作を行うようすを表すとき使います（例1, 2, 3, 4）。

Suisui denotes that something proceeds easily and without resistance, or that an action is carried out effortlessly and pleasantly (ex.1, 2, 3, 4).

1）子供たちは、プールですいすい泳いでいる。

Kodomotachiwa, puurude suisui oyoideiru.
The children are swimming like fish in the pool.

2) こんな簡単(かんたん)な計算(けいさん)なら、すいすいできる。
Konna kantanna keisannara, suisui dekiru.
If the calculation is this simple, I'll be able to solve it in no time.

3) とんぼが秋(あき)の空(そら)を、すいすい飛(と)んでいる。
Tonboga akino sorao, suisui tondeiru.
The dragonflies are flying about effortlessly in the autumn sky.

4) 私(わたし)の新(あたら)しい自転車(じてんしゃ)は、登(のぼ)り坂(ざか)でもすいすい走(はし)る。
Watashino atarashii jitenshawa, noborizakademo suisui hashiru.
I can even go uphill easily on my new bicycle.

すらすら

■ *surasura*
■ smoothly ; easily 

ものごとが**抵抗(ていこう)なくなめらかに**行(おこな)われるとき使(つか)います。とくに、話(はな)すこと・読(よ)むこと・書(か)くことによく使(つか)います（例(れい)5, 6, 7, 8)。

Surasura indicates that an action proceeds smoothly and without resistance. It is often used when referring to speaking, reading or writing (ex.5, 6, 7, 8).

---

5) その学生(がくせい)は、教授(きょうじゅ)の質問(しつもん)にすらすら答(こた)えた。
Sono gakuseiwa, kyoojuno shitsumonni surasura kotaeta.
The student was able to easily answer the professor's questions.

6) まだ３歳(さい)だというのに、その女(おんな)の子(こ)はすらすら童話(どうわ)を読(よ)んだ。
Mada sansaidato yuunoni, sono onnanokowa surasura doowao yonda.
Even though she is only three years old, she read the fairy tale without a problem.

7) はじめての海外旅行(かいがいりょこう)だったが、英語(えいご)がすらすらと口(くち)をついて出(で)た。
Hajimeteno kaigai-ryokoodattaga, eigoga surasurato kuchiotsuite deta.
Even though it was my first trip abroad, (I) was able to speak English without any trouble.

8) 犯人(はんにん)は取調室(とりしらべしつ)で犯行(はんこう)についてすらすらと話(はな)した。

Hanninwa torishirabe-shitsude hankoonitsuite surasurato hanashita.
The culprit poured out the details of the crime in the interrogation room.

すんなり

■ *sunnari*
■ easily ; smoothly 

ものごとを**抵抗**や**問題**なしに、**簡単**に 1 **回**で**終える**ことができるとき使います(例9, 10, 11)。

Sunnari is used to indicate that something is finished after only one try, and without resistance or difficulty (ex. 9, 10, 11).

9) 私の友人は、難しい試験に一度ですんなり受かった。
Watashino yuujinwa, muzukashii shikenni ichidode sunnari ukatta.
My friend passed the difficult test easily on his first try.

10) 社長は、社員の要求にすんなり応じた。
Shachoowa, shainno yookyuuni sunnari oojita.
The company president agreed to his employees' demands without argument.

11) 心配していた問題も、弁護士のおかげで、すんなりと解決した。
Shinpaishiteita mondaimo, bengoshino okagede, sunnarito kaiketsushita.
I was able to solve the troubling matter without a problem, thanks to my lawyer.

ずうずうしい/あつかましい

■ *zuuzuushii* ■ *atsukamashii*

ずうずうしい

■ *zuuzuushii*
■ cheeky ; impudent 

人の**良識**や**常識**を**気**にすることなく、**平気**なようす、**遠慮**のないようすをいいます。そのような行いに対して、非難・批判をこめて使います(例1, 2, 3, 4)。

The word *zuuzuushii* is used in a negative tone to describe a person with an attitude or behavior that is unreserved and inconsistent with what is considered appropriate (ex.1, 2, 3, 4).

---

1) あいつはずうずうしい男だなあ。金ばかりか、洋服まで借りていった。
Aitsuwa zuuzuushii otokodanaa. Kanebakarika, yoofukumade kariteitta.
He is a bold rascal. He borrowed not only my money but also my clothes.

2) あまり、ずうずうしいことばかりしていると、みんなにきらわれるよ。
Amari, zuuzuushii kotobakari shiteiruto, minnani kirawareruyo.
If you keep acting so cheeky, you are going to be disliked by everybody.

3) 知り合ったばかりの人の家に、泊めてくれだなんてずうずうしい。
Shiriatta bakarino hitono ieni, tometekure-danante zuuzuushii.
It's rude to ask someone you've just met to put you up for the night.

4) 彼は仕事もしないで、ずうずうしくも、給料を上げてもらおうとした。
Karewa shigotomo shinaide, zuuzuushikumo, kyuuryoo-o agetemoraooto shita.
Even though he didn't even do his job, he is so impudent he tried to get a raise in salary.

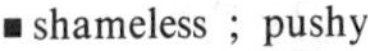

あつかましい

■ *atsukamashii*
■ shameless ; pushy

こんなことをしては**恥ずかしいという気持ち**や、**他人に悪いからやめよう**という心づかいなどが、**まったくない**ようすをいいます（例5, 6, 7, 8)。「恥知らず」という点が強調されています。

This describes a person who has absolutely no sense of modesty or reservation (ex.5, 6, 7, 8). A sense of *hajishirazu* (being shameless) is emphasized.

---

5) あんなあつかましい人は見たこともない。
Anna atsukamashii hitowa mitakotomo nai.
(I) have never seen such a shameless person.

6) 4人がけの席を一人じめして、何とあつかましいやつだ。
Yoningakeno sekio hitorijimeshite, nanto atsukamashii yatsuda.
The nerve of that man! He is taking up a seat for four all by himself.

7) あいさつもしないで、上がり込むなんて、なんてあつかましいんでしょう。

Aisatsumo shinaide, agarikomunante, nante atsukamashiin-deshoo.
He came into my house without saying anything. How rude!

8) あつかましいお願いですが、借金の返済を、もう少し待っていただけないでしょうか。

Atsukamashii onegaidesuga, shakkinno hensaio, moosukoshi matte itadakenai-deshooka?
(I) may be asking too much, but would you please defer the due date of my loan a little longer?

ずきずき／ひりひり／がんがん

■*zukizuki* ■*hirihiri* ■*gangan*

ずきずき ■*zukizuki* ■throb 大

傷や頭、または骨折したところが**脈を打つように痛む**ようすです（例1, 2)。腹痛には使いません。

Zukizuki describes a continuing, stabbing pain in a wound, head or broken bone area; it is a sharp, pounding or throbbing pain, like a pulse beat (ex.1, 2). *Zukizuki* is not used to describe a stomachache.

1) 指がずきずきする。傷口が化膿したらしい。

Yubiga zukizukisuru. Kizuguchiga kanooshitarashii.
(My) finger is throbbing. It seems that the wound is infected.

2) ゆうべは、頭がずきずき痛くて、一晩中眠れなかった。

Yuubewa, atamaga zukizuki itakute, hitobanjuu nemurenakatta.
Last night (I) had a throbbing headache and I couldn't sleep at all.

ひりひり ■*hirihiri* ■burn ; smart 大

すりむいたりやけどをしたり、あるいは薬品が**しみたり**などで**皮膚の表面が痛い**ようすを表します（例3, 4, 5)。

Hirihiri is used to describe the pain of a skin injury caused by scraping, burning, or the effects of a chemical substance (ex.3, 4, 5).

3) 日に焼けた肌がひりひりする。
Hini yaketa hadaga hirihirisuru.
(My) sunburnt skin smarts.

4) 風邪をひいたらしい。のどがひりひりする。
Kazeo hiitarashii. Nodoga hirihirisuru.
(I) think I caught a cold. My throat is scratchy.

5) ころんですりむいたところがひりひり痛い。
Koronde surimuita tokoroga hirihiri itai.
The place where (I) skinned myself when I fell stings. (The scratch I got from my fall stings).

がんがん ■*gangan* ■ache 大

頭が絶えず殴られるように痛むことです（例6, 7）。強い痛みで、「割れるように痛い」と同じように使われます。

Gangan describes a throbbing or ringing type of pain, as of the head or ears (ex.6, 7). It expresses strong pain, and is used in the same manner as *wareru yoo ni itai*, which literally means 'my head hurts so much that it feels as if it is breaking up'.

6) 二日酔いで頭ががんがんする。
Futsukayoide atamaga gangansuru.
My head is splitting because of my hangover.

7) そんなに大きな声を出さないでください。
耳ががんがんするから。
Sonnani ookina koeo dasanaide kudasai.
Mimiga gangansurukara.
Don't talk so loud. (My) ears are ringing.

すくなくとも／せめて

■*sukunakutomo* ■*semete*

すくなくとも［少なくとも］ ■*sukunakutomo* ■at least

どう見積もっても**最低これぐらいは**、という数量や程度の限度を表します。「～だろう・かもしれない」などの**推量表現**や「～たい・～てほしい」などの**希望表現**に使います（例1, 2, 3, 4, 5）。

Sukunakutomo indicates the lowest limit of a number or degree of something, which does not change no matter how evaluated. *Sukunakutomo* may be used in expressions of speculation, such as ~*daroo* and ~*kamoshirenai*, or expressions of desire, such as ~*tai* and ~*te hoshii* (ex.1, 2, 3, 4, 5).

1) 彼女は毎日、少なくとも２時間はピアノの練習をします。
Kanojowa mainichi, sukunakutomo nijikanwa pianono renshuuo shimasu.
She practices the piano for at least two hours every day.

2) このホールには、少なくとも1000人は入るだろう。
Kono hooruniwa, sukunakutomo senninwa hairudaroo.
This hall will probably hold at least 1,000 people.

3) 彼のけががすっかりよくなるまでに、少なくとも１か月はかかるだろう。
Kareno kegaga sukkari yokunarumadeni, sukunakutomo ikkagetsuwa kakarudaroo.
It will probably take at least one month for his wound to heal completely.

4) 少なくとも年に１回ぐらいは、のんびりと旅行がしたい。
Sukunakutomo nenni ikkaiguraiwa, nonbirito ryokooga shitai.
(I) would like to take a relaxing trip at least once a year.

5) この実験には、助手が少なくとも３人必要だ。
Kono jikkenniwa, joshuga sukunakutomo sannin hitsuyooda.
(We) will need at least three assistants to help with this experiment.

せめて ■*semete* ■at least

望んでいることのすべてを達成するのが無理ならば、**最低これだけは**という限界を表すとき使います。心の底から強く「〜たい・〜てほしい・〜ならいいのに」と願う最低の限度を表す使い方です（例6, 7, 8, 9）。**自分の願望**を述べるときに使い、「せめて100人はいるだろう」のような推量表現には使いません。

Semete indicates the minimum limit that is acceptable if the desired level is unattainable. It may be used when speaking of the minimum limit of a strong desire, and is often used in sentences which include *〜tai*, *〜te hoshii*, or *〜nara ii noni* (ex.6, 7, 8, 9). It may not be used when making suppositions, i.e., you cannot say '*Semete hyaku-nin wa iru daroo.* (There must be at least 100 people there.)'

---

6) 私は、せめて50メートル泳げるようになりたい。
Watashiwa, semete gojuumeetoru oyogeruyooni naritai.
I want to get so I am able to swim at least 50 meters.

7) せめて病気の時ぐらい、仕事のことは忘れてください。
Semete byookino tokigurai, shigotono kotowa wasuretekudasai.
Please forget about work, at least while (you're) sick.

8) せめてあと1週間あれば、もっといいレポートが書けたのに……。
Semete ato isshuukan-areba, motto ii repootoga kaketanoni...
(I) would have been able to write a better report if I had had at least another week until the due date.

9) 外国で暮らすんだったら、せめて日常会話ぐらいはできたほうがいい。
Gaikokude kurasundattara, semete nichijoo-kaiwaguraiwa dekitahooga ii.
If (you're) going to live abroad you should at least be able to handle everyday conversation in the local language.

すこし／ちょっと

■ *sukoshi* ■ *chotto*

すこし［少し］ ■ *sukoshi* ■ few ; a little 

ものごとの**数**や**量**・**程度**などが、**わずかだ**というようすを表します（例1, 2, 3, 4, 5）。

Sukoshi is used to indicate that the number, amount, or degree of something is small (ex.1, 2, 3, 4, 5).

1) この推理小説は、少し読んだだけで犯人がわかってしまった。
すいりしょうせつ　すこ　よ　はんにん
Kono suirishoosetsuwa, sukoshi yondadakede hanninga wakatteshimatta.
(I) was able to figure out who the criminal was in this mystery story after reading just a short bit.

2) 給料日前なので、お金が少ししかない。
きゅうりょうびまえ　かね　すこ
Kyuuryoobimae-nanode, okanega sukoshishika nai.
It's just before payday so (I) don't have much money.

3) 魚をたくさん釣ってきたので、少し隣にあげました。
さかな　つ　すこ　となり
Sakanao takusan tsuttekitanode, sukoshi tonarini agemashita.
(I) caught a lot of fish so I gave some to my neighbor.

4) 朝から体がだるくて、少し熱もある。
あさ　からだ　すこ　ねつ
Asakara karadaga darukute, sukoshi netsumo aru.
(I've) been feeling tired and have had a slight fever since this morning.

5) その件については、少し考えさせてください。
けん　すこ　かんが
Sono kennitsuitewa, sukoshi kangaesasete-kudasai.
Please let me think about the matter a bit.

ちょっと

■ *chotto*
■ a little ; a moment 

①ものごとの数や量・程度などが**わずかだ**、というようすを表します（例6, 7, 8)。「すこし」よりも「**ほんのわずか・もっと少ない**」という感じがあり、話しことばでよく使われます。

Chotto indicates that the number, amount, or degree of something is small (ex.6, 7, 8). It implies an even smaller amount than does *sukoshi*, and is often used in conversation.

②「ちょっとわからない」のように、動詞の否定形といっしょに使うときは「すぐには・簡単には」の意味を表します（例9, 10)。例11、12のように、はっきりとは答えたくない・あいまいにしたい、などの理由で、表現をやわらげるとき、また例13のように軽く呼びかけるとき使います。

When used together with a verb in its negative form, as in *chotto wakaranai*, it means 'soon' or 'easily' (ex.9, 10). As in Examples 11 and 12, *chotto* may be used to soften an expression when one does not want to answer precisely or provide details. Also, as in Example 13, it is used when casually calling for someone's attention.

---

6) このバッグはちょっと傷(きず)がついているので、安(やす)く買(か)えた。

Kono bagguwa chotto kizuga tsuiteirunode, yasuku kaeta.
(I) was able to buy this handbag at a discount because it has a small tear in it.

7) 私(わたし)がちょっと目(め)を離(はな)したすきに、息子(むすこ)は迷子(まいご)になってしまった。

Watashiga chotto meo hanashita sukini, musukowa maigoni natteshimatta.
My son got lost when I took my eyes off him for just a second.

8) 私(わたし)は、紅茶(こうちゃ)にブランデーをちょっとたらして飲(の)むのが好(す)きです。

Watashiwa, koochani burandeeo chotto tarashite nomunoga sukidesu.
I like drinking tea with just a touch of brandy added to it.

9) A：ご主人(しゅじん)は何時(なんじ)ごろお帰(かえ)りになりますか。

B：さあ、ちょっとわかりません。

A： *Goshujinwa nanjigoro okaerini narimasuka?*
What time will your husband return home?
B： *Saa, chotto wakarimasen.*
Hmm, (I) really don't know.

10) あの人(ひと)の顔(かお)に見覚(みおぼ)えはあるのに、名前(なまえ)がちょっと思(おも)い出(だ)せない。

Ano hitono kaoni mioboewa arunoni, namaega chotto omoidasenai.
(I) remember his face, but I just can't recall his name.

11) 彼(かれ)は人(ひと)はいいんだけれど、恋人(こいびと)にはちょっと……（向(む)かない）。

Karewa hitowa iindakeredo, koibitoniwa chotto...(mukanai).
He's a nice guy, but as a boyfriend (I) don't know...(there's something about him I don't like).

12) この薬(くすり)はちょっと苦(にが)いかもしれませんが、よく効(き)きます。

Kono kusuriwa chotto nigaikamo shiremasenga, yoku kikimasu.
This medicine may be a bit bitter, but it is very effective.

13) ちょっと、誰(だれ)か手伝(てつだ)ってくれない。

Chotto, dareka tetsudattekurenai?
Hey, can somebody give (me) a hand?

すっかり／そっくり

■ *sukkari* ■ *sokkuri*

すっかり

■ *sukkari*
■ all ; completely

ものの数量(すうりょう)やことがらの程度(ていど)について、「**残(のこ)らず・全部(ぜんぶ)・完全(かんぜん)に・全(まった)く**」というようすを表(あらわ)すとき使(つか)います（例(れい)1, 2, 3, 4, 5, 6）。

When referring to the quantity or degree of something, *sukkari* means 'wholly', 'all', 'completely', or 'thoroughly' (ex.1, 2, 3, 4, 5, 6).

1) 20匹(ぴき)いた熱帯魚(ねったいぎょ)を、すっかり猫(ねこ)にとられてしまった。
Nijuppiki ita nettaigyoo, sukkari nekoni torarete-shimatta.
The cat got all twenty of my tropical fish.

2) きのうのカレーは、すっかり食(た)べてしまって少(すこ)しも残(のこ)っていない。
*Kinoono karee**wa*, sukkari tabeteshimatte sukoshimo nokotteinai.* *p.702
(I) ate up all of yesterday's curry, so nothing is left.

3) 話(はなし)に夢中(むちゅう)になっている間(あいだ)に、アイスクリームがすっかり溶(と)けてしまった。
Hanashini muchuuni natteiru aidani, aisukuriimuga sukkari toketeshimatta.
While (I) was absorbed in the conversation, my ice cream melted completely.

4) かえでの葉(は)が赤(あか)くなりました。もうすっかり秋(あき)ですね。
Kaedeno haga akaku narimashita. Moo sukkari akidesune.
The maple leaves have turned red. Autumn is here in full.

5) あまり仕事(しごと)が忙(いそが)しかったので、友(とも)だちと会(あ)う約束(やくそく)をすっかり忘(わす)れてしまった。
Amari shigotoga isogashikattanode, tomodachito au yakusokuo sukkari wasurete-shimatta.
Because (I) was so busy with my work, I completely forgot about my appointment with my friend.

6) 病気(びょうき)がすっかりよくなったら、遊園地(ゆうえんち)に行(い)こうね。
Byookiga sukkari yokunattara, yuuenchini ikoone.
Let's go to an amusement park when (you) have completely recovered from your illness.

そっくり

■ *sokkuri*
■ completely

①ひとかたまりになったものや、**ひとつにまとまっているものを**、そのままの状態で**全部・残らず**というようすを表します。「そっくりそのまま」という使い方もあります（例7, 8, 9)。

Sokkuri indicates that things which constitute a single group or which have been organized into a unit are considered in their entirety, with nothing excluded or omitted. We may say *sokkuri sonomama*, which means 'everything exactly as is' (ex.7, 8, 9).

②とてもよく似ているようすを表すとき使います（例10, 11)。

It is used also to indicate that two or more things or people look very much alike (ex.10, 11).

---

7) どろぼうに、金庫の中のお金や宝石をそっくり盗まれた。
Dorobooni, kinkono nakano okaneya hoosekio sokkuri nusumareta.
The thief stole all of the money and jewelry in the safe.

8) 彼は親の遺産を、がん研究センターにそっくり寄付した。
Karewa oyano isan-o, gan-kenkyuusentaani sokkuri kifushita.
He donated all of his inheritance from his parents to a cancer research center.

9) この湖の底に沈んだ遺跡は、今もそっくりそのまま残っています。
Kono mizuumino sokoni shizunda isekiwa, imamo sokkuri sonomama nokotteimasu.
The ruins that now lay at the bottom of this lake are still perfectly preserved.

10) 母と姉は声がそっくりです。
Hahato anewa koega sokkuridesu.
My mother and older sister have exactly the same voice (sound exactly the same).

11) 彼女の作るろう人形は、本物そっくりだ。
Kanojono tsukuru rooningyoowa, honmono sokkurida.
The wax dolls she makes look just like the real thing.

どろぼうが指輪をとりました

ヘレンの部屋にどろぼうが入りました。大切にしていた指輪がありません。かけつけた警官に言いました。「どろぼうが指輪をとりました」ちょっと変です。確かに指輪をとったのはどろぼうですが、このようなとき日本語では、迷惑を受けたという形を使って「どろぼうに指輪をとられました」と言います。つまりヘレンが迷惑を受けたのです。同様に「物をこわされた、犬にかまれた、雨に降られた」などの使い方があります。どれも「困った」という迷惑が表れています。

Doroboo ga yubiwa o torimashita[1]

A burglar broke into Helen's room and stole a ring that she valued. When the police rushed over she told them, "*Doroboo ga yubiwa o torimashita.*" Unfortunately, her sentence was a bit strange. Although it is certain that the person who stole the ring was a burglar, in this case a passive form of the verb indicating trouble or annoyance is used in Japanese. In other words, Helen was aggrieved by the theft of her ring, therefore *doroboo ni yubiwa o toraremashita*[2] is a better expression.

Expressions such as *mono o kowasareta*[3], *inu ni kamareta*[4], and *ame ni furareta*[5] are used in the same way. Each implies that the speaker has been caused nuisance or trouble.

1 *A thief took (my) ring.*
2 *The ring was taken by the thief (and I was upset).*
3 *Something was broken (and it affected me adversely).*
4 *I was bitten by the dog (and I suffered).*
5 *It rained (and I got wet).*

ずっと／じっと／ひたすら

■ *zutto* ■ *jitto* ■ *hitasura*

ずっと

■ *zutto*
■ all the time ; by far

①**長い間その状態が続く**とき、その時間や距離を強調して使います（例1, 2, 3, 4, 5, 6）。

Zutto indicates that a certain state continues, and is used to emphasize length of time or distance (ex.1, 2, 3, 4, 5, 6).

②はるかに・かなりのように、**程度の高さ**を表して使います（例7, 8, 9, 10）。

Zutto is also used to indicate a high degree (ex.7, 8, 9, 10).

1) 私は生まれてからずっと東京に住んでいる。
Watashiwa umaretekara zutto Tookyooni sundeiru.
I have lived in Tokyo ever since I was born.

2) 彼は20年間ずっと日記をつけている。
Karewa nijuunenkan zutto nikkio tsuketeiru.
He has been keeping a diary for 20 years.

3) あの子はさっきからずっと泣いている。
Ano kowa sakkikara zutto naiteiru.
That child has been crying for quite some time.

4) 私は、これからもずっとテニスを続けるつもりです。
Watashiwa, korekaramo zutto tenisuo tsuzukeru tsumoridesu.
I intend to keep playing tennis even in the future.

5) このままずっと行くと駅です。
Konomama zutto ikuto ekidesu.
If (you) go straight down this street, you'll get to the station.

6) この道はずっと海まで続いている。
Kono michiwa zutto umimade tsuzuiteiru.
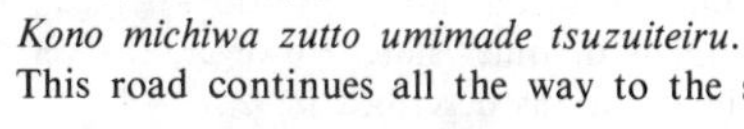
This road continues all the way to the sea.

7) A：この本を読んだことがありますか。

B：ずっと前に読みました。

A： *Kono hon-o yondakotoga arimasuka?*
Have (you) ever read this book?

B： *Zutto maeni yomimashita.*
(I) read it a long time ago.

8) ずっと遠くに富士山が見える。

Zutto tookuni Fujisanga mieru.
Mt. Fuji can be seen in the distance.

9) あなたには、この服のほうがずっと似合う。

Anataniwa, kono fukuno hooga zutto niau.
This dress (rather than the other one) looks much more becoming on you.

10) 前のゲームより今度のゲームのほうが、ずっとおもしろい。

Maeno geemuyori kondono geemuno hooga, zutto omoshiroi.
This game is far more interesting than the previous one.

じっと ■*jitto* ■fixedly ; intently 

---

①**視線**や**考え**を、ひとつのものごとから**そらさない**で見続けたり考え続けたりするようすを表すとき使います（例11, 12）。

Jitto denotes the continuation of a single action, such as looking at or thinking about something, in an unwavering, fixed manner (ex.11, 12).

②**動かないでおとなしくしているようす**を表すとき使います（例13, 14, 15, 16）。

It is also used to denote staying quiet and motionless (ex.13, 14, 15, 16).

③「じっとがまんする・じっと耐える」のように、**感情を抑える**とき使います（例17）。①②③のすべてに共通するのは、「続ける・動きがない・おとなしい」ということですが、「じっとする」という形で使えるのは、②の場合だけです。

Jitto is used in expressions which denote suppression of emotions, as in *jitto gamansuru* or *jitto taeru* (ex.17). Common to all three definitions (①, ②, ③) is the notion of a continuing motionless or quiet state. However, the verb form *jitto suru* may only be used in situations described in ②.

---

11) 彼は目を閉じたまま、じっと考えていた。
Karewa meo tojitamama, jitto kangaeteita.
With his eyes kept closed, he concentrated hard.

12) そんなにじっと見つめないで。恥ずかしいから……。
Sonnani jitto mitsumenaide. Hazukashiikara...
Don't keep staring at (me) like that. I feel embarrassed.

13) きのうは、頭が痛かったので、一日中じっと寝ていた。
Kinoowa, atamaga itakattanode, ichinichijuu jitto neteita.
(I) rested in bed all day long yesterday because I had a headache.

14) レントゲンを撮るときは、じっとしていなければならない。
Rentogen-o toru tokiwa, jittoshite inakerebanaranai.
(You'll) have to keep still when (I) take your X-ray.

15) 子供というのは、少しもじっとしてはいられない。
Kodomoto yuunowa, sukoshimo jittoshitewa irarenai.
Children cannot stay still even for a short while.

16) その犬は、主人の帰りをじっと待っていた。
Sono inuwa, shujinno kaerio jitto matteita.
The dog waited patiently for his master to return.

17) その生徒は、友達にどんなにいじめられても、じっとがまんした。
Sono seitowa, tomodachini donnani ijimeraretemo, jitto gamanshita.
No matter how much his friends teased him, that student patiently put up with it.

ひたすら ■ *hitasura* ■ single-mindedly 

ただひとつのことだけを考えてやりぬこうとする**一途で動かない気持ち**を表すとき使います。たとえ周りがどんな状況でも、自分の考えを**信じて行動し続ける**という**意志**を含んでいます（例18, 19, 20, 21）。

Hitasura expresses an earnestness or feeling of determination while engaged in doing something. It includes the sense that no matter how circumstances may change, one believes in one's own ideas and acts on them (ex.18, 19, 20, 21).

---

18) 彼は、ゴールをめざして、ひたすら走り続けた。

Karewa, gooruo mezashite, hitasura hashiritsuzuketa.
He kept running intently toward the goal.

19) 彼(かれ)は寝(ね)る時間(じかん)も惜(お)しんで、ひたすら研究(けんきゅう)に打(う)ち込(こ)んだ。
Karewa neru jikanmo oshinde, hitasura kenkyuuni uchikonda.
He was fervently wrapped up in his research, and did not even want to take the time to sleep.

20) 彼(かれ)は自分(じぶん)が悪(わる)かったと、ひたすら謝(あやま)った。
Karewa jibunga warukattato, hitasura ayamatta.
He kept apologizing, saying it was all his fault.

21) 両親(りょうしん)は、息子(むすこ)が無事(ぶじ)に帰(かえ)れるようにひたすら祈(いの)った。
Ryooshinwa, musukoga bujini kaereruyooni hitasura inotta.
The parents prayed fervently for their son's safe return.

すばらしい／すてき

■ *subarashii* ■ *suteki*

すばらしい ■ *subarashii* ■ wonderful 

ものごとの本質(ほんしつ)が**非常(ひじょう)にすぐれている・価値(かち)がある・感動的(かんどうてき)だ**というようすを表(あらわ)します（例(れい)1, 2, 3, 4, 5）。

Subarashii describes an object as having superior qualities, or as being impressive, remarkable, or of high value (ex.1, 2, 3, 4, 5).

---

1) きょうは、空(そら)がまっ青(さお)ですばらしい天気(てんき)だ。
Kyoowa, soraga massaode subarashii tenkida.
The weather today is fantastic, with clear blue skies.

2) 南(みなみ)の島(しま)の夕焼(ゆうや)けはすばらしかった。
Minamino shimano yuuyakewa subarashikatta.
The sunset on the southern islands was fantastic.

3) 彼(かれ)は、きのうの野球(やきゅう)ですばらしい活躍(かつやく)をした。
Karewa, kinoono yakyuude subarashii katsuyakuo shita.
Yesterday, he played a great baseball game.

4）砂漠の緑化に、わが国の科学技術が役立つなんて、すばらしいことだ。
Sabakuno ryokkani, wagakunino kagakugijutsuga yakudatsunante, subarashii kotoda.
Our country's scientific technology was useful in the transformation of desert to verdant land. It was a marvelous thing.

5）彼は、患者たちに献身的につくしたすばらしい医師だった。
Karewa, kanjatachini kenshintekini tsukushita subarashii ishidatta.
He was a wonderful doctor who devoted himself to his patients.

すてき

■ *suteki*
■ wonderful ; lovely 

ものやことがらを、**いいと感じるようす**を表します。**しゃれていて心がひかれる**という感じを含み、見た目について多く使います（例6, 7, 8）。例9は女性の言い方です。

Suteki is used to express a favorable impression of a matter or thing. It includes a sense of being captivated by something stylish, thus, it is frequently used when speaking of something visible (ex.6, 7, 8). The usage seen in Example 9 would mainly be used by women.

6）彼女はいつもすてきな服を着ている。
Kanojowa itsumo sutekina fukuo kiteiru.
She is always dressed beautifully.

7）あの映画に出てきた刑事は、とてもすてきだった。
Ano eigani detekita keijiwa, totemo sutekidatta.
The detective who appeared in that movie was really splendid.

8）彼女の恋人は、とてもすてきな人です。
Kanojono koibitowa, totemo sutekina hitodesu.
Her boyfriend is a really splendid person.

9）A：新婚旅行は世界一周にしよう。
B：わあ、すてき。うれしいわ。

A： *Shinkon-ryokoowa sekaiisshuuni shiyoo!*
Let's take a trip around the world for our honeymoon!
B： *Waa, suteki! Ureshiiwa!* Wow, fantastic! (I'd) love to!

すむ／くらす／すごす

■*sumu* ■*kurasu* ■*sugosu*

すむ［住む］

■*sumu*
■to reside ; to dwell in

人が場所や家を定めて、そこで生活することです（例1, 2, 3, 4, 5)。「巣を作ってそこで生活する」「そこに生息している」という意味で「この森に、狼がすんでいる」と使うこともあります。けれども「私の家には猫がすんでいる」は変で、ふつうは「いる」を使います。人間については「住む」と書き、動物については「棲む」と書きますが、ひらがなでかまいません。

Sumu means to reside at a certain place or house (ex.1, 2, 3, 4, 5). When speaking about animals, *sumu* can be used to mean 'to make a nest and live in it.' For example, we could translate *kono mori ni, ookami ga sunde iru* as 'the wolf makes its habitat in these woods.' However, if one has a pet cat, instead of saying *watashi no ie ni wa neko ga sunde iru* (an awkward sentence that would be translated as 'a cat lives in my house'), one should use the verb *iru*, as in *neko ga iru*. When referring to people, *sumu* is written with the *kanji* 住む, and when referring to animals, 棲む is used. In the latter case, however, simple *hiragana* may be used.

1) 私のうちの隣に、有名な作家が住んでいる。
Watashino uchino tonarini, yuumeina sakkaga sundeiru.
A famous writer lives next door to me.

2) 私は、海の近くに住みたい。
Watashiwa, umino chikakuni sumitai.
I want to live somewhere close to the sea.

3) この島には、だれも住んでいない。
Kono shimaniwa, daremo sundeinai.
Nobody lives on this island.

4) この川は魚もすまないほど汚れてしまった。
Kono kawawa sakanamo sumanaihodo yogoreteshimatta.
This river is so polluted that there aren't even any fish living in it.

5) この森の中には、オランウータンがすんでいる。

Kono morino nakaniwa, oran-uutanga sundeiru.
Orangutans live in this jungle.

くらす［暮らす］

■ *kurasu*
■ to live ; to earn a livelihood 

人が毎日毎日をおくることです（例6, 7, 8)。「住む」のように、ただ場所や家を定めているというのではなく、「**寝たり、笑ったり、働いたり**」といったいろいろな人間的な行動を伴っています。また、例9, 10のように、経済的なことも含んでいます。

Kurasu denotes living life day by day (ex.6, 7, 8). Unlike *sumu*, it does not only mean to establish a residence in a certain place or house, but it also encompasses various human behaviors, such as to sleep, laugh, or work. Also, as in examples 9 and 10, it may refer to financial livelihood.

---

6) 私の両親は、いなかで暮らしています。
Watashino ryooshinwa, inakade kurashiteimasu.
My parents live in the countryside.

7) 毎日、楽しく暮らしたい。
Mainichi, tanoshiku kurashitai.
(I) want to enjoy living every day.

8) 私は寒がりなので、とても北国では暮らせない。
Watashiwa samugarinanode, totemo kitagunidewa kurasenai.
I can't live in the north because I'm very sensitive to cold.

9) 彼は親の仕送りで暮らしている。
Karewa oyano shiokuride kurashiteiru.
He lives off the money his parents send him.

10) うちは子供が多いので、夫の給料だけではとても暮らせない。
Uchiwa kodomoga ooinode, ottono kyuuryoo dakedewa totemo kurasenai.
Because we have many children, my husband's salary is not enough to support all of us.

すごす［過ごす］

■ *sugosu*
■ to spend (time)  

人が、ある**一定の時間をおくる**ことです。時間の長さに関係はなく、例11、12、13のような短い時間から、例14、15のような長い時間も表します。何かしながら、時間を費やす・その時をおくるという意味です。

To spend a certain amount of time. The length of time is not important because as seen in Examples 11,12 and 13 it may be a short amount of time, or, as in Examples 14 and 15, it may be long. It implies that one spends the time doing something.

---

11) 久し振りに学生時代の友達と会って、楽しいひとときを過ごした。
Hisashiburini gakuseijidaino tomodachito atte, tanoshii hitotokio sugoshita.
(I) had a very good time getting together with some of my school friends from long ago.

12) 今日は、1日何もしないでなまけて過ごした。
Kyoowa, ichinichi nanimo shinaide namakete sugoshita.
Today, (I) lazily spent the whole day doing nothing.

13) 彼は山で道に迷い、岩かげで一夜を過ごした。
Karewa yamade michini mayoi, iwakagede ichiyao sugoshita.
He got lost on the mountain, so he spent the night next to a big rock for protection.

14) 私は少年時代、京都で過ごした。
Watashiwa shoonenjidai, Kyootode sugoshita.
I spent my boyhood in Kyoto.

15) 彼女は、一生ひとりで幸せに過ごした。
Kanojowa, isshoo hitoride shiawaseni sugoshita.
She lived the whole of her life very happily alone.

せいぜい／たかだか

■ *seizei* ■ *takadaka*

せいぜい

■ *seizei*
■ at most / best ; to the utmost

---

①ものごとの程度や数量が、「多く見積もっても、良くても**このぐらいだろう**」

ということを述べるとき使います（例1, 2, 3, 4)。

Seizei is used to state that the degree or quantity of something is 'probably about this much at the largest or best approximation' (ex.1, 2, 3, 4).

②「**できるだけ**」という意味で使います（例5, 6)。

It is also used to mean 'as (much) as possible' (ex.5, 6).

---

1) 今年の夏休みは、せいぜい４日ぐらいしかとれそうもない。
Kotoshino natsuyasumiwa, seizei yokkaguraishika toresoomo nai.
It looks like (I) can only take at most about four days for summer vacation this year.

2) 急行で行っても、せいぜい５分早く着くだけだ。
Kyuukoode ittemo, seizei gofun hayaku tsukudakeda.
Even if (you) go by express train you'll arrive only five minutes earlier.

3) 私が、今貸してあげられるのは、せいぜい２万円です。
Watashiga, ima kashite-agerarerunowa, seizei niman-endesu.
All I can lend you now would be at most ¥20,000.

4) ペットを飼いたくても、マンションでは、せいぜい小鳥ぐらいしかだめだ。
Pettoo kaitakutemo, manshondewa, seizei kotori-guraishika dameda.
In a condominium, even if (you) wanted to have a pet, you wouldn't be allowed anything more than some little birds at most.

5) 前からやりたかった研究なので、せいぜい頑張ろうと思います。
Maekara yaritakatta kenkyuunanode, seizei ganbarooto omoimasu.
Since it's research (I've) wanted to do for some time, I intend to give it my best.

6) 私で役に立つことがあれば、遠慮なく言ってください。せいぜい協力しますから。
Watashide yakuni tatsu kotoga areba, enryonaku ittekudasai. Seizei kyooryoku shimasukara.
If there's anything I can do to help, please feel free to tell me. I'll do all I can.

たかだか

■ *takadaka*
■ at most / best ; no more than 

「そのくらいなら**大したことはない・問題になるほどではない**」という、数

量や程度を表すとき使います（例7, 8, 9, 10)。

Takadaka means 'if that's about it, then it's not a great matter', or 'it doesn't amount to a problem' when speaking of a given quantity or degree (ex.7, 8, 9, 10).

---

7) こんどの家は、駅から歩いてもたかだか10分です。

Kondono iewa, ekikara aruitemo takadaka juppundesu.
(My) new house is at most ten minutes from the station, even on foot.

8) たかだか2000円の違いなら、気に入ったブラウスを買ったほうがいい。

Takadaka nisen-enno chigainara, kiniitta burausuo kattahooga ii.
As long as it's at most only ¥2,000 more, (you) should buy the blouse you like.

9) 社長といっても、たかだか従業員6人の零細企業ですから、大したことはありません。

Shachooto ittemo, takadaka juugyooin rokuninno reisaikigyoo-desukara, taishita kotowa arimasen.
(He) may be 'president', but it's just a small business with six employees, so it's no big deal.

10) たかだか半年や1年暮らしたぐらいでは、その国の伝統や文化を知りつくすことはできない。

Takadaka hantoshiya ichinen kurashita guraidewa, sono kunino dentooya bunkao shiritsukusu kotowa dekinai.
There's no way (you) can know all about a country's traditions and culture by just living there a mere six months or a year.

せっかく／わざわざ

■ *sekkaku* ■ *wazawaza*

せっかく

■ *sekkaku*
■ with a great deal of trouble (time, effort) 

ある目的のために努力をしたり、多少無理をしたのが、無駄になるのは残念だ・不満だという気持ちを表すとき使います。また、やっと手に入れた・苦

労してその状態に持ってきた・めったにないようなというようすを表すとき使います。「せっかく〜のに・けれど・が」などのように、逆接の助詞をいっしょに使うことが多いです（例1, 2, 3, 4, 5, 6）。「せっかくの」+「名詞（句）」という形でも使います。

Sekkaku is used to express a feeling of regret, dissapointment or dissatisfaction when something one put a great deal of effort into does not turn out desirably. It is also used to indicate that one has spent time, effort or hardship to obtain something, or to reach a certain state. It is often used with particles such as ～ *noni, keredo* and *ga*. The form '*sekkaku no* +noun (phrase)' is also used (ex.1, 2, 3, 4, 5, 6).

1）せっかく行ったのに、彼女は留守だった。

Sekkaku ittanoni, kanojowa rusudatta.
Although (I) went out of my way to see her, she was not home.

2）せっかく休みをとって旅行に来たのに、天気が悪いなんて……。

Sekkaku yasumio totte ryokooni kitanoni, tenkiga waruinante...
(I) went through the trouble off getting time off to make this trip, just to get awful weather.

3）せっかくのごちそうが冷めないうちに食べましょう。

Sekkakuno gochisooga samenai uchini tabemashoo.
Let's eat this fantastic meal (which she took the trouble to prepare) before it gets cold.

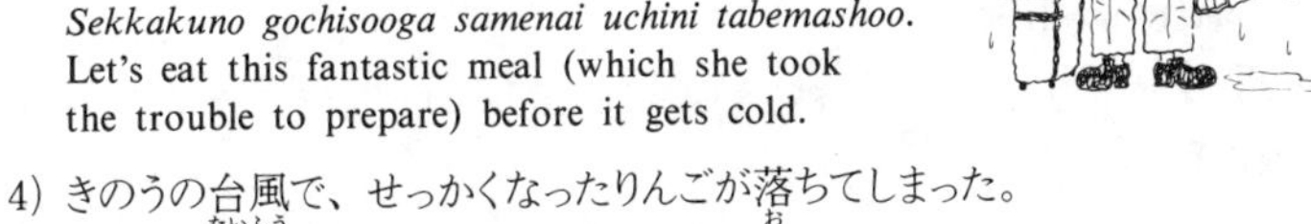

4）きのうの台風で、せっかくなったりんごが落ちてしまった。

Kinoono taifuude, sekkaku natta ringoga ochiteshimatta.
The apples, which took so much trouble to grow, ended up falling on the ground in yesterday's typhoon.

5）せっかくの休みだから、ゆっくり本を読みたい。

Sekkakuno yasumidakara, yukkuri hon-o yomitai.
Since it's a well-earned vacation, (I'd) like to spend the time reading a book leisurely.

6）せっかく昔の仲間が集まったんだから、記念写真を撮ろう。

Sekkaku mukashino nakamaga atsumattandakara, kinenshashin-o toroo.
Let's take some pictures, now that (we've) finally got the old group together.

わざわざ

■ *wazawaza*
■ on purpose ; taking the trouble (to do); especially 

①ものごとのついでや、ほかのことといっしょにではなく、**特別にそのことのために時間や、労力を使う**ようすを表すとき使います（例7, 8, 9）。

Wazawaza denotes taking time and / or effort to do something specifically. The action is not incidental to or done together with another action (ex.7, 8, 9).

②何かをするとき、必要以上に手間のかかる方法をとったり、しなくてもいいことを、好んでするようすを表すとき使います（例10, 11）。

It also denotes doing something in a way that takes more time than necessary, or purposely doing something that isn't necessary (ex.10, 11).

---

7) わざわざ行かなくても、電話で用事は済む。

Wazawaza ikanakutemo, denwade yoojiwa sumu.
(You) don't have to go out of your way—just complete the business by phone.

8) お忙しいところ、わざわざいらしてくださいましてありがとうございました。

Oisogashiitokoro, wazawaza irashite-kudasaimashite arigatoo gozaimashita.
Thank you very much for taking time from (your) busy schedule to come to see (me).

9) わざわざ届けてくれなくても、こちらに来る用事のあるときに持って来てくれればいいんですよ。

Wazawaza todokete-kurenakutemo, kochirani kuru yoojino aru tokini motte-kite kurereba iindesuyo.
(You) don't have to bother making a special trip to deliver it—just bring it when you come by next time.

10) 子供は、わざわざ水たまりを歩くのが好きだ。

Kodomowa, wazawaza mizutamario arukunoga sukida.
Children like to walk through rain puddles on purpose.

11) まっすぐ行けば近いのに、わざわざ遠回りをするなんて変な人だ。

Massugu ikeba chikainoni, wazawaza toomawario surunante henna hitoda.
(He) certainly is an oddball to take the long way around when it's shorter just to go straight.

ぜひ／どうか／なんとか／どうぞ

■ *zehi* ■ *douka* ■ *nantoka* ■ *douzo*

ぜひ［是非］

■ *zehi*
■ by all means

強い願望や**希望・依頼の気持ちを表す**とき使います。「〜てほしい・〜てもらいたい・〜てください・〜たい・〜しよう」などといっしょに使います（例1, 2, 3, 4)。「ぜひとも」は「ぜひ」よりも強い意味で使います（例５）。

Zehi indicates strong feelings of desire, hope or reliance on someone. It is often used together with such words as *〜te hoshii* (I want someone to〜), *〜te moraitai* (I want to have someone do), *〜te kudasai* (please〜), *〜tai* (I want to〜) and, *〜shiyou* (let's〜, or I shall〜) (ex.1, 2, 3, 4). *Zehi tomo* is a more emphatic way of saying *zehi* (ex.5).

1) 今度ぜひ私の家に遊びに来てください。
Kondo zehi watashino ieni asobini kite kudasai.
By all means come to visit me sometime.

2) 今年こそは、ぜひ泳げるようになりたい。
Kotoshikosowa, zehi oyogeruyooni naritai.
(I) really want to be able to swim by the end of this year.

3) 私もぜひ旅行の仲間に入れてください。
Watashimo zehi ryokoono nakamani irete kudasai.
Please allow me to join your tour group.

4) この試合には、ぜひ勝ちたい。
Kono shiainiwa, zehi kachitai.
(I) want to win this game by any means.

5) 今度の仕事は、ぜひとも成功させたい。
Kondono shigotowa, zehitomo seikoosasetai.
(I) really hope to make this project a success.

どうか

■ *douka*
■ please

心の底から強く願ったり頼んだりするとき使います。「どうぞ」よりも、「無理かもしれないけれど、それでも……」と願う気持ちが強く含まれています（例6, 7, 8, 9, 10）。

Douka is used when one wholeheartedly wishes or asks for something. It expresses a much stronger feeling of desire or hope than *douzo*, as in 'it might be unreasonable, but I still hope...' (ex.6, 7, 8, 9, 10).

---

6) お願いです、どうか私の言い分を聞いてください。
Onegaidesu, dooka watashino iibun-o kiite kudasai.
I beg you, please listen to what I have to say.

7) 神様、どうか娘の病気を治してください。
Kamisama, dooka musumeno byookio naoshite kudasai.
Oh, God, please cure my daughter's illness.

8) どうか試験に合格しますように。
Dooka shikenni gookaku-shimasuyooni.
(I) pray that I will pass the examination.

9) 今回のことは、すべて私が悪いのです。どうか許してください。
Konkaino kotowa, subete watashiga waruinodesu. Dooka yurushite kudasai.
Everything that happened this time was my fault. Please do forgive me.

10) どうかお願いだから、少し静かにしてくれませんか。
Dooka onegaidakara, sukoshi shizukani shite-kuremasenka?
I'm asking you, would you please be a little quieter?

なんとか［何とか］

■ *nantoka*
■ somehow

---

①ものごとをするのが**無理だったり、困難な状態にある**ことはわかっている**けれども**、それでも**良い方向に**行くことを**強く願う**気持ちを表します（例11, 12, 13）。

Nantoka is used to indicate that, although the speaker knows that it may be impossible or extremely difficult, he still wishes to somehow improve a situation or the condition of something (ex.11, 12, 13).

②大変だったり困難だったりしたけれど終えることができたということを表します（例14, 15）。

It is also used to indicate that, although it was hard or troublesome, the speaker was able to finish something (ex.14, 15).

11) なんとか今日中にこの仕事を終わらせたい。
Nantoka kyoojuuni kono shigotoo owarasetai.
(I) would like to finish this work by the end of the day, no matter what.

12) なんとか少し体重を減らさないと、このままでは太りすぎだ。
Nantoka sukoshi taijuuo herasanaito, kono mamadewa futorisugida.
I must lose some weight one way or another—(I) am too fat now.

13) 学生のうちに、なんとか運転免許をとりたい。
Gakuseino uchini, nantoka untenmenkyoo toritai.
One way or another, (I) want to get my driver's license while I am still a student.

14) 2年かかって、論文をなんとか書き上げた。
Ninen kakatte, ronbun-o nantoka kakiageta.
(I) somehow managed to finish writing my thesis in two years.

15) 寝ぼうしてしまったけれど、なんとかいつもの電車に間に合った。
Nebooshite-shimattakeredo, nantoka itsumono denshani maniatta.
Although (I) overslept, I was somehow able to catch my usual train.

どうぞ
■ *douzo*
■ please ; go ahead 

相手にものを**ていねいに頼む**ときや**願望**を表すとき使います(例16, 17)。また、何かを**勧めたり許可したり**するとき使います(例18, 19, 20, 21, 22)。「どうぞ」は、言い方をていねいで、やわらかい感じにします。

Douzo is used when one politely asks for something, or when one expresses a wish (ex.16, 17). It is also used when offering something or giving permission (ex.18, 19, 20, 21, 22). *Douzo* softens one's statement and makes it sound politer.

16) 初めまして。どうぞよろしく。
Hajimemashite. Doozo yoroshiku.
How do you do? (lit. Please treat me favorably.)

17) どうぞいつまでもお元気で。

Doozo itsumademo ogenkide.
May (you) always be in good health.

18) A：窓を開けてもいいですか。

B：ええ、どうぞ。

A： *Madoo aketemo iidesuka?* May (I) open the window?
B： *Ee, doozo.* Yes, you may.

19) A：ペンを貸していただけますか。

B：はい、どうぞ。

A： *Pen-o kashite itadakemasuka?* May (I) borrow your pen?
B： *Hai, doozo.* Sure, here you are.

20) どうぞお大事に。

Doozo odaijini.
(to a sick person) Please take care of yourself.

21) どうぞ召し上がってください。

Doozo meshiagatte kudasai.
Please help yourself.

22) 次の方、どうぞお入りください。

Tsugino kata, doozo ohairikudasai.
Next person, please come in.

そして／それから／すると

■ *soshite* ■ *sorekara* ■ *suruto*

そして ■ *soshite* ■ then ; and 

つぎつぎと、ことがらを重ねてあげていくときや、関連して起こることがらを述べるとき使います。最後のものや、結論・結果を述べるという感じを含みます（例1, 2, 3, 4, 5）。

Soshite is used when referring to a number of events or matters and describing each of them in succession. It includes a feeling that the speaker is expressing the last of the matters, or the conclusion or result (ex.1, 2, 3, 4, 5).

1) きょうの時間割り(じかんわ)は、英語(えいご)・数学(すうがく)・音楽(おんがく)、そして物理(ぶつり)です。
Kyoono jikanwariwa, Eigo, suugaku, ongaku, soshite butsuridesu.
My class schedule for today is English, math, music, and then physics.

2) この間(あいだ)、鎌倉(かまくら)に行(い)きました。大仏(だいぶつ)やお寺(てら)を見(み)て、そして夜(よる)は、海辺(うみべ)を散歩(さんぽ)しました。
Konoaida, Kamakurani ikimashita. Daibutsuya oterao mite, soshite yoruwa, umibeo sanposhimashita.
(I) went to Kamakura a few days ago. I saw the Great Buddha statue and some temples, and then I took a walk by the sea.

3) 私(わたし)の希望(きぼう)は、法学部(ほうがくぶ)に行(い)って勉強(べんきょう)して、そして裁判官(さいばんかん)になることです。
Watashino kiboowa, hoogakubuni itte benkyooshite, soshite saibankanni naru kotodesu.
My hope is to study in the department of law and after that become a judge.

4) 収穫(しゅうかく)したぶどうを絞(しぼ)って、発酵(はっこう)させ、ねかせて……そしてワインを作(つく)ります。
Shuukakushita budoo-o shibotte, hakkoosase, nekasete...soshite wain-o tsukurimasu.
The harvested grapes are crushed, fermented and aged—that's how we make wine.

5) 彼(かれ)らは、長(なが)い間(あいだ)調査(ちょうさ)を続(つづ)け、そしてついに、古代(こだい)の遺跡(いせき)を発見(はっけん)した。
Karerawa, nagai aida choosao tsuzuke, soshite tsuini, kodaino isekio hakkenshita.
They continued their exploration for many years, and finally discovered the ancient ruins.

それから

■ *sorekara*
■ after that ; then

①あることがらの、後(あと)(その次(つぎ))のことがらを述(の)べるとき使(つか)います。ことがらの順番(じゅんばん)を、はっきり表(あらわ)します。「その時以来(ときいらい)」という意味(いみ)でも使(つか)います(例(れい)6, 7, 8, 9)。

After describing the occurrence of a given matter, this term is used when mentioning the aftermath or a subsequent event. It clearly expresses the sequence of events. It can also be used to mean *sono toki irai* (from that time forward) (ex.6, 7, 8, 9).

②ことがらを順にあげていって、そのほかにもう1つ2つ、付け加えるときに使います（例10, 11）。

Sorekara is also used when, after describing a sequence of events or matters, the speaker then supplements the prior discourse with one or two items (not necessarily in any order) (ex.10, 11).

---

6) きょうは、午前中に銀行へ行って、それから大学に行きます。
Kyoowa, gozenchuuni ginkooe itte, sorekara daigakuni ikimasu.
This morning (I'll) go to the bank, and then I'll go to the university.

7) 私は朝起きるとまずシャワーをあびます。それから食事をします。
Watashiwa asa okiruto mazu shawaao abimasu. Sorekara shokujio shimasu.
The first thing I do after waking up is take a shower. Then I have breakfast.

8) 私は子供のころ犬にかまれた。それから犬が大きらいになった。
Watashiwa kodomono koro inuni kamareta. Sorekara inuga daikiraini natta.
I was bitten by a dog when I was a child. Since then I've hated dogs.

9) A：来月会社を辞めて、田舎へ帰ります。
B：それからどうするの。

A： *Raigetsu kaishao yamete, inakae kaerimasu.*
Next month (I'm) going to quit my job (the company) and go back to my hometown.
B： *Sorekara doosuruno?* Then, what will (you) do?

10) きのうデパートに行って、セーターとシャツと、それからネクタイを買いました。
Kinoo depaatoni itte, seetaato shatsuto, sorekara nekutaio kaimashita.
(I) went to the department store yesterday and bought a sweater, shirt and necktie.

11) 私の好きな食べ物は、おすしと焼き肉と、それからうどんです。
*Watashino sukina tabemonowa, osushi*to yakinikuto, sorekara udon**desu.*
*p.410 **p.500
My favorite foods are *sushi*, *yakiniku* and *udon*.

すると ■*suruto* ■whereupon ; then

①あることがらに続いて、起こったことがらを述べるための**つなぎのことば**です。初めのことがらが原因や要因になっています。「そして・それから」が、1つのことがらが終わって次に別のことがらが起こるという時間の経過に重点があるのに対し、「すると」は、「**思いもよらない結果になった、考えてもいなかったのに**」、という**軽い驚き**を含むこともあります。ですから、未来のことや話し手の意志を表すことには使いません（例12, 13, 14, 15）。

Suruto indicates that some action or event occurs following a previous action or event. The first action is considered to be the cause of second. *Soshite* and *sorekara* emphasize the temporal sequence between one event and the following one, whereas *suruto* includes an element of slight surprise at the unexpected or unthought-of results. Thus, *suruto* cannot be used when speaking of future events or to express one's own will (ex.12, 13, 14, 15).

②それまでに話題になったことから考えられることを述べるときに使います。「それならば」「それでは」という意味です（例16, 17）。

It may be used to mention something which can be considered as deriving from the immediately preceding topic of conversation, as in saying 'Well then,...' or 'If that's the case,...' (ex.16, 17).

---

12) 夜が明けはじめた。するといろいろな鳥の声がきこえてきた。
Yoga akehajimeta. Suruto iroirona torino koega kikoetekita.
Day began to break, whereupon all kinds of birds could be heard.

13) 男の子が口笛を吹きました。すると犬がとんで来ました。
Otokonokoga kuchibueo fukimashita. Suruto inuga tondekimashita.
The boy whistled, and his dog came running up.

14) 暑いので窓を開けた。すると明かりにつられて虫がたくさん入ってきた。
Atsuinode madoo aketa. Suruto akarini tsurarete mushiga takusan haittekita.
It was hot so (I) opened the window, whereupon lots of bugs came in, attracted by the light.

15) 40階で会議をしていたら大きな地震があった。すると人々はとっさに机の下に入った。
Yonjukkaide kaigio shiteitara ookina jishinga atta. Suruto hitobitowa tossani tsukueno shitani haitta.

(We) were in conference on the 40th floor when there was a big earthquake, whereupon everybody instantly got under the table.

16) A：台風が日本の上を通るそうです。

B：すると明日は東京も雨ですね。

A：*Taifuuga Nihonno ueo tooru soodesu.*
The typhoon is going to pass over Japan, (I) hear.

B：*Suruto ashitawa Tookyoomo amedesune.*
That means it's going to rain in Tokyo tomorrow, doesn't it?

17) A：来週、青森に出張になったんです。

B：すると久しぶりに、ご両親に会えるわけですね。

A：*Raishuu, Aomorini shutchooni nattandesu.*
(I'm) going on a business trip to Aomori next week.

B：*Suruto hisashiburini, goryooshinni aeru wakedesune?*
Really? Then (you'll) have a chance to see your folks, won't you?

そそぐ／つぐ

■ ***sosogu*** ■ ***tsugu***

そそぐ［注ぐ］ ■ *sosogu* ■ to pour ; to flow 

①ある目標に**液体を**、とぎれないように**ていねいに流したり、かけたりする**ことです（例1, 2）。

To carefully allow a liquid to flow without interruption for a certain purpose (ex.1, 2).

②川が、海や湖に流れていくことです（例３）。

Sosogu may be used to describe the flowing of a river into an ocean or lake (ex.3).

③**視線・愛情・情熱**などを**集中させる**とき使います（例4, 5）。

To direct things such as a gaze, affection, or passion at something or someone (ex.4, 5).

---

1) 私は洗面器に水を注いだ。

Watashiwa senmenkini mizuo sosoida.
I poured water into the washbowl.

2) カップ麺(めん)は、熱湯(ねっとう)を注(そそ)いでから少(すこ)し待(ま)たなければ食(た)べられません。

Kappumenwa, nettoo-o sosoidekara sukoshi matanakereba taberaremasen.
For instant (cup) noodles, (you) have to wait a short while after you pour the hot water before you can eat them.

3) 信濃川(しなのがわ)は、日本海(にほんかい)に注(そそ)いでいる。

Shinanogawawa, Nihonkaini sosoide iru.
The Shinano River flows into the Sea of Japan.

4) 両親(りょうしん)は、私(わたし)たち兄弟(きょうだい)に深(ふか)い愛情(あいじょう)を注(そそ)いでくれた。

Ryooshinwa, watashi-tachi kyoodaini fukai aijoo-o sosoide kureta.
Our parents showered their deep affection on all of us children.

5) 彼女(かのじょ)は、野生動物(やせいどうぶつ)の保護(ほご)に情熱(じょうねつ)を注(そそ)いでいる。

Kanojowa, yaseidoobutsuno hogoni joonetsuo sosoide iru.
She is very passionate about protecting wild animals.

つぐ ■*tsugu* ■to pour (into)

水(みず)やお茶(ちゃ)などの**飲(の)みものを**、コップや湯(ゆ)のみなど、飲(の)むための**器(うつわ)に入(い)れる**ことです（例(れい)6, 7, 8）。

To put a liquid such as water or tea into a container such as a cup or glass in order to drink it (ex.6, 7, 8).

---

6) きゅうすから湯(ゆ)のみにお茶(ちゃ)をつぐ。

Kyuusukara yunomini ochao tsugu.
Pour the tea from the teapot into the tea cups.

7) 神道(しんとう)の結婚式(けっこんしき)では、新郎新婦(しんろうしんぷ)は杯(さかずき)につがれた酒(さけ)を飲(の)む。

Shintoono kekkonshikidewa, shinroo-shinpuwa sakazukini tsugareta sakeo nomu.
In *Shinto* weddings, the newlyweds drink *sake* which has been poured into a *sakazuki* (*sake* cup).

8) ウエイターは、客(きゃく)のグラスにワインをついでまわった。

Ueitaawa, kyakuno gurasuni wain-o tsuide mawatta.
The waiter went around the room pouring wine into the guests' glasses.

そだてる／やしなう

■ *sodateru* ■ *yashinau*

そだてる［育てる］

■ *sodateru*
■ to raise (children, animals)

人間や動物、植物の**世話をして成長させる**ことです（例1, 2, 3, 4）。**才能や能力などを身につけさせ**たり、**伸びるように**したりするときにも使います（例5, 6）。しつけをして、正しい方向に成長させるという意味を含みます。

To take care of a person, animal, plant, etc., so that it may grow and mature (ex.1, 2, 3, 4). It may also be used to mean to teach a skill or allow someone to gain ability in something (ex.5, 6). It suggests that one uses training or discipline to cause someone or something to develop in the proper way.

1）母は子供を５人育てた。
Hahawa kodomoo gonin sodateta.
My mother raised five children.

2）子供を育てるのは、苦労でもあり喜びでもある。
Kodomoo sodaterunowa, kuroodemo ari yorokobidemo aru.
There is both suffering and joy in raising children.

3）このライオンは、人間に育てられた。
Kono raionwa, ningenni sodaterareta.
This lion was raised by humans.

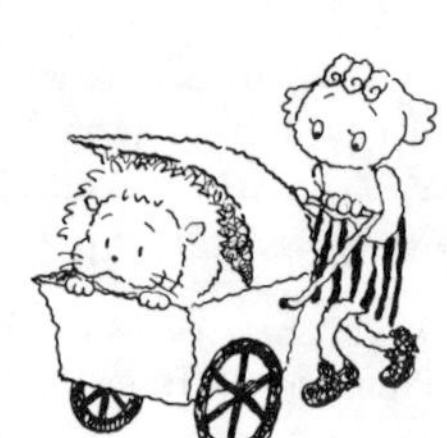

4）これは私が育てたゆりです。
Korewa watashiga sodateta yuridesu.
This is the lily that I grew.

5）彼は、多くの俳優を育ててきた。
Karewa, ookuno haiyuuo sodatetekita.
He has trained many actors.

6）彼女の両親は、彼女のピアノの才能を育てるために、留学させた。
Kanojono ryooshinwa, kanojono pianono sainoo-o sodaterutameni, ryuugakusaseta.
Her parents sent her abroad to develop her piano skills.

やしなう［養う］ ■ *yashinau* ■ to support

①人や動物の食べ物や住むところなど、**経済的な生活の面倒を見る**ことです（例7, 8）。

To look after a person or animal in economic sense, providing e.g., food, housing, etc. (ex.7, 8).

②**能力**や**気力**などを身につけて、**豊かに**していくことです（例9, 10）。

To better oneself by enriching one's own abilities or will (ex.9, 10).

---

7) 彼女は、病気の夫と３人の子供を養うために、夜おそくまで働いている。
Kanojowa, byookino ottoto sanninno kodomoo yashinau tameni, yoru osokumade hataraiteiru.
She works until late at night every day in order to support her sick husband and three children.

8) 私は子供のころ、叔父に養ってもらった。
Watashiwa kodomono koro, ojini yashinatte-moratta.
I was supported by my uncle when I was a child.

9) 彼は、空手によって体力を養ったそうです。
Karewa, karateni yotte tairyokuo yashinatta soodesu.
(I) hear he developed his body strength through *karate*.

10) 絵画に対する確かな目を養うには、良い作品をたくさん見ることです。
Kaigani taisuru tashikana meo yashinauniwa, yoi sakuhin-o takusan mirukotodesu.
It takes looking at a lot of good works to develop an eye for paintings.

コーヒーは２杯か２つか

ものを数えるときに使う単位の、助数詞には「（えんぴつ）１本・（車）２台・（本）３さつ…」などたくさんあります。コーヒーはどうでしょうか。「１杯・２杯…」と数えます。スパゲティは…？　「１本・２本…」とも数えますし、料理として出てくれば「１皿・２皿…」と言います。それなのに…。

レストランでビルが直人の分も含めて「コーヒー２杯」と言ったらウェイトレスは、ビルの前に２杯置くかもしれません。２人分のつもりならふつうは「コーヒー２つ」と言います。レストランや喫茶店などで注文するときは、助数詞にこだわらずに「（１つ、２つ、のように）～つ」を使うのです。ただ、もしもビルが本当にコーヒーを一度に２杯飲みたければ「コーヒー２杯」と注文していいのです。

Coffee-2 cups or a double order

In Japanese, there are many different words used for counting, depending on the objects being counted; for example, *ippon* (a pencil), *nidai* (two cars), and *sansatsu* (three books). What about coffee? A cup of coffee is counted as *ippai, nihai.* Well then, what about spaghetti? Spaghetti noodles are counted as *ippon, nihon*, but if they are prepared as a meal then *hitosara*[1], *futasara*[2] is used. However...

Say Bill and Naoto go to a restaurant together. If Bill orders coffee for both Naoto and himself by saying, "*Koohii nihai,*" the waitress may place two cups of coffee in front of Bill. Ordinarily, when ordering for two at a restaurant or coffee shop one would say "*Koohii futatsu,*" as the generic counting form ~*tsu* (e.g., *hitotsu*[3], *futatsu*[4]) is used regardless of the proper counting word. However, if Bill really wanted to drink two cups of coffee at one time, then it would be all right to say "*Koohii nihai.*"

1 *One plate.* 2 *Two plates.* 3 *One order.* 4 *Two orders.*

それぞれ／おのおの／めいめい

■ *sorezore* ■ *onoono* ■ *meimei*

それぞれ

■ *sorezore*
■ each ; respectively 

いくつかの物やことがら、あるいは何人かの人の中での、**一つ一つ、一人一人を指す**とき使います（例1, 2, 3, 4, 5）。例３のように、何人かが集まってできているグループを一つの単位としてとらえることもあります。例5のような使い方をするのは「それぞれ」だけです。「それぞれ」は「おのおの・めいめい」よりも日常的に使われることばです。

Sorezore is used to designate each person or object that belongs to a group of people or objects (ex.1, 2, 3, 4, 5). As in Example 3, it may also be used when referring to a group of people as one. In expressions like the one in Example 5, *sorezore* is the only word of the three words listed above that may be used. *Sorezore* is more commonly used in conversation than are *onoono* and *meimei.*

---

1) 人はそれぞれ考え方がちがう。
Hitowa sorezore kangaekataga chigau.
Each person has his own way of thinking.

2) 彼女は、ピンクのバラと白いバラをそれぞれ３本ずつ買った。
Kanojowa, pinkuno barato shiroi barao sorezore sanbonzutsu katta.
She bought three each of the pink and white roses.

3) どこの家庭にもそれぞれ悩みはあるものだ。
Dokono kateinimo sorezore nayamiwa arumonoda.
Every family has its problems.

4) 私には兄が２人いて、それぞれ会社員と公務員です。
Watashiniwa aniga futariite, sorezore kaishainto koomuindesu.
I have two (elder) brothers; one is an office worker and the other is a civil servant.

5) このお皿の上のケーキは、左からそれぞれチーズケーキ、アップルパイ、チョコレートケーキです。
Kono osarano ueno keekiwa, hidarikara sorezore chiizu-keeki, appuru-pai, chokoreeto-keekidesu.
The cakes on this plate are, from the left, cheesecake, apple pie, and chocolate cake.

おのおの ■*onoono* ■each 

何人かの人の内の、一人一人を指します。基本的には人について使いますが(例6, 7, 8)、特徴や独特な特色などを言う時には人以外のものにも使います

(例9, 10)。「それぞれ」よりも**改まった**語で、**かたい**言い方です。

Onoono is used to designate every individual of a group of people. Although primarily used when speaking of people (ex.6, 7, 8), it may also be used when speaking of the special characteristics of things other than people (ex.9, 10). *Onoono* is used in more formal expressions than *sorezore*.

---

6) 私たちは、おのおの自分の荷物をロッカーに入れた。
Watashitachiwa, onoono jibunno nimotsuo rokkaani ireta.
We each put our baggage in our own locker.

7) 友達がおのおの料理を１品ずつ持ってわが家に集まることになった。
Tomodachiga, onoono ryoorio ippinzutsu motte wagayani atsumaru kotoni natta.
It's been decided that my friends will gather at my house, each bringing a dish with them.

8) この病院には８人医者がいて、おのおの専門が違う。
Kono byooinniwa hachinin ishaga ite, onoono senmonga chigau.
This hospital has eight doctors, each with his own specialty.

9) 漢字は表意文字で、おのおの意味を持っている。
Kanjiwa hyooimojide, onoono imio motteiru.
Kanji characters are ideographs, each with its own meaning.

10) 包丁には種類がたくさんあって、おのおの用途が違う。
Hoochooniwa shuruiga takusan atte, onoono yootoga chigau.
There are many kinds of kitchen knives, each one with a different use.

めいめい

■ *meimei*
■ each (person) 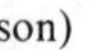 

何人かの集まりの中での**個人個人**を指します（例11, 12, 13）。その人自身、個人に判断や行為が任されるという感じがあります。

Meimei is used to refer to each person in a group of people (ex.11, 12, 13). A sense that each person is left to make his own judgments, or determine his own actions, is implied.

---

11) 中華料理は、めいめいが大皿から自分の小皿に取って食べます。
Chuukaryooriwa, meimeiga oozarakara jibunno kozarani totte tabemasu.

Chinese food is served on one large plate, and each person takes the amount (he) wants on his own small plate to eat.

12) 自分の食器は、めいめい自分で洗ってください。
Jibunno shokkiwa, meimei jibunde aratte kudasai.
Please wash your own dishes.

13) うちは子供が4人いて、めいめいが一部屋ずつほしがっている。
Uchiwa kodomoga yonin ite, meimeiga hitoheyazutsu hoshigatteiru.
There are four children in our family, and each wants (his) own room.

それに／そのうえ／しかも

■ *soreni* ■ *sonoue* ■ *shikamo*

それに ■ *soreni* ■ besides

今述べたことに、また**似たようなことをつけ加える**とき使います（例1, 2, 3)。くだけた会話の中で使います。

Soreni is used when adding something of a similar nature to a statement one has just made (ex.1, 2, 3). It is often used in informal conversation.

1) 今日は暑い、それに湿度も高い。
Kyoowa atsui, soreni shitsudomo takai.
It's hot today, and besides that the humidity is high.

2) この店は安い、それに品物も揃っている。
Kono misewa yasui, soreni shinamonomo sorotteiru.
This shop is inexpensive, and on top of that they have a large selection.

3) のどが痛いし、それに少し熱っぽい。どうもかぜをひいたらしい。
Nodoga itaishi, soreni sukoshi netsuppoi. Doomo kazeo hiitarashii.
(I) have a sore throat and a slight fever as well. It feels like I'm coming down with a cold.

そのうえ ■ *sonoue* ■ besides ; moreover 

ことがらや状況を説明するのに、もう一つのことがらや状況をつけ加えるとき使います（例4, 5, 6, 7）。「**それだけでも十分なのに、さらに**」の意味です。「そのうえ」は、改まった少しかたいことばです。

This is used when, after explaining a matter or condition, one adds a further matter or condition (ex.4, 5, 6, 7). It is used when the speaker wishes to say that, although the original statement was sufficient, there is more to add. *Sonoue* is a slightly formal expression.

4）卵は安い、そのうえ栄養もある。

Tamagowa yasui, sonoue eiyoomo aru.
Eggs are cheap and, moreover, they are nutritious.

5）道に迷ってしまった。日は暮れてくるし、そのうえ雨まで降りだした。

Michini mayotteshimatta. Hiwa kuretekurushi, sonoue amemade furidashita.
(I) got lost. The sun was setting, and to make things worse it started to rain.

6）おばがセーターを編んで送ってくれた。そのうえ、おそろいのマフラーと手袋まで入っていた。

Obaga seetaao ande okuttekureta. Sonoue, osoroino mafuraato tebukuromade haitteita.
My aunt sent (me) a sweater she had knitted. And on top of that, she included some matching gloves and a muffler.

7）今日、私は友達のお母さんに食事をごちそうになった。そのうえ、おみやげまでいただいた。

Kyoo, watashiwa tomodachino okaasanni shokujio gochisooni natta. Sonoue, omiyage made itadaita.
Today, my friend's mother treated me to a meal. On top of that, I also received a present from her.

しかも

■ *shikamo*
■ besides ; furthermore 

あることがらや状態にもう一つのことがらや状態を重ねて述べるとき使います（例8, 9, 10）。「**それだけでなく・そのうえさらに**」の意味です。「おどろき・よろこび・困惑」などの感情が含まれている感じです。

Shikamo is used when adding a second statement to a first (ex.8, 9, 10), and means the same as *sore dake de naku* (not only that, but～) and *sonoue sarani* (furthermore). Feelings such as surprise, happiness, or embarrassment may be implied.

8) 彼は、もう結婚している。しかも、子供が３人もいる。
Karewa, moo kekkonshiteiru. Shikamo, kodomoga sanninmo iru.
He's already married. Furthermore, he has three children.

9) きょうから連休で、しかも天気がいいので行楽地はどこも混雑している。
Kyookara renkyuude, shikamo tenkiga iinode koorakuchiwa dokomo konzatsushiteiru.
Today is the first day of the long holiday, and on top of that, it's a beautiful day, so all the resort areas are crowded.

10) この洗剤は、今までのものより汚れがよく落ち、しかも半分の量ですむ。
Kono senzaiwa, imamadeno monoyori yogorega yoku ochi, shikamo hanbunno ryoode sumu.
This detergent gets clothes cleaner than the detergent (I) have been using, and I use only half the amount.

そろえる／まとめる

■ *soroeru* ■ *matomeru*

そろえる

■ *soroeru*
■ to gather ; to arrange

①ばらばらになっているものを、**きちんと**正しく**並べたり置いたりする**ことです（例1, 2）。

To place or line up in proper order objects that are scattered (ex.1, 2).

②**種類**や**大きさ**、**調子**などを同じように**統一する**ことです（例3, 4）。

To standardize things according to type, size, condition, etc. (ex.3, 4)

③**必要なもの**を**集めたり準備したりする**ことです。本来一組になっているものを集めるという意味も含みます（例5, 6, 7）。

To collect or prepare things that will be necessary. It is implied that the objects collected belong together (ex.5, 6, 7).

1) 靴をぬいだら、きちんとそろえてください。
Kutsuo nuidara, kichinto soroete kudasai.
Please arrange (your) shoes properly after you take them off.

2) 床に紙が散らばっていたので、そろえて机の上に置いた。
Yukani kamiga chirabatteitanode, soroete tsukueno ueni oita.
The papers were scattered about on the floor, so (I) gathered them together and put them on the desk.

3) ひもは、長さを２メートルにそろえて切っておいてください。
Himowa, nagasao nimeetoruni soroete kitteoite kudasai.
Please cut the string in equal lengths of two meters.

4) 家具の色をそろえると、部屋の感じがすっきりする。
Kaguno iroo soroeruto, heyano kanjiga sukkirisuru.
The room will look tidy if (you) make all the furniture the same color.

5) 鍋料理は、材料さえそろえておけば簡単にできる。
*Nabe-ryoori*wa, zairyoosae soroeteokeba kantanni dekiru.*
It's easy to cook *nabe-ryoori* if (you) gather the ingredients beforehand.
—— * *Nabe-ryoori* is a dish consisting of meat and/or fish, vegetables, and *tofu* that is cooked on a small stove placed in the middle of the dinner table. A popular form of *nabe-ryoori* is *sukiyaki.*

6) 彼は日曜大工が趣味なので、工具をいろいろそろえている。
Karewa nichiyoo-daikuga shuminanode, kooguo iroiro soroeteiru.
He's a do-it-yourselfer, so he has collected many kinds of tools.

7) 私は、シェークスピア全集をそろえようと思っている。
Watashiwa, Sheekusupia-zenshuuo soroeyooto omotteiru.
I'm thinking about collecting the complete works of Shakespeare.

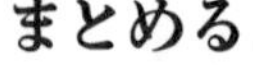

■ *matomeru*
■ to gather ; to collect 

ものを**１か所に集めたり**、**１つにする**ことです（例8, 9, 10）。いろいろな意見を１つに決めたり合意させるとき（例11, 12）、考えやものごとの内容を**整理**したり**要約する**とき（例13, 14, 15）、また「まとめて」の形で、何回分かを一度にという意味で使います（例16, 17）。

To collect things together in one place in order to form a group (ex.8, 9, 10). It may be used to mean to form a consensus from many opinions (ex.11, 12), to sum up things such as one's thoughts by arranging them (ex.13, 14, 15), or in the form *matomete*, to do something at once instead of over several times (ex.16, 17).

---

8) この市では、再利用できる新聞や雑誌を、まとめて決められた日に出します。

Kono shidewa, sairiyoodekiru shinbun-ya zasshio, matomete kimerareta hini dashimasu.
In this town (we) collect our recyclable newspapers and magazines, and put them out on the designated day.

9) 彼女は、長い髪をうしろで1つにまとめて、リボンで結んでいる。
Kanojowa, nagai kamio ushirode hitotsuni matomete, ribonde musundeiru.
She gathered her long hair back into a pony tail, and tied it with a ribbon.

10) 私のうちでは、電気製品などの保証書を、なくさないように1か所にまとめてとってある。
Watashino uchidewa, denki-seihinnadono hoshooshoo, nakusanai yooni ikkashoni matomete totte aru.
At our house, (we) keep the warranties for our appliances and such all together in one place so we won't lose them.

11) 大勢の意見を1つにまとめるのは、とても難しいことだ。
Oozeino iken-o hitotsuni matomerunowa, totemo muzukashii kotoda.
It's very difficult to get many people to agree on one thing.

12) 彼はサッカー部の主将として、この1年間部員をよくまとめてきた。
Karewa sakkaabuno shushootoshite, kono ichinenkan buin-o yoku matometekita.
He did a good job of leading the team during his year as captain of the soccer club.

13) アンケートの結果をまとめて、報告書を書かなければならない。
Ankeetono kekkao matomete, hookokushoo kakanakereba-naranai.
(I) have to put together the results of the survey and write a report.

14) 私は教授から、今までの研究をまとめて論文を書くようにと言われた。
Watashiwa kyoojukara, imamadeno kenkyuuo matomete ronbun-o kakuyoonito iwareta.

I've been told by my professor to organize all of my research to date and write it up in a paper.

15) まわりが騒々しいので、考えをまとめることができない。
Mawariga soozooshiinode, kangaeo matomeru kotoga dekinai.
With all of this noise around I can't concentrate.

16) 彼女は勤めているので、食料品は週に1回まとめて買う。
Kanojowa tsutometeirunode, shokuryoohinwa shuuni ikkai matomete kau.
She works, so she does all of her grocery shopping once a week.

17) 掃除や洗濯は、まとめてするより毎日少しずつするほうが楽だ。
Soojiya sentakuwa, matometesuruyori mainichi sukoshizutsu suruhooga rakuda.
It's easier to do things such as house cleaning and laundry if (you) do a little every day, instead of all at once.

そろそろ／やがて／そのうち

■ *sorosoro* ■ *yagate* ■ *sonouchi*

そろそろ

■ *sorosoro*
■ soon ; almost

ものごとを始めたり、ものごとが起こったりするのに、ちょうどよい時期が近づいたようすを表します（例1, 2, 3, 4）。

Sorosoro indicates that the appropriate time to begin something, or for something to occur, has approached (ex.1, 2, 3, 4).

1) おなかがすいたでしょう。そろそろ食事にしましょう。
Onakaga suitadeshoo? Sorosoro shokujini shimashoo.
(I'll) bet (you're) hungry. It's about time we got something to eat.

2) 暗くなってきたから、そろそろ帰らなくちゃ。
Kuraku nattekitakara, sorosoro kaeranakucha.
It's gotten dark so (I) should head back home now.

3) まだ10時だけど、朝5時に起きなくてはならないから、そろそろ寝よう。
Mada juujidakedo, asa gojini okinakutewa naranaikara, sorosoro neyoo.

Although it's only ten o'clock, (I) have to get up at five tomorrow, so I guess I'll go to bed soon.

4) 芝居が6時に始まるから、そろそろ出かけましょう。
Shibaiga rokujini hajimarukara, sorosoro dekakemashoo.
The play starts at 6 o'clock, so let's get going soon.

やがて ■ *yagate* ■ soon

①1つの**ことがらが終わって次に・まもなく**、というようすを表します（例5,6）。

This expresses that something occurs shortly after the previous event is finished (ex.5, 6).

②ものごとが、**続いていった結果**を述べるときに、「将来」の意味で使います（例7, 8, 9, 10）。この場合は「やがては～」と使うこともあります。

When speaking of an action that will lead to an outcome, it is used to mean 'the future' (ex.7, 8, 9, 10), and is often used in the form *yagate wa*～.

---

5) 長かった冬ももうじき終わり、やがて春が来ます。
Nagakatta fuyumo moojiki owari, yagate haruga kimasu.
The long winter is almost over and spring will soon begin.

6) 夜中に降りだした雨は、やがて雪になった。
Yonakani furidashita amewa, yagate yukini natta.
In the middle of night the rain soon turned to snow.

7) ものを大切にしないと、やがて地球の資源はなくなってしまうだろう。
Monoo taisetsuni shinaito, yagate chikyuuno shigenwa nakunatte shimaudaroo.
If (we) don't take care of things now, we will one day lose all of our natural resources.

8) 平均寿命が延びるいっぽう、子供の数は年々減っている。このままでは、やがて老人ばかりになってしまう。
Heikinjumyooga nobiru ippoo, kodomono kazuwa nennen hetteiru. Kono mamadewa, yagate roojinbakarini natteshimau.
The average life expectancy is increasing while people are having fewer children each year. At this rate, society will be full of old people some-

day.

9) 静かだったこの村にも観光客が来るようになった。やがては自然が失われてしまうだろう。

Shizukadatta kono muranimo kankookyakuga kuruyooni natta. Yagatewa shizenga ushinawarete shimaudaroo.
This once quiet town has become full of tourists. It won't be long until the natural scenery is lost.

10) 医学の研究が進めば、やがてはどんな病気でも治せる日が来るだろう。

Igakuno kenkyuuga susumeba, yagatewa donna byookidemo naoseru higa kurudaroo.
If medical research continues to progress, the day will probably come when all diseases will be curable.

そのうち

■ *sonouchi*
■ soon ; someday

「**近いうちに・少し時間がたってから**・ある程度の時間がたてば」という意味で使います（例11, 12, 13）。ここで言う、時間の長さは、何らかの基準や経験に基づいていて、話し手や聞き手が、だいたい判断できる程度のものです。また、はっきりと日時を決めないで、**あいまいに**するとき使います（例14, 15）。

Sonouchi is used to mean 'soon', 'after a short time', or 'after a certain period of time' (ex.11, 12, 13). The period of time referred to is based on things such as a standard or one's experience, so that both the speaker and the listener are able to judge its length. It is also used when making a vague reference to the future, i.e., not deciding on a specific date or time (ex.14, 15).

---

11) 西の空が明るくなってきたから、そのうち雨も止むでしょう。

Nishino soraga akaruku nattekitakara, sonouchi amemo yamudeshoo.
The western sky has brightened some, so the rain will probably stop soon.

12) 講演を聴きながら、はじめはメモを取っていたけれど、そのうち面倒になってやめてしまった。

Kooen-o kikinagara, hajimewa memoo totteitakeredo, sonouchi mendooni natte yameteshimatta.
(I) began taking notes while listening to the lecture, but after a while it became troublesome so (I) stopped.

13) しばらく傷あとが残りますが、そのうち目立たなくなりますから心配はいりません。

Shibaraku kizuatoga nokorimasuga, sonouchi medatanaku narimasukara shinpaiwa irimasen.
(You'll) have a scar for a while, but it will eventually disappear so don't worry about it.

14) あの店のてんぷらはとてもおいしいから、そのうちあなたにごちそうします。

Ano miseno tenpurawa totemo oishiikara, sonouchi anatani gochisooshimasu.
That restaurant serves great *tempura*, so (I'll) treat you to dinner there sometime.

15) きょうは忙しいからだめだけど、そのうちゆっくり会いましょう。

Kyoowa isogashiikara damedakedo, sonouchi yukkuri aimashoo.
(I'm) busy so today is out, but let's meet some other day when we'll have plenty of time.

たいくつ／あきる

■ *taikutsu* ■ *akiru*

たいくつ ■ *taikutsu* ■ boring 

①なにも**することがなく**、時間をもてあましていて**おもしろくない**ようすを表します（例1,2）。

Taikutsu indicates that one has nothing to do, has time to spare, and is not amused (ex.1, 2).

②興味の対象にならなくて、**つまらない**ようすを表します（例3,4,5）。

It may also describe something as uninteresting (ex.3, 4, 5).

1) きょうは一日中何もすることがなく、たいくつな日だった。

Kyoowa ichinichijuu nanimo suru kotoga naku, taikutsuna hidatta.
Today was boring because there was nothing to do all day.

2) たいくつだから、テレビでも見ようかな。

Taikutsudakara, terebidemo miyookana.

(I'm) bored so maybe I'll watch some TV.

3) きょうの芝居(しばい)はたいくつだった。

Kyoono shibaiwa taikutsudatta.
Today's play was boring.

4) あの教授(きょうじゅ)の講義(こうぎ)はたいくつで、あくびがでる。

Ano kyoojuno koogiwa taikutsude, akubiga deru.
(I) end up yawning during that professor's lectures because they are so dull.

5) 彼(かれ)はたいくつで魅力(みりょく)のない男(おとこ)だ。

Karewa taikutsude miryokuno nai otokoda.
He is a boring man with absolutely no charm.

あきる［飽(あ)きる］ ■ *akiru* ■ to be tired of 

ものごとに対(たい)して**興味(きょうみ)を失(うしな)ってしまったり**、十分(じゅうぶん)すぎて**うんざりしたり**、いやになったりするようすを表(あらわ)します（例(れい)6, 7, 8, 9）。

Akiru indicates that one loses interest in something, or that something becomes tiresome because one has had one's fill (ex.6, 7, 8, 9).

---

6) 子供(こども)たちは、新(あたら)しいゲームにもすぐにあきてしまった。

Kodomotachiwa, atarashii geemunimo suguni akiteshimatta.
The children soon became bored with the new game, too.

7) 生徒(せいと)たちは校長先生(こうちょうせんせい)の長(なが)い話(はなし)にあきて、おしゃべりを始(はじ)めた。

Seitotachiwa koochoosenseino nagai hanashini akite, oshaberio hajimeta.
The students grew weary of the principal's long speech and began chatting among themselves.

8) 私(わたし)はおすしが大好(だいす)きで、毎日(まいにち)食(た)べてもあきない。

*Watashiwa osushi*ga daisukide, mainichi tabetemo akinai.*
I love *sushi*, and could eat it every day without getting tired of it.
—— * *Sushi* is vinegared rice formed into the shape of a ball and topped with slices of raw fish, shellfish, fish eggs, or other foods.

9) もう彼(かれ)の自慢話(じまんばなし)は、聞(き)きあきた。

Moo kareno jimanbanashiwa, kikiakita.
(I'm) tired of listening to his boasting.

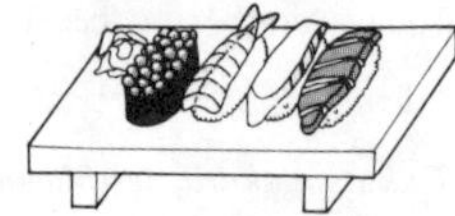

たおれる／ひっくりかえる

■ *taoreru* ■ *hikkurikaeru*

たおれる［倒れる］ ■ *taoreru* ■ to fall down

①**立っていたものが、横になってしまう**とき使います（例1, 2, 3, 4）。「倒れる」ものは、はばよりも高さがあるものです。

Taoreru is used when an upright object becomes horizontal (ex.1, 2, 3, 4). Things that *taoreru* must be taller than they are wide.

②政府・会社など、組織がだめになるとき（例5, 6）、また、重い病気になったときや、死んだとき（例7, 8, 9）にも使います。

It may express the downfall of an organization such as a government or company (ex.5, 6). It is also used when a person comes down with a serious illness or dies (ex.7, 8, 9).

1) 台風で木が倒れた。
Taifuude kiga taoreta.
Trees fell from the typhoon.

2) 地震で棚の上の花びんが、倒れて割れた。
Jishinde tanano ueno kabinga, taorete wareta.
A flower vase that was on the shelf fell and broke in the earthquake.

3) 川島君は朝礼のとき、貧血を起こして倒れた。
*Kawashima-kun***wa chooreino toki, hinketsuo okoshite taoreta.*
My friend Kawashima had an anemic attack and collapsed during morning services.
—— * *Kun* is commonly added to the given or family name of boys or young men by friends as a way of referring to or addressing them.

4) ボウリングで、ピンが一回で全部倒れるとストライクです。
Booringude, pinga ikkaide zenbu taoreruto sutoraikudesu.
In bowling, if all the pins fall over, it's a strike.

5) 新しい内閣は、わずか半年で倒れた。
Atarashii naikakuwa, wazuka hantoshide taoreta.
The new cabinet fell in a mere six months.

6) 不景気で、彼の会社は倒れてしまった。
Fukeikide, kareno kaishawa taoreteshimatta.
His company went bankrupt in the recession.

7) あまり働きすぎて倒れないようにしてください。
Amari hatarakisugite taorenaiyooni shite kudasai.
Please don't overwork yourself into a collapse.

8) 私の父は、心臓発作で倒れた。
Watashino chichiwa, shinzoohossade taoreta.
My father collapsed from a heart attack.

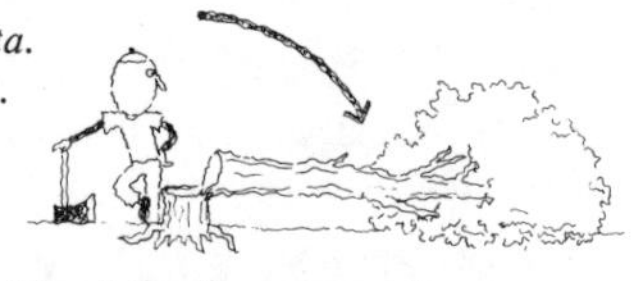

9) 彼は演説中、凶弾に倒れた。
Karewa enzetsuchuu, kyoodanni taoreta.
He was killed by (an assassin's) bullet while delivering a speech.

ひっくりかえる［ひっくり返る］

■ *hikkurikaeru*
■ to overturn

---

①立っていたものが、**勢いよく横になってしまったり**、表を向いているものが**裏を向いてしまう**とき（例10, 11, 12, 13）使います。
Hikkurikaeru is used when an upright object suddenly falls over or when something that is face-up turns over (ex.10, 11, 12, 13).

②ある状態が、**全く逆の状態になる**とき（例14, 15）使います。
It is also used when a certain state or condition is completely reversed (ex.14, 15).

---

10) かめは、ひっくり返るとなかなか自分では起き上がれない。
Kamewa, hikkurikaeruto nakanaka jibundewa okiagarenai.
When a turtle gets turned upside-down it can't right itself very well.

11) すべってあお向けにひっくり返ったので、頭を打った。
Subette aomukeni hikkurikaettanode, atamao utta.
(I) hit my head when I slipped and fell flat on my back.

12) ボートがひっくり返って、乗っていた２人は川に落ちた。
Bootoga hikkurikaette, notteita futariwa kawani ochita.
The boat capsized and the two people in it fell into the river.

13) 彼女は、ひっくり返って大笑いしている。
Kanojowa, hikkurikaette oowarai shiteiru.
She has collapsed with laughter.

14) ゆうべの野球の試合は、９回裏で得点がひっくり返った。
Yuubeno yakyuuno shiaiwa, kyuukaiurade tokutenga hikkurikaetta.
There was a come-from-behind victory in the bottom of the ninth of last night's baseball game.

15) 最高裁で判決がひっくり返って、有罪が無罪になった。
Saikoosaide hanketsuga hikkurikaette, yuuzaiga muzaini natta.
The verdict was overturned by the Supreme Court. 'Guilty' was changed to 'not guilty'.

～だけ／～ばかり／～しか(～)ない

■ *～dake* ■ *～bakari* ■ *～shika(～)nai*

～だけ ■ *dake* ■ only

ものやことがらを「それ以外の何ものでもない」、「そのほかのものはない」と**限定する**とき使います（例1, 2, 3, 4）。

～dake limits a thing or event by saying that there is 'nothing more added or different', or 'there is no other' (ex.1, 2, 3, 4).

1) ひらがなだけの文は意外と読みにくいものだ。
Hiraganadakeno bunwa igaito yominikui monoda.
Passages written in *hiragana* only are harder to read than (you) might think.

2) 安売りのいちごを一山買ってきたが、傷んでいたのは２粒だけだった。
Yasuurino ichigoo hitoyama kattekitaga, itandeitanowa futatsubu dakedatta.
(I) bought a heap of strawberries on sale and only two of them were bruised.

3) 生の魚を食べるのは日本人だけではない。
Namano sakanao taberunowa Nihonjindakedewa nai.

It's not only the Japanese who eat raw fish.

4) 5分だけでいいから、私の話を聞いてください。
Gofundakede iikara, watashino hanashio kiite kudasai.
Just five minutes is enough; please listen to what (I) have to say.

~ばかり
■ *~bakari*
■ only~ ; about~

---

①あることがらが、「**とても多い・例外はほとんどない**」ということを表すとき使います（例5, 6, 7, 8, 9）。「～だけ」は限定を表しますが、「～ばかり」は、**多さや頻度**の高さを表します。したがって「私だけ叱られる」は、私以外の人は叱られないという意味ですが、「私ばかり叱られる」は、私以外の人が叱られることもあるけれど、私が叱られることがとても多いことを表しています。

~bakari is used when stating that some thing or state occurs very frequently or without exception (ex.5, 6, 7, 8, 9). *~dake* expresses a limit, while *~bakari* expresses abundance or frequency. Thus, *watashi dake shikarareru* means 'I'm the only one that gets scolded', while *watashi bakari shikarareru* means there may be others who get scolded, but 'I get scolded all the time'.

②例10、11のように数といっしょに使うときは、「～ぐらい・約～」と、**だいたいの数量**を表します。
①は、話しことばでは「～ばっかり」と言うこともあります。

As in Examples 10 and 11, *~bakari* may also be used with a number to express an approximate quantity, as in 'about~', or 'approximately~'. In spoken language, the *~bakari* of definition ① may be pronounced *~bakkari*.

---

5) 最近、雨の日ばかり続いている。
Saikin, amenohibakari tsuzuiteiru.
These days there's nothing but one rainy day after another.

6) 肉ばかり食べるのも体に悪いが、野菜ばかり食べるのも良くない。
Nikubakari taberunomo karadani waruiga, yasaibakari taberunomo yokunai.
Eating nothing but meat is not good for (you), but eating nothing but vegetables is no good either.

7) 弟は小さい頃、気が弱くて、いつも泣いてばかりいた。
Otootowa chiisai koro, kiga yowakute, itsumo naitebakari ita.
My little brother was a crybaby as a child and bawled all the time.

8) 週末(しゅうまつ)、天気(てんき)が良(よ)かったので一日中(いちにちじゅう)テニスばかりしていた。
Shuumatsu, tenkiga yokattanode ichinichijuu tenisubakari shiteita.
The weather was good on the weekend, so (I) just played tennis all day.

9) お菓子(かし)ばかり食(た)べていると、虫歯(むしば)になるよ。
Okashibakari tabeteiruto, mushibani naruyo.
If (you) eat nothing but sweets you'll get cavities!

10) ちょっと用事(ようじ)があるので、２時間(じかん)ばかり出(で)かけてきます。
Chotto yoojiga arunode, nijikanbakari dekaketekimasu.
(I) have something to do, so I'll be gone about two hours or so.

11) この牧場(ぼくじょう)には牛(うし)が500頭(とう)ばかりいるそうです。
Kono bokujooniwa ushiga gohyaku-toobakari irusoodesu.
(I) hear there are some 500 head of cattle on this ranch.

～しか(～)ない

■～*shika* (～) *nai*
■only～ ; no more than ; nothing but～

---

①「～だけ」と同(おな)じように、あるものや、ことがら以外(いがい)のものは存在(そんざい)しないというとき使(つか)いますが、「～だけ」よりも**強(つよ)く限定(げんてい)する**言(い)い方(かた)です（例(れい)12, 13, 14, 15)。

This expression is used like ～*dake* to state that there is no other thing or event than the one mentioned. It is somewhat more forceful than ～*dake* (ex.12, 13, 14, 15).

②数量(すうりょう)といっしょに使(つか)うときは、ほかにも何(なに)かあるだろうと期待(きたい)していたのに、実際(じっさい)には数(かず)や量(りょう)が少(すく)なく、**それ以上(いじょう)はない**ことに対(たい)しての、不満(ふまん)や失望(しつぼう)が表(あらわ)れています（例(れい)16, 17, 18)。

When used with a number, it expresses disappointment or dissatisfaction that the number or quantity is actually less than was expected (ex.16, 17, 18).

---

12) コアラはユーカリの葉(は)しか食(た)べない。
Koarawa yuukarino hashika tabenai.
Koalas eat nothing but eucalyptus leaves.

13) 朝(あさ)は食欲(しょくよく)がないので、ジュースしか飲(の)まない。
Asawa shokuyokuga nainode, juusushika nomanai.
I don't have much of an appetite in the morning, so (I) just drink juice.

14) 最終(さいしゅう)バスが出(で)てしまったので、歩(ある)いて帰(かえ)るしかない。
Saishuu-basuga deteshimattanode, aruite kaerushika nai.
The last bus has left, so there's nothing left to do but to walk home.

15) この島(しま)には、ここでしか見(み)られない植物(しょくぶつ)がたくさんあります。
Kono shimaniwa, kokodeshika mirarenai shokubutsuga takusan arimasu.
On this island there are lots of plants that can be seen nowhere else but here.

16) 買(か)い物(もの)をしようと思(おも)ったけれど、さいふには1000円(えん)しかなかった。
Kaimonoo shiyooto omottakeredo, saifuniwa sen-enshika nakatta.
(I) wanted to go shopping, but there was only ¥1,000 in my wallet.

17) 姉(あね)の部屋(へや)は広(ひろ)いのに、私(わたし)の部屋(へや)は３畳(じょう)しかない。
*Aneno heyawa hiroinoni, watashino heyawa sanjoo** *shikanai.* *p.592
My big sister's room is big, but mine is only three *tatami* mats.

18) 出発(しゅっぱつ)の時間(じかん)までに１分(ぷん)しかないのに、彼(かれ)はまだ来(こ)ない。
Shuppatsuno jikanmadeni ippunshika nainoni, karewa mada konai.
There's only one minute till departure, but he's not here yet.

たすける／すくう／てつだう

■*tasukeru* ■*sukuu* ■*tetsudau*

たすける［助(たす)ける］ ■*tasukeru* ■to help

困(こま)っていたり危険(きけん)な状態(じょうたい)にある人(ひと)やものが良(よ)い状態(じょうたい)や安全(あんぜん)な状態(じょうたい)になるように、力(ちから)を貸(か)すことです（例(れい)1, 2, 3, 4, 5, 6)。「助(たす)ける」は「手伝(てつだ)う」を意味(いみ)する、**ちょっと力(ちから)を貸(か)す程度(ていど)から**、「救(すく)う」を意味(いみ)する、**全面的(ぜんめんてき)な救助(きゅうじょ)まで**広(ひろ)く使(つか)えることばです。

To help a person or thing which is in difficulty or danger achieve a safe or improved state (ex.1, 2, 3, 4, 5, 6). *Tasukeru* is a word encompassing a range of meanings, from *tetsudau* (to lend a hand) to *sukuu* (to rescue).

---

1) 彼(かれ)は、川(かわ)で溺(おぼ)れている子供(こども)を助(たす)けて表彰(ひょうしょう)された。

Karewa, kawade oboreteiru kodomoo tasukete hyooshoosareta.
He was commended for rescuing a drowning child in the river.

2) 猟師は、わなにかかった子ぎつねを助けてやった。
Ryooshiwa, wanani kakatta kogitsuneo tasuketeyatta.
The hunter rescued a baby fox caught in a trap.

3) 「助けて」と叫ぶ声が聞こえたので行ってみると、女の子が犬に追いかけられていた。
"*Tasukete*" *to sakebu koega kikoetanode ittemiruto, onnanokoga inuni oikakerareteita.*
(I) heard a scream for help, so when I went to look I found a girl was being chased by a dog.

4) 何か困ったことがあると、いつも家族が助けてくれた。
Nanika komatta kotoga aruto, itsumo kazokuga tasuketekureta.
Whenever (I) had difficulty my family would always help me out.

5) 彼女は高校を卒業すると、就職して家計を助けた。
Kanojowa kookoo-o sotsugyoosuruto, shuushokushite kakeio tasuketa.
After graduating from high school she got a job to help out with the family finances.

6) 大根には、消化を助ける成分がたくさん含まれている。
Daikonniwa, shookao tasukeru seibunga takusan fukumareteiru.
A *daikon* radish contains many elements which aid digestion.

すくう［救う］

■ *sukuu*
■ to save ; to rescue 

かなり危険な状態にある人やものを、安全な状態に移らせることです。特に危険な状態の命や、精神面に多く使います（例7, 8, 9, 10）。「助けられる人」は、まだ少し本人にも力は残っていますが、「救われる人」は全く自分ではどうしようもない・力が残っていないという感じです。

To help a person or thing in extreme danger attain safety. It is used often especially with respect to a life or mental condition that is in danger (ex.7, 8, 9, 10). A *tasukerareru hito* (a person that is helped) has some strength, whereas a *sukuwareru hito* (a person that is saved) no longer has the power to help himself.

---

7) 医師の適切な処置が、患者の命を救った。

Ishino tekisetsuna shochiga, kanjano inochio sukutta.
The doctor's timely measures saved the patient's life.

8) 私は去年の冬、山で遭難して、捜索隊に救われた。
Watashiwa kyonenno fuyu, yamade soonanshite, soosakutaini sukuwareta.
Last winter I had an accident in the mountains and was rescued by a search party.

9) 彼は、私の子供を火の中から救ってくれた。
Karewa, watashino kodomoo hino nakakara sukuttekureta.
He rescued my child from the fire.

10) 彼のユーモアで、その場の気まずい雰囲気が救われた。
Kareno yuumoade, sonobano kimazui fun-ikiga sukuwareta.
His good sense of humor relieved the awkward atmosphere of the moment.

てつだう［手伝う］ ■*tetsudau* ■to help out

人の仕事や作業などの負担が軽くなるように、**手を貸す**ことです（例11, 12, 13, 14)。「助ける」や「救う」のように危険から脱出させるという感じはありません。

To lend a hand in order to lighten the burden of someone's work or labor (ex.11, 12, 13, 14). It does not include the sense of helping someone escape from danger found with *tasukeru* or *sukuu*.

---

11) 部屋をかたづけるのを手伝ってください。
Heyao katazukerunoo tetsudatte kudasai.
Please help (me) tidy up the room.

12) 先週の日曜日、友達の引っ越しを手伝った。
Senshuuno nichiyoobi, tomodachino hikkoshio tetsudatta.
(I) helped my friend move last Sunday.

13) 私は、着物を着るときは、いつも母に手伝ってもらいます。
Watashiwa, kimonoo kirutokiwa, itsumo hahani tetsudatte-moraimasu.
I always have my mom help me when I put on a *kimono*.

14) 彼は、父が経営する喫茶店を手伝っている。
Karewa, chichiga keieisuru kissaten-o tetsudatteiru.
He helps out at the coffee shop that his father runs.

ものの数え方（かぞ かた） COUNTER SUFFIXES

	本 ほん hon / pon / bon	杯 はい hai / pai / bai	匹 ひき hiki / piki / biki	個 こ ko
1	いっぽん	いっぱい	いっぴき	いっこ
2	にほん	にはい	にひき	にこ
3	さんぼん	さんばい	さんびき	さんこ
4	よんほん	よんはい	よんひき	よんこ
5	ごほん	ごはい	ごひき	ごこ
6	ろっぽん	ろっぱい	ろっぴき	ろっこ
7	ななほん	ななはい	ななひき	ななこ
8	はっぽん	はっぱい	はっぴき	はっこ
9	きゅうほん	きゅうはい	きゅうひき	きゅうこ
10	じっぽん	じっぱい	じっぴき	じっこ
?	なんぼん	なんばい	なんびき	なんこ

	軒 けん ken / gen	足 そく soku / zoku	人 にん nin	つ tsu
1	いっけん	いっそく	ひとり	ひとつ
2	にけん	にそく	ふたり	ふたつ
3	さんげん	さんぞく	さんにん	みっつ
4	よんけん	よんそく	よにん	よっつ
5	ごけん	ごそく	ごにん	いつつ
6	ろっけん	ろくそく	ろくにん	むっつ
7	ななけん	ななそく	しちにん	ななつ
8	はっけん	はっそく	はちにん	やっつ
9	きゅうけん	きゅうそく	きゅうにん	ここのつ
10	じっけん	じっそく	じゅうにん	とお
?	なんげん	なんぞく	なんにん	いくつ

	枚 まい mai	台 だい dai	冊 さつ satsu	頭 とう tou
1	いちまい	いちだい	いっさつ	いっとう
2	にまい	にだい	にさつ	にとう
⋮	⋮	⋮	⋮	⋮
8	はちまい	はちだい	はっさつ	はっとう
⋮	⋮	⋮	⋮	⋮
10	じゅうまい	じゅうだい	じっさつ	じっとう
?	なんまい	なんだい	なんさつ	なんとう

たびに／そのつど

■*tabi ni*　　■*sono tsudo*

たびに

■*tabi ni*
■every time ; whenever 

何度か起こる、あるいは**くり返して起こる**ことがらのそのときどきを**指し、回数の多さ**や、回数を重ねることを表します（例1,2,3,4）。

Tabi ni refers to every instance in which a frequent or repeating action or event occurs, and indicates that the number of occurrences is great or repeated (ex.1, 2, 3, 4).

1) あの２人は、婚約しているのに会うたびにけんかをしている。
Ano futariwa, kon-yaku shiteirunoni autabini kenkao shiteiru.
Even though they're engaged, those two fight every time they see each other.

2) 波が寄せるたびに、子供たちは声をあげて走りまわる。
Namiga yoserutabini, kodomotachiwa koeo agete hashirimawaru.
Every time a wave comes near the kids scream and run about.

3) 季節が変わるたびに、衣類の出し入れをしなければならない。
Kisetsuga kawarutabini, iruino dashi-ireo shinakereba naranai.
With every change of season (we) have to put away and take out (seasonal) clothing.

4) 子供の頃、よく兄弟げんかをしたが、そのたびに私がしかられた。
Kodomono koro, yoku kyoodaigenkao shitaga, sonotabini watashiga shikarareta.
I often got into fights with my brothers as a child, but every time I did I got in trouble.

そのつど

■*sono tsudo*
■at any time that ; each time 

何かをしたり、何かが起きたりするとき、その１回ずつを指して使います（例5,6,7,8）。**その場その時における対処**を述べる時に多く使います。

This expression is used to refer to any single instance of, or encounter with, some action or event (ex.5, 6, 7, 8). It is often used to mention that one will deal with something at such time or place as it should occur.

---

5) わからないところがあったら、そのつど先生(せんせい)に聞(き)きなさい。
Wakaranai tokoroga attara, sonotsudo senseini kikinasai.
If there's anything (you) don't understand, ask your teacher as the occasion arises.

6) 困(こま)ったことがあったら、そのつど解決(かいけつ)したほうがいい。
Komatta kotoga attara, sonotsudo kaiketsushita hooga ii.
(You) should resolve your problems as they arise, should there be any.

7) 部屋(へや)を出(で)る時(とき)は、そのつど電気(でんき)を消(け)してください。
Heyao deru tokiwa, sonotsudo denkio keshite kudasai.
Please turn off the lights every time (you) leave the room.

8) 私(わたし)は買(か)い置(お)きはしないで、必要(ひつよう)に応(おう)じてそのつど買(か)うことにしています。
Watashiwa kaiokiwa shinaide, hitsuyooni oojite sonotsudo kau kotoni shiteimasu.
I don't stock up; I make it a practice to buy things as the need arises.

たぶん／おそらく／どうやら

■ *tabun* ■ *osoraku* ■ *douyara*

たぶん［多分(たぶん)］

■ *tabun*
■ probably ; perhaps 

主観的(しゅかんてき)にかなり**確実性**(かくじつせい)**が高**(たか)**い**と思(おも)われる**推量**(すいりょう)を表(あらわ)します。はっきりとした根拠(こんきょ)がなくても、自分(じぶん)の判断(はんだん)ではそう思(おも)うということです。話(はな)しことばでよく使(つか)います(例(れい)1, 2, 3, 4, 5)。

Tabun is used when one feels subjectively that something has a fairly high probability of occurring. The speaker bases his statement on his own judgment rather than on actual grounds. It is often used in spoken Japanese (ex.1, 2, 3, 4, 5).

---

1) たいしたけがではないので、たぶん1週間(しゅうかん)ぐらいで治(なお)るだろう。

Taishita kegadewa nainode, tabun isshuukan-guraide naorudaroo.
It's not a bad injury, so it will probably heal in a week.

2) 来年の今ごろはたぶん日本にいないだろう。

Rainenno imagorowa tabun Nihonni inaidaroo.
At this time next year (I) probably won't be in Japan.

3) A：あしたのパーティー、行く。

B：うん、たぶん。

A： *Ashitano paatii, iku?* Are (you) going to the party tomorrow?
B： *Un, tabun.* Uh huh, probably.

4) たぶん1万円で足りると思うけど、もし足りなかったら、立て替えておいてください。

Tabun ichiman-ende tariruto omoukedo, moshi tarinakattara, tatekaeteoite kudasai.
(I) think ¥10,000 will probably be enough, but please lend (me) some money in case it isn't.

5) もし私が鈴木さんの立場にいたら、たぶん同じことをしたでしょう。

Moshi watashiga Suzukisanno tachibani itara, tabun onaji kotoo shitadeshoo.
If I were in Mr. Suzuki's position, I'd probably have done the same thing.

おそらく［恐らく］ ■ *osoraku* ■ probably 

確実性の高い推量を表すときに使う、**ていねいな、あらたまった表現**です。ふつう「～でしょう・～と思います・～と思われます」などといっしょに使います（例6, 7, 8, 9）。

Osoraku is a formal, polite way of expressing that one speculates there is a high probability (of something happening). It is ordinarily used together with expressions such as *～deshoo*, *～to omoimasu*, and *～to omowaremasu* (ex.6, 7, 8, 9).

---

6) あの家はおそらく1億円はするだろう。

Ano iewa osoraku ichiokuenwa surudaroo.
That house probably costs around ¥100,000,000.

7) 夜9時過ぎなら、おそらくうちにいると思いますので、そのころ、お電話をくださいませんか。

Yoru kujisuginara, osoraku uchini iruto omoimasunode, sonokoro, odenwao kudasaimasenka?
(I) think I'll probably be home after nine o'clock, so would you mind calling me around then?

8) どろぼうはおそらくこの窓から入ったものと思われます。

Doroboowa osoraku kono madokara haittamonoto omowaremasu.
It seems that the burglar probably entered through this window.

9) 森林がこんなに広く自然のままで残されているのは、日本国内ではおそらくここだけでしょう。

Shinringa konnani hiroku shizenno mamade nokosarete-irunowa, Nihon-kokunai-dewa osoraku kokodakedeshoo.
This is probably the only place in Japan that still has large forests like this left in their natural state.

どうやら ■*douyara* ■apparently 

まだはっきりしていないけれど、これまでに得られた**さまざまな情報からある程度わかってきた**というときに使います（例10, 11, 12）。多くの場合「～らしい・～ようだ・～そうだ」などや「～と思われる」などと共に使われます。

Douyara means that, although still not completely clear, one is able to gain somewhat of an understanding of something by looking at the information gathered so far (ex.10, 11, 12). In most cases it is used together with expressions such as ～*rashii*, ～*youda*, ～*souda*, or ～*to omowareru*.

---

10) 寒気がする。どうやら風邪をひいたようだ。

Samukega suru. Dooyara kazeo hiitayooda.
(I) have the chills. It seems as if I've caught a cold.

11) ノックをしても返事がない。どうやら彼女は留守らしい。

Nokkuo shitemo henjiga nai. Dooyara kanojowa rusurashii.
(I've) knocked but there's no reply. Apparently she's out.

12) 約束の時間を30分も過ぎたのに、山田さんはまだ来ていない。どうやら約束を忘れているようだ。

Yakusokuno jikan-o sanjuppunmo sugitanoni, Yamadasanwa mada kiteinai.

Dooyara yakusokuo wasureteiruyooda.
Even though it is now 30 minutes past our meeting time, Mr. Yamada has not yet arrived. It seems he has forgotten our appointment.

だます／ごまかす

■ *damasu* ■ *gomakasu*

だます ■ *damasu* ■ to deceive

①**うそをついて**、相手に本当だと思わせて**信用**させることです（例1, 2, 3, 4)。

To deceive others into believing that one's story or statement is true (ex.1, 2, 3, 4).

②「だましだまし」は、調子や状態の良くない体や機械を、少しずつようすを見ながらうまく使うことです（例5, 6)。

The expression *damashi-damashi* means to try to keep a machine or body that is in poor condition working by watching it carefully (ex.5, 6).

1) その男は「お母さんが病気だ」とだまして、少女を誘拐した。
Sono otokowa "Okaasanga byookida" to damashite, shoojoo yuukaishita.
That man kidnapped the girl by lying to her that her mother was sick.

2) 10万円が1年で100万円になるなんて、そんなうまい話があるわけない。きっとだまされたんだよ。
Juuman-enga ichinende hyakuman-enni narunante, sonna umai hanashiga aruwakenai. Kitto damasaretandayo.
It's impossible to make ¥100,000 increase to ¥1,000,000 in one year. (I'm) sure that (you) were lied to.

3) 私はダイヤモンドだとだまされて、偽物を買わされた。
Watashiwa daiyamondodato damasarete, nisemonoo kawasareta.
To my regret, I bought a fake diamond because I was tricked into believing it was a genuine diamond.

4) 人をだますのは良くない。
Hitoo damasunowa yokunai.

To deceive others is wrong.

5) この機械は古いので時々調子が悪くなるけれど、だましだまし使えば、まだ使える。

Kono kikaiwa furuinode tokidoki chooshiga waruku-narukeredo, damashi-damashi tsukaeba, mada tsukaeru.

Because this machine is old so we sometimes have problems with it, but we can still use it if we handle it skillfully.

6) 私も年をとって体があちこち悪くなってきたけれど、だましだましどうにかやっています。

Watashimo toshio totte karadaga achikochi warukunatte-kitakeredo, damashi-damashi doonika yatteimasu.

I am getting old and starting to have all kinds of health problems, but I somehow coax my body into getting me around.

ごまかす

■ *gomakasu*
■ to deceive ; to cheat 

---

①本当のことを言いたくないときや、自分に**都合の悪い話題**のときに、ちょっとうそをついたり**適当な**ことを言って**あいまいにする**ことです（例7, 8）。また、適当な態度でその場の話題からのがれたり（例 9）、ものごとをいいかげんにすませるとき使います（例10, 11）。

Gomakasu is used when a speaker does not want to tell the truth or disclose a matter that is not favorable for him. The speaker may tell a lie or avoid going into details in order to be vague or unclear (ex.7, 8). It may also mean to take a nonchalant attitude in order to avoid a serious situation or discussion of an uncomfortable topic (ex.9), or to do a halfway job (ex.10, 11).

②人の気がつかないところで、自分の利益になるように他人や会社などのものや**お金の数や計算をいいかげんにする**ことです（例12, 13）。

To intentionally pocket a company or person's money or property by handling it in a sneaky manner (ex.12, 13).

---

7) 彼女はいつも年齢を２つ３つ若くごまかす。

Kanojowa itsumo nenreio futatsu mittsu wakaku gomakasu.

She always lies about how her age, saying she's a couple of years younger than she really is.

8) Ａ：この間貸した１万円返して。

B：え、１万円(まんえん)も借(か)りたかなあ、2000円(えん)じゃなかったっけ。

A：ごまかさないで。

A： *Konoaida kashita ichiman-en kaeshite.*
Give me back the ¥10,000 that I loaned you the other day.
B： *E? ichiman-enmo karitakanaa, nisen-enja nakattakke?*
¥10,000? That much?! Wasn't it ¥2,000?
A： *Gomakasanaide!* Oh, come on. Stop pretending!

9) 彼(かれ)は、「彼女(かのじょ)にふられたんだって」と聞(き)かれて笑(わら)ってごまかした。
Karewa, "Kanojoni furaretandatte?" to kikarete waratte gomakashita.
When he was asked, "I heard that she left you, is that true?" he laughed to evade the question.

10) 食事(しょくじ)を作(つく)るのが面倒(めんどう)なので、インスタントのものでごまかした。
Shokujio tsukurunoga mendoonanode, insutantono monode gomakashita.
Cooking was troublesome, so (I) just ate some instant food.

11) 映画(えいが)の背景(はいけい)は、写真(しゃしん)や絵(え)でごまかすことが多(おお)いという。
Eigano haikeiwa, shashin-ya ede gomakasu kotoga ooito yuu.
(I) heard that the background scenes in movies are often created using photos and paintings.

12) 彼(かれ)は頼(たの)まれた買(か)い物(もの)のおつりをごまかして、自分(じぶん)のポケットに入(い)れた。
Karewa tanomareta kaimonono otsurio gomakashite, jibunno pokettoni ireta.
He lied about how much change he received from the shopping he was asked to do, and pocketed the money himself.

13) 会計士(かいけいし)が帳簿(ちょうぼ)をごまかしていたのが分(わ)かって、問題(もんだい)になった。
Kaikeishiga chooboo gomakashite-itanoga wakatte, mondaini natta.
When it was found out that the accountant had been falsifying on the books, it became a big issue.

たりない／ふそくする／かける

■ *tarinai* ■ *fusoku suru* ■ *kakeru*

たりない［足(た)りない］

■ *tarinai*
■ not enough ; lacking 

十分ではないこと・目的を達するために**必要な数量に満たない**ようすを表すとき使います（例1, 2, 3, 4, 5）。

Tarinai indicates that something is inadequate, or does not reach the amount required (ex.1, 2, 3, 4, 5).

1）きのう買い物をしておつりをもらったら、100円足りなかった。

Kinoo kaimonoo shite otsurio morattara, hyakuen tarinakatta.
(I) was shortchanged ¥100 when I went shopping yesterday.

2）数学の試験で、時間が足りずに全問解くことはできなかった。
Suugakuno shikende, jikanga tarizuni zenmon toku kotowa dekinakatta.
(I) didn't have enough time to solve all of the problems on the math test.

3）この魚は焼き方が足りなくて、中まで火が通っていない。
Kono sakanawa yakikataga tarinakute, nakamade higa tootteinai.
This fish hasn't been cooked enough——the heat hasn't reached the center (the center is still raw).

4）このみかんは甘みが足りない。
Kono mikanwa amamiga tarinai.
This *mikan* (mandarin orange) isn't sweet enough.

5）きみのように乱暴な運転をしていたら、命がいくつあっても足りないよ。
*Kiminoyooni ranboona unten-o shiteitara, inochiga ikutsu attemo tarinai**yo.*
If you keep driving like that, you'll end up dead someday soon.
——* The expression *inochi ga ikutsu atte mo tarinai* (even if you have several lives they won't be enough) is used when warning someone of dangerous behavior. It literally means that a person's conduct is so reckless that he would quickly use up many lives if he had them.

ふそくする［不足する］

■*fusoku suru*
■to be lacking ; to be short 

「足りない」と同様に、**十分ではない**こと・必要な数量に**満たない**ようすを表します。「足りない」よりも**少しかたい感じ**で、「〜不足」の形で使うことが多

いです（例6, 7, 8, 9）。

Fusoku is similar to *tarinai* in meaning that something is inadequate or less than the quantity required. However, it is a slightly more formal expression and is often used in compound words such as *suimin-busoku* (lack of sleep) and *undoo-busoku* (lack of exercise)(ex.6, 7, 8, 9).

---

6) 今、建設業界では人手が不足しているらしい。
Ima, kensetsu-gyookaidewa hitodega fusokushite-irurashii.
There seems to be a shortage of labor in the construction industry now.

7) ビタミンAが不足すると、目が疲れやすくなるそうです。
Bitamin-eega fusokusuruto, mega tsukareyasuku narusoodesu.
(I) hear that if (you) don't get enough Vitamin A, your eyes will become tired easily.

8) 試合に負けたのは、練習不足が原因だ。
Shiaini maketanowa, renshuu-busokuga gen-inda.
The reason (we) lost the game is because we didn't practice enough.

9) ゆうべ遅く寝たので睡眠不足です。
Yuube osoku netanode suiminbusoku-desu.
(I) didn't get enough sleep because I went to bed late last night.

かける［欠ける］

■ *kakeru*
■ to be lacking ; to be missing 

---

①もの（多くの場合、かたいもの）の**一部分が、こわれてとれる**ことです（例10, 11）。

Kakeru indicates that an object (in most cases something hard) is broken in one place (ex.10, 11).

②**完全なもの・本来あるはずのもの**・まとまっていたものの**一部がない**ことです（例12, 13, 14, 15）。「足りない・不足する」は、それがないために完全なものにならないという意味で、「欠ける」は本来完全であるはずのものから、一部分がなくなるという意味を表します。

It also expresses that something that should be or is by nature complete is missing a part (ex.12, 13, 14, 15). *Tarinai* and *fusoku suru* refer to the idea that something is insufficient and therefore incomplete, while *kakeru* indicates something that was originally complete is now missing a part.

10) この包丁(ほうちょう)は、刃(は)が欠(か)けている。
Kono hoochoowa, haga kaketeiru.
The blade of this knife is nicked.

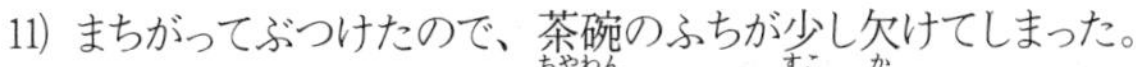

11) まちがってぶつけたので、茶碗(ちゃわん)のふちが少(すこ)し欠(か)けてしまった。
Machigatte butsuketanode, chawanno fuchiga sukoshi kaketeshimatta.
(I) accidently knocked the tea cup (against something) and chipped the rim.

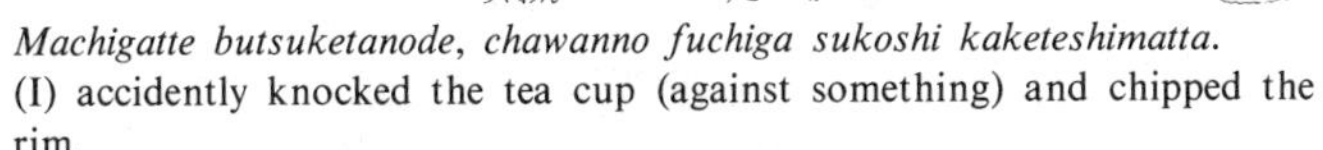

12) 私達(わたしたち)のだれか1人(ひとり)でも欠(か)けると、試合(しあい)には出(で)られない。
Watashi-tachino dareka hitoridemo kakeruto, shiainiwa derarenai.
We can't play the game if even one person is missing.

13) この論文(ろんぶん)は、ポイントが欠(か)けている。
Kono ronbunwa, pointoga kaketeiru.
This paper (thesis) doesn't have a point.

14) 夜(よる)おそく人(ひと)のうちを訪(たず)ねるなんて、あの人(ひと)は常識(じょうしき)に欠(か)けている。
Yoru osoku hitono uchio tazunerunante, ano hitowa jooshikini kaketeiru.
He is lacking in common sense, going that late to a person's house.

15) 今回(こんかい)のことは、教師(きょうし)として配慮(はいりょ)に欠(か)けていたと反省(はんせい)しています。
Konkaino kotowa, kyooshitoshite hairyoni kaketeitato hanseishiteimasu.
Being a teacher, (I) regret my lack of consideration during the incident.

たりる/まにあう/じゅうぶん

■*tariru* ■*maniau* ■*juubun*

たりる［足(た)りる］ ■*tariru* ■to be enough

①**必要(ひつよう)な数(すう)や量(りょう)を満(み)たす**ことができるというとき使(つか)います（例(れい)1, 2, 3, 4)。
Tariru indicates that something is sufficient to meet a necessary number or quantity (ex.1, 2, 3, 4).

②**ことがらの程度(ていど)**などのように、はっきりとした数量(すうりょう)や必要量(ひつようりょう)が示(しめ)せないものについても使(つか)います（例(れい)5, 6, 7)。
It is used also when no definite number or quantity is specified, as in when

speaking about the extent or degree of a situation or event (ex.5, 6, 7).

---

1) 交通費は1000円で足りますか。
Kootsuuhiwa sen-ende tarimasuka?
Will ¥1,000 cover (your) transportation costs?

2) 野球をしようと思ったけれど、人数が足りないのでだめだった。
Yakyuuo shiyooto omottakeredo, ninzuuga tarinainode damedatta.
(We) wanted to play baseball, but there weren't enough people so we couldn't.

3) 数学の試験の時、時間が足りなくて、1問残ってしまった。
Suugakuno shikenno toki, jikanga tarinakute, ichimon nokotteshimatta.
(I) didn't have enough time on the math test so I left one problem (unsolved).

4) うちではみんなパンが好きなので、米は1か月3キロ買えば足ります。
Uchidewa minna panga sukinanode, komewa ikkagetsu sankiro kaeba tarimasu.
Everyone in our house likes bread, so if we buy (only) three kilograms of rice a month it's enough.

5) 私が提出した企画書は、工夫が足りないということで採用されなかった。
Watashiga teishutsushita kikakushowa, kufuuga tarinaito yuu kotode saiyoo-sarenakatta.
The plan I submitted wasn't accepted because it wasn't sufficiently innovative.

6) 彼らが別れたのは、お互いに思いやりが足りなかったからだと思う。
Kareraga wakaretanowa, otagaini omoiyariga tarinakatta-karadato omou.
(I) think the reason they separated was that they didn't have enough consideration for each other's feelings.

7) 彼の猫は栄養が足りているせいか、毛並みが美しくコロコロと太っている。
Kareno nekowa eiyooga tariteiruseika, kenamiga utsukushiku korokoroto futotteiru.
His cat is plump and has beautiful fur. He must be getting plenty of nourishment.

まにあう [間に合う]

■ *maniau*
■ to be enough ; to be in time (for)

---

①**なんとか**その場は、必要な数や量を**満たす**ことができるときや、その場の役に立つことができるとき（例 8, 9, 10, 11）使います。

Maniau is used when indicating that something will be adequate to fulfill a required number or quantity, or to serve a purpose at hand (ex.8, 9, 10, 11).

②決められた**日や時間に遅れない・遅刻しない**というとき使います（例12, 13, 14）。

To not be late for or miss an appointed day or time (ex.12, 13, 14).

---

8) パンと牛乳だけなら、500円で間に合うでしょう。
Panto gyuunyuu-dakenara, gohyakuende maniaudeshoo.
If you're getting only bread and milk, ¥500 should be enough.

9) 10人の会議なので、この部屋で間に合う。
Juuninno kaiginanode, kono heyade maniau.
There'll be 10 people at the meeting so this room should be adequate.

10) シチューに入れる赤ワインがなかったので、日本酒で間に合わせたが、おいしかった。
Shichuuni ireru akawainga nakattanode, nihonshude maniawasetaga, oishikatta.
(I) didn't have any red wine to put in the stew so I made do with *sake*. However, the stew turned out tasting good.

11) 来週の友達の結婚式は、兄のスーツで間に合わせます。
Raishuuno tomodachino kekkonshikiwa, anino suutsude maniawasemasu.
(I) will make do by wearing my brother's suit to my friend's wedding next week.

12) 今すぐにうちを出れば、９時のバスに間に合う。
Ima suguni uchio dereba, kujino basuni maniau.
(I) can make the nine o'clock bus if I leave the house right now.

13) 寝坊してしまったので、１時間目の授業に間に合わなかった。
Nebooshite-shimattanode, ichijikanmeno jugyooni maniawanakatta.
(I) overslept this morning so I wasn't able to make my first class.

14) 終電に間に合わなければ、タクシーで帰るかどこかに泊まるしかない。
Shuudenni maniawanakereba, takushiide kaeruka dokokani tomarushikanai.
If (I) miss the last train, I'll have to go home by taxi or find some place to stay (for the night).

じゅうぶん［十分］ ■*juubun* ■ample ; enough

物やことがらの量や程度に余裕があって、満足できるほどだというようすを表します（例15, 16, 17）。「足りる」「間に合う」につけて、必要を満たしてさらにたくさんあるようすも表します（例18, 19）。

This denotes a state of having enough or more than enough of something to fulfill a need or desire (ex.15, 16, 17). When combined with *tariru* or *maniau* it emphasizes that an amount is much greater than what is necessary (ex.18, 19).

15) スピードを出しすぎないよう、十分注意して運転してください。
Supiidoo dashisuginaiyoo, juubun chuuishite untenshite kudasai.
Please pay extra-special attention to (your) driving so you don't speed.

16) ゆうべは十分寝たので、疲れがとれた。
Yuubewa juubun netanode, tsukarega toreta.
(I) was able to get over my fatigue because I got plenty of sleep last night.

17) ぬれた靴は十分乾かさないと、かびが生えることがある。
Nureta kutsuwa juubun kawakasanaito, kabiga haeru kotoga aru.
If (you) don't dry out your wet shoes thoroughly, mildew may grow on them.

18) 3日間の旅行だから、1人10万円あれば十分足ります。
Mikkakanno ryokoodakara, hitori juuman-en areba juubun tarimasu.
It's (only) a three-day trip, so if each person has ¥100,000 it should be plenty.

19) 映画が始まる時間には十分間に合うから、お茶を飲んでいきませんか。
Eigaga hajimaru jikanniwa juubun maniaukara, ochao nonde ikimasenka?
We'll be there in plenty of time for the start of the movie, so why don't we have something to drink before we go?

たるむ／ゆるむ

■*tarumu* ■*yurumu*

たるむ

■ *tarumu*
■ to sag ; to slack off 

①強く**ピンと張っていたもの**が、伸びて**だらりと下がる**とき使います（例1, 2)。

Tarumu indicates that something that was taut has stretched and begins to droop (ex.1, 2).

②緊張している気持ちがなくなって、**だらしなくなった**とき使います（例３)。

To relax to the point of laziness or sloppiness (ex.3).

1) 洗濯のロープが、古くなってたるんでいる。
Sentakuno roopuga, furukunatte tarundeiru.
The clothesline is sagging because it's old.

2) ふとって、おなかの肉がたるんできた。
Futotte, onakano nikuga tarundekita.
(My) belly has begun to sag since I've gained weight.

3) ぼくたちは、試合の後で「たるんでいるから負けるんだ」と、コーチにしかられた。
Bokutachiwa, shiaino atode "Tarundeirukara makerunda!" to, koochini shikarareta.
The coach scolded us after the game, saying "We lost the game because you guys were slacking off."

ゆるむ

■ *yurumu*
■ to loosen ; to abate ; to slack off 

①きつく締めていたり、**強く引っ張っていたものの力が弱くなったり**するとき使います（例4, 5)。

Yurumu indicates that something that was tight or strongly stretched (pulled) has gradually loosened (ex.4, 5).

②**注意力を欠いたり**、**油断**したりするとき使います（例6, 7)。例８は、ゆるやかになる・おだやかになるという意味です。

It also denotes losing one's concentration or letting down one's guard (ex.6, 7). In Example 8 it means 'to become mild'.

4) 私の結び方が悪いのか、ネクタイがすぐにゆるむ。
Watashino musubikataga waruinoka, nekutaiga suguni yurumu.
Probably because I am not good at tying it, my necktie gets loose very easily.

5) めがねのねじがゆるんで、つるがはずれた。
Meganeno nejiga yurunde, tsuruga hazureta.
A screw in (my) eye glasses became loose and the stem came off.

6) 警戒が、ゆるんだすきに、強盗は逃げた。
Keikaiga, yurunda sukini, gootoowa nigeta.
The burglar escaped the moment security slackened.

7) 車の運転に慣れて気がゆるむと、事故を起こしやすい。
Kurumano untenni narete kiga yurumuto, jikoo okoshiyasui.
When (you) get used to driving a car and let down your guard, it becomes more likely that you'll cause an accident.

8) 寒さがゆるんで梅の花が咲き始めた。
Samusaga yurunde umeno hanaga sakihajimeta.
The cold spell has lifted and the plum trees have started to bloom.

ちがう／まちがえる／まちがう

■ *chigau* ■ *machigaeru* ■ *machigau*

ちがう［違う］ ■ *chigau* ■ wrong ; different 

①「誤っている・正しくない」という意味です（例1, 2, 3)。
Chigau means 'mistaken' or 'not correct' (ex.1, 2, 3).

②ほかと比べて、「それと同じではない・別だ」ということを表します（例4, 5, 6)。また例7、8は、程度が上で、すぐれているという意味です。
It is also used to indicate that one thing 'is not the same as', or 'is distinct from' some other thing (ex.4, 5, 6). Examples 7 and 8 illustrate how this term can be used to indicate that something is at a higher level than, or is superior to, something else.

1) A：失礼(しつれい)ですが、山本(やまもと)さんですか。

B：いいえ、違(ちが)います。

A： *Shitsureidesuga, Yamamotosan desuka?*
Excuse me. Are you Mr. Yamamoto?
B： *Iie, chigaimasu.* No, I'm not.

2) 住所(じゅうしょ)が違(ちが)っていたので、手紙(てがみ)が戻(もど)ってきてしまった。
Juushoga chigatteitanode, tegamiga modottekite-shimatta.
The address was wrong, so the letter came back.

3) 後(うし)ろ姿(すがた)がジョンに似(に)ていたので声(こえ)をかけたら、違(ちが)う人(ひと)だった。
Ushirosugataga Jonni niteitanode koeo kaketara, chigau hitodatta.
(I) called out to him because he looked like John from the back, but it was someone else.

4) 彼(かれ)のセーターと彼女(かのじょ)のは色(いろ)も柄(がら)も同(おな)じだが、大(おお)きさは全然(ぜんぜん)違(ちが)う。
Kareno seetaato kanojonowa iromo garamo onajidaga, ookisawa zenzen chigau.
His sweater and hers are the same color and design, but they are completely different sizes.

5) たまには違(ちが)う店(みせ)で昼(ひる)ごはんを食(た)べませんか。
Tamaniwa chigau misede hirugohan-o tabemasenka?
Why don't (you) try going to a different restaurant for lunch once in a while?

6) 10年(ねん)ぶりに友人(ゆうじん)に会(あ)ったら、彼(かれ)は前(まえ)とはまるで違(ちが)う人(ひと)のように明(あか)るかった。
Juunenburini yuujinni attara, karewa maetowa marude chigau hitono yooni akarukatta.
When (I) saw my friend after not seeing him for ten years, he was bright and cheerful—it was as if he were a completely different person from before.

7) 同(おな)じ犬小屋(いぬごや)でも大工(だいく)さんが作(つく)ったのと、私(わたし)が作(つく)ったのではまるで違(ちが)います。
Onaji inugoyademo daikusanga tsukuttanoto, watashiga tsukuttanodewa marude chigaimasu.
The dog house that the carpenter built is completely different from the one that I built.

8) 君(きみ)は慣(な)れているから手際(てぎわ)が違(ちが)うね。
Kimiwa nareteirukara tegiwaga chigaune.
You're experienced, so your workmanship is special.

まちがえる［間違(まちが)える］ ■ *machigaeru* ■ to make a mistake 

わざとではなく、**正(ただ)しくないことをしたり、とりちがえたりする**ことです（例(れい)9, 10, 11, 12, 13）。

To unintentionally do something wrong, misunderstand, or mistake one thing for another (ex.9, 10, 11, 12, 13).

9) 私(わたし)はＬとＲの発音(はつおん)をよく間違(まちが)える。
Watashiwa eruto aaruno hatsuon-o yoku machigaeru.
I frequently confuse the pronunciation of 'L' and 'R'.

10) 私(わたし)は英語(えいご)の試験(しけん)で３か所(しょ)も間違(まちが)えてしまった。
Watashiwa Eigono shikende sankashomo machigaete-shimatta.
I made three mistakes on the English exam.

11) 誰(だれ)かが自分(じぶん)のと間違(まちが)えて私(わたし)のかばんを持(も)って行(い)ってしまった。
Darekaga jibunnoto machigaete watashino kaban-o motteitteshimatta.
Someone mistook my bag for his and walked away with it.

12) ゆうべ遅(おそ)く、道(みち)を歩(ある)いていたら、おまわりさんにどろぼうと間違(まちが)えられた。
Yuube osoku, michio aruiteitara, omawarisanni dorobooto machigaerareta.
(I) was mistaken for a thief by a policeman while I was out walking late last night.

13) 歯医者(はいしゃ)の予約(よやく)の時間(じかん)を間違(まちが)えて、１時間(じかん)おくれてしまった。
Haishano yoyakuno jikan-o machigaete, ichijikan okurete shimatta.
(I) mistook the actual time of my appointment with the dentist and arrived an hour late.

まちがう［間違(まちが)う］ ■ *machigau* ■ to be wrong 

正(ただ)しくないものを選(えら)んでしまうことや、ものごとを**とりちがえ**てしまうことです（例(れい)14, 15）。

This is used when one selects the wrong thing or when one mistakes one thing for another (ex.14, 15).

「まちがった（考(かんが)え……）・まちがっている」などの形(かたち)で使(つか)うときは、誤(あやま)っている・正(ただ)しくない・公正(こうせい)でないなどの意味(いみ)を表(あらわ)します（例(れい)16, 17）。

The form *machigatta* (*kangae*...) or *machigatte iru* indicates that something is wrong or unjust (ex.16, 17).

---

14) 私(わたし)は初(はじ)めてケーキを作(つく)ったとき、塩(しお)と砂糖(さとう)を間違(まちが)っていれてしまった。
Watashiwa hajimete keekio tsukutta toki, shioto satoo-o machigatte ireteshimatta.
The first time I baked a cake I confused the salt and sugar.

15) 間違(まちが)って覚(おぼ)えてしまった発音(はつおん)は、なかなか直(なお)せない。
Machigatte oboeteshimatta hatsuonwa, nakanaka naosenai.
It's difficult to correct (your) pronunciation once you learn it the wrong way.

16) きのう友達(ともだち)に間違(まちが)った住所(じゅうしょ)を教(おし)えてしまった。
Kinoo tomodachini machigatta juushoo oshieteshimatta.
(I) gave my friend the wrong address yesterday.

17) 君(きみ)の考(かんが)えは間違(まちが)っている。
Kimino kangaewa machigatteiru.
Your thinking is incorrect.

つかう／もちいる

■*tsukau* ■*mochiiru*

つかう［使(つか)う］ ■*tsukau* ■to use

①何(なに)かの目的(もくてき)のために人(ひと)や物(もの)を**働(はたら)かせたり**、**役立(やくだ)てる**ことです（例(れい)1, 2, 3, 4, 5）。利用(りよう)するという意味(いみ)もあります。

To make use of or put to work someone or something for a certain purpose (ex.1, 2, 3, 4, 5). *Tsukau* often has the same meaning as *riyou suru*.

②時間(じかん)やお金(かね)、物(もの)などを**消費(しょうひ)する**ことです（例(れい)6, 7）。

To spend things such as money or time (ex.6, 7).

③「気(き)をつかう（遣(つか)う）」は、まわりのことに**こまかい配慮(はいりょ)**をするという意味(いみ)です（例(れい)8, 9）。

The expression *ki o tsukau* means to take careful consideration of one's surroundings (ex.8, 9).

---

1) 私は手紙を書く時、このペンを使います。
わたし てがみ か とき つか
Watashiwa tegamio kaku toki, kono pen-o tsukaimasu.
I use this pen whenever I write letters.

2) はさみは、物を切るのに使う道具です。
もの き つか どうぐ
Hasamiwa, monoo kirunoni tsukau doogudesu.
A pair of scissors is a tool used for cutting things.

3) この電話は故障中なので使えません。
でんわ こしょうちゅう つか
Kono denwawa koshoochuunanode tsukaemasen.
(You) can't use this phone because it's out of order.

4) 彼の工場では、人を500人も使っている。
かれ こうじょう ひと にん つか
Kareno koojoodewa, hitoo gohyakuninmo tsukatteiru.
His factory employs 500 people.

5) 日本語の授業中は、日本語しか使ってはいけません。
にほんご じゅぎょうちゅう にほんご つか
Nihongono jugyoochuuwa, Nihongoshika tsukattewa ikemasen.
During Japanese class (we) must speak only Japanese.

6) 忙しい人ほど時間の使い方がじょうずだ。
いそが ひと じかん つか かた
Isogashii hitohodo jikanno tsukaikataga joozuda.
Busy people are better at using their time than others.

7) きのう、遊園地に行って、１日で２万円も使ってしまった。
ゆうえんち い にち まんえん つか
Kinoo, yuuenchini itte, ichinichide niman-enmo tsukatteshimatta.
Yesterday (I) went to the amusement park and spent ¥20,000.

8) 彼は私だけではなく、私の家族にもとても気をつかってくれた。
かれ わたし わたし かぞく き
Karewa watashidake-dewanaku, watashino kazokunimo totemo kio tsukattekureta.
He was attentive to not only me, but my whole family as well.

9) そんなに気をつかわないでください。
き
Sonnani kio tsukawanaide kudasai.
Please don't worry about (me) so much.

もちいる ［用いる］
もち

■ *mochiiru*
■ to utilize ; to use

物（道具）や方法・人などを**何かの目的で、役立て**たり**利用したり**することです。「使う」よりもかたい表現で、日常の会話ではあまり使いません（例10, 11, 12, 13）。そのものが本来持っている「機能や能力を生かして」という意味を強く含みます。

To employ such things as a tool, method, or person for a certain purpose. *Mochiiru* is a more formal expression than *tsukau*, and is only rarely used in casual conversation (ex.10, 11, 12, 13). It is implied that one is utilizing an inherent ability or function the object or person possesses.

---

10) これは、当時の公式行事に用いられた服装です。

Korewa, toojino kooshikigyoojini mochiirareta fukusoodesu.
This is a costume that was used in official functions of the period.

11) 今では多くの電気製品に、マイコン技術が用いられている。

Imadewa ookuno denkiseihinni, maikon-gijutsuga mochiirareteiru.
Most of today's electrical products make use of microcomputers.

12) 最近では、天然木材を用いた建築が少なくなっている。

Saikindewa, tennenmokuzaio mochiita kenchikuga sukunakunatteiru.
These days, the number of buildings built using real wood is decreasing.

13) この計画を成功させるには有能な専門家を用いる必要がある。

Kono keikakuo seikoosaseruniwa yuunoona senmonkao mochiiru hitsuyoo-gaaru.
(We) will need to employ the services of a qualified expert to make this plan succeed.

1さつの本

「『彼は1さつの本を持って旅行に行った』という文と、『彼は本を1さつ持って旅行に行った』は全く同じ意味ですか」とミッシェルが聞きました。同じようですが実は違います。「1さつの本」は「ある本」という意味で、その本がどういう本なのか、なぜ持って行ったのかなどの説明が続き、1さつという数を問題にしているのではありません。そして、「本を1さつ持って旅行に行きました」の方は、ほかには何も持って行かなかったのかもしれません。旅行の荷物や本の数を説明しているだけです。

同じように、「その家には1人の子供がいました」は、ほかにも子供がいるかもしれないけれどその内の1人を特にとりあげていることを表し、「子供が1人いました」は、その家にいる子供の数は1人だということを表しています。

Issatsu no hon

Michelle asked, "Are the sentences *Kare wa issatsu no hon o motte ryokoo ni itta*[1], and *Kare wa hon o issatsu motte ryokoo ni itta*[2] exactly the same?" They appear the same but are actually different. *Issatsu no hon* refers to a particular book, with an explanation as to the kind of book it is or why it is being taken to follow. It does not mean that there is only one book. *Hon o issatsu motte ryokoo ni ikimashita* may mean that a book, and nothing else, was taken. It simply refers to the number of belongings or books that were taken on the trip.

In the same manner, *sono ie niwa hitori no kodomo ga imashita*[3] is used when speaking specifically of one child, although there may have been other children in the house. *Kodomo ga hitori imashita*[4] indicates that only one child was in the house.

1 *He took a book with him on the trip.*
2 *He took one book with him on the trip.*
3 *There was a child in the house.*
4 *There was one child (in the house).*

つかまえる／とらえる

■ *tsukamaeru* ■ *toraeru*

つかまえる［捕まえる］ ■ *tsukamaeru* ■ to catch 

何かが**逃げないように**、どこかへ行ってしまわないように**とりおさえる**ことです（例1, 2, 3)。用事があって**捜していた人を見つけたり**、連絡をとること

（例4, 5）や、タクシーをよびとめること（例6, 7）にも使います。

To capture and keep something from escaping or moving away (ex.1, 2, 3). This expression may also be used when speaking of finding a person one has been looking for, making contact with someone (ex.4, 5), or stopping a taxi (ex.6, 7).

1）猫はねずみを捕まえるのがうまい。
Nekowa nezumio tsukamaerunoga umai.
Cats are good at catching mice.

2）あの青年は、どろぼうを追いかけて捕まえた。
Ano seinenwa, doroboo-o oikakete tsukamaeta.
That young man chased and caught the burglar.

3）野鳥を捕まえてはいけません。
Yachoo-o tsukamaetewa ikemasen.
(You) must not catch wild birds.

4）彼は忙しいので、なかなか捕まえることができない。
Karewa isogashiinode, nakanaka tsukamaeru kotoga dekinai.
He's been so busy that (I) haven't been able to get hold of him.

5）何度も電話をかけて、やっと彼女を捕まえることができた。
Nandomo denwao kakete, yatto kanojo-o tsukamaeru kotoga dekita.
(I) was finally able to get hold of her after calling several times.

6）夜、雨がふりだしたので、タクシーを捕まえるのに苦労した。
Yoru, amega furidashitanode, takushiio tsukamaerunoni kurooshita.
It suddenly started raining last night and (I) had a hard time catching a taxi.

7）広い通りに出れば、すぐタクシーが捕まえられます。
Hiroi toorini dereba, sugu takushiiga tsukamaeraremasu.
(You'll) be able to get a taxi quickly if you go to a main road.

とらえる［捕らえる］

■ *toraeru*
■ to catch ; to capture 

---

①動物・犯人などをとりおさえることです。「捕まえる」よりもかたいことばで、**大がかり**・**大変な感じ**がします。日常的なことにはあまり使いません（例8, 9, 10）。

To capture something such as an animal or criminal. It is a more formal expression than *tsukamaeru*, and carries a feeling that the action is an extensive or difficult undertaking. It is not used when speaking of ordinary daily matters (ex.8, 9, 10).

②特徴・要点などを正しくしっかり理解すること（例11, 12）や、**人の心をひきつけること**（例13, 14）です。

To completely and correctly understand the characteristics or point of something (ex.11, 12), or to charm or attract someone (ex.13, 14).

---

8) 動物園から逃げたライオンは、２時間後に捕らえられた。
Doobutsuenkara nigeta raionwa, nijikangoni toraerareta.
The lion that escaped from the zoo was captured two hours later.

9) 銀行強盗を捕らえた女性の記事が、新聞にのっている。
Ginkoo-gootoo-o toraeta joseino kijiga, shinbunni notteiru.
There is an article about the woman who captured the bank robber in the newspaper.

10) 警察は、せっかく捕らえた犯人を、証拠不十分で釈放した。
Keisatsuwa, sekkaku toraeta hannin-o, shooko-fujuubunde shakuhooshita.
The man the police took so much trouble in capturing was released due to insufficient evidence.

11) この似顔絵は、彼の特徴をよくとらえている。
Kono nigaoewa, kareno tokuchoo-o yoku toraeteiru.
This portrait really captures his features well.

12) 彼の話は、要点をとらえていてわかりやすい。
Kareno hanashiwa, yooten-o toraeteite wakariyasui.
What he has to say captures the essential points and is easy to understand.

13) 彼女の美しい顔が、ぼくの心をとらえてしまった。
Kanojono utsukushii kaoga, bokuno kokoroo toraeteshimatta.
Her beautiful face has captured my heart.

14) すすり泣くようなバイオリンの音色は、聴衆の心をとらえた。
Susurinakuyoona baiorinno neirowa, chooshuuno kokoroo toraeta.
The weeping tone of the violin captivated the audience.

つかむ／にぎる

■*tsukamu*　■*nigiru*

つかむ ■*tsukamu* ■to seize ; to grasp 

ものの一部（小さいものは、全部のこともある）を手のひらで**しっかりと持ち、押さえる**ことです（例1, 2, 3）。そのものが、**逃げたりどこかへ行ってしまわないようにする・離さない**ようにするという意味を含みます。「握る」よりも瞬間的であることが多く、乱暴だ・雑だなどの感じがすることもあります。また、チャンスや情報・要点などをとらえたり理解したりするときにも使います（例4, 5, 6）。

To strongly grasp part of something (or all of something small) with one's hand (ex.1, 2, 3). It is implied that the purpose of the action is to keep the object from escaping or moving away. *Tsukamu* may sometimes suggest violent or forceful action, and is often a more brief action than is *nigiru*. Furthermore, it may be used when speaking of obtaining things such as information, a chance, or the point of something (ex.4, 5, 6).

1) 子供が車道に飛び出そうとしたので、あわてて腕をつかんだ。

Kodomoga shadooni tobidasooto shitanode, awatete udeo tsukanda.

My child was about to dash into the road, so (I) quickly grabbed his arm.

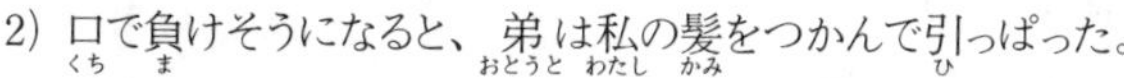

2) 口で負けそうになると、弟は私の髪をつかんで引っぱった。

Kuchide makesooni naruto, otootowa watashino kamio tsukande hippatta.

When it seemed my little brother was about to lose the argument, he grabbed and pulled my hair.

3) 電車が急停車したので、私はとっさにつり革をつかんだ。

Denshaga kyuuteisha-shitanode, watashiwa tossani tsurikawao tsukanda.

The train breaked suddenly so I instinctively grabbed the safety strap.

4) 彼は、ドラマの主役に選ばれるという幸運をつかんだ。

Karewa, doramano shuyakuni erabareruto yuu kooun-o tsukanda.

He was fortunate enough to be named lead in the drama.

5) 彼女は、話の要点をつかんで短くまとめるのがうまい。
Kanojowa, hanashino yooten-o tsukande mijikaku matomerunoga umai.
She is good at grasping the main points of an issue and summing it up briefly.

6) 災害のときは、はやく正確な情報をつかむことが必要だ。
Saigaino tokiwa, hayaku seikakuna joohoo-o tsukamu kotoga hitsuyooda.
In times of disaster it is necessary to get accurate information quickly.

にぎる［握る］
■ *nigiru*
■ to grasp ; to clasp ; to seize 

手の**指を内側に強く曲げること**です。何も持っていなければ、握りこぶしを作ることになりますし（例7）、ものを持っているときは、しっかりと持ったりさらに力を入れたり圧力を加えたりすることです（例8, 9, 10）。

To firmly bend one's fingers inward so that if there is nothing in the hand a fist would be formed (ex.7), or if something is in the hand it would be held tightly, with pressure applied to it (ex.8, 9, 10).

例11, 12は、自分のものにして離さない・押さえておく、という意味です。

In Examples 11 and 12, *nigiru* means to take and keep something for one's own, without letting go of it.

---

7) 言い争いをしているうちにかっとなって、彼は握ったこぶしを振り上げた。
Iiarasoio shiteiru uchini kattonatte, karewa nigitta kobushio furiageta.
He became so angry during the argument that he began shaking his fist.

8) 別れぎわに彼は私の手を強く握った。
Wakaregiwani karewa watashino teo tsuyoku nigitta.
He held my hand tightly as we said good-bye.

9) 息子は小さいころ、どこへ行くときでも気に入ったおもちゃを握って放さなかった。
Musukowa chiisai koro, dokoe iku tokidemo kiniitta omochao nigitte hanasanakatta.
When (my) son was little, wherever we went he would grab on to toys he liked and wouldn't let go.

10) 運転免許をとったばかりなので、ハンドルを握る手に力が入ってしまう。

Untenmenkyoo tottabakari-nanode, handoruo nigiru teni chikaraga haitteshimau.
(I've) just gotten my driver's license so I instinctively hold onto the steering wheel with all my might.

11) 私は、彼が真犯人だという証拠を握っている。
Watashiwa, karega shinhannindato yuu shookoo nigitteiru.
I have gotten hold of solid proof that he is the criminal.

12) あの会社の実権を握っているのは、社長の夫人だ。
Ano kaishano jikken-o nigitteirunowa, shachoono fujinda.
The person who is actually in charge of that company is the president's wife.

つかれる／くたびれる

■ *tsukareru* ■ *kutabireru*

つかれる［疲れる］ ■ *tsukareru* ■ to get ／ to be tired 大 

体や気を遣いすぎて負担がかかり、**力や元気がなくなる**ことです（例1, 2, 3）。また、例4のように何かを長く続けすぎていやになる、という意味を含むときにも使い、例5、6のようにほかの動詞の後につけて使うこともあります。

To lose energy or spirit through excessive physical or mental exertion (ex.1, 2, 3). It may also mean to be fed up with something that has gone on too long (ex.4). *Tsukareru* is occasionally used following another verb (ex.5, 6).

---

1) 彼女は病人の世話で疲れている。
Kanojowa byooninno sewade tsukareteiru.
She's tired out from nursing the sick.

2) 細かい字ばかり読んでいると、目が疲れる。
Komakai jibakari yondeiruto, mega tsukareru.
My eyes get tired when (I) read small print all the time.

3) 新幹線が混んでいて、東京から新大阪まで立ちっぱなしだったので疲れた。

Shinkansenga kondeite, Tookyookara Shin-oosakamade tachippanashi datta-node tsukareta.
The *Shinkansen* was so crowded (I) ended up standing all the way from Tokyo to Shin-osaka, so I'm really tired.

4) 失業、借金、離婚……彼は人生に疲れてしまった。
Shitsugyoo, shakkin, rikon...karewa jinseini tsukarete-shimatta.
He's unemployed, in debt, and divorced——he's worn out from life.

5) おかあさんにしかられた男の子は、泣き疲れて眠ってしまった。
Okaasanni shikarareta otokonokowa, nakitsukarete nemutte-shimatta.
A little boy, scolded by his mother, fell asleep all worn out from crying.

6) 京都の寺をあちこち見てまわり、歩き疲れてホテルにもどった。
Kyootono terao achikochi mitemawari, arukitsukarete hoteruni modotta.
(I) went all around Kyoto looking at temples and returned to the hotel completely worn out from walking.

くたびれる

■ *kutabireru*
■ to be exhausted ; to be worn out

---

①体や気を遣いすぎたために、**力や元気がなくなる**ことです。「疲れる」より、くだけた感じのすることばです（例7, 8, 9）。「くたびれる」は多くの場合、どちらかというと**肉体的な疲れ**を表します。

To lose energy or spirit through excessive physical or mental exertion. *Kutabireru* is a more colloquial expression than *tsukareru* (ex.7, 8, 9). In most cases, *kutabireru* expresses physical tiredness.

②長く使ったために、**物が古くなったりみすぼらしく**なったりすることです（例10, 11）。

To be old or worn out to the point of shabbiness from long use (ex.10, 11).

---

7) きょうは、一日中デパートを歩きまわったので、くたびれた。
Kyoowa, ichinichijuu depaatoo arukimawatta-node, kutabireta.
(I) walked around (many) department stores all day today and I'm dead beat.

8) 山歩きは気持ちがよかったけれど、帰り道ですっかりくたびれてしまった。
Yamaarukiwa kimochiga yokattakeredo, kaerimichide sukkari kutabirete shi-matta.

It felt good walking in the mountains, but (I) got completely worn out on the way back.

9) 彼女は約束の時間に30分も遅れて来たので、私は待ちくたびれてしまった。
Kanojowa yakusokuno jikanni sanjuppunmo okurete kitanode, watashiwa machikutabirete-shimatta.
She came a whole 30 minutes later than the time we set, and I got tired of waiting.

10) この靴は、長いことはいたのでくたびれている。
Kono kutsuwa, nagaikoto haitanode kutabireteiru.
These shoes are shabby because (I've) worn them so long.

11) 彼はくたびれたコートを着ている。
Karewa kutabireta kootoo kiteiru.
He's wearing a worn-out coat.

つぎ／こんど

■*tsugi*　■*kondo*

つぎ［次］ ■*tsugi* ■next 

基準となっているものの、**すぐ後にくるもの**や、**続くもの**を指すとき使います(例1, 2, 3, 4, 5, 6, 7)。順番や順位が決まっているものやことがら、あるいは並んでいるものを、その順番どおりに取りあげるときの表現です。

Tsugi refers to the idea that an object or event is next, following the original point of reference (ex.1, 2, 3, 4, 5, 6, 7). It indicates that things are ordered and are taken or occur in a certain succession.

1) 月曜日の次は火曜日です。
Getsuyoobino tsugiwa kayoobidesu.
After Monday comes Tuesday.

2) 次は、あなたが答える番です。
Tsugiwa, anataga kotaeru bandesu.
Next is your turn to answer (my questions).

3) この資料は次の会議までにまとめておいてください。

Kono shiryoowa tsugino kaigimadeni matometeoite kudasai.
Please put this data in order before the next meeting.

4) 私は、定期を買った次の日に失くしてしまった。

*Watashiwa, teiki*o katta tsugino hini nakushite-shimatta.* *p.198
I bought my commuter's pass, but unfortunately I lost it the next day.

5) この道をまっすぐ行って、次の角を左に曲がると図書館があります。

Kono michio massugu itte, tsugino kadoo hidarini magaruto toshokanga arimasu.
Continue straight on this street and turn left at the next corner. There (you'll) see a library.

6) 私は家族の中で、兄の次に背が高い。

Watashiwa kazokuno nakade, anino tsugini sega takai.
I'm the next tallest in my family, after my (elder) brother.

7) いちばん上の姉は司書で、次の姉は通訳です。

Ichiban ueno anewa shishode, tsugino anewa tsuuyakudesu.
My oldest sister is a librarian and the second oldest is an interpreter.

こんど［今度］

■ *kondo*
■ this (next) time ; sometime 

---

①「今回・このたび」のように、**現在にいちばん近い未来**に起こること（例8, 9）や**現在**起こっていること（例10, 11）、また**いちばん近い過去**に起こったこと（例12）を指すとき使います。「次」は順番に重点がありますが「今度」は、「現在に近い」という、時期に重点があります。したがって、単に順番を表す使い方はしません。

Kondo is used like the expressions *konkai* and *konotabi* to refer to something which is happening at the present (ex.8, 9), is going to happen imminently (ex.10, 11), or has just happened (ex.12). In the case of *tsugi*, the focus is on the order in which an event occurs, however with *kondo*, the focus is on a certain time (e.g., 'this time' or 'next time') ; therefore, it is not used to indicate order.

②「**いつか**」という意味で、特に決まっていない近い将来を表します（例13, 14）。

Kondo may indicate an indefinite point of time in the future, in the same way as the word *itsuka* (someday) (ex.13, 14).

8) 今度の土曜日に国から母が来ます。
Kondono doyoobini kunikara hahaga kimasu.
My mother is coming from our hometown next Saturday.

9) 今度彼は、大阪に転勤することになった。
Kondo karewa, Oosakani tenkinsuru kotoni natta.
It has been decided that he will be transfered to Osaka this time.

10) 彼女の作った今度の曲は、なかなか評判がいい。
Kanojono tsukutta kondono kyokuwa, nakanaka hyoobanga ii.
The song she composed this time has been quite well received.

11) 今度の公演は大成功だった。
Kondono kooenwa daiseikoodatta.
The performance was very successful this time.

12) 今度隣に越して来た人は、大きな犬を飼っている。
Kondo tonarini koshitekita hitowa, ookina inuo katteiru.
The person who just moved in next door has a big dog.

13) 今度、私のうちに遊びに来てください。
Kondo, watashino uchini asobini kite kudasai.
Please come to visit me sometime (at the next opportunity).

14) この話の続きは、また今度にしましょう。
Kono hanashino tsuzukiwa, mata kondoni-shimashoo.
Let's continue our conversation about this matter some other time.

つぎつぎ／ぞくぞく／ひっきりなしに

■ *tsugitsugi* ■ *zokuzoku* ■ *hikkirinashi ni*

つぎつぎ

■ *tsugitsugi*
■ one after another

1つが終わると、また後から**続いてことがらが起こるようす**を表します（例1,2,3）。

Tsugitsugi expresses the successive occurrence of an event or thing closely following another (ex.1, 2, 3).

---

1) 彼はつぎつぎ珍しい発明をして、世間をおどろかせている。
Karewa tsugitsugi mezurashii hatsumeioshite, seken-o odorokaseteiru.
He's astounding the world with one unusual invention after another.

2) このごろ、つぎつぎと新しい雑誌が出版されている。
Konogoro, tsugitsugito atarashii zasshiga shuppansareteiru.
These days new magazines are being published one after the other.

3) 昼寝をしようと思ったのに、つぎつぎと電話がかかって寝られなかった。
Hiruneo shiyooto omottanoni, tsugitsugito denwaga kakatte nerarenakatta.
(I) was going to take a nap, but I got one phone call after another and I wasn't able to get to sleep.

ぞくぞく

■ *zokuzoku*
■ one after another 

ことがらが続けて起こるようすを表します。「つぎつぎ」よりも回数が多く、どんどんたまっていく・いっぱいになっていくという意味を含みます（例4, 5, 6, 7）。

This expresses the repeated occurrence of an event. The frequency of events is greater than with *tsugitsugi* and it includes the idea of rapid accumulation or filling up (ex.4, 5, 6, 7).

---

4) 桜が咲き始めると、その公園にはお花見の人がぞくぞくつめかけた。
*Sakuraga sakihajimeruto, sono kooenniwa ohanami*no hitoga zokuzoku tsumekaketa.*
Once the cherry blossoms began blooming, people began to pour into the park to see them.
——* *ohanami* Among the most popular of the seasonal events in Japan is *hanami*. At the beginning of spring, people of all ages gather beneath the blossoming cherry trees to eat and drink.

5) 外務大臣の就任祝いに、祝電や花束がぞくぞく届いた。
Gaimudaijinno shuunin-iwaini, shukudenya hanatabaga zokuzoku todoita.
Congratulatory telegrams and bouquets arrived in a steady stream for the foreign minister' inaugural celebration.

6) 火事の現場にやじ馬がぞくぞくと集まってきた。
Kajino genbani yajiumaga zokuzokuto atsumattekita.

Curious onlookers gathered at the scene of the fire one after the other.

7) 発掘された遺跡から、当時の装飾品がぞくぞくと出てきた。
Hakkutsusareta isekikara, toojino sooshokuhinga zokuzokuto detekita.
Personal ornaments from the period kept turning up one after another from the excavated ruins.

ひっきりなしに ■*hikkirinashi ni* ■unceasingly 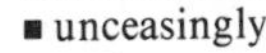 

同じことがらが、切れ目なしに立て続けに起こるようすを表します（例8, 9, 10)。
This expression denotes the continued occurrence of an event without a break (ex.8, 9, 10).

8) この道は狭いのに、車がひっきりなしに通るので危ない。
Kono michiwa semainoni, kurumaga hikkirinashini toorunode abunai.
This street is dangerous because it's narrow, yet cars drive through it incessantly.

9) 事故の後、航空会社には問い合わせの電話がひっきりなしにかかってきた。
Jikono ato, kookuugaishaniwa toiawaseno denwaga hikkirinashini kakattekita.
After the accident, calls for information flooded into the airline.

10) 彼は、何か約束でもあるらしく、さっきからひっきりなしに時計を見ている。
Karewa, nanika yakusokudemo arurashiku, sakkikara hikkirinashini tokeio miteiru.
He's been looking at the clock constantly for a while now——as if he's got an appointment or something.

つく／つつく／さす
■*tsuku* ■*tsutsuku* ■*sasu*

つく［突く］ ■*tsuku* ■to poke ; to stab 

①先の細いものやとがっているもので、一気に強い衝撃を与えることです

（例1, 2)。

To thrust at something with a pointed or sharp object in order to create impact (ex.1, 2).

②弱点・問題点・要点などを**鋭く指摘する**とき使います（例3, 4)。例5、6は、「支えにする」という意味です。

To clearly point out a weakness, problem area, or the gist of something (ex.3, 4). In Examples 5 and 6 *tsuku* is used to mean 'to support'.

---

1) 青年は海にもぐると、魚をもりで突いてとってきた。
Seinenwa umini moguruto, sakanao moride tsuite tottekita.
The boys brought back fish they had speared with gaffs while diving in the ocean.

2) 兄は、木の枝にひっかかったボールを、棒で突いて落としてくれた。
Aniwa, kino edani hikkakatta booruo, boode tsuite otoshitekureta.
My brother knocked my ball out of the tree by poking it with a stick.

3) 彼の質問は、核心を突いている。
Kareno shitsumonwa, kakushin-o tsuiteiru.
His question got to the heart of the problem.

4) きのうの柔道の試合で、彼は相手の弱点を突いて、みごとに優勝した。
Kinoono juudoono shiaide, karewa aiteno jakuten-o tsuite, migotoni yuushoo shita.
He scored a brilliant victory at yesterday's judo tournament by attacking his opponent's weakness.

5) 食事中に、ひじを突いてはいけません。
Shokujichuuni, hijio tsuitewa ikemasen.
(You) mustn't rest your elbows on the table while eating.

6) おじいさんは、つえを突いて歩いて来た。
Ojiisanwa, tsueo tsuite aruite kita.
My grandfather walked toward us, using a cane for support.

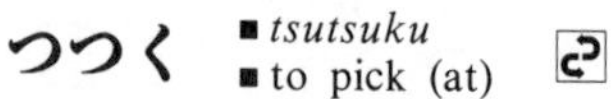

つつく ■*tsutsuku* ■to pick (at)

棒のように**先の細いものや指先**などで、**軽い衝撃を何度か与える**ことです

(例7, 8)。あやまちや欠点などを、とり上げて非難するときにも使います(例9)。「つっつく」は話しことばで、少し強い感じです(例10)。

To repeatedly and lightly poke at something with a narrow-tipped object like a stick or finger (ex.7, 8). *Tsutsuku* may be used when one points out and criticizes a mistake or deficiency (ex.9). In spoken language, this may be pronounced *tsuttsuku* with a slightly stronger meaning (ex.10).

---

7) 授業中にいねむりをしていたら、友達に後ろからつつかれた。
Jugyoochuuni inemurio shiteitara, tomodachini ushirokara tsutsukareta.
When (I) was dozing off in class, my friend poked me from behind.

8) にわとりが、くちばしで地面をつついている。
Niwatoriga, kuchibashide jimen-o tsutsuiteiru.
The chicken is pecking at the ground with its beak.

9) 記事に問題があったと、新聞社がつつかれている。
Kijini mondaiga attato, shinbunshaga tsutsukareteiru.
The newspaper is being criticized for a problem in one of its articles.

10) からすにつっつかれて、けがをした。
Karasuni tsuttsukarete, kegao shita.
A crow pecked at (me) and hurt me.

さす[刺す]

■ *sasu*
■ to pierce ; to bite ; to prick 

先の鋭いものやとがったものを、**つき立てたりつき通したりする**ことです(例11, 12, 13, 14)。

To thrust at and pierce something with a pointed or sharp instrument (ex.11, 12, 13, 14).

11) ししゅうをしている時に、指に針を刺してしまった。
Shishuuo shiteiru tokini, yubini hario sashiteshimatta.
(I) pricked my finger with a needle while doing embroidery.

12) 山で、いっぱい蚊に刺された。
Yamade, ippai kani sasareta.
(I) was bitten by a lot of mosquitos while in the mountains.

13) 蜂の巣があるから、刺されないように気をつけて。

Hachinosuga arukara, sasarenaiyooni kio tsukete.
There's a beehive near here, so be careful not to get stung.

14) 彼はナイフで人を刺して、警察につかまった。
Karewa naifude hitoo sashite, keisatsuni tsukamatta.
He was captured by the police after stabbing a person with a knife.

つくづく／しみじみ

■*tsukuzuku* ■*shimijimi*

つくづく

■*tsukuzuku*
■thoroughly ; deeply ♥

ものごとに対して、深く考えさせられたり、感心したり、**ほんとうにそうだと心から思う**ようなとき使います（例1, 2, 3, 4）。

This word is used when someone is deeply impressed by, made to think seriously about, or is deeply convinced of something (ex1, 2, 3, 4).

---

1) 最近の若い人たちと話していると、自分の世代との考え方の違いをつくづく感じる。
Saikinno wakai hitotachito hanashiteiruto, jibunno sedaitono kangaekatano chigaio tsukuzuku kanjiru.
When (I) talk with young people nowadays, I keenly feel the difference in the way our generations think.

2) 外国で暮らしていると、自分の国との文化の違いをつくづく考えさせられる。
Gaikokude kurashiteiruto, jibunno kunitono bunkano chigaio tsukuzuku kangae saserareru.
When one lives in a foreign country, one is forced to reflect seriously upon the differences there are in culture from one's native country.

3) 飛行機に乗ると、つくづく世の中は便利になったと感じる。
Hikookini noruto, tsukuzuku yononakawa benrini nattato kanjiru.
Whenever (I) fly, I am deeply impressed by how convenient this world has become.

4) 毎日残業ばかりで、もう働くのがつくづくいやになった。

Mainichi zangyoobakaride, moo hatarakunoga tsukuzuku iyaninatta.
Every day (I) have to do overtime ; I've really become fed up with working.

しみじみ

■ *shimijimi*
■ keenly ; thoroughly 

ものごとの良(よ)さ、**ありがたさなどを心(こころ)の底(そこ)から**身(み)にしみて**感(かん)じる**とき使(つか)います(例(れい)5, 6, 7, 8)。**感慨深(かんがいぶか)い**という気持(きも)ちや、感傷的(かんしょうてき)な気持(きも)ちあるいはおだやかで落(お)ちついた雰囲気(ふんいき)を含(ふく)んでいます。

Shimijimi is used when someone feels deep appreciation and gratitude for the quality of something (ex.5, 6, 7, 8). It imparts a sense of deep emotional, sentimental or calm feelings.

---

5) 久(ひさ)しぶりに田舎(いなか)に帰(かえ)り、懐(なつ)かしいふるさとの料理(りょうり)をしみじみと味(あじ)わった。
Hisashiburini inakani kaeri, natsukashii furusatono ryoorio shimijimito ajiwatta.
When (I) returned to my hometown after a long absence, I really enjoyed the home cooking that I had been longing for.

6) はなれて暮(く)らしてみて、母(はは)のありがたみをしみじみと感(かん)じた。
Hanarete kurashitemite, hahano arigatamio shimijimito kanjita.
Having lived away from my mother, (I) now deeply appreciate her.

7) おじいさんは、若(わか)いころの思(おも)い出(で)を孫(まご)たちにしみじみと語(かた)って聞(き)かせた。
Ojiisanwa, wakai korono omoideo magotachini shimijimito katatte kikaseta.
The old man sentimentally told his grandchildren about his childhood memories.

8) ゆうべは、学生時代(がくせいじだい)の友(とも)だちと、一晩中(ひとばんじゅう)しみじみ語(かた)り明(あ)かした。
Yuubewa, gakusei-jidaino tomodachito, hitobanjuu shimijimi katariakashita.
Last night, (I) spent the whole night with my old school friends talking sentimentally.

身につける表現 'HOW TO DRESS' EXPRESSIONS

In the diagram above, please note the differences in terms within the parentheses next to each article of attire. The words to the left of the ↔ symbol describe 'putting on' or 'wearing' the piece and the words to the right of the ↔ symbol describe 'taking off' the article.

つける／とりつける／はる

■ *tsukeru* ■ *toritsukeru* ■ *haru*

つける［付ける・着ける］

■ *tsukeru*
■ to attach ; to fix 

あるものを、ほかのものに**離れないように留めたり、加えたりする**ことです(例1,2,3,4,5,6)。また、液体やクリーム状のものなどを何かの表面に塗ったりするというときにも使い、粉などにも使います（例7,8,9)。漢字は「付ける・着ける」の2つがあり、着る物やアクセサリーなどは、「着ける」を使いますが、ほとんどの場合ひらがなで書いてかまいません。

To fasten or add something to something else in a such way that it doesn't come off or become separated (ex.1, 2, 3, 4, 5, 6). Also, to cover the surface of something with a substance that is in a liquid, cream, or powdered state (ex.7, 8, 9). *Tsukeru* is written with either the *kanji* 付ける or 着ける, the latter is used when speaking of clothes or accessories, however in most cases *hiragana* may also be used.

1) 先週、どろぼうに入られたので、玄関にもう1つかぎをつけた。
Senshuu, dorobooni hairaretanode, genkanni moo hitotsu kagio tsuketa.
A burglar broke in here last week, so (I) put another lock on the front door.

2) ワイシャツのボタンがとれそうですよ。つけてあげましょうか。
Waishatsuno botanga toresoodesuyo. Tsukete agemashooka?
The button on (your) shirt looks like it will fall off. Shall I reattach it (sew it back on) for you?

3) スーツケースにちゃんと名札をつけていたのに、だれかがまちがって持っていった。
Suutsukeesuni chanto nafudao tsuketeitanoni, darekaga machigatte motteitta.
Even though (I) put a name tag on my suitcase, somebody took it by mistake.

4) 私は子猫の首輪に鈴をつけた。
Watashiwa konekono kubiwani suzuo tsuketa.
I attached a bell to my kitten's collar.

5) 彼女は、プレゼントにもらったブローチをさっそくつけてみた。

Kanojowa, purezentoni moratta buroochio sassoku tsuketemita.
She immediately tried on the broach she had received as a present.

6) 非常の場合は、救命具をつけて船から避難してください。

Hijoono baaiwa, kyuumeiguo tsukete funekara hinanshite kudasai.
In case of emergency, please put on a life preserver and evacuate the ship.

7) 彼女は、毎晩顔や首にたっぷりクリームをつけてから寝る。

Kanojowa, maiban kaoya kubini tappuri kuriimuo tsuketekara neru.
Every night, she applies plenty of beauty cream to her face and neck before going to bed.

8) 私はダイエットのため、パンにバターやジャムをつけないことにした。

Watashiwa daiettono tame, panni bataaya jamuo tsukenai kotoni shita.
Because I'm on a diet, I've decided not to put butter or jam on my bread anymore.

9) たいした傷ではありません。病院に行かなくても、何か薬をつけておけばすぐ治りますよ。

Taishita kizudewa arimasen. Byooinni ikanakutemo, nanika kusurio tsuketeo-keba sugu naorimasuyo.
It's not a bad cut. Even if you don't go to the hospital, it will soon heal if you just apply some medicine to it.

とりつける［取り付ける］ ■*toritsukeru* ■to install 

ねじやくぎなどで**器具や部品などを**ある場所に**設置したり、固定したり**して使えるようにすることです（例10, 11, 12）。

To secure a machine or part in a position with screws, nails, etc., so that it may be used (ex.10, 11, 12).

10) きのう引っ越してきたばかりで、まだ電話は取り付けてない。

Kinoo hikkoshite-kitabakaride, mada denwawa toritsuketenai.
(I) just moved yesterday, so my phone hasn't been installed yet.

11) この銀行では、天井に取り付けた防犯カメラで、店内を監視している。

Kono ginkoodewa, tenjooni toritsuketa boohankamerade, tennaio kanshishiteiru.
The inside of this bank is watched over by a security camera installed on the ceiling.

12) このファックスは、電話につなぐだけで使えます。特別な取り付け工事は必要ありません。
Kono fakkusuwa, denwani tsunagudakede tsukaemasu. Tokubetsuna toritsukekoojiwa hitsuyooarimasen.
This fax may be used by simply connecting it to a phone. No special installation is required.

はる［張る］

■ *haru*
■ to attach ; to stick 

紙などのような**薄くて平たいものを**平らな面に、のり・テープ・画びょうなどで、動いたりはがれたりしないように**密着させる**ことです（例13, 14, 15, 16)。

To firmly affix a flat, thin object to the surface of something with glue, tape, thumbtacks, etc., so that it doesn't move or come off (ex.13, 14, 15, 16).

---

13) 店の主人は、アルバイト募集のポスターを作って店の入り口にはった。
Miseno shujinwa, arubaito-boshuuno posutaao tsukutte miseno iriguchini hatta.
The shop owner made a 'part-time help wanted' poster and stuck it up at the entrance to his shop.

14) ついうっかりして、切手をはらないでポストに手紙を入れてしまった。
Tsui ukkarishite, kitteo haranaide posutoni tegamio ireteshimatta.
(I) absentmindedly put a letter into the mail box without putting a stamp on it.

15) 足首をねんざしたので、湿布薬をはった。
Ashikubio nenzashitanode, shippuyakuo hatta.
(I) sprained my ankle so I applied a compress to it.

16) 週末に、この部屋の壁紙をはりかえるつもりだ。
Shuumatsuni, kono heyano kabegamio harikaeru tsumorida.
(I'm) planning to replace the wallpaper in this room this weekend.

つける／ひたす

■*tsukeru*　■*hitasu*

つける［漬ける］

■*tsukeru*
■to soak ; to steep ; to pickle

①**液体の中に物を入れる**ことです（例1, 2, 3）。入れた物の**状態を変える**、または**保存する**などの**目的**があります。「ひたす」よりも、物に対して**液体の量は多く**、**比較的長い時間**入れておくときに使います。

To immerse something in a liquid (ex.1, 2, 3), for the purpose of changing its appearance or to preserve it. In contrast to *hitasu*, the proportion of liquid to the object immersed is greater, and the object is left in for a relatively longer period of time.

②くだもの・野菜・魚・肉などを、調味料の中に入れてしっかりと味をつけたり、保存したりすることです（例4, 5）。

To put fruits, vegetables, fish, meat, or the like into a seasoning medium to flavor or preserve it (ex.4, 5).

1）汚れた服は、洗剤の入った水に一晩漬けておくといい。
Yogoreta fukuwa, senzaino haitta mizuni hitoban tsuketeokuto ii.
It's a good idea to soak dirty clothes overnight in soapy water.

2）糸を染料に漬けて染める。
Itoo senryooni tsukete someru.
Dye the yarn by soaking it in the dye solution.

3）りんごをむいたら、塩水に一度漬けると、色が変わらない。
Ringoo muitara, shiomizuni ichido tsukeruto, iroga kawaranai.
If (you) dip an apple briefly in salt water after (you) peel it, it won't change color.

4）梅干しは、梅を塩で漬けてから干したものです。
Umeboshiwa, umeo shiode tsuketekara hoshita monodesu.
Umeboshi are plums pickled in salt and then dried.

5）魚を油に漬けて保存する方法は昔からある。
Sakanao aburani tsukete hozonsuru hoohoowa mukashikara aru.

The method of preserving fish by soaking it in oil has been around for a long time.

ひたす［浸す］ ■*hitasu* ■to immerse ; to dip in

ものを、**全体がかくれる程度の量の液体の中に入れる**ことです（例6, 7, 8）。**水分を含ませる**という意味を持ち、保存ではありません。

To put something into enough liquid so that it is entirely covered (ex.6, 7, 8). It is used in the meaning of restoring moisture content, not of preserving.

---

6) 妹は、トーストをココアに浸して食べるのが好きです。
Imootowa, toosutoo kokoani hitashite taberunoga sukidesu.
My (little) sister likes to dip her toast in hot chocolate.

7) 日本や中国には、干した野菜や魚介類を水に浸して、もどしてから使う料理がたくさんある。
Nihonya Chuugokuniwa, hoshita yasaiya gyokairuio mizuni hitashite, modoshitekara tsukau ryooriga takusan aru.
In Japan and China, there are many dishes using dried vegetables or seafoods which have been reconstituted in water.

8) 消毒薬に浸したガーゼで傷口をふいた。
Shoodoku-yakuni hitashita gaazede kizuguchio fuita.
(I) swabbed the wound with gauze dipped in disinfectant.

つつむ／くるむ

■*tsutsumu* ■*kurumu*

つつむ［包む］ ■*tsutsumu* ■to wrap ; to envelop

①ものを**紙や布などでおおう**とき使います（例1, 2, 3）。包むものと包まれるものがぴったりとくっついて「くるむ」よりも、おおい方が整ってきれいです。例1, 2では助詞が「AをBで包む」ですが例3では「AをBに包む」となります。紙

や布(ぬの)など、包(つつ)むものに重点(じゅうてん)があるときは、「〜で」となり、包(つつ)まれている状態(じょうたい)に重点(じゅうてん)があるときは「〜に」となることが多(おお)いです。

To cover something very neatly with paper, cloth, etc. (ex.1, 2, 3). *Tsutsumu* implies more of a feeling that the wrapping is done more neatly and covers all sides of the object than does *kurumu*. In Examples 1 and 2, the grammatical particles are structured *A o B de tsutsumu*, while in Example 3 the structure is *A o B ni tsutsumu*. In the former, the wrapping material (paper, cloth, etc.) is in focus, while in the latter, the condition of being wrapped is usually in focus.

②煙(けむり)・霧(きり)・炎(ほのお)などが回(まわ)りを囲(かこ)むとき、あるいはなんらかの雰囲気(ふんいき)があるとき「〜に包(つつ)まれる」の形(かたち)で使(つか)います(例(れい)4, 5)。このときの包(つつ)むものは抽象的(ちゅうしょうてき)なものの場合(ばあい)が多(おお)いです。

Tsutsumu may be used when something, such as smoke, mist or flames, surrounds something, or when something is enveloped in such abstract things as emotions or mystery (ex.4, 5).

---

1) プレゼントを、きれいな紙(かみ)で包(つつ)む。

Purezentoo, kireina kamide tsutsumu.
(I) will wrap the present with some pretty paper.

2) 昔(むかし)は物(もの)を風呂敷(ふろしき)で包(つつ)んで持(も)ち運(はこ)んだ。

Mukashiwa monoo furoshiki de tsutsunde mochihakonda.*
In the old days, (people) carried things around in a *furoshiki*.
—— * *Furoshiki* is a square cloth, that is used to carry things.

3) ガムは、紙(かみ)に包(つつ)んで捨(す)てましょう。

Gamuwa, kamini tsutsunde sutemashoo.
Please wrap (your) chewing gum in paper and throw it away.

4) 山(やま)の頂上(ちょうじょう)は、濃(こ)い霧(きり)に包(つつ)まれていた。

Yamano choojoowa, koi kirini tsutsumareteita.
The summit of the mountain was wrapped in dense fog.

5) あの事件(じけん)は、まだなぞに包(つつ)まれている。

Ano jikenwa, mada nazoni tsutsumareteiru.
That incident still remains unsolved (wrapped in mystery).

くるむ ■*kurumu* ■to wrap 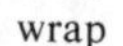 

ものを、紙や布などで**ざっとおおう**とき使います。ものを**保護する**という意味を含むことが多く、「包む」ほどていねいではなく、**大ざっぱに巻く**という感じです。したがってものの一部分が出ていてもかまいません（例6, 7, 8)。

To roughly wrap something with paper (often for purposes of protection). There is a feeling that since the object is not as neatly wrapped as it would be with *tsutsumu*, a part of the contents may be exposed (ex.6, 7, 8,).

6) 八百屋は、大根を新聞紙でくるんで客に渡した。
Yaoyawa, daikon-o shinbunshide kurunde kyakuni watashita.
The man at the vegetable store wrapped the *daikon* radish in newspaper and handed it to the customer.

7) 寒いので、赤ちゃんを毛布でくるんででかけた。
Samuinode, akachan-o moofude kurunde dekaketa.
It was cold, so (I) bundled my baby up in a blanket before taking him out.

8) 私は、アーモンドをチョコレートでくるんだお菓子が好きです。
Watashiwa, aamondoo chokoreetode kurunda okashiga sukidesu.
I love chocolate-covered almonds.

つぶす／くだく

■*tsubusu* ■*kudaku*

つぶす ■*tsubusu* ■to crush

①ものに上や横から**圧力を加えて、形をくずしたり変えたりしてしまうこと**です（例1, 2, 3)。

Tsubusu means to break down or change the shape of something by applying force to it from the top or side (ex.1, 2, 3).

②すでに成立していることがら，たとえば「会社・顔（名誉）・計画」などを、だめにしてなくすことです（例4, 5, 6)。また例7の「ひま（時間）をつぶす」は、空いている時間に何かをして過ごすことです。

To destroy and lose something that had already been established, e.g., a company, a plan, or one's honor (ex.4, 5, 6). The expression *hima* (*jikan*) *o tsubusu* indicates that one fills a period of spare time by doing something (ex.7).

1) ゆでたじゃがいもをつぶして、コロッケを作(つく)ります。

Yudeta jagaimoo tsubushite, korokkeo tsukurimasu.
(You) make croquettes by mashing boiled potatoes.

2) ビールやジュースの空(あ)き缶(かん)は、つぶして捨(す)てたほうがいい。

Biiruya juusuno akikanwa, tsubushite suteta hooga ii.
(You) should crush your empty beer and juice cans before you throw them away.

3) がけくずれで、家(いえ)が一軒(いっけん)つぶされた。

Gakekuzurede, iega ikken tsubusareta.
A house was crushed in the landslide.

4) 春休(はるやす)みに、友達(ともだち)と北海道(ほっかいどう)に行(い)く計画(けいかく)は、親(おや)の反対(はんたい)でつぶされてしまった。

Haruyasumini, tomodachito Hokkaidooni iku keikakuwa, oyano hantaide tsubusarete-shimatta.
(My) plan to go to Hokkaido with my friends during spring break was wrecked by my parent's objections.

5) 彼(かれ)が苦労(くろう)して作(つく)り上(あ)げた会社(かいしゃ)を、2代目(だいめ)の社長(しゃちょう)になった息子(むすこ)がつぶしてしまった。

Karega kurooshite tsukuriageta kaishao, nidaimeno shachooni natta musukoga tsubushite-shimatta.
The company he worked so hard to build went bankrupt when his son took over as president.

6) 彼(かれ)は友達(ともだち)を、知(し)り合(あ)いの会社(かいしゃ)に紹介(しょうかい)したのに、すぐに辞(や)めてしまったので、顔(かお)をつぶされたと怒(おこ)っている。

Karewa tomodachio, shiriaino kaishani shookaishitanoni, suguni yameteshimatta-node, kaoo tsubusaretato okotteiru.
He is angry because he lost face when the friend whom he had persuaded the company to hire soon quit.

7) 待(ま)ち合(あ)わせの時間(じかん)まで、1時間(じかん)もあったので、喫茶店(きっさてん)で紅茶(こうちゃ)を飲(の)んで時間(じかん)をつぶした。

Machiawaseno jikanmade, ichijikanmo attanode, kissatende koochao nonde jikan-o tsubushita.

There was an hour left until (I) had to meet my friend, so I went to a coffee shop and had some tea to kill time.

くだく［砕く］

■ *kudaku*
■ to break into pieces 

①ものを**たたいたりして**、元の形が分からないくらいに、**こなごなにすることです**（例8, 9, 10)。「つぶす」は、ものの形をくずしたり変えたりすることですが、「砕く」は、ものを「割る」よりももっと**数多くの細かいかけらにしてしまいます**。したがって、「砕く」は、「氷・石・角ざとう」などのような**比較的固いものや**、**かたまり**になっているものに使います。

Kudaku means to hit something so that it breaks into pieces and it's original shape is no longer recognizable (ex.8, 9, 10). While *tsubusu* means to break or change the shape of something, *kudaku* suggests that the object is broken into many pieces or fragments, and is a stronger expression than *waru* (to break). Therefore, it is used with relatively hard or solidified objects, such as ice, rock, or sugar cubes.

②望み・野望などを、かなうまえにこわすことです（例11)。

To destroy one's hopes or ambitions before they are fulfilled (ex.11).

8) 彼は失敗作の茶わんを、たたきつけてこなごなに砕いた。
Karewa shippaisakuno chawan-o, tatakitsukete konagonani kudaita.
He threw down the tea bowl that he failed to make properly and smashed it to smithereens.

9) 南極観測船は、厚い氷を砕きながら進んで行く。
Nankyoku-kansokusenwa, atsui koorio kudakinagara susundeiku.
The Antarctic research ship moves through the sea by breaking the thick ice before it.

10) ダイナマイトは、大きな岩を一瞬のうちに砕いた。
Dainamaitowa, ookina iwao isshunno uchini kudaita.
The dynamite blasted the huge boulder to bits in a flash.

11) 彼の野望は、民衆の力によって砕かれた。
Kareno yaboowa, minshuuno chikarani yotte kudakareta.
His ambitions were dashed by the power of the people.

つまらない／くだらない

■ *tsumaranai*　　■ *kudaranai*

つまらない

■ *tsumaranai*
■ trifling ; boring ♥

①「**おもしろくない・退屈だ・楽しくない**」という満たされない気持ちを表します（例1, 2, 3)。

Tsumaranai expresses feelings of dissatisfaction because something is uninteresting, boring, or not enjoyable (ex.1, 2, 3).

②**重要ではないささいなことや、値打ちがない**ことを表します。無駄になる・もったいない・ばからしいの意味も含みます（例4, 5, 6)。「つまらない物」は、人に贈り物をするときなどに、けんそんして言う決まった使い方です。話しことばで「つまんない」とも言います。

It also means that something is unimportant or of no value. It may also imply that something is a waste (of time, energy, etc.) or is meaningless (ex.4, 5, 6). *Tsumaranai mono* (an unimportant thing) is a humble expression used when one offers something such as a gift. *Tsumaranai* is often pronounced as *tsumannai* in spoken language.

---

1) A：映画おもしろかった。
　B：ううん。つまらなくてあくびが出たよ。

　A： *Eiga omoshirokatta?* Was the movie interesting?
　B： *Uun. Tsumaranakute akubiga detayo.*
　　No, it was so boring it made me yawn.

2) ぼくだけ留守番だなんてつまんない。

Bokudake rusubandanante tsumannai.
This is no fun at all; (everybody is going and) I have to stay home.

3) あの女の子は、ひとりでつまらなそうに遊んでいる。

Ano onnanokowa, hitoride tsumaranasooni asondeiru.
That girl looks so bored playing all by herself.

4) 趣味を持たないなんて、つまらない人だ。

Shumio motanainante, tsumaranai hitoda.

(You) mean he doesn't have any hobbies? What a boring person!

5) つまらないことにこだわっていないで、済んだことはさっさと忘れなさい。
Tsumaranai kotoni kodawatteinaide, sunda kotowa sassato wasurenasai.
Don't dwell on such trivial matters; (you) should quickly forget about things that are over and done with.

6) これ、つまらない物ですが、どうぞ皆様でお召し上がりください。
Kore, tsumaranai monodesuga, doozo minasamade omeshiagari kudasai.
This is just something (I) picked up. Everybody eat some, please.

くだらない

■ *kudaranai*
■ silly ; trivial

価値がない・低俗だ・内容の程度が低い・ばかばかしいということです（例7,8,9)。「つまらない」は対象となるものに対する関心の低さを表し、「くだらない」は内容の程度が低いことに対する軽蔑の気持ちを表します。
Kudaranai means that something or someone is worthless, unsophisticated, of a low-level, or is a waste of time or energy (ex.7, 8, 9).
Tsumaranai suggests that the speaker does not have much interest in something, while *kudaranai* suggests the quality of the thing itself is low; and implies the speaker's feelings of contempt.

7) あんなに下品でくだらない番組を、おもしろがって見る人もいるんだね。
Annani gehinde kudaranai bangumio, omoshirogatte miru hitomo irundane.
(I) am amazed that there are people who enjoy watching such vulgar, idiotic programs.

8) くだらないマンガばかり読んでいないで、少しは勉強しなさい。
Kudaranai mangabakari yondeinaide, sukoshiwa benkyooshinasai.
Don't just read those stupid comic books ; at least spend a little time studying!

9) うそつきで思いやりがない、そんなくだらない男はつき合う価値がない。
Usotsukide omoiyariga nai, sonna kudaranai otokowa tsukiau kachiga nai.
He is not worth hanging around with; he is a liar and has no concern for others.

つもり／~ようとおもう

■*tsumori*　■*~you to omou*

つもり

■*tsumori*
■intention 

①**自分の気持ちや考えを述べる**とき使います。自分なりの判断や確信を表します（例1, 2, 3）。これから~するという意志や決意を述べるときに「動詞の辞書形＋つもり」の形で使います（例4, 5, 6）。「~ようと思う」よりも**強い意志**を表し、**具体的な計画や予定がはっきりとしている**感じです。

Tsumori is used when stating one's feelings and thoughts. It expresses personal judgment or conviction (ex.1, 2, 3).
When used in the form 'V-dict. form + *tsumori*', it states one's resolve or intention to do something in the future (ex.4, 5, 6). It expresses intention much more clearly than 'V-*you to omou*', and suggests that concrete plans or arrangements have been made.

②実際はそうではないのに、そうであるかのような気持ちだというとき使います（例7, 8）。

Tsumori is also used to indicate one's belief in something which is contrary to the truth (ex.7, 8).

---

1) あなたは正しいつもりかもしれないけれど、ほかの人はそうは思わないでしょう。

Anatawa tadashii tsumorikamo shirenaikeredo, hokano hitowa soowa omowanaideshoo.
You may think you're correct, but the others probably don't think so.

2) 冗談のつもりで言ったことが、彼を傷つけてしまった。

Joodanno tsumoride itta kotoga, kareo kizutsukete-shimatta.
What (I) said to him as a joke ended up hurting him.

3) こんな忙しい時にのんびりお茶を飲んでいるなんて、いったいどういうつもりですか。

Konna isogashii tokini nonbiri ochao nondeirunante, ittai dooyuu tsumoridesuka?
What do (you) think you're doing having a leisurely cup of tea at such

a busy time as this?

4) 今度(こんど)の日曜日(にちようび)は、屋根(やね)のペンキ塗(ぬ)りをするつもりです。
Kondono nichiyoobiwa, yaneno penkinurio suru tsumoridesu.
Next Sunday (I) intend to paint the roof.

5) きょうはかぜをひいて学校(がっこう)を休(やす)みましたが、あすは休(やす)まないつもりです。
Kyoowa kazeo hiite gakkoo-o yasumimashitaga, asuwa yasumanai tsumori-desu.
(I) caught a cold and stayed home from school today, but I definitely intend not to be absent tomorrow.

6) どんなに彼女(かのじょ)に頼(たの)まれても、いっしょに買(か)い物(もの)に行(い)くつもりはありません。
Donnani kanojoni tanomaretemo, isshoni kaimononi iku tsumoriwa arimasen.
No matter how much she begs me, (I) have no intention of going shopping with her.

7) 設計図(せっけいず)を書(か)いただけで、もう彼(かれ)は家(いえ)を建(た)てたつもりでいる。
Sekkeizuo kaitadakede, moo karewa ieo tateta tsumorideiru.
Just by drawing the blueprints, he thinks he's already built the house.

8) 王様(おうさま)は裸(はだか)なのに、服(ふく)を着(き)ているつもりで人々(ひとびと)の前(まえ)に出(で)て行(い)きました。
Oosamawa hadakananoni, fukuo kiteiru tsumoride hitobitono maeni deteiki-mashita.
Though the king was naked, he went out in public thinking he was wearing clothes.

〜ようとおもう［〜思(おも)う］

■ 〜*you to omou*
■ to think (one) will〜

自分(じぶん)が**これから〜する**という**考**(かんが)**え**や**意志**(いし)を**述**(の)**べる**とき使(つか)います（例(れい)9, 10, 11, 12, 13)。まだそれほどはっきり決(き)まっていないときや、ものごとを**ひかえめに言**(い)**うとき**にも使(つか)います。

This expression is used when stating one's will or intention to do something (ex.9, 10, 11, 12, 13). It is also used when one's plans are not yet firmly decided, or when one is speaking with reserve or restraint.

---

9) 今度(こんど)の休(やす)みには、京都(きょうと)へ旅行(りょこう)に行(い)こうと思(おも)っています。
Kondono yasuminiwa, Kyootoe ryokooni ikooto omotteimasu.
On my next holiday (I'm) planning to take a trip to Kyoto.

10) 健康のために、水泳を始めようと思います。
Kenkoono tameni, suieio hajimeyooto omoimasu.
(I'm) thinking of taking up swimming for my health.

11) テレビを見るのは好きだけれど、一日中見ていようとは思いません。
Terebio mirunowa sukidakeredo, ichinichijuu miteiyootowa omoimasen.
(I) like to watch TV, but I wouldn't think of watching it all day.

12) 時間なので、そろそろ帰ろうと思います。
Jikannanode, sorosoro kaerooto omoimasu.
It's time, so (I) think I'll be going along home.

13) 次の会議は３日後に開こうと思います。
Tsugino kaigiwa mikkagoni hirakooto omoimasu.
(I'm) thinking of holding the meeting three days from now.

つよい／じょうぶ

■*tsuyoi* ■*joubu*

つよい［強い］ ■*tsuyoi* ■strong 

①ほかのものより、**力がある**ようすを表します（例1, 2）。

Tsuyoi indicates that something or someone has greater strength or power than others (ex.1, 2).

②体や心、あるいはものがしっかりしていて、**耐える力がある・こわれにくい**というようすを表します（例3, 4, 5）。

Tsuyoi also indicates that one's body or mind, or an object is sound or firm (in character or construction) and long-lasting, i.e., not easily broken or destroyed (ex.3, 4, 5).

③勢いや程度などが、**激しい・きびしい**というようすを表します（例6, 7）。

It also expresses a violent or severe force or degree (ex.6, 7).

1) 私たちの学校は野球が強い。
Watashitachino gakkoowa yakyuuga tsuyoi.

Our school is strong in baseball.

2) 兄(あに)は握力(あくりょく)が強(つよ)い。
Aniwa akuryokuga tsuyoi.
My (elder) brother has a strong grip.

3) 彼(かれ)は責任感(せきにんかん)が強(つよ)いので、みんなに信頼(しんらい)されている。
Karewa sekininkanga tsuyoinode, minnani shinraisareteiru.
He has a strong sense of responsibility, so we have confidence in him.

4) 彼女(かのじょ)は意志(いし)が強(つよ)くて、一度(いちど)決(き)めたことはやり通(とお)す。
Kanojowa ishiga tsuyokute, ichido kimeta kotowa yaritoosu.
She's so strong-willed that once she's made up her mind to do something she sees it through to the end.

5) 熱(ねつ)に強(つよ)いガラスが開発(かいはつ)されている。
Netsuni tsuyoi garasuga kaihatsusareteiru.
A kind of glass is being developed that is resistant to heat.

6) ウオッカは強(つよ)いお酒(さけ)です。
Uokkawa tsuyoi osakedesu.
Vodka is a strong liquor.

7) きょうは風(かぜ)が強(つよ)い。
Kyoowa kazega tsuyoi.
The wind is strong today. (It's windy today.)

じょうぶ［丈夫(じょうぶ)］

■*joubu*
■healthy ; strong 

からだが**健康(けんこう)だ**というようすを表(あらわ)します。また、もののつくりがしっかりしていて、**こわれにくい**ようすも表(あらわ)します（例(れい)8, 9, 10, 11）。

Joubu indicates that one is in good health. Also, when speaking of an object, it indicates that the object is well-made so as to be not easily broken or destroyed (ex.8, 9, 10, 11).

---

8) 祖父(そふ)はとても丈夫(じょうぶ)で、大(おお)きい病気(びょうき)をしたことがありません。
Sofuwa totemo joobude, ookii byookio shita kotoga arimasen.
My grandfather is very healthy and has never had a serious illness.

9) 私(わたし)は、水泳(すいえい)を始(はじ)めてからとても丈夫(じょうぶ)になりました。

Watashiwa, suieio hajimetekara totemo joobuni narimashita.
I've gotten very fit since I started swimming.

10) 彼は子供のころ、山道を２キロも歩いて学校に通ったので、足が丈夫だ。
Karewa kodomono koro, yamamichio nikiromo aruite gakkooni kayottanode, ashiga joobuda.
He walked over two kilometers to school over mountain roads as a child, so his legs are sturdy.

11) 綱引きには、太くて丈夫なロープを使う。
Tsunahikiniwa, futokute joobuna roopuo tsukau.
(You) have to use a thick, strong rope for tug-of-war.

～てき／～ふう
■～ *teki*　■～ *fuu*

～てき［的］ ■～ *teki* ■～ like

「名詞＋的」という形で使います。

～*teki* is attached to nouns, in the form 'noun＋*teki*'.

①「～である条件をかなり満たしている・**まさしくそうだ**」というようすを表します（例1, 2, 3)。

The expression is used to indicate that the object or situation described fulfills the definition of, or is very similar to, the noun (ex.1, 2, 3).

②「**～に関する・～に基づいた・～としての**」というようすを表します（例4, 5, 6)。

It is also used to express that something is related to, based on, or equivalent to the noun (ex.4, 5, 6).

---

1) この映画は、義理と人情を描いた極めて日本的な内容だ。
Kono eigawa, girito ninjoo-o egaita kiwamete Nihontekina naiyooda.
This movie has a very Japanese theme depicting humanity and duty.

2) 彼は日焼けして、健康的に見える。

Karewa hiyakeshite, kenkootekini mieru.
He looks so healthy with his suntan.

3) 日本(にほん)の着物(きもの)には、古典的(こてんてき)な柄(がら)が多(おお)い。
Nihonno kimononiwa, kotentekina garaga ooi.
Classical designs are the most common in the Japanese *kimono.*

4) 私(わたし)は基本的(きほんてき)には、彼(かれ)の意見(いけん)に賛成(さんせい)です。
Watashiwa kihontekiniwa, kareno ikenni sanseidesu.
Basically, I am in agreement with his views.

5) フラメンコは情熱的(じょうねつてき)な踊(おど)りです。
Furamenkowa joonetsutekina odoridesu.
Flamenco is a passionate style of dancing.

6) 私(わたし)は、あなたの個人的(こじんてき)な問題(もんだい)に口(くち)を出(だ)すつもりはありません。
Watashiwa, anatano kojintekina mondaini kuchio dasu tsumoriwa arimasen.
I have no intention of intruding into your personal problems.

～ふう ［風(ふう)］ ■*fuu* ■appearance ; style

「名詞(めいし)＋ふう」の形(かたち)で、「～のような・～のように見(み)える」という、人(ひと)やことがらのようす・型(かた)・やりかた・状態(じょうたい)に使(つか)います（例(れい)7, 8, 9, 10）。「学者的(がくしゃてき)な考(かんが)え」は、学者(がくしゃ)としての立場(たちば)からの当然(とうぜん)の考(かんが)えという意味(いみ)ですが、「学者風(がくしゃふう)の人(ひと)」は、一見学者(いっけんがくしゃ)のように見(み)えるけれど、そうではないかもしれません。

In expressions in which *fuu* is attached to a noun, it describes the condition, appearance, or methods of a person or object as being similar to, or in the style of the noun (ex.7, 8, 9, 10). *Gakusha-teki na kangae* (a scholarly opinion) means 'an opinion which is in keeping with the position of a scholar', while *gakusha-fuu no hito* (a person who looks like a scholar) refers to a person who appears at a glance to be a scholar, but may not be.

---

7) 交差点(こうさてん)で、サラリーマン風(ふう)の男(おとこ)に道(みち)をきかれた。
Koosatende, sarariiman-fuuno otokoni michio kikareta.
(I) was asked for directions at the intersection by a man who appeared to be a salaried office worker.

8) あの人(ひと)、一見学生風(いっけんがくせいふう)だけれど、実(じつ)は医者(いしゃ)なんですよ。
Anohito, ikken gakusei-fuudakeredo, jitsuwa ishanandesuyo.

At first glance he looks like a student, but he's really a doctor.

9) 北欧風(ほくおうふう)の白木(しらき)の食器棚(しょっきだな)がほしい。
Hokuoofuuno shirakino shokkidanaga hoshii.
(I) want a Scandinavian-style unfinished china cupboard.

10) きれいな字(じ)ですね。私(わたし)はとてもこんな風(ふう)には書(か)けません。
Kireina jidesune. Watashiwa totemo konna fuuniwa kakemasen.
What lovely writing! I can't write like this at all.

できるだけ／なるべく

■ *dekirudake* ■ *narubeku*

できるだけ

■ *dekirudake*
■ to the extent possible

自分(じぶん)の持(も)っている力(ちから)を出(だ)し切(き)って、あるいは**努力(どりょく)をして可能(かのう)な限(かぎ)り**何(なに)かをする、というとき使(つか)います。「できるかぎり」は、もう少(すこ)し「すべて」と強調(きょうちょう)した言(い)い方(かた)です（例(れい)1, 2, 3, 4)。

This expression is used when one exerts strength or effort to do something to the fullest extent possible.
Dekiru kagiri is used to stress the idea 'completely' (ex.1, 2, 3, 4).

---

1) きょうお願(ねが)いした仕事(しごと)は、できるだけ急(いそ)いでやってください。
Kyoo onegaishita shigotowa, dekirudake isoide yattekudasai.
Please do all you can to rush that job I asked you to do today.

2) ふだんは、仕事(しごと)で忙(いそが)しいので、休(やす)みの日(ひ)はできるだけ家族(かぞく)と過(す)ごしたい。
Fudanwa, shigotode isogashiinode, yasumino hiwa dekirudake kazokuto sugoshitai.
Ordinarily (I'm) busy with work, so I want to spend my days off with my family as much as possible.

3) 雪(ゆき)が降(ふ)っているから、できるだけ暖(あたた)かい格好(かっこう)で出(で)かけた方(ほう)がいい。
Yukiga futteirukara, dekirudake atatakai kakkoode dekaketa hooga ii.
It's snowing so you'd better go out in as warm an outfit as you can.

4) 友達(ともだち)が困(こま)っているときには、できるだけのことをしてあげなさい。

Tomodachiga komatteiru tokiniwa, dekirudakeno koto-o shiteagenasai.
When your friends are in trouble, do all you can for them.

なるべく ■ *narubeku* ■ if possible 

「**もしできたら・もしそのことが可能なら**」という意味を表します(例5, 6, 7, 8)。「できるだけ」と同じような使い方をしますが、「できるだけ」が「自分の力を出し切る」というような緊迫感や努力を伴うのに対して、「なるべく」は「**もしできたら**」という程度で、そんなに強くはありません。たとえば、貸したお金を「できるだけ早く返してください」は、早く返すことを強く望んでいることになりますが、「なるべく早く返してください」は、もう少し時間にゆとりがある感じで、やさしい言い方になります。「どちらかといえば」という意味も含んでいます。

Narubeku is used to express the meanings 'if you can' or 'if that is possible' (ex.5, 6, 7, 8). It is used in the same way as *dekirudake*, but whereas *dekirudake* carries a sense of effort or pressure, i.e., 'to the extent of one's ability', *narubeku* is not as forceful, and merely implies 'if possible'. For example, if you ask for repayment of a loan saying *dekirudake hayaku kaeshite kudasai*, you are emphasizing the early return of the money. *Narubeku hayaku kaeshite kudasai*, however, includes a feeling that some leeway is being allowed, and is a softer expression. It may also include a sense of *dochira ka to ieba*, meaning 'if anything'.

---

5) 今晩見たい番組があるので、仕事が終わったらなるべく早く帰るつもりです。
Konban mitai bangumiga arunode, shigotoga owattara narubeku hayaku kaeru tsumoridesu.
There's a TV program (I) want to see today, so I intend to go home as early as possible after work.

6) 健康のために、ふだんからなるべくたくさん歩くようにしている。
Kenkoono tameni, fudankara narubeku takusan arukuyooni shiteiru.
(I) make it a point to walk as much as possible for my health.

7) 私は早口なので、なるべくゆっくり話すように気をつけています。
Watashiwa hayakuchinanode, narubeku yukkuri hanasuyooni kiotsuketeimasu.
(I) tend to speak fast, so I'm taking care to speak as slowly as possible.

8) なるべくなら、あしたはずっと家に居たいのですが……。

Narubekunara, ashitawa zutto ieni itainodesuga…
If at all possible, (I'd) like to stay home all day tomorrow.

~て(~くて)/~し

■ *~te (~kute)*　　■ *~shi*

~て(~くて)　■ *~te (~kute)* ■ ~and

関連のある**A**、**B** 2つ以上のことがらを**並べて言う表現**ですが、Aのことがらを述べて、すぐBのことを言うときや、**初めから、全体がわかっていて、順に言う**ときに使います(例1, 2, 3)。AがBの理由を表すこともあります(例4, 5, 6)。
This expression is used when one mentions two or more items (item A, item B) in the same sentence.
It may be that one just happens to mention item B after saying item A, or that A and B are part of an ordered list of things (ex.1, 2, 3). There may be times when A is the reason for B (ex.4, 5, 6).

1) A：彼はどんな人ですか。
B：頭がよくて、優しい人です。
A： *Karewa donna hitodesuka?*　What kind of person is he?
B： *Atamaga yokute, yasashii hitodesu.*　He's very smart and nice.

2) このカメラは、古くて重い。
Kono kamerawa, furukute omoi.
This camera is old and heavy.

3) 地下鉄は、安くて便利な乗り物です。
Chikatetsuwa, yasukute benrina norimonodesu.
The subway is an inexpensive and convenient mode of transportation.

4) 休みの日の新宿は、人が多くて疲れる。
Yasumino hino Shinjukuwa, hitoga ookute tsukareru.
Walking in Shinjuku on holidays is tiring because there are so many people.

5) うちの子は生まれたときの体重が少なくて、育てるのが大変でした。

Uchino kowa umareta tokino taijuuga sukunakute, sodaterunoga taihende-shita.
Our son was underweight when he was born, and (we) had a lot of difficulty raising him.

6) 工事の音がうるさくて眠れない。
Koojino otoga urusakute nemurenai.
The construction noise is so loud that (I) can't sleep.

〜し ■〜*shi* ■〜and

いくつか**理由をあげて言うときの表現**として使います（例7, 8, 9, 10, 11）。その言い方も、全部わかっていて言うのではなく、Aのことがらを頭で考えながら、**思いつくままに、つぎ**のBのことを述べるというようなとき使います。したがって、考えがまとまらず、途中でやめたような言い方（例10）のようになることもあります。しかし、基本的には、「だから……だ」というとらえ方がかくれているときの表現です。

This expression is used when one is listing several reasons for something (ex.7, 8, 9, 10, 11). It may also be used when the speaker doesn't have his thoughts perfectly in order, and is saying things as they occur to him. Therefore, when the speaker cannot think of anything further to add, his sentence may sound incomplete (ex.10). As a basic rule, however, this expression is used as an indirect way of saying 'because...'.

---

7) あの子はなんでも食べるし、スポーツもするから体がじょうぶだ。
Ano kowa nandemo taberushi, supootsumo surukara karadaga joobuda.
That child eats anything, and what's more he plays sports, so he is healthy.

8) 東京は人も車も多いし、物の値段も高い。（だから嫌いだ）
Tookyoowa hitomo kurumamo ooishi, monono nedanmo takai. (Dakara kiraida.)
(I don't like Tokyo, because) there are many people and cars, and on top of that, things are expensive.

9) A：どうして三島由紀夫の小説が好きなんですか。
B：そうですね、感性がすばらしいし、文章もうまいし、小説のねらいもおもしろいんです。

A : *Dooshite Mishima Yukiono shoosetsuga sukinandesuka?*
Why do (you) like Yukio Mishima's novels?

B : *Soodesune, kanseiga subarashiishi, bunshoomo umaishi, shoosetsuno neraimo omoshiroindesu.*
Well, they are wonderfully sensitive, well-written, and his themes are interesting.

10) A : 休暇(きゅうか)は、またヨーロッパですか。

B : ええ、美術館(びじゅつかん)や博物館(はくぶつかん)がおもしろいし、町(まち)の風景(ふうけい)がすてきだし……。

A : *Kyuukawa, mata Yooroppadesuka?*
Are (you) going to spend your vacation in Europe again?

B : *Ee, bijutsukan-ya hakubutsukanga omoshiroishi, machino fuukeiga sutekidashi...*
Yes, (because I think) the art galleries and museums are interesting, the scenery is beautiful...

11) くしゃみは出(で)るし、頭(あたま)は痛(いた)いし、熱(ねつ)もある。

Kushamiwa derushi, atamawa itaishi, netsumo aru.
(I) keep sneezing, I have a headache, and I have a fever, too.

いい男(おとこ)はいい人(ひと)か

近(ちか)くのスーパーに強盗(ごうとう)が入(はい)りました。目撃者(もくげきしゃ)が警官(けいかん)に「犯人(はんにん)は、30歳(さい)ぐらいのちょっといい男(おとこ)だった」と言(い)うのを聞(き)いて、ピーターはおかしいなと思(おも)いました。強盗(ごうとう)は悪(わる)い人(ひと)に決(き)まっているのに「いい男(おとこ)」だなんて…。「ピーター、いい男(おとこ)というのはね、ハンサムな男性(だんせい)のことですよ」とルームメイトの正夫(まさお)が教(おし)えてくれました。

いい男(おとこ)が悪(わる)い人(ひと)の場合(ばあい)もあるという日本語(にほんご)のおもしろさを、ピーターはまた1(ひと)つ覚(おぼ)えました。

Does *ii otoko* mean *ii hito*?

A burglar broke into a supermarket near Peter's house. Later, when he overheard a witness tell the police, "The burglar was about 30 years old and he was *chotto ii otoko*,[1]" Peter thought, "Something sounds funny." He wondered why the witness would say *ii otoko* when talking about a burglar, when burglars are usually thought of as bad. Masao, his roommate, kindly explained, "Peter, *ii otoko* refers to a man who is handsome or good-looking."

Peter has learned another interesting thing about the Japanese language. There are some cases where *ii otoko* can refer to a bad guy.

1 *a rather good-looking man*

でる／でかける

■ *deru* ■ *dekakeru*

でる［出る］ ■ *deru* ■ to go out ; to leave

今いる場所や空間から外に行くことです（例1, 2, 3, 4)。所属している団体や組織を抜けることも表し、「学校を出る」は「卒業する」という意味です（例5, 6)。「出る」には人の行動に関するものだけでも「テレビに出る・電話に出る」などいろいろな使い方がありますが、ここでは「入る」に対応する「～から出る・～を出る」についてとりあげます。

To go outside, i.e., leave one's present location or space (ex.1, 2, 3, 4), or to leave a group or organization. The expression *gakkou o deru* means 'to graduate from school' (ex.5, 6). There are many expressions with *deru*, even when counting only those concerning human behavior: e.g., *terebi ni deru* (to appear on TV) and *denwa ni deru* (to answer the phone); however, the examples listed below are limited to the expressions ~*kara deru* and ~*o deru*, which are the counterparts of the verb *hairu* (to enter).

1) 私は毎朝7時に家を出ます。
Watashiwa maiasa shichijini ieo demasu.
I leave home at seven every morning.

2) 駅の改札を出て右の方へ行くと、交番があります。
Ekino kaisatsuo dete migino hooe ikuto, koobanga arimasu.
Go out through the wickets of the train station,

turn right, and then (you'll) see a police box.

3) 山下さんは、1時間ぐらい前に外へ出て、まだ会社には戻ってきません。
Yamashitasan-wa, ichijikangurai maeni sotoe dete, mada kaishaniwa modotte kimasen.
Mr. Yamashita went out about an hour ago and hasn't come back to the office yet.

4) 父はお風呂から出ると、必ずビールを1杯飲む。
Chichiwa ofurokara deruto, kanarazu biiruo ippai nomu.
My father always drinks a glass of beer when he gets out of the bath.

5) 姉は家を出て、ひとり暮らしをしたがっている。
Anewa ieo dete, hitorigurashio shitagatteiru.
My older sister wants to leave home and live on her own.

6) 私は高校を出てからすぐ車の免許を取った。
Watashiwa kookoo-o detekara sugu kurumano menkyoo totta.
I obtained my driver's license soon after graduating from high school.

でかける［出かける］

■ *dekakeru*
■ to go out ; to leave 

家や職場など長い時間過ごすところ、また現在居場所としているところから、仕事や買い物・旅行など**ある目的のために外に行く**ことで、また**帰ってくる**という**前提**があります（例7, 8, 9, 10)。「出る」は「入る」と対応し、「出かける」は「帰る」と対応します。例11は訪問するという意味です。

To leave a place where one spends a lot of one's time every day (for example, a home or work place), for a certain purpose, such as to go to work, to go shopping, or to travel. It is assumed that the person will eventually return to that same place (ex.7, 8, 9, 10). While *deru* is the opposite of *hairu*, *kaeru* is that of *dekakeru*. In Example 11 it means to 'visit'.

---

7) 母は、今出かけていますが、夕方には戻ります。
Hahawa, ima dekakete imasuga, yuugataniwa modorimasu.
My mother is out now, but she will come back this evening.

8) 私は来週、船でヨーロッパへ出かける予定です。
Watashiwa raishuu, funede Yooroppae dekakeru yoteidesu.
I am planning to leave by ship for Europe next week.

9) 今(いま)出(で)かけるところなので、話(はなし)は後(あと)にしてください。
Ima dekakeru tokoronanode, hanashiwa atoni shite kudasai.
(I) am going out right now, so please talk to me later.

10) 彼女(かのじょ)は出(で)かけるのが大好(だいす)きで、昼間(ひるま)はほとんど家(いえ)にいない。
Kanojowa dekakerunoga daisukide, hirumawa hotondo ieni inai.
She loves going out, so she is almost never at home during the day.

11) 今度(こんど)ぜひ私(わたし)のうちにもお出(で)かけください。
Kondo zehi watashino uchinimo odekake kudasai.
Please come and visit us at the next opportunity.

ときどき/ときおり/たまに

■ *tokidoki* ■ *tokiori* ■ *tamani*

ときどき ■ *tokidoki* ■ sometimes

ものごとが、**「いつも」ではなく間(あいだ)をおいて起(お)こる**、あるいは間(あいだ)をおいてものごとをするとき使(つか)います。「ときおり・たまに」よりも間隔(かんかく)が短(みじか)く、回数(かいすう)が多(おお)いです(例(れい)1, 2, 3, 4)。

Tokidoki indicates that something occurs or is done at certain intervals. Each interval is shorter and recurs more frequently than those expressed by *tokiori* or *tamani* (ex.1, 2, 3, 4).

---

1) 私(わたし)は仕事(しごと)で、ときどき海外(かいがい)へ行(い)く。
Watashiwa shigotode, tokidoki kaigaie iku.
I sometimes go abroad on business.

2) あしたの天気(てんき)は、晴(は)れときどき曇(くも)りです。
Ashitano tenkiwa, hare tokidoki kumoridesu.
Tomorrow's weather will be sunny with occasional clouds.

3) 引(ひ)っ越(こ)しても、ときどき手紙(てがみ)をください。
Hikkoshitemo, tokidoki tegamio kudasai.

Even after (you) move, please write to (me) sometimes.

4) 私は健康のために、ときどきスイミングプールに行きます。
Watashiwa kenkoono tameni, tokidoki suimingupuuruni ikimasu.
I sometimes go to the swimming pool for the sake of my health.

ときおり

■ *tokiori*
■ on occasion

「ときどき」よりも間隔があるとき使います。忘れたころに・思いがけないころに、という感じを含み、**文学的**な言い方です。現在では多くの場合「ときおり」の代わりに「ときどき」が使われます（例5, 6, 7）。

Tokiori expresses a greater interval of time separating events than does *tokidoki*. It includes a sense that one has forgotten a matter or that something unexpected occurs. *Tokiori* is a literary form of expression. Nowadays, in most instances *tokidoki* is used in place of *tokiori* (ex.5, 6, 7).

---

5) 遠くでときおり雷が鳴っている。
Tookude tokiori kaminariga natteiru.
There's the occasional sound of thunder in the distance.

6) このあたりでは、ときおりうぐいすの鳴き声が聞こえます。
Kono ataridewa, tokiori uguisuno nakigoega kikoemasu.
We occasionally hear the call of the bush warbler around here.

7) 台風が近づいたらしく、ときおり強い風が吹く。
Taifuuga chikazuitarashiku, tokiori tsuyoi kazega fuku.
There are occasional strong winds, as if a typhoon is approaching.

たまに

■ *tamani*
■ once in a while ; at times

かなりの間隔をおいて、ものごとが起こったり起こしたりするとき使います（例8, 9, 10, 11）。久し振り・めずらしいといった意味を含むこともあります。

Tamani indicates that something happens or is done at quite long intervals (ex.8, 9, 10, 11). It may imply a sense of *hisashiburi* (after a long time) or *mezurashii* (rarely).

---

8) 私は、たまにディスコに行く。
Watashiwa, tamani disukoni iku.
I go to a disco every now and then.

9) 彼は、たまに連絡をしてくる。
Karewa, tamani renrakuo shitekuru.
He gets in touch with me every once in a while.

10) 私はいつも８時ごろ家に帰りますが、たまにもっと遅くなることもあります。
Watashiwa itsumo hachijigoro ieni kaerimasuga, tamani motto osokunaru kotomo arimasu.
I usually get home around 8:00, but there are times when I arrive later.

11) 忙しいでしょうが、たまには遊びに来てください。
Isogashii-deshooga, tamaniwa asobini kite kudasai.
(I) know (you're) busy, but please come to visit us once in a while.

とく／とかす

■ *toku* ■ *tokasu*

とく［溶く］ ■ *toku* ■ to dissolve

粉やかたまっているものなどを、水や油などの液体で**液状や糊状にうすめたりやわらかくする**とき使います（例1, 2, 3）。

This word describes the process whereby a powder or solid substance is softened, or is dissolved in water or oil and made into a liquid or paste (ex.1, 2, 3).

---

1) 粉ミルクをお湯で溶いて、子犬に飲ませた。
Kona-mirukuo oyude toite, koinuni nomaseta.
(I) dissolved the powdered milk in warm water and fed it to the puppy.

2) 小麦粉を卵と牛乳で溶いて、パンケーキを焼いた。
Komugikoo tamagoto gyuunyuude toite, pankeekio yaita.
(I) mixed flour and eggs in milk and made some pancakes.

3) 油絵の具がかたまってしまっても、オイルで溶けば使える。
Aburaenoguga katamatte-shimattemo, oirude tokeba tsukaeru.
Even if the oil paint hardens, (you) can still use it if you thin it with some oil.

とかす［溶かす・解かす］ ■*tokasu* ■to melt

ものを加熱したりして、液状にするとき使います（例4, 5, 6）。例7、8は液体に混ぜ合わせて、もとの形がなくなるようにするという意味です。

Tokasu describes the process by which something is heated until it melts and changes to liquid form (ex.4, 5, 6). Examples 7 and 8 are usages of the term whereby something is mixed with another liquid substance so that it loses its original form.

漢字は、氷や雪には「解かす」を使います。

The *kanji* character describing ice or snow melting is 解かす.

4) この工場では、回収した空きびんを溶かして再生している。
Kono koojoodewa, kaishuushita akibin-o tokashite saiseishiteiru.
They are recycling the returned bottles by melting them down at this factory.

5) ケーキの種に、溶かしたバターを加えた。
Keekino taneni, tokashita bataao kuwaeta.
(I) mixed in melted butter with the basic cake ingredients.

6) 南極では氷を溶かして水をつくるそうです。
Nankyokudewa koorio tokashite mizuo tsukurusoodesu.
(They) say that people in Antarctica make water by melting ice.

7) この粉薬は水に溶かしてから子供に飲ませてください。
Kono konagusuriwa mizuni tokashitekara kodomoni nomasete kudasai.
Give this powdered medicine to (your) child after dissolving it in water.

8) 油のよごれはベンジンで溶かしておとします。
Aburano yogorewa benjinde tokashite otoshimasu.
Oily stains can be (broken down and) removed with benzine.

とくべつ／とくに

■ *tokubetsu* ■ *tokuni*

とくべつ［特別］ ■ *tokubetsu* ■ special

いつもとは違う・普通とはちがう、というような**例外を表す**とき使います（例1, 2, 3, 4, 5, 6, 7)。

Tokubetsu describes something as an exception to the norm or different from what is considered usual (ex.1, 2, 3, 4, 5, 6, 7).

1) この話はないしょだけれど、あなたにだけ特別に教えてあげる。
Kono hanashiwa naishodakeredo, anatanidake tokubetsuni oshieteageru.
This is a secret, but I'll make an exception and tell only you.

2) これは病人用の特別な食事です。
Korewa byoonin-yoono tokubetsuna shokujidesu.
This is a special meal for sick people.

3) 若さを保つために何か特別なことをしていますか。
Wakasao tamotsu tameni nanika tokubetsuna kotoo shiteimasuka?
Are (you) doing anything in particular to maintain your youth?

4) あの仏像は非公開だが、研究のために特別に見せてもらった。
Ano butsuzoowa hikookaidaga, kenkyuuno tameni tokubetsuni misetemoratta.
That statue of Buddha is ordinally not displayed to the public, but (we) were allowed to see it for research purposes.

5) そのデザイナーは、出身校のために特別に制服をデザインした。
Sono dezainaawa, shusshinkoono tameni tokubetsuni seifukuo dezainshita.
That fashion designer created a new school uniform specially for his alma mater.

6) 特別な理由がないかぎり、給料の前払いは認められない。
Tokubetsuna riyuuga naikagiri, kyuuryoono maebaraiwa mitomerarenai.
Except for special cases, pay advances are not granted.

7) キャンプではみんなの協力がたいせつだ。子供だからといって、特別扱いする必要はない。

Kyanpudewa minnano kyooryokuga taisetsuda. Kodomodakara-toitte, tokubetsu-atsukaisuru hitsuyoowa nai.
When camping, everyone's cooperation is important. There is no need to give children special treatment.

とくに［特に］ ■ *tokuni* ■ especially 

いくつかのものやことがらの中で、それだけを**取り立てたり強調したりする**ときや、ほかのものと比べると**程度がとびぬけているようす**を表すとき使います（例8, 9, 10, 11, 12）。

Tokuni is used to specify or place emphasis on a single part of a group, or to describe something as far better than others it is being compared to (ex.8, 9, 10, 11, 12).

---

8) 食事のあとにかならず歯をみがきなさい。特に奥歯は念入りに。
Shokujino atoni kanarazu hao migakinasai. Tokuni okubawa nen-irini!
After eating be sure to brush (your) teeth. Be especially careful to get the molars.

9) 京都の冬は寒いといわれているが、今年は特に寒い。
Kyootono fuyuwa samuito iwareteiruga, kotoshiwa tokuni samui.
Winter in Kyoto is always (said to be) cold, but this year is especially cold.

10) 私は本が好きですが、特に推理小説が好きです。
Watashiwa honga sukidesuga, tokuni suirishoosetsuga sukidesu.
I like (all kinds of) books, but I especially like mystery stories.

11) 私は牛乳が特に好きではないけれど、健康のために毎日飲んでいます。
Watashiwa gyuunyuuga tokuni sukidewa-naikeredo, kenkoono tameni mainichi nondeimasu.
It's not that I like milk so much; I drink it every day because it's good for my health.

12) 非常ベルが鳴ったので調べてみたが、特に異常はみつからなかった。
Hijooberuga nattanode shirabetemitaga, tokuni ijoowa mitsukaranakatta.
The emergency bell rang so (I) went to investigate, but I couldn't find anything especially out of the ordinary.

どちら／どれ／なに

■ *dochira* ■ *dore* ■ *nani*

どちら ■ *dochira* ■ which (of two) 

①**2(ふた)つのうちの1(ひと)つを選(えら)ぶとき**、あるいは**選(えら)ばせるとき**に使(つか)うことばです(例(れい)1, 2, 3, 4)。「どっち」は、くだけた使(つか)い方(かた)です。

Dochira is used when choosing, or having someone choose, one of two things (ex.1, 2, 3, 4). *Dotchi* is a shortened colloquial form.

②**たくさんあるうちの1(ひと)つ**という意味(いみ)で使(つか)います。「どちら」は「どれ」「どこ」のていねいな言(い)い方(かた)です。また、相手(あいて)の名前(なまえ)などをたずねるときの、「どちら様(さま)」は「だれ・どなた」のていねいな言(い)い方(かた)です（例(れい)5, 6, 7, 8)。

It also is a polite way of asking *dore* (which) or *doko* (where) when the selection is from among many items. *Dochira sama*, which is a politer expression than *dare* or *donata*, is used when asking someone for their name (ex.5, 6, 7, 8).

1) うどんとそばと、どちらが好(す)きですか。

*Udonto soba*to, dochiraga sukidesuka?* * p.500
Which would (you) prefer, *udon* or *soba*?

2) A：鉄(てつ)1キログラムと綿(わた)1キログラムと、どちらが重(おも)いですか。
B：どちらも同(おな)じです。

A： *Tetsu ichikiroguramuto wata ichikiroguramuto, dochiraga omoidesuka?*
Which is heavier, a kilogram of iron or a kilogram of cotton?
B： *Dochiramo onajidesu.* They're both the same.

3) お茶(ちゃ)かお花(はな)が習(なら)いたいんだけど、どっちがいいか迷(まよ)っています。

Ochaka ohanaga naraitaindakedo, dotchiga iika mayotteimasu.
(I) want to study either tea ceremony or flower arrangement. I can't make up my mind which would be better.

4) 博多(はかた)へ行(い)くのに、飛行機(ひこうき)と新幹線(しんかんせん)とどっちが速(はや)いかなあ。

Hakatae ikunoni, hikookito Shinkansento dotchiga hayaikanaa?
To go to Hakata, which would be faster, a plane or the *Shinkansen*?

5) A：ご出身(しゅっしん)はどちらですか。

B：北海道(ほっかいどう)です。

A： *Goshusshinwa dochiradesuka?* Where are (you) from?
B： *Hokkaidoodesu.* Hokkaido.

6) A：これから、どちらへいらっしゃいますか。

B：まっすぐうちへ帰(かえ)ります。

A： *Korekara, dochirae irasshaimasuka?* Where are (you) going now?
B： *Massugu uchie kaerimasu.* (I'm) going straight home.

7) A：どちらが岡田(おかだ)さんですか。

B：はい。私(わたし)です。

A： *Dochiraga Okadasan desuka?* Which one of you is Mr. Okada?
B： *Hai. Watashidesu.* That's me.

8) 失礼(しつれい)ですが、どちら様(さま)でしょうか。

Shitsureidesuga, dochirasama-deshooka?
Excuse me, who might you be? (May I have your name, please?)

どれ

■ *dore*
■ which (of three or more) 

3つ(みっつ)**以上**(いじょう)あるもの**の中**(なか)**から**、**1つ**(ひとつ)を選(えら)ぶときたずねることばです（例(れい)9, 10, 11）。
This is a word used when asking 'which' when choosing from among three or more choices (ex.9, 10, 11).

---

9) あなたの荷物(にもつ)はどれですか。

Anatano nimotsuwa doredesuka? Which bags are yours?

10) ここにある本(ほん)のなかで、どれが一番(いちばん)おもしろいですか。

Kokoni aru honno nakade, dorega ichiban omoshiroidesuka?
Which is the most interesting of the books that are here?

11) 飲(の)み物(もの)は、コーヒーと紅茶(こうちゃ)と日本茶(にほんちゃ)がありますけれど、どれにしますか。

Nomimonowa, koohiito koochato nihonchaga arimasukeredo, doreni shimasuka?
For drinks, we have coffee, tea or green tea. Which will you have?

なに ［何］ ■ *nani* ■ what 

わからないものやことがらをさすときや、**たずねる**ときに使うことばです（例12, 13, 14, 15, 16）。「どちら」や「どれ」のように特定のものの中から1つを選ぶのではありません。また、「なに」は後ろに「ですか・だ・でも」などがつくと「なん」になります。「何本・何人」「何色・何語」などのように数や種類をたずねるときにも使います。

Nani is used when asking about or referring to some thing or event that is not known (ex.12, 13, 14, 15, 16). It is not used like *dochira* and *dore* to select one from among many specified objects. When followed by ～*desu ka*, ～*da*, or ～*demo*, *nani* becomes *nan*.
It is also used to ask about quantity or type in such expressions as *nan-bon*, *nan-nin*, *nani-iro*, and *nani-go*.

---

12) A：これは何ですか。
B：これは珍しい貝の化石なんですよ。

A： *Korewa nandesuka?* What is this?
B： *Korewa mezurashii kaino kasekinandesuyo.* This is the fossil of a very rare shellfish.

13) A：今晩、何が食べたい。
B：何でもいいよ。
A： *Konban, naniga tabetai?* What do you want to eat tonight?
B： *Nandemo iiyo.* Anything's OK with me.

14) すごい人だかりですね。何があったのでしょうか。
Sugoi hitodakari-desune. Naniga attanodeshooka?
What a crowd! What could have happened?

15) お金さえあれば何でも買えるのに。
Okanesae areba nandemo kaerunoni.
(I) could buy anything if only I had money!

16) あなたは子供の頃、大きくなったら何になりたいと思っていましたか。
Anatawa kodomono koro, ookiku nattara nanni naritaito omotte-imashitaka?
When you were a child, what did you want to be when you grew up?

とても／たいへん／ひじょうに

■ *totemo*　　■ *taihen*　　■ *hijou ni*

とても

■ *totemo*
■ completely ; very

①ことがらの**程度の強調**を表すときに使います。話し手の判断による表現で、**話しことば**に多く使われます（例1, 2, 3)。また、「とっても」は程度をさらに強調するときによく使います（例4, 5)。

Totemo is used when emphasizing the degree of something. It expresses the speaker's judgment, and is used mainly in spoken language (ex.1, 2, 3). *Tottemo* is often used when stressing an even greater degree (ex.4, 5).

②「〜ない」・「無理」などといっしょに使い、**どんなに努力しても**、気持ちや能力の点で限界があって**できない**という話し手の気持ちを表します（例6, 7, 8, 9)。

When used with negative expressions such as ～*nai* or *muri*, it expresses that the speaker feels that, no matter how much he may try, it is impossible to do something because it is beyond his emotional or physical capabilities (ex.6, 7, 8, 9).

---

1) きのうのパーティーはとても楽しかった。

Kinoono paatiiwa totemo tanoshikatta.
The party yesterday was a lot of fun.

2) A：元気がないね。どうかしたの。

B：うん。ゆうべとても変な夢を見たんだ。

A： *Genkiga naine. Dookashitano?*
(You) look kind of down. Is something wrong?
B： *Un. Yuube totemo henna yumeo mitanda.*
Uh, huh. Last night I had a really strange dream.

3) 運転をしていたら、突然人が道に飛び出してきたので、とてもびっくりした。

Unten-o shiteitara, totsuzen-hitoga michini tobidashite-kitanode, totemo bikkurishita.
(I) was really startled because when I was driving, someone suddenly ran out into the street.

4) この指輪、とっても高かったんだよ。
Kono yubiwa, tottemo takakattandayo.
This ring was very expensive!

5) A：このケーキ、私が作ったの。どう、おいしい。
B：うん、とってもおいしいよ。

A： *Kono keeki, watashiga tsukuttano. Doo, oishii?*
I made this cake. How is it? Good?
B： *Un, tottemo oishiiyo.*
Umm, really delicious!

6) この計算問題はむずかしすぎて、私にはとても解けない。
Kono keisanmondaiwa muzukashisugite, watashiniwa totemo tokenai.
This calculation is too hard; I can't possibly solve it.

7) 今の私の収 入では、うちを買うのはとても無理だ。
Imano watashino shuunyuudewa, uchio kaunowa totemo murida.
With my current income, buying a house is absolutely impossible.

8) あんなにまじめな人がどろぼうをするなんて、とても信じられない。
Annani majimena hitoga doroboo-o surunante, totemo shinjirarenai.
That such an upstanding person as he should commit a burglary is totally unbelievable.

9) あの人は若々しくて、とても80歳には見えない。
Ano hitowa wakawakashikute, totemo hachijussainiwa mienai.
She looks so young; she doesn't at all look 80.

たいへん［大変］

■ *taihen*
■ terribly ; very ; terrible 

①ことがらの程度の強 調を表すときに使います。**丁寧で改まった言い方**です。また、ただごとではない、**重 大だ**という意味も含みます（例10, 11, 12, 13)。

Taihen, like *totemo*, is also used when emphasizing the degree of something. However, it is a more polite and formal expression. It also includes the meanings of 'out of the ordinary' or 'very serious' (ex.10, 11, 12, 13).

②何かよくないことや重 大なことなどが起こって、**驚いたり、困ったり**している**ようす**や、何かをするのに**努力や苦労が必要**であるようすを表します（例14, 15, 16, 17, 18)。

Taihen also expresses dismay or perplexity at something serious or bad which happens, or denotes that a great deal of effort or suffering is necessary to do something (ex.14, 15, 16, 17, 18).

---

10) お目にかかれて大変光栄です。
Omeni kakarete taihen kooeidesu.
It is a great privilege to make your acquaintance.

11) 先日はお越しくださったのに、留守にしておりまして、大変失礼しました。
Senjitsuwa okoshi-kudasattanoni, rusuni shiteorimashite, taihen shitsurei shimashita.
(I) have to apologize for being out when (you) kindly came to call the other day.

12) このコンピューター・ゲームは、今、子供たちの間で大変な人気だ。
Kono konpyuutaa-geemuwa, ima, kodomotachino aidade taihenna ninkida.
This computer game is extremely popular among children right now.

13) この橋の建設には大変な費用がかかった。
Kono hashino kensetsuniwa taihenna hiyooga kakatta.
An incredible amount was spent on the construction of this bridge.

14) 彼は何か大変な実験をしているらしい。
Karewa nanika taihenna jikken-o shiteirurashii.
He seems to be conducting a difficult experiment of some sort.

15) 大変だ。もう８時。急がないと遅刻してしまう。
Taihenda. Moo hachiji. Isoganaito chikoku-shiteshimau.
Oh no! It's eight o'clock already. If (I) don't hurry I'll be late.

16) かばんを忘れたり、課長に怒られたり、きょうは大変な１日だった。
Kaban-o wasuretari, kachooni okoraretari, kyoowa taihenna ichinichidatta.
(I) forgot my briefcase and I got yelled at by my supervisor. Today was an awful day.

17) 満員電車で毎日２時間も通勤するのは大変だ。
Man-indenshade mainichi nijikanmo tsuukinsurunowa taihenda.
Commuting to and from work two whole hours every day on a packed train is terrible.

18) 朝から晩まで勉強ばかりで、受験生も大変だ。
Asakara banmade benkyoobakaride, jukenseimo taihenda.
Students preparing for exams have it hard, too; with nothing but study,

study, study from morning till night.

ひじょうに［非常に］ ■*hijou ni* ■extremely 

ことがらの**程度の強調**を表すときに使い、**ふつうとは違っている**という意味があります。丁寧で改まった言い方です。**客観的な**感じがします（例19, 20, 21, 22）。

This is also used when emphasizing the degree of something. However, it includes the meaning 'different from the usual'. It is a polite, formal expression, and gives a feeling of objectivity (ex.19, 20, 21, 22).

19) 先週の竜巻で農作物に非常に大きな被害が出た。
Senshuuno tatsumakide noosakubutsuni hijooni ookina higaiga deta.
There was a great amount of damage to crops from last week's tornado.

20) この賞は非常に優れた作品に対してあたえられます。
Kono shoowa hijooni sugureta sakuhinni taishite ataeraremasu.
This prize is awarded for extremely outstanding works.

21) スタントマンは、非常に危険な仕事です。
Sutantomanwa, hijooni kikenna shigotodesu.
A stuntman's job is extremely dangerous.

22) 非常にまれではあるが、ＡＢ型の血液の両親からＯ型の子供が生まれることがある。
Hijooni maredewa aruga, eebiigatano ketsuekino ryooshinkara oogatano kodomoga umareru kotoga aru.
It occurs extremely rarely, but sometimes a child with type O blood is born to type AB parents.

とどく／つく／たっする
■*todoku* ■*tsuku* ■*tassuru*

とどく［届く］ ■*todoku* ■to reach ; to arrive 

①荷物や手紙など、**送られたものが受け取る側に来る**ことです（例1, 2, 3）。「着く」は単に物が受け取る側に「来た」ということを表すだけですが、「届く」は送る側のことが意識されています。

Todoku is used when a package, letter, or other sent object comes to the receiving side (ex.1, 2, 3). While *tsuku* means only that the object arrives at the receiving end, *todoku* refers also to the fact that a person has sent the object.

②手や足またはものの一方などが、**目的のところにふれる**ことができることです（例4, 5, 6, 7）。「のびていってふれる」という感じがあります。①、②共に、電波・音声・数値など具体的な形のないものについても使います（例8, 9）。例10の「手が届く」は「自分のものにすることができる」という意味です。

It is also used when a hand, foot, or end of an object is able to touch an objective (ex.4, 5, 6, 7). It is suggested that the hand, foot, etc. touches after it is extended. In both definitions ① and ② *todoku* may refer to radio waves, sound, numbers or other abstract, shapeless things (ex.8, 9). In Example 10 *te ga todoku* is used to mean 'to be able to have something for oneself'.

---

1) さっき、母から手紙が届いた。
Sakki, hahakara tegamiga todoita.
I received a letter from my mother a little while ago.

2) 本屋に図鑑を注 文してあるのに、まだ届きません。
Hon-yani zukan-o chuumonshite arunoni, mada todokimasen.
(I've) ordered an illustrated book at the bookstore, but it hasn't arrived yet.

3) 地震で大きな被害を受けた国に、世界 中から救 援物資が届いた。
Jishinde ookina higaio uketa kunini, sekaijuukara kyuuenbusshiga todoita.
Relief goods have arrived from all around the world in the country so damaged by the earthquake.

4) 薬は、小さい子の手が届かないところにしまっておきましょう。
Kusuriwa, chiisai kono tega todokanai tokoroni shimatte okimashoo.
Let's put the medicine in a place out of the reach of children.

5) いすが高すぎて、床に足が届かない。
Isuga takasugite, yukani ashiga todokanai.
(My) feet don't reach the floor because this chair is too high.

6) 彼の髪は、肩まで届きそうだ。

Kareno kamiwa, katamade todokisooda.
His hair looks like it reaches his shoulders.

7) 電気スタンドのコードが短くて、枕元まで届かない。
Denkisutandono koodoga mijikakute, makuramotomade todokanai.
The cord for the lamp is too short to reach the bedside.

8) このあたりは山に囲まれているので、電波が届かない。
Kono atariwa yamani kakomarete irunode, denpaga todokanai.
Radio waves don't reach this area because it is surrounded by mountains.

9) 寄付を募ったけれど、目標の１億円には届かなかった。
Kifuo tsunottakeredo, mokuhyoono ichiokuenniwa todokanakatta.
(We) had a fund-raiser but fell short of our 100 million yen goal.

10) そんな高い車には、手が届きません。
Sonna takai kurumaniwa, tega todokimasen.
There's no way (I'll) be able to buy such an expensive car.

つく［着く］ ■*tsuku* ■to arrive ; to reach 

---

①人やものが、**目的とする場所に来る**ことです（例11, 12, 13, 14）。
To arrive at one's destination (ex.11, 12, 13, 14).

②体の一部分やものの一方などが、**目的のところにふれる**ことができることです（例15, 16, 17）。「高い所に手が届く」は、高い所のものを取ったりすることができるという意味を含み、「高い所に手がつく」は指先でちょっとさわることができるという程度でもかまいません。

Tsuku may indicate that a part of the body or the end of an object touches its goal (ex.15, 16, 17). The expression *takai tokoro ni te ga todoku* means that one is able to take something from a high place, while *takai tokoro ni te ga tsuku* may mean that one is only able to touch the object with one's finger tips.

---

11) この列車は、10時15分に東京駅に着く。
Kono resshawa, juuji juugofunni Tookyooekini tsuku.
This train arrives at Tokyo station at 10:15.

12) 港に船が着いて、乗客がぞろぞろ降りてきた。

Minatoni funega tsuite, jookyakuga zorozoro oritekita.
The ship arrived in port, and the passengers disembarked in a steady stream.

13) ホテルに着いたら、うちに電話しよう。
Hoteruni tsuitara, uchini denwashiyoo.
Let's call home when (we) reach the hotel.

14) おととい娘に送った荷物が、きょう着いたそうだ。
Ototoi musumeni okutta nimotsuga, kyoo tsuitasooda.
It seems the things (I) sent to my daughter two days ago arrived today.

15) このプールは、深くて足がつかない。
Kono puuruwa, fukakute ashiga tsukanai.
This pool is so deep that my feet don't reach the bottom.

16) 屋根裏部屋は天井が低いので、立つと頭がついてしまう。
Yaneurabeyawa tenjooga hikuinode, tatsuto atamaga tsuiteshimau.
The attic ceiling is so low that if (I) stand up my head will touch.

17) 立ったまま体を前に曲げて、手のひらが床につきますか。
Tattamama karadao maeni magete, tenohiraga yukani tsukimasuka?
Can (you) bend over and touch the floor with the palms of your hands?

たっする［達する］

■ *tassuru*
■ to reach ; to attain

ものごとや人の行為がだんだん進んでいって、**目的とする地点や数量・水準に行きつく**ことです（例18, 19, 20, 21, 22)。「大したことだ・かなりなことだ」という意識を含んでいます。

Tassuru indicates that the action of a person or thing gradually progresses so that a specific goal, volume, or level is reached (ex.18, 19, 20, 21, 22).
An amount of importance or significance is implied.

---

18) 正午現在、東京の気温は32度に達した。
Shoogo genzai, Tookyoono kionwa sanjuunidoni tasshita.
As of noon, the temperature in Tokyo had reached 32°C.

19) あの人の無責任な態度に、私のがまんも限界に達した。
Ano hitono musekininna taidoni, watashino gamanmo genkaini tasshita.

I've reached the end of my patience with his irresponsible attitude.

20) 犯人の撃ったピストルの弾は、被害者の心臓に達していた。
Hanninno utta pisutoruno tamawa, higaishano shinzooni tasshiteita.
The bullet fired by the criminal hit the victim in the heart.

21) この遊園地では、きょう1日の入場者が5000人に達した。
Kono yuuenchidewa, kyoo ichinichino nyuujooshaga gosenninni tasshita.
Today's attendance at the amusement park reached 5,000 people.

22) 登山隊は、けさ早く山頂に達した。
Tozantaiwa, kesa hayaku sanchooni tasshita.
The mountaineering party reached the top of the mountain early this morning.

とどける/おくる/だす

■ *todokeru* ■ *okuru* ■ *dasu*

とどける［届ける］ ■ *todokeru* ■ to deliver 

ものを**相手の所や目的の所まで持って行って渡す**ことです。自分で直接持って行って、相手に渡す場合と、また人や輸送機関などに頼んで渡してもらうことの両方があります（例1, 2, 3, 4, 5）。

To take something and carry it to another person's location or a destination. It is used both when going in person to hand something over to someone, or when having something delivered by another person or a delivery service (ex. 1, 2, 3, 4, 5).

1) 彼は女優の楽屋にファンからの花束を届けた。
Karewa joyuuno gakuyani fankarano hanatabao todoketa.
He delivered the flower bouquets from the actress' fans to her dressing room.

2) ご注文の品は日曜日までにお届けいたします。
Gochuumonno shinawa nichiyoobimadeni otodoke-itashimasu.

(We) will deliver your order by Sunday.

3) すみませんが、この書類を総務課の田中さんに届けてくれませんか。

Sumimasenga, kono shoruio soomukano Tanakasanni todokete kuremasenka?
Excuse me, would (you) please deliver these documents to Mr. Tanaka in the general affairs office?

4) 私はそば屋にきつねうどんを届けてくれるように電話した。

Watashiwa sobayani kitsuneudon o todokete kureruyooni denwashita.*
I called the noodle shop to have them deliver me a bowl of *kitsune-udon*.

—— * *Kitsuneudon* is Japanese soup noodle *udon* served with a deep fried bean curd. * p.500

5) 私の留守中に届けられた荷物を管理人が預かっていてくれた。

Watashino rusuchuuni todokerareta nimotsuo kanrininga azukatte-itekureta.
The (building) manager took care of the package that arrived for me while I was away.

おくる［送る］ ■*okuru* ■to send

郵便や**宅配便**などの**輸送機関を使って、相手にものが行くようにする**ことです（例6, 7, 8, 9, 10, 11）。

To send something to someone by means of mail, a shipping agent, or a delivery service (ex.6, 7, 8, 9, 10, 11).

---

6) お中元やお歳暮は、宅配便で送る人が多い。

Ochuugenya oseibowa, takuhaibinde okuru hitoga ooi.
A lot of people send midyear and year-end gifts by delivery service.

7) 私は大阪に転勤のため、荷物をさきにトラックで送った。

Watashiwa Oosakani tenkinno tame, nimotsuo sakini torakkude okutta.
I was transferred to Osaka so I sent my belongings ahead by truck.

8) 北海道のおじが、今年もかにを送ってくれた。

Hokkaidoono ojiga, kotoshimo kanio okuttekureta.
(My) uncle in Hokkaido sent us crabs again this year.

9) 商品の代金は、郵便局から現金書留で送ればいい。

Shoohinno daikinwa, yuubinkyokukara genkinkakitomede okurebaii.
(You) can send payment for the merchandise in cash by registered mail through the post office.

10) 見積書は、ファックスで送ります。
Mitsumorishowa, fakkusude okurimasu.
(I'll) send the estimate by fax.

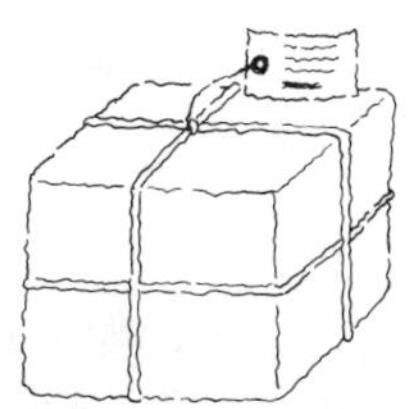

11) 私は、友人を駅まで車で送っていった。
Watashiwa, yuujin-o ekimade kurumade okutteitta.
I took my friend to the station in my car.

だす［出す］ ■ *dasu* ■ to send 

ものを**ある場所から、ほかの場所へ行かせること**です。郵便や宅配便などを使います（例12, 13, 14）。「届ける・送る」は、目的地に着くまでを強く意識していますが、「出す」は相手に届けてくれるように、郵便局や輸送機関に渡すこと、つまり**送る人の手を離れること**に重点があります。

To send an object from one place to another by means of a postal or delivery service (ex.12, 13, 14). *Todokeru* and *okuru* emphasize arrival of the object at its final destination, while *dasu* is the entrusting of something to a post office or shipping agent to deliver it. The focus is on the object leaving the sender's possession.

---

12) きのう、田舎の母に手紙を出した。
Kinoo, inakano hahani tegamio dashita.
Yesterday, (I) sent a letter to my mom back home.

13) 彼に返事を書いたのに、うっかりして出すのを忘れていた。
Kareni henjio kaitanoni, ukkarishite dasunoo wasureteita.
(I) wrote him my reply, but I completely forgot to send it.

14) ちょっと郵便局まで、小包を出しに行ってきます。
Chotto yuubinkyokumade, kozutsumio dashini ittekimasu.
(I'm) just going out to the post office to send a small package.

めん類

日本では、軽い食事としてめん類が人気です。主なものに「そば」「うどん」「ラーメン」があります。

そばは、そば粉を水などで練ったものをひも状にしてゆでて、ねぎなどと熱いつゆに入れて食べます。また、冷たいつゆにつけながら食べるのも好まれています。

うどんは、小麦粉を練ったものを、そばよりも太いひも状にして、そばと同じようにして食べます。

また、ラーメンは中国風のめんを、中国風の熱いスープに入れて食べるものです。「そば」「うどん」「ラーメン」共に、いろいろなバリエーションがあり、すすって音を立てて食べます。

Noodles

A popular form of light meal in Japan is noodles, the most common of which are *soba*, *udon*, and *raamen*.

Soba noodles are made of buckwheat flour, which is kneaded and formed into thin, string-like noodles. The noodles are boiled and served in a hot broth topped with onions or other vegetables. *Soba* noodles are also enjoyed dipped in a cold broth.

Udon noodles are made from kneaded flour, and are thicker than *soba* noodles, but served the same way.

Raamen noodles are Chinese style noodles which are served in a hot Chinese style soup. There are numerous variations and ways to serve all three types, but all are eaten in a slurping style.

となり／よこ

■*tonari* ■*yoko*

となり［隣］ ■*tonari* ■neighbor ; next (door)

①**ものや人を正面から見たときその両わき**、つまり右か左に並んで存在するものや人の位置を示すとき使います。「隣」に存在するのは、同じ質や種類のもので、対等だという感じがあります。ですから「彼は机の隣に立っている」という言い方はしません（例1, 2, 3)。

Tonari is used to indicate the position of an object or person which exists at the side of something ; that is, parallel to and either on the left or right of another object or person as viewed from the front. Things that are *tonari* must be of the same quality or type and be perceived as equal in some respect. Thus one cannot say *Kare wa tsukue no tonari ni tatte iru* to mean 'He is standing beside the desk' (ex.1, 2, 3).

②距離が近くても離れていても、**同種のいちばん近くにあるもの**を指します（例4, 5)。また、隣の家や、その家の人を指して「隣」「お隣」と言います。

It is also used to refer to the nearest object of the same type, regardless of whether the actual distance is near or far (ex.4, 5). Also, a neighboring house, or a person living in a neighboring house, is referred to as *tonari* or *otonari.*

---

1) うちの隣は幼稚園です。
Uchino tonariwa yoochiendesu.
A kindergarten is next to (my) house.

2) 彼女は小学校1年生のとき、私の隣の席だった。
Kanojowa shoogakkoo-ichinenseino toki, watashino tonarino sekidatta.
Her desk was next to mine when we were first grade students.

3) あのめがねをかけた人の隣にいるのが、高野さんです。
Ano meganeo kaketa hitono tonarini irunoga, Takanosandesu.
Mr. Takano is the one standing next to the person wearing glasses.

4) 東京の隣の駅は神田です。
Tookyoono tonarino ekiwa Kandadesu.
The next station from Tokyo is Kanda.

5) ここは山の中なので、隣の家まで１キロもある。
Kokowa yamano nakananode, tonarino iemade ichikiromo aru.
This is a mountainous area, so neighbors may be as much as one kilometer apart.

よこ［横］ ■*yoko* ■side ; width ; horizontal

---

①ものや人を正面から見たときの**その両わき**、つまり**右や左の場所**を示すとき使います（例6, 7, 8, 9, 10)。「Aの横にB」は、まず主となるものがあり、そのすぐそばにほかのものがあるという感じを含みます。また、そのもの**自体の側面を指して**使います（例11)。

Yoko is used to indicate a position on either side of something, that is, to the left or right of an object or person as viewed from the front (ex.6, 7, 8, 9, 10). A *no yoko ni* B includes the sense that some other object is right next to object A, which is the focus. It is used also to refer to the surface of the side of an object (ex.11).

②ものの「**たて**」**に対して水平の方向**を表します（例12, 13, 14)。

It also indicates horizontal or flat position or direction, as opposed to vertical (ex.12, 13, 14).

---

6) 公園の天使の像の横に、水飲み場がある。
Kooenno tenshino zoono yokoni, mizunomibaga aru.
There's a drinking fountain next to the statue of an angel in the park.

7) さっき、あなたの横にいたのはだれですか。
Sakki, anatano yokoni itanowa daredesuka?
Who was that person next to you a little while ago?

8) 親犬の横に子犬がいる。
Oyainuno yokoni koinuga iru.
There are some puppies next to their mother.

9) 人が話をしているのに、横を向いているのは失礼だ。
Hitoga hanashio shiteirunoni, yokoo muiteirunowa shitsureida.
It's rude to look away (to the side) when (I'm) talking.

10) 彼は、横から見たところが父親にそっくりだ。
Karewa, yokokara mita tokoroga chichioyani sokkurida.

He looks just like his father when (you) see him in profile.

11) チョコレートの箱(はこ)の横(よこ)のところに、ベルギー製(せい)と書(か)いてあった。
Chokoreetono hakono yokono tokoroni, Berugiiseito kaiteatta.
It said 'Made in Belgium' on the side of the box of chocolates.

12) この紙(かみ)の大(おお)きさは、たて15センチ、よこ20センチです。
Kono kamino ookisawa, tate juugosenchi, yoko nijussenchidesu.
This paper is 15cm long by 20cm wide.

13) 英語(えいご)は左(ひだり)から右(みぎ)へと横(よこ)に書(か)く。
Eigowa hidarikara migieto yokoni kaku.
English is written horizontally from left to right.

14) 疲(つか)れたので、横(よこ)になって少(すこ)し休(やす)んだ。
Tsukaretanode, yokoni natte sukoshi yasunda.
(I) was tired, so I lay down and rested a bit.

どのくらい／どれほど

■ *dono kurai* ■ *dore hodo*

どのくらい

■ *dono kurai*
■ how much (long, far, etc.) 

いま問題(もんだい)になっているものや、ことがらの**だいたいの数量(すうりょう)をきく**ときに使(つか)います（例(れい)1, 2, 3, 4）。

Dono kurai is used when asking for an approximation of the quantity of objects, or the amount of time, distance, degree, etc. in question (ex.1, 2, 3, 4).

---

1) A：ここからあなたの家(いえ)まで、どのくらいかかりますか。

B：１時間(じかん)くらいかかります。

A: *Kokokara anatano iemade, donokurai kakarimasuka?*
How long does it take from here to your house?
B: *Ichijikankurai kakarimasu.* It takes about an hour.

2) 新(あたら)しいスタジアムはどのくらいの人(ひと)が入(はい)るのでしょう。
Atarashii sutajiamuwa donokuraino hitoga hairunodeshoo?
(I) wonder how many people the new stadium will hold?

3) 私の英語がどのくらい通じるか、わかりませんが、頑張ってみます。
Watashino Eigoga donokurai tsuujiruka, wakarimasenga, ganbattemimasu.
I don't know how much my English will be understood, but I'll do my best.

4) どのくらい寝たのか、目が覚めたらもう窓の外は暗くなっていた。
Donokurai netanoka, mega sametara moo madono sotowa kurakunatteita.
How long could (I) have been asleep? When I woke up it was already dark outside (the window).

どれほど ■*dore hodo* ■how much

「どのくらい」と同じ意味で使います。また「どれほど～ても」の形で**数量や回数や程度がとても大きく（小さく）ても**、という意味で使います（例5, 6, 7, 8, 9)。
This expression is used in the same way as *dono kurai*. It may also be used in the form *dore hodo～te mo* to emphasize the greatness (or smallness) of a quantity, number of times, degree, etc. (ex.5, 6, 7, 8, 9).

---

5) こんどの台風でどれほどの被害がでたか心配です。
Kondono taifuude dorehodono higaiga detaka shinpaidesu.
(We're) worried about how bad was the damage in this last typhoon.

6) 彼は仲良しの友達が転校してしまい、どれほどがっかりしていることだろう。
Karewa nakayoshino tomodachiga tenkoo-shiteshimai, dorehodo gakkarishiteiru kotodaroo.
How unhappy he must be that his friend has moved to another school.

7) 私は学生時代、あの人にどれほど世話になったかしれません。
Watashiwa gakuseijidai, ano hitoni dorehodo sewani nattaka shiremasen.
I was indebted to him for so much during my school days that it can't even be told.

8) 火の始末はどれほど注意しても、しすぎることはありません。
Hino shimatsuwa dorehodo chuuishitemo, shisugiru kotowa arimasen.
You can't be too careful about extinguishing fires.

9) どれほど着飾ってみても、その人の内容が変わるものではない。
Dorehodo kikazattemitemo, sono hitono naiyooga kawaru monodewa nai.
No matter how much one tries to dress oneself up, the person inside doesn't change.

とる／ぬく／はずす

■*toru* ■*nuku* ■*hazusu*

とる［取る］

■*toru*
■to remove ; to take off 

ついているもの・ついてしまったものを除いて、ついていない状態にすることです（例1, 2, 3, 4, 5）。

To remove something which was attached to or part of something (ex.1, 2, 3, 4, 5).

1）古いセーターの毛玉を取った。
Furui seetaano kedamao totta.
(I) shaved the pile off an old sweater.

2）母は、鍋のふたを取って、肉が煮えているかどうかを見た。
Hahawa, nabeno futao totte, nikuga nieteiruka dookao mita.
Mother removed the lid of the pot to check if the meat was cooked yet.

3）白いシャツについたよごれを、きれいに取るのはむずかしい。
Shiroi shatsuni tsuita yogoreo, kireini torunowa muzukashii.
It is difficult to completely remove stains from a white shirt.

4）彼は、ぼうしを取ってあいさつをした。
Karewa, booshio totte aisatsuo shita.
He took off his hat and greeted (me).

5）この本のカバーを取らないでください。
Kono honno kabaao toranaide kudasai.
Please don't take the dust jacket off this book.

ぬく［抜く］

■*nuku*
■to pull (take) out ; to extract 

はえているもの・刺さっているものを引っぱって外に出すときや、入っているもの・混ざっているものを外に出してなくしてしまうとき使います（例6, 7, 8, 9, 10）。

To pull out and remove something that is sticking out or sprouting. Also, to remove a substance that is contained or mixed into another substance (ex.6, 7, 8, 9, 10).

---

6) あした庭(にわ)の雑草(ざっそう)を抜(ぬ)きます。
Ashita niwano zassoo-o nukimasu.
(I'm) going to pull the weeds in my yard tomorrow.

7) 午前中(ごぜんちゅう)歯医者(はいしゃ)で、歯(は)を2本(ほん)抜(ぬ)きました。
Gozenchuu haishade, hao nihon nukimashita.
This morning (I) had two teeth pulled at the dentist.

8) 指(ゆび)に刺(さ)さったとげが抜(ぬ)けない。
Yubini sasatta togega nukenai.
(I) can't get the thorn that's stuck in my finger out.

9) 脂肪(しぼう)を抜(ぬ)いたミルクを、スキムミルクといいます。
Shiboo-o nuita mirukuo, sukimumirukuto iimasu.
Milk that has had the fat removed is called skim milk.

10) テーブルクロスについたしみが抜(ぬ)けない。
Teeburukurosuni tsuita shimiga nukenai.
The stain in the tablecloth won't come out.

はずす [外(はず)す] ■ *hazusu* ■ to remove ; to unfasten ; to undo 

組(く)み合(あ)わさっているものを、分(わ)かれた状態(じょうたい)にすることです(例(れい)11, 12, 13, 14, 15, 16)。

To cause something which is attached to another thing to become separated or loosened (ex.11, 12, 13, 14, 15, 16).

---

11) 彼(かれ)はそで口(ぐち)のボタンを外(はず)して、腕(うで)まくりをした。
Karewa sodeguchino botan-o hazushite, udemakurio shita.
He unbuttoned his sleeves and rolled them up.

12) 門(もん)のかけがねが、外(はず)したままになっていた。
Monno kakeganega, hazushita-mamani natteita.
The gate had been left unlatched.

13) キーホルダーから家のかぎを外しておいたら、なくなってしまった。
Kiihorudaakara ieno kagio hazushiteoitara, nakunatte-shimatta.
(I) took my house key off my key ring and lost it.

14) 原っぱで、犬をくさりから外して、自由に走りまわらせた。
Harappade, inuo kusarikara hazushite, jiyuuni hashiri-mawaraseta.
(I) took the leash off my dog and let him run free in the open field.

15) 彼がめがねを外した顔を、見たことがない。
Karega meganeo hazushita kaoo, mita kotoga nai.
(I) have never seen him with his glasses off.

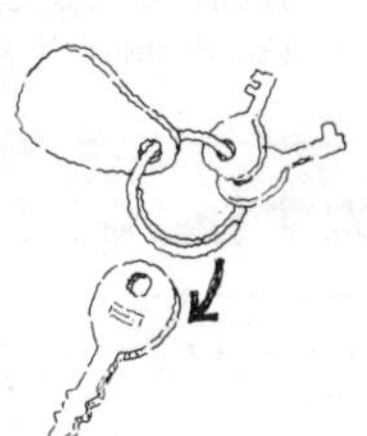

16) 私は、いつでも結婚指輪は外さない。
Watashiwa, itsudemo kekkon-yubiwawa hazusanai.
I never remove my wedding ring.

とる/ぬすむ

■*toru* ■*nusumu*

とる［取る］ ■*toru* ■to take ; to steal 

ほかのひとのものを自分のものにすることです。相手に気づかれないようにこっそりするときと、また相手から直接むりやり奪うときの両方があります（例1, 2, 3, 4）。

To make someone else's belongings one's own. It is used both to mean to take something stealthily while the other person doesn't notice, or to steal directly from someone by force (ex.1, 2, 3, 4).

1) 妹は、私が人形を取ったと言って泣いた。
Imootowa, watashiga ningyoo-o tottato itte naita.
My (younger) sister was crying, saying I had taken her doll.

2) 昔、その島は、戦争でほかの国に取られてしまったことがあったそうだ。
Mukashi, sono shimawa, sensoode hokano kunini torarete shimattakotoga attasooda.
It is said that in the past that island was seized by another country dur-

ing a war.

3) 人込みでさいふを取られた。
Hitogomide saifuo torareta.
(My) wallet was stolen in the crowd.

4) 人のものを取ってはいけない。
Hitono monoo tottewa ikenai.
(You) mustn't take other people's things.

ぬすむ［盗む］ ■*nusumu* ■to steal 

他人の持ちものを、**持ち主にわからないように持ち出し**て、自分のものにしてしまうことです（例5, 6, 7)。「～の目を盗んで」は「人に気づかれないように・気づかないうちに」という意味です（例8, 9)。

To take someone else's belongings without the owner's noticing, and make it one's own (ex.5, 6, 7). The expression ～*no me o nusunde* means 'while ～ isn't looking', or 'so ～ doesn't notice' (ex.8, 9).

---

5) 男はその牧場から、1頭の馬を盗んだ。
Otokowa sono bokujookara, ittoono umao nusunda.
A man stole a horse from the ranch.

6) だれも知らないうちに、美術館から多数の絵画が盗まれていた。
Daremo shiranai uchini, bijutsukankara tasuuno kaigaga nusumareteita.
A great number of paintings were stolen from the art museum before anyone knew about it.

7) 彼は本を1冊盗んでつかまった。
Karewa hon-o issatsu nusunde tsukamatta.
He stole a book and was caught.

8) 上司の目を盗んで、彼女はしばしば仕事中に私用の電話をかけた。
Jooshino meo nusunde, kanojowa shibashiba shigoto-chuuni shiyoono denwao kaketa.
She often made personal phone calls at the office while her boss wasn't looking.

9) 親の目を盗んで、その子供は真夜中に家を抜け出した。
Oyano meo nusunde, sono kodomowa mayonakani ieo nukedashita.
That child snuck out of the house in the middle of the night without his parents noticing.

（手に）とる／（手に）もつ

■ (*te ni*) *toru* ■ (*te ni*) *motsu*

（手に）とる

■ (*te ni*) *toru*
■ to take ; to hold (in the hands)

よく見る・人に渡すなどなんらかの**目的のために**、そこにある**ものを**まず**一度自分の手にする**ことです（例1, 2, 3, 4）。したがって、ほとんどの場合「（手に）とって〜する」という形で使います。

To put something in one's hands for some purpose, i.e., to examine it or to pass it to someone else (ex.1, 2, 3, 4). Thus, it is used in most cases in the form (*te ni*) *totte〜suru*.

---

1) この博物館では、展示物を手にとって見ることができる。
Kono hakubutsukan-dewa, tenjibutsuo teni totte miru kotoga dekiru.
At this museum you can pick up the objects on display with your hands and look at them.

2) 彼女は店先のキャベツをいくつか手にとって、重さを比べた。
Kanojowa misesakino kyabetsuo ikutsuka teni totte, omosao kurabeta.
She picked up several cabbages (on sale) in front of the store and compared their weights.

3) すみませんが、その本をとっていただけますか。
Sumimasenga, sono hon-o totte itadakemasuka?
Excuse me, could you hand me that book?

4) 私はテーブルの上のこしょうをとって兄にわたした。
Watashiwa teeburuno ueno koshoo-o totte anini watashita.
I picked up the pepper on the table and gave it to my (elder) brother.

(手に)もつ［持つ］ ■(*te ni*) *motsu* ■to hold (in the hand)

運ぶなどの目的で、ものを手にすることです（例5, 6, 7, 8）。「（手に）とる」よりも長い時間手にしていたり、かかえていたりします。例7は、持ち歩いている・携帯しているの意味です。この場合は直接手にしていなくても、かばんなどの中に入れてあってもかまいません。

To take something in the hand in order to carry it someplace (ex.5, 6, 7, 8). The object is kept in the hands or supported for a longer time than with (*te ni*) *toru*. In Example 7 it means 'to carry with or have on one's person'. In this case the object may be contained in a bag or other such container and not held in the hand directly.

5) 荷物が重そうですね、1つ持ってあげましょうか。
Nimotsuga omosoodesune, hitotsu motte-agemashooka?
(Your) bundles look so heavy, why don't (I) carry one for you.

6) 両手に荷物を持っているときに転んで、顔にけがをした。
Ryooteni nimotsuo motteiru tokini koronde, kaoni kegao shita.
I fell and hurt my face when (I) was holding luggage in both hands.

7) 私はいつも、かばんの中に折りたたみがさを持っています。
Watashiwa itsumo, kabanno nakani oritatamigasao motteimasu.
I always have a folding umbrella in my briefcase.

8) 姉の赤ちゃんは、いつもタオルを持って寝る。
Aneno akachanwa, itsumo taoruo motte neru.
My (elder) sister's baby always goes to sleep holding a towel.

~ないで／~なくて

■*~naide* ■*~nakute*

~ないで ■*~naide* ■without ~ing

いつもしたり、するのがあたりまえになっていることをぬきにして何かをすることを表します（例1, 2, 3, 4）。「～ずに」という形でも使われます（例5, 6）。

This expression indicates that one does something without performing an action that is usual or expected (ex.1, 2, 3, 4). The form ～*zu ni* is also used (ex. 5, 6).

1）私はこの問題を一晩寝ないで解いた。
Watashiwa kono mondaio hitoban nenaide toita.
I went without sleep all night and solved this problem.

2）朝食をとらないで出かけるのは、体に良くない。
Chooshokuo toranaide dekakerunowa, karadani yokunai.
It's not good for (you) to go out without eating breakfast.

3）きょうは寄り道をしないで、まっすぐうちに帰ろう。
Kyoowa yorimichio shinaide, massugu uchini kaeroo.
Today, let's go straight home without stopping off anywhere.

4）彼はよく考えないで、思ったことをすぐ行動に移してしまう。
Karewa yoku kangaenaide, omotta kotoo sugu koodooni utsushiteshimau.
He puts his ideas right into action without giving them careful consideration.

5）この薬は、かまずに口の中でゆっくり溶かして飲んでください。
Kono kusuriwa, kamazuni kuchino nakade yukkuri tokashite nonde kudasai.
Please let the medicine dissolve slowly in your mouth without chewing it.

6）父は、わけも聞かずに兄をどなりつけた。
Chichiwa, wakemo kikazuni anio donaritsuketa.
My dad yelled at my brother without even listening to his excuse.

～なくて

- ～*nakute*
- without～ ; therefore～

ことがらの**原因や理由が、あることが行われていない・ある状態ではない**というとき使います（例7, 8, 9, 10）。

～*nakute* is used when the non-occurrence of an action, or the non-fulfillment of a state or condition, is the cause or reason for another event or action (ex.7, 8, 9, 10).

7）私は、上田さんの住所がわからなくて困っています。

Watashiwa, Uedasanno juushoga wakaranakute komatteimasu.
I'm really in trouble—I don't know Mr. Ueda's address.

8) 暑(あつ)さで食欲(しょくよく)がなくて、冷(つめ)たいものばかり飲(の)んでいる。
Atsusade shokuyokuga nakute, tsumetai monobakari nondeiru.
Because of the heat, (I) have no appetite and I drink nothing but cold things.

9) 気(き)に入(い)ったコートがあったけれど、お金(かね)が足(た)りなくて買(か)えなかった。
Kiniitta kootoga attakeredo, okanega tarinakute kaenakatta.
There was a coat (I) liked, but I didn't have enough money so I couldn't buy it.

10) 私(わたし)が乗(の)る予定(よてい)だった船(ふね)が遭難(そうなん)したとの知(し)らせを聞(き)いて、「乗(の)らなくて助(たす)かった」と思(おも)った。
Watashiga noru yoteidatta funega soonanshitatono shiraseo kiite, 'noranakute tasukatta' to omotta.
When I heard the news that the boat I was to have taken had had an accident, I thought (to myself) 'Thank God I didn't get on it!'

なおる／かいふくする

■ *naoru* ■ *kaifuku suru*

なおる［直(なお)る・治(なお)る］

■ *naoru*
■ to be repaired ; to get well

---

①故障(こしょう)やまちがいなど、よくない状態(じょうたい)だったものが、また**元(もと)の良(よ)い・正(ただ)しい状態(じょうたい)にもどる**ことです（例(れい)1, 2, 3）。

Naoru indicates that something that is broken, wrong, or otherwise in bad condition returns to its original or correct condition (ex.1, 2, 3).

②**病気(びょうき)やけが**などの状態(じょうたい)から、**健康(けんこう)な状態(じょうたい)にもどる**ことにも使(つか)い、この場合(ばあい)は「治(なお)る」と書(か)きます（例(れい)4, 5, 6）。

Naoru may also be used when speaking of an illness or injury being cured, and in this case the *kanji* 治る is written (ex.4, 5, 6).

---

1) 電話(でんわ)の故障(こしょう)は、すぐに直(なお)るそうです。

Denwano koshoowa, suguni naorusoodesu.
They say the problem with the telephone can be easily repaired.

2) 修理に出していた車が、直ってもどってきた。
Shuurini dashiteita kurumaga, naotte modottekita.
The car (I) took in to be repaired came back running well (fixed).

3) 彼のなまけぐせは、いくつになっても直らない。
Kareno namakegusewa, ikutsuni nattemo naoranai.
He'll never mend his lazy ways no matter how old he gets.

4) このぐらいのけがなら、3日もすれば治るよ。
Kono guraino keganara, mikkamo sureba naoruyo.
A wound like this should heal in about three days.

5) かぜが治っても、すぐに無理をしないほうがいいですよ。
Kazega naottemo, suguni murio shinai hooga iidesuyo.
Even after you get over your cold (you) should take it easy for a while, you know.

6) 彼の病気はもう治らないと、医者から聞いた。
Kareno byookiwa moo naoranaito, ishakara kiita.
(I) heard from the doctor that his sickness is incurable. (The doctor told me that...)

かいふくする［回復する］ ■*kaifuku suru* ■to recover

①病気やけがが良くなり**元通りの健康を取りもどす**ことです（例7, 8, 9)。
To return to health after illness or injury (ex.7, 8, 9).

②よくない状態になっていたものが、**元の状態を取りもどす**ことです（例10, 11)。「なおる」よりも時間がかかっている・大事だという感じがあります。例12, 13のように、**失っていたものを取りもどす**という意味もあります。
To return something that was in a bad condition to a normal one (ex.10, 11). *Kaifuku suru* suggests the condition is more serious and takes more time to recover from than does *naoru*. As in Examples 12 and 13, it may be used to denote recovering something that was lost.

7) 父の健康が回復したら、家族で旅行に行きます。

Chichino kenkooga kaifukushitara, kazokude ryokooni ikimasu.
When my father's health improves, we'll take a family trip together.

8) 若いうちは、疲れても回復するのが早い。
Wakai uchiwa, tsukaretemo kaifukusurunoga hayai.
People quickly recover from fatigue when they're young.

9) 彼の病状は、少しずつ回復に向かっているそうです。
Kareno byoojoowa, sukoshizutsu kaifukuni mukatteirusoodesu.
He appears to be recovering from his illness little by little.

10) 私たちは天候が回復するのを待って、漁に出かけた。
Watashi-tachiwa tenkooga kaifukusurunoo matte, ryooni dekaketa.
We waited for the weather to improve and then went fishing.

11) 落雷による停電のため、電車のダイヤは回復の見とおしがたたない。
Rakurainiyoru teidenno tame, denshano daiyawa kaifukuno mitooshiga tata-nai.
Lightning caused a power failure, and there's no way of telling when the trains will get back on schedule.

12) 手術のあと、彼女の意識が回復するまでまる１日かかった。
Shujutsuno ato, kanojono ishikiga kaifukusurumade maru ichinichi kakatta.
It took one full day for her to regain consciousness after the operation.

13) 一度失った信用を回復するのは、大変なことだ。
Ichido ushinatta shinyoo-o kaifukusurunowa, taihenna kotoda.
It's very difficult to regain someone's trust once it's been lost.

なかなか／けっこう／わりと

■ *nakanaka* ■ *kekkou* ■ *warito*

なかなか

■ *nakanaka*
■ quite ; rather

①ようすや程度を表すことばとともに使い、その**度合いが高い**ことを表します。**感心したり、ほめたりする気持ち**を含んでいます（例1, 2, 3, 4, 5）。

Nakanaka is used together with descriptive words to express that the degree or level of something is high. A feeling of admiration or praise is implied (ex.

1, 2, 3, 4, 5).

②「なかなか〜ない」という形で、そうすることが困難だ・簡単にはその状態にならないというようすを表します（例6, 7, 8)。

The expression *nakanaka〜nai* means that something is difficult to do, or that a situation does not easily come about (ex.6, 7, 8).

---

1) この車はなかなか乗り心地がいいですね。
Kono kurumawa nakanaka norigokochiga iidesune.
This car is quite comfortable to ride in.

2) あの店のインテリアはなかなかしゃれている。
Ano miseno interiawa nakanaka shareteiru.
The interior of that shop is quite elegant.

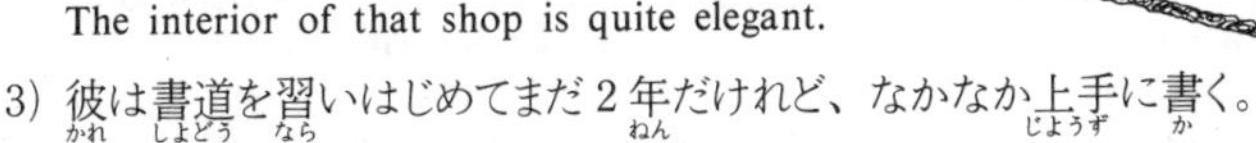

3) 彼は書道を習いはじめてまだ２年だけれど、なかなか上手に書く。
Karewa shodoo-o naraihajimete mada ninendakeredo, nakanaka joozuni kaku.
Although he has been studying calligraphy for only two years, he is rather good at it.

4) あの歌手の今度出たアルバムは、なかなか評判がいいようだ。
Ano kashuno kondo deta arubamuwa, nakanaka hyoobanga iiyooda.
That singer's latest album seems to have been quite well received.

5) 次の首相にだれがなるのか予想するのは、なかなかむずかしい。
Tsugino shushooni darega narunoka yosoosurunowa, nakanaka muzukashii.
It's difficult to imagine who might become the next Prime Minister.

6) 今回の会議は、各国の利害がからんでいるので、なかなか合意に達しないようだ。
Konkaino kaigiwa, kakkokuno rigaiga karandeirunode, nakanaka gooini tasshinaiyooda.
(We) just can't seem to achieve a consensus at this conference because the interests of each country are involved.

7) 地価が高くて、首都圏ではなかなかマイホームを持つことができない。
Chikaga takakute, shutokendewa nakanaka maihoomuo motsu kotoga dekinai.
The price of land is so high that it's very difficult to own (your) own home in the metropolitan area.

8) 事故のため電車がなかなか来なかったので、遅刻してしまった。
Jikono tame denshaga nakanaka konakattanode, chikokushite-shimatta.
Because of an accident, the train just didn't come and (I) ended up being late.

けっこう ■*kekkou* ■quite ; rather 

ものごとの**程度が予想していたものより上だ、一応満足できる**ということを表します。はじめの予想が低いものであったという印象を与えることがあるので、使うときは注意が必要です。口語的な表現です（例9, 10, 11, 12, 13）。

Kekkou describes something as being at a higher level than was first anticipated, and that for the moment one is satisfied with it. Care must be exercised when using it, because there are times when the listener may take it to mean that the speaker's original expectations were low. It is a colloquial expression (ex.9, 10, 11, 12, 13).

9) この仕事は大変かと思ったが、やってみるとけっこう簡単だった。
Kono shigotowa taihenkato omottaga, yattemiruto kekkoo kantandatta.
(I) thought this work would be difficult, but once I tried it, I found it was rather simple.

10) ここはまわりに緑も多いし、静かだし、けっこういい所だね。
Kokowa mawarini midorimo ooishi, shizukadashi, kekkoo ii tokorodane.
There's a lot of green around here, and it's quiet—it's really a nice area, isn't it?

11) 夜10時なのに、電車はけっこう込んでいた。
Yoru juujinanoni, denshawa kekkoo kondeita.
The train was rather crowded, even though it was ten o'clock at night.

12) 彼はいつもは無口だが、お酒を飲むと、けっこうおしゃべりになる。
Karewa itsumowa mukuchidaga, osakeo nomuto, kekkoo oshaberini naru.
He usually doesn't talk much, but when he drinks he gets quite talkative.

13) ここに引っ越してきて１年になるが、駅も店も近くて便利なので、けっこう気に入っている。
Kokoni hikkoshitekite ichinenni naruga, ekimo misemo chikakute benrinanode, kekkoo kiniitteiru.

It's been a year now since (I) moved here. I've come to like it quite a lot because it's so convenient, with the station and shops nearby.

わりと ■ *warito* ■ rather ; fairly 

程度が、きわだってはいないが、**比較的良い**とか、**悪い**ということを表します（例14, 15, 16, 17）。**控え目に表す**ために使われることもあります（例18）。

Warito expresses that, although not conspicuous, the level of something is comparatively good (or bad) (ex.14, 15, 16, 17). There are cases in which it is used to make a statement sound modest or reserved (ex.18).

---

14) きょうは12月にしては、わりと暖かい。

Kyoowa juunigatsuni shitewa, warito atatakai.
It is rather warm for December today.

15) あの映画は、題名はおもしろそうだけど、見たらわりとつまらなかった。

Ano eigawa, daimeiwa omoshirosooda-kedo, mitara warito tsumaranakatta.
That movie has an interesting title, but it was actually a bit boring.

16) あの子は、生まれたときはわりと小さかったが、今では家中で一番大きくなってしまった。

Ano kowa, umareta tokiwa warito chiisakattaga, imadewa iejuude ichiban ookiku natteshimatta.
He was somewhat small when he was born, but now he's the biggest in the family.

17) きょうは道がすいていたので、わりと早く目的地に着くことができた。

Kyoowa michiga suiteitanode, warito hayaku mokutekichini tsuku kotoga dekita.
Today the streets weren't crowded so (we) were able to get to our destination fairly quickly.

18) 今年うちのチームには、わりといい選手が多いので、優勝できるかもしれませんよ。

Kotoshi uchino chiimuniwa, warito ii senshuga ooinode, yuushoo dekirukamo shiremasenyo.
Our team has a lot of pretty good players on it this year, so maybe we can win the championship.

なげる／ほうる

■*nageru*　■*houru*

なげる［投げる］ ■*nageru* ■to throw

手に持ったものを**力をこめて遠くへ飛ばす**ことです。多くの場合受け取ったり的となったりする目標があります（例1, 2, 3）。

To forcefully hurl an object one is holding in one's hand through the air toward a distant area. In most cases an objective, i.e., a target or a person that will catch the object, is aimed at (ex.1, 2, 3).

1) あのピッチャーは、とても速い球を投げる。
Ano pitchaawa, totemo hayai tamao nageru.
That pitcher throws a very fast ball.

2) 彼は、的をよくねらって、ダーツの矢を投げた。
Karewa, matoo yoku neratte, daatsuno yao nageta.
He carefully aimed and threw the dart at the target.

3) 彼は石を投げてからすを追い払った。
Karewa ishio nagete karasuo oiharatta.
He drove the crows away by hurling stones at them.

ほうる［放る］ ■*houru* ■to toss ; to throw

①手に持ったものを**軽く向こうへ**、あるいは上のほうへ**飛ばす**ことです。時として、「投げる」と同じように使うこともあります（例4, 5）。

To make an object one is holding in one's hand fly lightly up and away from oneself. There are cases in which *houru* is used with the same meaning as *nageru* (ex.4, 5).

②「放っておく」は、そのままにしておく・好きにさせておくという意味です（例6, 7）。

The expression *houtteoku* means to leave something as it is, or to allow someone to do as he or she pleases (ex.6, 7).

4) 人に物を放って渡すなんて失礼だ。
Hitoni monoo hootte watasunante shitsureida.
It is impolite to pass things to people by tossing them.

5) 池に石を放ると、一面に水の輪が広がった。
Ikeni ishio hooruto, ichimenni mizuno waga hirogatta.
When (I) threw a rock into the pond, ripples spread out across the surface of the water.

6) 子供のけんかは、放っておくほうがいい。
Kodomono kenkawa, hootteoku hooga ii.
It's better to ignore children's arguments.

7) もう私のことは、放っておいてください。
Moo watashino kotowa, hootteoite kudasai.
Please, leave me alone.

なさけない／たよりない

■ *nasakenai* ■ *tayorinai*

なさけない［情けない］

■ *nasakenai*
■ shameful

「**恥ずべきことだ・嘆かわしい**」または「**みじめだ**」というようすを表します。他人のことにも自分のことにも使います（例1, 2, 3, 4, 5)。

Nasakenai describes a situation or condition as embarrassing, regrettable or miserable. It may be used when speaking of oneself or others (ex.1, 2, 3, 4, 5).

1) 友達を裏切るなんて、情けないやつだ。
Tomodachio uragirunante, nasakenai yatsuda.
What a despicable man, to double-cross (his) friend like that.

2) 今回のテストの成績は、自分でも情けなくなるほどひどかった。
Konkaino tesutono seisekiwa, jibundemo nasakenaku-naruhodo hidokatta.
My grade on this test was so bad (I) have to feel ashamed of myself.

3) 人を信じられないなんて情けない世の中だ。
Hitoo shinjirarenainante nasakenai yononakada.
What a pitiful state of affairs it is when (you) can't believe in anyone.

4) 情けないことに、今月はもうほとんどお金がないんです。
Nasakenai kotoni, kongetsuwa moo hotondo okanega naindesu.
To my embarrassment (I) have practically no money left this month.

5) 雨には降られるし、おなかはすくし、なんだか情けなくなってきた。
Ameniwa furarerushi, onakawa sukushi, nandaka nasakenaku nattekita.
(I) got rained on, I'm hungry, and all in all I feel pretty wretched.

たよりない［頼りない］ ■ *tayorinai* ■ unreliable 

ものの作りや人などに対して、「**しっかりしていない・信頼できない・あてにならない**」などの理由で、心細いという不安を感じるようすを表します（例6, 7, 8, 9）。

Tayorinai describes a condition in which one feels insecure or uneasy because the construction of an object, or a person, is unreliable or undependable (ex. 6, 7, 8, 9).

6) 彼は経験が浅くて、まだ医者として頼りない。
Karewa keikenga asakute, mada ishatoshite tayorinai.
He's inexperienced, so (you) can't trust him as a doctor yet.

7) この川を下るのに、こんなに小さなボートでは、ちょっと頼りない。
Kono kawao kudarunoni, konnani chiisana bootodewa, chotto tayorinai.
This small boat seems a bit unstable to take down this river.

8) この地図だけでは頼りないから、行く前に電話で場所を確認してください。
Kono chizudakedewa tayorinaikara, iku maeni denwade bashoo kakuninshite kudasai.
This map alone won't be reliable enough; please call before (you) leave and make sure of the location.

9) 彼女はふだんおとなしくて頼りなく見えるが、意外に気が強い。
Kanojowa fudan otonashikute tayorinaku mieruga, igaini kiga tsuyoi.
That girl usually appears quiet and meek, but she is unexpectedly strong in spirit.

なでる／さする／こする

■*naderu*　■*sasuru*　■*kosuru*

なでる　■*naderu* ■to stroke

人間や動物の体を、手のひらですべらせるようにやさしくさわることです。何度かくり返しても、一度でもかまいません。**相手をかわいいと思う気持ちや、やさしさ・いたわりなど愛情**がこもっています（例1, 2, 3, 4)。

To stroke or pet a human or animal with the palm of the hand. It may or may not be a repeated movement, and it expresses a person's affection or feelings of concern or tenderness (ex.1, 2, 3, 4).

1) 彼女は「なんてかわいいんでしょう」と、赤ちゃんの頭をやさしくなでた。
Kanojowa "Nante kawaiindeshoo" to, akachanno atamao yasashiku nadeta.
She said, "How cute!" and gently patted the baby on his head.

2) 猫ののどをなでると、気持ち良さそうにゴロゴロいう。
Nekono nodoo naderuto, kimochi-yosasooni gorogoro yuu.
When (you) stroke a cat's throat, it purrs contentedly.

3) 彼は、子犬をなでてやった。
Karewa, koinuo nadeteyatta.
He petted the puppy.

4) そよ風が、そっとほおをなでていった。
Soyokazega, sotto hoo-o nadeteitta.
The breeze gently brushed across (my) cheeks.

さする　■*sasuru* ■to rub

「なでる」とほとんど同じ動作ですが、一度だけではなく**しばらくの時間続ける動作**です。**苦痛をやわらげたり安心させたりする気持ちで**行います（例5, 6, 7)。

Sasuru has almost the same meaning as *naderu*, but is not a one-time event;

the rubbing may continue for a while. This action is done in order to ease one's pain or to offer relief (ex.5, 6, 7).

5) 「ああ痛い」と彼は、いすにぶつけた足をさすった。
"Aa itai" to karewa, isuni butsuketa ashio sasutta.
He shouted "Ouch!" and rubbed the leg he knocked against the chair.

6) お母さんは、子供のせきが止まるまで背中をさすってやった。
Okaasanwa, kodomono sekiga tomarumade senakao sasutteyatta.
The mother rubbed the child's back until he stopped coughing.

7) 気分が悪いんですか。背中をさすりましょうか。
Kibunga waruindesuka? Senakao sasurimashooka?
Are (you) feeling lousy? Shall I rub (your) back?

こする
■ *kosuru*
■ to rub ; to scrub

あるものを何かに**強く押しつけるように**して、前後あるいは左右に**何度も動かす動作**です（例8, 9, 10）。こするものは、手でも道具を使ってもかまいません。例11のように一度だけというときもあります。

To repeatedly move something back and forth or left and right, while pressing it hard against something else (ex.8, 9, 10). The rubbing object may be a part of the body, i.e., a hand or an instrument. As in Example 11, it may be a one-time movement.

8) 男の子は、眠そうに目をこすった。
Otokonokowa, nemusooni meo kosutta.
The boy rubbed his eyes sleepily.

9) つめでガラスをこするといやな音がする。
Tsumede garasuo kosuruto iyana otoga suru.
If (you) scratch the surface of glass with your fingernails, it makes a very unpleasant sound.

10) 原始時代、人は木をこすって火をおこした。
Genshi-jidai, hitowa kio kosutte hio okoshita.
In primitive times, people made fire by rubbing wood together.

11) ガードレールにこすったので、車(くるま)にきずがついた。
Gaadoreeruni kosuttanode, kurumani kizuga tsuita.
(I) scraped my car against a guardrail, and it got scratched.

私(わたし)はコーヒーでいいです

和田(わだ)さんの家(いえ)に、健(けん)と恵美子(えみこ)と耕平(こうへい)が遊(あそ)びに行(い)きました。

「コーヒーでもいれましょうか。それとも紅茶(こうちゃ)がいいですか」と和田(わだ)さんが聞(き)きました。「コーヒーはいいです」と健(けん)が言(い)いました。「コーヒーでいいです」と恵美子(えみこ)。そして「コーヒーがいいです」と耕平(こうへい)が言(い)いました。みんな似(に)ている答(こた)えですが、意味(いみ)はそれぞれちがいます。「～はいい」は「いらない」という断(ことわ)りで、「～でいい」は遠慮(えんりょ)して、いちばん手間(てま)のかからなそうなものを頼(たの)むとき、または自分(じぶん)の希望(きぼう)をはっきりと言(い)わないで、遠慮(えんりょ)して言(い)うときに使(つか)います。「～がいい」は、「ほしいのはコーヒーだ」という自分(じぶん)の希望(きぼう)をはっきりと述(の)べています。

～の部分(ぶぶん)には、時間(じかん)・場所(ばしょ)・人(ひと)などいろいろなことばが入(はい)りますが、今回(こんかい)のようなとき「～はいい」は「断(ことわ)り」を、「～でいい」は「遠慮(えんりょ)しながらの希望(きぼう)や許可(きょか)・妥協(だきょう)」を、そして「～がいい」は「希望(きぼう)・意志(いし)」を表(あらわ)します。

Watashi wa koohii de ii desu[1]

Ken, Emiko, and Kohei went to visit Ms. Wada's house. Ms. Wada asked, "*Koohii demo iremashoo ka? Soretomo koocha ga ii desu ka*[2]?" Ken replied, "*Koohii wa ii desu,*[3]" Emiko said, "*Koohii de ii desu,*[4]" and Kohei said, "*Koohii ga ii desu.*[5]"

These answers appear to be very similar, but each has a different meaning. ~*wa ii* means 'I don't want ~', ~*de ii* is used when you don't want the other person to go to too much trouble, or you wish not to say what you really want because you know it is troublesome, and ~*ga ii* is used when you are clearly stating a preference.

The word before *wa*, *de*, or *ga* may refer to a variety of things, including time, place, or people. In these cases as well, *wa ii* expresses refusal, *de ii* indicates permission or compromise with hesitation, while *ga ii* expresses desire.

1 *As for me, coffee will do (I'll make do with coffee).*
2 *Shall I make some coffee, or would you prefer tea?*
3 *As for coffee, I'm fine (I don't need it).*
4 *I'll settle for coffee.*
5 *I would like some coffee.*

なまける／サボる／おこたる

■ *namakeru* ■ *saboru* ■ *okotaru*

なまける［怠ける］ ■ *namakeru* ■ to be lazy 

「面倒だ・楽をしたい」などの理由で、**やるべきことをやらない**ことです（例1,2,3,4）。また、ものごとを一生懸命にやらない、まじめではないときにも使います。

To not do what one should do because it is troublesome, or one wants to take it easy (ex.1, 2, 3, 4); it also means to not do things seriously or eagerly.

1) 彼は仕事中、なまけていねむりばかりしている。
Karewa shigotochuu, namakete inemuribakari shiteiru.
In the office, he doesn't work seriously; (in fact) he does nothing but doze off.

2) 休みの間、なまけて何もしなかったので太ってしまった。

Yasumino aida, namakete nanimo shinakattanode futotteshimatta.
(I) ended up gaining weight because I was lazy and didn't do anything during my vacation.

3) 予習(よしゅう)をなまけると、あしたの授業(じゅぎょう)で困(こま)りますよ。
Yoshuuo namakeruto, ashitano jugyoode komarimasuyo.
If (you) slack off on preparing, you'll have trouble in tomorrow's class.

4) 若(わか)いときになまけてばかりいると、いつか後悔(こうかい)する。
Wakai tokini namakete-bakariiruto, itsuka kookaisuru.
If (you) don't do anything but fool around when you're young, you'll be sorry someday.

サボる
■ *saboru*
■ to cut a class (meeting, etc.)

しなければならないことを、楽(らく)をしたいために**わざとしなかったり**、仕事(しごと)や授業(じゅぎょう)などを**無断(むだん)で**、あるいは**正当(せいとう)な理由(りゆう)なしに休(やす)む**ことです（例(れい)5, 6, 7, 8)。
To not do what should be done because one wants to take it easy; also means to be absent from school or work without permission or proper reasons (ex.5, 6, 7, 8).

---

5) 彼(かれ)は試験(しけん)があると、ときどき仮病(けびょう)を使(つか)って学校(がっこう)をサボる。
Karewa shikenga aruto, tokidoki kebyoo-o tsukatte gakkoo-o saboru.
When he has an examination, he sometimes pretends to be sick and skips school.

6) 私(わたし)は学生時代(がくせいじだい)、よく授業(じゅぎょう)をサボって映画(えいが)を見(み)に行(い)った。
Watashiwa gakuseijidai, yoku jugyoo-o sabotte eigao mini itta.
When I was a student, I often cut classes and went to see a movie.

7) 彼(かれ)は仕事(しごと)をサボって競馬(けいば)に行(い)ったのが見(み)つかって、会社(かいしゃ)を首(くび)になった。
Karewa shigotoo sabotte keibani ittanoga mitsukatte, kaishao kubininatta.
He was fired because the company found out that he skipped work and went to the horse races.

8) 私(わたし)はピアノの練習(れんしゅう)をサボって母(はは)にしかられた。
Watashiwa pianono renshuuo sabotte hahani shikarareta.
My mother scolded me because I skipped out on my piano lesson.

おこたる［怠る］ ■*okotaru* ■to neglect

当然しなければならないことを、**しない**ことです（例9, 10, 11, 12)。うっかりしていた、ぼんやりしていた、など油断が原因であることが多いです。おこたることにより、自分が困ったり他人に迷惑がかかるという意味を含みます。

To not carry out a responsibility (ex.9, 10, 11, 12); in many cases, carelessness, negligence or absent-mindedness are the reasons. It is implied that the negligence results in trouble for oneself or others.

9) あの事故は、彼が一時停止をおこたったのが原因だ。
Ano jikowa, karega ichijiteishio okotattanoga gen-inda.
The cause of the accident was his failure to stop.

10) 泳ぐ前に、準備運動をおこたってはいけない。
Oyogu maeni, junbiundoo-o okotattewa ikenai.
(You) mustn't neglect to do your warm-up exercises before you swim.

11) 彼は税金の申告をおこたったので、罰金をとられた。
Karewa zeikinno shinkokuo okotattanode, bakkin-o torareta.
He neglected to send in his tax report, so he had to pay a fine.

12) 何事も上達するためには、常に努力をおこたってはいけない。
Nanigotomo jootatsusuru tameniwa, tsuneni doryokuo okotattewa ikenai.
At anything you do if you want to improve, you cannot stop putting forth effort.

なやむ／こまる／まよう

■*nayamu* ■*komaru* ■*mayou*

なやむ［悩む］ ■*nayamu* ■to worry 

①**問題**や**心配ごと**を、どうしたら良いのだろうと**いろいろ考え込む**とき使います。解決法がなかったりなかなか見つからずに心を痛めたりします（例1, 2, 3)。

To brood about how to handle a problem or worrisome matter. To feel mental anguish because a solution is difficult to find or is nonexistent (ex.1, 2, 3).

②「～に悩む」というのは、病気・公害などの悪い状態がなかなか良い状態にならなくて苦しんでいるということです（例4, 5, 6）。

～ni nayamu means to be distressed because an adverse condition such as illness, pollution, etc. is not improving (ex.4, 5, 6).

1）彼は、いくら勉強しても成績が上がらないので悩んでいる。
Karewa, ikura benkyooshitemo seisekiga agaranainode nayandeiru.
He is worried because, no matter how much he studies, his grades don't improve.

2）若いころは、つまらないことでくよくよと悩むものだ。
Wakai korowa, tsumaranai kotode kuyokuyoto nayamu monoda.
When (you) are young, you always worry about trivial matters.

3）彼女は娘の将来のことで悩んでいる。
Kanojowa musumeno shooraino kotode nayandeiru.
She is worried about her daughter's future.

4）父は関節炎に悩んでいる。
Chichiwa kansetsuenni nayandeiru.
(My) father suffers from arthritis.

5）彼の会社は人手不足に悩んでいる。
Kareno kaishawa hitodebusokuni nayandeiru.
His company is suffering from a shortage of manpower.

6）私の家は国道沿いなので、車の騒音に悩まされています。
Watashino iewa kokudoozoinanode, kurumano soo-onni nayamasareteimasu.
My house is next to a national highway, so we are bothered by the noise of cars.

こまる［困る］

■ *komaru*
■ to be in trouble ; to be annoyed 

---

①**どうしたら良いのかわからない**・解決するのがむずかしい・大変なことになったというときや、苦労や不自由を感じるとき使います（例7, 8, 9）。

This verb is used when one feels uncertainty or difficulty in solving a problem, has a feeling that a situation has become serious, or feels hardship or constraint (ex.7, 8, 9).

②**良くない**ことだ、**迷惑だ**というとき使います（例10, 11）。また、本心は迷惑だとは思っていないのに、恥ずかしかったり遠慮を表したりするとき使うこともあります（例12, 13）。また「困った人」は、その人が困っているのではなく、他人を困らせる人という意味です（例14）。

It is also used to describe something as bad or bothersome (ex.10, 11). In addition, it may indicate that something is not necessarily a bother, however the speaker feels embarrassed or modest about it (ex.12, 13). The expression *komatta hito* refers to a person that is a bother to others, not one who is himself disturbed (ex.14).

---

7) 旅行中、さいふをなくして困った。
Ryokoochuu, saifuo nakushite komatta.
(I) was in a fix because I lost my wallet while travelling.

8) 都会では多くの人が住宅難で困っている。
Tokaidewa ookuno hitoga juutakunande komatteiru.
A lot of people are having trouble finding housing in the city.

9) 困ったことに重要な書類をなくしてしまった。
Komatta kotoni juuyoona shoruio nakushiteshimatta.
(I) am in a terrible fix because I lost some important documents.

10) こんなところに車を止めては困ります。
Konna tokoroni kurumao tometewa komarimasu.
Parking (your) car here will cause problems for others.

11) 風邪をひくと困るから、あたたかくして出かけよう。
Kazeo hikuto komarukara, atatakakushite dekakeyoo.
(I) don't want to catch a cold, so I'd better bundle up before I go out.

12) こんなに高価なものをくださるなんて……困りますよ。
Konnani kookana mono-o kudasarunante...komarimasuyo.
(You've) given me such an expensive gift. (I) don't know what to say.

13) 突然好きだなんて言われて、困っちゃった。
Totsuzen sukidanante iwarete, komatchatta.
(I) didn't know what to do when he suddenly told me he likes me.

14) 会えばいつもけんかばかりして困った人たちだ。
Aeba itsumo kenkabakari shite komatta hitotachida.
(They) are a bit of a problem because they fight whenever they meet.

まよう［迷う］ ■*mayou* ■to be at a loss ; to get lost 

①いくつかのものごとの中から、どれを選んだらよいのかわからないときや、**決められない**とき使います（例15, 16, 17）。

To have difficulty deciding or choosing from several choices (ex.15, 16, 17).

②初めての場所や複雑なところで、正しい行き方がわからなくなったとき「道に迷う」と使います（例18）。

The expression *michi ni mayou* means to be unable to find one's way through a new or confusing place, i.e., to be lost (ex.18).

---

15) 私は、どの大学に行こうか迷っている。
Watashiwa, dono daigakuni ikooka mayotteiru.
I'm not sure which university to choose.

16) 靴を買いに行ったけれど、どれにしようか迷ってしまった。
Kutsuo kaini ittakeredo, doreni shiyooka mayotteshimatta.
(I) went shopping for shoes but had difficulty picking a pair I liked.

17) 自分が正しいと思ったことは、迷わず実行したほうがいい。
Jibunga tadashiito omotta kotowa, mayowazu jikkooshita hooga ii.
When you feel sure about something, you should proceed without hesitation.

18) 初めての土地ですっかり道に迷い、3時間も歩き回ってしまった。
Hajimeteno tochide sukkari michini mayoi, sanjikanmo arukimawatte-shimatta.
(I) got completely lost in an unfamiliar area and walked in circles for three hours.

~なれる/~つける

■ *~nareru* ■ *~tsukeru*

~なれる [~慣れる] ■ *~nareru* ■ V + be used to 

何度も経験したので、「熟練した・身についた・なじんでいる・抵抗感や違和感がない」というとき使います(例1, 2, 3, 4)。「住み慣れた家・はき慣れた靴」などのように名詞を修飾すると、安心していたりなじんだりしている状態を表します(例5, 6)。

This expression is used to convey a sense of familiarity, comfort, skill, adaptation, etc., that is achieved through long experience doing something (ex.1, 2, 3, 4). It may indicate an absence of resistance or discomfort in doing something. When used to modify nouns, as in *suminareta ie* (a familiar house) or *hakinareta kutsu* (old, comfortable shoes), it indicates a sense of security or comfort imparted by that object (ex.5, 6).

1) ぜいたくな料理より、食べ慣れた家庭料理のほうがいい。

Zeitakuna ryooriyori, tabenareta kateiryoorino hooga ii.
(I'd) rather have the home cooking that I'm used to than some fancy meal.

2) この道は学生のころから通い慣れているので、目をつぶっても歩けるくらいです。

Kono michiwa gakuseino korokara kayoinarete-irunode, meo tsubuttemo arukeru kuraidesu.
(I've) been taking this street ever since my school days, so I could almost walk it with my eyes closed.

3) 旅慣れている人は、荷物が少ない。

Tabinareteiru hitowa, nimotsuga sukunai.
A seasoned traveler has little luggage.

4) 玄関に見慣れない靴がある。だれが来ているのだろう。

Genkanni minarenai kutsuga aru. Darega kiteirunodaroo.
There are some shoes (I) don't recognize at the front door. Who do (you) suppose is here?

5) 住み慣れた町を離れるのはさびしい。
Suminareta machio hanarerunowa sabishii.
Leaving the town (you've) always lived in makes you feel forlorn.

6) はき慣れない靴で出かけたら、靴ずれができてしまった。
Hakinarenai kutsude dekaketara, kutsuzurega dekiteshimatta.
When (I) went out in shoes that weren't broken-in, I got blisters.

〜つける ▪〜*tsukeru* ▪V＋be used to 

いつもしていることだ・**ふだんからしていること**だ、というとき使います（例7,8,9)。「〜慣れる」ほど、ことがらに対する安心感や心地良さは、感じられません。単に、「経験する機会が多かったので特殊なことではなくなった」という感じです。「行きつけの店・かかりつけの医者」は、本人の意志で選んだという意識を含み、「いつも行くことに決めている」という意味で使います。

This is used when speaking of an action that one always does or has habitually done (ex.7, 8, 9). It does not convey the sense of comfort or security found with 〜*nareru*, but merely expresses the idea that something becomes customary through much experience. It also includes a sense of consciously having selected or decided on something, as in, *ikitsuke no mise* (the shop we always go to) or *kakaritsuke no isha* (our regular doctor), and means 'the one we have chosen to go to regularly'.

7) 彼は持ちつけない大金を持ったばかりに、人が変わってしまった。
Karewa mochitsukenai taikin-o mottabakarini, hitoga kawatteshimatta.
Just coming into possession of a much larger sum of money than he's used to having has made him a different person.

8) ふだんやりつけない運動をしたので、体じゅう痛くてたまらない。
Fudan yaritsukenai undoo-o shitanode, karadajuu itakute tamaranai.
(My) body is so sore all over from doing exercises I'm not used to doing regularly.

9) 日ごろ使いつけない敬語を使うと、まちがえて恥をかくことになる。
Higoro tsukaitsukenai keigoo tsukauto, machigaete hajio kaku kotoni naru.
Whenever (I) use honorific language, which I don't ordinarily use, I make mistakes and embarrass myself.

~にくい／~づらい／~がたい

■ *~nikui* ■ *~zurai* ■ *~gatai*

~にくい

■ *~nikui*
■ hard (to do)

何かの原因や理由により、ものごとを**快適に行えない**、普通よりも大変だということです（例1, 2, 3, 4, 5)。その原因や理由は、多くの場合、「かかとが高すぎる・ペン先が悪い・苦い……」など**外的状況**です。

This expression indicates that, because of some reason or cause, something cannot be done comfortably, or is more difficult to do than usual (ex.1, 2, 3, 4, 5). In many cases this is due to an external situation, for example, 'the heel of one's shoes are too high', 'the tip of a pen is bad', or 'a food tastes bitter'.

1) このペンは書きにくい。
Kono penwa kakinikui.
This pen is hard to write with.

2) 苦い薬は飲みにくい。
Nigai kusuriwa nominikui.
It's hard to swallow bitter-tasting medicine.

3) 席が舞台のななめ前だったので、劇がとても見にくかった。
Sekiga butaino nanamemaedattanode, gekiga totemo minikukatta.
(My) seat was off to the side of the stage so it was very hard to see the play.

4) この靴は、かかとが高すぎて歩きにくい。
Kono kutsuwa, kakatoga takasugite arukinikui.
These shoes are hard to walk in because the heels are too high.

5) ちょっと言いにくいのですが、先日貸したお金を返していただけませんか。
Chotto iinikuinodesuga, senjitsu kashita okaneo kaeshite itadakemasenka?
(I) hate to say this, but would you please pay back the money I lent you the other day?

~づらい

■ *~zurai*
■ difficult (to do) 

ものごとを行うのが**大変だ・困難だ**ということです（例6, 7, 8, 9, 10）。「～にくい」よりも**困難の度合いが強く**感じられ、**肉体的・精神的苦痛**を表します。
This expression indicates that doing something is troublesome or difficult (ex.6, 7, 8, 9, 10). ～*zurai* suggests a stronger degree of difficulty than ～*nikui* and implies an amount of physical or psychological pain.

---

6) 最近歯が悪くなったので、かたいものは、食べづらい。
Saikin haga warukunattanode, katai monowa, tabezurai.
Recently (my) teeth have become bad, so it's difficult for me to eat anything hard.

7) 雨で手紙の文字がにじんで読みづらい。
Amede tegamino mojiga nijinde yomizurai.
The writing on the letter is blurred because of the rain, so it's hard to read.

8) 高いビルのたっている地域では、電波がじゃまされて、テレビが見づらくなることがあります。
Takai biruno tatteiru chiikidewa, denpaga jamasarete, terebiga mizurakunaru kotoga arimasu.
In areas with high rise buildings there are times when TV reception becomes bad because high frequency waves are blocked.

9) 新しい靴をはいたら、足にまめができて歩きづらい。
Atarashii kutsuo haitara, ashini mamega dekite arukizurai.
(I) got a blister on my foot after wearing new shoes, so it's painful to walk.

10) 親が失敗をしたなんて、子供には話しづらい。
Oyaga shippaio shitanante, kodomoniwa hanashizurai.
It's difficult to tell (your) children that their parents have failed.

～がたい
■ ～*gatai*
■ difficult (to do)

ものごとをするのが**とてもむずかしく、ほとんどできない**ことです（例11, 12, 13, 14, 15）。「信じる・耐える・理解する・得る・捨てる・離れる」などの語と使うことが多く、現実の行為ではなく**精神的行為**として使います。つまり「捨てがたい」は、思い出や愛着、なにか良い点があって離れたくない、とい

う気持ちが含まれているのです。

~*gatai* suggests that something is extremely difficult or nearly impossible to do (ex.11, 12, 13, 14, 15). It is often used with words such as *shinjiru* (to believe), *taeru* (to endure), *rikaisuru* (to understand), *eru* (to obtain), *suteru* (to discard), and *hanareru* (to be separated from), and refers to mental activity instead of actual deeds. For example, *sutegatai* implies that one finds it difficult to part with a memory or something one is attached to.

---

11) 彼が宝くじで1億円あてたなんて、すぐには信じがたい話だ。
Karega takarakujide ichiokuen atetanante, suguniwa shinjigatai hanashida.
He won ¥100,000,000 in the lottery? (I) find it hard to believe such a story.

12) 論文もなくて、学者だなんて、とても信じがたい。
Ronbunmo nakute, gakushadanante, totemo shinjigatai.
(I) can't believe that he is a scholar; he has never even published a paper.

13) A：森博士が亡くなったそうですね。
B：ええ、我々は得がたい人を失ってしまいました。
A： *Morihakasega nakunatta soodesune.*
I heard Dr. Mori passed away.
B： *Ee, warewarewa egatai hitoo ushinatte-shimaimashita.*
Yes, we've lost a one-of-a-kind person.

14) この勝負は白黒つけがたい。
Kono shoobuwa shirokuro tsukegatai.
It's hard to decide who the winner of this match is.

15) 彼女は、とてもえらくなってしまって、近寄りがたい。
Kanojowa, totemo erakunatteshimatte, chikayorigatai.
She's become difficult to approach since being promoted to her new high position.

にげる／のがれる

■ *nigeru* ■ *nogareru*

にげる［逃げる］ ■ *nigeru* ■ to escape ; to run away (from)

追いかけてくるものにつかまらないように、遠くに離れようとすることです。つかまっているところから脱出したり、目の前にせまっている危険なことやいやなことを避けて遠ざかるときにも使います（例1, 2, 3, 4, 5, 6）。

To try to distance oneself from something that is in pursuit in order not to be caught. It may be used when speaking of escaping from a place in which one is detained, or avoiding something dangerous or unpleasant (ex.1, 2, 3, 4, 5, 6).

1）うさぎは、猟犬に追われて巣に逃げた。

Usagiwa, ryookenni owarete suni nigeta.
The rabbit, with hounds after it, escaped into its burrow.

2）私は、つかまえたすりを交番に連れて行く途中で逃げられた。

Watashiwa, tsukamaeta surio koobanni tsureteiku tochuude nigerareta.
The pickpocket I caught escaped as I was taking him to a police box.

3）ライオンが動物園から逃げて大騒ぎになった。

Raionga doobutsuenkara nigete oosawagini natta.
A lion escaped from the zoo and caused a panic.

4）この公園のりすは人間に慣れているので、近づいても逃げない。

Kono kooenno risuwa ningenni nareteirunode, chikazuitemo nigenai.
The squirrels in the park are quite tame and won't run away even if (you) approach them.

5）「困難から逃げようとするな、進んで立ち向かえ」と、先生は私たちに言った。

"*Konnankara nigeyooto suruna, susunde tachimukae*" *to, senseiwa watashitachini itta.*
Our teacher told us, "Stop running away from your troubles. Stand up and confront them!"

6）私たちは現実の問題から逃げることはできない。

Watashitachlwa genjitsuno mondaikara nigeru kotowa dekinai.
We cannot run away from the problems of the real world.

のがれる［逃れる］

■ *nogareru*
■ to escape ; to evade

危険な状態や災難などにあわないように**未然に避けたり遠ざかったり**、ぬけ

出したりすることです。また、責任や義務などいやなことをしないでいようとしたり、怠ったりすることです（例7, 8, 9, 10, 11）。

To take steps to avoid, separate oneself from, or slip away from danger or misfortune. It may also denote avoiding or neglecting to do an unpleasant job or responsibility (ex.7, 8, 9, 10, 11).

---

7) 彼は誘拐犯の手から無事に逃れて、家族のもとに帰ってきた。
Karewa yuukaihanno tekara bujini nogarete, kazokuno motoni kaettekita.
He safely escaped from the kidnappers and returned to his family.

8) 彼は火事があったときその建物にいなかったので、難を逃れた。
Karewa kajiga atta toki sono tatemononi inakattanode, nan-o nogareta.
He wasn't in the building at the time of the fire and therefore escaped injury.

9) 彼は都会の騒がしさを逃れて、山奥の村で暮らすことにした。
Karewa tokaino sawagashisao nogarete, yamaokuno murade kurasu kotoni shita.
He decided to live in a remote mountain village to escape the bustle of the city.

10) 私たちは戦火を逃れて、国外に脱出した。
Watashitachiwa senkao nogarete, kokugaini dasshutsushita.
We escaped the war by fleeing to a foreign country.

11) 彼女が車を運転していたのだから、事故の責任を逃れることはできない。
Kanojoga kurumao untenshite itanodakara, jikono sekinin-o nogareru kotowa dekinai.
She can't shirk responsibility for the accident because she was (the one) driving the car.

にこにこ／にやにや

■ *nikoniko* ■ *niyaniya*

にこにこ

■ *nikoniko*
■ smile (pleasantly) 

楽しいときや**うれしい**とき・**機嫌のいい**ときの**表情**で、相手にいい印象を与える**笑顔**です（例1, 2, 3）。

Nikoniko refers to a smiling face one gets when one is happy, and which makes a positive impression on other people (ex.1, 2, 3).

---

1) 就職が決まったと、彼はにこにこしながら言った。
Shuushokuga kimattato, karewa nikoniko-shinagara itta.
With a smile on his face, he said that he had found a job.

2) あの会社の受付は、いつもにこにこしていて感じがいい。
Ano kaishano uketsukewa, itsumo nikoniko-shiteite kanjiga ii.
(I) get a pleasant feeling from that company's receptionist because she's always smiling.

3) その赤ちゃんは今までにこにこ笑っていたのに、私が抱くと泣きだした。
Sono akachanwa imamade nikoniko waratteitanoni, watashiga dakuto nakidashita.
The baby was smiling until a minute ago, but when I held her she started crying.

にやにや ■ *niyaniya* ■ smirk 

おもしろいことや下品なことなどを想像したり思い出したりして、**ひとりで満足したり楽しんだりしているときの表情**です。多くの場合、相手にあまりいい印象を与えません（例4, 5, 6）。

Niyaniya describes the facial expression that appears when one is thinking or imagining something interesting or vulgar, and enjoying it all by himself. A facial expression described with *niyaniya* does not usually make a very good impression on other people (ex.4, 5, 6).

---

4) 彼は失敗をすると照れかくしににやにや笑う。
Karewa shippaio suruto terekakushini niyaniya warau.
Whenever he makes a mistake he grins to hide his embarrassment.

5) 彼はやっと500万円貯めた。毎晩１人でにやにやしながら通帳の０の数を数えている。
Karewa yatto gohyakuman-en tameta. Maiban hitoride niyaniya-shinagara

tsuuchoono zerono kazuo kazoeteiru.
He's finally saved ¥5,000,000. Now every night he grins to himself as he counts the zeros in his bankbook.

6) 犯人は刑事に問いつめられても、にやにや笑うだけで、肝心なことは何も話さなかった。
Hanninwa keijini toitsumeraretemo, niyaniya waraudakede, kanjinna kotowa nanimo hanasanakatta.
The criminal was questioned by the police detective, but he just smirked and said nothing of value.

ぬれる／しみる

■ *nureru* ■ *shimiru*

ぬれる ■ *nureru* ■ to get wet

水などの**液体が表面につく**ときや、**ついて水分を含む**とき使います（例1, 2, 3, 4）。

Nureru means that a liquid, such as water, adheres to the surface of something or that something is moist (ex.1, 2, 3, 4).

1) 川で遊んで服がぬれた。
Kawade asonde fukuga nureta.
(My) clothes got wet while I was playing in the river.

2) ゆうべ雨が降ったので道路がぬれている。
Yuube amega futtanode dooroga nureteiru.
It rained last night, so the streets are wet.

3) ぬれた手でコンセントをさわると危ない。
Nureta tede konsentoo sawaruto abunai.
It's dangerous to touch an electric outlet with wet hands.

4) 犬の鼻はいつもぬれている。
Inuno hanawa itsumo nureteiru.
Dogs' noses are always wet.

しみる

■ *shimiru*
■ to soak into ; to smart ; to sting ; to irritate 

①水(みず)などの**液体(えきたい)が**、ものに**少(すこ)しずつ入(はい)っていく**とき使(つか)います（例(れい)5, 6）。

Shimiru means that a liquid, such as water, penetrates slowly into something (ex.5, 6).

②**薬(くすり)・煙(けむり)**などで体(からだ)に**刺激(しげき)**を感(かん)じるとき（例(れい)7, 8, 9）、やさしさなどが、心(こころ)に深(ふか)く感(かん)じられるとき（例(れい)10, 11）使(つか)います。

It also means that one feels physical irritation from things such as medicine or smoke (ex.7, 8, 9). It can also mean a person is deeply moved by someone else's kindness (ex.10, 11).

---

5) ひどい雨(あめ)だったので、レインコートを着(き)ていたのに中(なか)までしみてしまった。
Hidoi ame dattanode, reinkootoo kiteitanoni nakamade shimiteshimatta.
The rain was so heavy that (I) got wet even though I wore a raincoat.

6) こぼれたミルクは、カーペットにしみていった。
Koboreta mirukuwa, kaapettoni shimiteitta.
The spilt milk soaked into the carpet.

7) 冷(つめ)たい水(みず)が、歯(は)にしみる。
Tsumetai mizuga, hani shimiru.
Cold water causes (my) teeth to ache.

8) 薬(くすり)が、傷口(きずぐち)にしみて痛(いた)い。
Kusuriga, kizuguchini shimite itai.
The medicine makes (my) wound hurt.

9) 煙(けむり)が目(め)にしみる。
Kemuriga meni shimiru.
The smoke irritates (my) eyes.

10) 本当(ほんとう)に困(こま)ったときには、他人(たにん)の親切(しんせつ)が身(み)にしみる。
Hontooni komatta tokiniwa, taninno shinsetsuga mini shimiru.
When (one) is really in trouble, he deeply appreciates the kindness of others.

11) 外国(がいこく)で1人(ひとり)で暮(く)らしていると、家族(かぞく)の大切(たいせつ)さが身(み)にしみてわかる。
Gaikokude hitoride kurashiteiruto, kazokuno taisetsusaga mini shimite wakaru.

Since (I) have lived alone in a foreign country, I have really come to understand the importance of family.

ねじる／ひねる

■*nejiru* ■*hineru*

ねじる

■*nejiru*
■to twist ; to screw ; to warp

ものの両端を、それぞれ**反対の方向に力を入れてまわす**ことです。片方の端を動かさないで、もう一方をまわすこともあります（例1, 2, 3, 4）。

To turn opposite sides of something in opposite directions, applying force. Also, to turn one side of something without moving the other (ex.1, 2, 3, 4).

1）座ったまま体をねじって後ろの戸棚の物をとったら、腰が痛くなってしまった。
Suwattamama karadao nejitte ushirono todanano monoo tottara, koshiga itaku natteshimatta.
When (I) twisted around to get something from the shelf behind me without getting up, my lower back started hurting.

2）古いくぎをペンチで抜こうとしてねじったら、折れてしまった。
Furui kugio penchide nukooto shite nejittara, oreteshimatta.
When (I) tried to twist out an old nail with a pair of pliers, it broke off.

3）針金を切るカッターがなかったので、ぐるぐるまわしてねじって切った。
Hariganeo kiru kattaaga nakattanode, guruguru mawashite nejitte kitta.
Since I didn't have a wire cutter, I twisted and twisted the wire until it broke.

4）警官は、つかまえた泥棒のうでをねじり上げて連行していった。
Keikanwa, tsukamaeta doroboono udeo nejiriagete renkooshiteitta.
The police officer twisted the arm of the thief he had caught and hauled him off to the police station.

ひねる ■ *hineru* ■ to rotate ; to twist 

ものの一部をまわすように、向きを変えることです。「ねじる」よりも軽い動作だという感じがあります（例5, 6, 7）。例８は考え込む・よくわからないというようすを表します。例９は、よく考えなければできないように工夫した問題のことです。

To adjust something by turning a part of it. The impression is that of a gentler action than *nejiru* (ex.5, 6, 7). In Example 8, it denotes puzzlement or having to think deeply. In Example 9, it describes a problem that is contrived so that one can't solve it without a lot of careful or involved thought.

5) このスイッチを右にひねると電気がつきます。
Kono suitchio migini hineruto denkiga tsukimasu.
If (you) rotate this switch to the right, the lights will come on.

6) 寒い日には水道管が凍って、蛇口をひねっても水が出ないことがあります。
Samui hiniwa suidookanga kootte, jaguchio hinettemo mizuga denai kotoga arimasu.
Sometimes on cold days the water pipes freeze, and water doesn't come out (even) when (you) turn the faucet.

7) このびんは栓抜きはいりません。ひねればあきます。
Kono binwa sennukiwa irimasen. Hinereba akimasu.
(You) don't need a bottle opener for this bottle. It'll open if you just twist (the cap).

8) 事故の原因はよくわからず、専門家も首をひねっている。
Jikono gen-inwa yoku wakarazu, senmonkamo kubio hinetteiru.
They haven't identified the cause of the accident;
even the specialists are racking their brains over it.

9) きょうの試験は、ひねった問題だったので、
成績はあまりよくないと思う。
Kyoono shikenwa, hinetta mondaidattanode,
seisekiwa amari yokunaito omou.
The questions on today's exam were tricky,
so (I) don't think I got a very good score.

ねっしん／ねっちゅう／むちゅう

■*nesshin* ■*netchuu* ■*muchuu*

ねっしん［熱心］

■*nesshin*
■eager ; earnest ; devoted 

仕事や**勉強**、あるいは何か**ものごと**を、**一生懸命にする**ようすを表します。「まじめさ・勤勉さ・意欲・熱意」などが感じられます。他人へのほめことばや評価に使い、自分には使いません（例1, 2, 3, 4, 5）。

Nesshin is used when one does something (work, study, etc.) the best one can. Feelings of seriousness, diligence, ambition, and enthusiasm are implied. It is used to compliment others, and therefore cannot be used to describe oneself (ex.1, 2, 3, 4, 5).

1) その講演会では、だれもが熱心に話を聞いていた。
Sono kooenkaidewa, daremoga nesshinni hanashio kiiteita.
Everybody at the lecture meeting listened intently to the speeches.

2) 彼は熱心な学生で、分からないところはすぐ聞きに来る。
Karewa nesshinna gakuseide, wakaranai tokorowa sugu kikini kuru.
He is a very eager student. Whenever he doesn't understand something, he quickly comes to ask about it.

3) 彼女は教育熱心で、息子をいい学校に入れたいと必死だ。
Kanojowa kyooiku-nesshinde, musukoo ii gakkooni iretaito hisshida.
She is very concerned about her son's education and is desperate to get him into a good school.

4) 彼女は難民へのボランティア活動に熱心だ。
Kanojowa nanmin-eno borantia-katsudooni nesshinda.
She is very involved in her volunteer work with refugees.

5) 彼女はまじめで何事にも熱心にとりくむ性格だ。
Kanojowa majimede nanigotonimo nesshinni torikumu seikakuda.
She is the type of person that does everything 100%.

ねっちゅう［熱中］

■*netchuu*
■absorbed in ; enthusiastic about 

ものごとに対して、「**好きだ・楽しい・興味**がある」などの理由で一生懸命になったり**集中**したりするようすを表します。「熱中している」の形で、多く使われます（例6, 7, 8, 9）。

This indicates that one strives to do well in or concentrates on something because he or she finds it pleasurable, fun, or interesting. The phrase *netchuu shiteiru* is commonly used (ex.6, 7, 8, 9).

---

6) 妹は今、お菓子作りに熱中している。
Imootowa ima, okashizukurini netchuushiteiru.
My sister is absorbed in making cakes now.

7) 父がテレビの野球に熱中しているときは、話しかけてもだめだ。
Chichiga terebino yakyuuni netchuushiteiru tokiwa, hanashikaketemo dameda.
It's no use talking to my father when he is concentrating on the baseball broadcast.

8) うちの子供は、ごはんも食べずにテレビゲームに熱中している。
Uchino kodomowa, gohanmo tabezuni terebi-geemuni netchuushiteiru.
My child is so engrossed in the video game that he has forgotton to eat.

9) 何か熱中してできるような趣味を持ちなさい。
Nanika netchuushite dekiruyoona shumio mochinasai.
(You) should find a hobby that you can really get interested in.

むちゅう［夢中］ ■*muchuu* ■crazy about 

何か一つのことに**心を奪われて**、ほかのことを考える余裕がない、**頭に入らない**という状態になってしまうようすを表します。**冷静さや理性的判断を失っている**という意味を含みます（例10, 11, 12, 13, 14）。「〜に熱中している」と「〜に夢中だ・夢中になっている」は趣味などについては同じように使います。

Muchuu indicates that one is so engrossed by one thing that he or she cannot think about anything else. It implies a loss of rationality or reason (ex. 10, 11, 12, 13, 14). The expressions *~ni netchuu shite iru*, *~ni muchuu da*, and *muchuu ni natte iru* are used in the same way when referring to a person's hobbies or interests.

---

10) 読書(どくしょ)に夢中(むちゅう)だったので、兄(あに)が部屋(へや)に入(はい)って来(き)たのに、気(き)がつかなかった。
Dokusyoni muchuu-dattanode, aniga heyani haittekitanoni, kigatsukanakatta.
(I) was so engrossed in reading that I didn't notice that my (elder) brother had come into the room.

11) 話(はなし)に夢中(むちゅう)で、つい電車(でんしゃ)を乗(の)り過(す)ごしてしまった。
Hanashini muchuude, tsui denshao norisugoshite-shimatta.
(I) was so involved in a conversation that I forgot to get off at my station.

12) 料理中(りょうりちゅう)に火(ひ)がカーテンに燃(も)えうつってしまい、私(わたし)は夢中(むちゅう)で火(ひ)を消(け)した。
Ryoorichuuni higa kaatenni moeutsutte-shimai, watashiwa muchuude hio keshita.
While I was cooking the curtain caught fire and I desperately put it out.

13) 彼女(かのじょ)は彼(かれ)に夢中(むちゅう)だ。
Kanojowa kareni muchuuda.
She is crazy about him.

14) 私(わたし)はただ逃(に)げるのに夢中(むちゅう)だったので、
足(あし)にけがをしているのも気(き)づかなかった。
Watashiwa tada nigerunoni muchuu-dattanode,
ashini kegao shiteirunomo kizukanakatta.
All I could think about was running away, so I didn't even notice that I had hurt my leg.

ねむる／ねる

■*nemuru* ■*neru*

ねむる［眠(ねむ)る］ ■*nemuru* ■to sleep

①人間(にんげん)やその他(た)の生物(せいぶつ)が目(め)を閉(と)じて、体(からだ)も心(こころ)も休(やす)んで意識(いしき)がない状態(じょうたい)のとき使(つか)います（例(れい)1, 2, 3, 4, 5）。
Nemuru denotes the unconscious state that human beings and animals enter when both eyes are closed and the body and mind are very relaxed (ex. 1,

2, 3, 4, 5).

②まだ**発見されていない・見出されていない**という意味です（例6, 7）。

It also means that something has not been discovered yet (ex.6, 7).

1）人間や多くの動物は、夜眠る。

Ningen-ya ookuno doobutsuwa, yoru nemuru.

Human beings and many animals sleep at night.

2）ゆりかごの中で赤ちゃんは、気持ち良さそうに眠っている。

Yurikagono nakade akachanwa, kimochi-yosasooni nemutteiru.

A baby is sleeping comfortably in the cradle.

3）一晩ぐっすり眠れば、疲れはとれる。

Hitoban gussuri nemureba, tsukarewa toreru.

If (you) sleep well all night, you'll feel as good as new.

4）ゆうべは暑くてよく眠れなかった。

Yuubewa atsukute yoku nemurenakatta.

Last night, it was so hot that (I) couldn't sleep well.

5）私は眠れない夜は、睡眠薬を飲む。

Watashiwa nemurenai yoruwa, suimin-yakuo nomu.

I take sleeping pills on nights when I can't sleep.

6）眠っている才能を訓練で呼びさますことができるという。

Nemutteiru sainoo-o kunrende yobisamasu kotoga dekiruto yuu.

It is said that undiscovered talents can be uncovered through practice.

7）海の底に難破船の宝が眠っている。

Umino sokoni nanpasenno takaraga nemutteiru.

The treasures of ancient shipwrecks are lying undiscovered on the bottom of the sea.

ねる［寝る］

■ *neru*
■ to go to bed, to (go to) sleep ; to lie down

---

①「眠る」と同じ意味で使います（例8, 9）。

Neru is used in the same sense as *nemuru* (ex.8, 9).

②**床につく**・「眠る」状態にもっていくとき使います（例10, 11）。

To go to bed; that is, the process of moving into the *nemuru* stage (ex.10, 11).

③体(からだ)を横(よこ)たえるとき使(つか)います（例(れい)12, 13）。②③は眠(ねむ)くなくてもよいのです。

To lie down (ex.12, 13). In definitions ② and ③, the subject does not have to be sleepy.

---

8) 私(わたし)は、毎日(まいにち)8時間(じかん)寝(ね)ます。
Watashiwa, mainichi hachijikan nemasu.
I sleep eight hours every day.

9) 寝(ね)ているときは、起(お)こさないでください。
Neteiru tokiwa, okosanaide kudasai.
Please don't wake me when (I) am sleeping.

10) 私(わたし)は、毎晩(まいばん)12時(じ)に寝(ね)る。
Watashiwa, maiban juunijini neru.
I go to bed at 12 o'clock every night.

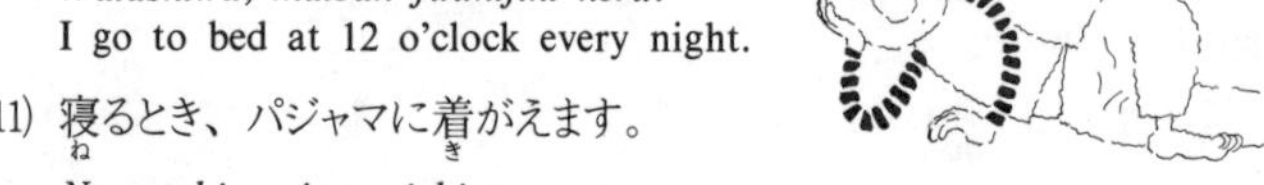

11) 寝(ね)るとき、パジャマに着(き)がえます。
Neru toki, pajamani kigaemasu.
(I) change into my pajamas before going to bed.

12) 寝(ね)ながらテレビを見(み)るのは目(め)に悪(わる)い。
Nenagara terebio mirunowa meni warui.
Watching TV while lying down is bad for (your) eyes.

13) 草(くさ)の上(うえ)に寝(ね)て、空(そら)を見(み)ていたら、眠(ねむ)くなった。
Kusano ueni nete, sorao miteitara, nemukunatta.
(I) lay down on the grass, and while looking at the sky, I became sleepy.

のんびり／ゆっくり

■ *nonbiri* ■ *yukkuri*

のんびり

■ *nonbiri*
■ peacefully ; leisurely 

心(こころ)や体(からだ)を休(やす)めて、何(なに)もしないで過(す)ごすようすを表(あらわ)します（例(れい)1, 2, 3, 4, 5）。緊張(きんちょう)がほぐれて、くつろいでいるようすです。「ゆっくり」が主(おも)に時間的(じかんてき)なことを

表すのに対し、「のんびり」は**精神的**なことを表します。「あの人はのんびりした人だ」と人の性格についても使いますが、時には「のろい・ぼんやりしている」などの感じがするので、あまり面と向かって言うのは失礼です。

Nonbiri is used when one rests one's mind or body by spending time not doing anything (ex.1, 2, 3, 4, 5), and generally refers to a tension-free, relaxed condition. While *yukkuri* is principally an expression of time, *nonbiri* refers to one's mental state. The expression *ano hito wa nonbiri shita hito da* may be used to describe a person's personality. However, it may be taken to mean 'slow-witted'; therefore, there are times when it should not be said directly to someone.

---

1) 休みの日は何もしないで、のんびりすごすことにしている。
Yasumino hiwa nanimo shinaide, nonbiri sugosu kotoni shiteiru.
(I've) decided that I'm not going to do anything and just relax on my day off.

2) 年をとったら、田舎でのんびり暮らしたいと思います。
Toshio tottara, inakade nonbiri kurashitaito omoimasu.
When (I) get old, I think I'd like to live quietly in the country.

3) 今朝はのんびりテレビを見ているひまはない。
Kesawa nonbiri terebio miteiru himawa nai.
I'm busy this morning, so (I) never have time to watch TV.

4) 川で釣りをしていると、のんびりした気分になります。
Kawade tsurio shiteiruto, nonbirishita kibunni narimasu.
When (I) go fishing at the river I feel carefree.

5) 彼女はのんびりしているけれど、仕事の期日は守ります。
Kanojowa nonbiri-shiteirukeredo, shigotono kijitsuwa mamorimasu.
She works leisurely but always gets her work done on time.

ゆっくり ■*yukkuri* ■slowly 

何かをするのに**時間をかける**ようすを表します（例6, 7, 8, 9, 10）。**時間的にゆとり**があるようすや、落ちついてくつろぐようすも表します。

Yukkuri is used when one takes his time doing something (ex.6, 7, 8, 9, 10). It implies that a lot of time is available or that one is unhurried.

6) 私の家から地下鉄の駅まで、ゆっくり歩いて７分です。
Watashino iekara chikatetsuno ekimade, yukkuri aruite nanafundesu.
It's just a seven minute stroll from my house to the subway station.

7) 疲れているときは、ゆっくりおふろに入って早く休んだほうがいい。
Tsukareteiru tokiwa, yukkuri ofuroni haitte hayaku yasunda hooga ii.
When (you're) tired, you should take a leisurely bath and go to bed early.

8) あわてないで、落ちついてゆっくり説明してください。
Awatenaide, ochitsuite yukkuri setsumei-shite kudasai.
Don't rush. Just quietly and slowly explain it to me, please.

9) 久しぶりにいらっしゃったんですから、どうぞゆっくりしていってください。
Hisashiburini irasshattan-desukara, doozo yukkurishiteitte kudasai.
It's been a long time since you've visited, so please make yourself at home for a while.

10) きょうは仕事の途中で寄っただけなので、ゆっくりしていられないんです。
Kyoowa shigotono tochuude yottadakenanode, yukkurishite-irarenaindesu.
I've dropped by while still on company time, so (I) can't stay long.

楽になってください

清水さんは、バーンズさんの家に招待されました。バーンズさんはソファーに腰をかけるように勧めると、こう言いました。「清水さん、よくいらっしゃいました。どうぞ楽になってください」

清水さんは考えました。「楽になる」は「苦労から解放されること」で、「生活が楽になる」は「貧乏だったのに、余裕が出てくること」です。清水さんは、生活が苦しいわけではありません。バーンズさんは何を気の毒だと思ったのでしょうか…？

「あ、そうか」と清水さんは気づきました。バーンズさんが言いたかったのは「どうぞ楽にしてください」つまり「くつろいでください」ということだったのです。まじめな顔でもう一度「どうぞ楽になってください」と言うバーンズさんに清水さんは、大笑いしながら「楽にしてください」か「お楽に（なさってください）」と言わなければならないことを教えてあげました。

Raku ni natte kudasai[1]

Mr. Shimizu was invited to the Burns' home. While showing him to the sofa Mr. Burns said, "Welcome Mr. Shimizu. *Doozo raku ni natte kudasai.*" Mr. Shimizu thought for a bit. *Raku ni naru*[2] means to be released from hardship; for example, *seikatsu ga raku ni naru*[3] means that one who was poor begins to live easier. Mr. Shimizu's life was not so difficult and he wondered why Mr. Burns felt sorry for him.

Then he suddenly realized what Mr. Burns meant. What he wanted to say was *raku ni shite kudasai,* which means 'please make yourself at home'. When Mr. Burns again said with a straight face, "*Doozo raku ni natte kudasai,*" Mr. Shimizu laughed out loud and told him he must say either "*Raku ni shite kudasai*" or "*O-raku ni* (*nasatte kudasai*)".

1 *please feel relieved* 2 *be relieved, at ease* 3 *living becomes easier*

はがす／はぐ／むく

■ *hagasu* ■ *hagu* ■ *muku*

はがす

■ *hagasu*
■ to peel ; to tear off 

ものの表面に、ぴったりとはりついている、紙や布などの薄いものを取りさることです（例1, 2, 3, 4）。

To take a thin and firmly attached object, for example, paper or cloth, off the surface of something (ex.1, 2, 3, 4).

1) 私は、アルバムから小さいころの写真を１枚はがした。
Watashiwa, arubamukara chiisai korono shashin-o ichimai hagashita.
I took a picture of myself when I was little out from a photo album.

2) きょう壁紙をはがして、あした新しい壁紙をはります。
Kyoo kabegamio hagashite, ashita atarashii kabegamio harimasu.
I'll peel off the old wallpaper today and put on the new wallpaper tomorrow.

3) 選挙のポスターをはがしてはいけません。
Senkyono posutaao hagashitewa ikemasen.
You mustn't tear down political campaign posters.

4) 看護婦は、傷のばんそうこうをそっとはがしてとりかえた。
Kangofuwa, kizuno bansookoo-o sotto hagashite torikaeta.
The nurse gently peeled the Band-Aid from the wound and replaced it.

はぐ

■ *hagu*
■ to peel ; to tear off 

もの の表面の薄いものを手で取りさることです（例5, 6, 7, 8)。**本来は取れないもの・一体になっているものを、乱暴に無理やり取る**ことです。

To remove the thin surface of something with one's hand (ex.5, 6, 7, 8). The surface being peeled is an original part of or has become one with the object ; therefore force is required.

---

5) 木の皮をはいで紙のかわりにした時代もある。
Kino kawao haide kamino kawarini shita jidaimo aru.
There was a time when the peeled bark of a tree was used as paper.

6) 原始人は、獣の皮をはいで敷物や衣服にした。
Genshijinwa, kemonono kawao haide shikimonoya ifukuni shita.
Primitive humans skinned large animals and used the hides for floor coverings and clothing.

7) どんなに起こしても起きないので、彼女は息子のふとんをはいだ。
*Donnani okoshitemo okinainode, kanojowa musukono futon**o *haida.* *p.611
Her son wouldn't get up no matter how many times she told him to, so she pulled the *futon* off him.

8) 彼(かれ)は、逃(に)げようとする男(おとこ)の仮面(かめん)をはいだ。
Karewa, nigeyooto suru otokono kamen-o haida.
He tore off the mask of the man who was attempting to flee.

むく ■*muku* ■to peel

中(なか)にあるものを取(と)り出(だ)すために、**外側(そとがわ)をおおっているものを取(と)りさる**ことです（例(れい)9, 10, 11, 12）。くだものや野菜(やさい)の皮(かわ)のように、「むく」ことに**無理(むり)や不(ふ)自然(しぜん)さを感(かん)じないもの**に使(つか)います。

To remove the outside of something in order to get to the middle (ex.9, 10, 11, 12). *Muku* is used when speaking of taking the skin off things like fruit or vegetables in which little force is required.

---

9) オレンジの皮(かわ)をむくと、部屋中(へやじゅう)にいい香(かお)りが広(ひろ)がった。
Orenjino kawao mukuto, heyajuuni ii kaoriga hirogatta.
When (I) peeled the orange its scent filled the room.

10) じゃがいもは、ゆでてから皮(かわ)をむくほうがおいしい。
Jagaimowa, yudetekara kawao muku hooga oishii.
Potatoes taste better if (you) peel them after boiling.

11) この工場(こうじょう)では、カキのからをむいて缶詰(かんづめ)にしています。

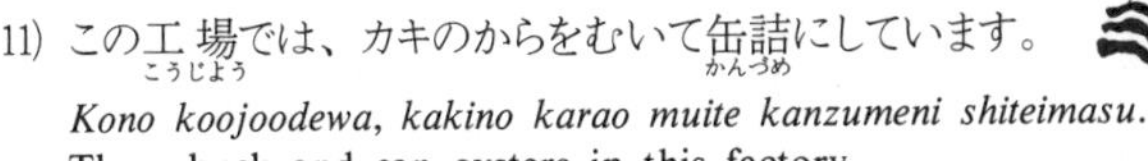

Kono koojoodewa, kakino karao muite kanzumeni shiteimasu.
They shuck and can oysters in this factory.

12) 私(わたし)は、りんごの皮(かわ)をむかないで丸(まる)かじりする。
Watashiwa, ringono kawao mukanaide marukajiri-suru.
I eat apples as they are, without peeling them.

（～た）ばかり／（～た）ところ

■(～*ta*) *bakari* ■(～*ta*) *tokoro*

（～た）ばかり ■(～*ta*) *bakari* ■just ～ed

ものごとが**行(おこな)われてから**、あまり**時間(じかん)が経(た)っていない**ということを表(あらわ)すとき使(つか)います。「さっき・今・たった今・３日前に・先月……」など過去のある時を指す語をいっしょに使うことがあり、「~たばかりだから~だ」という意味が、かくされている感じがあります（例1, 2, 3, 4）。

This expression indicates that something has just been done a short while ago. Words that refer to a certain time point, such as *sakki* (a little while ago), *ima* (now), *tatta ima* (just now), *mikka mae ni* (three days ago), and *sengetsu* (last month) are commonly used together with (~*ta*) *bakari* to imply that 'something has just been done, that's why...' (ex.1, 2, 3, 4).

1）電車は、さっき行ったばかりです。だからすぐには来ません。
Denshawa, sakki ittabakaridesu. Dakara suguniwa kimasen.
The train has just left, so another one won't come for a while.

2）彼らは、最近結婚したばかりです。
Karerawa, saikin kekkonshita-bakaridesu.
They have just gotten married (recently).

3）スミスさんは、日本に来たばかりで東京の地理はよくわかりません。
Sumisusanwa, Nihonni kitabakaride Tookyoono chiriwa yoku wakarimasen.
Mr. Smith has just come to Japan, that's why he is not familiar with the layout of Tokyo.

4）この靴は、買ったばかりです。
Kono kutsuwa, kattabakaridesu.
(I) have just bought these shoes.

（~た）ところ　■(~*ta*) *tokoro*　■have just ~ed

ものごとが行われた**すぐ後**である、ということを表すとき使います（例5, 6, 7）。「**たった今・今・ちょうど**」を、いっしょに使うことが多いです。そのことが行われた場所からそう離れてはいないという感じを含みます。

(~*ta*) *tokoro* indicates that something has just been done or finished (ex.5, 6, 7). Words such as *tatta ima* (just now), *ima* (now), and *choudo* (at this moment) are often used together with (~*ta*) *tokoro*. It is implied that the speaker is not far from the place where the action occurred.

5）乗客：８時30分発の新宿行きの電車は何番線ですか。
駅員：その電車なら、今行ったところですよ。

Jookyaku : *Hachiji sanjuppun-hatsuno Shinjukuyukino denshawa nanban-sendesuka?*
Passenger : What platform does the 8:30 train for Shinjuku leave from?
Ekiin : *Sono denshanara ima itta tokorodesuyo.*
Station employee : That train has just left.

6) A：食事(しょくじ)に行(い)きませんか。
B：たった今(いま)、食(た)べたところなんです。
A： *Shokujini ikimasenka?*
Would you like to go out to eat?
B： *Tattaima, tabeta tokoronandesu.*
I've just eaten.

7) スミス氏(し)：もしもし、ブラウンさんはいらっしゃいますか。
ブラウン夫人(ふじん)：ちょうど今(いま)、帰(かえ)って来(き)たところです。少(すこ)しお待(ま)ちください。
Sumisu-shi : *Moshimoshi, Buraunsanwa irasshaimasuka?*
Mr. Smith : Hello, is Mr. Brown in?
Braun-fujin : *Choodo ima kaettekita tokorodesu. Sukoshi omachi kudasai.*
Mrs. Brown : He has just come in. One moment, please.

はげしい／ひどい

■ *hageshii* ■ *hidoi*

はげしい［激(はげ)しい］ ■ *hageshii* ■ hard ; violent

ものごとの勢(いきお)いが、ひじょうに強(つよ)いようすを表(あらわ)します（例(れい)1, 2, 3, 4, 5）。程度(ていど)がふつうではないほどだという意味(いみ)を含(ふく)みます。

Hageshii indicates that the force of something is extremely strong (ex.1, 2, 3, 4, 5). It is implied that the level of strength is not normal.

1) 台風(たいふう)が近(ちか)づき、雨(あめ)と風(かぜ)が激(はげ)しくなった。
Taifuuga chikazuki, ameto kazega hageshiku natta.
As the typhoon approached the rain became much heavier.

2) ラグビーの試合(しあい)では、選手(せんしゅ)たちが激(はげ)しくぶつかり合(あ)う。
Ragubiino shiaidewa, senshutachiga hageshiku butsukariau.

In rugby games, the players fiercely collide into one another.

3) 彼女は、約束を守らなかった私を激しくせめた。
Kanojowa, yakusokuo mamoranakatta watashio hageshiku semeta.
She severely criticized me for breaking my promise.

4) あいかわらず、首都圏の人口増加が激しい。
Aikawarazu, shutokenno jinkoozookaga hageshii.
The population of the capital is increasing as dramatically as ever.

5) 夜中に、激しい腹痛で救急車を呼んだ。
Yonakani, hageshii fukutsuude kyuukyuushao yonda.
In the middle of the night (I) had severe stomach pains, so I called for an ambulance.

ひどい ■ *hidoi* ■ terrible

ものごとの状態や程度が、**度を超して悪い**ようすを表します（例6, 7, 8, 9, 10）。

Hidoi describes the condition or degree of something as being extremely bad (ex.6, 7, 8, 9, 10).

---

6) 私は先週、ひどい風邪をひきました。
Watashiwa senshyuu, hidoi kazeo hikimashita.
I had a terrible cold last week.

7) 雪がひどくなって、電車が止まってしまいました。
Yukiga hidoku natte, denshaga tomatte-shimaimashita.
The train stopped because the snow became worse.

8) 私は今回のテストの成績があまりにもひどかったので、がっかりしました。
Watashiwa konkaino tesutono seisekiga amarinimo hidokattanode, gakkari-shimashita.
I was disappointed because I did so poorly on the last test.

9) この地方は先日の台風で、ひどい被害をうけました。
Kono chihoowa senjitsuno taifuude, hidoi higaio ukemashita.
This area was heavily damaged in the last typhoon.

10) あなたにいじわるをするなんて、ほんとうにあの人はひどい人ですね。

Anatani ijiwaruo surunante, hontooni anohitowa hidoi hitodesune.
He really is a terrible person to tease you like that.

はじめて／はじめに／はじめは

■ *hajimete* ■ *hajime ni* ■ *hajime wa*

はじめて ［初(はじ)めて］ ■ *hajimete* ■ first time ; first

今(いま)までにない経験(けいけん)だ、今回(こんかい)が1回目(かいめ)だというようすを表(あらわ)すとき使(つか)います（例(れい)1, 2, 3, 4, 5, 6, 7, 8, 9）。

Hajimete states that some event or situation has not occurred or been experienced previously, and that this is the first time (ex.1, 2, 3, 4, 5, 6, 7, 8, 9).

1) 私(わたし)がスキーをするのは、きょうが初(はじ)めてです。
Watashiga sukiio surunowa, kyooga hajimetedesu.
Today is the first time I've ever skied.

2) 日本(にほん)へはなんども来(き)たが、名古屋(なごや)は初(はじ)めてだ。
Nihon-ewa nandomo kitaga, Nagoyawa hajimeteda.
(I've) been to Japan many times, but Nagoya is a first.

3) 私(わたし)は両親(りょうしん)にとって、初(はじ)めての子供(こども)です。
Watashiwa ryooshinnitotte, hajimeteno kodomodesu.
I am the first child for my parents.

4) きょう東京(とうきょう)に今年(ことし)初(はじ)めての雪(ゆき)が降(ふ)りました。
Kyoo Tookyooni kotoshi hajimeteno yukiga furimashita.
The first snow of the year fell in Tokyo today.

5) 彼(かれ)は外国人(がいこくじん)として初(はじ)めて大関(おおぜき)になった。
*Karewa gaikokujintoshite hajimete oozeki*ni natta.*
He is the first foreigner to become *oozeki.*
——* *Oozeki* is the second highest rank a wrestler can achieve in sumo, following *yokozuna.* *p.698

6) 彼女(かのじょ)は世界(せかい)で初(はじ)めて宇宙(うちゅう)に行(い)った女性(じょせい)だ。
Kanojowa sekaide hajimete uchuuni itta joseida.

She is the first woman to have been in space.

7) あなたに初めて会った時のことを、今でも覚えています。
Anatani hajimete atta tokino kotoo, imademo oboeteimasu.
Even now, (I) remember the first time I met you.

8) 初めて飛行機に乗った時は、とても緊張した。
Hajimete hikookini notta tokiwa, totemo kinchooshita.
The first time (I) flew in an airplane I was very nervous.

9) 病気になって初めて健康のありがたさがわかった。
Byookini natte hajimete kenkoono arigatasaga wakatta.
(I) came to appreciate good health for the first time after falling seriously ill.

はじめに［初めに］

■ *hajime ni*
■ in the beginning ; at first 

「なによりも前に・まず先に」ということを表すとき使います（例10, 11, 12, 13)。

Hajime ni indicates that something comes first and before anything else (ex.10, 11, 12, 13).

---

10) ブラジルのサッカーチームが11月の初めに来日する予定です。
Burajiruno sakkaachiimuga juuichigatsuno hajimeni rainichisuru yoteidesu.
The Brazilian soccer team is scheduled to come to Japan at the beginning of November.

11) けさの役員会では初めに新社長のあいさつがあった。
Kesano yakuinkaidewa hajimeni shinshachoono aisatsuga atta.
This morning's board of director's meeting began with a greeting from the new president.

12) きのうの入試では初めに論文試験が、次に面接が行われた。
Kinoono nyuushidewa hajimeni ronbunshikenga, tsugini mensetsuga okonawareta.
At yesterday's entrance exam there was an essay exam first, and then interviews.

13) その火事に初めに気がついたのは、わが家の犬だった。

Sono kajini hajimeni kigatsuitanowa, wagayano inudatta.
The first one to notice the fire was our dog.

はじめは［初めは］ ■hajime wa ■at first

順番や段階があることがらにおいて、**一番に行われる**ことがらを述べるとき使います（例14, 15, 16）。

This is used when mentioning an event that occurs first in a sequence or ordered set of events (ex.14, 15, 16).

14) どんな仕事も初めはむずかしいけれど、だんだん慣れてくるものだ。
Donna shigotomo hajimewa muzukashiikeredo, dandan naretekurumonoda.
Any job is difficult at first, but (you) get used to it gradually.

15) 私は初めはめがねをかけていましたが、今はコンタクトレンズをしています。
Watashiwa hajimewa meganeo kaketeimashitaga, imawa kontakutorenzuo shiteimasu.
At first I wore glasses, but these days I'm wearing contact lenses.

16) 初めは広く感じたこの家も、家族が増えて狭く感じるようになった。
Hajimewa hiroku kanjita kono iemo, kazokuga fuete semaku kanjiruyooni natta.
This house, which felt spacious at first, has come to feel small as the family has grown.

～はじめる／～だす

■*～hajimeru* ■*～dasu*

～はじめる［～始める］ ■*～hajimeru* ■to begin (doing)

それまでと**ちがう動作や行動にとりかかる**ことです。「暗くなり始める」のように、ちがう状態になりつつあるときにも使います（例1, 2, 3, 4, 5, 6, 7）。

To begin to do something different from the previous activity or behavior. As in *kuraku nari hajimeru* (to start to become dark), it is also used to show a change in a state or condition (ex.1, 2, 3, 4, 5, 6, 7).

1) 父は夕食の後、新聞を読み始めた。
Chichiwa yuushokuno ato, shinbun-o yomihajimeta.
My father began reading the newspaper after supper.

2) 音楽に合わせて、彼らは踊り始めた。
Ongakuni awasete, karerawa odorihajimeta.
They began to dance in time to the music.

3) うちの子供は、1歳になる前に歩き始めました。
Uchino kodomowa, issaini naru maeni arukihajime-mashita.
My child started to walk before he reached the age of one.

4) 私は先月からお花を習い始めました。
Watashiwa sengetsukara ohanao naraihajime-mashita.
I began to learn the art of flower arrangement last month.

5) 秋になり、木々の葉が色づき始めた。
Akini nari, kigino haga irozukihajimeta.
Autumn has come and the tree leaves have started to change color.

6) 太陽の光を受けて、屋根の雪がとけ始めた。
Taiyoono hikario ukete, yaneno yukiga tokehajimeta.
The snow on the roof began to melt after it was exposed to sunlight.

7) そろそろ電車が込み始める時間だ。
Sorosoro denshaga komihajimeru jikanda.
It's about the time that trains start to get crowded.

～だす [～出す]

■ *~dasu*
■ to begin (doing)

それまでと**ちがう動作や行動にとりかかる**ことや**ちがう状態になる**ことです(例8, 9, 10, 11, 12, 13)。「～始める」と同じように使いますが、「～出す」は「～始める」よりも**客観的**で、自分の意志での動作や行動には使いません。また「～始める」は単に、ある動作・行動・状態の初期だということですが、「～出す」は、その動作・行動・状態を予想していなかったという「**軽い驚きやとまどい**」の感情を含んでいます。

～dasu indicates that a new action starts which is different from the previous one, or that a new situation occurs (ex.8, 9, 10, 11, 12, 13). It has the same meaning as *～hajimeru*; however, it is used in more objective statements and, therefore, cannot be used to describe something one does willfully. Also, *～hajimeru* simply indicates that an action or situation is in its initial stage, whereas *～dasu* suggests that the speaker did not expect the action or situation to occur, and is therefore slightly surprised by it.

---

8) スタートの合図が鳴り、彼らはいっせいに走り出した。
Sutaatono aizuga nari, karerawa isseini hashiridashita.
The starting signal sounded, and they all started to run at the same time.

9) 彼の謝りかたが、あまりにもおかしかったので、初めは怒っていた彼女も笑い出してしまった。
Kareno ayamarikataga, amarinimo okashikattanode, hajimewa okotteita kanojomo waraidashite-shimatta.
Although she was angry in the beginning, the way he apologized was so funny that she burst into laughter.

10) 朝は晴れていたのに、午後になって急に雨が降り出した。
Asawa hareteitanoni, gogoni natte kyuuni amega furidashita.
In the morning the sky was clear, but in the afternoon it suddenly started to rain.

11) 迷子になっていた男の子は、お母さんの顔を見たとたんに泣き出した。
Maigoni natteita otokonokowa, okaasanno kaoo mitatotanni nakidashita.
The little boy who had been lost started to cry the minute he saw his mother.

12) オルゴールのふたを開けると、きれいな曲が流れ出した。
Orugooruno futao akeruto, kireina kyokuga nagaredashita.
As soon as (I) opened the lid of the music box, a beautiful melody began playing.

13) さっきから急に歯が痛み出した。早く歯医者に行かなくちゃ。
Sakkikara kyuuni haga itamidashita. Hayaku haishani ikanakucha.
A little while ago (my) tooth suddenly started hurting. I have to get to the dentist right away.

はたらく／しごと

■ *hataraku*　　■ *shigoto*

はたらく［働く］ ■ *hataraku* ■ to work

①**お金を得る**ためや生活していくために、人がそれぞれの役割を果たすことです（例1, 2, 3）。

To carry out a duty or job in order to earn money or to make a living (ex.1, 2, 3).

②**活動**する（例４）、**作用**する、**機能**する（例5, 6）ことです。例７は、悪いことをするという特別な使い方です。

Also, to be active, to function, or to operate (ex.4, 5, 6). Example 7 is a special use meaning 'to commit a crime'.

1) 彼女は朝から晩までよく働く。
Kanojowa asakara banmade yoku hataraku.
She works very hard from morning till night.

2) 私の父は大使館で働いている。
Watashino chichiwa taishikande hataraiteiru.
My father is working at the embassy.

3) 彼は、親の遺産が入ったので働かなくても食べていけるそうだ。
Karewa, oyano isanga haittanode hatarakanakutemo tabeteikerusooda.
It is said that he can live without working because he received an inheritance from his parents.

4) 私は朝、あまり頭が働かない。
Watashiwa asa, amari atamaga hatarakanai.
My head does not function very well in the morning. (I don't think well in the morning.)

5) 物が落ちるのは、引力が働いているからです。
Monoga ochirunowa, inryokuga hataraite-irukaradesu.
The reason things fall downward is because gravity is at work. (Things fall downward due to the effects of gravity.)

6) 天井のスプリンクラーが働いて、火事を消した。
Tenjoono supurinkuraaga hataraite, kajio keshita.
The sprinklers on the ceiling came on and extinguished the fire.

7) 彼は、盗みをはたらいて警察に捕まった。
Karewa, nusumio hataraite keisatsuni tsukamatta.
He was arrested by the police because he committed theft.

しごと［仕事］ ■ *shigoto* ■ work ; job

①職業や、人それぞれが受け持っているしなければならないこと・**労働**・**役割**のことです（例8, 9, 10)。
Shigoto refers to labor, duties, or work that someone is responsible for and must carry out (ex.8, 9, 10).

②「仕事をする」の形で、動詞として使います（例11, 12, 13)。
It is used as a verb in the form *shigoto o suru* (ex.11, 12, 13).

---

8) 私の仕事は看護婦です。
Watashino shigotowa kangofudesu.
I'm a nurse by occupation.

9) 学生は、勉強するのが仕事です。
Gakuseiwa, benkyoosurunoga shigotodesu.
A student's job is to study.

10) あしたは日曜日ですが、仕事があるので事務所へ行きます。
Ashitawa nichiyoobidesuga, shigotoga arunode jimushoe ikimasu.
Even though tomorrow is Sunday, (I) will go to the office because I have some work to do.

11) 兄は、朝9時から夕方5時まで、会社で仕事をします。
Aniwa, asa kujikara yuugata gojimade, kaishade shigotoo shimasu.
My (elder) brother works at his company from 9:00 am to 5:00 pm.

12) 仕事をしているときは、じゃまをしないでください。
Shigotoo shiteiru tokiwa, jamao shinaide kudasai.
Don't bother (me) when I'm working.

13) 彼は、仕事をしていないので収入がない。
Karewa, shigotoo shiteinainode shuunyuuga nai.
Because he doesn't have a job, he doesn't have any income.

はなす／いう／しゃべる

■ *hanasu* ■ *iu* ■ *shaberu*

はなす［話す］ ■ *hanasu* ■ to speak ; to talk

①内容のあることを**口に出して伝える**とき使います。伝えることが目的なので**必ず相手があり**、その相手が「聞こう・答えよう」という態度をとることを前提としています（例1, 2, 3）。

To speak about a particular subject. It is implied that the speaking is for the purpose of communication. Therefore, there needs to be a listener, who it is assumed is willing to listen or respond (ex.1, 2, 3).

②ある国の言語を理解し、口に出すとき「〜語を話す」と使います（例4, 5）。

In the form '(language) *~go o hanasu*' it means to be able to comprehend and converse in a particular language (ex.4, 5).

1) 彼はいつも、小さい声で話す。
Karewa itsumo, chiisai koede hanasu.
He always speaks softly.

2) もっとゆっくり話してください。
Motto yukkuri hanashite kudasai.
Please speak more slowly.

3) 母は、私の生まれた時のことを話してくれた。
Hahawa, watashino umareta tokino kotoo hanashitekureta.
My mother told me about the time when I was born.

4) 彼は、ドイツ語と日本語を話す。
Karewa, Doitsugoto Nihongoo hanasu.
He speaks German and Japanese.

5) 私は、ガーナ人の友だちと英語で話します。
Watashiwa, Gaanajinno tomodachito Eigode hanashimasu.
I speak in English with my Ghanaian friend.

いう［言う］ ■*iu* ■to say ; to speak

①ものごとを**ことば**（言語）**で表現する**ことです。ことばや音声を口に出すときは、**必ずしも相手がいなくてもかまいません**。相手がいるときは結果的にものごとを伝えることになりますし、一方的に告げるという意味も強く含みます（例6, 7, 8, 9, 10）。したがって、「話し合い」が、どうしようかと発展的に意見を出し合うのに対し、「言い合い」は自分の意見や考えを一方的にぶつける「口げんか」を意味します。

To express something with words. Unlike *hanasu*, a listener is not required. If there is a listener, communication may occur; however *iu* implies 'speaking to' rather than 'speaking with' a person (ex.6, 7, 8, 9, 10). Therefore, *hanashi-ai* would mean a discussion where the participants exchange ideas, while *ii-ai* would be an argument, where the participants speak out their own (opposing) opinions.

②ものごとを客観的に述べるときや説明するとき、「〜ということ（もの）」などのように使います（例11, 12）。

Iu is also used in expressions like ～*to iu koto* (*mono*) to state or explain something objectively (ex.11, 12).

③音を出すことです（例13, 14）。

To make a sound or a noise (ex.13, 14).

---

6) 彼はときどきひとりごとを言う。
Karewa tokidoki hitorigotoo yuu.
He sometimes talks to himself.

7) あの歌手がテレビに出ると妹はキャーキャー言う。
Ano kashuga terebini deruto imootowa kyaakyaa yuu.
Whenever that singer appears on TV, my younger sister screams in excitement.

8) そんなことはやめろと言ったのに……。

Sonna kotowa yameroto ittanoni…
(I) told (you) to stop it, and yet…

9) 「きみの顔など二度と見たくない。」と彼は言った。
"*Kimino kaonado nidoto mitakunai.*" *to karewa itta.*
He said, "(I) never want to see your face again."

10) 天気予報では、あしたは雨になると言っていた。
Tenkiyohoodewa, ashitawa ameni naruto itteita.
The weather forecast said it will rain tomorrow.

11) 人の心というのは不思議なものだ。
Hitono kokoroto yuunowa fushigina monoda.
What we call 'the heart' is a mysterious thing.

12) あの部屋にゆうれいが出るという話を信じますか。
Ano heyani yuureiga deruto yuu hanashio shinjimasuka?
Do (you) believe the story about a ghost that appears in that room?

13) 私の自転車はブレーキをかけるとキーキーいう。
Watashino jitenshawa bureekio kakeruto kiikii yuu.
The brakes of my bicycle go 'squeak, squeak'.

14) この家は古いので、ちょっとの風でも窓がガタガタいう。
Kono iewa furuinode, chottono kazedemo madoga gatagata yuu.
This house is old, so even when there is only a slight wind the windows rattle loudly.

しゃべる

■ *shaberu*
■ to converse ; to chat

---

①たいして**内容のない**ことを、あまり考えもなく口にするとき使います。自分が**楽しむ**その場限りのことです（例15, 16）。時には、**うるさい**と感じられることもあります。

To casually utter something that has not much content, often only to pass the time (ex.15, 16).
It may sometimes be seen as annoying by other people.

②**言ってはいけないことを他人に言って**しまうとき使います（例17, 18）。

To gossip or say something that must not be said to others (ex.17, 18).

---

15) 授業中しゃべってばかりいて、うるさい学生だ。

Jugyoochuu shabette bakariite, urusai gakuseida.
That student is so annoying because he is constantly chattering during class.

16) 映画館で、前の人がずっとしゃべっていたので、よく聞こえなかった。

Eigakande, maeno hitoga zutto shabette itanode, yoku kikoenakatta.
At the movie theater, (I) couldn't hear the movie very well because the person in front of me was constantly chatting.

17) これはここだけの話です。誰にもしゃべらないでください。

Korewa kokodakeno hanashidesu. Darenimo shaberanaide kudasai.
This is only between you and me. Please don't tell anybody.

18) あんなに口止めされていたのに、ついうっかり人にしゃべってしまった。

Annani kuchidomesarete itanoni, tsui ukkari hitoni shabette-shimatta.
(I) was told again and again not to talk about it, but being careless, I let it slip out.

はねる/はずむ

■ *haneru* ■ *hazumu*

はねる［跳ねる］ ■ *haneru* ■ to jump 

ものが、**とびあがること**です。そのもの自体にとびあがる力がある場合（例1, 2, 3）と液体などが、とび散る場合があります（例4, 5, 6）。自動車が人などをひいてしまうことも「はねる」と言います（例7）。

To jump or spring up. *Haneru* is used when an object jumps under its own power (ex.1, 2, 3), or when a liquid or other substance splashes (ex.4, 5, 6). Also, to hit or knock down someone or something with a vehicle (ex.7).

1) かえるがはねて、池にとびこんだ。

Kaeruga hanete, ikeni tobikonda.

The frog sprang up and jumped into the pond.

2) 野原を歩いていたら、足もとでバッタがはねた。
Noharao aruiteitara, ashimotode battaga haneta.
As (I) walked through the field, grasshoppers flew up about my feet.

3) ポップコーンは、はねる音がしなくなったらできあがりです。
Poppukoonwa, haneru otoga shinakunattara dekiagaridesu.
Popcorn is done when the popping sound stops.

4) 天ぷらを揚げていたら、油がはねて手にやけどをした。
Tenpurao ageteitara, aburaga hanete teni yakedoo shita.
When (I) was frying *tempura*, the oil splattered and I burned my hand.

5) 食器を洗っていたら、水がはねて服がぬれてしまった。
Shokkio aratteitara, mizuga hanete fukuga nureteshimatta.
While (I) was washing the dishes, water splashed and my clothes got wet.

6) 雨の日は、泥水をはねないように気をつけて運転してください。
Ameno hiwa, doromizuo hanenaiyooni kiotsukete untenshite kudasai.
Please be careful on rainy days to drive so you don't splatter mud (on anyone).

7) 息子は、バイクにはねられてけがをした。
Musukowa, baikuni hanerarete kegao shita.
My son was hit by a motorcycle and injured.

はずむ［弾む］

■ *hazumu*
■ to bounce ; to spring 

---

①ボールなどのように**弾力のあるものが**、かたいものにぶつかって、**上にはね返る**ことです（例8, 9）。

To bounce or spring up or back after hitting a hard surface. It is used especially for resilient objects, such as balls (ex.8, 9).

②とてもうれしくて、明るく活気づいているとき、例10, 11, 12のように使います。

Hazumu is also used, as in Examples 10, 11 and 12, to express liveliness, cheerfulness, or exhilaration.

---

8) 彼のけったボールは、大きく弾んで柵の外へとんでいった。

Kareno ketta booruwa, ookiku hazunde sakuno sotoe tondeitta.
The ball he kicked bounced high and flew over the fence.

9) 空気の抜けたボールは、弾まない。
Kuukino nuketa booruwa, hazumanai.
A deflated ball doesn't bounce.

10) 帰って来ると息子は、「試合に勝ったよ」と、弾んだ声でいった。

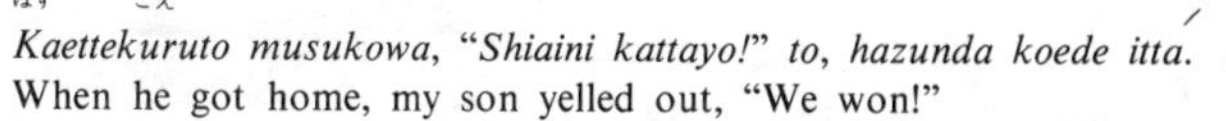

Kaettekuruto musukowa, "Shiaini kattayo!" to, hazunda koede itta.
When he got home, my son yelled out, "We won!"

11) 夕食の食卓を囲んで家族で話が弾んでいる。
Yuushokuno shokutakuo kakonde kazokude hanashiga hazundeiru.
The whole family is having a lively conversation gathered around the dinner table.

12) あしたはデートだと思うと、心が弾む。
Ashitawa deetodato omouto, kokoroga hazumu.
Just thinking about (my) date tomorrow makes me all excited.

はやい／すばやい／すばしっこい

■ *hayai* ■ *subayai* ■ *subashikkoi*

はやい ［速い・早い］ ■ *hayai* ■ fast ; early 

①ものごとをする**時間が短い・時間がかからない**というようすを表します。**動作**や**行動**に使います（例1, 2, 3)。

Hayai indicates that little or no time is required to do something. It may be used for action or behavior (ex.1, 2, 3).

②時刻・時期について使い、「まだその時刻・時期ではない」（例4, 5)、「時間が遅くない」（例6, 7)、「簡単だ・手間がかからない」（例８）などのようすを表します。例9, 10は、「今すぐに・急いで」の意味です。
①は「速い」と書き、②は「早い」と書きます。

When referring to time or a period of time, it indicates "it's not yet time..."

(ex.4, 5), 'it's not late (early)' (ex.6, 7), or 'it's simple and does not take time to do' (ex.8). In Examples 9 and 10, it means 'right now', or 'in a hurry (as soon as possible)'.
In definition ① the *kanji* 速い is used, while in ② 早い is used.

---

1) 私より兄のほうが足が速い。
Watashiyori anino hooga ashiga hayai.
My (older) brother runs faster than I do.

2) これは、世界一速い飛行機です。
Korewa, sekaiichi hayai hikookidesu.
This is the world's fastest airplane.

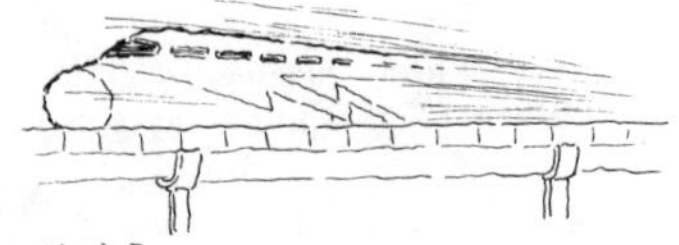

3) もっと速く歩かないと、電車に乗り遅れてしまう。
Motto hayaku arukanaito, denshani noriokureteshimau.
If (you) don't walk faster, you will be late for the train.

4) 庭のいちごはまだ赤くなっていないから、食べるには早い。
Niwano ichigowa mada akakunatteinaikara, taberuniwa hayai.
The strawberries in (our) yard have not turned red yet, so it is too early to eat them.

5) しゃべれるようになったばかりの子供に、字を教えようなんて、まだ早いよ。
Shabereruyooni nattabakarino kodomoni, jio oshieyoonante, mada hayaiyo.
It's too early to teach the alphabet to a child who has just started to talk.

6) うちのそばのパン屋は、朝早くから店を開けている。
Uchino sobano pan-yawa, asa hayakukara miseo aketeiru.
The bakery near my house is open from early in the morning.

7) あしたは遠足だから、早く寝て早く起きよう。
Ashitawa ensokudakara, hayaku nete hayaku okiyoo.
(I) will go to bed early tonight and wake up early in the morning, because tomorrow I'm going on an outing.

8) この仕事なら、人に頼むより自分でやったほうが早い。
Kono shigotonara, hitoni tanomuyori jibunde yatta hooga hayai.
With this job, it's faster to do it myself than to ask someone else to do it.

9) 火事だ、早く逃げろ。

Kajida, hayaku nigero!
Fire! Get away quickly!

10) 早(はや)く元気(げんき)になってください。
Hayaku genkini nattekudasai.
Please get well soon.

すばやい
■ *subayai*
■ quick 

一瞬(いっしゅん)だと感(かん)じるほど、**動作(どうさ)や行動(こうどう)が速(はや)い・機敏(きびん)だ**というようすを表(あらわ)します（例(れい)11, 12, 13, 14, 15）。

This indicates that someone's action or behavior is so quick that it looks 'momentary' or 'split-second' (ex.11, 12, 13, 14, 15).

11) カメレオンは、虫(むし)をすばやく舌(した)でつかまえる。
Kamereonwa, mushio subayaku shitade tsukamaeru.
The chameleon catches insects swiftly with its tongue.

12) どろぼうは、塀(へい)をすばやく乗(の)り越(こ)えて逃(に)げていった。
Doroboowa, heio subayaku norikoete nigeteitta.
The thief quickly climbed over the wall and ran away.

13) 彼(かれ)は計算(けいさん)がすばやい。
Karewa keisanga subayai.
He is very fast at calculating.

14) 彼女(かのじょ)は、先生(せんせい)の質問(しつもん)にすばやく答(こた)えた。
Kanojowa, senseino shitsumonni subayaku kotaeta.
She promptly answered the teacher's question.

15) 彼(かれ)はものごとの決断がすばやいと評判(ひょうばん)だ。
Karewa monogotono ketsudanga subayaito hyoobanda.
He has a reputation for having a quick decision.

すばしっこい
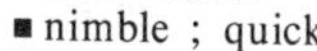
■ *subashikkoi*
■ nimble ; quick 

とても身軽(みがる)に、**あちらこちらと動(うご)き回(まわ)ったり逃(に)げ回(まわ)ったりする**ようすを表(あらわ)しま

す。比較的小さい人間や動物の動きについて使います（例16, 17, 18)。

Subashikkoi indicates that someone or something moves or runs around very swiftly. It refers to the movements of humans or animals that are relatively small (ex.16, 17, 18).

---

16) ぼくがつかまえようとしたら、ねずみはすばしっこく逃げてしまった。

Bokuga tsukamaeyooto-shitara, nezumiwa subashikkoku nigeteshimatta.
When I tried to catch the mouse, it nimbly fled.

17) 少年は、サッカーチームの中でいちばん小柄だけれど、すばしっこいのですぐにボールをうばう。

Shoonenwa, sakkaa-chiimuno nakade ichiban kogarada-keredo, subashikkoinode suguni booruo ubau.
Although that boy is the smallest on the soccer team, he is very quick so he steals the ball easily.

18) 子猿は、木から木へすばしっこくとび移って遊んでいる。

Kozaruwa, kikara kie subashikkoku tobiutsutte asondeiru.
The baby monkeys are playing by jumping swiftly from tree to tree.

はやる／にんき

■ *hayaru* ■ *ninki*

はやる

■ *hayaru*
■ to spread ; to be popular 

---

①世の中の人びとの間で**好かれている、広まっている**という意味で、一時的なものです（例1, 2, 3)。

This word means that something is liked and widely used for a brief period (ex.1, 2, 3).

②**病気が**多くの人の間にうつって**広がる**ことです（例４)。

(Of a disease) to spread among a large number of people (ex.4).

③店や病院などの評判がよく、客や患者などがたくさん来ることです（例5, 6, 7)。「はやり」は名詞です（例８)。名詞としての「はやり」は③の意味には使

いません。また「〜さんは、はやっている」などと人については使いません。

Hayaru describes places such as stores or hospitals as having a very good reputation and that many people come to visit (ex.5, 6, 7). *Hayari* is the noun form (ex.8), but it cannot be used in the meaning of definition ③. Also, *hayatte iru* cannot be used when speaking of people.

---

1) 今年の秋は、茶色がはやるらしい。
Kotoshino akiwa, chairoga hayarurashii.
Brown seems to be the popular color this fall.

2) 今、若い人たちの間でテニスがはやっている。
Ima, wakai hitotachino aidade tenisuga hayatteiru.
These days, tennis is popular among young people.

3) 10年前にはやった歌が、このごろまたはやっている。
Juunenmaeni hayatta utaga, konogoro mata hayatteiru.
Songs that were popular ten years ago are now popular again.

4) 悪い風邪がはやっているから、気をつけたほうがいい。
Warui kazega hayatteirukara, kio tsuketa hooga ii.
Be careful; a terrible flu is going around.

5) このすし屋は安くておいしいのでとてもはやっている。
Kono sushiyawa yasukute oishiinode totemo hayatteiru.
This *sushi* shop is very popular because its *sushi* is cheap and delicious.

6) あの歯医者はとてもはやっている。きっと腕がいいのでしょう。
Ano haishawa totemo hayatteiru. Kitto udega iinodeshoo.
That dentist is very popular. He must be very good.

7) 駅前のラーメン屋はあまりはやらなかったので、つぶれてしまった。
Ekimaeno raamen-yawa amari hayaranakatta-node, tsuburete-shimatta.*
The *raamen* shop in front of the station didn't get much business, so it closed up. *p.129

8) 彼女はいつもはやりの服を着ている。
Kanojowa itsumo hayarino fukuo kiteiru.
She is always wearing fashionable clothes.

にんき［人気］ ■ *ninki* ■ be popular 

世の中の**多くの人が好き**だと思っていること、**もてはやされている**ことです。人にも使います（例9,10,11,12,13,14）。したがって病気など悪いことには使いません。

Ninki indicates that something is liked by many people ; *ninki* may also be used when speaking of people being well liked (ex.9, 10, 11, 12, 13, 14), but it is not used when speaking of bad things such as diseases.

---

9) 動物園のコアラは、子供たちに人気がある。
Doobutsuenno koarawa, kodomotachini ninkiga aru.
The koalas in the zoo are very popular with the children.

10) あの歌手は歌はへただけれど人気がある。
Ano kashuwa utawa hetadakeredo ninkiga aru.
That singer does not sing very well but is very popular.

11) 今、日本で一番人気があるスポーツは何ですか。
Ima, Nihonde ichiban ninkiga aru supootsuwa nandesuka?
What is the most popular sport in Japan now?

12) モーツァルトの作品は、いつの世でも人気がある。
Mootsuarutono sakuhinwa, itsuno yodemo ninkiga aru.
Mozart's music has always been popular throughout the generations.

13) あの先生は、学生に人気がない。
Ano senseiwa, gakuseini ninkiga nai.
That teacher is not popular with students.

14) 犬のタローは、我が家の人気者だ。
Inuno Taroowa, wagayano ninkimonoda.
Our dog, Taro, is the favorite in our family.

ごはんを食べましたか？

サムが下宿している家の奥さんはとても親切で、彼をほんとうの息子のようにかわいがってくれます。彼がこの家に来たばかりのことです。「おはよう、サム。ちゃんとごはんを食べましたか」「いいえ」とサムは答えました。それを聞いた奥さんは、「じゃあ、ごはんを作ってあげましょう」と言いました。するとサムは困った顔をして、「でもおなかがいっぱいです」と言いました。奥さんは心配そうに「だってまだごはんを食べていないのでしょう、気分が悪いのですか」と聞きました。「あのう…ごはんは食べていないけれど、パンを食べました」奥さんは笑い出しました。日本では、炊いたお米のことを「ごはん」と言いますが、「食事をする」ことも「ごはんを食べる」というのです。「さあ、ごはんを食べましょう」と言っても「ごはんつぶ」のことではなく、パンやスパゲティを食べることもあるのです。

「酒を飲む」と言うときの「酒」が、ビール、ワイン、ウイスキー、日本酒など全てのアルコール飲料を指すのと同じことですね。

Have you eaten yet?

The landlady of the boarding house Sam is staying at is very kind and takes care of him as if he were her own son.

Soon after he moved in she said, "Good morning, Sam. *Chanto gohan o tabemashita ka*[1]*?*" "No," Sam replied. Then she said, "*Jaa, gohan* *o tsukutte agemashoo.*[2]" Sam, with a perplexed look, said, "But I am full." She then asked, "*Datte mada gohan o tabete inai no deshoo*[3]. Are you OK?" Sam answered, "*Anoo... gohan wa tabete inai keredo, pan o tabemashita*[4]." She started to laugh after realizing what was wrong. In Japan, cooked rice is called *gohan*, but to have a meal is also expressed as *gohan o taberu*.

Therefore, if someone says "*Saa, gohan o tabemashoo*[5]," they may not necessarily mean rice. What they may mean is bread, spaghetti or any kind of food.

The same meaning is taken when one says *sake o nomu*[6], as they may want to drink beer, wine or whiskey. The word *sake* refers to all kinds of alcoholic beverages.

1 *Have you eaten yet?*
2 *Well, I'll prepare something for you to eat.*
3 *You haven't eaten yet, right?*
4 *I didn't eat rice. I ate some bread.*
5 *Let's eat (some food).*
6 *to drink (an alcoholic beverage).*

はんせいする／こうかいする

■*hansei suru* ■*koukai suru*

はんせいする［反省する］

■*hansei suru*
■to reflect on

自分のしたことが悪くなかったかどうかを、振り返ったり、**まちがっていた点や悪かった点を**よく考えて、**くり返さないように**しようと思うことです（例1, 2, 3, 4）。

This is used when a person thinks back on something he has done to determine if it was wrong (bad) or not. *Hansei suru* means to think hard about a mistake or a wrong one has committed so as not to repeat it in the future (ex.1, 2, 3, 4).

1）試合の後で私たちのチームは、きょうの試合の反省をした。
Shiaino atode watashitachino chiimuwa, kyoono shiaino hanseio shita.
Our team reflected on our play after the game.

2) 自分がまちがっていたら、すなおに反省して謝るべきだ。
Jibunga machigatteitara, sunaoni hanseishite ayamarubekida.
If (you've) made a mistake, then you should think about it frankly, and then apologize.

3) あれだけ大きなミスを犯したのに、彼は反省しているようには見えない。
Aredake ookina misuo okashitanoni, karewa hanseishiteiru yooniwa mienai.
Even though he committed such a big error, he doesn't seem to regret it at all.

4) 今回のできごとで、いかに自分の考えが甘かったか大いに反省させられた。
Konkaino dekigotode, ikani jibunno kangaega amakattaka ooini hanseisa-serareta.
This latest incident has made me think hard that maybe (I) was too optimistic.

こうかいする［後悔する］

■ *koukai suru*
■ to regret

そのことがら自体が良いことか悪いことか、というのではなく、このような結果になる道を選んだことを**残念だ・しまった・ああすればよかった**、などと思うことです（例5, 6, 7）。

To regret a choice one has made, i.e., to think 'I should have acted differently' (ex.5, 6, 7). *Koukai suru* does not mean to consider whether an act or event was in itself good or bad.

---

5) 若いうちにたくさん勉強しておかないと、いつか後悔する。
Wakaiuchini takusan benkyooshite-okanaito, itsuka kookaisuru.
If (you) don't study hard while you're young, you are going to regret it someday.

6) こんなに値が上がるのなら、あのときもっとたくさん株を買っておけば良かったと、後悔している。
Konnani nega agarunonara, ano toki motto takusan kabuo katteokeba yokattato, kookaishiteiru.
Stock prices have really gone up, so now (I) regret not buying more stock back then.

7) 今さら自分の犯した罪を後悔しても、もうとりかえしがつかない。

Imasara jibunno okashita tsumio kookaishitemo, moo torikaeshiga tsukanai.
It doesn't matter that (you) now regret your crime, because what's done is done.

はんたい／ぎゃく

■*hantai* ■*gyaku*

はんたい［反対］ ■*hantai* ■opposite

---

①「大きい」と「小さい」、「暑い」と「寒い」などのように、**対になっているものの**一方と他方との**関係**を表します（例1, 2, 3, 4）。

Hantai expresses an opposing relationship between two things, as in 'big and small' or 'hot and cold' (ex.1, 2, 3, 4).

②相手の意見や考え方に、**賛成しない**という意味を表します（例5, 6）。

It also expresses that one does not agree with the opinions or way of thinking of his partner (ex.5, 6).

③「反対に」の形で、「逆に」と同様に、期待されることとは異なった状態になったことへの意外さ・驚きを表します（例７）。

When used in the form *hantai ni* it has the same meaning as *gyaku ni*, i.e.. to indicate that something has turned out differently from what one had anticipated (ex.7).

---

1) 「広い」の反対は「狭い」です。
'Hiroi' no hantaiwa 'semai' desu.
The opposite of wide is narrow.

2) 道路のこちら側は空いているのに、反対車線はずいぶん込んでいる。
Doorono kochiragawawa suiteirunoni, hantaishasenwa zuibun kondeiru.
Although this side of the road is empty, the opposite lane is quite crowded.

3) 私は小さい頃、よく靴を左右反対にはいた。
Watashiwa chiisai koro, yoku kutsuo sayuu hantaini haita.
When I was a child I often put my shoes on the wrong feet.

4) 乾電池(かんでんち)は、プラスとマイナスを反対(はんたい)に入(い)れないように気(き)をつけてください。
Kandenchiwa, purasuto mainasuo hantaini irenaiyooni kiotsukete kudasai.
Please be careful not to put the batteries in with their plus and minus signs switched.

5) 私(わたし)は、あなたの意見(いけん)には反対(はんたい)です。
Watashiwa, anatano ikenniwa hantaidesu.
I don't agree with your opinion.

6) 私(わたし)はだれに反対(はんたい)されても、決(き)めたことはやり通(とお)すつもりです。
Watashiwa dareni hantaisaretemo, kimeta kotowa yaritoosu tsumoridesu.
I don't care who opposes me, I'll do things the way I want to.

7) 病気(びょうき)の友達(ともだち)のお見舞(みま)いに行(い)ったら、反対(はんたい)に元気(げんき)づけられた。
Byookino tomodachino omimaini ittara, hantaini genkizukerareta.
(I) went to visit my sick friend to comfort him, but he ended up encouraging me instead.

ぎゃく［逆(ぎゃく)］ ■*gyaku* ■reverse ; converse ; opposite

ものごとの**順序(じゅんじょ)・方向(ほうこう)・位置(いち)**などが、**本来(ほんらい)あるべき状態(じょうたい)ではなく**、左(ひだり)が右(みぎ)になったり、後(うし)ろが前(まえ)になったりしているようすを表(あらわ)します（例(れい)8, 9, 10)。また、期待(きたい)していたことや**当然(とうぜん)そうなるはず**のこととは、**ちがう状態(じょうたい)**になったとき使(つか)います（例(れい)11, 12)。

Gyaku indicates that the order, direction, position, etc. of something is not the way it should be; as in, left is where right should be, or the back is now the front (ex.8, 9, 10). It may also mean that something that was expected to turn out one way actually turns out differently (ex.11, 12).

---

8) 車(くるま)を買(か)ってから免許(めんきょ)をとるなんて、順序(じゅんじょ)が逆(ぎゃく)です。
Kurumao kattekara menkyoo torunante, junjoga gyakudesu.
(You) bought a car before you got your license? That's doing things backwards.

9) 一方通行(いっぽうつうこう)の道(みち)を逆(ぎゃく)に走(はし)って、パトカーにつかまった。
Ippootsuukoono michio gyakuni hashitte, patokaani tsukamatta.
A police car caught me when (I) drove the wrong way down a one-way street.

10) 鏡に映ったものは、左右が逆になる。
Kagamini utsutta monowa, sayuuga gyakuni naru.
Things reflected in a mirror are reversed.

11) 彼にごちそうしようと思っていたのに、逆にごちそうになってしまった。
Kareni gochisooshiyooto omotteitanoni, gyakuni gochisooni natteshimatta.
(I) had planned to treat him to a meal, but I ended up being treated by him.

12) もうけようと思って株に手を出したら、逆に損をしてしまった。
Mookeyooto omotte kabuni teo dashitara, gyakuni son-o shiteshimatta.
(I) bought some stock expecting to make a profit, but I wound up losing money.

ひかる／かがやく

■ *hikaru* ■ *kagayaku*

ひかる［光る］ ■ *hikaru* ■ to shine ; to flash 

①暗いところにあるものが、**一瞬でも明るくなる**ことです。まわりよりも**ひときわ目立ったり、まぶしいほど明るくなる**という意味です。反射して光ることも含みます（例1, 2, 3, 4）。
To give off light or become bright in the dark, even if only for a moment. Also, to become bright to the point of brilliance, so as to stand out from the surroundings; this includes reflected light (ex.1, 2, 3, 4).

②人の**才能**や**技術**など、すぐれているところが特に**きわ立って目立つ**ようすを表します（例5, 6）。
It is also used to indicate that a person has a special feature, e.g., talent, skill, etc., that is particularly outstanding and notable (ex.5, 6).

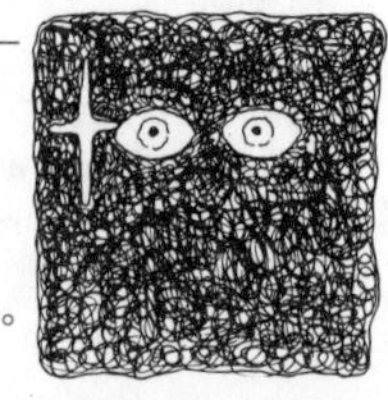

1) くさむらで、ほたるがたくさん光っている。
Kusamurade, hotaruga takusan hikatteiru.
There are many fireflies sparkling in the grass.

2) 外はひどい嵐で、ときおりいなずまが光るのが見える。

Sotowa hidoi arashide, tokiori inazumaga hikarunoga mieru.
There's a terrible storm out—(you) can see occasional flashes of lightning.

3) からすは、光るものを巣に集める習性がある。

Karasuwa, hikaru monoo suni atsumeru shuuseiga aru.
Crows have the habit of accumulating glittery objects in their nests.

4) 彼の靴は、いつもよくみがいてあって光っている。

Kareno kutsuwa, itsumo yoku migaiteatte hikatteiru.
His shoes are always well shined and sparkling.

5) 展覧会では彼の作品がいちばん光っていた。

Tenrankaidewa kareno sakuhinga ichiban hikatteita.
His works were the most brilliant at the exhibition.

6) 彼の最後の一言が光っていた。

Kareno saigono hitokotoga hikatteita.
His final words shone.

かがやく［輝く］

■ *kagayaku*
■ to shine ; to sparkle 

---

①ものが**光を受けて**強く**反射する**ことです。「光る」は一瞬でもかまいませんが、「輝く」は光が**きらきらとまぶしいように**継続的に反射しているという感じがあります（例7, 8, 9）。

To shine with reflected light. The light of *hikaru* may last only a moment, but *kagayaku* imparts the meaning that light sparkles brilliantly for an extended period of time (ex.7, 8, 9).

②いきいきとして**喜びにあふれている表情**を表すときにも使います（例10）。また、注目されるようなすばらしい名誉や賞などを受けるということを表します（例11）。

Kagayaku is also used to describe a facial expression that is vital and bursting with joy (ex.10), or to denote being awarded a noteworthy prize or honor (ex.11).

---

7) 空から見た東京の夜景は、きらきらと輝いていた。

Sorakara mita Tookyoono yakeiwa, kirakirato kagayaiteita.

The night view of Tokyo from the air sparkled brilliantly.

8) 冬の夜空の星は輝いている。
Fuyuno yozorano hoshiwa kagayaiteiru.
The stars in the wintry night sky are sparkling.

9) 朝日をあびて、木々の若葉が輝いた。
Asahio abite, kigino wakabaga kagayaita.
The young leaves of the trees sparkled, bathed in the morning sunlight.

10) 婚約指輪をもらった彼女の顔は、喜びに輝いていた。
Kon-yakuyubiwao moratta kanojono kaowa, yorokobini kagayaiteita.
Having just received her engagement ring, her face was radiant with happiness.

11) 彼の小説は、今年の最優秀賞に輝いた。
Kareno shoosetsuwa, kotoshino saiyuushuu-shooni kagayaita.
His novel was honored (shone) with this year's top prize.

ひく／えんそうする

■*hiku* ■*ensou suru*

ひく［弾く］ ■*hiku* ■to play (a stringed instrument) 

ピアノ・バイオリン・ギターなどの**鍵盤楽器や弦楽器をならす**ことです(例1, 2, 3)。

To make sound from a piano, violin, guitar or other keyboard or stringed instrument (ex.1, 2, 3).

---

1) 私の趣味はピアノを弾くことです。
Watashino shumiwa pianoo hiku kotodesu.
My hobby is playing the piano.

2) 友達のギターをちょっと弾いてみたら、いい音がした。
Tomodachino gitaao chotto hiitemitara, ii otoga shita.
When (I) tried playing my friend's guitar, it made a good sound.

3) 私の姉は、琴を弾くのが上手です。

Watashino anewa, kotoo hikunoga joozudesu.
My (elder) sister is good at playing the *koto*.

えんそうする［演奏する］ ■*ensou suru* ■to perform

ひとに音楽を聞かせるために楽器をならすことです。**すべての楽器**について使います（例4, 5, 6）。

To play an instrument in order to create music for others to hear. It is used when referring to all kinds of musical instruments (ex.4, 5, 6).

4) あんなにたくさんの人の前でバイオリンを演奏するのは初めてだったので、とても緊張した。
Annani takusanno hitono maede baiorin-o ensoosurunowa hajimete-dattano-de, totemo kinchooshita.
(I) was very nervous because it was the first time I had ever played the violin in front of so many people.

5) 晩餐会で、弦楽四重奏が演奏された。
Bansankaide, gengaku-shijuusooga ensoosareta.
A string quartet performed at the banquet.

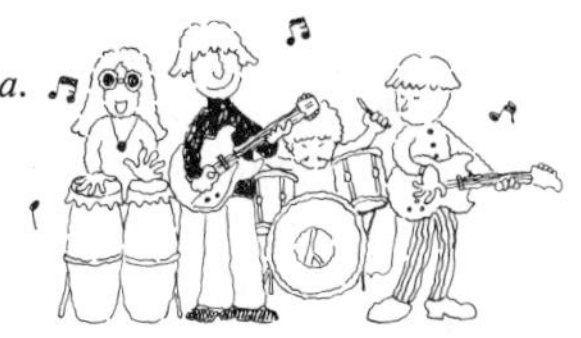

6) 私はスコットランドに行ったとき、初めてバグパイプの演奏を聞いた。
Watashiwa Sukottorandoni itta toki, hajimete bagupaipuno ensoo-o kiita.
I heard a bagpipe performance for the first time when I went to Scotland.

びくびく／どきどき／おどおど
■*bikubiku* ■*dokidoki* ■*odoodo*

びくびく ■*bikubiku* ■to be afraid or nervous 

心配・不安・おそれなどで**気持ちが**少しも**落ち着かない**ようすや態度を表すと

き使います。自分にとって、不利なことにならないかという気持ちの表れです（例1, 2, 3, 4）。

This expression indicates that because of worry, fear or nervousness, a person is entirely unable to relax. It is implied that the speaker is worried or afraid that something will happen to his disadvantage (ex.1, 2, 3, 4).

---

1) どろぼうは、いつつかまるかと、びくびくしている。

Doroboowa, itsu tsukamarukato, bikubikushiteiru.
The thief waits in fear, wondering when they will get him.

2) 銀行から大金をおろして帰る途中、だれかがつけてくるような気がして、びくびくした。

Ginkookara taikin-o oroshite kaeru tochuu, darekaga tsuketekuruyoona kiga shite, bikubikushita.
After withdrawing a large sum of money from the bank, (I) suddenly became afraid that somebody was following me as I walked home.

3) 犬が嫌いな郵便配達員は、配達のとき犬にかまれないかとびくびくしている。

Inuga kiraina yuubin-haitatsuinwa, haitatsuno toki inuni kamarenaikato bikubikushiteiru.
The mailman, who hates dogs, is nervous because he's afraid he might be bitten by one.

4) 窓ガラスを割った子供たちは、家の人に怒られないかとびくびくしていた。

Madogarasuo watta kodomotachiwa, ieno hitoni okorarenaikato bikubikushiteita.
The children who broke the window were afraid that someone might come out and scold them.

どきどき

■ *dokidoki*
■ to throb ; to pound 

心臓が脈打つようすからきたことばです。走ったり、興奮したり、不安だったりすることから、心臓が、いつもよりはやく打ったとき使います（例5, 6, 7, 8）。

This word is an onomatopoeic expression for the sound of a rapidly beating heart, and is used when one runs, gets excited or becomes uneasy (ex.5, 6, 7, 8).

---

5) 12時ちょうどの電車に乗ろうと走ったので、心臓がどきどきしている。

Juuniji choodono denshani norooto hashittanode, shinzooga dokidokishiteiru.
(I) ran to catch the 12:00 train, so my heart is pounding.

6) 私にとって初めてのコンサートだったので、どきどきしました。

Watashinitotte hajimeteno konsaatodattanode, dokidokishimashita.
Because it was my first concert, I was nervous.

7) 面接で、えらい人の前でいろいろ答えなくてはならず、どきどきした。

Mensetsude, eraihitono maede iroiro kotaenakutewa narazu, dokidokishita.
(I) was very nervous at the job interview because I had to answer various questions in front of executives.

8) あした恋人に会えると思うと、胸がどきどきする。

Ashita koibitoni aeruto omouto, munega dokidokisuru.
When (I) think of meeting my boyfriend tomorrow, my heart begins to flutter.

おどおど

■ *odoodo*
■ to be nervous ; to have the jitters 

自分に自信がなかったり、慣れない人の前に出たりしたときや、何らかの心理的な圧力が加わったときなどに感じる**不安やおびえのようす**です。「びくびくする」より落ち着かないようすに見えます（例9, 10, 11）。「**びくびくする**」は、**こわさが原因**で、「**おどおどする**」は**自信のなさ**が原因です。

Odoodo indicates a feeling of uneasiness or fear caused by psychological pressure or a lack of self-confidence. Compared with *bikubiku suru*, *odoodo suru* suggests a higher degree of anxiety (ex.9, 10, 11), and while *bikubiku suru* is caused by fear, *odoodo suru* is caused by insecurity or diffidence.

---

9) どんなえらい人の前でも、おどおどしないで、自信を持っていなさい。

Donna erai hitono maedemo, odoodoshinaide, jishin-o motteinasai.
Even in front of people of high rank, don't be timid and stay confident.

10) なぜあの人は人前に出るとおどおどするのだろう。

Naze ano hitowa hitomaeni deruto odoodo-surunodaroo?
Why is he so nervous whenever he gets in front of other people?

11) 証人はまるで犯人のようにおどおどしながら検事の質問に答えた。

Shooninwa marude hanninno yooni odoodo-shinagara kenjino shitsumonni kotaeta.
The witness nervously answered the prosecutor's questions, as if he were the culprit himself.

ひそかに／こっそり

■ *hisoka ni*　■ *kossori*

ひそかに

■ *hisoka ni*
■ secretly ; stealthily

計画(けいかく)や事業(じぎょう)などを、ほかの人(ひと)に**知(し)られたり気(き)づかれたりしない**ように行(おこな)うようすを表(あらわ)します（例(れい)1, 2, 3, 4, 5）。

Hisoka ni expresses a manner of carrying out plans or conducting business in such a way that others do not know or take notice (ex.1, 2, 3, 4, 5).

---

1) 新製品(しんせいひん)の開発(かいはつ)が、ひそかに進(すす)められている。
Shinseihinno kaihatsuga, hisokani susumerareteiru.
Development of the new product is proceeding in secrecy.

2) 夜明(よあ)け前(まえ)、密航者(みっこうしゃ)はひそかに船(ふね)にもぐりこんだ。
Yoakemae, mikkooshawa hisokani funeni mogurikonda.
Just before dawn, the stowaways crept unseen aboard the ship.

3) 美術館(びじゅつかん)の名画(めいが)が、何者(なにもの)かによってひそかに持(も)ち出(だ)されてしまった。
Bijutsukanno meigaga, nanimonokani yotte hisokani mochidasarete-shimatta.
A famous painting that had been on exhibit in the art museum was stealthily stolen by someone.

4) 私(わたし)は子供(こども)たちに見(み)つからないように、ひそかにクリスマスプレゼントを用意(ようい)した。
Watashiwa kodomotachini mitsukaranai-yooni, hisokani kurisumasu-purezentoo yooishita.
I got the Christmas presents all ready in secret so the kids wouldn't find them.

5) 高校時代、私にはひそかに憧れた先生がいた。
こうこうじだい わたし あこが せんせい
Kookoojidai, watashiniwa hisokani akogareta senseiga ita.
In my high school days, there was a teacher on whom I secretly had a crush.

こっそり

■ *kossori*
■ stealthily ; sneakily ; secretly 

ほかの人に気づかれないように、何かをするようすを表します（例6, 7, 8, 9, 10）。「ひそかに」は、「計画や情報がほかの人にもれないように、何かをする」という意味ですが、「こっそり」は「**物音や声でほかの人に気づかれないように**」という意味を強く含んでいます。
ひと き なに あらわ れい けいかく じょうほう ひと なに いみ ものおと こえ ひと き いみ つよ ふく

This denotes doing something in such a way that others don't notice (ex.6, 7, 8, 9, 10), i.e., stealthily, secretly, or on the sly. *Hisoka ni* means 'do something so that plans or information do not leak out to others,' but *kossori* includes a strong nuance of 'not making a sound that would be noticed by others'.

---

6) 私は、姉の日記をこっそり読んでしまった。
わたし あね にっき よ
Watashiwa, aneno nikkio kossori yondeshimatta.
I secretly read my (elder) sister's diary.

7) 彼は授業中にこっそり教室を抜けだして、パンを買いに行った。
かれ じゅぎょうちゅう きょうしつ ぬ か い
Karewa jugyoochuuni kossori kyooshitsuo nukedashite, pan-o kaini itta.
He snuck out during class and went to get some rolls.

8) どろぼうは、窓からこっそり忍びこんだ。
まど しの
Doroboowa, madokara kossori shinobikonda.
The thief snuck in stealthily through a window.

9) 彼女は大家にだまって、アパートでこっそり猫を飼っている。
かのじょ おおや ねこ か
Kanojowa ooyani damatte, apaatode kossori nekoo katteiru.
She's secretly keeping a cat in her apartment without telling her landlord.

10) 弟は、悪い点の答案用紙を、引き出しの奥にこっそりかくしている。
おとうと わる てん とうあんようし ひ だ おく
Otootowa, warui tenno tooanyooshio, hikidashino okuni kossori kakushiteiru.
My (little) brother is keeping his bad exam papers tucked out of sight in the back of a drawer.

ひとりで／じぶんで

■*hitori de*　■*jibun de*

ひとりで ■*hitori de* ■alone 

①だれかといっしょに、ではなく単独でというとき使います（例1, 2, 3）。

Hitori de means to be alone, that is, not with other people (ex.1, 2, 3).

②例4, 5は、ほかの人の助けを借りずにその人自身の力でという意味を強く表します。

In Examples 4 and 5 it emphasizes that one does something without help from others.

1) 彼はあの家にひとりで住んでいる。
Karewa ano ieni hitoride sundeiru.
He lives alone in that house.

2) 食事はひとりで食べるより大勢で食べるほうがおいしい。
Shokujiwa hitoride taberuyori oozeide taberu hooga oishii.
Food tastes better when (you) eat with a lot of people than when you eat alone.

3) たまにはひとりで旅行するのもいいものだ。
Tamaniwa hitoride ryokoosurunomo iimonoda.
Once in a while, it's good to travel alone.

4) 3歳になった娘は、何でもひとりでやりたがる。
Sansaini natta musumewa, nandemo hitoride yaritagaru.
My three-year-old daughter wants to do everything by herself.

5) 彼は、あれだけの仕事をたったひとりでやりとげた。
Karewa, aredakeno shigotoo tattahitoride yaritogeta.
He completed all of that work all by himself.

じぶんで［自分で］ ■*jibun de* ■by oneself 

その人本人だけで、という意味で使います。独力で、という意味ですが「ひとりで」の①とは異なり、「自分で」のほうが「**その人自身の責任で**」という感じを強く含みます（例6, 7, 8, 9）。

Jibun de means to do something oneself or unaided. In contrast with definition ① of *hitori de*, *jibun de* does not focus on the number of people involved, but rather implies that something will be done on the person's own responsibility (ex.6, 7, 8, 9).

6）これは私自身の問題なので、自分で解決します。
Korewa watashijishinno mondainanode, jibunde kaiketsushimasu.
This is my problem so I'll solve it myself.

7）卒業後の進路は、よく考えて自分で決めたほうがいい。
Sotsugyoogono shinrowa, yoku kangaete jibunde kimetahooga ii.
(You'd) better think carefully and decide on your own the course you will take after graduating.

8）自分のことは自分でしなさい。
Jibunno kotowa jibunde shinasai.
Do (your) own things yourself.

9）自分で言ったことには責任を持つべきだ。
Jibunde itta kotoniwa sekinin-o motsubekida.
(You) should take responsibility for what you have said.

ひとりでに／しぜんに

■ *hitorideni* ■ *shizen ni*

ひとりでに

■ *hitorideni*
■ automatically ; by itself 

本来は、何らかの力や働きかけによって動くはずのものが、**何もしなくても動いた・そうなったというとき**使います。なぜそうなるのか、原因が分からないときにも（例1, 2, 3）、「用意しておけばあとで自動的に」「いちいち手をわずらわさずに」というときにも使います（例4, 5, 6）。また、**自分の意志とは関係**

なく、何らかの条件で体が動いてしまうときにも使います（例7, 8)。

Hitorideni denotes that something that is supposed to move by some kind of power or stimulus moves by itself; it is used when the reason or cause of the movement is not clear (ex.1, 2, 3). It may also be used when saying that once its mechanism is set, a device will do something automatically (ex.4, 5, 6). *Hitorideni* is also used when one's body moves by itself or unconsciously in certain situations (ex.7, 8).

---

1) ドアが突然、ひとりでに開いた。

Doaga totsuzen, hitorideni aita.
The door suddenly opened by itself.

2) 部屋の電気がひとりでに消えた。

Heyano denkiga hitorideni kieta.
The room light went out by itself.

3) 地震でもないのに、棚の上の花びんがひとりでに落ちてきた。

Jishindemo nainoni, tanano ueno kabinga hitorideni ochitekita.
Although there was no earthquake, a flower vase on the shelf fell off all by itself.

4) このビデオは、終わるとひとりでに巻き戻る。

Kono bideowa, owaruto hitorideni makimodoru.
This video tape will rewind automatically when it is finished.

5) 朝6時に、ひとりでに暖房が入ります。

Asa rokujini, hitorideni danbooga hairimasu.
At six o'clock in the morning the heater will turn on by itself.

6) 部屋に人が入ると、センサーがそれを感知して、ひとりでに電気がつく。

Heyani hitoga hairuto, sensaaga soreo kanchishite, hitorideni denkiga tsuku.
When someone enters the room, the sensor senses it and the light comes on automatically.

7) 音楽を聞いていると、ひとりでに体が動き出す。

Ongakuo kiiteiruto, hitorideni karadaga ugokidasu.
When (I) listen to music my body unconsciously begins to move.

8) 彼女の話を聞いているうちに、ひとりでに涙が出てきた。

Kanojono hanashio kiiteiru uchini, hitorideni namidaga detekita.
While listening to her story, tears started welling up in (my) eyes.

しぜんに［自然に］ ■ *shizen ni* ■ naturally 

特に何もしないのに・手を加えたわけでもないのに、じょじょに時間をかけて、ものごとが起こるようすを表すとき使います（例9, 10, 11, 12）。「放っておくと**無理なく・何の抵抗もなく・成り行きで**」という意味を表します。

Shizen ni expresses the idea that some event occurs gradually over time, although no one has done anything special to bring it about (ex.9, 10, 11, 12). It expresses the meaning that something occurs if left to itself 'without any strain', 'with no resistance' or 'as a matter of course'.

---

9) 何度もくり返して聞くうちに、自然にその曲を覚えてしまった。
Nandomo kurikaeshite kiku uchini, shizenni sono kyokuo oboeteshimatta.
(I) just learned that song unconsciously, while listening to it over and over.

10) その程度の傷なら、放っておいても自然に治るよ。
Sono teidono kizunara, hootteoitemo shizenni naoruyo.
A wound like that will heal by itself if (you) just leave it alone.

11) 私たちは、自然に友達になっていった。
Watashitachiwa, shizenni tomodachini natteitta.
We became friends very naturally.

12) 無理に教えなくても、赤ちゃんは自然にことばを覚えるものだ。
Murini oshienakutemo, akachanwa shizenni kotobao oboeru monoda.
Babies learn how to speak naturally, even if (you) don't go to any trouble to teach them.

ひらたい／たいらな／へいたんな

■ *hiratai* ■ *taira na* ■ *heitan na*

ひらたい［平たい］ ■ *hiratai* ■ flat ; level

ものの形全体が、**凹凸がないようす**を表します。**厚みや深さがほとんどな**

い形です（例1, 2, 3）。「平たく言う」は、わかりやすく身近な表現で言うという意味です（例４）。

Hiratai indicates that the shape of something is even and does not have much thickness or depth (ex.1, 2, 3). The expression *hirataku iu* means 'to say something in an easily understandable way using familiar words' (ex.4).

1）この料理は平たいお皿にのせてください。
Kono ryooriwa hiratai osarani nosete kudasai.
Please serve this on a flat dish.

2）この平たい箱には、ハンカチが入っている。
Kono hiratai hakoniwa, hankachiga haitteiru.
There is a handkerchief in this flat box.

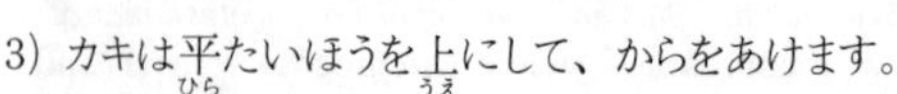

3）カキは平たいほうを上にして、からをあけます。
Kakiwa hiratai hoo-o ueni shite, karao akemasu.
(You) shuck an oyster by first putting its flat side up.

4）彼の提案を平たくいえば、労働時間を減らして、ゆとりのある生活をしようということだ。
Kareno teian-o hirataku ieba, roodoojikan-o herashite, yutorino aru seikatsuo shiyooto yuu kotoda.
To put his suggestion simply, (we) should lessen our work hours and live more leisurely.

たいらな［平らな］

■ *taira na*
■ flat ; smooth ; horizontal 

ものや土地の表面に凹凸がないようすを表します（例5, 6, 7, 8, 9）。「平たい」は、ものの形のようすで、「平らな」は、ものや土地の表面のようすです。

Taira na indicates that the surface of something is not bumpy (ex.5, 6, 7, 8, 9). *Hiratai* refers to the shape of something, while *taira na* refers to the condition of the surface of an object or land.

5）ブルドーザーは、土地を平らにする機械です。
Burudoozaawa, tochio tairanisuru kikaidesu.
A bulldozer is a machine used to level the earth.

6）彼らは明日の試合のために、テニスコートをローラーで平らにした。

Karerawa asuno shiaino tameni, tenisukootoo rooraade tairanishita.
They leveled the tennis court with a roller in preparation for the game tomorrow.

7) 私たちは、海辺の平らな石をテーブルがわりにして、おべんとうを食べた。
Watashitachiwa, umibeno tairana ishio teeburugawarini-shite, obentoo-o tabeta.
At the seaside we used a flat rock for a table and ate our lunches.

8) パイ生地をめん棒で平らにのばすのは、わりとむずかしい。
Paikijio menboode tairani nobasunowa, warito muzukashii.
Rolling out pie dough with a rolling pin is rather difficult.

9) はかりは狂いやすいので、平らな所に置きます。
Hakariwa kuruiyasuinode, tairana tokoroni okimasu.
A scale is easy to upset, so put it in a flat place.

へいたんな

■ *heitan na*
■ even ; flat

山や丘、谷などがなく、**上り下りの変化のほとんどない土地**のようすを表します。「平らな」で言いかえられますが、「へいたんな」は、土地、道などにしか使いません（例10, 11）。

Heitan na indicates that an area of land does not have features such as mountains, hills, valleys, or other changes in elevation. Although *heitan na* and *taira na* are interchangeable in this sense, *heitan na* may only be used to describe geographic features, such as an area of land or a road (ex.10, 11).

---

10) 私が通った小学校は、山のふもとのへいたんな所にあります。
Watashiga kayotta shoogakkoowa, yamano fumotono heitanna tokoroni arimasu.
The elementary school I used to go to is in a flat area at the foot of a mountain.

11) へいたんな田舎道を、車で1時間も走り続けると、飽きてくる。
Heitanna inakamichio, kurumade ichijikanmo hashiri-tsuzukeruto, akitekuru.
(I) get bored after driving about an hour on flat country roads.

日本の住宅

日本では部屋の広さを表すのに「～畳」という言い方をします。畳はたたみのことで、その部屋がたたみ何枚分の広さかを表します。たたみ１枚の大きさは一般には90㎝×180㎝ぐらいですが、多少の大小はあり、近ごろは昔より小さいようです。主な部屋の広さは、４畳半・６畳・８畳・10畳などです。

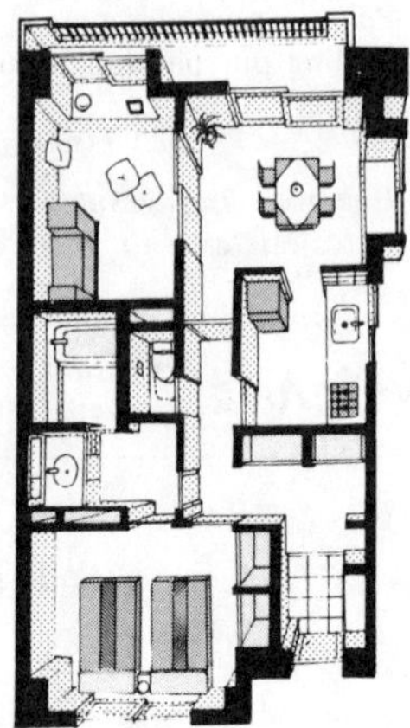

また不動産屋の広告などで、２ＬＤＫ・３ＤＫなどとある場合、Ｌは、家族が集まったり、くつろいだりする居間で、ソファーを置いたりします。Ｄは食事をするところで、テーブルやいすを置きます。そしてＫは、キッチンのことです。２や３などの数字は、それ以外の部屋の数を表します。しかし実際は、見てみないとわかりません。２ＬＤＫのほうが３ＬＤＫよりも広いということだってあるのですから。

Housing in Japan

In Japan, the size of a room is measured in *joo*, which is the Chinese reading of the *kanji* character for *tatami* (or straw) mat. The number of these mats placed in a room indicates the size of the room. Generally, a *tatami* mat measures 90 cm × 180 cm, although there may be some differences. In recent times the mats have become smaller than their traditional size. Rooms most often come in sizes of 4½ mats (*yo-joo-han*), 6 mats (*roku-joo*), 8 mats (*hachi-joo*), 10 mats (*juu-joo*), or more.

Also, real estate agencies often describe apartments in their advertisements as 2LDK, 3DK, etc. Under this system, the L stands for a living room in which a sofa may be placed and a family may gather, D indicates that there is a dining area in which a table and chairs may be placed, and K stands for a kitchen. The 2 or 3 refers to the number of bedrooms in the apartment. However, the true size of an apartment cannot be determined without actually seeing it, because a 2LDK may in fact be larger than a 3LDK.

ひろがる／ひろまる

■ *hirogaru* ■ *hiromaru*

ひろがる［広がる］ ■ *hirogaru* ■ to spread 

面積・幅・範囲が大きくなっていくことです（例1, 2, 3, 4, 5）。**中心から、まわりに広く**なっていく感じがあります。

Hirogaru indicates that the area, width, or scope of something becomes larger (ex.1, 2, 3, 4, 5). It suggests that the growth occurs from the center.

1) 風が強かったので、火事はあっという間に広がった。
Kazega tsuyokattanode, kajiwa atto yuu mani hirogatta.
Because the wind was strong, the fire quickly spread.

2) 服についた染みは、こするとよけい広がる。
Fukuni tsuita shimiwa, kosuruto yokei hirogaru.
The stains on your clothing will only get bigger if (you) rub them.

3) ヘリコプターから見ると、下流へ行くほど川幅が広がっているのがわかる。
Herikoputaakara miruto, karyuue ikuhodo kawahabaga hirogatte irunoga wakaru.
From a helicopter, the widening of the river as it flows downstream is clearly visible.

4) 山のふもとには、れんげ畑が広がっている。
Yamano fumotoniwa, rengebatakega hirogatteiru.
Fields of milk vetch flowers extend across the base of the mountain.

5) 池に小石を投げたら、水面に波紋が広がった。
Ikeni koishio nagetara, suimenni hamonga hirogatta.
When (I) threw a pebble into the pond,
ripples spread out on the surface of the water.

ひろまる［広まる］ ■ *hiromaru* ■ to spread ; to be disseminated 

話や考え、評判やうわさなどが、多くの人々に知られて、普及していくことです（例6, 7, 8, 9)。

Hiromaru denotes that something, such as a story, idea, reputation or rumor, becomes widely known, popular, or widespread (ex.6, 7, 8, 9).

---

6) 悪いうわさは、すぐに広まる。
Warui uwasawa, suguni hiromaru.
A bad rumor spreads quickly.

7) あの家におばけが出るというううわさが、子供たちの間で広まっている。
Ano ieni obakega deruto yuu uwasaga, kodomotachino aidade hiromatte-iru.
A rumor that a ghost lives in that house is spreading among the children.

8) バランスのとれた食事をしようという考え方が広まってきている。
Baransuno toreta shokujio shiyooto yuu kangaekataga hiromatte-kiteiru.
The idea that (we) should eat well-balanced meals is becoming popular.

9) 彼女は歌がうまいという評判が広まった。
Kanojowa utaga umaito yuu hyoobanga hiromatta.
Her reputation for being a good singer spread.

ふいに／ふと

■ *fui ni* ■ *futo*

ふいに［不意に］ ■ *fui ni* ■ unexpectedly ; suddenly 

目の前で起こった、**予告や前ぶれなしの思いがけない**、他人の**動作や行動**に使います（例1, 2, 3, 4, 5)。そのできごとに**出会った人の驚き**を含みます。ですから、意志的な自分の行動には使いません。例5は、その気持ちを自分の意志ではどうすることもできない、つまり意志的行動ではないから使えるのです。

Fui ni is used to describe the suddenness of a person's behavior, or a happening without notice or warning (ex.1, 2, 3, 4, 5). It suggests that the observer was surprised by the unexpected incident ; therefore, *fui ni* is not used when speaking of one's own intentional behavior. The sentence in Example 5 is possible because the speaker's feelings are unexpected.

---

1) 彼女は、ふいに立ち止まると、こちらを振り返った。
Kanojowa, fuini tachidomaruto, kochirao furikaetta.
Suddenly, she stopped walking and looked back.

2) 物理の先生は、ふいにテストをするので、学生たちに恐れられている。
Butsurino senseiwa, fuini tesutoo surunode, gakuseitachini osorerareteiru.
The physics teacher gives pop quizes, so the students dread his classes.

3) 彼はいつも、予告もなしに、ふいに訪ねてくる。
Karewa itsumo, yokokumo nashini, fuini tazunetekuru.
He always comes to visit (me) without giving prior notice.

4) 物かげから、ふいに人が飛び出してきたので、もうすこしでぶつかるところだった。
Monokagekara, fuini hitoga tobidashite kitanode, moosukoshide butsukaru tokorodatta.
(I) almost ran into a person because he suddenly rushed out of a shadow (into view).

5) 夜中に目がさめて、ふいに不安な気持ちに襲われた。
Yonakani mega samete, fuini fuanna kimochini osowareta.
(I) woke up in the middle of the night, and all of a sudden, I felt uneasy.

■ *futo*
■ suddenly ; by chance ; accidentally 

そうしようと考えたわけではないのに、なぜかしてしまったというときに使います（例6, 7, 8, 9）。今していることと必ずしも関連のないことが突然頭に浮かんだり、無意識のうちに違う動作をしてしまうときに使います。「ふいに」は、そのできごとの影響を受けた側から見た「おどろき」を表し、「ふと」は、その動作は無意識の瞬間的な行動なのだということを表します。「ふとしたこと」は「ちょっとしたきっかけで・思いがけない理由で」という意味です（例10）。

Futo indicates that one does something unconsciously or spontaneously without any particular reason (ex.6, 7, 8, 9). It suggests that one suddenly does or thinks of something unrelated to his previous action. *Fui ni* indicates a feeling of surprise on the part of the person affected by an event or experience, while *futo* expresses that the behavior or action was suddenly and unconsciously done; a *futo shita koto* is somewhat that happened 'by mere chance' or 'because of an unexpected matter' (ex.10).

---

6) あるとき、ふと小学校のころの友達のことを思い出した。
Aru toki, futo shoogakkoono korono tomodachino kotoo omoidashita.
One time, out of the blue, (I) remembered one of my friends from my elementary school days.

7) 散歩の途中で、ふと足もとを見ると、すみれの花が咲いていた。
Sanpono tochuude, futo ashimotoo miruto, sumireno hanaga saiteita.
While (I) was taking a walk, I looked down by chance and saw violets in bloom.

8) 今は楽しく暮らしているけれど、ふと将来が不安になることがある。
Imawa tanoshiku kurashite-irukeredo, futo shooraiga fuanni naru kotoga aru.
Although (I) am enjoying my life at this time, there are times when I feel uneasy about the future.

9) 推理小説を読むのに夢中になっていて、ふと気がつくと夜が明けていた。
Suirishoosetsuo yomunoni muchuuni natteite, futo kiga tsukuto yoga aketeita.
(I) was absorbed in reading a detective novel, and before I knew it, it was already morning.

10) ふとしたことから彼女と知りあいになった。
Futoshita kotokara kanojoto shiriaini natta.
(I) became acquainted with her by chance.

ふく／ぬぐう

■*fuku* ■*nuguu*

ふく ■*fuku* ■to wipe

ほこりやよごれ・水気などがついたところを、布や紙などで**こすってきれいにする**ことです。きれいにされるものに重点があります（例1, 2, 3, 4, 5）。

To clean the surface of something that is dusty, dirty, or wet by wiping it with cloth or paper. The focus is on (the surface of) the object that is cleaned (ex.1, 2, 3, 4, 5).

1) きのう、家中の窓ガラスをふきました。

Kinoo, iejuuno madogarasuo fukimashita.
Yesterday, (I) cleaned all the windows in my house.

2) 洗った食器は、きれいにふいてしまってください。

Aratta shokkiwa, kireini fuite shimatte kudasai.
Please dry the washed dishes well, and put them away.

3) このタオルで汗をふいてもいいですよ。

Kono taorude aseo fuitemo iidesuyo.
(You) may use this towel to wipe off your perspiration.

4) あとは、廊下をふけばそうじは終わりです。

Atowa, rookao fukeba soojiwa owaridesu.
After mopping the hallway, (I'll) be done with the cleaning.

5) めがねのレンズは、乾いたやわらかい布でふいて、きれいにします。

Meganeno renzuwa, kawaita yawarakai nunode fuite, kireini shimasu.
(You) clean eyeglass lenses by wiping with a soft, dry cloth.

ぬぐう ■*nuguu* ■to wipe off

汗や水・よごれなどを紙や布・手などで**取り去ること**です（例6, 7, 8）。「ふく」は、こすってきれいにすることを表すので、乾いたものをふくこともあります。

また「ぬぐう」は、取り去るものに重点があるので、例4, 5のような広い範囲については使いません。このごろは例9のような慣用表現以外はほとんどの場合、「ふく」で置きかえられます。

To remove sweat, water, or stains by wiping it with paper or cloth (ex.6, 7, 8). *Fuku* means to clean something by scrubbing or wiping, so it's possible to use it to mean 'to wipe a dry object', while *nuguu* focuses on the thing to be removed, and cannot be used when cleaning large areas like those in Examples 4 and 5. Nowadays *fuku* is used interchangeably with *nuguu*, except in idiomatic expressions like that in Example 9.

---

6) 彼は、汗をぬぐいながら試合を続けた。
Karewa, aseo nuguinagara shiaio tsuzuketa.
He continued the match, repeatedly wiping perspiration (from his brow).

7) 彼女は、指先についたソースをナプキンでぬぐった。
Kanojowa, yubisakini tsuita soosuo napukinde nugutta.
She wiped the sauce off her finger with a napkin.

8) 彼女は、あふれる涙をぬぐおうともせずに、映画を見ていた。
Kanojowa, afureru namidao nuguootomo sezuni, eigao miteita.
She watched the movie without even bothering to wipe away the tears that came welling up.

9) あの事件について私たちは、何も知らないかのように口をぬぐいとおした。
Ano jikenni tsuite watashitachiwa, nanimo shiranaikanoyooni kuchio nuguitooshita.
We kept silent about the incident, pretending we didn't know anything.

ふくらむ／ふくれる／はれる

■*fukuramu* ■*fukureru* ■*hareru*

ふくらむ［膨らむ］

■*fukuramu*
■to swell ; to bulge

ものの**体積**が、**初めよりも大きくなる**ことです。時期がくれば、いずれはふくらむようにできているものについて使います（例1, 2, 3, 4, 5）。

ふくらんだものは、やわらかい・ふわふわしている、気持ちが良いなどの雰囲気があります。例6のように夢や希望が大きくなるようすも表します。「ふくらんだ状態」にすることを、「ふくらませる」といいます。

Fukuramu denotes that the size of something becomes larger than it originally was. It is used when speaking of objects that always grow naturally under certain conditions or after a specific period of time passes (ex.1, 2, 3, 4, 5). Something described as *fukuranda mono* has a pleasant feeling of softness or fluffiness. As in Example 6, *fukuramu* may be used to mean that one's aspirations or expectations become greater. The verb *fukuramaseru* means 'to cause something to swell or expand'.

---

1) 熱風を送りこむと、熱気球はどんどんふくらんだ。
Neppuuo okurikomuto, netsukikyuuwa dondon fukuranda.
The hot-air balloon became larger and larger as it filled with hot air.

2) パン屋はオーブンから、よくふくらんでおいしそうに焼けたパンをとり出した。
Pan-yawa oobunkara, yoku fukurande oishisooni yaketa pan-o toridashita.
The baker took the soft, puffy, tasty-looking bread out of the oven.

3) 彼は、風船ガムをふくらませるのが得意だ。
Karewa, fuusengamuo fukuramaseru-noga tokuida.
He is very good at blowing up bubble gum.

4) 春になって、花のつぼみがふくらんだ。
Haruninatte, hanano tsubomiga fukuranda.
Spring has come, and the flower buds have swelled.

5) かえるはのどをふくらませて鳴きます。
Kaeruwa nodoo fukuramasete nakimasu.
A frog croaks by inflating its throat.

6) 学生達は卒業式のあと、希望に胸をふくらませて、それぞれの道を進んで行った。
Gakuseitachiwa sotsugyooshikino ato, kibooni muneo fukuramasete, sorezoreno michio susundeitta.
After the graduation ceremony, the students set off on their different ways with hearts filled with hope.

ふくれる ■*fukureru* ■to swell

①ものの一部(いちぶ)や全体(ぜんたい)が、中(なか)から押(お)されるような感(かん)じで大(おお)きくなることです(例(れい)7, 8, 9, 10)。「ふくれる」は、本来(ほんらい)は大(おお)きくならないはずのものが、何(なに)かの原因(げんいん)で大(おお)きくなった、という感(かん)じを含(ふく)みます。

This word indicates that an object expands entirely or partially, as if being pushed out from the center (ex.7, 8, 9, 10). *Fukureru* implies that an object which does not ordinarily grow larger has expanded due to some cause.

②機嫌(きげん)を悪(わる)くしたり、すねたりするようすを表(あらわ)します。子供(こども)っぽいという感(かん)じがします(例(れい)11)。

It may be used to describe someone's behavior as sulky or cross, and somewhat childish (ex.11).

7) おもちを焼(や)くとふくれる。

Omochio yakuto fukureru.
Japanese rice cakes swells as they roast.

8) 柱(はしら)にぶつけたおでこがふくれて、こぶになってしまった。

Hashirani butsuketa odekoga fukurete, kobuni natteshimatta.
I bumped my forehead on a pole, and the swelling became a big bump.

9) ピーナツは胃(い)の中(なか)でふくれるから、食(た)べすぎないほうがいい。

Piinatsuwa ino nakade fukurerukara, tabesuginai hooga ii.
Peanuts expand in your stomach, so you shouldn't eat too many.

10) おなかがふくれると眠(ねむ)くなる。

Onakaga fukureruto nemukunaru.
(I) get sleepy when I have a full stomach.

11) 彼女(かのじょ)は、注意(ちゅうい)されるとすぐふくれる。

Kanojowa, chuuisareruto sugu fukureru.
She quickly gets huffy if she is admonished.

はれる ■*hareru* ■to swell

人間(にんげん)や動物(どうぶつ)の体(からだ)の一部(いちぶ)が、病気(びょうき)やけがなどのために、もり上(あ)がったり大(おお)き

くなったりすることです（例12, 13, 14, 15）。

Hareru indicates that a part of a person's or animal's body swells and becomes larger because of illness or injury (ex.12, 13, 14, 15).

---

12) はちに刺されて、足がはれた。

Hachini sasarete, ashiga hareta.
My instep swelled up because (I) was stung by a bee.

13) 彼女はゆうべ泣いたので、目がはれている。

Kanojowa yuube naitanode, mega hareteiru.
She cried last night, so now her eyes are puffy.

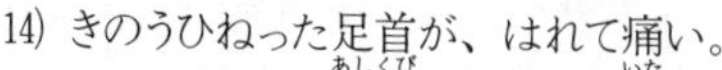

14) きのうひねった足首が、はれて痛い。

Kinoo hinetta ashikubiga, harete itai.
The ankle (I) twisted yesterday is swollen and painful.

15) 彼は肝臓がはれているので、医者に酒をとめられている。

Karewa kanzooga hareteirunode, ishani sakeo tomerareteiru.
His doctor has ordered him to stop drinking because his liver is swollen.

ふさぐ／めいる／おちこむ

■*fusagu* ■*meiru* ■*ochikomu*

ふさぐ

■*fusagu*
■to be depressed

悲しみや苦しみなどで、**暗い気持ち**になって**元気がなくなってしまうようす**を表します。「私はふさいでいる」のように、現在の自分のようすを表す使い方はしません（例1, 2, 3, 4）。

This verb expresses that one has a dark, cheerless feeling caused by sadness, hardship, etc. It cannot be used to describe one's own feelings at the moment, therefore the sentence *watashi wa fusaideiru* is not said (ex.1, 2, 3, 4).

---

1) 彼女は息子が家を出てから、すっかりふさいでいる。

Kanojowa musukoga ieo detekara, sukkari fusaideiru.

She has been depressed ever since her son left home.

2) 会社が倒産して、彼は気がふさいでいるようすだ。
Kaishaga toosanshite, karewa kiga fusaideiru yoosuda.
He's been depressed ever since his business went bankrupt.

3) A：何をそんなにふさいだ顔をしているんですか。
B：仕事がうまくいかなくて……。
A： *Nanio sonnani fusaida kaoo shiteirundesuka?*
Why do (you) look so glum?
B： *Shigotoga umaku ikanakute...*　(My) work isn't going so well.

4) 何度論文を書いても認めてもらえず、彼女はふさぎこんでいる。
Nando ronbun-o kaitemo mitometemoraezu, kanojowa fusagikondeiru.
She is depressed because her thesis hasn't been accepted even though she's rewritten it many times.

めいる

■ *meiru*
■ to feel gloomy ; to be depressed 

気が進まないことをしなければならない・あるいは**うんざりするほど面倒なことがある**などの原因で、ゆううつになったり気持ちが暗くなるときに使います（例5, 6, 7, 8)。「気がめいる」と使うことが多いです。

Meiru is used when a person becomes downcast because of something he has to but would rather not do, or something troublesome and boring (ex.5, 6, 7, 8). It is often used in the expression *ki ga meiru*.

---

5) いくら不景気だといっても、10人もの部下の首を切らなければならないかと思うと、気がめいる。
Ikura fukeikidato ittemo, juuninmono bukano kubio kiranakereba naranaikato omouto, kiga meiru.
(I) understand the economy is bad, but whenever I think about having to lay off ten of my employees, I get depressed.

6) 夏休みに田舎に帰るのは楽しみだが、列車の混雑を思うと気がめいる。
Natsuyasumini inakani kaerunowa tanoshimi-daga, resshano konzatsuo omouto kiga meiru.
(I'm) looking forward to going home for summer vacation, but when I think about how crowded the trains will be I am less than excited.

7) 毎日暗いニュースばかりで気がめいる。
Mainichi kurai nyuusubakaride kiga meiru.
Seeing such bad news everyday makes (me) depressed.

8) ぐちばかり聞かされていると、こちらまでめいってしまう。
Guchibakari kikasareteiruto, kochiramade meitteshimau.
By making (me) listen to (his) complaining, he's made me become depressed, too.

おちこむ［落ち込む］ ■ *ochikomu* ■ to feel down 

失敗などで、**自信や元気を失っている**ようすを表します。話しことばでよく使われ、目上の人には使いません（例9, 10, 11, 12）。

To feel down or lose confidence in oneself because of failure, etc. Although *ochikomu* is often used in casual conversation, it is not used when speaking to a superior or senior person (ex.9, 10, 11, 12).

---

9) 彼女は、自信があった数学のテストの点が悪かったので落ち込んでいる。
Kanojowa, jishinga atta suugakuno tesutono tenga warukattanode ochikondeiru.
She's feeling down because she got a low score on the math test she thought she would do well on.

10) 彼は恋人にふられてから、すっかり落ち込んでいるようだ。
Karewa koibitoni furaretekara, sukkari ochikondeiru yooda.
Ever since he was dumped by his girl friend he has seemed quite depressed.

11) A：どうしたんですか、今日は元気がないですね。
B：企画が採用されなかったので、落ち込んでいるんです。
A : *Dooshitandesuka? Kyoowa genkiga naidesune.*
What's wrong? (You) look depressed today.
B : *Kikakuga saiyoo sarenakattanode, ochikonde-irundesu.*
(I'm) feeling down because my plan wasn't accepted (by my boss).

12) あれぐらいの失敗で、そんなに落ち込まなくてもいいのに。
Areguraino shippaide, sonnani ochikomanakutemo iinoni.
There's no need to be so depressed over such a little failure.

へいき／だいじょうぶ

■ *heiki*　■ *daijoubu*

へいき［平気］ ■ *heiki* ■ calm

何かいやなことや、問題などがあっても気にしないで、ふつうの精神状態でいられるというようすを表します（例1, 2, 3, 4, 5)。

Heiki indicates that one is not worried about a particular trouble or problem, and maintains a normal state of mind (ex.1, 2, 3, 4, 5).

1) 彼女は自分に自信があるので、人にいくら悪く言われても平気だ。
Kanojowa jibunni jishinga arunode, hitoni ikura waruku iwaretemo heikida.
She's got confidence in herself, so no matter how poorly people speak of her, she doesn't care.

2) 彼は毎日のように遅刻して、先生に注意されても平気でいる。
Karewa mainichinoyooni chikokushite, senseini chuuisaretemo heikideiru.
He is late almost every day, and doesn't care if the teacher scolds him.

3) 子供も高校生にもなれば、親が１週間ぐらい留守をしても平気ですよ。
Kodomomo kookooseinimo nareba, oyaga isshuukangurai rusuo shitemo heikidesuyo.
Parents can be away from home for a week or so without worry once their children become high school students.

4) 彼は正義感が強いので、困っている人を平気で見ていることはできない。
Karewa seigikanga tsuyoinode, komatteiru hitoo heikide miteiru kotowa dekinai.
He has a strong sense of justice, so he can't ignore people in need.

5) 彼は平気な顔をしているけど、実は仕事がうまくいかなくて大変らしい。
Karewa heikina kaoo shiteirukedo, jitsuwa shigotoga umaku ikanakute taihenrashii.
He looks calm, but it seems that he is actually having a difficult time because his work is not going well.

だいじょうぶ［大丈夫］ ■ *daijoubu* ■ all right 

病気やけがなど、体の**調子が悪い**ときや、何か**困難**があっても、それほど問題はない・**耐えられる**というとき使います（例6, 7, 8, 9）。ものの調子や状態にも使います（例10, 11）。ものごとがうまくいく、安心して見ていられる・心配がないという意味を含みます。

Daijoubu is used to indicate that one is able to endure, or does not feel too inconvenienced by, things such as sickness, the condition of one's body, or other problems (ex.6, 7, 8, 9). *Daijoubu* may also be used when speaking of a situation or the condition of an object (ex.10, 11). It is implied that something will (or is expected to) go well, and therefore there is no need to worry about it.

---

6) きのうまで熱があったけれど、もう大丈夫です。
あしたは起きられるでしょう。
Kinoomade netsuga attakeredo, moo daijoobudesu.
Ashitawa okirarerudeshoo.
(I) had a fever until yesterday, but I'm fine now.
I'm sure I'll be able to get out of bed tomorrow.

7) 気分が悪そうですね、大丈夫ですか。
Kibunga warusoodesune, daijoobudesuka?
(You) don't look well. Are you all right?

8) 難しい仕事だけれども、彼だったら任せても大丈夫だろう。
Muzukashii shigotodakeredomo, karedattara makasetemo daijoobudaroo.
It's a difficult job, but if he's doing it (I'm) sure we can trust him to do it right.

9) 冷凍食品が十分買ってあるので、いつお客が来ても大丈夫だ。
Reitoo-shokuhinga juubun kattearunode, itsu okyakuga kitemo daijoobuda.
(I) bought a lot of frozen food, so we'll be all right no matter when a guest might come.

10) この金庫に入れておけば、どんな火事になっても中の物は大丈夫です。
Kono kinkoni ireteokeba, donna kajini nattemo nakano monowa daijoobu-desu.
If (you) put your valuables in this safe, they will be protected from even the biggest fire.

11) この時計は古いけど、部品を取りかえれば大丈夫だそうです。

Kono tokeiwa furuikedo, buhin-o torikaereba daijoobuda-soodesu.
This is an old clock, but (they) said that if you replace some of the parts, it should work fine.

へこむ／くぼむ／ひっこむ

■ *hekomu* ■ *kubomu* ■ *hikkomu*

へこむ ■ *hekomu* ■ to be dented 

ものののある部分に、何らかの**力が加わって内側に入りこんだ形**になることです(例1, 2, 3, 4)。また「へこむ」は、「ボール・缶・やかん」など比較的薄いものや、それほどかたくないものの変形について使います。

Hekomu indicates that the shape of a part of something is pushed in because of pressure applied to it (ex.1, 2, 3, 4). In addition, *hekomu* is used to describe changes in the shape of relatively soft or thin objects, such as a ball, can, or kettle.

---

1) 追突されて、バンパーがへこんだ。
Tsuitotsusarete, banpaaga hekonda.
(My) bumper was dented when someone ran into me.

2) 紅茶の缶を落としたらへこんでしまった。
Koochano kan-o otoshitara hekonde-shimatta.
(I) dropped the can of tea and it dented.

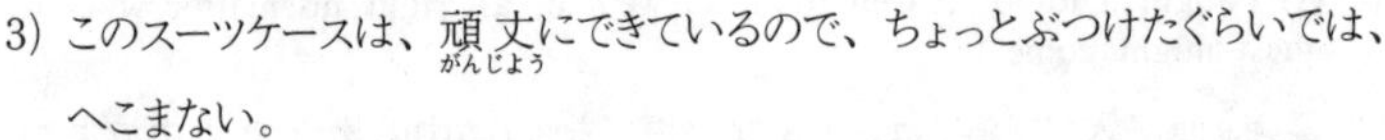

3) このスーツケースは、頑丈にできているので、ちょっとぶつけたぐらいでは、へこまない。
Kono suutsukeesuwa, ganjooni dekiteirunode, chotto butsuketa guraidewa, hekomanai.
This suitcase is strongly made so it won't dent even if it is bumped around a little.

4) この缶づめはちょっとへこんでいるから安くなっている。
Kono kanzumewa chotto hekondeirukara yasukunatteiru.
The price of this can has been marked down because it's dented.

くぼむ ■*kubomu* ■to sink

ものの一部が内側に入りこんでいる、つまり**落ち込んだ状態**になることです(例5, 6, 7)。「へこむ」と違って瞬間的な変形には使わず、ある**程度の時間**を必要とします。また外部からの**力が加わらなくても**かまいません。結果の状態を表す「くぼんだ目」「くぼんでいる所」などのような使い方がほとんどです。

Kubomu is used when a part of something bends inward or is depressed (ex. 5, 6, 7). Unlike *hekomu*, *kubomu* does not refer to momentary changes in shape, but instead requires a certain amount of time. Also, pressure applied from the outside is not necessarily required. It is most often used in expressions such as *kubonda me* (hollow eyes) or *kubondeiru tokoro* (a sunken area) that show resultant change.

5) 潮が引いた後、岩のくぼんだ所に魚が１匹いた。
Shioga hiita ato, iwano kubonda tokoroni sakanaga ippiki ita.
After the tide went out a fish was caught in a depression in a rock.

6) お寺の石段は、何百年ものあいだ、人が上り下りするうちに、すり減ってくぼんでしまった。
Oterano ishidanwa, nanbyakunen-mono aida, hitoga noboriori-suruuchini, surihette kubondeshimatta.
The steps to the temple are worn down from people going up and down them over hundreds of years.

7) 彼は仕事で徹夜が続いたので、疲れて目がくぼんでしまった。
Karewa shigotode tetsuyaga tsuzuitanode, tsukarete mega kubondeshimatta.
His eyes are sunken because he has been continually working late nights.

ひっこむ［引っこむ］ ■*hikkomu* ■to withdraw

①つき出ているものや**とび出しているものが、元の状態にもどる**こと(例8, 9, 10, 11)、あるいは前よりもより奥まったところに入ることです。

Hikkomu is used when something that sticks out or jumps out returns to it's original condition or position (ex.8, 9, 10, 11). It may imply that the object moves back to a more recessed position than before.

②**表立っていたものが目立たない状態になる**ことです(例12, 13)。また、

目立たない奥まった場所も表します。「へこむ・くぼむ」は形の変化ですが、「引っこむ」は移動です。

It also indicates that something that is exposed becomes less conspicuous, or moves to a secluded place (ex.12, 13). While *hekomu* and *kubomu* refer to a change in the shape of something, *hikkomu* refers to movement.

---

8) 彼は、出っぱったおなかが引っこむようにと、毎晩腹筋運動をしている。
Karewa, deppatta onakaga hikkomuyoonito, maiban fukkin undoo-o shiteiru.
He is doing sit-ups every night in order to reduce his bulging stomach.

9) シャープペンシルがこわれて、芯が引っこまなくなった。
Shaapupenshiruga kowarete, shinga hikkomanaku natta.
This mechanical pencil is broken and the lead won't retract.

10) かたつむりをつついたら、殻の中に引っこんでしまった。
Katatsumurio tsutsuitara, karano nakani hikkondeshimatta.
When (I) touched the snail, it retreated into its shell.

11) 出かけたくしゃみが引っこんでしまうのは、気持ちが悪い。
Dekaketa kushamiga hikkonde-shimaunowa, kimochiga warui.
It feels weird to suppress a sneeze.

12) 彼は退職して、田舎に引っこんだ。
Karewa taishokushite, inakani hikkonda.
After retiring he moved to the country.

13) この店は表通りからちょっと引っこんでいるので、知らない人が多い。
Kono misewa omotedoorikara chotto hikkonde-irunode, shiranai hitoga ooi.
This shop is a bit off the main street, so a lot of people don't know of it.

ほか／べつ

■ *hoka* ■ *betsu*

ほか

■ *hoka*
■ another ; other ; else 

「あるもの」に対して「**それ以外のもの**」を指すことばです（例1, 2, 3, 4）。「あ

るもの」と「それ以外のもの」の間には、何らかの基準や目的など、共通するものがあります。

Hoka is used to refer to something that is other than the original subject (ex.1, 2, 3, 4). Although different, there is a commonality in standard or purpose between the two things.

---

1) 彼は、日本語と英語のほかにスペイン語も話せる。
Karewa, Nihongoto Eigono hokani Supeingomo hanaseru.
Besides Japanese and English, he can also speak Spanish.

2) 彼のほかに、こんなに細かい仕事ができる職人はいない。
Kareno hokani, konnani komakai shigotoga dekiru shokuninwa inai.
Besides him, there is no other craftsman that can do such detailed work.

3) 私にはよくわからないので、だれかほかの人に聞いてください。
Watashiniwa yoku wakaranainode, dareka hokano hitoni kiitekudasai.
I don't know much about this, so please ask somebody else about it.

4) 宿題を終えてしまうと、ほかにすることがなかったので、テレビを見た。
Shukudaio oeteshimauto, hokani surukotoga nakattanode, terebio mita.
(I) didn't have anything else to do after finishing my homework, so I watched TV.

べつ［別］

■ *betsu*
■ another ; other 

ことがらや状態などが、同じではない違うものや、**分けられたもの・区別されたもの**を指します（例5, 6, 7, 8, 9, 10)。「ほか」は「それ以外のもの」を表し、「別」は、「ちがうもの」「分けられたもの」を表します。例10の「別に～ない」は「特に（は）～ない」という意味です。

Betsu is used when referring to a thing or condition that is different, divided from, or classified differently from the original subject (ex.5, 6, 7, 8, 9, 10). While *hoka* means 'something other than', *betsu* refers to something that is different or separated. In Example 10, the expression *betsu ni ～nai* means the same as *toku ni ～nai* (nothing in particular).

---

5) 理論と実践とは別のことだ。
Rironto jissentowa betsuno kotoda.

Theory and application are different matters.

6) 私は講義を聞きながら、別のことを考えていた。
Watashiwa koogio kikinagara, betsuno kotoo kangaeteita.
My mind was somewhere else during the lecture. (I was thinking about something else while listening to the lecture.)

7) 新幹線に乗るときは、運賃とは別に特急料金を払わなければならない。
Shinkansenni noru tokiwa, unchintowa betsuni tokkyuu-ryookin-o harawanakereba naranai.
When (you) ride on the *Shinkansen*, you must buy an express ticket in addition to the regular fare.

8) この地区では空き缶を出すとき、アルミ缶とスチール缶を別にしなければならない。
Kono chikudewa akikan-o dasutoki, arumikanto suchiirukan-o betsuni shinakereba naranai.
In this area, (you) must separate your empty steel and aluminum cans when you throw them away.

9) 私たちの学校では、成績別にクラスが分けられている。
Watashitachino gakkoodewa, seisekibetsuni kurasuga wakerareteiru.
In our school, classes are divided according to the grades of the students.

10) 今日は別にすることがない。
Kyoowa betsuni suru kotoga nai.
(I) don't have anything special to do today.

ほす／かわかす

■*hosu* ■*kawakasu*

ほす［干す］ ■*hosu* ■to dry ; to hang out to dry ; to air

ものの湿気やいらない水分を無くすために、**つるしたり広げたり**して、しばらくの間、**日光や風にあてる**とき使います（例1, 2, 3)。例4、5のように、ぬれていないものを干すこともあります。「干す」という**行為や動作に重点**があるので、干したものが必ずしも完全に乾かなくて、水分が残っていてもかまいません。
To expose something to the sun or wind by hanging or spreading it out in order to dry it (ex.1, 2, 3). As in Examples 4 and 5, *hosu* also means to air out something (a quilt, blanket, etc.). The focus is on the action itself, and not on the dryness of the object. Therefore, it does not matter if the object is not fully dried.

1) 洗濯物を庭に干す。
Sentakumonoo niwani hosu.
Hang laundry out in their yard.

2) ぶどうを干して、干しぶどうを作る。
Budoo-o hoshite, hoshibudoo-o tsukuru.
Raisins are made by drying grapes.

3) 食品を干して保存する方法は昔からある。
Shokuhin-o hoshite hozonsuru hoohoowa mukashikara aru.
The method of preserving food by dehydration has been around for a long time.

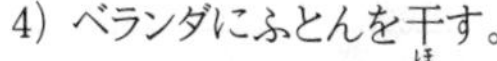
4) ベランダにふとんを干す。
Berandani futon-o hosu.*
Air out the *futon* on the veranda.
—— * A *futon* is Japanese bedding stuffed with cotton wadding, down or other filling. A *futon* set consists of two *futons*, one which is used to cover oneself and one that is laid down as a mattress underneath.

5) 長い間たんすに入れておいた服を日かげに干す。
Nagai aida tansuni ireteoita fukuo hikageni hosu.
Air out clothes that have been kept in the chest of drawers for a long time in the shade.

かわかす [乾かす] ■*kawakasu* ■to dry 

ぬれたものを、ぬれる前の状態にもどすときや、ものの**中まで完全に湿気や水分が無くなるようにする**とき使います（例6, 7, 8, 9）。手段は日光・風・熱など何を使ってもかまいません。したがって乾燥機を使うのは、「洗濯物を乾かす」で「干す」ではありません。

To get the moisture out of something in order to make it dry, or to completely dehydrate something (ex.6, 7, 8, 9). Various methods can be used, such as using sunlight, wind, or heat. Thus *kawakasu*, not *hosu*, is used to express 'to dry' laundry in a dryer.

6) 洗濯物を干して乾かす。
Sentakumonoo hoshite kawakasu.
Hang laundry out to dry.

7) 雨なので、洗濯物を乾燥機で乾かした。
Amenanode, sentakumonoo kansookide kawakashita.
Because it was raining, (I) dried my laundry in the dryer.

8) 雨にぬれた髪は、すぐ乾かしたほうがいい。
Ameni nureta kamiwa, sugu kawakashita hooga ii.
(You'd) better dry your rain-soaked hair immediately.

9) ペンキを速く乾かすには、どうすればいいでしょうか。
Penkio hayaku kawakasuniwa, doosureba iideshooka?
How can (I) make the paint dry quickly?

ほぼ／だいたい／およそ

■*hobo* ■*daitai* ■*oyoso*

ほぼ

■*hobo*
■about ; almost

もう少しで目標となる数量や程度になるようすを表します。「大部分・ほとんど・百パーセントに近い」という意味を含みます（例1, 2, 3, 4）。

Hobo indicates a condition in which an additional small amount is required to reach a desired amount or level. It includes the meanings of the words *daibubun* (the majority), *hotondo* (nearly), and *hyaku-paasento ni chikai* (nearly 100%) (ex.1, 2, 3, 4).

1) 貯金がほぼ100万円になった。
Chokinga hobo hyakuman-enni natta.
(My) savings have nearly reached ¥1,000,000.

2) 長い間かかったこのビルもほぼ完成に近づいた。
Nagai aida kakatta kono birumo hobo kansei ni chikazuita.
This building, which has taken so long to build, is near completion.

3) この公会堂は隣にある教会とほぼ同じころに建てられた。
Kono kookaidoowa tonarini aru kyookaito hobo onaji koroni taterareta.
This public hall was built about the same time as the church next door.

4) こんど買った家は前の家とほぼ同じ広さです。
Kondo katta iewa maeno ieto hobo onaji hirosadesu.
The house (we've) just bought is about as large as our old house.

だいたい

■ *daitai*
■ about ; roughly

基準となる数量や程度から大きくはずれてはいないようすや、ものごとの**大筋**（**要点**）を表します。**おおざっぱ**なきりのいい単位をのべたり、かなり近い程度の例をひいてのべるときに使います（例5, 6, 7, 8)。

Daitai indicates that the amount or level of something is not far from the standard. It may also be used when speaking of a summary or the point of something, when speaking in approximate terms of something, or when mentioning something else that is nearly of the same level (ex.5, 6, 7, 8).

---

5) あなたの言いたいことはだいたいわかりました。
Anatano iitai kotowa daitai wakarimashita.
(I) basically understand what you are trying to say.

6) このりんごは直径がだいたい10センチぐらいです。
Kono ringowa chokkeiga daitai jussenchi guraidesu.
The diameter of this apple is around ten centimeters.

7) 私は朝のしたくにだいたい30分かかります。
Watashiwa asano shitakuni daitai sanjuppun kakarimasu.
It takes me about 30 minutes to get ready in the morning.

8) 次の仕事についてはだいたいのことは田中さんに話してあります。
Tsugino shigotoni tsuitewa daitaino kotowa Tanakasanni hanashite-arimasu.
Most of the details concerning the next project have been mentioned to Mr. Tanaka.

およそ ■ *oyoso* ■ roughly ; approximately 

ものごとの**要点**(ようてん)をのべたり、数量(すうりょう)などをきりのいい単位(たんい)にまとめていうときに使(つか)います。**だいたい**と同(おな)じように使(つか)われますが、「およそ」のほうが**やや改**(あらた)**まった表現**(ひょうげん)です(例(れい)9, 10, 11, 12)。また例(れい)13は「まったく〜ない」という意味(いみ)です。

Oyoso is used when speaking of the gist of something, or an approximate amount. It is used similarly to *daitai*, but is a slightly more formal expression (ex.9, 10, 11, 12). In Example 13, *oyoso* takes the meaning 'not at all'.

9) この駅(えき)の利用者(りようしゃ)は1日(にち)におよそ1万人(まんにん)ぐらいです。
Kono ekino riyooshawa ichinichini oyoso ichimannin guraidesu.
Approximately 10,000 people a day use this station.

10) 事件(じけん)のあらましはおよそ次(つぎ)の通(とお)りです。
Jikenno aramashiwa oyoso tsugino tooridesu.
The incident occured something like this.

11) およそのことはわかりましたが、細(こま)かいことをもう一度(いちど)説明(せつめい)してください。
Oyosono kotowa wakarimashitaga, komakai kotoo mooichido setsumeishite kudasai.
(I) basically understand, but would you mind explaining the details again.

12) 来月(らいげつ)になれば事件(じけん)のおよその見当(けんとう)がつきます。
Raigetsuni nareba jikenno oyosono kentooga tsukimasu.
(I) can give a rough guess as to what will happen next month.

13) 山(やま)が動(うご)いたなんて、およそ聞(き)いたことがありません。
Yamaga ugoitanante, oyoso kiita kotoga arimasen.
(I've) never heard of mountains moving before.

体(からだ)が沈没(ちんぼつ)するんです

いつもむずかしいことばを使(つか)いたがるエディが、きょうもまたおかしなことを言(い)いました。「ぼくは水泳(すいえい)が得意(とくい)じゃないんです。いっしょうけんめい水(みず)をかいているつもりなのに、すぐに

体(からだ)が沈没(ちんぼつ)するんです」

ちょっと待(ま)ってください。たしかに「沈没(ちんぼつ)する」も「沈(しず)む」もどちらも、何(なに)かが水(みず)の底(そこ)に行(い)くことですけれど…。「沈没(ちんぼつ)する」は船(ふね)についてだけ使(つか)うことばです。ですから「このあたりの海(うみ)で、昔(むかし)海賊船(かいぞくせん)が沈没(ちんぼつ)した」とは言(い)えますが、「体(からだ)が沈没(ちんぼつ)する」はおかしな言(い)い方(かた)です。

Karada ga chinbotsu suru n desu

Eddie likes using difficult Japanese words, but unfortunately he often misuses them. Today, he said something odd again ; "I'm not good at swimming. I try my hardest to paddle but... *sugu ni karada ga chinbotsu suru n desu*[1]."

Now just a moment. Certainly, *chinbotsu suru* means the same as *shizumu*, i.e., to go to the bottom of the water. However, *chinbotsu suru* is only used when speaking of ships. Therefore, it may be used when saying, 'In these waters, *mukashi kaizokusen ga chinbotsu shita*,[2]' but when speaking of a person's body it sounds strange.

1 *my body soon sinks (This expression is actually incorrect in Japanese.)*
2 *A pirate ship that sank a long time ago is resting.*

まえ／さき

■ *mae* ■ *saki*

まえ［前(まえ)］ ■ *mae* ■ (in) front ; before 

①**現在(げんざい)より**も、または過去(かこ)の一時点(いちじてん)よりも**過去(かこ)を指(さ)して**使(つか)います（例(れい)1, 2, 3）。

Mae is used to indicate a time in the past, either prior to the present moment or a point of time in the past (ex.1, 2, 3).

②あることがらよりも**早(はや)い時期(じき)**を表(あらわ)します（例(れい)4, 5）。

It may indicate a time prior to a certain event (ex.4, 5).

③ものの**正面**の**位置**や**方向**を表すとき使います（例6, 7）。

Mae is also used to express a position or direction that is directly in front of something (ex.6, 7).

④**並んでいるものの初めのほう**を表すとき使います（例8, 9）。

劇場や教室などでは、ステージや教壇に近いところ、そして乗り物では、進行方向（運転席）に近いところをそれぞれ「前」といいます。

In addition, it is used to indicate the beginning portion of objects that are arranged in a line (ex.8, 9).

In a theater or classroom, *mae* refers to the area near the stage or podium, and with vehicles it refers to a place near the driver's seat, facing the direction of travel.

---

1) この絵は、前に見たことがある。
Kono ewa, maeni mitakotoga aru.
(I've) seen this painting before.

2) 私は、3週間前に田中さんに会いました。
Watashiwa, sanshuukanmaeni Tanakasanni aimashita.
I saw Mr. Tanaka three weeks ago.

3) 去年のクリスマスの2日前に、子犬をもらいました。
Kyonenno kurisumasuno futsukamaeni, koinuo moraimashita.
(We) were given a puppy two days before last Christmas.

4) 彼は食事の前に必ずお祈りをする。
Karewa shokujino maeni kanarazu oinorio suru.
He always says grace before meals.

5) 私は寝る前にコーヒーを飲むと、眠れなくなるんです。
Watashiwa nerumaeni koohiio nomuto, nemurenaku narundesu.
Whenever I drink coffee before I go to bed I can't get to sleep.

6) 12時に、交番の前で友達と会うことになっています。
Juunijini, koobanno maede tomodachito au kotoni natteimasu.
(We've) arranged to meet our friends at 12 o'clock in front of the police box.

7) 授業中はよそ見をしないで、ちゃんと前を向いていなさい。
Jugyoochuuwa yosomio shinaide, chanto maeo muiteinasai.
Don't look off to the side during class; face the front properly.

8) 私の名前は青野なので、いつも出席簿では前のほうです。
Watashino namaewa Aononanode, itsumo shussekibodewa maeno hoodesu.
My name is Aono so I'm always toward the top of the attendance list.

9) この列車の、前２両は禁煙車です。
Kono resshano, mae niryoowa kin-enshadesu.
The first two cars of this train are no-smoking cars.

さき［先］

■ *saki*
■ (in) the future ; earlier ; previous

---

①**将来**や**未来**を指して使います（例10, 11）。
Saki is used to refer to the future (ex.10, 11).

②**進んで行くところ・もっと向こう**という意味で使います（例12, 13）。
It may also be used when speaking of a place further beyond, or up ahead in the direction of motion (ex.12, 13).

③ものごとの**順序が、より早い・最初だ**という意味で使います（例14, 15, 16）。
Saki also specifies that something is earlier than or at the beginning of an ordered sequence of events (ex.14, 15, 16).

④ナイフ・棒・針などの**とがった部分**や長いものの**はし**、あるいは突き出たもののはしなどを指します（例17）。
位置についていうとき「前」は「すぐ正面」を指し、「先」は「もう少し行ったところ・向こう」を指します。
Saki also refers to the pointed end of a knife, stick, needle, etc., or the tip of something long or protruding (ex.17).
When referring to position, *mae* indicates 'immediately in front', while *saki* indicates a position 'further ahead' or 'beyond'.

---

10) １か月先までテニスコートの予約は、いっぱいです。
Ikkagetsu sakimade tenisukootono yoyakuwa, ippaidesu.
The tennis court is booked up (reservations are filled up) until a month from now.

11) この仕事の先は、まだ見えない。
Kono shigotono sakiwa, mada mienai.
There is still no end in sight for this job.

12) 100メートル先にある建物が、私の会社です。

Hyaku-meetoru-sakini aru tatemonoga, watashino kaishadesu.
The building 100 meters ahead is my company.

13) この先は行き止まりです。

Kono sakiwa ikidomaridesu.
There is a dead-end ahead.

14) ここはセルフサービスなので、先に食券を買ってください。

Kokowa serufusaabisunanode, sakini shokken-o kattekudasai.
This is a self-service place so please purchase a meal ticket first.

15) どうぞお先に。

Doozo osakini. Please go ahead. (After you.)

16) お先に失礼します。

Osakini shitsureishimasu.
Excuse me for leaving before you. (Good-bye.)

17) ボールが木にひっかかったので、棒の先でつついて落とした。

Booruga kini hikkakattanode, boono sakide tsutsuite otoshita.
The ball got stuck in a tree so (we) poked it with the end of a stick and knocked it down.

まがる／そる／しなう

■*magaru* ■*soru* ■*shinau*

まがる［曲がる］ ■*magaru* ■to curve ; to bend ; to turn 

①もともとまっすぐなものが、**まっすぐでなくなる**とき使います（例1,2）。

Magaru is used to indicate that something which was originally straight becomes bent or curved (ex.1, 2).

②**方向を変えて進む**とき使います（例3,4）。

To change direction while moving, i.e., to turn left or right (ex.3, 4).

③正しい**位置からずれる**とき使います（例5,6）。

To deviate from a proper location or position (ex.5, 6, 7).

例7の「曲がったこと」は、不誠実なことという意味です。

In Example 7, *magatta koto* means dishonesty.

---

1) その超能力者が投げたスプーンは皆、曲がってしまった。
Sono choonooryoku-shaga nageta supuunwa mina, magatteshimatta.
The spoons that the man with telekinetic powers threw in the air were all bent.

2) 最近は、腰の曲がったお年寄りをあまり見なくなった。
Saikinwa, koshino magatta otoshiyorio amari minakunatta.
Nowadays, (we) seldom see old people with curvature of the spine.

3) 次の角を左に曲がると、すぐに私の家がある。
Tsugino kadoo hidarini magaruto, suguni watashino iega aru.
Turn left at the next corner and you'll see my house right away.

4) 川は、ジャングルの中をくねくねと曲がって流れている。
Kawawa, janguruno nakao kunekuneto magatte nagareteiru.
The river winds through the jungle.

5) きみのネクタイは、いつも曲がっているよ。
Kimino nekutaiwa, itsumo magatteiruyo.
Your necktie is always crooked.

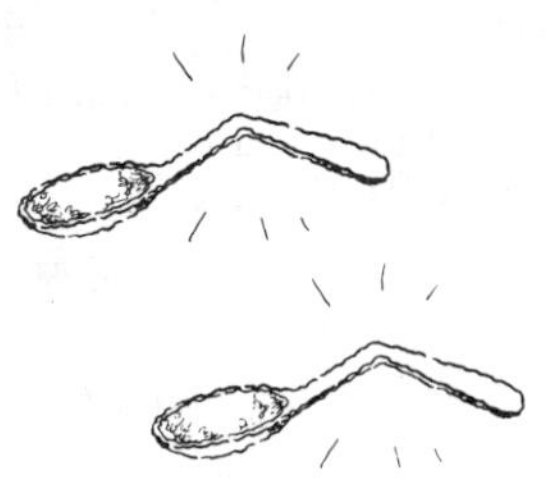

6) 壁にかけた絵が曲がっている。
Kabeni kaketa ega magatteiru.
The picture on the wall is crooked.

7) 私は曲がったことは大きらいだ。
Watashiwa magatta kotowa daikiraida.
I hate dishonesty.

そる「反る」 ■ *soru*
■ to be warped ; to be curved 

平らなものが，**弓のようにカーブした形になる**とき使います（例8, 9）。人間の体（手・指）については、本来一方向にしか曲がらないものを、あえて逆の方向に曲げるとき（例10）使います。

Soru is used to indicate that something flat becomes curved (ex.8, 9). When used in speaking about a part of the human body (i.e., a hand, finger, etc.), *soru* means to bend backward in an unnatural fashion (ex.10).

---

8) 窓(まど)ぎわに置(お)いておくと、本(ほん)の表紙(ひょうし)は、すぐにそる。
Madogiwani oite okuto, honno hyooshiwa, suguni soru.
The cover of a book placed by a window will soon warp.

9) 日(ひ)なたに置(お)いておいたら、板(いた)がそってしまった。
Hinatani oiteoitara, itaga sotteshimatta.
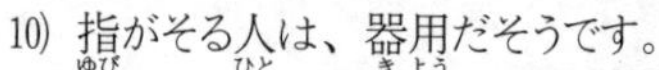
When (I) left the board in the sun it got warped.

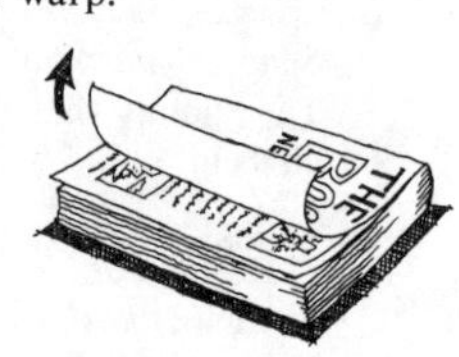

10) 指(ゆび)がそる人(ひと)は、器用(きよう)だそうです。
Yubiga soruhitowa, kiyoodasoodesu.
(They) say that a person who can bend his fingers backwards is skillful (in handywork).

しなう
- *shinau*
- to bend ; to be supple ; to be pliant

細長(ほそなが)く弾力性(だんりょくせい)のあるものが、力(ちから)を加(くわ)えられて**曲(ま)がり**、力(ちから)をぬくと**また元(もと)の形(かたち)にもどる**とき使(つか)います（例(れい)11, 12, 13, 14)。

Shinau denotes that something long, slender, and flexible bends when pressure is applied to it, and returns to its original position when the pressure is removed (ex.11, 12, 13, 14).

---

11) 風(かぜ)で竹(たけ)がしなっている。
Kazede takega shinatteiru.
The bamboo is bending in the wind.

12) 大(おお)きい魚(さかな)がかかったので、つりざおがしなった。
Ookii sakanaga kakattanode, tsurizaoga shinatta.
My fishing pole bent because (I) hooked a big fish.

13) 棒高飛(ぼうたかと)びの棒(ぼう)は、よくしなう材質(ざいしつ)でできている。
Bootakatobino boowa, yoku shinau zaishitsude dekiteiru.
The pole used in pole-vaulting is made of flexible materials.

14) 柳(やなぎ)の枝(えだ)は、しなうので折(お)れにくい。
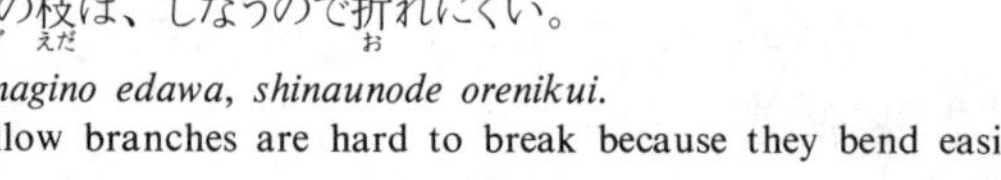
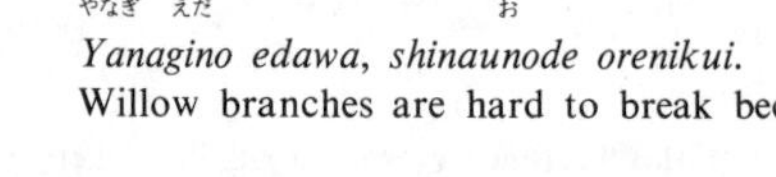
Yanagino edawa, shinaunode orenikui.
Willow branches are hard to break because they bend easily.

まじる／まざる

■*majiru*　　■*mazaru*

まじる［混じる・交じる］ ■*majiru* ■to (be) mix(ed)

あるものの中に、**少量の異なった種類のものが入りこんでいる**・まぎれこんでいるというとき使います（例1, 2, 3, 4, 5)。それぞれの性質・形などは残っていて、見分けることができるという感じを含みます。

This indicates that a small amount of some substance has gotten into or is intermingled with a different substance (ex.1, 2, 3, 4, 5). It includes a sense that the respective properties, form, etc., of the mixed objects are preserved and can be individually discerned.

1) 浜では大人に交じって子供たちも網を引いていた。
Hamadewa otonani majitte kodomotachimo amio hiiteita.
On the shore, mingled among the adults, children were also pulling on the nets.

2) この犬にはコリーの血が混じっているらしい。
Kono inuniwa koriino chiga majitteiru rashii.
This dog seems to have some collie (breed) blood (mixed) in him.

3) 雑音が混じってしまって放送が聞きとれない。
Zatsuonga majitteshimatte hoosooga kikitorenai.
There's a lot of static mixed in the broadcasts and it's hard to hear.

4) 食品工場でミルクに機械油が混じるという事故があった。
Shokuhinkoojoode mirukuni kikaiaburaga majirutoyuu jikoga atta.
There was an accident at a food processing plant, in which some machine oil was mixed in with milk.

5) 彼も白髪が交じる年齢になった。
Karemo shiragaga majiru nenreini natta.
He, too, has reached the age when gray hairs start to creep in.

まざる［混ざる・交ざる］ ■*mazaru* ■to mix and blend

あるものに**別(べつ)のもの**が**加(くわ)わって**、**一(ひと)つの状態(じょうたい)になる**ことです。**とけあう・一体化(いったいか)する**という意味(いみ)で、違和感(いわかん)がない状態(じょうたい)です（例(れい)6, 7, 8, 9）。

Mazaru indicates that one substance is added to another, resulting in a single substance. It is implied that the substances melt or integrate into a single unit, creating a state free of discord or incompatibility (ex.6, 7, 8, 9).

---

6) A：水(みず)と油(あぶら)は混(ま)ざりますか。
B：いいえ、混(ま)ざりません。

A： *Mizuto aburawa mazarimasuka?* Do water and oil mix?
B： *Iie, mazarimasen.* No, they don't.

7) ドレッシングは、酢(す)と油(あぶら)がよく混(ま)ざっていないとおいしくない。
Doresshinguwa, suto aburaga yoku mazatteinaito oishikunai.
Salad dressing isn't good unless the oil and vinegar are well mixed.

8) 白(しろ)い絵(え)の具(ぐ)に赤(あか)い絵(え)の具(ぐ)が混(ま)ざって、ピンクになってしまった。
Shiroi enoguni akai enoguga mazatte, pinkuni natteshimatta.
Some red paint got mixed into the white paint, and it turned out pink.

9) このシャツには少(すこ)し麻(あさ)が交(ま)ざっている。
Kono shatsuniwa sukoshi asaga mazatteiru.
There's a little hemp mixed in this shirt.

ます／ふやす／ためる

■*masu* ■*fuyasu* ■*tameru*

ます［増(ま)す］ ■*masu* ■to increase

ものごとの**数(すう)・量(りょう)・程度(ていど)**がそれまでよりも**多(おお)くなる**とき、また多(おお)くするとき使(つか)います（例(れい)1, 2, 3, 4, 5）。多(おお)くなるときは自動詞(じどうし)で「～が増(ま)す」と使(つか)い、多(おお)くするときは他動詞(たどうし)で「～を増(ま)す」と使(つか)います。「信用(しんよう)、人気(にんき)、興味(きょうみ)、親(した)しみ」など抽象的(ちゅうしょうてき)なことには「増(ま)す」しか使(つか)いません。

Masu is used when the number, amount or degree of something becomes, or is made, larger than it was before (ex.1, 2, 3, 4, 5). When it indicates that something becomes larger it is used as an intransitive verb, i.e., *~ga masu*, and when it is used to mean to make something larger it takes the transitive verb form, i.e., ~*o masu*. When speaking of an increase in an abstract matter such as trust, popularity, interest, or friendship *masu* is the only verb that may be used.

---

1) 大雨のあと、川は水かさが増す。
Ooameno ato, kawawa mizukasaga masu.
After a heavy rain, the river's water level rises.

2) 秋になると食欲が増す。
Akini naruto shokuyokuga masu.
In autumn, (my) appetite increases.

3) 彼が来てから、パーティーの楽しさが一段と増した。
Karega kitekara, paatiino tanoshisaga ichidanto mashita.
After he came, the party became much more enjoyable.

4) この駐車場の料金は1時間500円で、あとは30分増すごとに200円です。
Kono chuushajoono ryookinwa ichijikan gohyakuende, atowa sanjuppun masu gotoni nihyakuendesu.
The fee at this parking lot is ¥500 for up to one hour ; after that, it is an additional ¥200 for every 30 minutes.

5) 列車は駅を出るとじょじょにスピードを増していった。
Resshawa ekioderuto jojoni supiidoo mashiteitta.
The train gradually increased its speed after leaving the station.

ふやす［増やす・殖やす］ ■*fuyasu* ■ to increase 

数、量をそれまでよりも多くすることです（例6, 7, 8, 9）。具体的に**数えられるもの**にしか使いません。自動詞は「増える」です。財産、資産などは「殖やす」と書きます。

To increase a number or quantity (ex.6, 7, 8, 9). *Fuyasu* can be used only for countable objects. The intransitive form is *fueru*. When referring to things such as fortune, assets, etc., the *kanji* 殖やす is written.

---

6) 外国の首相が来るので警備の人数を増やした。
Gaikokuno shushooga kurunode keibino ninzuuo fuyashita.

Because the Prime Minister of a foreign country is coming, (they) increased the number of guards on duty.

7) 外国語が自由に話せるようになるには、語彙を増やさなければならない。
Gaikokugoga jiyuuni hanaseruyooni naruniwa, goio fuyasanakereba-naranai.
To be able to speak a foreign language fluently, (you) must increase your vocabulary.

8) 私の母はこれ以上体重を増やさないように気をつけています。
Watashino hahawa koreijoo taijuuo fuyasanaiyooni kiotsuketeimasu.
My mother is being careful not to gain any more weight.

9) 彼は、株で資産を殖やしたそうです。
Karewa, kabude shisan-o fuyashitasoodesu.
(They) say that he increased his assets with stock.

ためる ■ *tameru* ■ to save ; to pile up

---

①少しずつ量を加えていって、ある程度まとまった量にすることです。**目標となる量や目的**がはっきりしていることが多いです。「増す・増やす」はすでに元になる量があるのに対し「ためる」は**初めはゼロでもかまいません**（例10, 11)。

To save something bit by bit in order to reach a certain amount or quantity. Usually, a desired amount or purpose for saving is clear. In the cases of *masu* and *fuyasu* there already exists a certain amount of the object, but with *tameru*, there may be nothing at the beginning (ex.10, 11).

②結果的に量を多くしてしまうことです（例12, 13, 14)。人数には使いません。自動詞は「たまる」です。

To end up accumulating something (ex.12, 13, 14). *Tameru* cannot be used when speaking of people. The intransitive equivalent is *tamaru*.

---

10) 弟は新しい自転車が買いたくて、お金をためている。
Otootowa atarashii jitenshaga kaitakute, okaneo tameteiru.
My younger brother is saving money because he wants to buy a new bicycle.

11) ここでは雨水をためて飲み水にしている。
Kokodewa amamizuo tamete nomimizuni shiteiru.
Here, people keep rain water and use it as drinking water.

12) 彼(かれ)は故郷(こきょう)を離(はな)れるとき、目(め)にいっぱい涙(なみだ)をためていた。
Karewa kokyoo-o hanareru toki, meni ippai namidao tameteita.
When he left his hometown, his eyes were filled with tears.

13) 疲(つか)れをためるのは、体(からだ)に悪(わる)い。
Tsukareo tamerunowa, karadani warui.
It's bad for (one's) health to let fatigue build up.

14) 宿題(しゅくだい)をためてしまったので、今夜(こんや)は徹夜(てつや)でやらなくてはならない。
Shukudaio tameteshimatta-node, kon-yawa tetsuyade yaranakutewa naranai.
Since (I) let my homework accumulate I must stay up all night long and study.

まずしい／びんぼう

■ *mazushii* ■ *binbou*

まずしい［貧(まず)しい］ ■ *mazushii* ■ poor ; needy 

①金(かね)や物(もの)などが無(な)くて、**生活(せいかつ)が苦(くる)しい**ようすを表(あらわ)すとき使(つか)います（例(れい)1, 2）。
Mazushii describes the state of not having money or possessions, and, therefore, one has difficult life (ex.1, 2).

②**才能(さいのう)・心(こころ)などが、豊(ゆた)かではない**・粗末(そまつ)であるというようすを表(あらわ)すとき使(つか)います。したがって金持(かねも)ちでも、いつも金(かね)のことばかり考(かんが)えていて他人(たにん)に思(おも)いやりや、やさしさのない人(ひと)は、「心(こころ)の貧(まず)しい人(ひと)」と使(つか)います（例(れい)3, 4）。
It is also used to denote a deficiency of talent or compassion. Therefore, a rich person who thinks only of money and is not caring towards others is said to be *kokoro no mazushii hito* (ex.3, 4).

1) 子供(こども)の頃(ころ)、私(わたし)の家(いえ)は貧(まず)しかったので、お米(こめ)が買(か)えない日(ひ)もあった。
Kodomono koro, watashino iewa mazushikattanode, okomega kaenai himo atta.
When I was a child my family was poor, so that somedays we couldn't even buy rice.

2) 戦争(せんそう)直後(ちょくご)は、日本(にほん)も貧(まず)しい国(くに)だった。

Sensoo-chokugowa, Nihonmo mazushii kunidatta.
Right after the war, Japan was a poor country, too.

3) どんなに貧乏でも、心までまずしくなってはいけない。
Donnani binboodemo, kokoromade mazushiku nattewa ikenai.
No matter how poor (you) are, you should never be poor at heart.

4) 私の貧しい才能では、入選するのはとても無理だ。
Watashino mazushii sainoodewa, nyuusensurunowa totemo murida.
With my lack of ability, it is impossible for me to win.

びんぼう［貧乏］ ■ *binbou* ■ poverty 

金や物などが無くて、**生活が苦しい**ようすを表すとき使います（例5, 6, 7, 8）。使い方としては「貧しい」の①と同じですが、例3, 4のような才能・心といった精神的な面には使いません。

This expresses the condition of being on hard times due to a lack of money or things (ex.5, 6, 7, 8). In this regard it is interchangeable with *mazushii*, however it cannot be used in sentences like those in Examples 3 and 4 to describe a mental or spiritual condition.

---

5) 彼は貧乏な家に生まれたが、努力して大金持ちになった。
Karewa binboona ieni umaretaga, doryokushite ooganemochini natta.
He was born into a poor family, but through his efforts, he became very wealthy.

6) 私の家は貧乏だったけれど、奨学金をもらって大学に行った。
Watashino iewa binboodatta-keredo, shoogaku-kin-o moratte daigakuni itta.
My family was poor, but I received a scholarship and was able to attend college.

7) 貧乏暇なしとは、よく言ったものだ。
Binboohimanashi-towa, yoku ittamonoda.
The expression 'poor people have no leisure time' is well stated.

8) 貧乏でも心が豊かな人はいる。
Binboodemo kokoroga yutakana hitowa iru.
There are people who are poor, yet rich at heart.

～ませんか／～ましょうか

■～*masen ka*　　■～*mashou ka*

～ませんか

■～*masen ka*
■won't you...? ; shall we...?

①**誘い**や**提案をする**とき使います（例1, 2, 3)。相手の答えや意向を聞いています。

This expression is used when extending an invitation or making a suggestion (ex.1, 2, 3). It is used when asking for the listener's response or inquiring about their intentions.

②「～てくれませんか」は人に**ていねいに**ものを**頼む**ときに使います（例4, 5)。

～*te kuremasen ka* is used when one asks somebody to do something politely (ex.4, 5).

1) あした、神田の古本屋に行きませんか。
Ashita, Kandano furuhon-yani ikimasenka?
Won't you go (with me) to the used bookstores in Kanda tomorrow?

2) きょうはもう遅いので、この話の続きはあしたにしませんか。
Kyoowa moo osoinode, kono hanashino tsuzukiwa ashitani shimasenka?
It's getting late, so why don't (we) continue our conversation tomorrow?

3) 風が強くなってきましたね、窓を閉めませんか。
Kazega tsuyokunatte-kimashitane, madoo shimemasenka?
It's getting windy, isn't it? Shall (we) close the windows?

4) すみませんが、電卓を貸してくれませんか。
Sumimasenga, dentakuo kashite kuremasenka?
Excuse me, could (you) lend me your calculator, please?

5) 部屋をかたづけるのを手伝ってくれませんか。
Heyao katazukerunoo tetsudatte kuremasenka?
Won't (you) help me clean up the room, please?

～ましょうか

■～*mashou ka*
■shall we...? ; shall I...? 

①いっしょに何かをしようと**誘うとき**使います（例6, 7, 8）。

This expression is used when extending an invitation or making a suggestion which includes the listener's participation (ex.6, 7, 8).

②「私がします・してあげます」という申し出を、**ひかえめでていねいに言う**とき使います（例9, 10）。

It is also used when making a polite, modest offer to do something for someone (ex.9, 10).

---

6) そろそろお昼にしましょうか。
Sorosoro ohiruni shimashooka?
It's about time (we) went to lunch. (Let's go to lunch.)

7) 花壇にチューリップを植えましょうか。
Kadanni chuurippuo uemashooka?
Shall (we) plant tulips in the flower bed?

8) あとで買い物に行きましょうか。
Atode kaimononi ikimashooka?
Shall (we) go shopping later?

9) 何かお手伝いしましょうか。
Nanika otetsudai shimashooka?
Is there something (I) can do to help?

10) 駅まで車でお送りしましょうか。
Ekimade kurumade ookuri-shimashooka?
Why don't (I) take (you) to the station by car?

また／もういちど／ふたたび

■*mata* ■*mou ichido* ■*futatabi*

また［又］ ■*mata* ■again

同じことが、さらに**くり返される**とき使います（例1, 2, 3, 4）。

Mata denotes the repetition of some event (ex.1, 2, 3, 4).

---

1) きょうはこれで帰(かえ)ります。あしたまた来(き)ます。

Kyoowa korede kaerimasu. Ashita mata kimasu.
(I'll) go home now. I'll come again tomorrow.

2) 彼(かれ)はきょうもまた遅刻(ちこく)だ。

Karewa kyoomo mata chikokuda.
He was late again today.

3) インド旅行(りょこう)は楽(たの)しかった。ぜひまた行(い)きたい。

Indoryokoowa tanoshikatta. Zehi mata ikitai.
(My) trip to India was a lot of fun. I'd really like to go again someday.

4) またどろぼうに入(はい)られた。これで３回目(かいめ)だ。

Mata dorobooni hairareta. Korede sankaimeda.
A burglar broke in here again. This is the third time.

もういちど［もう一度(いちど)］

■ *mou ichido*
■ one more time ; again

同(おな)じことをくり返(かえ)すとき使(つか)います。まだ**足(た)りない・不十分(ふじゅうぶん)**だ、などの理由(りゆう)で、「もう一度(いちど)」とはっきり回数(かいすう)を限(かぎ)って希望(きぼう)したり要求(ようきゅう)したり頼(たの)んだりする気持(きも)ちが強(つよ)く含(ふく)まれています（例(れい)5, 6, 7, 8)。

Mou ichido is used when one repeats an action. It implies that one is requesting, demanding, or hoping for something to be done one more time because the previous time was insufficient or unsatisfactory (ex.5, 6, 7, 8).

---

5) よく聞(き)こえません。もう一度(いちど)大(おお)きい声(こえ)で言(い)ってください。

Yoku kikoemasen. Moo ichido ookii koede ittekudasai.
(I) can't hear you. Would you say it again louder, please?

6) あの映画(えいが)、とても良(よ)かった。もう一度(いちど)見(み)たい。

Ano eiga, totemo yokatta. Moo ichido mitai.
That was a very good movie. (I'd) like to see it again.

7) もう一度(いちど)、学生時代(がくせいじだい)にもどりたい。

Moo ichido, gakuseijidaini modoritai.
(I'd) like to return to my student days again.

8) もう一度(いちど)呼(よ)んでみても返事(へんじ)がなければ、帰(かえ)ろう。

Moo ichido yondemitemo henjiga nakereba, kaeroo.

Call him again, and if (he) doesn't answer, let's go home.

ふたたび［再び］ ■*futatabi* ■again

前と同じことが、**さらにくり返される**とき使います（例9, 10）。「**二度目だ**」という意味を持ち「また」と同じように使いますが、「また」よりも少しかたい表現で、ふつうの会話ではあまり使いません。「決して〜ない」と強い否定を表すとき、「二度と再び〜ない」のように使います（例11, 12）。

This word is used when something is repeated the same way as before (ex.9, 10). Like *mata*, it is used to mean 'a second time', however it is a slightly more formal expression and is only rarely used in conversation. It may be used in strong negative statements in the form *nido to futatabi* 〜*nai* (never 〜again) (ex.11, 12).

9) アンコールの後、再び大きな拍手がわきおこった。
Ankooruno ato, futatabi ookina hakushuga wakiokotta.
After the encore, (the audience) broke into enthusiastic applause once again.

10) 古いアルバムを見ていたら、懐かしい思い出が再びよみがえってきた。
Furui arubamuo miteitara, natsukashii omoidega futatabi yomigaettekita.
While looking at the old photo album, (I) began to recall fond memories again.

11) あのような悲惨な戦争を二度と再び起こしてはならない。
Ano yoona hisanna sensoo-o nidoto futatabi okoshitewa naranai.
(We) must never cause such a tragic war again.

12) タイタニック号は海に沈んで、二度と再びその姿を現すことはなかった。
Taitanikkugoowa umini shizunde, nidoto futatabi sono sugatao arawasu kotowa nakatta.
The Titanic sank into the sea, never to be seen again.

まもる／ふせぐ

■*mamoru* ■*fusegu*

まもる［守る］ ■ *mamoru* ■ to protect ; to guard 

①**たいせつなもの**や、いまの**良い状態**がなくなったり壊れたりしないように**保つ**というとき使います（例1, 2, 3)。

To preserve or safeguard something important, or a favorable situation or condition (ex.1, 2, 3).

②**法則・規則・約束**などによって、決められていることを、**それに従って行動する**ときに使います（例4, 5)。

To act or behave in accordance with a law, rule, or promise (ex.4, 5).

1) カメレオンは敵から身を守るために体の色を変える。
Kamereonwa tekikara mio mamoru tameni karadano iroo kaeru.
A chameleon protects itself from enemies by changing colors.

2) 絶滅寸前の動物を守るためにワシントン条約がつくられた。
Zetsumetsu sunzenno doobutsuo mamoru tameni Washinton-jooyakuga tsukurareta.
The Washington Treaty was created in order to protect animals on the verge of extinction.

3) 世界各国で地球を守ろうという運動がさかんだ。
Sekaikakkokude chikyuuo mamorootoyuu undooga sakanda.
Movements to protect the earth have become more extensive throughout the world (in each of the countries of the world).

4) 彼女は必ず約束を守る人です。
Kanojowa kanarazu yakusokuo mamoru hitodesu.
She is a person who always keeps her promises.

5) 交通規則は守らなければなりません。
Kootsuu kisokuwa mamoranakereba narimasen.
(You) must follow the traffic rules.

ふせぐ［防ぐ］ ■ *fusegu* ■ to protect ; to defend 

悪い状態にならないように、いまの良い状態に変化や害を与えるものを**積**

極的に前もって避けるようにするとき使います（例6, 7, 8, 9, 10）。「守る」よりも、積極的である点がちがいます。

To try to prevent something that may cause harm or change in the present condition from doing so (ex.6, 7, 8, 9, 10). *Fusegu* suggests more active action to prevent something than does *mamoru*.

---

6) 海辺の家は松の木をたくさん植えて、砂や風を防ぎます。
Umibeno iewa matsunokio takusan uete, sunaya kazeo fusegimasu.
Many pine trees are planted by homes near the sea for protection from the sand and wind.

7) 病気を治すことだけでなく、病気を防ぐことも医者のだいじな仕事です。
Byookio naosu kotodakede naku, byookio fusegu kotomo ishano daijina shigotodesu.
An important task for doctors is not only to cure disease, but to prevent it as well.

8) ボクサーは、相手のパンチを両手で防いだ。
Bokusaawa, aiteno panchio ryootede fuseida.
The boxer defended himself from his opponent's punch with both hands.

9) ゴム手袋をはめて水仕事をすると、肌あれを防ぎます。
Gomutebukuroo hamete mizushigotoo suruto, hadaareo fusegimasu.
If (you) use rubber gloves when you do chores using water, you'll be able to prevent your hands from getting rough.

10) 野菜や果物を毎日ちゃんと食べていれば、ビタミン不足を防げます。
Yasaiya kudamonoo mainichi chanto tabeteireba, bitaminbusokuo fusegemasu.
If (you) eat vegetables and fruit everyday, you will avoid a vitamin deficiency.

まるで／ちょうど

■ *marude* ■ *choudo*

まるで

■ *marude*
■ just like ; (not) at all 

---

①ものごとの全体の雰囲気・状態・ようすなどを、その特徴をよく表している

ものや、**よく似ているものにたとえて**表現するときに使います。多くの場合、「〜ようだ・〜みたいだ」などといっしょに使い、軽い驚きなどを含んでいます（例1, 2, 3, 4）。

Marude is used in metaphorical expressions to liken the overall mood, condition, or appearance of something to something else that manifests precisely those particular characteristics, or to a very similar object. In most cases it is used with ~*youda* or ~*mitaida*, and includes a sense of slight surprise (ex.1, 2, 3, 4).

②「まるで〜ない・だめ」などのように使い、**完全な否定**を表します。また、**強調**の意味も含みます（例5, 6）。

When used in forms such as *marude~nai* or *marude~dame*, it denotes a completely negative situation, or is used for emphasis (ex.5, 6).

---

1) 彼は計算が速くて、まるでコンピューターのようだ。
Karewa keisanga hayakute, marude konpyuutaano yooda.
He is very quick at calculation—just like a computer.

2) 彼女は心が優しくて、まるで天使のような人だ。
Kanojowa kokoroga yasashikute, marude tenshino yoona hitoda.
She is so kind. It is as if she were an angel.

3) 薬を飲んだら、あんなに高かった熱がまるでうそのように下がった。
Kusurio nondara, annani takakatta netsuga marude usonoyooni sagatta.
It was amazing how my fever went down after I took the medicine.

4) おばさんの遺産がもらえるかもしれないなんて、まるで夢みたいなことを考えてないで、まじめに働きなさい。
Obasanno isanga moraeru-kamoshirenai-nante, marude yumemitaina kotoo kangaetenaide, majimeni hatarakinasai.
Don't think about (foolish) dreams like getting an inheritance from your aunt. Work hard (for yourself).

5) 彼は政治にはまるで関心がない。
Karewa seijiniwa marude kanshinga nai.
He is not at all interested in politics.

6) 姉はピアノはうまいが、歌はまるでだめだ。
Anewa pianowa umaiga, utawa marude dameda.
My sister is good at piano, but she is an absolutely terrible singer.

ちょうど ■*choudo* ■just like ; exactly

①ものごとがほかのものと**ほとんど同じ**だというようすを表し、同じような種類のものや、具体的な共通点を例に挙げて、詳しく説明するときに使います。全くかけ離れたものや具体的説明のできないものをたとえに使うことはありません。多くの場合、「～ようだ」といっしょに使います（例7, 8, 9)。

Choudo expresses that something is nearly the same as something else, and is used when clearly describing the two objects as being of the same type, or having something specific in common. It may not be used in sentences that refer to things which are very different, or cannot be explained concretely. In most cases it is used together with ～*youda* (ex.7, 8, 9).

②数量・大きさ・時刻などが、**ある目的や基準などとぴったり合っている**ようすを表すとき使います。切りの良さやタイミングの良さという意味も含みます（例10, 11, 12)。

Choudo may also be used to indicate that things, such as volume, size, or time, meet a certain objective or standard exactly. It may refer to a proper limit or suitable timing (ex.10, 11, 12).

---

7) ちょうど水が高いところから低いところへ流れるように、電流も電圧の高いほうから低いほうへ流れる。

Choodo mizuga takai tokorokara hikui tokoroe nagareruyooni, denryuumo den-atsuno takai hookara hikui hooe nagareru.

Just as water flows from a high place to a low place, electricity flows from high voltage to low voltage.

8) ちょうど乾いた土が水を吸収するように、彼は留学先で新しい知識をどんどん吸収した。

Choodo kawaita tsuchiga mizuo kyuushuu-suruyooni, karewa ryuugakusa-kide atarashii chishikio dondon kyuushuushita.

Just as parched earth soaks up water, he rapidly absorbed knowledge while studying abroad.

9) ちょうど私が学生時代にジャズに夢中になったように、息子もロックに夢中になっている。

Choodo watashiga gakuseijidaini jazuni muchuuni nattayooni, musukomo rokkuni muchuuni natteiru.

My son is as absorbed in rock music as I was in jazz when I was a student.

10) 彼は10時ちょうどの新幹線で仙台へ行った。
Karewa juuji choodono Shinkansende Sendaie itta.
He went to Sendai on the ten o'clock *Shinkansen.*

11) この靴は、大きさがちょうどいい。
Kono kutsuwa, ookisaga choodoii.
These shoes fit me perfectly.
(The size of these shoes is perfect for me.)

12) 駅に着くと、ちょうど急行が来た。
Ekini tsukuto, choodo kyuukooga kita.
The express train pulled in just as (I) arrived at the station.

火が出るところは？

マイクは日本語がかなりじょうずになり、いろいろな表現ができるようになってきました。

ある日のことです。公園を散歩していたマイクの顔に、男の子のけったボールがぶつかりました。「痛い！」思わずマイクは大声をあげました。「マイク、大丈夫？」弟のアダムが聞きました。「ああ痛い、顔から火が出た。これはね、頭や顔にものがぶつかったときに、すごく痛かったという表現なんだよ」と得意そうにマイクは説明しました。すると、いっしょにいた和人が言いました。「ねえ、それを言うのなら、『目から火が出た』でしょう。『顔から火が出る』っていうのは、とても恥ずかしい思いをするっていうことだよ」

アダムはマイクにこう言いました。「同じ、『火が出る』でも、どこから出るかによって全く意味が違うんですね。マイク、もっともっと日本語を勉強しないと、顔から火が出るような思いをするよ」そう言われたマイクは、ちょっと恥ずかしそうな顔をしました。

Where does fire come out from?

Mike has become quite good at Japanese and is now able to use many different expressions in his speech.

One day while Mike was walking in the park, he was hit in the face by a ball that was kicked by a boy, and shouted "Ouch!" His little brother, Adam, asked him, "Are you all right, Mike?" Mike said, "Ow, that hurts. *Kao kara hi ga deta*[1]." Then he ever so proudly explained to Adam that "You use this expression when you're in great pain after being hit on the head or in the face by something." After he finished saying this, his friend Kazuto remarked, "In that case, you should say *me kara hi ga deta*[2]. The expression *kao kara hi ga deru* is used by someone who is very embarrassed about something."

Adam said "That means that even though the *hi ga deru* part is the same, depending on where the fire comes from, the meaning is completely different. Hey Mike, unless you study Japanese a lot harder, you're going to have a lot of experience with *kao kara hi ga deru*." Mike looked embarrassed as he listened to his little brother's words of wisdom.

1 *Fire came out from the face* (*to burn with embarassment*).

2 *Fire came out from the eyes* (*to see stars after being hit on the head*).

みえる／みられる

■ *mieru* ■ *mirareru*

みえる［見える］ ■ *mieru* ■ to be visible ; to appear ; to seem 

①見ようとしなくても、**自然に目に入ってくる**・見ることができるというとき使います（例1, 2, 3)。

Mieru is used when an object enters one's field of vision naturally, or when one can see an object without making any special effort (ex.1, 2, 3).

②見たり聞いたりしたことをもとに、そのように思われたり、感じられるという、判断や推測を表します（例4, 5, 6, 7, 8)。

It also expresses an inference or conjecture based on something one has seen or heard (ex.4, 5, 6, 7, 8).

---

1) このホテルは、どのへやからも富士山が見える。

Kono hoteruwa, dono heyakaramo Fujisanga mieru.
At this hotel, Mount Fuji is visible from any room.

2) あそこに見えるのが、国会議事堂です。

Asokoni mierunoga, kokkaigijidoodesu.
What you can see over that way is the Diet Building.

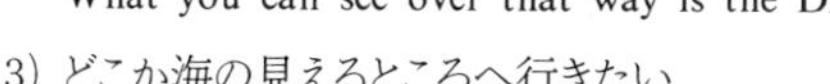

3) どこか海の見えるところへ行きたい。

Dokoka umino mieru tokoroe ikitai.
(I) want to go someplace where we can see the sea.

4) あの人は体格が立派で丈夫そうに見えるが、案外 体が弱いんですよ。

Ano hitowa taikakuga rippade joobusooni mieruga, angai karadaga yowaindesuyo.
He has a fantastic build and looks so robust, yet he's surprisingly frail.

5) この服を着るとやせて見える。

Kono fukuo kiruto yasete mieru.
When (I) wear this outfit, I look thin.

6) あの岩の形は、人の顔のように見えるんです。

Ano iwano katachiwa hitono kaono yooni mierundesu.
The shape of that rock looks like a person's face.

7) どうやら雨もあがったとみえて、外が明るくなった。

Dooyara amemo agattato miete, sotoga akarukunatta.
It seems the rain has stopped; it's gotten lighter outside.

8) あの子はとてもおなかがすいていたとみえて、ごはんを３杯もおかわりした。

Ano kowa totemo onakaga suiteitato miete, gohan-o sanbaimo okawarishita.
It looks like that child was very hungry; she ate three additional helpings of rice.

みられる［見られる］

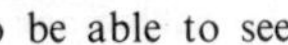
■ *mirareru*
■ to be able to see

①「**見ることができる**」という意味です（例9, 10）。

To be able to see (ex.9, 10).

②**現象**や**状態・ようす**などが**よくある**ということです（例11, 12）。

Mirareru may indicate that a phenomenon, situation, or circumstance occurs often (ex.11, 12).

③「～と見られている」の形で、まだはっきりとはわかっていないが、**そう考えられている・判断されている**という意味を表します（例13, 14）。

In the form ～*to mirareteiru*, it expresses that something can be considered or judged to be a certain way, although it is not yet completely understood (ex.13, 14).

---

9) こんどの皆既日食は、ハワイへ行けば見られる。
Kondono kaikinisshokuwa, Hawaie ikeba mirareru.
(You) will be able to see the next total solar eclipse if you go to Hawaii.

10) こんなにすばらしいショーは、めったに見られません。
Konnani subarashii shoowa, mettani miraremasen.
(You) can hardly ever see such a magnificent show as this.

11) 大地震のときには、地面の隆起や陥没などの現象が見られる。
Oojishinno tokiniwa, jimenno ryuukiya kanbotsunadono genshooga mirareru.
During a big earthquake (one) will see such phenomena as upheavals and collapsing of the ground.

12) 砂漠では、よく蜃気楼が見られるそうです。
Sabakudewa, yoku shinkirooga mirareru soodesu.
(They) say (you) can often see mirages in the desert.

13) 事故の原因は運転手の居眠り運転と見られている。
Jikono gen-inwa untenshuno inemuri-untento mirareteiru.
The cause of the accident appears to be the driver's having fallen asleep at the wheel.

14) 株価は今後も下がり続けるだろうと見られています。
Kabukawa kongomo sagaritsuzukeru-darooto mirareteimasu.
(They're) saying that stock prices are going to continue to decline from now on.

みち／とおり

■*michi*　■*toori*

みち［道］ ■*michi* ■road ; way

①人や車などが、どこかへ行くときに**通るところ**です。本来は自然にできたものですが、一般的には「通り・道路」などすべてに使えます（例1, 2, 3, 4）。

A road on which people, cars, etc., travel to somewhere. Originally, *michi* referred to a naturally-created pathway, but now it may be used to mean any kind of road, street, boulevard, etc. (ex.1, 2, 3, 4).

②**行き方**や**方法**、**人の生き方**などに使います（例5, 6, 7, 8, 9）。

It may also indicate a way to go, a way to live (one's life), or a way of doing something (ex.5, 6, 7, 8, 9).

1) この道をずっと登って行くと、頂上に着く。
Kono michio zutto nobotteikuto, choojooni tsuku.
If you keep hiking up this path, you'll reach the summit.

2) 川沿いの細い道で、とかげを見つけた。
Kawazoino hosoi michide, tokageo mitsuketa.
(I) saw (found) a lizard on the narrow pathway along the river.

3) この道は、車が多くて危ないから気をつけて。
Kono michiwa, kurumaga ookute abunaikara kio tsukete.
The traffic on the street is heavy and dangerous, so be careful.

4) いつもの道が工事中で通れなかった。
Itsumono michiga koojichuude toorenakatta.
The street (I) usually take is under repair, so I couldn't get through.

5) 知らない人に、美術館へ行く道を聞かれた。
Shiranai hitoni, bijutsukan-e iku michio kikareta.
A stranger asked (me) the way to the art museum.

6) ドライブの途中、道に迷ってしまった。
Doraibuno tochuu, michini mayotteshimatta.

(I) got lost while I was out for a drive.

7) 助(たす)かる道(みち)は一(ひと)つしかない。
Tasukaru michiwa hitotsushika nai.
There is only one way for (you) to be saved.

8) どうやったら彼(かれ)を悪(あく)の道(みち)から救(すく)い出(だ)すことができるだろうか。
Doo yattara kareo akuno michikara sukuidasu kotoga dekirudarooka.
How can (we) save him from the path of evil?

9) 私(わたし)は人(ひと)の道(みち)にはずれるようなことは大嫌(だいきら)いです。
Watashiwa hitono michini hazureruyoona kotowa daikiraidesu.
I hate to do anything that goes against morality.

とおり［通(とお)り］ ■ *toori* ■ street

人(ひと)や車(くるま)などが、どこかへ行(い)くときに**通(とお)るために作(つく)られたところ**です。おもに町(まち)の中(なか)のものを指(さ)し両側(りょうがわ)にある家(いえ)・店(みせ)などを含(ふく)んでいます（例(れい)10, 11, 12）。ですから山(やま)の中(なか)や畑(はたけ)の中(なか)のものは「通(とお)り」ではなく「道(みち)」です。

Toori refers to a passage or road purposely created for people or vehicles to travel on in order to go somewhere. Usually *toori* refers to roads in towns and cities and very often includes the houses and stores on both sides (ex.10, 11, 12). Paths found on mountains or in fields are not referred to as *toori* but *michi.*

---

10) 税務署(ぜいむしょ)は、この通(とお)りに面(めん)している。
Zeimushowa, kono toorini menshiteiru.
The tax office is on this street.

11) この通(とお)りは日曜日(にちようび)の昼間(ひるま)、歩行者専用道路(ほこうしゃせんようどうろ)になります。
Kono tooriwa nichiyoobino hiruma, hokoosha-sen-yoo-dooroni narimasu.
This street is (closed to traffic and used) for pedestrians only during the daytime on Sundays.

12) これが新宿(しんじゅく)でいちばんにぎやかな通(とお)りです。
Korega Shinjukude ichiban nigiyakana tooridesu.
This is the busiest street in Shinjuku.

みほん／てほん

■ *mihon*　　■ *tehon*

みほん［見本］ ■ *mihon* ■ sample 

それがどんなものであるかを知らせるために例として見せる**同じ種類のもの**をさします。**典型的**な例だ、という意味で**人**についても使います（例1, 2, 3, 4, 5)。

Mihon is something that is a representative sample of a product which shows what the product is like. It is also used to indicate that a person is a typical example (e.g., of a certain behavior) (ex.1, 2, 3, 4, 5).

1) 客　：この化粧水には香料が入っていますか。
店員：いいえ、これが見本です。どうぞお試しください。
Kyaku : Kono keshoo-suiniwa kooryooga haitteimasuka?
Customer : Is this lotion scented?
Ten-in : Iie, korega mihondesu. Doozo otameshikudasai.
Clerk : No, it isn't. Here's a sample. Please go ahead and try it.

2) これは新しい洗剤の見本です。どうぞお使いください。
Korewa atarashii senzaino mihondesu. Doozo otsukaikudasai.
This is a sample of a new detergent. Please try it.

3) 見本と実際の商品が、必ずしも同じだとは限らない。
Mihonto jissaino shoohinga, kanarazushimo onajidatowa kagiranai.
A sample is not necessarily exactly the same as the real product.

4) かけごとで人生を誤る人は多い。財産も家族も失った彼が、いい見本だ。
Kakegotode jinseio ayamaru hitowa ooi. Zaisanmo kazokumo ushinatta karega, ii mihonda.
There are many people who ruin their lives gambling. He's a good example, having lost both his wealth and his family.

5) 彼女は朝から晩までよく働く。働き者の見本のようだ。
Kanojowa asakara banmade yoku hataraku. Hataraki-monono mihonnoyooda.
She works hard from morning till night, just like a model worker.

てほん［手本］ ■*tehon* ■model

ものごとを学ぶときに、どのようにすればいいのか**見習ったりまねをしたり**する模範となるもののことです（例6, 7）。また、ほかの人が見習うべき立派な人やその行いに対しても使います（例８）。「お手本」と言うこともあります。

This is something that serves as a model to be copied or imitated when learning how to do something (ex.6, 7).
It is also used when saying that a person or a person's behavior is worthy of being imitated by others (ex.8). *Otehon* is also used.

6) 子供のころ、先生の字をお手本にして字の練習をした。
Kodomono koro, senseino jio otehonnishite jino renshuuo shita.
When (I) was a child I practiced handwriting using my teacher's writing as a model.

7) 体育の時間に、先生が鉄棒のお手本を見せてくれた。
Taiikuno jikanni, senseiga tetsuboono otehon-o misetekureta.
During PE (our) teacher showed us how to do the bars.

8) 親は子供の手本となるような生き方をしなければならない。
Oyawa kodomono tehonto naruyoona ikikatao shinakerebanaranai.
Parents must live in a way that sets an example for their children.

みる／みつめる／ながめる／のぞく

■*miru* ■*mitsumeru* ■*nagameru* ■*nozoku*

みる［見る］ ■*miru* ■to look (at) ; to see

①目で意識的に、**ものの形や色・状態**などを**感じとる**ことです（例1, 2, 3, 4）。

To consciously perceive the shape, color, condition, etc., of an object with the eyes (ex.1, 2, 3, 4).

②「**調べる・確かめる・判断する**」など**の意味で使います**（例5, 6, 7）。
また、「面倒を見る」は「世話をする」という意味です（例8, 9）。

To investigate, verify, or form a judgment (ex.5, 6, 7). The expression *mendou o miru* has the same meaning as *sewa o suru*, i.e., to take care of someone (ex.8, 9).

---

1) 私は水族館で、海蛇を見た。
わたし すいぞくかん うみへび み
Watashiwa suizokukande, umihebio mita.
I saw a sea snake at the aquarium.

2) 洞窟の中は暗くて何も見ることができなかった。
どうくつ なか くら なに み
Dookutsuno nakawa kurakute nanimo mirukotoga dekinakatta.
It was dark inside the cave and (we) couldn't see a thing.

3) あなたの子供の頃の写真が見たい。
こども ころ しゃしん み
Anatano kodomono korono shashinga mitai.
(I'd) like to see a picture of you as a child.

4) きのうデパートに行ったけれど、見ただけで何も買わなかった。
い み なに か
Kinoo depaatoni ittakeredo, mitadakede nanimo kawanakatta.
(I) went to the department store yesterday, but I just looked around and didn't buy anything.

5) 私はわからない単語があったらすぐに辞書を見ます。
わたし たんご じしょ み
Watashiwa wakaranai tangoga attara suguni jishoo mimasu.
When there are words I don't know, I look them up in the dictionary right away.

6) 玄関にだれか来たみたい。ちょっと見て来てください。
げんかん き み き
Genkanni dareka kitamitai. Chotto mitekite kudasai.
It sounds like someone is at the front door. Could (you) please go and look?

7) 私は、年内に国会の解散はないとみている。
わたし ねんない こっかい かいさん
Watashiwa, nennaini kokkaino kaisanwa naito miteiru.
The way I see it, the Diet won't dissolve within the year.

8) ちゃんと面倒を見られるのなら、犬を飼ってもいいと父が言った。
めんどう み いぬ か ちち い
Chanto mendoo-o mirarerunonara, inuo kattemo iito chichiga itta.
My dad said that if (I) could take care of it properly, I could have a dog.

9) 私が入院している間、母が子供の面倒を見てくれた。
わたし にゅういん あいだ はは こども めんどう み
Watashiga nyuuin-shiteiruaida, hahaga kodomono mendoo-o mite kureta.
While I was in the hospital, my mother took care of my child for me.

みつめる［見つめる］

■ *mitsumeru*
■ to gaze ; to stare

①人の顔などを、ほかのものに目を向けないで、**じっと見続ける**ことです（例10, 11, 12）。「見つめる」のは好奇心や興味・関心があるからです。

To look continuously at someone's face, etc., without looking away at anything else because of curiosity, interest, or admiration (ex.10, 11, 12).

②ことがらを**観察する・するどく追求する**という意味で使います（例13, 14）。

To closely observe or seriously pursue something (ex.13, 14).

10) 彼女は何か言いたそうに、私をじっと見つめていた。
Kanojowa nanika iitasooni, watashio jitto mitsumeteita.
She looked fixedly at me as if she had something she wanted to say.

11) 純心な子供に見つめられると、うそをつくことはできなかった。
Junshinna kodomoni mitsumerareruto, usoo tsuku kotowa dekinakatta.
It was impossible for (me) to tell a lie to my son with him gazing at me with those innocent eyes.

12) 少女は、器用に犬小屋を作っている父親の手元を、じっと見つめていた。
Shoojowa, kiyooni inugoyao tsukutteiru chichioyano temotoo, jitto mitsumeteita.
The girl gazed at their father's handiwork as he skillfully built a doghouse.

13) 時には、自分をよく見つめることも必要だ。
Tokiniwa, jibun-o yoku mitsumeru kotomo hitsuyooda.
It is necessary to take a good look at oneself from time to time.

14) 私達は現在の状況を見つめて、どのように自然を守っていったらいいか、考えなくてはならない。
Watashi-tachiwa genzaino jookyoo-o mitsumete, donoyooni shizen-o mamotte-ittara iika, kangaenakutewa naranai.
Mankind (we) must take a good look at the present state of affairs, and think about what should be done to protect the environment.

ながめる［眺める］

■ *nagameru*
■ to gaze at ; to look at

ものの**全体**や**広い範囲を見る**ことで、**景色・風景・絵画**などによく使います(例15, 16, 17, 18)。「少し離れたところのものを、ゆったりとした気分で見る」という客観的な感じがあります。

Nagameru is frequently used when looking at something in its entirety or from a wide perspective—especially scenery or art (ex.15, 16, 17, 18). It expresses an objective feeling that the object is being viewed from a somewhat distant location, and that the viewer is in a relaxed mood.

---

15) 窓の外を眺めていたら、珍しい鳥が飛んできて木にとまった。
Madono sotoo nagameteitara, mezurashii toriga tondekite kini tomatta.
As (I) was gazing out the window, an unusual bird flew by and landed in a tree.

16) 展望台の望遠鏡で眺めると、沖を行く船が見えた。
Tenboodaino booenkyoode nagameruto, okio iku funega mieta.
When (I) looked through the telescope on the observation platform, I could see some ships passing by offshore.

17) 父は日本画の大作を感心したように眺めていた。
Chichiwa Nihongano taisakuo kanshin-shitayooni nagameteita.
My father appeared to be greatly moved as he gazed at the Japanese art masterpiece.

18) 何も考えずにぼんやりと雲を眺めていると、時間を忘れてしまう。
Nanimo kangaezuni bonyarito kumoo nagameteiruto, jikan-o wasureteshimau.
When (I) lazily stare up at the clouds without a thought on my mind, I forget about the time.

のぞく

■ *nozoku*
■ to peep into ; to peek

---

①**小さい穴**や**すき間**などから、**向こう側を見る**とき使います(例19, 20, 21)。また高いところから身をのり出すように下の方を見るときや(例22)、ちょっと見てみるときも使い(例23, 24)、見てはいけないものを人にかくれて見てしまうという感じを含むこともあります(例25)。

To look through a small hole or crack at something on the other side (ex.19, 20, 21). Also, to look down from a high place with the body leaning forward (ex.22), or to take a quick peek at something (ex.23, 24). There may be a nuance that the viewer is hidden and is looking at something that he should not be (ex.25).

②「～がのぞく」の形(かたち)で、ものの全体(ぜんたい)ではなく一部分(いちぶぶん)が見(み)えたり表(あらわ)れたりするとき使(つか)います（例(れい)26, 27）。

When used in the form ～*ga nozoku*, it is implied that only a portion of the whole object is exposed to view (ex.26, 27).

---

19) 顕微鏡(けんびきょう)をのぞくと、細菌(さいきん)が動(うご)いているのが見(み)えた。
Kenbikyoo-o nozokuto, saikinga ugoiteirunoga mieta.
When (I) looked through the microscope, I could see bacteria moving around.

20) 庭(にわ)で、物音(ものおと)がしたので、カーテンのすき間(ま)からのぞいてみたら、猫(ねこ)だった。
Niwade, monootoga shitanode, kaatenno sukimakara nozoite mitara, nekodatta.
(I) heard a noise out in the garden, so I peeked out from between the curtains and saw it was a cat.

21) ドアのすき間(ま)から診察室(しんさつしつ)をのぞくと、看護婦(かんごふ)さんが注射(ちゅうしゃ)の準備(じゅんび)をしていた。
Doano sukimakara shinsatsushitsuo nozokuto, kangofusanga chuushano junbio shiteita.
When (I) peeked through the crack in the door into the examination room, I could see that the nurse was preparing an injection.

22) 崖(がけ)の上(うえ)から谷底(たにそこ)をのぞいたら足(あし)がふるえた。
Gakeno uekara tanisokoo nozoitara ashiga furueta.
(My) legs began to shake when I peered over the edge of the cliff at the bottom.

23) 私(わたし)は絵(え)が好(す)きなので、画廊(がろう)をのぞくのが楽(たの)しみです。
Watashiwa ega sukinanode, garoo-o nozokunoga tanoshimidesu.
Since I enjoy (looking at) paintings, I sometimes like to make a quick stop at the art gallery.

24) 果物屋(くだものや)をのぞいたら、季節(きせつ)はずれのさくらんぼがありました。
Kudamonoyao nozoitara, kisetsu-hazureno sakuranboga arimashita.
When (I) peeked into the fruit stand, (I found that) there were some cherries (even though they were) out of season.

25) 姉(あね)の机(つくえ)の引(ひ)き出(だ)しをのぞいたら、日記帳(にっきちょう)が入(はい)っていた。
Aneno tsukueno hikidashio nozoitara, nikkichooga haitteita.
(I) peeked into one of my older sister's desk drawers and saw her diary.

26) 彼(かれ)のズボンのポケットからさいふがのぞいていたので、注意(ちゅうい)した。

Kareno zubonno pokettokara saifuga nozoiteitanode, chuuishita.
His wallet was sticking out from his pants pocket so (I) called his attention to it.

27) 雲(くも)の切(き)れ間(ま)から月(つき)がのぞくと、夜道(よみち)が明(あか)るくなった。

Kumono kiremakara tsukiga nozokuto, yomichiga akaruku natta.
The (dark) path became brighter when the moon peeked out from between the clouds.

みんな／ぜんいん

■ *minna* ■ *zen-in*

みんな

■ *minna*
■ all ; everyone ; everything

---

①生活(せいかつ)や仕事(しごと)・趣味(しゅみ)・境遇(きょうぐう)など、それぞれの「場(ば)」で相手(あいて)となる人達(ひとたち)をまとめて指(さ)し、「**だれも残(のこ)らず、全部(ぜんぶ)**」という意味(いみ)です（例(れい)1, 2, 3, 4）。

Minna designates as a group all of the persons associated with a certain place or situation, e.g., the place one works, lives, pursues one's interests, etc. (ex.1, 2, 3, 4).

②「どの人(ひと)も・だれでも」という意味(いみ)で、**多(おお)くの人(ひと)や世間一般(せけんいっぱん)**を指(さ)して使(つか)います（例(れい)5, 6）。

In addition, it is used to mean 'anyone' or 'everyone' in a general sense (ex.5, 6).

③「すべて」「どれでも」「何(なん)でも」などの意味(いみ)で、物(もの)やものごとにも使(つか)います（例(れい)7, 8）。「みな（皆(みな)）」も同(おな)じ意味(いみ)ですが、多(おお)くの場合(ばあい)「みなさん・みなさま」のように敬語(けいご)として使(つか)います（例(れい)9）。

It is also used for objects, events, or abstract matters in the same way as the words *subete* (everything), *doredemo*, or *nandemo* (anything) (ex.7, 8).
Mina has the same meaning as *minna*, however, it is most often used in the formal expressions *minasan* and *minasama* (ex.9).

---

1) みんなの意見(いけん)を聞(き)いてから、結論(けつろん)を出(だ)すべきだと思(おも)うよ。

Minnano iken-o kiitekara, ketsuron-o dasubekidato omouyo.
I think we ought to make our conclusions after asking everyone's opinion.

2) おかげさまで、家族(かぞく)はみんな、元気(げんき)です。
Okagesamade, kazokuwa minna, genkidesu.
The family is all well, thank you.

3) これ、沖縄(おきなわ)のお菓子(かし)なんです。みんなで食べましょう。
Kore, Okinawano okashinandesu. Minnade tabemashoo.
Here are some sweets from Okinawa. Everyone please have some.

4) 次(つぎ)の日曜日(にちようび)に、家族(かぞく)みんなで潮干狩(しおひが)りに行(い)くことになった。
*Tsugino nichiyoobini, kazoku minnade shiohigari*ni iku kotoni natta.*
We (the family) are all going shellfish gathering next Sunday.
—— * *Shiohigari* is gathering of shellfish, especially clams, at low tide.

5) この世(よ)の中(なか)、だれもがみんな親切(しんせつ)だとは限(かぎ)りません。
Kono yononaka, daremoga minna shinsetsudatowa kagirimasen.
Not everyone in this world is necessarily kind.

6) 彼女(かのじょ)はまじめで、みんなに信頼(しんらい)されている。
Kanojowa majimede, minnani shinraisarete-iru.
She is honest and is (therefore) trusted by everybody.

7) お母(かあ)さん、きょうの宿題(しゅくだい)はもうみんな学校(がっこう)でやっちゃったよ。
Okaasan, Kyoono shukudaiwa moo minna gakkoode yatchattayo.
Mom, (I) already did all of today's homework at school.

8) 彼(かれ)の言(い)っていることは、みんな嘘(うそ)だよね。
Kareno itteiru kotowa, minna usodayone.
Everything he says is a lie.

9) ご家族(かぞく)は、みなさまお変(か)わりありませんか。
Gokazokuwa, minasama okawari arimasenka?
How has (your) family been?

ぜんいん［全員(ぜんいん)］

■ *zen-in*
■ all the members ; everyone

ある組織(そしき)・集団(しゅうだん)・境遇(きょうぐう)などにある、またはある場(ば)や問題(もんだい)などを共(とも)にする、す

べての人のことです（例10, 11, 12）。「みんな」は、必ずしも、百パーセントすべての人とは限りませんが、「全員」は、**1人も欠けていない**という意味が強く感じられます。

Zen-in refers to all of the people who are affiliated with some organization, group, or circumstance and who are involved with a specific location or issue (ex.10, 11, 12). While the term *minna* doesn't absolutely mean that each and every person is included, the term *zen-in* strongly implies that not one person is excluded.

---

10) その意見には、クラスの全員が賛成です。
Sono ikenniwa, kurasuno zen-inga sanseidesu.
Everyone in the class agrees with that opinion.

11) 事故にあったバスの乗客は、全員無事だった。
Jikoni atta basuno jookyakuwa, zen-in bujidatta.
All of the passengers on the bus were unharmed in the accident.

12) この研修には、新入社員全員が参加しなければならない。
Kono kenshuuniwa, shinnyuushain zen-inga sanka-shinakereba naranai.
All of the new employees have to participate in this training session.

〜むき［〜向き］ ■〜muki ■suitable for〜

〜に**適している・ふさわしい**ということです。必ずしも〜のために作られたものでなくても、〜に適していれば「〜向き」ということができます（例1, 2, 3, 4, 5）。

〜muki indicates that an object is fit or appropriate for something. It may be used if something is suitable for some purpose, even if it was not expressly made for that purpose (ex.1, 2, 3, 4, 5).

---

1) この車(くるま)のデザインは、若(わか)い人(ひと)向(む)きだ。
Kono kurumano dezainwa, wakaihito-mukida.
The design of this car is aimed at young people.

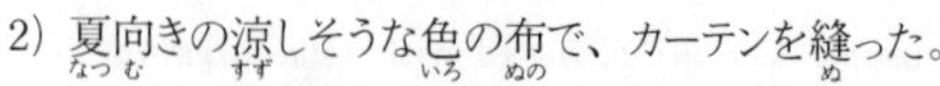

2) 夏(なつ)向(む)きの涼(すず)しそうな色(いろ)の布(ぬの)で、カーテンを縫(ぬ)った。
Natsumukino suzushisoona irono nunode, kaaten-o nutta.
(I) made curtains using fabric in a cool-looking color just right for summer.

3) このゲレンデは初心者(しょしんしゃ)向(む)きです。
Kono gerendewa shoshinsha-mukidesu.
This slope is for beginning skiers.

4) うちのカレーは，子供(こども)向(む)きの甘口(あまくち)です。
Uchino karee＊*wa, kodomomukino amakuchidesu.* ＊p.702
My curry is mild enough for children.

5) この掃除機(そうじき)は性能(せいのう)はいいが、重(おも)くて音(おと)が大(おお)きいので一般家庭(いっぱんかてい)向(む)きではない。
Kono soojikiwa seinoowa iiga, omokute otoga ookiinode ippankatei-mukidewa nai.
This vacuum cleaner is efficient, but it's heavy and noisy, so it's not suitable for common household use.

~むけ［~向(む)け］ ■~*muke* ■aimed at ; for 

ものを作(つく)ったり開発(かいはつ)するときに、**対象(たいしょう)となるものに、**目標(もくひょう)や照準(しょうじゅん)を**あわせる**ということです（例(れい)6, 7, 8, 9)。

This refers to the objective, target, or destination which is the aim of an object's development or manufacture (ex.6, 7, 8, 9).

---

6) この工場(こうじょう)では、輸出(ゆしゅつ)向(む)けの自動車(じどうしゃ)を作(つく)っています。
Kono koojoodewa, yushutsumukeno jidooshao tsukutteimasu.
At this factory they make cars destined for export.

7) 駅前(えきまえ)には、観光客(かんこうきゃく)向(む)けのみやげ物屋(ものや)がたくさんある。
Ekimaeniwa, kankookyaku-mukeno miyagemonoyaga takusan aru.
In front of the station there are a lot of souvenir shops aimed at tourists.

8) この番組は子供向けだけれど、大人が見てもおもしろい。
Kono bangumiwa kodomomuke-dakeredo, otonaga mitemo omoshiroi.
This TV program is for children, but it's of interest to adults, too.

9) 港の倉庫には、被災地向けの救援物資が山積みされている。
Minatono sookoniwa, hisaichimukeno kyuuenbusshiga yamazumisareteiru.
In the harbor warehouses, stacks of relief goods destined for disaster areas are piled up.

～よう［～用］

■ *～you*
■ for the use of～

用途が～に限定されていることを表します（例10, 11, 12, 13）。「～向き」や「～向け」とは異なり、**使用目的が限定されている**ので、それ以外の使い方をすると、おかしかったり不都合だったりします。

～you designates a limitation on the use of an object (ex.10, 11, 12, 13). Unlike *～muki* and *～muke*, when an object is used for purposes other than that indicated by *～you*, there is a sense of inappropriateness or strangeness.

---

10) 赤ちゃん用のベッドはすぐ使わなくなるから、買わないで借りた方がいい。
Akachan-yoono beddowa sugu tsukawanaku narukara, kawanaide karita hooga ii.
Because something like a baby crib becomes useless quickly, it's better to borrow rather than buy one.

11) 左きき用のはさみは、右ききの人には使いにくい。
Hidarikiki-yoono hasamiwa, migikikino hitoniwa tsukainikui.
Left-handed scissors are hard for right-handed people to use.

12) この黒いスーツは、冠婚葬祭用にもなる。
Kono kuroi suutsuwa, kankonsoosai-yoonimo naru.
This black suit will also be good for all formal occasions, too.

13) 最近、家庭用浄水器を取りつけるうちが増えている。
Saikin, kateiyoo-joosuikio toritsukeru uchiga fueteiru.
Lately, there's been an increase in the number of homes putting in household water purifiers.

むすぶ／しばる

■ *musubu*　■ *shibaru*

むすぶ［結(むす)ぶ］

■ *musubu*
■ to tie ; to connect

ひもなどをつなぐ、また、ものを**つないで一(ひと)つにする**ことです（例(れい)1, 2, 3, 4）。「つながるようにする・関係(かんけい)をつける」という意味(いみ)があります（例(れい)5, 6）。例(れい)7、8は鉄道(てつどう)や道路(どうろ)などが、いくつかの場所(ばしょ)をつなぐという意味(いみ)です。

To connect objects such as string, or to bundle a number of objects together so that they become one (ex.1, 2, 3, 4). It may also mean to form a relationship (ex.5, 6). In Examples 7 and 8 it is used to indicate that things like a road or railroad connect several places.

1）あの子(こ)は小(ちい)さいのに、じょうずに靴(くつ)ひもを結(むす)ぶ。
Ano kowa chiisainoni, joozuni kutsuhimoo musubu.
Although he is still small, that child ties his own shoestrings very well.

2）船(ふね)を岸(きし)につなぐときは、ロープをしっかり結(むす)びなさい。
Funeo kishini tsunagu tokiwa, roopuo shikkari musubinasai.
Make sure (you) tie the boat securely with a rope when you dock at the shore.

3）誕生日(たんじょうび)のプレゼントに、きれいなリボンが結(むす)んであった。
Tanjoobino purezentoni, kireina ribonga musundeatta.
There was a beautiful ribbon tied around the birthday present.

4）あの子(こ)は、いつも髪(かみ)にリボンを結(むす)んでいるね。
Ano kowa, itsumo kamini ribon-o musundeirune.
That child always wears her hair tied with a ribbon, doesn't she?

5）彼(かれ)と私(わたし)は、深(ふか)い友情(ゆうじょう)で結(むす)ばれている。
Kareto watashiwa, fukai yuujoode musubareteiru.
He and I have formed a strong friendship.

6）両国(りょうこく)は、平和条約(へいわじょうやく)を結(むす)んだ。
Ryookokuwa, heiwajooyakuo musunda.
The two nations concluded a peace treaty.

7) この飛行機は、成田とバンコクを３時間半で結んでいる。
Kono hikookiwa, Narita to Bankokuo sanjikan-han de musundeiru.
This airplane links Narita and Bangkok in three and a half hours.

8) 東京と名古屋を結ぶ東名高速道路は、いつも渋滞している。
Tookyooto Nagoyao musubu toomei-koosokudoorowa, itsumo juutai shiteiru.
The Tomei Expressway, which links Tokyo and Nagoya, is always jammed with cars.

しばる［縛る］

■ *shibaru*
■ to tie (up) ; to fasten ; to bundle 

---

①ひもなどで、ものを一つにまとめる・たばねることです（例9, 10）。**動かないように固定する**という意味も含みます。
「**結ぶ**」には、いくつかのものを**つなぐ**という意味があり、「**しばる**」には、**一つにまとめる・**動かないようにするという意味があります。

To tie together or bundle objects with string, etc. (ex.9, 10). While *musubu* means to connect several objects, *shibaru* means to gather the objects into one, or to fasten something so that it doesn't move.

②規則や強制などで、**他人の行動を制限する**意味で使います（例11, 12）。
To limit a person's actions through regulation or force (ex.11, 12).

---

9) ゴミは袋の口をしっかりしばって、決められた日に出してください。
Gomiwa fukurono kuchio shikkari shibatte, kimerareta hini dashite kudasai.
Please tie up (your) garbage bags securely and put them out on the designated day.

10) どろぼうに手や足をしばられて、とてもこわかった。
Dorobooni teya ashio shibararete, totemo kowakatta.
(I) was so scared when the burglar tied my hands and feet.

11) 私は、古い規則や慣習にはしばられたくない。
Watashiwa, furui kisokuya kanshuuniwa shibararetakunai.
I don't want to be bound by old rules and customs.

12) 私は子供がまだ小さいので、育児や家事にしばられて、なかなか自由にでかけられない。

Watashiwa kodomoga mada chiisainode, ikujiya kajini shibararete, nakanaka jiyuuni dekakerarenai.
My children are still little so I'm hardly ever free to go out, what with being tied down with housework and child-care.

むだ／もったいない

■*muda* ■*mottainai*

むだ［無駄(むだ)］ ■*muda* ■useless ; a waste 

①もの・時間(じかん)・お金(かね)などを、必要以上(ひつよういじょう)に消費(しょうひ)するようすを表(あらわ)します（例(れい)1, 2）。
Muda is used when one uses more effort, time, money, etc., than is necessary (ex.1, 2).

②効果(こうか)がない・役(やく)に立(た)たない・利益(りえき)がないというようすを表(あらわ)します（例(れい)3, 4, 5）。
It also may mean that something is fruitless, useless, or not profitable (ex.3, 4, 5).

1) 大切(たいせつ)な資源(しげん)をむだに使(つか)ってはいけない。
Taisetsuna shigen-o mudani tsukattewa ikenai.
(You) must not waste valuable resources.

2) 一日中(いちにちじゅう)テレビばかり見(み)ているなんて時間(じかん)のむだだ。
Ichinichijuu terebibakari miteirunante jikanno mudada.
To do nothing all day but watch TV is a waste of time.

3) 豚(ぶた)に真珠(しんじゅ)をやっても、まったくむだです。
Butani shinjuo yattemo, mattaku mudadesu.
It's useless to bestow pearls on swine (give pearls to a pig).

4) 彼(かれ)にいくら注意(ちゅうい)をしてもむだです。
Kareni ikura chuuio shitemo mudadesu.
No matter how many times (you) warn him, it's no use.

5) 彼女(かのじょ)は仕事中(しごとちゅう)、むだ話(ばなし)ばかりしている。
Kanojowa shigotochuu, mudabanashi-bakari shiteiru.
She does nothing but chat idly while she is working.

もったいない ■ *mottainai* ■ a waste 

①むだをすることを、惜しいと思ったり非難したりするとき使います（例6, 7）。
Mottainai is used when one is critical of, or feels regret for, something because it is a waste (ex.6, 7).

②人やものの価値を、十分に生かして使われないとき使います（例8, 9, 10）。
It is also used to express that a person or thing is not being utilized to maximum capacity (ex.8, 9, 10).

③おそれ多いことだというとき使います（例11）。
Mottainai is also used to express humble appreciation (ex.11).

---

6) 歯をみがくとき、水を出しっぱなしにするなんて水がもったいない。
Hao migakutoki, mizuo dashippanashini surunante mizuga mottainai.
Leaving the water running while (you) brush your teeth is such a waste!

7) A：まだ使える家具が捨ててあるよ。
B：もったいない。

A： *Mada tsukaeru kaguga sutete aruyo.*
Somebody threw away some furniture that is still usable.
B： *Mottainai.* What a waste!

8) こんな絵に100万円も払うのはもったいない。
Konna eni hyakuman-enmo haraunowa mottainai.
Paying ¥1,000,000 for this kind of painting is a waste of money.

9) 彼女は、あんな夫にはもったいないぐらいすばらしい人だ。
Kanojowa, anna ottoniwa mottainaigurai subarashii hitoda.
She is too good of a person to have that kind of husband.

10) こんなに高価な食器を、ふだん使うなんてもったいない。
Konnani kookana shokkio, fudan tsukaunante mottainai.
To use such expensive tableware as this for such an ordinary occasion is too much.

11) あのように偉い方からお礼を言われるなんて、もったいないことです。
Ano yooni eraikatakara oreio iwarerunante, mottainai kotodesu.
It's an honor for me to receive words of appreciation from such a great person.

めきめき／めっきり

■*mekimeki*　■*mekkiri*

めきめき

■*mekimeki*
■(to progress) remarkably 

ものごとの進歩がめざましく、**良い方向に向かう勢い**や**スピード**が感じられるようすを表すとき使います（例1, 2, 3, 4）。とくに、能力・技術・成長・回復などによく使います。

Mekimeki indicates that the progress of something is remarkable; i.e., the speed and force of improvement can be felt (ex.1, 2, 3, 4). *Mekimeki* is often used to describe progressing ability, technique, growth, recovery and the like.

1) 日本人の友だちが増えて、彼の日本語はめきめき上達した。
Nihonjinno tomodachiga fuete, kareno Nihongowa mekimeki jootatsushita.
His Japanese has shown remarkable progress since he made more Japanese friends.

2) 家庭教師をつけたら、めきめき成績が上がった。
Kateikyooshio tsuketara, mekimeki seisekiga agatta.
After (I) hired a tutor for (him), his grades markedly improved.

3) あの会社は社長が代わってから、売り上げがめきめき伸びた。
Ano kaishawa shachooga kawattekara, uriagega mekimeki nobita.
That company's sales rapidly increased after there was a change of company president.

4) 新しい薬を飲み始めてから、彼の病気はめきめき回復してきた。
Atarashii kusurio nomihajimetekara, kareno byookiwa mekimeki kaifukushitekita.
His recovery from his sickness has been remarkable since he started taking the new medicine.

めっきり

■*mekkiri*
■noticeably 

ものごとの程度が、**急に大きく変化する**ようすを表すとき使います（例5, 6, 7,

8)。**良く**変化したときにも**悪く**変化したときにも使います。

This indicates that the degree of something suddenly changes (ex.5, 6, 7, 8). *Mekkiri* can be used to refer to either a change for the better or worse.

5) 近頃めっきり春らしくなりましたね。
Chikagoro mekkiri harurashiku narimashitane.
Lately, the weather has become very much like spring, hasn't it?

6) この辺は日が暮れると、めっきり人通りが少なくなる。
Kono henwa higa kureruto, mekkiri hitodooriga sukunakunaru.
The pedestrian traffic in this area suddenly decreases after nightfall.

7) 彼は息子を亡くしてから、めっきり口数が減った。
Karewa musukoo nakushitekara, mekkiri kuchikazuga hetta.
He has become considerably withdrawn since his son died.

8) このごろめっきり視力が落ちてきたので、めがねをかけようと思います。
Konogoro mekkiri shiryokuga ochitekitanode, meganeo kakeyooto omoimasu.
(I) think I'll get glasses because my eyesight has become notably bad lately.

めんどう／やっかい

■ *mendou* ■ *yakkai*

めんどう［面倒］ ■ *mendou* ■ trouble ; bother ♥

①ものごとが**複雑だ・難しい・扱いにくい**など、**手間がかかるようす**を表します（例1, 2, 3）。「面倒くさい・めんどくさい（口語）」は、わずらわしくて、そのことをするのがいやだ・手数がかかるのはおっくうでいやだ、という気持ちを表します（例４）。

This indicates that something is complicated, difficult, or time consuming (ex.1, 2, 3). The expression *mendoukusai* (or *mendokusai* in spoken Japanese) expresses a feeling that something is troublesome or annoying (ex.4).

②「面倒を見る」「面倒をかける」のように、「**世話**」**の意味**でも使います

（例5, 6）。

In expressions like *mendou-o miru* and *mendou o kakeru*, *mendou* has the same meaning as *sewa* (care) (ex.5, 6).

---

1) 私はアイロンをかけるのが面倒なので、ワイシャツは洗濯屋に出す。
Watashiwa airon-o kakerunoga mendoonanode, waishatsuwa sentakuyani dasu.
I send my shirts to the cleaner's because it's a bother to iron them myself.

2) 手紙を書くのが面倒で、つい電話で用をすませてしまう。
Tegamio kakunoga mendoode, tsui denwade yoo-o sumaseteshimau.
It's troublesome to write letters, so (I) take care of matters by phone.

3) 公共料金の自動振替は、いちいち支払いに行く面倒がなくて便利だ。
Kookyoo-ryookinno jidoo-furikaewa, ichiichi shiharaini iku mendooga nakute benrida.
Having (my) utility charges taken automatically from my account sure beats having to go and pay each one separately.

4) 私は料理を作るのは好きだけれど、後片づけは面倒くさくてきらいです。
Watashiwa ryoorio tsukurunowa sukidakeredo, atokatazukewa mendookusakute kiraidesu.
I like cooking, but I hate the bother of cleaning up afterwards.

5) 彼女はまだ小学生ですが、弟や妹の面倒をよく見ます。
Kanojowa mada shoogakusei-desuga, otootoya imootono mendoo-o yoku mimasu.
Even though she is still an elementary school student herself, she often looks after her (younger) brother and sister.

6) 祖父は私たちに面倒をかけるのをいやがり、80歳を過ぎた今も1人で暮らしている。
Sofuwa watashitachini mendoo-o kakerunoo iyagari, hachijussaio sugita imamo hitoride kurashiteiru.
My grandfather doesn't want to trouble us, so he still lives by himself even though he is over 80 years old.

やっかい

■ *yakkai*
■ trouble ; troublesome 

①ものごとが**複雑**で、**解決するのが難しいようす**を表します。「困った」「できることならかかわりたくない・やりたくない」という気持ちを強く含みます（例7, 8, 9）。「面倒な問題」よりも「やっかいな問題」の方が、迷惑だ・解決するのが大変だ、という感じが強く表れています。

Yakkai indicates that a situation is complicated and therefore difficult to resolve. It strongly expresses feelings of difficulty, not wanting to do, or not wanting to be involved with a situation (ex.7, 8, 9). A problem described as *yakkai na mondai* is considered to be much more troublesome and difficult to solve than *mendou na mondai.*

②「**世話になる**」「**人の家に泊まる**」という意味で使います。自分や自分の身内のことで世話をかけることを遠慮している言い方です（例10, 11）。

It may be used to mean to 'be cared for by someone' or 'stay the night at someone's house' when speaking diffidently of one or one's family troubling others (ex.10, 11).

---

7) 高速道路で渋滞にまきこまれるとやっかいだ。
Koosokudoorode juutaini makikomareruto yakkaida.
It's a real pain to be caught in a traffic jam on the freeway.

8) 風邪をこじらせてひどくなるとやっかいだから、きょうは早く寝よう。
Kazeo kojirasete hidoku naruto yakkaidakara, kyoowa hayaku neyoo.
(I'll) be in a lot of trouble if I let my cold get worse, so I think I'll go to bed early today.

9) 弁護士である父は、やっかいな事件をかかえて疲れ気味だ。
Bengoshidearu chichiwa, yakkaina jiken-o kakaete tsukaregimida.
My father, who is a lawyer, seems to be tired out from his work on a difficult case.

10) 私は、上京するといつも彼の家にやっかいになる。
Watashiwa, jookyoosuruto itsumo kareno ieni yakkaini naru.
Whenever I come to Tokyo I stay at his house.

11) 彼は酔っぱらってけんかしたので、一晩警察のやっかいになった。
Karewa yopparatte kenkashitanode, hitoban keisatsuno yakkaini natta.
He was drunk and got into a fight, so he was put in jail for the night.

もぐ／むしる／つむ

■*mogu*　■*mushiru*　■*tsumu*

もぐ

■*mogu*
■to pick (fruits, vegetables)

りんごやトマトなど、比較的大きいくだものや野菜を、枝などから手でつかんでとるとき使います（例1, 2）。ねじったりひねったりして、少し無理にという感じがあります。

To pick relatively large fruits or vegetables, such as apples or tomatoes, from the branch by hand (ex.1, 2). It is suggested that twisting, turning, or other force is required.

1) 子供のころは、よく柿の実をもいで食べたものだ。
Kodomono korowa, yoku kakinomio moide tabetamonoda.
When (I) was young, I often picked persimmons (from the tree) and ate them.

2) 兄は、まっ赤なりんごを枝からもいで、私にくれた。
Aniwa, makkana ringoo edakara moide, watashini kureta.
My brother picked a bright red apple off the branch and gave it to me.

むしる

■*mushiru*
■to pluck ; to pull 

草や毛、羽などの細いものや束になっているものを、手や指で何本もつかんで引き抜くことです（例3, 4, 5）。「もぐ」はひとつずつ取りますが、「むしる」はいくつもいっぺんに無理につかみ取ってしまうことを表します。

To pull out several thin or bundled objects such as grass, hair, or feathers with one's hand or fingers (ex.3, 4, 5). While *mogu* means to take objects one at a time, *mushiru* means to take many objects at one time and by force.

3) 今度の休日に、庭の草をむしる予定です。
Kondono kyuujitsuni, niwano kusao mushiru yoteidesu.
(I) plan to pull the weeds in my garden on my next day off.

4) 子供たちがいたずらをして、咲いたばかりの花をむしってしまった。

Kodomotachiga itazuraoshite, saitabakarino hanao mushitteshimatta.
The children pulled out the newly bloomed flowers just to make mischief.

5) しめたにわとりの羽をむしるところを見てから、私は鶏肉が食べられなくなった。

Shimeta niwatorino haneo mushiru tokoroo mitekara, watashiwa torinikuga taberarenaku natta.
Ever since seeing a lifeless chicken being plucked, I haven't been able to eat chicken meat.

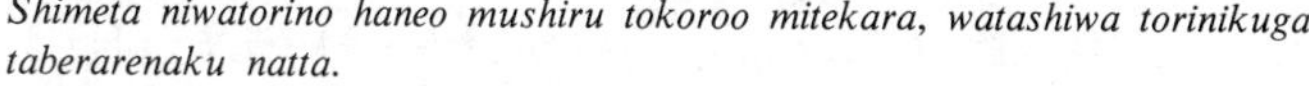

つむ［摘む］ ■ *tsumu*
■ to pick ; to snip 

草花や芽・葉など小さいものをひとつずつ**指先でつまんでとる**ことです（例6, 7, 8)。「摘む」のは伸びて来るものの先の方のものという感じがあります。

To pull off small objects such as a flower, a bud, or a leaf one by one with one's fingers (ex.6, 7, 8). *Tsumu* implies that what is being picked is the end of a long, growing object.

6) 赤くなったいちごをかごにいっぱい摘んだ。

Akaku natta ichigoo kagoni ippai tsunda.
(I) picked the ripe (red) strawberries and piled them in a basket.

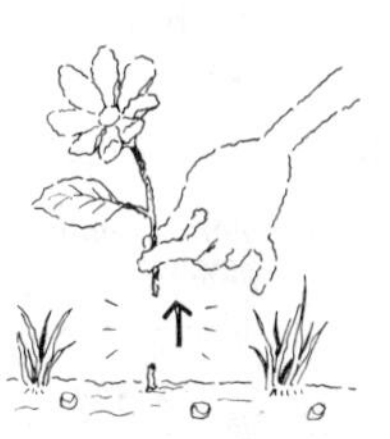

7) 庭の花を摘んできて、テーブルに飾りました。

Niwano hanao tsundekite, teeburuni kazarimashita.
(I) picked some flowers from my garden and decorated my table with them.

8) このあたりでは、初夏になると女の人たちがお茶の葉を摘む姿が見られる。

Kono ataridewa, shokani naruto onnano hitotachiga ochano hao tsumu sugataga mirareru.
In early summer, (you) can see women picking tea leaves around here.

もしかすると／ひょっとすると

■ *moshikasuruto* ■ *hyottosuruto*

もしかすると

■ *moshikasuruto*
■ possibly

確率(かくりつ)は低(ひく)いけれども、**起(お)こる可能性(かのうせい)のある**ことがらや、考(かんが)えられることがらを述(の)べるとき使(つか)います。多(おお)くの場合(ばあい)、「～かもしれない・～ではないだろうか」などといっしょに使(つか)います（例(れい)1, 2, 3, 4）。「もしかしたら・もしかして」も同じように使います。

This expression is used at such times as when indicating that something has a low likelihood of occurrence but that a valid possibility remains, or when expressing a conjecture or speculation. In many cases it is used together with expressions such as ～*kamo shirenai* (maybe) or ～*dewa naidarouka* (isn't it possible that～). *Moshikashitara* and *moshikashite* are also used in the same way (ex.1, 2, 3, 4).

1) もしかするときょうの集(あつ)まりは中止(ちゅうし)になるかもしれない。
Moshikasuruto kyoono atsumariwa chuushini narukamo shirenai.
There is a possibility that today's meeting will be called off.

2) もしかすると、今夜(こんや)あたり雪(ゆき)になるかもしれない。
Moshikasuruto, kon-yaatari yukini narukamo shirenai.
It looks like it just might snow tonight.

3) こんなに来(こ)ないなんて、もしかしたら彼(かれ)は約束(やくそく)を忘(わす)れたのかもしれない。
Konnani konainante, moshikashitara karewa yakusokuo wasuretanokamo shirenai.
He hasn't shown up yet—maybe he's forgotten about our appointment.

4) もしかしたらまた近(ちか)いうちに出張(しゅっちょう)があるかもしれない。
Moshikashitara mata chikai uchini shutchooga arukamo shirenai.
It looks like (I) might be taking another business trip soon.

ひょっとすると

■ *hyottosuruto*
■ possibly ; by some chance 

思いがけないできごとが起こるかもしれないというとき使います。その確率はかなり低く、もしほんとうにそうなったらびっくりする、という感じを含んでいます（例5, 6, 7, 8）。「ひょっとしたら・ひょっとして」も同じように使います。

Hyottosuruto expresses the possibility that something unexpected might happen. It is implied that the probability of occurrence is quite low, and that the speaker would be surprised if it actually does become reality (ex.5, 6, 7, 8). The expressions *hyottoshitara* and *hyottoshite* are used in the same way.

---

5) ひょっとすると、ここから温泉が出るかもしれません。

Hyottosuruto, kokokara onsenga derukamo shiremasen.
There might possibly be a hot spring here.

6) ひょっとすると、今年は宝くじに当たるかもしれない。

Hyottosuruto, kotoshiwa takarakujini atarukamo shirenai.
Maybe, by some chance, (I'll) win the lottery this year.

7) ひょっとすると、今度の公演の主役になれるかもしれない。

Hyottosuruto, kondono kooenno shuyakuni narerukamo shirenai.
It just might be that (I'll) be the lead in the next play.

8) ひょっとしたら、彼の消息がわかるかもしれない。

Hyottoshitara, kareno shoosokuga wakarukamo shirenai.
(I) might just have some news about his whereabouts.

もっと／ますます／さらに

■*motto* ■*masumasu* ■*sarani*

もっと ■*motto* ■more 

2つのものごとを比較して、量や程度などの違いや差を強調するとき使います（例1, 2, 3, 4, 5, 6）。

Motto is used to emphasize a difference in level or volume of two different things or conditions that are being compared (ex.1, 2, 3, 4, 5, 6).

---

1) もっとゆっくり話してください。

Motto yukkuri hanashite kudasai.
Please speak more slowly.

2) 来年は子供が生まれるので、もっと広い家に移りたい。
Rainenwa kodomoga umarerunode, motto hiroi ieni utsuritai.
Next year (we're) going to have a baby, so we would like to move into a larger house.

3) もっと速く歩かないと次の電車にまにあわないよ。
Motto hayaku arukanaito tsugino denshani maniawanaiyo.
If (you) don't walk faster, (we) aren't going to make the next train.

4) もっと上手な字で書いてください。これでは読めません。
Motto joozuna jide kaite kudasai. Koredewa yomemasen.
Please write more clearly. (I) can't read this.

5) これはおいしいお菓子だ、もっと食べたいね。
Korewa oishii okashida, motto tabetaine.
These sweets are delicious. (I) would like to have some more.

6) 富士山よりキリマンジャロのほうが高い。でもエベレストはもっと高い。
Fujisanyori Kirimanjarono-hooga takai. Demo Eberesutowa motto takai.
Mt. Kilimanjaro is taller than Mt. Fuji, but Mt. Everest is even taller.

ますます

■ *masumasu*
■ even more ; more and more

今までも**程度**や**量**が**変わってきたもの**が、その**変化**をどんどん**続けていくようす**を表します。「もっと」は、量や程度の比較ですが、「ますます」は、量や程度が**前よりもいっそう**変わっていくようすを表します（例7, 8, 9, 10）。

This is used in situations in which something that has changed in volume or level continues to change rapidly. *Motto* is used when making comparisons of volume or level, but *masumasu* is used in situations in which there is further and continuing change in the level or volume of something (ex.7, 8, 9, 10).

---

7) 二十歳をすぎて、彼女はますますきれいになりました。
Hatachio sugite, kanojowa masumasu kireini narimashita.
She has become even more beautiful since she turned twenty.

8) 車が多くなって、交通事故がますます増えてきました。

Kurumaga ooku natte, kootsuujikoga masumasu fuetekimashita.
As the roadways have become more crowded, the number of accidents has been on the increase.

9) 夜中(よなか)になって、雨(あめ)はますます激(はげ)しくなってきた。
Yonakani natte, amewa masumasu hageshiku nattekita.
It rained harder and harder as the night wore on.

10) あの女優(じょゆう)は年(とし)をとってからますます人気(にんき)がでた。
Ano joyuuwa toshio tottekara masumasu ninkiga deta.
That actress became increasingly popular as she aged.

さらに ■*sarani* ■still more

今(いま)までのことに加(くわ)える、あるいはその**上(うえ)に重(かさ)ねる・続(つづ)けるというようす**を表(あらわ)すとき使(つか)います（例(れい)11, 12, 13)。また、例(れい)14、15のように、加(くわ)える（減(へ)らす）数量(すうりょう)を述(の)べることもあります。

This is used when there is an addition to some condition or thing, or in situations in which things continue to pile up (ex.11, 12, 13). It can also be used when there is either an increase or a decrease in quantity, as in Examples 14 and 15.

---

11) 兄(あに)は食事(しょくじ)の後(あと)ケーキを食(た)べて、さらにチョコレートも食(た)べた。
Aniwa shokujino ato keekio tabete, sarani chokoreetomo tabeta.
After finishing his dinner, not only did my (older) brother eat a piece of cake, but after that he even ate a chocolate bar.

12) 彼女(かのじょ)はピアノとお花(はな)を習(なら)っていて、さらに英会話(えいかいわ)も始(はじ)めたそうだ。
Kanojowa pianoto ohanao naratteite, sarani eikaiwamo hajimetasooda.
Not only is she taking piano lessons and studying flower arrangement, but (I) hear that she also started studying English conversation.

13) 台風(たいふう)が近(ちか)づいているので、今夜(こんや)は風(かぜ)や雨(あめ)がさらに強(つよ)くなるだろう。
Taifuuga chikazuite-irunode, kon-yawa kazeya amega sarani tsuyoku narudaroo.
A typhoon is approaching so (we) expect stronger winds and rain tonight.

14) 彼(かれ)は学校(がっこう)から帰(かえ)って２時間(じかん)勉強(べんきょう)をして、食事(しょくじ)の後(あと)さらに２時間(じかん)勉強(べんきょう)した。

Karewa gakkookara kaette nijikan benkyoo-o shite, shokujino ato sarani nijikan benkyooshita.
He studied for two hours after coming home from school, then he studied for two more hours after dinner.

15) 先週彼にお金を貸したばかりなのに、きょうさらに5万円借りたいと言ってきました。

Senshuu kareni okaneo kashita bakarinanoni, kyoo sarani goman-en karitaito itte kimashita.
Even though (I) lent him some money just last week, he came asking to borrow another ¥50,000 today.

もどす／かえす

■*modosu* ■*kaesu*

もどす［戻す］ ■*modosu* ■to return ; to replace 

①ものを元あった所に置いたり、ものごとを**元のような状態にする**ことです（例1, 2, 3, 4）。

To place something back in its original location or condition (ex.1, 2, 3, 4).

②**進行方向とは逆の方向に進める**ことです（例5, 6）。吐くことを「もどす」というのは、このためです。例7, 8のように動詞と合わせて使うこともありますが、元の位置や状態に近づけるという基本的な意味は変わりません。

To go the opposite direction from the direction one was going (ex.5, 6). In this way *modosu* may be used to mean 'to vomit'. As in Examples 7 and 8, *modosu* may be used in conjunction with other verbs, however the basic meaning 'to restore to the original position or condition' does not change.

③例9は、**乾燥**させた食品を水や湯につけて**元の状態に近づける**ことです。

In Example 9 it means to rehydrate something dried.

---

1) 手に取った本をもう一度本棚に戻した。

Teni totta hon-o mooichido hondanani modoshita.
(I) put the book I had taken back on the bookshelf.

2) 彼女(かのじょ)はお金(かね)を払(はら)うと、またバッグにさいふを戻(もど)した。
Kanojowa okaneo harauto, mata bagguni saifuo modoshita.
She returned her wallet to her handbag after paying.

3) 使(つか)った道具(どうぐ)は、元(もと)の場所(ばしょ)に戻(もど)してください。
Tsukatta dooguwa, motono bashoni modoshite kudasai.
Please put the tools back after (you) use them.

4) 一度(いちど)こわれた友情(ゆうじょう)を元(もと)に戻(もど)すのはむずかしい。
Ichido kowareta yuujoo-o motoni modosunowa muzukashii.
It's difficult to restore a friendship once it has been lost.

5) 時計(とけい)の針(はり)は戻(もど)せるが、時間(じかん)を戻(もど)すことはできない。
Tokeino hariwa modoseruga, jikan-o modosu kotowa dekinai.
(You) can move back the hands of a clock, but you can never move back time.

6) 車(くるま)に酔(よ)って、戻(もど)してしまった。
Kurumani yotte, modoshite-shimatta.
(I) became carsick and threw up.

7) ビデオのテープを巻(ま)き戻(もど)しておいてください。
Bideono teepuo makimodoshiteoite kudasai.
Please rewind the video tape.

8) 霧(きり)で飛行機(ひこうき)が欠航(けっこう)したので、料金(りょうきん)を払(はら)い戻(もど)してもらった。
Kiride hikookiga kekkooshitanode, ryookin-o haraimodoshite-moratta.
(My) flight was cancelled due to fog so my money was refunded.

9) 干(ほ)ししいたけはぬるま湯(ゆ)で戻(もど)す。
Hoshi-shiitakewa nurumayude modosu.
Dried mushrooms are rehydrated with lukewarm water.

かえす［返(かえ)す・帰(かえ)す］ ■*kaesu* ■to return

①借(か)りたものや持(も)って来(き)たものを**本来(ほんらい)の持(も)ち主(ぬし)**に渡(わた)したり、**本来(ほんらい)の場所(ばしょ)**にもう一度(いちど)置(お)くことです(例(れい)10, 11, 12)。人(ひと)についても使(つか)い「帰(かえ)す」と書(か)きます(例(れい)13)。
To return something one has borrowed or taken to it's owner or original location (ex.10, 11, 12). When used to refer to people, as in, 'to send someone back home', the *kanji* 帰す is written (ex.13).

②相手が**働きかけ**てきたのと**同じ行為をする**ことです（例14）。この場合「やり返す、言い返す……」などのように、別の動詞と合わせて使うこともあります（例15）。単に**もう一度同じことをする**ときも同じように使います（例16, 17）。

To respond in kind to someone's action (ex.14). In this case it is often used in combination with another verb, such as *yarikaesu* (do back to someone) or *iikaesu* (say back to someone) (ex.15). It may also mean to simply do something again (ex.16, 17).

③**表**と**裏**を置きかえて、**逆**にすることです（例18）。

To turn something over, i.e., upside down or inside out; to reverse (ex.18).

---

10) 図書館に本を返す。
Toshokanni hon-o kaesu.
(I'll) return the book to the library.

11) 彼はいつも借りたお金を返さない。
Karewa itsumo karita okaneo kaesanai.
He never returns the money he borrows.

12) 借りたものは必ず返さなくてはいけない。
Karita monowa kanarazu kaesanakutewa ikenai.
(You) must always return things you borrow.

13) 台風が近づいたので、先生は生徒たちを家に帰した。
Taifuuga chikazuitanode, senseiwa seitotachio ieni kaeshita.
The teacher sent the students home because a typhoon was approaching.

14) そう言われては返すことばがありません。私が悪かったのですから。
Soo iwaretewa kaesu kotobaga arimasen. Watashiga warukattano-desukara.
(I) have no way to respond to what you say, because I know I was the one that was wrong.

15) あの子がぶったから、ぼくもぶち返したんだ。
Ano koga buttakara, bokumo buchikaeshitanda.
That kid punched me so I punched him back.

16) 私は母の手紙を何度も読み返した。
Watashiwa hahano tegamio nandomo yomikaeshita.
I read and re-read my mother's letter many times.

17) 彼は失敗をくり返してついに成功した。

Karewa shippaio kurikaeshite tsuini seikooshita.
He finally succeeded after repeated failure.

18) セーターが裏(うら)ですよ。ちゃんと表(おもて)に返(かえ)して着(き)なさい。
Seetaaga uradesuyo. Chanto omoteni kaeshite kinasai.
(Your) sweater is inside out. Turn it right side out.

(〜て) もらう／(〜て) くれる

■ (~*te*) *morau*　　■ (~*te*) *kureru*

(〜て) もらう

■ (~*te*) *morau*
■ to have (someone) do~

人(ひと)から**利益(りえき)になる行為(こうい)を受(う)ける**ことです。こちらから要求(ようきゅう)したり依頼(いらい)したりして、やらせることもあります（例(れい)1, 2, 3, 4, 5, 6)。「(〜て) いただく」は、ていねいな言(い)い方(かた)です。

This indicates that one has someone else do an action for one's own benefit. The beneficiary may have requested, demanded, or forced someone to do the action (ex.1, 2, 3, 4, 5, 6). ~*te itadaku* is a politer equivalent.

---

1) 私(わたし)は父(ちち)に自転車(じてんしゃ)を買(か)ってもらいました。
Watashiwa chichini jitenshao katte moraimashita.
I had my dad buy me a bicycle.

2) 私(わたし)は兄(あに)に、数学(すうがく)のわからないところを教(おし)えてもらいました。
Watashiwa anini, suugakuno wakaranaitokoroo oshiete morai-mashita.
I had my (elder) brother show me how to do the math I couldn't understand.

3) 彼(かれ)はスキーの道具(どうぐ)を、お兄(にい)さんに貸(か)してもらうそうです。
Karewa sukiino dooguo, oniisanni kashite morausoodesu.
He says he's going to have his (elder) brother lend him his ski equipment.

4) せきがひどいのなら、病院(びょういん)で診(み)てもらったほうがいいですよ。
Sekiga hidoinonara, byooinde mite moratta hooga iidesuyo.
If (your) cough gets bad you ought to have it examined at the clinic.

5) ちょっと荷物を運ぶのを手伝ってもらえませんか。
Chotto nimotsuo hakobunoo tetsudatte moraemasenka?
Could (I) have your help to carry my baggage?

6) この文章を英訳していただきたいのですが……。
Kono bunshoo-o eiyakushite itadakitai-nodesuga...
(I'd) like to have you translate this passage into English.

（～て）くれる

■ (~*te*) *kureru*
■ (someone) to do ～ for me (for us, etc.)

人が自分、あるいは、今話題になっている**人のために**何か**利益になることをする**ことです（例7, 8, 9, 10, 11）。「（～て）くださる」は、ていねいな言い方で、目上の人の行為に対して使います。

This indicates that someone does something that benefits the speaker or someone else closely associated with the speaker (ex.7, 8, 9, 10, 11). ~*te kudasaru* is a politer expression used when referring to the action of a person who is of superior or senior status.

---

7) 彼は私に、魚がよくつれる場所を教えてくれた。
Karewa watashini, sakanaga yoku tsureru bashoo oshiete kureta.
He told me about a place where a lot of fish can be caught.

8) これは私が子供の頃、母が作ってくれた人形です。
Korewa watashiga kodomono koro, hahaga tsukutte kureta ningyoodesu.
This is a doll my mother made for me when I was a child.

9) 彼女は、私が悩んでいるときはいつも、相談にのってくれる。
Kanojowa, watashiga nayandeiru tokiwa itsumo, soodanni notte kureru.
She always gives me advice whenever I'm distressed.

10) 姉は私にネックレスを貸してくれなかった。
Anewa watashini nekkuresuo kashite kurenakatta.
My (elder) sister wouldn't lend me her necklace.

11) きょうは、お忙しいところをいらしてくださって、ありがとうございました。
Kyoowa, oisogashii tokoroo irashite kudasatte, arigatoo-gozaimashita.
Thank you for being so kind as to come and see (me) today at such a busy time.

あなたに貸してあげる

急に雨に降られて困っていた大野教授に、学生のジョージが傘を差し出しながら言いました。「あなたに貸してあげる」親切はうれしいけれど、ちょっと変だぞと、教授は思いました。「あなた」は目上の人に使うのは失礼です。それに「貸してあげる」も同じです。「〜てあげる」は自分と同等以上の人に使うと、親切や行為を押し付けているようで失礼です。もしもジョージが、「先生、この傘をお貸しします」と言ったなら50点。「先生、どうぞお使いください」だったら、大野教授は「どうもありがとう、ジョージ」とすぐに喜んだはずです。

I'll lend this to you.

George, a student, in handing his umbrella to Professor Ono who was getting wet in the rain, said, "*Anata ni kashite ageru*[1]."

The professor appreciated George's kindness, but he was somewhat disappointed by the way it was offered.

Using *anata* to a person in a superior position than oneself is usually considered impolite, as is saying *kashite ageru*. The expression *~te ageru*, if used when speaking to a person who is the same rank as you or higher, may cause the other person to feel as if your kindness or goodwill is being pressed upon them.

If George had said, "*Sensei, kono kasa o okashi shimasu*[2]," he would have scored 50 points. If he had said, "*Sensei, doozo otsukai kudasai*[3]," Professor Ono would have replied, "Thank you, George," and would have been that much more grateful.

1 *I'll lend this to you.*
2 *I'll lend this to you* (*a more polite expression*).
3 *Please take this umbrella.*

もらす／こぼす

■ *morasu*　■ *kobosu*

もらす［漏らす］　■ *morasu* ■ to leak (out)

外に出してはいけない・あるいは出すべきではない液体や光、放射線などを、小さな穴やすき間から**少しずつ出**してしまうことです（例１）。

To slowly let things that should be kept inside, such as liquid, light, radiation, etc., leak out through a small hole or crack (ex.1).

秘密や**情報**についても使います（例2, 3）。またそのような状態になることを「〜がもれる」といいます（例4, 5, 6, 7, 8）。

Morasu is also used for the leaking out of secrets or information (ex.2, 3). The intransitive form of *morasu* is *moreru* (ex.4, 5, 6, 7, 8).

1）子供がおしっこをもらしてしまった。
Kodomoga oshikkoo morashiteshimatta.
The child unfortunately wet his pants.

2）これは会社の秘密だから、誰にももらしてはいけない。
Korewa kaishano himitsudakara, darenimo morashitewa ikenai.
This (information) is a company secret, so (you) must not tell it to anybody.

3）情報をもらしたのはだれか、調査中だ。
Joohoo-o morashitanowa dareka, choosachuuda.
(We) are investigating to find out who leaked the information.

4）原子力発電所で、放射線がもれるという事故があった。
Genshiryoku-hatsudenshode, hooshasenga moreruto yuu jikoga atta.
There was a radiation leakage accident at the atomic power plant.

5）もれたガスにストーブの火が引火して爆発した。
Moreta gasuni sutoobuno higa inkashite bakuhatsushita.
The flame from the stove ignited leaking gas, causing an explosion.

6）ドアのすき間から、部屋の明かりがもれてくる。

Doano sukimakara, heyano akariga moretekuru.
Light from the room is leaking out through an opening in the door.

7) 新製品の情報が、どこからかもれてしまった。
Shinseihinno joohooga, dokokaraka moreteshimatta.
Unfortunately, information about the new product has somehow leaked out.

8) 外国の要人が来日したので、警察では水ももらさぬ警備をしている。
Gaikokuno yoojinga rainichishitanode, keisatsudewa mizumo morasanu keibio shiteiru.
A VIP from a foreign country has come to Japan, and the police are providing tight security.

こぼす ■*kobosu* ■to spill

---

①入れ物に入っていたものの一部や全部を、入れ物を**かたむけたり揺らしたり**して、**外へ出**してしまうことです（例9, 10, 11, 12)。「もらす」は、小さな穴やすき間から少しずつ時間をかけて出しますが、「こぼす」は**一度に出**してしまいます。

To allow a part or all of something kept inside a container to spill out through tilting or shaking of the container (ex.9, 10, 11, 12). In the case of *morasu*, something is let out through a small hole or crack and over time, while *kobosu* means to let something out all at once.

②**不平**や**不満**をほかの**人に話す**ことです（例13, 14)。
To tell one's complaints or dissatisfaction to others (ex.13, 14).

---

9) いすの足につまずいて、持っていたコーヒーをこぼしてしまった。
Isuno ashini tsumazuite, motteita koohiio koboshiteshimatta.
(I) tripped on the chair leg and spilt my coffee.

10) 子供がごはんをこぼしながら食べている。
Kodomoga gohan-o koboshinagara tabeteiru.
The child keeps dropping rice while eating.

11) お客さんにお茶を運んでください。こぼさないように気をつけて。
Okyakusanni ochao hakonde kudasai. Kobosanaiyooni kiotsukete.
Please take this tea to (our) guest. Be careful not to spill it.

12) 母は、その話を聞いて、涙をこぼした。
はは　はなし　き　なみだ
Hahawa, sono hanashio kiite, namidao koboshita.
My mother cried when she heard that story.

13) 母は、このごろ物価が高くて困るとこぼしている。
はは　ぶっか　たか　こま
Hahawa, konogoro bukkaga takakute komaruto koboshiteiru.
My mother is complaining about how hard things are due to recent price-hikes.

14) 彼は会うたびに、仕事が忙しいとこぼしてばかりいる。
かれ　あ　しごと　いそが
Karewa autabini, shigotoga isogashiito koboshitebakari-iru.
Whenever (I) see him, he complains that his work is busy.

やくそくする／ちかう

■*yakusoku suru*　　■*chikau*

やくそくする［約束する］ ■*yakusoku suru* ■to promise ♥
やくそく

相手と、こうしようと決めることです（例1, 2, 3, 4, 5）。
あいて　き　れい
To make an agreement or promise to do something in the future (ex.1, 2, 3, 4, 5).

---

1) 私は、夏休みに子供たちを海に連れて行くと約束した。
わたし　なつやす　こども　うみ　つ　い　やくそく
Watashiwa, natsuyasumini kodomotachio umini tsureteikuto yakusokushita.
I promised to take my children to the beach during summer vacation.

2) 私と彼は結婚の約束をした。
わたし　かれ　けっこん　やくそく
Watashito karewa kekkonno yakusokuo shita.
He and I are engaged to be married.

3) 私は2時に駅で友達と会う約束をしている。
わたし　じ　えき　ともだち　あ　やくそく
Watashiwa nijini ekide tomodachito au yakusokuo shiteiru.
I've got an appointment to meet my friend at the station at two o'clock.

4) 父は必ず約束を守ります。
ちち　かなら　やくそく　まも
Chichiwa kanarazu yakusokuo mamorimasu.

My father always keeps his promises.

5) 約束の時間までに返さないと、兄はもう二度と車を貸してくれないでしょう。
Yakusokuno jikanmadeni kaesanaito, aniwa moo nidoto kurumao kashitekurenai-deshoo.
If (I) don't return my brother's car by the time I promised, he probably won't lend it to me again.

ちかう［誓う］ ■*chikau* ■to vow ; to swear 

相手や**自分自身**、あるいは**神聖なもの**（神仏）に対して、**必ずこうすると決める**ことです（例6, 7, 8, 9)。「やくそくする」には必ず相手がありますが、「ちかう」は自分自身で、かたく決心する場合にも使います。

To make a resolution to someone else, oneself, or a sacred being (God, Buddha, etc.) to do something without fail (ex.6, 7, 8, 9). There must be another party involved when *yakusoku suru* is used, but *chikau* may be used when making a firm resolve on one's own.

---

6) 私は母に、もう二度と危険な場所では遊ばないと誓った。
Watashiwa hahani, moo nidoto kikenna bashodewa asobanaito chikatta.
I swore to my mother that I would never play in a dangerous place again.

7) 一人前の役者になるまでは結婚をしないと、心に誓った。
Ichininmaeno yakushani narumadewa kekkon-o shinaito, kokoroni chikatta.
(I) made a vow not to get married until I became a full-fledged actor.

8) 証人は真実を述べることを誓った。
Shooninwa shinjitsuo noberu kotoo chikatta.
The witness swore to tell the truth.

9) 神に誓って、このことはだれにも言いません。
Kamini chikatte, kono kotowa darenimo iimasen.
(I) swear to God, I will not tell anyone about this.

やける/こげる/もえる

■*yakeru*　■*kogeru*　■*moeru*

やける［焼ける］

■*yakeru*
■to burn ; to fire (pottery) 

①**物質**が**火によって中まで変化する**ことです。火事で家などがだめになったときにも、料理や陶器などができあがるときにも使います（例1, 2, 3）。

To change some matter or substance completely by means of fire. It may refer to destruction of a house by fire, or to the making of things such as food or pottery (ex.1, 2, 3).

②**火や熱・光で人間の皮膚やものの色が変わる**ことです（例4, 5）。

The color of an object or a person's skin changes due to exposure to fire, heat, or light (ex.4, 5).

1) 薄く切った肉は早く焼ける。
Usuku kitta nikuwa hayaku yakeru.
Thinly sliced meat cooks quickly.

2) パンがおいしそうに焼けました。
Panga oishisooni yakemashita.
The bread looked delicious after baking.

3) ゆうべの火事で家が５軒焼けたらしい。
Yuubeno kajide iega goken yaketarashii.
It seems that five houses burned down in last night's fire.

4) 海で日に焼けて、鼻の頭が赤くなった。
Umide hini yakete, hanano atamaga akakunatta.
(I) got a sunburn at the beach, and the tip of my nose got red.

5) 白いレースのカーテンが、１年で黄色く焼けてしまった。
Shiroi reesuno kaatenga, ichinende kiiroku yaketeshimatta.
The white lace curtain became yellowed by the sun in one year.

こげる［焦げる］

■*kogeru*
■to burn ; to scorch 

火や**熱**で、ものの**表面**や**一部分**が**茶色**や**黒**っぽくなったり**炭**のようになることです。「焼ける」の程度が過ぎた状態です（例6, 7, 8, 9）。

Kogeru means that the surface or a part of something turns brownish or blackish because of fire or heat. The object may sometimes become charcoal-like. The degree of burning is stronger than with *yakeru* (ex.6, 7, 8, 9).

6）たき火に近づきすぎると服がこげるよ。

Takibini chikazukisugiruto fukuga kogeruyo.
If (you) get too close to the bonfire, you'll burn your clothes.

7）ガスの火が強すぎたので、魚の表面はまっくろにこげて、中は生だった。

Gasuno higa tsuyosugitanode, sakanano hyoomenwa makkuroni kogete, nakawa namadatta.
The gas flame was too high, so the outside of the fish burned completely black, but the inside was still raw.

8）なべを火にかけたまま長電話をしていたら、シチューがこげて食べられなくなった。

Nabeo hini kaketamama nagadenwao shiteitara, shichuuga kogete taberarenakunatta.
Forgetting about the pot on the stove, (I) talked on the phone for a long time, and the stew got so burned that (we) couldn't eat it.

9）A：何かこげているにおいがするよ。
　 B：あ、いけない。アイロンをかけている途中だったんだ。

A： *Nanika kogeteiru nioiga suruyo.*
　　I smell something burning.
B： *A, ikenai. Airon-o kaketeiru tochuudattanda.*
　　Oh, no! I was in the middle of ironing!

もえる［燃える］

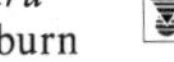

■ *moeru*
■ to burn

---

①そのもの**自体に火がついて炎が出る**ことです（例10, 11, 12, 13）。

To catch fire and burn (ex.10, 11, 12, 13).

②**希望・愛情・怒り**など**感情が激しく高まる**ことです（例14, 15）。

To experience a very strong feeling or emotion such as hope, affection, or anger (ex.14, 15).

10) このまきは、湿(しめ)っているのでよく燃(も)えない。
Kono makiwa, shimetteirunode yoku moenai.
This firewood is damp, so it won't burn well.

11) 燃(も)えるごみと燃(も)えないごみは、分(わ)けて出(だ)してください。
Moeru gomito moenai gomiwa, wakete dashitekudasai.
Please separate (your) burnable trash from your non-burnable trash before putting it out.

12) 暖炉(だんろ)の中(なか)で、まきが勢(いきお)いよく燃(も)えている。
Danrono nakade, makiga ikioiyoku moeteiru.
The firewood is burning well in the fireplace.

13) 火事(かじ)です！　私(わたし)の家(いえ)が燃(も)えているんです！
消防車(しょうぼうしゃ)を呼(よ)んでください！
Kajidesu! Watashino iega moeteirundesu!
Shoobooshao yonde kudasai!
Fire! My house is on fire! Call the fire department (for a fire engine)!

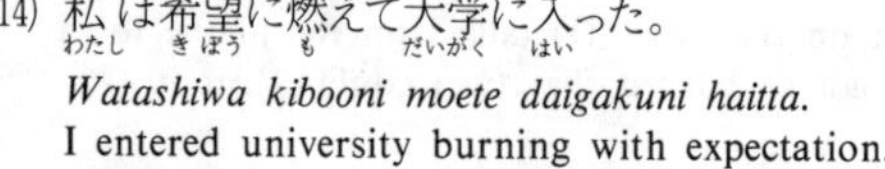

14) 私(わたし)は希望(きぼう)に燃(も)えて大学(だいがく)に入(はい)った。
Watashiwa kibooni moete daigakuni haitta.
I entered university burning with expectation.

15) 彼(かれ)は彼女(かのじょ)に対(たい)する燃(も)える思(おも)いを手紙(てがみ)に書(か)いた。
Karewa kanojoni taisuru moeru omoio tegamini kaita.
He expressed his burning love and admiration for her in a letter.

やさしい／かんたん

■ *yasashii*　■ *kantan*

やさしい［易(やさ)しい・優(やさ)しい］

■ *yasashii*
■ easy ; gentle 

①楽(らく)に理解(りかい)することができる・ものごとの程度(ていど)が高(たか)くなくて、むずかしくないようすを表(あらわ)します（例(れい)1, 2, 3)。

Yasashii indicates that something is easily understandable, not of a high level, or not difficult (ex.1, 2, 3).

②**おだやかで思(おも)いやり**がある・**あたたかみがある**・気持(きも)ちを落(お)ちつかせてくれる性格(せいかく)やようすを表(あらわ)します（例(れい)4, 5）。

It also describes the atmosphere of a place as friendly, or a person's personality as considerate and easy-going (ex.4, 5).

①は「易(やさ)しい」と書(か)き、②は「優(やさ)しい」と書(か)きます。

In definition ① the *kanji* 易しい is used, while 優しい is used in ②.

---

1) この本(ほん)は、易(やさ)しい日本語(にほんご)で書(か)いてある。
Kono honwa, yasashii Nihongode kaitearu.
This book is written in easy Japanese.

2) こんなに易(やさ)しい計算(けいさん)なら、小学生(しょうがくせい)でもできる。
Konnani yasashii keisannara, shoogakuseidemo dekiru.
If it is such an easy calculation as this, even an elementary school child could do it.

3) もう少(すこ)し易(やさ)しく説明(せつめい)してください。
Moosukoshi yasashiku setsumeishite kudasai.
Please explain this in a little simpler way.

4) 彼女(かのじょ)は優(やさ)しい人(ひと)です。
Kanojowa yasashii hitodesu.
She is a very kind person.

5) 母親(ははおや)は優(やさ)しい声(こえ)で子守歌(こもりうた)を歌(うた)った。
Hahaoyawa yasashii koede komoriutao utatta.
The mother sang a lullaby in a soft and tender voice.

かんたん［簡単(かんたん)］ ■*kantan* ■simple 

①「やさしい」の①と同(おな)じように、**むずかしくない**という意味(いみ)で使(つか)います（例(れい)6, 7, 8）。

Kantan has the same meaning as definition ① of *yasashii*, i.e., not difficult (ex.6, 7, 8).

②ものごとが**込(こ)みいっていない**・複雑(ふくざつ)でない・**時間(じかん)や手間(てま)がかからない**、あ

るいは、質素だ・粗末だというようすを表します（例9, 10）。したがって、例8の「かんたんな試験」は、「程度の低い試験」とも「問題が少なくて、時間がかからない試験」ともとれます。

It also indicates that something is not complex and does not require much time, or is plain and unpretentious (ex.9, 10). The *kantan na shiken* of example 8 may mean either 'an easy examination', or 'an examination that does not have many questions so it will not take much time to finish'.

---

6) 5×5なんて計算、簡単だよ。
Go kakeru go nante keisan, kantandayo.
A calculation like 5×5 is simple.

7) 車の運転なんて簡単です。
Kurumano untennante kantandesu.
Driving a car is easy.

8) 面接の後に、簡単な試験があります。
Mensetsuno atoni, kantanna shikenga arimasu.
After the interview, there is a short test.

9) 朝食は、コーヒーとトーストで簡単にすませました。
Chooshokuwa, koohiito toosutode kantanni sumasemashita.
(I) had a simple breakfast of coffee and toast.

10) えりもそでもない簡単なデザインの服なら、私にも作れます。
Erimo sodemo nai kantanna dezainno fukunara, watashinimo tsukuremasu.
If it is a simple design for a dress without sleeves or a collar, even I could make it.

やたらと／むやみに

■*yatara to*　■*muyami ni*

やたらと

■*yatara to*
■recklessly ; excessively

節度や深い考えなしに、何かをするようすや、ものごとの**程度をこえる**ようすを表すとき使います（例1, 2, 3, 4, 5）。

Yatara to indicates that someone does something without moderation or deep thought, or that something exceeds a limit (ex.1, 2, 3, 4, 5).

1) 最近、駅前にやたらと自転車を置く人が増えて困ったものだ。
Saikin, ekimaeni yatarato jitenshao oku hitoga fuete komatta monoda.
Recently, the number of people who carelessly leave their bicycles in front of the train station has increased, causing lots of problems.

2) このごろは、やたらと新しい雑誌が出ている。
Konogorowa, yatarato atarashii zasshiga deteiru.
These days, there is an unduly large number of new magazines being published.

3) 子供が少しぐらい失敗したって、やたらとさわぎ立てない方がいいですよ。
Kodomoga sukoshigurai shippai-shitatte, yatarato sawagi-tatenai hooga iidesuyo.
(Your) child made just a small mistake, so you shouldn't make too much fuss about it.

4) なんだか、やたらとのどがかわいてしようがない。昼食べたカレーが、辛かったからかな。
*Nandaka, yatarato nodoga kawaite shooga nai. Hiru tabeta karee*ga karakatta-karakana?* * p.702
(I) don't know why, but I'm extremely thirsty. I wonder if it's because the curry I ate for lunch was too spicy.

5) パーティーで彼女は、だれかれとなくやたらと愛敬をふりまいていた。
Paatiide kanojowa, darekareto naku yatarato aikyoo-o furimaiteita.
She was trying too hard to please anyone and everyone at the party.

むやみに

■ *muyami ni*
■ thoughtlessly ; unnecessarily 

結果を考えないで、計画性もなく不用意に何かをするようすを表すとき使います。また、必要以上に、という意味もあります（例6, 7, 8, 9)。

This indicates that one does something without thinking about results or consequences. It can also mean that something is beyond what is necessary (ex.6, 7, 8, 9).

6) 欲しい物を、次から次へと買うなんて……。むやみにお金を使うものではありませんよ。

Hoshii monoo, tsugikara-tsugieto kaunante.... Muyamini okaneo tsukau monodewa arimasen-yo.
(You) keep buying everything you want. You shouldn't use your money recklessly.

7) いくら害虫だからって、むやみに虫を殺してはいけない。

Ikura gaichuudakaratte, muyamini mushio koroshitewa ikenai.
Even if it is a harmful insect, (you) shouldn't kill it so thoughtlessly.

8) 薬は、むやみに飲まない方がいい。

Kusuriwa, muyamini nomanai hooga ii.
(You) shouldn't take medicine unnecessarily.

9) 人からむやみにお金を借りると、返すのが大変です。

Hitokara muyamini okaneo kariruto, kaesunoga taihendesu.
If (you) borrow money recklessly, it is hard to pay it back.

やっと／とうとう／ついに

■ *yatto* ■ *toutou* ■ *tsuini*

やっと

■ *yatto*
■ at last ; finally 

---

①待っていたことや望んでいたことが、苦労したり時間がかかったりして実現したとき、**かかった時間**や、**苦労に対する感情をこめて**使います（例1, 2, 3, 4）。

Yatto is used when emotionally expressing that something one has been looking forward to, waited a long time for, or taken a great deal of trouble to do has come to pass (ex.1, 2, 3, 4).

②なんとか・どうにかこの状態に達したときや、これでもう**精一杯だというようす**を表して使います。「～するのがやっとだ」という形でも使います（例5, 6, 7, 8）。「やっと」は、実現したことにだけ使い、否定形には使いません。

It may also indicate that it has been all one could do to somehow, in one way or another, achieve a certain state or condition; and may appear in the form ～*suru no ga yatto da* (ex.5, 6, 7, 8). *Yatto* is only used when speaking of things that have become reality, and not in negative statements.

---

1) 長い冬が終わり、やっと暖かい春が来た。
Nagai fuyuga owari, yatto atatakai haruga kita.
The long winter ended, and the warm spring finally came.

2) やっと100万円貯まった。
Yatto hyakuman-en tamatta.
At last, (I've) saved ¥1,000,000.

3) やっと間に合った。
Yatto maniatta.
(I) made it in the nick of time.

4) 急な山道を歩き続けて、やっと頂上に着いた。
Kyuuna yamamichio arukitsuzukete, yatto choojooni tsuita.
(We) kept walking up the steep mountain path,
and finally reached the summit.

5) 彼は疲れきっていて、歩くのがやっとだった。
Karewa tsukarekitteite, arukunoga yattodatta.
He was so exhausted that he could barely walk.

6) その夜は霧が濃くて、3メートル先のものがやっと見える程度だった。
Sono yoruwa kiriga kokute, sanmeetoru sakino monoga yatto mieru teido-datta.
That night, the fog was so dense that (we) could barely see things three meters ahead.

7) 彼女は事故のショックで口もきけず、立っているのがやっとだった。
Kanojowa jikono shokkude kuchimo kikezu, tatteirunoga yattodatta.
Because of the shock from the accident, she couldn't even talk ; in fact she was barely standing.

8) 母が亡くなったとき、私はやっと4歳になったばかりだった。
Hahaga nakunatta toki, watashiwa yatto yonsaini nattabakaridatta.
When my mother passed away, I was barely four years old.

とうとう

■ *toutou*
■ in the end ; finally 

---

①長い時間がかかったり、**苦労したり**、いろいろなことがあったけれど、**ある**

程度予想された結果になったとき、喜びや満足などの感情を表して使います。したがってよくない結果のときは、残念だなどの気持ちを含みます（例9, 10, 11, 12, 13）。

Toutou indicates that, although it has taken a long time or a great deal of trouble, a result which had been to a certain extent predicted is achieved. It expresses emotion such as joy or relief at a favorable outcome, or disappointment at an unfavorable outcome (ex.9, 10, 11, 12, 13).

②がまんしていたけれど、限界になって何かしてしまうようすを表して使います（例14, 15）。

It is also used when one cannot endure a situation any longer, and finally decides to do something about it (ex.14, 15).

---

9) 彼はとうとう金鉱を見つけた。
Karewa tootoo kinkoo-o mitsuketa.
He finally struck gold.

10) とうとう夢がかなって主役を演じることになった。
Tootoo yumega kanatte shuyakuo enjirukotoni natta.
At last my dream came true, and (I) got the leading role (in a play).

11) 彼は20年研究して、とうとうがんに効く薬を作りあげた。
Karewa nijuunen kenkyuushite, tootoo ganni kiku kusurio tsukuriageta.
After 20 years of research, he at last found a drug that was effective against cancer.

12) １か月待ったけれど、とうとう彼からの返事は来なかった。
Ikkagetsu mattakeredo, tootoo karekarano henjiwa konakatta.
(I) waited for a month, but in the end I didn't receive a response from him.

13) 彼は、病気で先月とうとう亡くなった。
Karewa, byookide sengetsu tootoo nakunatta.
He finally passed away last month after a long illness.

14) どのくらい息が続くか水にもぐっていたけれど、苦しくなってとうとう顔を出してしまった。
Donokurai ikiga tsuzukuka mizuni mogutteitakeredo, kurushikunatte tootoo

kaoo dashiteshimatta.
(I) stayed underwater to see how long I could hold my breath, but it got so painful that I had to come up for air at last.

15) 彼は事業に失敗して、自分の家をとうとう手放した。
Karewa jigyooni shippaishite, jibunno ieo tootoo tebanashita.
He failed in his business and, in the end, had to let his house go, too.

ついに ■*tsuini* ■in the end ; finally 

---

①**最終結果が出た**ときに使います。もうこの先はなくて、これまでの苦労・困難、あるいはかかった時間をこえて出た結果に対する強い感情を含んでいます(例16, 17, 18)。

Tsuini is used to express strong emotion when a final result is obtained. It expresses the idea that some degree of hardship, difficulty, or time has been overcome and that no further progress or action is possible (ex.16, 17, 18).

②最後まで・最後にはという意味で使います（例19, 20)。「ついに」はほとんどの場合、「とうとう」で言いかえられますが、「とうとう」は結果までの時間の長さ・苦労に重点があり、「ついに」は実現した瞬間とことがらに、より重点があります。そして少しかたい言い方です。

It may also mean 'until or in the end' (ex.19, 20). *Tsuini* can usually be replaced with *toutou*, but *toutou* emphasizes the length of time or amount of hardship involved in obtaining a result, while *tsuini* focuses on the instant or the fact that something is realized. *Tsuini* is a somewhat formal expression.

---

16) 人類は、ついに宇宙にまで行くようになった。
Jinruiwa, tsuini uchuunimade ikuyooni natta.
Humans have finally reached the point where they can go out into space.

17) ついに私の望みがかなった。
Tsuini watashino nozomiga kanatta.
At long last, my wishes have come true.

18) ついに私の理想の男性が現れた。
Tsuini watashino risoono danseiga arawareta.
At last, my ideal man has appeared.

19) ２時間も待ったのに、ついに彼女は来なかった。
Nijikanmo mattanoni, tsuini kanojowa konakatta.
(I) waited a whole two hours, but in the end she never showed up.

20) いくら注意をしても子供たちがけんかをやめないので、私はついに大声でどなりつけた。
Ikura chuuio shitemo kodomotachiga kenkao yamenainode, watashiwa tsuini oogoede donaritsuketa.
The children wouldn't stop fighting no matter how much I warned them, so I finally shouted at them.

やはり／さすが

■ *yahari* ■ *sasuga*

やはり

■ *yahari*
■ as expected ; as well 

---

①ものごとが**予想や判断と変わらない**とき使います（例1, 2）。

Yahari is used when something meets one's expectation or judgment (ex.1, 2).

②ものごとに対する**世間一般の考え方・常識をあらためて認める**とき使います（例3, 4）。

It is also used when acknowledging that something agrees with ideas that are generally held, or is common sense (ex.3, 4).

③過去と同じように今も・今度も、というとき使います（例5, 6）。

In other situations it is used to mean 'now, as in the past' (ex.5, 6).

④ほかの人・もの・場所などと同じように、というとき使います（例7, 8）。「やっぱり」は話しことばで、「やはり」と同じ使い方です。

It may also be used to indicate that something is similar to an other person, place, or thing (ex.7, 8). *Yappari* is a more colloquial expression which is used in the same way.

---

1) きのう電話をくれたのは、やはり桜井さんだそうです。

Kinoo denwao kuretanowa, yahari Sakuraisanda soodesu.
It was Mr. Sakurai that phoned (me) yesterday after all.

2) やはりきょうは雨(あめ)になった。

Yahari kyoowa ameni natta.
It did rain today after all.

3) やはり横綱(よこづな)は強(つよ)い。

Yahari yokozuna∗*wa tsuyoi.* ∗p.698
Yokozuna rank wrestlers are strong, indeed.
——∗ *Yokozuna* is the highest rank attainable in *sumoo* wrestling.

4) やはり我(わ)が家(や)が、一番(いちばん)落(お)ち着(つ)く。

Yahari wagayaga, ichiban ochitsuku.
Ah, nothing beats being at home for relaxation!

5) 今(いま)でもやはり、あなたのお父(とう)さんは銀行(ぎんこう)にお勤(つと)めですか。

Imademo yahari, anatano otoosanwa ginkooni otsutomedesuka?
(I) suppose your father is still working for the bank, isn't he?

6) 今年(ことし)の冬(ふゆ)も、やはりスキーに行(い)くつもりです。

Kotoshino fuyumo, yahari sukiini iku tsumoridesu.
Of course (I'm) going to go skiing this winter, too (as usual).

7) お兄(にい)さんも背(せ)が高(たか)いけれど、やっぱり弟(おとうと)も背(せ)が高(たか)い。

Oniisanmo sega takaikeredo, yappari ototomo sega takai.
The older brother is tall, but the younger brother is really tall.

8) フランス語(ご)も難(むず)かしいけれど、やっぱり中国語(ちゅうごくご)も難(むず)かしいね。

Furansugomo muzukashiikeredo, yappari Chuugokugomo muzukashiine.
Of course, French is difficult, but Chinese is really difficult.

さすが

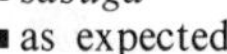

①**評判(ひょうばん)どおりだ・そういわれるだけのことはある**、というとき感心(かんしん)する気(き)持(も)ちを含(ふく)んで使(つか)います（例(れい)9, 10)。

Sasuga is used to express admiration for something or someone because it measures up to or is worthy of its reputation (ex.9, 10).

②そうなったのも当然(とうぜん)の結果(けっか)で、仕方(しかた)がないというとき使(つか)います（例(れい)11, 12)。

②には例13, 14のように、なりゆきの結果で納得できないがやむを得ないというものも含まれ「さすがに～ない」の形で使うことが多いです。

It also expresses the notion that some event or state is natural, expected, or unavoidable (ex.11,12). As shown in Examples 13 and 14, the expression *sasuga ni ～nai* is often used to imply that the resultant situation is not acceptable but was unavoidable.

---

9) あんな難しい問題を解くなんて、さすが秀才といわれるだけのことはある。
Anna muzukashii mondaio tokunante, sasuga shuusaito iwarerudakeno kotowa aru.
He solved a difficult problem like that?! He really is a genius.

10) さすが東京だね、人が多い。
Sasuga Tookyoodane, hitoga ooi.
Yep, this is Tokyo—full of people.

11) 10時間も山道を歩いたら、さすがに足が痛くなった。
Juujikanmo yamamichio aruitara, sasugani ashiga itakunatta.
After walking in the mountains for ten hours (my) feet started to hurt, as you can imagine.

12) ゆうべは徹夜で仕事をしたので、さすがにきょうは眠い。
Yuubewa tetsuyade shigotoo shitanode, sasugani kyoowa nemui.
(I) stayed up all night last night working, so it's no wonder I'm sleepy today.

13) 土地の価格がこう高くなっては、さすがに手が出せない。
Tochino kakakuga koo takaku nattewa, sasugani tega dasenai.
With the price of land going up like this, there's no way (I) can even touch it.

14) さすがに「100万円貸してほしい」とは言い出せなかった。
Sasugani "Hyakuman-en kashite hoshii" towa iidasenakatta.
Of course, (I) couldn't come out and say "Please lend me ¥1,000,000," after all.

ゆでる／にる／わかす

■*yuderu* ■*niru* ■*wakasu*

ゆでる ■*yuderu* ■to boil

野菜・卵・肉・魚などを**味をつけないお湯**に入れて**熱する**ことです（例1, 2, 3, 4）。塩を加えてゆでることを「塩ゆで」と言います（例5）。ゆで終わった状態になることを「ゆだる」と言います。

To cook vegetables, eggs, meat, fish, etc., in unseasoned boiling water (ex.1, 2, 3, 4). To cook in water to which salt has been added is called *shioyude* (ex.5). *Yudaru* is used to refer to the final, cooked state of something that has been boiled.

1) マカロニはゆで過ぎるとおいしくない。

Makaroniwa yudesugiruto oishikunai.
Macaroni isn't good if (you) boil it too long.

2) A：卵はどうしましょうか。

B：3分ゆでてください。

A： *Tamagowa dooshimashooka?* How should (I) do the eggs?
B： *Sanpun yudetekudasai.* Please boil them for three minutes.

3) このとうもろこしは今ゆでたばかりなので、熱くておいしいですよ。

Kono toomorokoshiwa ima yudetabakarinanode, atsukute oishiidesuyo.
This corn has just been boiled. It's hot and delicious.

4) ほうれん草は、ゆで過ぎないようにしてください。

Hoorensoowa, yudesuginai-yooni shitekudasai.
Please don't over-boil the spinach.

5) アスパラガスを塩ゆでにして食べる。

Asuparagasuo shioyudenishite taberu.
(I) eat asparagus boiled in salted water.

にる［煮る］ ■*niru* ■to stew ; to simmer 

野菜・肉・魚などの食品を、**味をつけた汁**の中に入れ、**味がつくまで**ある程度の時間、加熱調理することです（例6, 7, 8）。できあがった状態になることを「煮える」と言います（例9）。

To put vegetables, meat, fish, etc., into a seasoned broth and cook for a certain length of time until done (ex.6, 7, 8). The completed state is referred to with *nieru* (ex.9).

---

6) 冬(ふゆ)になると、母(はは)が煮(に)たシチューが食(た)べたくなる。
Fuyuni naruto, hahaga nita shichuuga tabetakunaru.
When winter comes (I) long for my mom's simmered stews.

7) 日本(にほん)の家庭(かてい)では、野菜(やさい)などをしょうゆ・さとう・酒(さけ)などで煮(に)て食(た)べる「煮物(にもの)」をよく作(つく)ります。
Nihonno kateidewa, yasainadoo shooyu, satoo, sakenadode nite taberu 'nimono'o yoku tsukurimasu.
In Japanese households they often make *nimono*, in which vegetables and other ingredients are stewed in a broth seasoned with soy sauce, sugar, *sake*, etc.

8) この肉(にく)はいくら煮(に)ても柔(やわ)らかくならない。
Kono nikuwa ikura nitemo yawarakaku naranai.
This meat won't get tender however much (you) stew it.

9) カレーが煮(に)えたらごはんにしましょう。
*Karee*ga nietara gohanni shimashoo.* *p.702
Let's eat as soon as the curry is done.

わかす ［沸(わ)かす］ ■ *wakasu* ■ to boil ; to heat 

水(みず)を熱(ねつ)してお湯(ゆ)にすることです（例(れい)10, 11, 12）。牛乳(ぎゅうにゅう)にも使(つか)います。
To heat water or milk until hot (ex.10, 11, 12).

お湯(ゆ)になることを「沸(わ)く」と言(い)います（例(れい)13）。
To reach the boiling state is called *waku* (ex.13).

---

10) お湯(ゆ)を沸(わ)かしてお茶(ちゃ)を入(い)れましょう。
Oyuo wakashite ochao iremashoo.
(I'll) boil some water and make tea.

11) 牛乳(ぎゅうにゅう)を沸(わ)かすときは、ふきこぼれないように気(き)をつけてください。
Gyuunyuuo wakasu tokiwa, fukikoborenai-yooni kiotsukete kudasai.
When (you) boil the milk, be careful not to let it boil over.

12) 今、お風呂を沸かしているところです。
Ima, ofuroo wakashiteiru tokorodesu.
(I'm) just now heating the bathwater.

13) お湯が沸いたらポットに入れておいてください。
Oyuga waitara pottoni ireteoite kudasai.
When the water boils, please fill the thermos pot.

ゆるす／きょかする

■*yurusu* ■*kyoka suru*

ゆるす［許す］ ■*yurusu* ■to forgive ; to allow

①人のあやまちや失敗、罪などを、とがめたり追及したりしないことです（例1, 2, 3）。
To refrain from blaming a person for their mistake, failure, crime, etc. (ex.1, 2, 3).

②願いや要求を認めて、その通りにさせることです（例4, 5）。
To grant a request or demand and allow it to proceed (ex.4, 5).

③可能な状況ならば、という意味で使います（例６）。
Yurusu is also used to mean 'if conditions permit' (ex.6).

---

1) 彼女は子供をはねた車の運転手を、決して許さないだろう。
Kanojowa kodomoo haneta kurumano untenshuo, kesshite yurusanaidaroo.
She will certainly never forgive the driver of the car that hit her child.

2) 彼は、待ち合わせの時間に遅れて来た彼女を、許してやった。
Karewa, machiawaseno jikanni okuretekita kanojoo, yurushiteyatta.
He forgave her for being late for their appointment.

3) 私は、彼女の嘘が許せない。
わたし かのじょ うそ ゆる
Watashiwa, kanojono usoga yurusenai.
I can't forgive her lie.

4) 父は私が16歳になったときに、はじめて1人で旅行するのを許してくれた。
ちち わたし さい ひとり りょこう ゆる
Chichiwa watashiga juurokusaini natta tokini, hajimete hitoride ryokoosuru-noo yurushite kureta.
My father allowed me to travel alone for the first time when I turned sixteen.

5) 彼が手術を受けてから3日後に、やっと面会が許された。
かれ しゅじゅつ う みっかご めんかい ゆる
Karega shujutsuo uketekara mikkagoni, yatto menkaiga yurusareta.
He was finally allowed visitors three days after his operation.

6) 時間が許す限り、話し合いを続けましょう。
じかん ゆる かぎ はな あ つづ
Jikanga yurusu kagiri, hanashiaio tsuzukemashoo.
Let's continue (our) discussion as long as time permits.

きょかする［許可する］ ■*kyoka suru* ■to permit 
きょか

願いや要求を認めてその通りにさせること、つまり「**～しても良い**」と認めることです（例7, 8, 9)。例10、11は名詞としての使い方です。
ねが ようきゅう みと とお よ みと れい れい めいし つか かた

To grant a request or demand and allow something to take place. In other words, to give approval by saying 'you may～' (ex.7, 8, 9). Examples 10 and 11 show the use of *kyoka* as a noun.

---

7) 校長は、生徒たちが放課後、会議室を使うのを許可した。
こうちょう せいと ほうかご かいぎしつ つか きょか
Koochoowa, seitotachiga hookago, kaigishitsuo tsukaunoo kyokashita.
The principal permitted the students to use the meeting room after school.

8) 彼女は、その高校への編入を許可された。
かのじょ こうこう へんにゅう きょか
Kanojowa, sono kookooeno hennyuuo kyokasareta.
She was allowed admission to the high school.

9) このお寺の中での撮影は許可されていない。
てら なか さつえい きょか
Kono oterano nakadeno satsueiwa kyokasareteinai.
Taking photographs is not permitted inside this temple.

10) 所長の許可がなければ、この研究所の中に入ることはできない。
しょちょう きょか けんきゅうじょ なか はい

Shochoono kyokaga nakereba, kono kenkyuujono nakani hairu kotowa dekinai.
(You) cannot enter this laboratory without the permission of the supervisor.

11) あの店は、脱税していたのがみつかって、営業許可を取り消された。
Ano misewa, datsuzei-shiteitanoga mitsukatte, eigyookyokao torikesareta.
That shop was stripped of its license to operate after it was found guilty of tax evasion.

(〜) よう (みたい)/ (〜) らしい

■(〜) *you* (*mitai*) ■(〜) *rashii*

(〜) よう (みたい)

■(〜) *you* (*mitai*)
■appearance ; manner 

---

①**不確か**だけれど、**たぶんそうだ**というとき使います。見たり聞いたりさわったりした、**自分の判断や推量**です(例1, 2)。断定をさけてやわらかく言う、という意味も含みます(例3, 4)。

(〜) *you* (*mitai*) denotes that something is vague but seems to be a certain way. It expresses one's personal judgment or conjecture based on having seen, heard, touched, etc., something (ex.1, 2). It is also used when saying something gently, without being conclusive (ex.3, 4).

②ほんとうはそうではないけれど、**あるものをほかのものに例えて**言うとき使います(例5, 6, 7, 8, 9)。

It may be used to liken some object or event to another (ex.5, 6, 7, 8, 9).

③**例として挙げるとき**使います(例10, 11)。
「みたい」はくだけた言い方で、日常よく使われますが、時には、あまり上品ではない・子供っぽいなどと感じられることがあります。

It is also used when mentioning something as an example (ex.10, 11).
Mitai is a frequently used colloquial expression, but can sound impolite, rough, or childish at times.

---

1) 疲れているようですね。顔色が悪いですよ。
Tsukareteiru-yoodesune. Kaoiroga waruidesuyo.
(You) look tired. Your face is pale.

2) あれ、地震かな。少しゆれたようだけど…。
Are, jishinkana? Sukoshi yuretayoodakedo...
Hey, was that an earthquake? It seemed like (we) were swaying.

3) この薬を飲んでも痛みがとれないようなら、また(病院に)来てください。
Kono kusurio nondemo itamiga torenaiyoonara, mata (byooinni) kitekudasai.
If the pain doesn't seem to go away even after (you've) taken this medicine, please come back (to the hospital).

4) 久しぶりに母校を訪れたら、とても立派になっていて、みちがえるようだった。
Hisashiburini bokoo-o otozuretara, totemo rippani natteite, michigaeru-yoodatta.
When, after some time, (I) paid a visit to my alma mater, I found it had changed so much for the better that it seemed as if I were seeing things.

5) 望遠鏡で見ると遠くの島がまるで目の前にあるようだ。
Booenkyoode miruto tookuno shimaga marude menomaeni aruyooda.
When (I) look through the telescope, the distant islands seem to be right in front of me.

6) 彼女の心は氷のように冷たい。
Kanojono kokorowa koorinoyooni tsumetai.
Her heart is as cold as ice.

7) 子供たちは子犬のように走りまわって遊んでいる。
Kodomotachiwa koinunoyooni hashirimawatte asondeiru.
The children are playing and running around like little puppies.

8) 彼はよほど疲れていたのか、死んだように眠っている。
Karewa yohodo tsukareteitanoka, shindayooni nemutteiru.
He must have been thoroughly tired out—he's sleeping like the dead.

9) 彼女は子供みたいに大声をあげて泣いた。
Kanojowa kodomomitaini oogoeo agete naita.
She cried, wailing like a child.

10) 将来は父のような立派な医者になりたい。

Shooraiwa chichinoyoona rippana ishani naritai.
I want to be a brilliant doctor like my father someday.

11) 私はにんにくのようににおいの強いものは苦手だ。
Watashiwa ninnikunoyooni nioino tsuyoi monowa nigateda.
I can't take strong-smelling foods like garlic.

(～) らしい

■(～) *rashii*
■seem ; appear ; ～like 

---

①不確かだけれど、自分が見たり聞いたりして**判断したこと**や**推量したこと**に使います（例12, 13）。あるいは、**外からの情報・伝聞**などを**客観的に述べる**とき使います（例14, 15）。責任を持たない感じです。

(～) *rashii* is used when making a judgment or conjecture based on something one has seen or heard oneself, though it may not be certain (ex.12, 13). It is also used when stating objectively some information or hearsay (ex.14, 15), and imparts a feeling of disavowal of responsibility.

②いかにもその**特性**や**特徴がよく表れている**というとき使います（例16, 17, 18)。

It is also used to indicate the manifestation of some typical characteristic or trait (ex.16, 17, 18).

---

12) 電気がついていないところをみると、彼はいないらしい。
Denkiga tsuiteinai tokoroo miruto, karewa inairashii.
He seems not to be in, judging from the fact that the lights are off.

13) 人だかりがしている。交通事故でもあったらしい。
Hitodakariga shiteiru. Kootsuujikodemo attarashii.
There's a crowd. It looks like there was an accident.

14) うわさによると、あの銀行は経営が苦しいらしい。
Uwasani yoruto, ano ginkoowa keieiga kurushiirashii.
From what (I) hear, that bank is in financial difficulty.

15) 天気予報によれば、午後から晴れるらしい。
Tenkiyohooni yoreba, gogokara harerurashii.
It seems it's going to clear up in the afternoon, according to the weather report.

16) きょうは忙(いそが)しくて、食事(しょくじ)らしい食事(しょくじ)をする暇(ひま)がなかった。

Kyoowa isogashikute, shokujirashii shokujio suru himaga nakatta.
Today (I) was so busy I didn't have time for anything you could call a 'meal'.

17) 私(わたし)は今(いま)まで病気(びょうき)らしい病気(びょうき)をしたことがない。

Watashiwa imamade byookirashii byookio shita kotoga nai.
Up to now I haven't been sick with a real illness.

18) こんなつまらない失敗(しっぱい)をするなんて、いつもの彼(かれ)らしくない。

Konna tsumaranai shippaio surunante, itsumono karerashiku nai.
It's not like him to have made such a silly mistake like this.

(～に) よって／(～に) おうじて

■ (～*ni*) *yotte* ■ (～*ni*) *oujite*

(～に) よって ■ (～*ni*) *yotte* ■ depending on～

いくつかの**条件(じょうけん)のひとつひとつに対応(たいおう)**することがらや状態(じょうたい)があるとき使(つか)います(例(れい)1, 2, 3, 4)。Aの場合(ばあい)にはX、Bの場合(ばあい)にはYというように、条件(じょうけん)とそれに対応(たいおう)することがらの種類(しゅるい)がいろいろあるということです。

(～*ni*) *yotte* is used to state a contingent situation or condition which will determine some state or course of action (ex.1, 2, 3, 4).
It is used to indicate that there are various possibilities available, which are brought about depending on the conditions, for example, if A then X, if B then Y, etc.

---

1) 風俗(ふうぞく)や習慣(しゅうかん)は、地方(ちほう)によって異(こと)なる。

Fuuzokuya shuukanwa, chihooniyotte kotonaru.
Manners and customs vary from region to region.

2) アメリカでは銀行(ぎんこう)によって預金(よきん)の金利(きんり)が違(ちが)います。

Amerikadewa ginkooniyotte yokinno kinriga chigaimasu.
The interest rate on deposits varies by bank in the U.S.

3) 人(ひと)によって言(い)うことがまちまちなので混乱(こんらん)した。

Hitoniyotte yuukotoga machimachi-nanode konranshita.
(I) became confused because each person gave me a different story.

4) 電車は一日中込んでいるわけではなく、時間によっては楽に座れます。
Denshawa ichinichijuu kondeiruwakedewa naku, jikanniyottewa rakuni suwaremasu.
It's not (true) that trains are crowded all day; depending on the time, you can easily find a seat.

（～に）おうじて ［（～に）応じて］ ■(～*ni*) *oujite* ■in response to～ 

条件の変化に合わせてものごとが行われるときに使います（例5, 6, 7, 8)。「～によって」が、対処や対応することがらの種類の多さを表し、「～に応じて」は、**よそからの働きかけに対処する・こたえる**という意味を強く表します。

This denotes that something happens in reaction to a change in some condition (ex.5, 6, 7, 8). The expression (～*ni*) *yotte* is used when there are specific conditions relating to specific situations; however (～*ni*) *oujite* implies responding to or dealing with a change in some condition.

---

5) 体力に応じて運動量や運動の種類を変えたほうがいい。
Tairyokuni oojite undooryooya undoono shuruio kaeta hooga ii.
(You) should adjust the type and intensity of exercise according to your physical strength.

6) この店では客の注文に応じていろいろなケーキを作ってくれる。
Kono misedewa kyakuno chuumonni oojite iroirona keekio tsukutte kureru.
This bakery will bake any kind of cake to meet customers' demands.

7) 医者は患者の病状に応じて薬を出す。
Ishawa kanjano byoojooni oojite kusurio dasu.
A doctor prescribes medication according to the patient's symptoms.

8) このホールは設備が整っているので、コンサートや国際会議など、目的に応じていろいろな使い方ができる。
Kono hooruwa setsubiga totonotte-irunode, konsaatoya kokusaikaiginado, mokutekini oojite iroirona tsukaikataga dekiru.
This assembly hall is set up so that it can be used for any sort of purpose—whether it be a concert or an international conference.

相撲

日本の国技で、古来からあり、現在のような形になったのは、18世紀初めか中頃からと言われています。相手の体（足の裏以外）を土俵につけたり、また土俵の外に出した方が勝ちです。決まり手と言われる70の技があります。

ランクは最高位が横綱で、以下、大関・関脇・小結・前頭などが続きます。大関で二場所連続優勝するなどの成績を収め、横綱審議委員会が安定した強さを認めた力士が、横綱になれます。

Sumoo

Sumoo is the national sport of Japan and has existed since ancient times, however the sport in its present form is said to have been developed sometime between the early to mid-18th century. The object of a *sumoo* match is to force one's opponent to touch the ground with a part of his body (except the soles of his feet) or to push him from the ring (*dohyoo*). There are 70 different techniques that may be employed to do this.

The highest *sumoo* rank is *yokozuna*, followed in descending order by *oozeki*, *sekiwake*, *komusubi* and *maegashira*. A wrestler who has attained the rank of *oozeki* may rise to the rank of *yokozuna* if he wins two consecutive *sumoo* tournaments, and has demonstrated consistent strength to the satisfaction of the Japan Sumo Federation.

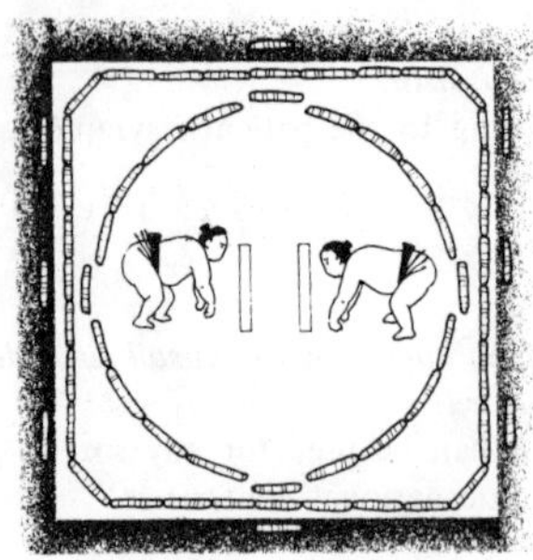

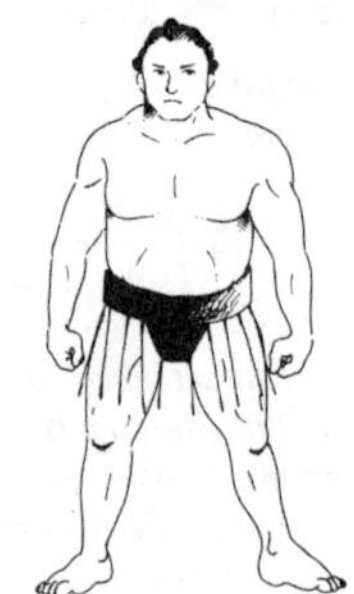

よぶ／まねく

■*yobu* ■*maneku*

よぶ［呼ぶ］ ■*yobu* ■to call ; to call (invite) over

①相手に**気づかせるために声をかける**ことです（例1, 2）。

To call out to someone in order to get their attention (ex.1, 2).

②自分のところに**来るように**させることです（例3, 4）。家に客として誘うときも使います（例5）。

To have someone come to where one is (ex.3, 4), or to invite someone as a guest to one's home (ex.5).

③名前を決める・称することです（例6, 7）。

To name or designate something (ex.6, 7).

④引き起こすという意味で使います（例8, 9, 10）。

Yobu is used also to mean 'to cause or bring about' (ex.8, 9, 10).

1）これからみなさんの名前を呼びます。呼ばれたら「はい」と返事をしてください。

Korekara minasanno namaeo yobimasu. Yobaretara "hai" to henjio shite kudasai.

Now (I) will call everyone's name. When (you) are called, please answer "Here".

2）「佐藤先生」と呼ばれて、私は後ろを振り向いた。

"Satoo sensei" to yobarete, watashiwa ushiroo furimuita.

I looked back when someone called out "Mr. Sato".

3）父のようすが変なので、私は急いで医者を呼んだ。

Chichino yoosuga hennanode, watashiwa isoide ishao yonda.

I hurried to call the doctor because my dad was looking ill.

4）私は社長に呼ばれて、社長室に行った。

Watashiwa shachooni yobarete, shachooshitsuni itta.

I was summoned by the president and went to his office.

5) 彼女は、きのう友達を３人食事に呼んだ。
Kanojowa, kinoo tomodachio sannin shokujini yonda.
She invited three friends over for a meal yesterday.

6) 彼は何でもよく知っているので、友達から「教授」と呼ばれている。
Karewa nandemo yoku shitteirunode, tomodachikara 'Kyooju' to yobareteiru.
He knows a lot about all kinds of things, so he's called 'Professor' by his friends.

7) ヒマラヤは、世界の屋根と呼ばれている。
Himarayawa, sekaino yaneto yobareteiru.
The Himalayas are called 'the roof of the world'.

8) 相撲は、海外でもたいへんな人気を呼んでいる。
Sumoo＊*wa, kaigaidemo taihenna ninkio yondeiru.* ＊ p.698
Sumo is even becoming very popular overseas.

9) その科学者の警告は、人びとの間に大きな反響を呼んだ。
Sono kagakushano keikokuwa, hitobitono aidani ookina hankyoo-o yonda.
The scientist's warning caused a great sensation among the people.

10) 四つ葉のクローバーは、幸運を呼ぶといわれている。
Yotsubano kuroobaawa, kooun-o yobuto iwareteiru.
(They) say that a four-leaf clover brings good luck.

まねく［招く］

■ *maneku*
■ to invite

①頼んだりして、**来てもらうこと**です。**客として誘う**ときにも使い、「呼ぶ」よりもていねいな言い方です（例11, 12, 13）。

To request someone to come to one's home, a party, etc. It is used also to invite someone as a guest and is a politer expression than *yobu* (ex.11, 12, 13).

②ある結果を引き起こすことです。多くの場合、よくない結果になるとき使います（例14, 15）。

To bring about a certain consequence. In many cases, the consequence will not be good (ex.14, 15).

---

11) 私達の研究会では、先日、専門家を招いて、日本経済の話をしてもらった。

Watashitachino kenkyuukaidewa, senjitsu, senmonkao maneite, Nihonkeizaino hanashio shitemoratta.
The other day, our research society invited an expert to speak to us about the Japanese economy.

12) 今年から私達の野球チームの監督として、元プロ野球選手の山田繁雄氏を招くことになった。
Kotoshikara watashitachino yakyuuchiimuno kantokutoshite, moto puro-yakyuusenshuno Yamada Shigeo-shio maneku kotoni natta.
We invited the former pro-baseball player Shigeo Yamada to be our team manager starting this year.

13) 彼女は、結婚式に小学校の恩師を招いた。
Kanojowa, kekkonshikini shoogakkoono onshio maneita.
She invited her old elementary school teacher to her wedding.

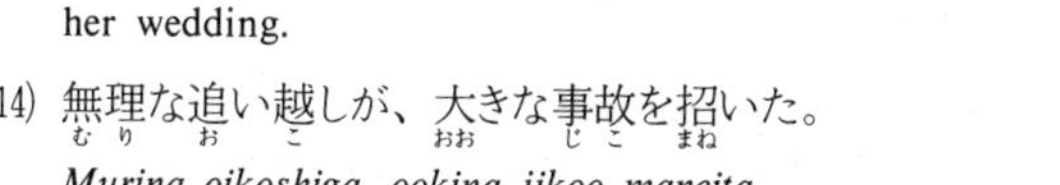

14) 無理な追い越しが、大きな事故を招いた。
Murina oikoshiga, ookina jikoo maneita.
It was an impossible attempt to pass that brought about the big accident.

15) 私の説明が足りなかったので、思わぬ誤解を招いてしまった。
Watashino setsumeiga tarinakatta-node, omowanu gokaio maneite-shimatta.
Because my explanation was insufficient, it unexpectedly invited misunderstanding.

～よりいい／～よりまし

■ *～yori ii* ■ *～yori mashi*

～よりいい ■ *～yori ii* ■ better than～

「AよりB（の方）がいい」の形で使い、単にAとBの**比較**です（例1, 2, 3, 4）。

This expression is used when comparing two things in the form *A yori B* (*no hoo*) *ga ii* (B is better than A) (ex.1, 2, 3, 4).

1) A：ピザを食(た)べに行(い)きませんか。

B：ピザよりカレーの方(ほう)がいいな。

A： *Pizao tabeni ikimasenka?*
Won't you come out for a pizza with me?

B： *Pizayori karee***nohooga iina.*
(I'd) rather have curry rice than pizza.

—— * 'Curry (rice)' is among the most popular dishes in Japan. It consists of a stew-like sauce that is seasoned with curry powder and served on rice.

2) きのうより顔色(かおいろ)がいいですね。

Kinooyori kaoiroga iidesune.
(Your) complexion looks better than it did yesterday. (You look better than you did yesterday.)

3) 私(わたし)は、飼(か)うのなら猫(ねこ)より犬(いぬ)の方(ほう)がいい。

Watashiwa, kaunonara nekoyori inunohooga ii.
If I'm going to keep a pet, I'd rather have a dog than a cat.

4) きょうは寒(さむ)いから、スカートよりズボンにした方(ほう)がいいよ。

Kyoowa samuikara, sukaatoyori zubonni shitahooga iiyo.
It's cold today so maybe pants would be better than a skirt.

～よりまし

■ *~yori mashi*
■ not good, but better than other options 

「AよりB（の方(ほう)）がまし」の形(かたち)で使(つか)います。AもBも**どちらも良(よ)くはないけれど、どちらかといえば、無理(むり)に選(えら)べば**Bの方(ほう)がいいというとき使(つか)います（例(れい)5, 6, 7, 8）。「～より」の部分(ぶぶん)は言(い)わないこともあります。

This is used in the form *A yori B* (*no hoo*) *ga mashi*. It is used when both options are not desirable, but if a choice must be made then B would be better (ex.5, 6, 7, 8). Sometimes the word *~yori* is left out of the expression.

---

5) A：具合(ぐあい)はどうですか。

B：きのうよりましですが、まだ頭痛(ずつう)がします。

A： *Guaiwa doodesuka?* How do you feel?

B： *Kinooyori mashidesuga, mada zutsuuga shimasu.*
Better than yesterday, but I still have a headache.

6) こんなまずいものを食べるくらいなら、何も食べない方がましだ。

Konna mazuimonoo taberukurainara, nanimo tabenaihooga mashida.
If (I) have to eat this stuff, I'd rather not eat at all.

7) A：どうしよう、きのうの数学のテスト、25点だった。

B：きみの方がましだよ。ぼくなんか20点だもの。

A： *Dooshiyoo, kinoono suugakuno tesuto, nijuugotendatta.*
What should (I) do? I only got 25 points on yesterday's math test.
B： *Kimino hooga mashidayo. Bokunanka nijuttendamono.*
You did better than I did. I only got 20.

8) 彼女の服装のセンスは、昔より少しましになったね。

Kanojono fukusoono sensuwa, mukashiyori sukoshi mashini nattane.
Her taste in clothes has improved somewhat from before, hasn't it?

よりかかる／もたれる

■ *yorikakaru* ■ *motareru*

よりかかる

■ *yorikakaru*
■ to lean (on, against)

自分の力だけで、立ったり座ったりしているのではなく、**体や、体の一部**、たとえば手や肩や背中などを、**人やものにあてててささえる**ことです（例1, 2, 3)。「頼りにする・補助してもらう」という意識が含まれているので、他人をあてにしたり頼ったりするときにも使います（例４)。

To support oneself by placing one's body, or a part of the body, e.g., hand, shoulder, back, etc., against another person or an object (ex.1, 2, 3). It includes a sense of dependence or of receiving assistance, so it is used also to mean 'to depend on' or 'to count on' someone (ex.4).

1) その塀はくずれかけているから、よりかかると危ない。

Sono heiwa kuzurekakete-irukara, yorikakaruto abunai.
That fence is about to fall apart, so it would be dangerous to lean on it.

2) 足をくじいたので、友達の肩によりかかって病院へ行った。

Ashio kujiitanode, tomodachino katani yorikakatte byooin-e itta.
(I) sprained my ankle, so I leaned on my friend's shoulder and went to the hospital.

3) 電車のドアによりかかっていると、開いたときに危ない。
Denshano doani yorikakatteiruto, aita tokini abunai.
Leaning against the doors of the train is dangerous because they may open on (you).

4) 二十歳を過ぎても親によりかかって生きているなんて、だらしがない。
Hatachio sugitemo oyani yorikakatte ikiteirunante, darashiganai.
It's shameful to be living off your parents once (you're) over 20.

もたれる

■ *motareru*
■ to lean (on, against) ; to recline 

「よりかかる」と同じように、自分の力だけで立っていたり座っていたりするのではなく、上半身を**人やものにあずけて**しまうことです。「よりかかる」よりも、「くつろいでいる・楽にしている・力をぬいている」という感じです（例5, 6, 7）。

Like *yorikakaru*, this means to entrust the support of the upper body to an object or person rather than standing or sitting under one's own power. However, it has more of a sense of leaning for relaxation, to be comfortable, or to relieve tension than *yorikakaru* (ex.5, 6, 7).

---

5) ソファーにもたれて音楽を聞いていたら、いつの間にか眠ってしまった。
Sofaani motarete ongakuo kiiteitara, itsunomanika nemutteshimatta.
When (I) was listening to music while reclining on the sofa, I just drifted off to sleep.

6) 私は子供のころ、木にもたれて雲をながめているのが好きだった。
Watashiwa kodomono koro, kini motarete kumoo nagameteirunoga sukidatta.
When I was a child, (I) used to like to lean back against a tree and gaze at the clouds.

7) いくら疲れていても、電車の中で人にもたれていねむりをするのは失礼だ。
Ikura tsukareteitemo, denshano nakade hitoni motarete inemurio surunowa shitsureida.
It's rude to lean against someone on the train and nap, no matter how tired (you) are.

よわい／もろい

■ *yowai*　　■ *moroi*

よわい［弱い］ ■ *yowai* ■ weak 

力がたりない・小さいというようすを表します。丈夫ではないという意味も含みます（例1, 2, 3, 4）。例5は、**得意ではない**という意味です。

Yowai indicates that something or someone is lacking in strength or is small. It is implied that the object or person is not of sturdy build (ex.1, 2, 3, 4). In Example 5, *yowai* is used to mean that one is not skilled at something.

1) 私は腕の力が弱いので、腕相撲では負けてばかりいる。
Watashiwa udeno chikaraga yowainode, udezumoodewa maketebakariiru.
My arms are not very strong so I always lose in arm-wrestling.

2) 車にばかり乗っていると、足が弱くなる。
Kurumanibakari notteiruto, ashiga yowakunaru.
If (you) always travel by car, your legs will lose their strength.

3) 彼は意志が弱いので、何をやっても長続きしない。
Karewa ishiga yowainode, nanio yattemo nagatsuzuki-shinai.
He is very weak-willed so he has trouble sticking with things for long.

4) アルコール分の弱いカクテルなら飲めます。
Arukoorubunno yowai kakuterunara nomemasu.
(I) can drink cocktails if they don't contain much alcohol.

5) 私は機械に弱いんです。
Watashiwa kikaini yowaindesu.
I am terrible with machines.

もろい ■ *moroi* ■ fragile ; brittle 

一見かたく丈夫そうに見えるものが、実はくずれやすく、こわれやすいというようすを表します（例6, 7, 8, 9）。

Moroi indicates that something is easily broken although it appears strong (ex.6, 7, 8, 9).

---

6) A：この石は手でもくずれるよ。

B：ずいぶん、もろい石だね。

A： *Kono ishiwa tedemo kuzureruyo.*
This stone can be crumbled even by hand.

B： *Zuibun, moroi ishidane.* It is very brittle stone, isn't it?

7) カルシウムが不足すると骨がもろくなる。

Karushiumuga fusokusuruto honega morokunaru.
If (you) are deficient in calcium, your bones will become brittle.

8) そんなことで別れるなんて、２人の愛はもろいものだったのね。

Sonna kotode wakarerunante, futarino aiwa moroimono-dattanone.
(I'm) surprised they separated over something so trivial. Their love must not have been very strong.

9) 母はとても涙もろくて、かわいそうな話を聞いただけで涙をこぼす。

Hahawa totemo namidamorokute, kawaisoona hanashio kiita dakede namidao kobosu.
My mother is moved to tears easily, so she cries whenever she hears a sad story.

りゃくす／はぶく／しょうりゃくする

■*ryakusu* ■*habuku* ■*shooryaku suru*

りゃくす［略す］

■*ryakusu*
■to abbreviate ; to shorten

ものごとの**大切な部分だけを残して**、あとは取って**短くする**ことです（例1, 2, 3)。会社や組織の名称や、外来語などを縮めていうときに、よく使います。

To shorten something by removing what is unnecessary and keeping only the important part (ex.1, 2, 3). It is often used when referring to the shortening of the name of a company, organization, etc., or foreign loan words.

---

1) 「リモコン」というのは、「リモートコントロール」を略したことばです。

'Rimokon' to yuunowa, 'rimooto-kontorooru' o ryakushita kotobadesu.
Rimokon is an abbreviation of the words 'remote control'.

2) 「国際連合」を略して「国連」という。
'Kokusai-rengoo' o ryakushite 'Kokuren' to yuu.
Kokusairengoo (the United Nations) is abbreviated as *Kokuren.*

3) 「U・F・O」というのは、「unidentified flying object（未確認飛行物体）」を略したものです。
'Yuufoo' to yuunowa, unidentified flying object *o ryakushita monodesu.*
'UFO' is an abbreviation of 'unidentified flying object'.

はぶく［省く］

■ *habuku*
■ to omit ; to cut out

ものごとの余分な部分や**いらない部分を取り除く**ことです（例4, 5, 6）。
To leave out or remove something that is extra or unnecessary (ex.4, 5, 6).

---

4) 日本語は、主語を省くことが多い。
Nihongowa, shugoo habuku kotoga ooi.
In Japanese, the subject of a sentence is often left out (not stated).

5) いろいろな電気製品のおかげで、家事の手間がだいぶ省けるようになった。
Iroirona denkiseihinno okagede, kajino temaga daibu habukeruyooni natta.
Thanks to all sorts of electrical appliances, a lot of the trouble of housework has been cut out.

6) 文章を書くときは、よぶんな修飾は省いた方がわかりやすい。
Bunshoo-o kaku tokiwa, yobunna shuushokuwa habuita hooga wakariyasui.
When writing, it (what you say) will be clearer if (you) omit any unnecessary modification.

しょうりゃくする［省略する］

■ *shooryaku suru*
■ to omit ; to abbreviate

時間や手間がかからないように、ものごとやことがらの一部を取り除いて、**簡単にする**ことです（例7, 8）。手続きや文章、仕事の手順などに多く使います。
To simplify something by removing or omitting some part, so as to save time

or trouble (ex.7, 8). It is often used when speaking of such things as procedures, or the steps involved in a job or writing process.

7) 履歴書の学歴の欄は、最終学歴以外は省略することもある。
Rirekishono gakurekino ranwa, saishuu-gakureki igaiwa shooryakusuru kotomo aru.
Some people only put their most recent school record on their résumés, and leave out the rest.

8) 細かい説明は省略して、だいたいの経過だけ報告します。
Komakai setsumeiwa shooryakushite, daitaino keikadake hookokushimasu.
(I'll) omit the details and report only on the overall progress.

わがまま／かって

■ *wagamama* ■ *katte*

わがまま ■ *wagamama* ■ selfish 

ほかの人の迷惑を考えないで、**自分の好きなようにやりたがる性格**をいいます（例1, 2, 3, 4）。また、自分の好きなようにやりたがることを「わがままを言う」といいます（例5, 6）。

Wagamama describes a person as selfish, i.e., doing only what he or she wishes, without thinking of how it may annoy others (ex.1, 2, 3, 4). Also, the phrase *wagamama o iu* may be used when speaking of a person who wants to do exactly as he or she pleases (ex.5, 6).

1) 彼はわがままなので、何でも自分の思うとおりにやりたがる。
Karewa wagamamananode, nandemo jibunno omoutoorini yaritagaru.
He's a selfish person, so he only wants to do things his own way.

2) いくら子供がかわいいからといって、言うことを聞いてばかりいると、わがままな子供になってしまうよ。
Ikura kodomoga kawaiikarato itte, yuukotoo kiitebakari iruto, wagamamana kodomoni natteshimauyo.
No matter how much (you) love your children, if you

let them have everything they want, they'll become selfish.

3) そのわがままな性格を直さないと、親友なんかできないと思うよ。

Sono wagamamana seikakuo naosanaito, shin-yuunanka dekinaito omouyo.
Unless (you) change your selfish personality, (I) don't think you can make close friends.

4) 自分だけ良ければいいなんて、そんなわがままは団体生活では許されません。

Jibundake yokereba iinante, sonna wagamamawa dantaiseikatsu-dewa yurusaremasen.
Selfish behavior, such as thinking only of oneself, will not be allowed within the group.

5) わがままを言うと、みんなに嫌われる。

Wagamamao yuuto, minnani kirawareru.
If (you're) always saying selfish things, nobody will like you.

6) お菓子を1人で食べたいなんて、そんなわがままを言ってはいけません。

Okashio hitoride tabetainante, sonna wagamamao ittewa ikemasen.
(You) mustn't be so selfish and say you want to eat all of the sweets yourself.

かって［勝手］ ■ *katte* ■ one's own way 

①仕事や人生、人とのつきあいなどを、**自分の思うとおりにやる**こと、あるいはそのやり方のことです（例7, 8, 9, 10）。「勝手な人」のことを「自分勝手な人」とも言います。

Katte indicates that one does as he wants at work, in life, or in dealing with people; it may also refer to actions done in such a manner (ex.7, 8, 9, 10). *Kattena hito* may also be expressed as *jibun katte na hito.*

②仕事などを、**許可を受けないでやること**です（例11, 12, 13）。

To do work, etc., without permission (ex.11, 12, 13).

主に「**わがまま**」は**性格**に使い、「**勝手**」は**行動**に使います。また「勝手」には、「この家の勝手をよく知っている」のように、ようすや方法などを表す使い方もあります。

Katte is generally used to describe actions, while *wagamama* is used to describe personality.
Also, *katte* may used to mean 'circumstances or methods', as in *kono ie no*

katte o yoku shitteiru (I know this house well).

---

7) 彼女は人の意見も聞かないで勝手にやるから、いっしょに仕事をしたくない。
Kanojowa hitono ikenmo kikanaide katteni yarukara, isshoni shigotoo shitakunai.
(I) don't want to work with her because she never listens to other people and only does what she wants.

8) 今度の旅行に参加するのもしないのも、きみの勝手だ。
Kondono ryokooni sankasurunomo shinainomo, kimino katteda.
It's up to you whether you go on the next trip or not.

9) そんなに私の忠告が聞けないのなら、もう勝手にしなさい。
Sonnani watashino chuukokuga kikenainonara, moo katteni shinasai.
If (you) can't take my advice, then go ahead and do as you like.

10) 団体旅行なんだから、自分勝手な行動は許されない。
Dantairyokoo-nandakara, jibun-kattena koodoowa yurusarenai.
It's a group tour, so they won't let (me) go off on my own.

11) 図書館の本を勝手に持ち出さないでください。
Toshokanno hon-o katteni mochidasanaide kudasai.
Please don't take books out of the library without permission.

12) 誰ですか、私の引き出しを勝手に開けたのは。
Daredesuka, watashino hikidashio katteni aketanowa?
Who opened my drawer without my permission?

13) 研究室に勝手に入ってはいけません。
Kenkyuushitsuni katteni haittewa ikemasen.
(You) may not enter the laboratory unless you have permission.

わずか／たった／ほんの

■*wazuka* ■*tatta* ■*honno*

わずか

■*wazuka*
■few ; little

数量や時間、程度などが**とても少ない**ようすを表します（例1, 2, 3)。また、

「1日・100円・5人」などのような具体的な数量の前につけて、少なさを強調します（例4）。

This expression indicates that a volume, level, amount of time, etc., is extremely small (ex.1, 2, 3). Also, by placing *wazuka* in front of a concrete number (e.g., one day, ¥100, five people) the smallness of the amount is emphasized (ex.4).

---

1) 楽しかった学生生活も残りはわずかだ。
Tanoshikatta gakusei-seikatsumo nokoriwa wazukada.
There's only a little left of (our) carefree student days.

2) 彼女は、わずかな時間も惜しんで働いている。
Kanojowa, wazukana jikanmo oshinde hataraiteiru.
She works hard every single minute.

3) 人が寝静まった夜中は、わずかな音でも大きく感じることがある。
Hitoga neshizumatta yonakawa, wazukana otodemo ookiku kanjiru kotoga aru.
People are sometimes startled by even slight sounds late at night when everyone else is asleep.

4) 新しくできた店が、わずか1か月でつぶれてしまった。
Atarashiku dekita misega, wazuka ikkagetsude tsuburete-shimatta.
That new shop closed up after just one short month of business.

たった

■ *tatta*
■ only ; mere

「1日・2人・5万円」などの具体的に示された数量や、「このくらい・今」などのように相手に分かる量や時間を表す語の前につけて、**「これだけで」と少なさを強調する**とき使います（例5, 6, 7, 8）。「わずか・ほんの」よりも量の少なさや時間の短さに対する驚きが含まれています。「たった今、出かけた人」は追いかければ間に合いますが、「ほんの今、出かけた人」には追いつけない場合もあります。

When placed in front of concrete numbers (e.g., one day, two people, ¥50,000) or amounts of time, it emphasizes to the listener how small the amount is, as in 'only this much' (ex.5, 6, 7, 8). It implies more of a feeling of surprise than do *wazuka* or *honno*. A person who has *tatta ima dekaketa* may be chased and caught up with, while a person who has *honno ima dekaketa* may be too far away to be caught.

---

5) あれだけの仕事をたった２日で終わらせるなんて、彼は大したものだ。
Aredakeno shigotoo tatta futsukade owaraserunante, karewa taishita monoda.
He must be something special to be able to finish all that work in just two days.

6) 彼女は、あんなに広い家にたった１人で住んでいる。
Kanojowa, annani hiroi ieni tatta hitoride sundeiru.
She's living all by herself in that big house.

7) こんなに駅に近いアパートが、たった９万円で借りられるなんて安い。
Konnani ekini chikai apaatoga, tatta kyuuman-ende karirarerunante yasui.
It's amazing that (you) are able to rent an apartment so near the station for only ¥90,000.

8) A：山口さんは。
B：たった今出て行ったばかりだから、まだその辺にいると思うよ。
A: *Yamaguchisanwa?* Where's Mr. Yamaguchi?
B: *Tattaima deteittabakari-dakara, mada sonohenni iruto omouyo.*
He just left a second ago, so he must be over there somewhere.

ほんの

■ *honno*
■ just ; only

「少し・小さい・わずか」などの意味を表す語の前につけて少なさを強 調するとき使います（例9, 10, 11, 12）。「少しお酒が飲める人」は「ほんの少し飲める人」よりも多く飲めます。例13は、**ひかえめな表 現**です。

Honno adds emphasis when placed in front of words like *sukoshi*, *chiisai*, and *wazuka* (ex.9, 10, 11, 12). An example of its usage may be; a person who is described as being a *sukoshi osake ga nomeru hito* can drink a little more than a person who is *honno sukoshi* (*osake ga*) *nomeru hito*. In Example 13, *honno* is used to make the speaker sound more humble or modest.

---

9) 父はほんの２、３分前に帰って来ました。
Chichiwa honno nisanpunmaeni kaettekimashita.
My father came home just two or three minutes ago.

10) 私は紅茶にブランデーをほんの少し入れて飲むのが好きだ。

Watashiwa koochani burandeeo honno sukoshi irete nomunoga sukida.
I like drinking tea with just a touch of brandy added.

11) ほんの小さな出来事がこんなに大きな事件になるとは、誰も考えなかった。
Honno chiisana dekigotoga konnani ookina jikenni narutowa, daremo kangaenakatta.
Nobody thought that tiny incident would turn into such a big problem.

12) ほんのひとにぎりの人びとが起こした平和運動が、全世界に広がった。
Honno hitonigirino hitobitoga okoshita heiwaundooga, zensekaini hirogatta.
The peace movement, which was started by just a handful of people, has now spread throughout the world.

13) 彼女は「ほんのお礼のしるしです」とチョコレートを持って来た。
Kanojowa "Honno oreino shirushidesu" to chokoreetoo mottekita.
She brought some chocolate, saying "It's just a token of my gratitude."

わる／こわす

■*waru* ■*kowasu*

わる［割る］ ■*waru* ■to break

①卵のから、ガラス・陶器・板などを、ぶつけたり手や物でたたいたりして**2つ以上にする**ことです（例1, 2, 3, 4）。
To break an object, such as an eggshell, glass, pottery, or a board, into two or more pieces by striking it with a hand or object (ex.1, 2, 3, 4).

②**割り算**をすることです（例5, 6）。
To mathematically divide a number (ex.5, 6).

③数量が、**ある基準より低い**ことです（例7, 8）。
To show that something is less than the designated level (ex.7, 8).

④液体にほかの**液体を混ぜて薄める**ことです（例９）。
To dilute a liquid by adding another liquid (ex.9).

1) ごめんなさい。ガラスを割(わ)ったのは私(わたし)です。

Gomennasai. Garasuo wattanowa watashidesu.
I am sorry. I am the one who broke the glass.

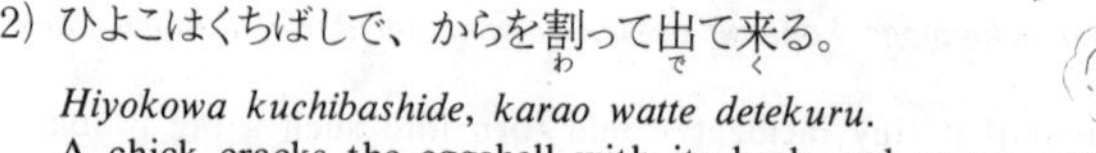

2) ひよこはくちばしで、からを割(わ)って出(で)て来(く)る。

Hiyokowa kuchibashide, karao watte detekuru.
A chick cracks the eggshell with its beak and comes out.

3) 私(わたし)の兄(あに)は空手(からて)が得意(とくい)なので、手(て)で厚(あつ)い板(いた)を割(わ)ることができます。

Watashino aniwa karatega tokuinanode, tede atsui itao waru kotoga dekimasu.
My (elder) brother is an expert in *karate*, so he is able to break thick wooden boards with his hand.

4) このワイングラスは大切(たいせつ)なので、割(わ)らないように気(き)をつけてください。

Kono waingurasuwa taisetsunanode, waranaiyooni kiotsukete kudasai.
This is a valuable wine glass, so be careful not to break it, please.

5) 6割(わ)る2は3です。(6 ÷ 2 = 3)

Roku waru niwa sandesu.
Six divided by two equals three.

6) 余(あま)った5000円(えん)を4人(にん)で割(わ)って、1250円(えん)ずつ分(わ)けた。

Amatta gosen-en-o yoninde watte, sennihyaku-gojuuenzutsu waketa.
(We) divided the remaining ¥5,000 four ways, giving each person ¥1,250.

7) 会議(かいぎ)の出席者(しゅっせきしゃ)が過半数(かはんすう)を割(わ)ったので、採決(さいけつ)ができなかった。

Kaigino shussekishaga kahansuuo wattanode, saiketsuga dekinakatta.
Because attendance at the meeting was less than 50%, a vote could not be taken.

8) 今年(ことし)の大学(だいがく)入試(にゅうし)の受験者数(じゅけんしゃすう)が、定員(ていいん)を割(わ)ったそうだ。

Kotoshino daigaku-nyuushino jukenshasuuga, teiin-o wattasooda.
(They) say that the number of students who took the college entrance examination this year was less than the limit.

9) 私(わたし)はウイスキーを水(みず)で割(わ)って飲(の)む。

Watashiwa uisukiio mizude watte nomu.
I drink whisky diluted with water.

こわす [壊(こわ)す]

- *kowasu*
- to break ; to destroy 

---

①正常な状態にあるものを、力を加えたり、きずつけたりして**使えない状態にする**ことです。**だめにする**という意味です（例10, 11, 12）。ことがらにも使います（例13, 14）。

To make something which is in a normal condition useless through force or injury (ex.10, 11, 12). It may also be used when speaking of abstract matters (ex.13, 14).

②**健康状態が悪くなる**ことです（例15, 16）。

The condition of one's health becomes bad (ex.15, 16).

---

10) どろぼうは、窓のかぎを壊して入ったらしい。

Doroboowa, madono kagio kowashite haittarashii.
It seems that the thief broke the lock on the window and entered the house.

11) 買ったばかりの時計を落として壊してしまった。

Kattabakarino tokeio otoshite kowashiteshimatta.
(I) dropped the watch that I just bought and broke it (to my regret).

12) ビデオをいたずらして壊さないでください。

Bideoo itazurashite kowasanaide kudasai.
Please don't play around with the VCR and break it.

13) 彼の失言が、せっかくまとまりかけた話を壊した。

Kareno shitsugenga, sekkaku matomarikaketa hanashio kowashita.
His slip of the tongue destroyed our agreement that, after much difficulty, was about to be finalized.

14) 彼らのけんかのおかげで、楽しい雰囲気が壊された。

Karerano kenkano okagede, tanoshii fun-ikiga kowasareta.
The pleasant mood was destroyed by their fight.

15) そんなにたくさんアイスクリームを食べると、おなかをこわすよ。

Sonnani takusan aisukuriimuo taberuto, onakao kowasuyo.
If (you) eat so much ice cream, you'll get a stomachache.

16) 彼女の夫は、働きすぎて体をこわしてしまった。

Kanojono ottowa, hatarakisugite karadao kowashite-shimatta.
Her husband became ill due to overwork.

動詞活用表

（1）子音動詞 Consonant Verbs（五段活用 Five-Step Conjugation）

例 Ex.	英訳 Eng.	語幹 Stem	辞書形 Dict.	丁寧形 Pol.	否定形 Neg.	過去形 Past
書く	write	kak-	kaku	kakimasu	kakanai	kaita
行く	go	ik-	iku	ikimasu	ikanai	itta
泳ぐ	swim	oyog-	oyogu	oyogimasu	oyoganai	oyoida
出す	put out	das-	dasu	dashimasu	dasanai	dashita
読む	read	yom-	yomu	yomimasu	yomanai	yonda
死ぬ	die	shin-	shinu	shinimasu	shinanai	shinda
呼ぶ	call	yob-	yobu	yobimasu	yobanai	yonda
打つ	hit	ut-	utsu	uchimasu	utanai	utta
切る	cut	kir-	kiru	kirimasu	kiranai	kitta
洗う	wash	araw-	arau	araimasu	arawanai	aratta

（2）母音動詞 Vowel Verbs（一段活用 One-Step Conjugation）

例 Ex.	英訳 Eng.	語幹 Stem	辞書形 Dict.	丁寧形 Pol.	否定形 Neg.	過去形 Past
着る	put on	ki-	kiru	kimasu	kinai	kita
寝る	sleep	ne-	neru	nemasu	nenai	neta

（3）不規則動詞 Irregular Verbs

例 Ex.	英訳 Eng.	語幹 Stem	辞書形 Dict.	丁寧形 Pol.	否定形 Neg.	過去形 Past
来る	come	ku-	kuru	kimasu	konai	kita
する	do	su-	suru	shimasu	shinai	shita

Ex. : Example
Eng. : English
Dict. : Dictionary
Pol. : Polite

Neg. : Negative
Cond. : Conditional
Volit. : Volitional
Imper.: Imperative

Potent.: Potential
Pass. : Passive
Caus. : Causative

て形 *te*-form	仮定形 Cond.	意志形 Volit.	命令形 Imper.	可能形 Potent.	受身形 Pass.	使役形 Caus.
kaite	kakeba	kakoo	kake	kakeru	kakareru	kakaseru
itte	ikeba	ikoo	ike	ikeru / ikareru	ikareru	ikaseru
oyoide	oyogeba	oyogoo	oyoge	oyogeru	oyogareru	oyogaseru
dashite	daseba	dasoo	dase	daseru	dasareru	dasaseru
yonde	yomeba	yomoo	yome	yomeru	yomareru	yomaseru
shinde	shineba	shinoo	shine	shineru	shinareru	shinaseru
yonde	yobeba	yoboo	yobe	yoberu	yobareru	yobaseru
utte	uteba	utoo	ute	uteru	utareru	utaseru
kitte	kireba	kiroo	kire	kireru	kirareru	kiraseru
aratte	araeba	araoo	arae	araeru	arawareru	arawaseru

て形 *te*-form	仮定形 Cond.	意志形 Volit.	命令形 Imper.	可能形 Potent.	受身形 Pass.	使役形 Caus.
kite	kireba	kiyoo	kiro	kirareru	kirareru	kisaseru
nete	nereba	neyoo	nero	nerareru	nerareru	nesaseru

て形 *te*-form	仮定形 Cond.	意志形 Volit.	命令形 Imper.	可能形 Potent.	受身形 Pass.	使役形 Caus.
kite	kureba	koyoo	koi	korareru / koreru	korareru	kosaseru
shite	sureba	shiyoo	shiro	(dekiru)	sareru	saseru

動詞対応表

【 ～が 】をとる動詞		【 ～を 】をとる動詞	
あがる	rise	あげる	raise
あく	open	あける	open
あたる	hit	あてる	hit
あつまる	gather	あつめる	gather
あらわれる	appear	あらわす	show
あれる	be rough	あらす	damage
うかぶ	float	うかべる	float
うく	float	うかす	float
うごく	move	うごかす	move
うつる	move; be reflected	うつす	move; copy; project
うまれる	be born	うむ	give birth
うれる	sell	うる	sell
おきる	get up	おこす	wake; get up
おちる	fall	おとす	drop
おどろく	be surprised	おどろかす	surprise
おりる	go; come down	おろす	lower
おれる	break	おる	break
おわる	come to an end	おえる	end; complete
かえる	return	かえす	return; repay
かかる	cost; take	かける	spend
かくれる	hide (one self)	かくす	hide (something)
かさなる	be piled up	かさねる	pile up
かたまる	become hard	かためる	harden
かぶる	wear	かぶせる	cover
かわく	dry (up)	かわかす	dry
かわる	change	かえる	change
きえる	disappear	けす	make disappear
きこえる	be audible	きく	hear; listen
きまる	be decided	きめる	decide
きれる	break	きる	cut
くるしむ	suffer	くるしめる	make suffer
くわわる	participate	くわえる	add
こげる	scorch	こがす	scorch
こぼれる	spill	こぼす	spill
ころがる	roll	ころがす	roll
こわれる	break	こわす	break

【 ～が 】をとる動詞		【 ～を 】をとる動詞	
さがる	come down	さげる	lower
さける	rip	さく	tear
ささる	stick; be stuck	さす	stick
さめる	become cool	さます	cool
しずむ	sink	しずめる	sink
しまる	close	しめる	close
すぎる	pass; exceed	すごす	spend (time)
そだつ	grow (up)	そだてる	raise; rear
そる	bend	そらす	bend (backward)
そろう	become complete	そろえる	make complete
たおれる	fall	たおす	fell
たすかる	be saved	たすける	save; help
たつ	stand	たてる	make stand
たまる	accumulate	ためる	save
ちぢむ	shrink	ちぢめる	shrink
ちる	scatter	ちらす	scatter
つく	be attached	つける	attach
つたわる	be transmitted	つたえる	transmit
つながる	be connected	つなぐ	connect
つぶれる	be crushed	つぶす	crush
でる	come out	だす	take out
とおる	go through	とおす	pass through
とける	melt; thaw	とかす	melt; dissolve (in)
とける	become loose	とく	loosen
とどく	reach; be delivered	とどける	deliver
とまる	stop	とめる	stop
とれる	be taken; come off	とる	take
なおる	be fixed	なおす	fix
ながれる	flow	ながす	flush
なくなる	disappear	なくす	lose
ならぶ	line up	ならべる	line up
なる	ring	ならす	ring
にえる	be boiled	にる	boil
にげる	escape	にがす	let escape
ぬける	come off	ぬく	pull out
ぬげる	come off	ぬぐ	take off
ぬれる	get wet	ぬらす	wet
ねる	lie down; sleep	ねかす	lay; make sleep

【 ～が 】をとる動詞		【 ～を 】をとる動詞	
のこる	remain	のこす	leave
のびる	become longer	のばす	lengthen
のる	get on; ride	のせる	put on; give a ride
はえる	grow	はやす	grow
はがれる	peel off	はがす	peel off
はじまる	begin	はじめる	begin
はずれる	become loose	はずす	loosen
はなれる	separate	はなす	separate
ひえる	become cool	ひやす	cool
ひっくりかえる	be turned over	ひっくりかえす	turn over
ひっこむ	draw back	ひっこめる	draw in
ひろがる	be widened	ひろげる	widen
ふえる	increase	ふやす	increase
ふくらむ	become inflated	ふくらます	inflate
ぶつかる	hit	ぶつける	hit
へる	decrease	へらす	decrease
ほどける	become untied	ほどく	untie
まがる	bend	まげる	bend
まける	lose	まかす	make lose (=win)
まざる	mix	まぜる	mix
まじる	be mixed	まぜる	mix
まとまる	be brought together	まとめる	bring together
まわる	turn; revolve	まわす	turn
みえる	be visible	みる	see; look; watch
みだれる	be disarranged	みだす	disturb
みつかる	be found	みつける	find
もえる	burn	もやす	burn
もどる	return	もどす	return
もれる	leak	もらす	leak
やける	be burned	やく	burn
やすむ	rest	やすめる	make rest
やぶれる	rip	やぶる	rip
ゆるむ	become loose	ゆるめる	loosen
よごれる	become dirty	よごす	make dirty
よわまる	be weakened	よわめる	weaken
わかれる	be separated	わける	separate
わく	boil	わかす	boil
われる	break	わる	break

ひらがな項目索引

［あ］

あいだに・うちに　1
あがる・のぼる　3
あき・から　7
あきらか・たしか　9
あける・ひらく　11
～あげる・～きる・～おわる　14
あせる・さめる　16
あそこ・あちら・むこう　18
あたかも・いかにも　21
あたたかい・ぬるい　23
あたり・へん　26
あたる・ぶつかる　28
あっさり・さっぱり・からっと　31
あつまる・まとまる　33
あつめる・よせる　35
あてる・ぶつける　37
あと・もう　40
あとで・のちほど　42
あふれる・こぼれる　44
あまり～ない・たいして～ない　46
あまる・のこる　49
あらためる・かえる・なおす　52
ある・いる　56
あれる・すさむ　58
あんがい・いがい・おもったより　60

［い］

いいかげん・てきとう　62
いえ・うち　64
いく・くる　66
いくら～ても・どんなに～ても　68
いじめる・いびる・ぎゃくたいする　70
いそがしい・せわしい・あわただしい　74
いそぐ・あわてる・あせる　76
いたい・うずく　78
いちいち・ひとつひとつ　80
いちおう・とりあえず　82
いちじ・ひととき・いっこく　84
いちだんと・いっそう・ひときわ　86
いちどに・いっぺんに　89
いちばん・もっとも　90
いっきに・ひといきに　93
いっけん・ひとめ・いちべつ　95
いっせいに・どうじに　98
いっそ・おもいきって　100
いったん・ひとまず　101
いっぽう・かたほう　103
いつも・いつでも・しょっちゅう　105
いぶす・くすぶる・けむる　108
いま・げんざい・ただいま　110
いまから・これから　113
いる・かかる・ひつよう　115
いれもの・うつわ・ようき　119
いろいろ・さまざま　121

［う］

うく・うかぶ　123
うつ・たたく　125
うっかり・つい　127
うまい・おいしい　129
うらむ・にくむ　130
うる・ばいきゃくする・うりはらう　132
うるさい・さわがしい・にぎやか　135
うれしい・たのしい・ゆかい　138

［お］

おう・おいかける　140
おおい・たくさん・いっぱい　143
おかげ・せい・ため　146

おきに・ごとに　149
(〜て)おく・(〜て)ある　151
おく・のせる・つむ・かさねる　153
おこる・しかる　157
おしえる・しらせる　159
おす・おさえる　160
おそい・のろい　162
おそろしい・こわい　166
おそわる・ならう・まなぶ・べんきょうする　168
おだてる・ちやほやする　171
おとす・すてる　172
おなじ・ひとしい　175
おもいだす・おぼえる　178
おもう・かんがえる　179
おもしろい・おかしい・へん・かわっている　182
おもわず・おもいがけない　185
おりる・くだる　187
おわる・やめる・すむ　192

［か］

かえって・むしろ　194
かえる・もどる　196
〜かかる・〜かける・〜そうだ　199
かける・はしる　201
かこむ・とりまく　203
かじる・かむ　205
がっかり・しつぼうする・きをおとす　207
かど・すみ　210
かなしい・さびしい　213
かならず・きっと・きまって・ぜったい　215
かなり・だいぶ　219
かぶせる・おおう　220
かり・いちじてき・りんじ　223
〜がる・〜ぶる・ふりをする　225
かわす・よける・さける　229
かんしん・かんどう　231
がんばる・いっしょうけんめい・ひっし　234

［き］

きく・こたえる　237
きこえる・きかれる　239
きたない・きたならしい　241
きちんと・ちゃんと・しっかり　243
きつい・かたい　246
きにする・きになる　249
きのどく・かわいそう　251
〜ぎみ・〜がち　253
きめる・けっていする　255
きもち・きぶん　258
きゅうに・とつぜん・いきなり　261
きらい・いや　263
(〜た)きり・(〜た)まま　265
きる・さく・たつ　267
きれい・うつくしい　270

［く］

ぐうぜん・たまたま・まぐれ　272
くぎる・しきる　275
くさる・いたむ　277
くすくす・げらげら　279
くるくる・ぐるぐる・ころころ　280
くわえる・たす　284
くわしい・こまかい　286

［け］

けいけん・たいけん　288
けっきょく・とにかく　290
けなげ・いじらしい　292
けれども・〜のに・〜ても　294

［こ］

こえる・こす・すぎる　298
このごろ・ちかごろ・さいきん　301
こむ・こんざつする　304
こらえる・がまんする　307

～ごろ・～ぐらい(くらい) 309
ころぶ・ころがる 311

［さ］

さいごまで・あくまで 313
～さえ・～だって 315
さがす・さぐる・あさる 317
さかんに・しきりに 320
さけぶ・どなる 321
さげる・かける・つる・つるす 323
さぞ・よほど 326
さっそく・すぐ 329
さむい・つめたい・すずしい 330
さりげない・なにげない 334
さわる・ふれる 336
ざんねん・おしい 338

［し］

しずか・おだやか 340
しつもん・ぎもん 342
しばらく・とうぶん 344
しまう・かたづける 346
じめじめ・むしむし 348
しめる・とじる・ふさぐ 350
じゅんばんに・こうたいで・かわるがわる 354
じょうず・とくい 356
じょじょに・じわじわ 358
しる・わかる 360

［す］

すいすい・すらすら・すんなり 362
ずうずうしい・あつかましい 364
ずきずき・ひりひり・がんがん 366
すくなくとも・せめて 368
すこし・ちょっと 369
すっかり・そっくり 372
ずっと・じっと・ひたすら 375
すばらしい・すてき 378
すむ・くらす・すごす 380

［せ］

せいぜい・たかだか 382
せっかく・わざわざ 384
ぜひ・どうか・なんとか・どうぞ 387

［そ］

そして・それから・すると 390
そそぐ・つぐ 394
そだてる・やしなう 396
それぞれ・おのおの・めいめい 398
それに・そのうえ・しかも 401
そろえる・まとめる 403
そろそろ・やがて・そのうち 406

［た］

たいくつ・あきる 409
たおれる・ひっくりかえる 411
～だけ・～ばかり・～しか～ない 413
たすける・すくう・てつだう 416
たびに・そのつど 420
たぶん・おそらく・どうやら 421
だます・ごまかす 424
たりない・ふそくする・かける 426
たりる・まにあう・じゅうぶん 429
たるむ・ゆるむ 432

［ち］

ちがう・まちがえる・まちがう 434

［つ］

つかう・もちいる 437
つかまえる・とらえる 440
つかむ・にぎる 443
つかれる・くたびれる 445
つぎ・こんど 447
つぎつぎ・ぞくぞく・ひっきりなしに 449

つく・つつく・さす　451
つくづく・しみじみ　454
つける・とりつける・はる　457
つける・ひたす　460
つつむ・くるむ　461
つぶす・くだく　463
つまらない・くだらない　466
つもり・～ようとおもう　468
つよい・じょうぶ　470

［て］

～てき・～ふう　472
できるだけ・なるべく　474
～て(～くて)・～し　476
でる・でかける　479

［と］

ときどき・ときおり・たまに　481
とく・とかす　483
とくべつ・とくに　485
どちら・どれ・なに　487
とても・たいへん・ひじょうに　490
とどく・つく・たっする　493
とどける・おくる・だす　497
となり・よこ　501
どのくらい・どれほど　503
とる・ぬく・はずす　505
とる・ぬすむ　507
(手に)とる・(手に)もつ　509

［な］～［の］

～ないで・～なくて　510
なおる・かいふくする　512
なかなか・けっこう・わりと　514
なげる・ほうる　518
なさけない・たよりない　519
なでる・さする・こする　521
なまける・サボる・おこたる　524
なやむ・こまる・まよう　526
～なれる・～つける　530
～にくい・～づらい・～がたい　532
にげる・のがれる　534
にこにこ・にやにや　536
ぬれる・しみる　538
ねじる・ひねる　540
ねっしん・ねっちゅう・むちゅう　542
ねむる・ねる　544
のんびり・ゆっくり　546

［は］

はがす・はぐ・むく　549
(～た)ばかり・(～た)ところ　551
はげしい・ひどい　553
はじめて・はじめに・はじめは　555
～はじめる・～だす　557
はたらく・しごと　560
はなす・いう・しゃべる　562
はねる・はずむ　565
はやい・すばやい・すばしっこい　567
はやる・にんき　570
はんせいする・こうかいする　574
はんたい・ぎゃく　576

［ひ］

ひかる・かがやく　578
ひく・えんそうする　580
びくびく・どきどき・おどおど　581
ひそかに・こっそり　584
ひとりで・じぶんで　586
ひとりでに・しぜんに　587
ひらたい・たいらな・へいたんな　589
ひろがる・ひろまる　593

［ふ］

ふいに・ふと　594
ふく・ぬぐう　597
ふくらむ・ふくれる・はれる　598

ふさぐ・めいる・おちこむ　601

［へ］

へいき・だいじょうぶ　604
へこむ・くぼむ・ひっこむ　606

［ほ］

ほか・べつ　608
ほす・かわかす　610
ほぼ・だいたい・およそ　612

［ま］

まえ・さき　615
まがる・そる・しなう　618
まじる・まざる　621
ます・ふやす・ためる　622
まずしい・びんぼう　625
～ませんか・～ましょうか　627
また・もういちど・ふたたび　628
まもる・ふせぐ　630
まるで・ちょうど　632

［み］

みえる・みられる　636
みち・とおり　639
みほん・てほん　641
みる・みつめる・ながめる・のぞく　642
みんな・ぜんいん　647

［む］～［め］

～むき・～むけ・～よう　649
むすぶ・しばる　652
むだ・もったいない　654
めきめき・めっきり　656
めんどう・やっかい　657

［も］

もぐ・むしる・つむ　660
もしかすると・ひょっとすると　662
もっと・ますます・さらに　663
もどす・かえす　666
（～て）もらう・（～て）くれる　669
もらす・こぼす　672

［や］～［よ］

やくそくする・ちかう　674
やける・こげる・もえる　676
やさしい・かんたん　678
やたらと・むやみに　680
やっと・とうとう・ついに　682
やはり・さすが　686
ゆでる・にる・わかす　688
ゆるす・きょかする　691
（～）よう（みたい）・～らしい　693
（～に）よって・（～に）おうじて　696
よぶ・まねく　699
～よりいい・～よりまし　701
よりかかる・もたれる　703
よわい・もろい　705

［り］～［わ］

りゃくす・はぶく・しょうりゃくする　706
わがまま・かって　708
わずか・たった・ほんの　710
わる・こわす　713

ひらがな語索引

［あ～お］

あいだに　1
あがる　3
あき　7
あきらか　9
あきる　410
あくまで　314
あける　11
～あげる　14
あさる　319
あせる　16
あせる　77
あそこ　18
あたかも　21
あたたかい　23
あたり　26
あたる　28
あちら　19
あつかましい　365
あっさり　31
あつまる　33
あつめる　35
あてる　37
あと　40
あとで　42
あふれる　44
あまり～ない　46
あまる　49
あらためる　52
ある　56
(～て)ある　152
あれる　58
あわただしい　75
あわてる　77
あんがい　60
いいかげん　62
いう　563
いえ　64
いがい　61
いかにも　22
いきなり　262
いく　66
いくら～ても　68
いじめる　70
いじらしい　293
いそがしい　74
いそぐ　76
いたい　78
いたむ　277
いちいち　80
いちおう　82
いちじ　84
いちじてき　224
いちだんと　86
いちどに　89
いちばん　90
いちべつ　97
いっきに　93
いっけん　95
いっこく　86
いっしょうけんめい　235
いっせいに　98
いっそ　100
いっそう　87
いったん　101
いつでも　106
いっぱい　145
いっぺんに　90
いっぽう　103
いつも　105
いびる　71
いぶす　108
いま　110
いまから　113
いや　264
いる　57
いる　115
いれもの　119
いろいろ　121
うかぶ　124
うく　123
うずく　79
うち　65
うちに　2
うつ　125
うっかり　127
うつくしい　271
うつわ　119
うまい　129
うらむ　131
うりはらう　134
うる　133
うるさい　135
うれしい　138
えんそうする　581
おいかける　141
おいしい　130
おう　140
(～に)おうじて　697
おおい　143
おおう　222
おかげ　146
おかしい　183
おきに　149
おく　153
(～て)おく　151
おくる　498
おこたる　526
おこる　157
おさえる　161
おしい　339
おしえる　159

おす　160
おそい　162
おそらく　422
おそろしい　166
おそわる　168
おだてる　171
おだやか　341
おちこむ　603
おどおど　583
おとす　172
おなじ　175
おのおの　399
おぼえる　178
おもいがけない　186
おもいきって　101
おもいだす　178
おもう　179
おもしろい　182
おもったより　62
おもわず　185
およそ　614
おりる　187
おわる　192
〜おわる　15

［か〜こ］

かいふくする　513
かえす　667
かえって　194
かえる　53
かえる　196
かがやく　579
かかる　116
〜かかる　199
かける　201
かける　324
かける　428
〜かける　199
かこむ　203
かさねる　156
かじる　205
かたい　247
〜がたい　533
かたづける　347
かたほう　104
〜がち　254
がっかり　207
かって　709
かど　210
かなしい　213
かならず　215
かなり　219
かぶせる　220
がまんする　308
かむ　206
から　8
からっと　33
かり　223
〜がる　225
かわいそう　252
かわかす　611
かわす　229
かわっている　184
かわるがわる　355
かんがえる　181
がんがん　367
かんしん　231
かんたん　679
かんどう　232
がんばる　234
きをおとす　208
きかれる　240
きく　237
きこえる　239
きたない　241
きたならしい　242
きちんと　243
きつい　246
きっと　216
きにする　249
きになる　250
きのどく　251
きぶん　259
きまって　217
〜ぎみ　253
きめる　255
きもち　258
ぎもん　343
ぎゃく　577
ぎゃくたいする　72
きゅうに　261
きょかする　692
きらい　263
(〜た)きり　265
きる　267
〜きる　14
きれい　270
ぐうぜん　272
くぎる　275
くさる　277
くすくす　279
くすぶる　109
くだく　465
くたびれる　446
くだらない　467
くだる　189
くぼむ　607
〜ぐらい(くらい)　310
くらす　381
くる　67
くるくる　280
ぐるぐる　281
くるむ　462
(〜て)くれる　670
くわえる　284
くわしい　286
けいけん　288
けっきょく　290
けっこう　516
けっていする　256

けなげ　293
けむる　110
げらげら　279
けれども　294
げんざい　111
こうかいする　575
こうたいで　354
こえる　298
こげる　676
こす　299
こする　522
こたえる　238
こっそり　585
ごとに　150
このごろ　301
こぼす　673
こぼれる　45
こまかい　287
ごまかす　425
こまる　527
こむ　304
こらえる　307
これから　114
〜ごろ　309
ころがる　312
ころころ　282
ころぶ　311
こわい　167
こわす　714
こんざつする　305
こんど　448

［さ〜そ］

さいきん　303
さいごまで　313
〜さえ　315
さがす　317
さかんに　320
さき　617
さく　268
さぐる　318
さけぶ　321
さける　230
さげる　323
さす　453
さすが　687
さする　521
さぞ　327
さっそく　329
さっぱり　32
さびしい　214
サボる　525
さまざま　122
さむい　330
さめる　17
さらに　665
さりげない　334
さわがしい　136
さわる　336
ざんねん　338
〜し　477
〜しか(〜)ない　415
しかも　402
しかる　158
しきりに　320
しきる　276
しごと　561
しずか　340
しぜんに　589
しっかり　245
じっと　376
しつぼうする　208
しつもん　342
しなう　620
しばらく　344
しばる　653
じぶんで　586
しまう　346
しみじみ　455
しみる　539
じめじめ　348
しめる　350
しゃべる　564
じゅうぶん　432
じゅんばんに　354
じょうず　356
じょうぶ　471
しょうりゃくする　707
じょじょに　358
しょっちゅう　107
しらせる　160
しる　360
じわじわ　359
すいすい　362
ずうずうしい　364
ずきずき　366
すぎる　300
すぐ　329
すくう　417
すくなくとも　368
すこし　369
すごす　381
すさむ　59
すずしい　332
すっかり　372
ずっと　375
すてき　379
すてる　174
すばしっこい　569
すばやい　569
すばらしい　378
すみ　212
すむ　193
すむ　380
すらすら　363
すると　393
すんなり　364
せい　147
せいぜい　382
せっかく　384

ぜったい　217
ぜひ　387
せめて　368
せわしい　75
ぜんいん　648
〜そうだ　200
ぞくぞく　450
そして　390
そそぐ　394
そだてる　396
そっくり　373
そのうえ　401
そのうち　408
そのつど　420
そる　619
それから　391
それぞれ　398
それに　401
そろえる　403
そろそろ　406

［た〜と］

たいくつ　409
たいけん　290
たいして〜ない　47
だいじょうぶ　604
だいたい　613
だいぶ　220
たいへん　491
たいらな　590
たおれる　411
たかだか　383
たくさん　144
〜だけ　413
たしか　10
たす　285
だす　499
〜だす　558
たすける　416
ただいま　112
たたく　126
たつ　269
たっする　496
たった　711
〜だって　316
たのしい　139
たびに　420
たぶん　421
だます　424
たまたま　273
たまに　482
ため　148
ためる　624
たよりない　520
たりない　426
たりる　429
たるむ　433
ちかう　675
ちがう　434
ちかごろ　302
ちやほやする　171
ちゃんと　244
ちょうど　634
ちょっと　370
つい　128
ついに　685
つかう　437
つかまえる　440
つかむ　443
つかれる　445
つぎ　447
つぎつぎ　449
つく　451
つく　495
つぐ　395
つくづく　454
つける　457
つける　460
〜つける　531
つつく　452
つつむ　461
つぶす　463
つまらない　466
つむ　155
つむ　661
つめたい　331
つもり　468
つよい　470
〜づらい　532
つる　325
つるす　326
〜て(〜くて)　476
でかける　480
〜てき　472
てきとう　63
できるだけ　474
てつだう　418
てはん　642
〜ても　296
でる　479
どうか　387
どうじに　99
どうぞ　389
とうとう　683
とうぶん　345
どうやら　423
とおり　640
とかす　484
ときおり　482
ときどき　481
どきどき　582
とく　483
とくい　357
とくに　486
とくべつ　485
(〜た)ところ　552
とじる　350
どちら　487
とつぜん　262
とても　490

とどく 493
とどける 497
となり 501
どなる 322
とにかく 291
どのくらい 503
とらえる 441
とりあえず 83
とりつける 458
とりまく 204
とる 505
とる 507
(手に)とる 509
どれ 488
どれほど 504
どんなに〜ても 69

［な〜の］

〜ないで 510
なおす 54
なおる 512
なかなか 514
ながめる 644
〜なくて 511
なげる 518
なさけない 519
なでる 521
なに 489
なにげない 335
なまける 524
なやむ 526
ならう 168
なるべく 475
〜なれる 530
なんとか 388
にぎやか 137
にぎる 444
〜にくい 532
にくむ 132
にげる 534
にこにこ 536
にやにや 537
にる 689
にんき 572
ぬく 505
ぬぐう 597
ぬすむ 508
ぬるい 24
ぬれる 538
ねじる 540
ねっしん 542
ねっちゅう 542
ねむる 544
ねる 545
のがれる 535
のこる 51
のせる 154
のぞく 645
のちほど 43
〜のに 296
のぼる 5
のろい 163
のんびり 546

［は〜ほ］

ばいきゃくする 133
はがす 549
〜ばかり 414
(〜た)ばかり 551
はぐ 550
はげしい 553
はじめて 555
はじめに 556
はじめは 557
〜はじめる 557
はしる 202
はずす 506
はずむ 566
はたらく 560
はなす 562
はねる 565
はぶく 707
はやい 567
はやる 570
はる 459
はれる 600
はんせいする 574
はんたい 576
ひかる 578
ひく 580
びくびく 581
ひじょうに 493
ひそかに 584
ひたす 461
ひたすら 377
ひっきりなしに 451
ひっくりかえる 412
ひっこむ 607
ひっし 236
ひつよう 117
ひどい 554
ひといきに 93
ひときわ 88
ひとしい 177
ひとつひとつ 81
ひととき 85
ひとまず 102
ひとめ 96
ひとりで 586
ひとりでに 587
ひねる 541
ひょっとすると 662
ひらく 12
ひらたい 589
ひりひり 366
ひろがる 593
ひろまる 594
びんぼう 626
ふいに 594
〜ふう 473

ふく　597
ふくらむ　598
ふくれる　600
ふさぐ　351
ふさぐ　601
ふせぐ　631
ふそくする　427
ふたたび　630
ぶつかる　30
ぶつける　39
ふと　595
ふやす　623
ふりをする　227
〜ぶる　226
ふれる　337
へいき　604
へいたんな　591
へこむ　606
べつ　609
へん　27
へん　184
べんきょうする　170
ほうる　518
ほか　608
ほす　610
ほぼ　612
ほんの　712

［ま〜も］

まえ　615
まがる　618
まぐれ　274
まざる　621
〜ましょうか　627
まじる　621
ます　622
まずしい　625
ますます　664
〜ませんか　627
また　628
まちがう　436
まちがえる　436
まとまる　34
まとめる　404
まなぶ　169
まにあう　430
まねく　700
(〜た)まま　266
まもる　631
まよう　529
まるで　632
みえる　636
みち　639
みつめる　644
みほん　641
みられる　638
みる　642
みんな　647
〜むき　649
むく　551
〜むけ　650
むこう　20
むしむし　349
むしる　660
むしろ　195
むすぶ　652
むだ　654
むちゅう　543
むやみに　681
めいめい　400
めいる　602
めきめき　656
めっきり　656
めんどう　657
もう　41
もういちど　629
もえる　677
もぐ　660
もしかすると　662
もたれる　704
もちいる　438
(手に)もつ　510
もったいない　655
もっと　663
もっとも　92
もどす　666
もどる　197
(〜て)もらう　669
もらす　672
もろい　705

［や〜よ］

やがて　407
やくそくする　674
やける　676
やさしい　678
やしなう　397
やたらと　680
やっかい　659
やっと　682
やはり　686
やめる　192
ゆかい　139
ゆっくり　547
ゆでる　689
ゆるす　691
ゆるむ　433
〜よう　651
(〜)よう(みたい)　693
ようき　120
〜ようとおもう　469
よける　229
よこ　502
よせる　36
(〜に)よって　696
よぶ　699
よほど　327
〜よりいい　701
よりかかる　703
〜よりまし　702

よわい　705

［ら～ろ］

(～)らしい　695
りゃくす　706
りんじ　224

［わ］

わかす　690
わがまま　708
わかる　361
わざわざ　386
わずか　710
わりと　517
わる　713

〔日本文化の生活語〕

お花見　27　450
カレー　117　372
　650　690　702
ラーメン　129　571
～くん　130　411
暴走族　135
成人式　181
定期券　198　448
おせんべい　206
歌舞伎　303
源氏物語　313
すし　410
うどん　487　498　500
鍋料理　404
命がいくつあっても足り
　ない　427
風呂敷　462
そば　487　500
ふとん　550　611
大関　555　698
潮干狩り　648
横綱　343　687　698

〔読み物学習コラム〕

「～で」と「～に」　25
お願いします　48
お兄ちゃんて誰？　72
すみません　94
私の家族・親族　118
お忘れ物ですよ　142
「お待ちどおさま」と「お待たせし
　ました」　164
下がる　191
「来なくていい」は来てはいけない？
　209
すごい!!　233
けっこうです　256
良かったじゃない　283
どこで食べますか？　306
天気が寒い　333
さようなら　352
どろぼうが指輪をとりました　374
コーヒーは２杯か２つか　397
ものの数え方　419
１さつの本　439
身につける表現　456
いい男はいい人か　478
めん類　500
私はコーヒーでいいです　523
楽になってください　548
ごはんを食べましたか？　573
日本の住宅　592
体が沈没するんです　614
火が出るところは？　635
あなたに貸してあげる　671
相撲　698

ローマ字索引英語つき

[**a**]

achira———(over) there　19
afureru———to overflow　44
agaru———to rise ; to go up　3
～ageru———to finish　14
aida ni———during ; between　1
akeru———to open　11
aki———empty ; vacant　7
akiraka———obvious ; clear　9
akiru———to be tired of　410
akumade———to the last　314
amari～nai———not very... ; not so... 46
amaru———to be left over ; to be too much　49
angai———unexpectedly　60
aratameru———to change ; to revise　52
areru———to be rough　58
aru———to be ; to exist　56
asaru———to hunt for ; to scrounge 319
aseru———to fade　16
aseru———to hurry ; to fret　77
asoko———(over) there　18
assari———light ; easy　31
atakamo———just as if　21
atari———neighborhood ; around (here)　26
ataru———to hit ; to touch ; to win (a lottery)　28
atatakai———warm　23
ateru———to hit ; touch ; to expose to　37
ato———still ; remaining ; later　40
ato de———later ; after　42
atsukamashii———shameless ; pushy　365
atsumaru———to gather ; to assemble　33
atsumeru———to collect ; to gather 35
awatadashii———hurried　75
awateru———to panic ; to get flustered ; to rush　77

[**b**]

baikyaku suru———to sell　133
～bakari———only～ ; about～ 414
benkyou suru———to study　170
betsu———another ; other　609
bikubiku———to be afraid or nervous　581
binbou———poverty　626
～buru———to pretend ; to pose as 226
butsukaru———to hit (against) ; to run (into)　30
butsukeru———to hit (against...) ; to crash (into)　39

[**c**]

chanto———neatly ; correctly　244
chigau———wrong ; different　434
chikagoro———recently ; these days 302
chikau———to vow ; to swear 675
chiyahoya suru———to pamper 171
chotto———a little ; a moment　370
choudo———just like ; exactly　634

[**d**]

daibu———much ; very 220
daijoubu———all right 604
daitai———about ; roughly 613
dake———only 413
damasu———to deceive 424
dasu———to send 499
～*dasu*———to begin (doing) 558
～*datte*———too ; either 316
dekakeru———to go out ; to leave 480
dekirudake———to the extent possible 474
deru———to go out ; to leave 479
dochira———which (of two) 487
dokidoki———to throb ; to pound 582
donaru———to yell (at) ; to scold 322
donna ni～*temo*———no matter how 69
dono kurai———how much (long, far, etc.) 503
dore———which (of 3 or more) 488
dore hodo———how much 504
doujini———at the same time 99
douka———please 387
douyara———apparently 423
douzo———please ; go ahead 389

[**e**]

ensou suru———to perform 581

[**f**]

fui ni———unexpectedly ; suddenly 594
fuku———to wipe 597
fukuramu———to swell ; to bulge 598
fukureru———to swell 600
fureru———to touch 337
furi o suru———to pretend 227
fusagu———to close (up) ; to plug (up) 351
fusagu———to be depressed 601
fusegu———to protect ; to defend 631
fusoku suru———to be lacking ; to be short 427
futatabi———again 630
futo———suddenly ; by chance ; accidentally 595
fuu———appearance ; style 473
fuyasu———to increase 623

[**g**]

～*gachi*———tendency ; inclination 254
gakkari———to be disappointed 207
gaman suru———to withstand ; to make do 308
ganbaru———to persist 234
gangan———ache 367
～*garu*———to want ; to seem 225
～*gatai*———difficult (to do) 533
genzai———the present time 111
geragera———laugh (out loud) 279
～*gimi*———tendency 253
gimon———doubt ; question 343
gomakasu———to deceive ; to cheat 425

~goro——around~ 309
goto ni——every ; each 150
~gurai (*kurai*) ——around~ ; about 310
guruguru——(turn/go) round and round 281
guuzen——by chance ; by coincidence 272
gyaku——reverse ; converse ; opposite 577
gyakutai suru——to mistreat 72

[**h**]

habuku——to omit ; to cut out 707
hagasu——to peel ; to tear off 549
hageshii——hard ; violent 553
hagu——to peel ; to tear off 550
hajime ni——in the beginning ; at first 556
~hajimeru——to begin (doing) 557
hajimete——first time ; first 555
hajime wa——at first 557
hanasu——to speak ; to talk 562
haneru——to jump 565
hansei suru——to reflect on 574
hantai——opposite 576
hareru——to swell 600
haru——to attach ; to stick 459
hashiru——to run 202
hataraku——to work 560
hayai——fast ; early 567
hayaru——to spread ; to be popular 570
hazumu——to bounce ; to spring 566
hazusu——to remove ; to unfasten ; to undo 506
heiki——calm 604
heitan na——even ; flat 591
hekomu——to be dented 606
hen——area ; neighborhood 27
hen——strange ; odd 184
hidoi——terrible 554
hijou ni——extremely 493
hikaru——to shine ; to flash 578
hikkiri nashi ni——unceasingly 451
hikkomu——to withdraw 607
hikkurikaeru——to overturn 412
hiku——to play (a stringed instrument) 580
hineru——to rotate ; to twist 541
hiraku——to open ; to start 12
hiratai——flat ; level 589
hirihiri——burn ; smart 366
hirogaru——to spread 593
hiromaru——to spread ; to be disseminated 594
hisoka ni——secretly ; stealthily 584
hisshi——desperate(ly) 236
hitasu——to immerse ; to dip in 461
hitasura——single-mindedly 377
hitoikini——at a breath ; at once 93
hitokiwa——especially ; remarkably 88
hitomazu——for the time being 102

hitome———at a glance ; at first sight 96
hitori de———alone 586
hitorideni———automatically ; by itself 587
hitoshii———equivalent 177
hitotoki———a brief time 85
hitotsu hitotsu———one by one ; each 81
hitsuyou———to need ; to require 117
hobo———about ; almost 612
hoka———another ; other ; else 608
honno———just ; only 712
hosu———to dry ; to hang out to dry ; to air 610
houru———to toss ; to throw 518
hyottosuruto———possibly ; by some chance 662

[**i**]

ibiru———to be mean to ; to be hard on 71
ibusu———to smoke (something) 108
ichiban———number one ; the most ; best 90
ichibetsu———(at) a glance 97
ichidanto———(a step) further ; greater 86
ichido ni———at once 89
ichiichi———one by one ; in detail 80
ichiji———a brief period ; once 84
ichijiteki———temporary 224
ichiou———just in case ; for the time being 82
ie———house ; family 64
igai———unexpectedly 61
iikagen———irresponsible ; groundless ; limit 62
ijimeru———to tease ; to pick on 70
ijirashii———touching ; pathetic ; lovable 293
ikanimo———as if ; really 22
ikinari———suddenly 262
ikken———(at) a glance 95
ikkini———at a breath 93
ikkoku———a short time 86
iku———to go 66
ikura～temo———no matter how much (many...) 68
ima———now 110
ima kara———starting from now 113
ippai———a lot of ; full 145
ippen ni———at once 90
ippou———one side 103
iremono———container 119
iroiro———various 121
iru———to be ; to exist 57
iru———to need ; to require 115
isogashii———busy 74
isogu———to hurry 76
isseini———at once ; all together 98
isshoukenmei———(work / play) hard 235
isso———(I) would rather 100
issou———all the more 87
itai———painful ; sore 78
itamu———to be damaged ; to ache 277
itsu demo———always ; at any time 106

itsumo——always 105
ittan——once 101
iu——to say ; to speak 563
iya——to dislike 264

［**j**］

jibun de——by oneself 586
jimejime——moist ; damp 348
jitto——fixedly ; intently 376
jiwajiwa——gradually ; steadily 359
jojoni——gradually 358
joubu——healthy ; strong 471
jouzu——skill ; proficiency 356
junban ni——in order 354
juubun——ample ; enough 432

［**k**］

kabuseru——to cover 220
kado——corner 210
kaeru——to change 53
kaeru——to return ; to go home 196
kaesu——to return 667
kaette——contrary (to one's expectation) 194
kagayaku——to shine ; to sparkle 579
kaifuku suru——to recover 513
kajiru——to bite ; to gnaw 205
kakaru——to take ; to require 116
kakaru——to be about to ～ ; almost 199
kakeru——to start to ～ ; to be about to 199
kakeru——to run 201
kakeru——to hang ; to hook (on) 324
kakeru——to be lacking ; to be missing 428
kakomu——to surround ; to encircle 203
kamu——to bite ; to chew 206
kanarazu——certainly ; without fail 215
kanari——quite ; extremely ; very 219
kanashii——sad ; sorrowful 213
kandou——impression ; to be impressed 232
kangaeru——to think about ; to consider 181
kanshin——admiration 231
kantan——simple 679
kara——empty 8
karatto——clear ; crisp 33
kari——temporary 223
kasaneru——to pile on ; to layer 156
katahou——one side ; one of two 104
katai——hard ; strong ; tight 247
katazukeru——to clean up ; to straighten up 347
katte——one's own way 709
kawaisou——pitiful 252
kawakasu——to dry 611
kawarugawaru——in turns 355
kawasu——to evade ; to dodge 229
kawatte iru——unusual ; different 184
keiken——experience 288
kekkou——quite ; rather 516
kekkyoku——eventually ; in the

end 290
kemuru——to smoke ; to be hazy 110
kenage——admirable ; brave 293
keredomo——but ; however 294
kettei suru——to decide 256
kibun——mood ; feeling 259
kichinto——properly ; exactly 243
kikareru——to hear ; to be heard 240
kikoeru——(can) hear ; to sound (like) 239
kiku——to be effective ; to work 237
kimatte——invariably ; without fail 217
kimeru——to decide 255
kimochi——feeling 258
ki ni naru——to bother ; to worry ; to feel anxious 250
ki ni suru——to worry 249
kinodoku——unfortunate ; pitiable 251
ki o otosu——to lose heart 208
kirai——to dislike ; to hate 263
kirei——beautiful ; clean 270
～*kiru*——to use up ; run out of 14
kiru——to cut 267
kitanai——dirty ; filthy 241
kitanarashii——dirty 242
kitsui——tight ; hard 246
kitto——(almost) certainly 216
koboreru——to spill ; to drop 45
kobosu——to spill 673
koeru——to go over ; to exceed 298
kogeru——to burn ; to scorch 676
komakai——detailed ; minute 287
komaru——to be in trouble ; to be annoyed 527
komu——to be crowded ; to be congested 304
kondo——this (next) time ; sometime 448
konogoro——nowadays ; these days 301
konzatsu suru——to be crowded ; to be congested 305
koraeru——to endure 307
korekara——starting now ; from now (on) 114
korobu——to fall down ; to tumble over 311
korogaru——to roll 312
korokoro——roll over and over 282
kossori——stealthily ; sneakily ; secretly 585
kosu——to be more than ; to pass 299
kosuru——to rub ; to scrub 522
kotaeru——to have an effect on ; to be hard on 238
koukai suru——to regret 575
koutai de——in turns 354
kowai——scary ; fearful 167
kowasu——to break ; to destroy 714
kubomu——to sink 607
kudaku——to break into pieces 465
kudaranai——silly ; trivial 467

kudaru———to descend ; to issue 189
kugiru———to divide 275
kurasu———to live ; to earn a livelihood 381
kuru———to come 67
kurukuru———(go/turn) round and round 280
kurumu———to wrap 462
kusaru———to go bad ; to decay 277
kusuburu———to smolder 109
kusukusu———giggle ; chuckle 279
kutabireru———to be exhausted ; to be worn out 446
kuwaeru———to add (to) 284
kuwashii———detailed 286
kyoka suru———to permit 692
kyuuni———suddenly 261

[**m**]

machigaeru———to make a mistake 436
machigau———to be wrong 436
mae———(in) front ; before 615
magaru———to curve ; to bend ; to turn 618
magure———by chance ; a fluke 274
majiru———to (be) mix(ed) 621
mamoru———to protect ; to guard 631
manabu———to learn ; to study 169
maneku———to invite 700
maniau———to be enough ; to be in time (for) 430
marude———just like ; (not) at all 632
~masen ka———won't you...? ; shall we...? 627
~mashou ka———shall we...? ; shall I...? 627
masu———to increase 622
masumasu———even more ; more and more 664
mata———again 628
matomaru———to be collected ; to be united 34
matomeru———to gather ; to collect 404
mayou———to be at a loss ; to get lost 529
mazaru———to mix and blend 621
mazushii———poor ; needy 625
meimei———each (person) 400
meiru———to feel gloomy ; to be depressed 602
mekimeki———(to progress) remarkably 656
mekkiri———noticeably 656
mendou———trouble ; bother 657
michi———road ; way 639
mieru———to be visible ; to appear ; to seem 636
mihon———sample 641
minna———all ; everyone ; everything 647
mirareru———to be able to see 638
miru———to look (at) ; to see 642
mitsumeru———to gaze ; to stare 644
mochiiru———to utilize ; to use 438

modoru———to return 197
modosu———to return ; to replace 666
moeru———to burn 677
mogu———to pick (fruits, vegetables) 660
morasu———to leak (out) 672
moroi———fragile ; brittle 705
moshikasuruto———possibly 662
motareru———to lean (on, against) ; to recline 704
mottainai———a waste 655
motto———more 663
mottomo———most ; extremely 92
mou———more ; already 41
mou ichido———one more time ; again 629
muchuu———crazy about 543
muda———useless ; a waste 654
～muke———aimed at ; for 650
～muki———suitable for～ 649
mukou———beyond ; (on) the other side 20
muku———to peel 551
mushimushi———humid ; muggy 349
mushiro———rather (than...) 195
mushiru———to pluck ; to pull 660
musubu———to tie ; to connect 652
muyami ni———thoughtlessly ; unnecessarily 681

［**n**］

naderu———to stroke 521
nagameru———to gaze at ; to look at 644
nageru———to throw 518
～naide———without ～ing 510
nakanaka———quite ; rather 514
～nakute———without～ ; therefore～ 511
namakeru———to be lazy 524
nani———what 489
nanigenai———casual 335
nantoka———somehow 388
naoru———to be repaired ; to get well 512
naosu———to repair ; to cure 54
narau———to learn ; to study ; to take lessons 168
～nareru———V＋be used to 530
narubeku———if possible 475
nasakenai———shameful 519
nayamu———to worry 526
nejiru———to twist ; to screw ; to warp 540
nemuru———to sleep 544
neru———to go to bed, to (go to) sleep ; to lie down 545
nesshin———eager ; earnest ; devoted 542
netchuu———absorbed in ; enthusiastic about 542
nigeru———to escape ; to run away (from) 534
nigiru———to grasp ; to clasp ; to seize 444
nigiyaka———bustling 137
nikoniko———smile (pleasantly) 536
～nikui———hard (to do) 532
nikumu———to hate 132
ninki———be popular 572
(～*ni*) *oujite*———in response to～ 697
niru———to stew ; to simmer 689

niyaniya———smirk 537
(*～ni*) *yotte*———depending on～ 696
noboru———to climb ; to go up 5
nochihodo———later 43
nogareru———to escape ; to evade 535
nokoru———to remain 51
nonbiri———peacefully ; leisurely 546
～noni———～although ; but 296
noroi———slow 163
noseru———to put (load) on 154
nozoku———to peep into ; to peek 645
nuguu———to wipe off 597
nuku———to pull (take) out ; to extract 505
nureru———to get wet 538
nurui———lukewarm 24
nusumu———to steal 508

[**o**]

oboeru———to memorize ; to remember 178
ochikomu———to feel down 603
odateru———to flatter (someone into) 171
odayaka———calm 341
odoodo———to be nervous ; to have the jitters 583
oikakeru———to chase (in order to catch) 141
oishii———delicious 130
okage———thanks to ; owe～ (to～) 146
okashii———amusing ; strange ; odd 183
oki ni———every (other) 149
okoru———to be angry ; to scold 157
okotaru———to neglect 526
oku———to put ; to set (down) 153
okuru———to send 498
omoidasu———to recall ; to remember 178
omoigakenai———unexpected 186
omoikitte———to finally decide to 101
omoshiroi———interesting ; amusing 182
omotta yori———unexpectedly 62
omou———to think 179
omowazu———unconsciously 185
onaji———same 175
onoono———each 399
ooi———many ; much ; a lot of 143
oou———to wrap ; to cover 222
oriru———to descend ; to go down 187
osaeru———to hold down ; to suppress 161
oshieru———to teach ; to tell 159
oshii———regrettable 339
osoi———slow ; late 162
osoraku———probably 422
osoroshii———frightening ; terrible 166
osowaru———to learn (from) 168
osu———to push 160
otosu———to drop ; to lose 172
ou———to follow ; to chase 140
～owaru———to finish ; to end 15
owaru———to end ; to finish 192
oyoso———roughly ; approximately

614

[r]

(～) *rashii*———seem ; appear ; ～like 695
rinji———special ; extra ; temporary 224
ryakusu———to abbreviate ; to shorten 706

[s]

sabishii———lonely 214
saboru———to cut a class (meeting, etc.) 525
～*sae*———even 315
sagasu———to look for 317
sageru———to hang 323
saguru———to search for ; to feel for ; to explore 318
saigomade———until the end 313
saikin———recently 303
sakan ni———greatly ; vigorously 320
sakebu———to shout ; to scream 321
sakeru———to avoid 230
saki———(in) the future ; earlier ; previous 617
saku———to rip ; to tear apart 268
samazama———various ; diverse ; all kinds 122
sameru———to fade ; to cool down 17
samui———cold 330
sappari———refreshing ; neat ; completely 32
sarani———still more 665
sarigenai———casual ; unconcerned 334
sassoku———at once 329
sasu———to pierce ; to bite ; to prick 453
sasuga———as expected 687
sasuru———to rub 521
sawagashii———noisy ; boisterous 136
sawaru———to touch ; to feel 336
sazo———surely ; must 327
sei———blame 147
seizei———at most / best ; to the utmost 382
sekkaku———with a great deal of trouble (time, effort) 384
semete———at least 368
sewashii———busy ; restless 75
shaberu———to converse ; to chat 564
～*shi*———～and 477
shibaraku———for a (little) while 344
shibaru———to tie (up) ; to fasten ; to bundle 653
shigoto———work ; job 561
shikamo———besides ; furthermore 402
～*shika (～) nai*———only～ ; no more than ; nothing but～ 415
shikaru———to scold 158
shikirini———frequently ; repeatedly 320
shikiru———to divide ; to partition 276
shikkari———firm ; reliable 245
shimau———to store ; to keep 346
shimeru———to close 350

shimijimi———keenly ; thoroughly 455
shimiru———to soak into ; to smart ; to sting ; to irritate 539
shinau———to bend ; to be supple ; to be pliant 620
shiraseru———to let ～know ; to tell 160
shiru———to know 360
shitsubou suru———to despair ; to lose hope 208
shitsumon———question 342
shizen ni———naturally 589
shizuka———quiet 340
shooryaku suru———to omit ; to abbreviate 707
shotchuu———often 107
sodateru———to raise (children, animals) 396
sokkuri———completely 373
sono tsudo———at any time that ; each time 420
sonouchi———soon ; someday 408
sonoue———besides ; moreover 401
sorekara———after that ; then 391
soreni———besides 401
sorezore———each ; respectively 398
soroeru———to gather ; to arrange 403
sorosoro———soon ; almost 406
soru———to be warped ; to be curved 619
soshite———then ; and 390
sosogu———to pour ; to flow 394
～sou da———almost ; appear as if 200
subarashii———wonderful 378
subashikkoi———nimble ; quick 569
subayai———quick 569
sugiru———to go beyond ; to pass 300
sugosu———to spend (time) 381
sugu———immediately ; at once 329
suisui———smoothly ; easily 362
sukkari———all ; completely 372
sukoshi———few ; a little 369
sukunakutomo———at least 368
sukuu———to save ; to rescue 417
sumi———corner 212
sumu———to end ; to finish ; to be over 193
sumu———to reside ; to dwell in 380
sunnari———easily ; smoothly 364
surasura———smoothly ; easily 363
suruto———whereupon ; then 393
susamu———to become desolate 59
suteki———wonderful ; lovely 379
suteru———to discard ; to throw away 174
suzushii———cool 332

[**t**]

(*～ta*) *bakari*———just ～ed 551
tabi ni———every time, whenever 420
tabun———probably ; perhaps

421
tadaima———just now 112
taihen———terribly ; very ; terrible 491
taiken———experience 290
taikutsu———boring 409
taira na———flat ; smooth ; horizontal 590
taishite~nai———not very... ; not much... 47
takadaka———at most / best ; no more than 383
(*~ta*) *kiri*———since 265
takusan———many ; much ; a lot of 144
(*~ta*) *mama*———as (something) is 266
tamani———once in a while ; at times 482
tamatama———by chance 273
tame———reason ; cause 148
tameru———to save ; to pile up 624
tanoshii———fun ; cheerful 139
taoreru———to fall down 411
tarinai———not enough ; lacking 426
tariru———to be enough 429
tarumu———to sag ; to slack off 433
tashika———certain ; reliable 10
tassuru———to reach ; to attain 496
tasu———to add 285
tasukeru———to help 416
tataku———to hit ; to knock ; to beat 126
(*~ta*) *tokoro*———have just ~ed 552
tatsu———to cut 269
tatta———only ; mere 711
tayorinai———unreliable 520
(*~te*) *aru*———to remain ; to keep 152
tehon———model 642
~ teki———~ like 472
tekitou———suitable ; irresponsible 63
(*~te*) *kureru*———(someone) to do ~ for me (for us, etc.) 670
~te (*~kute*) ———~and 476
~temo———even (though / if) ; but 296
(*~te*) *morau*———to have (someone) do~ 669
(*te ni*) *motsu*———to hold (in the hand) 510
(*te ni*) *toru*———to take ; to hold (in the hands) 509
(*~te*) *oku*———to leave ; to keep 151
tetsudau———to help out 418
todokeru———to deliver 497
todoku———to reach ; to arrive 493
tojiru———to close 350
tokasu———to melt 484
tokidoki———sometimes 481
tokiori———on occasion 482
toku———to dissolve 483
tokubetsu———special 485
tokui———specialty ; forte ; pride 357
tokuni———especially 486
tonari———neighbor ; next (door) 501
tonikaku———anyway 291
toori———street 640

toraeru——to catch ; to capture 441
toriaezu——for the time being 83
torimaku——to surround ; to gather around 204
toritsukeru——to install 458
toru——to remove ; to take off 505
toru——to take ; to steal 507
totemo——completely ; very 490
totsuzen——suddenly 262
toubun——for a while 345
toutou——in the end ; finally 683
tsubusu——to crush 463
tsugi——next 447
tsugitsugi——one after another 449
tsugu——to pour (into) 395
tsui——by habit ; without thinking 128
tsuini——in the end ; finally 685
tsukamaeru——to catch 440
tsukamu——to seize ; to grasp 443
tsukareru——to get / to be tired 445
tsukau——to use 437
tsukeru——to attach ; to fix 457
tsukeru——to soak ; to steep ; to pickle 460
~tsukeru——V + be used to 531
tsuku——to poke ; to stab 451
tsuku——to arrive ; to reach 495
tsukuzuku——thoroughly ; deeply 454
tsumaranai——trifling ; boring 466
tsumetai——cold 331
tsumori——intention 468
tsumu——to pile up ; to load 155
tsumu——to pick ; to snip 661
tsuru——to hang ; to suspend ; to sling 325
tsurusu——to hang ; to suspend 326
tsutsuku——to pick (at) 452
tsutsumu——to wrap ; to envelop 461
tsuyoi——strong 470

[**u**]

uchi——house ; home 65
uchi ni——while ; before 2
ukabu——to float 124
ukkari——careless 127
uku——to float 123
umai——good ; skilled 129
uramu——to hold a grudge (against) 131
ureshii——happy ; glad 138
uriharau——to sell off ; to dispose of 134
uru——to sell 133
urusai——noisy ; bothersome 135
utsu——to hit ; to strike 125
utsukushii——beautiful 271
utsuwa——container ; receptacle 119
uzuku——to ache 79

［w］

wagamama———selfish 708
wakaru———to understand ; to know 361
wakasu———to boil ; to heat 690
warito———rather ; fairly 517
waru———to break 713
wazawaza———on purpose ; taking the trouble (to do); especially 386
wazuka———few ; little 710

［y］

yagate———soon 407
yahari———as expected ; as well 686
yakeru———to burn ; to fire (pottery) 676
yakkai———trouble ; troublesome 659
yakusoku suru———to promise 674
yameru———to quit ; to stop 192
yasashii———easy ; gentle 678
yashinau———to support 397
yatara to———recklessly ; excessively 680
yatto———at last ; finally 682
yobu———to call ; to call (invite) over 699
yohodo———greatly ; much 327
yokeru———to avoid ; to evade 229
yoko———side ; width ; horizontal 502
～yori ii———better than～ 701
yorikakaru———to lean (on, against) 703
～yori mashi———not good, but better than other options 702
yoseru———to draw near ; to collect 36
～you———for the use of～ 651
youki———container 120
（～） *you* （*mitai*） ———appearance ; manner 693
～you to omou———to think (one) will～ 469
yowai———weak 705
yuderu———to boil 689
yukai———amusing ; fun ; cheerful 139
yukkuri———slowly 547
yurumu———to loosen ; to abate ; to slack off 433
yurusu———to forgive ; to allow 691

［z］

zannen———regrettable 338
zehi———by all means 387
zen———*in*-all the members ; everyone 648
zettai———absolute(ly) 217
zokuzoku———one after another 450
zukizuki———throb 366
～zurai———difficult (to do) 532
zutto———all the time ; by far 375
zuuzuushii———cheeky ; impudent 364

ことばの意味分類索引

程度や量を表すことば

あくまで　314
あたかも　21
あと　40
あまり〜ない　46
あんがい　60
いがい　61
いかにも　22
いくら〜ても　68
いちいち　80
いちおう　82
いちだんと　86
いちばん　90
いっそ　100
いっそう　87
いっぱい　145
いっぺんに　90
いろいろ　121
おおい　143
おなじ　175
おのおの　399
おもいきって　101
おもったより　62
およそ　614
かえって　194
〜がたい　533
かならず　215
かなり　219
きまって　217
きゅうに　261
〜きる　14
〜ぐらい(くらい)　310
けっこう　516
さいごまで　313
〜さえ　315
さかんに　320
さぞ　327
さまざま　122
さらに　665
〜しか(〜)ない　415
しきりに　320
じゅうぶん　432
すくなくとも　368
すこし　369
すっかり　372
せいぜい　382
せっかく　384
ぜったい　217
せめて　368
ぜんいん　648
そっくり　373
そのつど　420
それぞれ　398
たいして〜ない　47
だいたい　613
だいぶ　220
たいへん　491
たかだか　383
たくさん　144
〜だけ　413
たった　711
〜だって　316
たびに　420
たりる　429
ちょうど　634
ちょっと　370
ついに　685
〜づらい　532
できるだけ　474
とうとう　683
とくに　486
とくべつ　485
とても　490
どのくらい　503
とりあえず　83
どれほど　504
どんなに〜ても　69
なかなか　514
なるべく　475
〜にくい　532
〜ばかり　414
はげしい　553
ひじょうに　493
ひときわ　88
ひとしい　177
ひとつひとつ　81
ひとめ　96
ふたたび　630
ほぼ　612
ほんの　712
ますます　664
また　628
まにあう　430
みんな　647
むしろ　195
むやみに　681
めいめい　400
もう　41
もういちど　629
もっと　663
もっとも　92
やたらと　680
やっと　682

よほど　327
〜よりいい　701
〜よりまし　702
わざわざ　386
わずか　710
わりと　517

時間や場所、位置を表すことば

あいだに　1
〜あげる　14
あそこ　18
あたり　26
あちら　19
あと　40
あとで　42
いちじ　84
いちじてき　224
いちどに　89
いっこく　86
いっせいに　98
いったん　101
いっぽう　103
いま　110
いまから　113
うちに　2
おきに　149
〜おわる　15
かたほう　104
かど　210
かり　223
ぎゃく　577
げんざい　111
ごとに　150
このごろ　301
これから　114
〜ごろ　309
こんど　448
さいきん　303
さき　617
さっそく　329
しばらく　344
すぐ　329
ずっと　375
すみ　212
そのうち　408
そろそろ　406
ただいま　112
たまに　482
ちかごろ　302
つぎ　447
どうじに　99
とうぶん　345
とおり　640
ときおり　482
ときどき　481
(〜た)ところ　552
となり　501
のちほど　43
(〜た)ばかり　551
はじめて　555
はじめに　556
はじめは　557
はんたい　576
ひととき　85
ひとまず　102
へん　27
まえ　615
みち　639
むこう　20
やがて　407
よこ　502
りんじ　224

動きを表すことば

あがる　3
あける　11
あさる　319
あたる　28
あつまる　33
あつめる　35
あてる　37
あらためる　52
いう　563
いく　66
いじめる　70
いそぐ　76
いびる　71
いぶす　108
うつ　125
うりはらう　134
うる　133
えんそうする　581
おいかける　141
おう　140
おおう　222
(〜て)おく　151
おく　153
おくる　498
おこたる　526
おこる　157
おさえる　161
おしえる　159
おす　160
おそわる　168

おとす 172
おりる 187
かえす 667
かえる 53
かえる 196
かける 201
かける 324
かこむ 203
かさねる 156
かじる 205
かたづける 347
かぶせる 220
かむ 206
かわかす 611
かわす 229
きめる 255
ぎゃくたいする 72
きょかする 692
きる 267
くぎる 275
くだく 465
くだる 189
くらす 381
くる 67
くるむ 462
(〜て)くれる 670
くわえる 284
けっていする 256
こえる 298
こす 299
こする 522
こぼす 673
ごまかす 425
ころがる 312
ころぶ 311
こわす 714
さがす 317
さく 268
さぐる 318
さけぶ 321
さける 230
さげる 323
さす 453
さする 521
サボる 525
さわる 336
しかる 158
しきる 276
しごと 561
しばる 653
しまう 346
しめる 350
しゃべる 564
しょうりゃくする 707
しらせる 160
すぎる 300
すくう 417
すごす 381
すてる 174
すむ 380
そそぐ 394
そだてる 396
そろえる 403
たおれる 411
たす 285
だす 499
たすける 416
たたく 126
たつ 269
だます 424
ためる 624
ちかう 675
ちやほやする 171
つかう 437
つかまえる 440
つかむ 443
つく 451
つぐ 395
つける 457
つける 460
つつく 452
つつむ 461
つぶす 463
つむ 155
つむ 661
つる 325
つるす 326
でかける 480
てつだう 418
でる 479
とかす 484
とく 483
とじる 350
とどける 497
どなる 322
とらえる 441
とりつける 458
とりまく 204
とる 505
とる 507
(手に)とる 509
(手に)もつ 510
なおす 54
ながめる 644
なげる 518
なでる 521
なまける 524
ならう 168
にぎる 444
にげる 534
にる 689
ぬく 505
ぬぐう 597
ぬすむ 508

ねじる　540
ねむる　544
ねる　545
のがれる　535
のせる　154
のぞく　645
のぼる　5
ばいきゃくする　133
はがす　549
はぐ　550
はしる　202
はずす　506
はずむ　566
はたらく　560
はなす　562
はねる　565
はぶく　707
はる　459
ひく　580
ひたす　461
ひっくりかえる　412
ひねる　541
ひらく　12
ふく　597
ふさぐ　351
ふせぐ　631
ぶつかる　30
ぶつける　39
ふやす　623
ふりをする　227
ふれる　337
べんきょうする　170
ほうる　518
ほす　610
ます　622
まちがう　436
まちがえる　436
まとまる　34
まとめる　404
まなぶ　169
まねく　700
まもる　631
みつめる　644
みる　642
むく　551
むしる　660
むすぶ　652
もぐ　660
もたれる　704
もちいる　438
もどす　666
もどる　197
(〜て)もらう　669
もらす　672
やしなう　397
やめる　192
ゆでる　689
ゆるす　691
よける　229
よせる　36
よぶ　699
よりかかる　703
りゃくす　706
わかす　690
わる　713

◎ ようすを表すことば

あき　7
あきらか　9
あつかましい　365
あっさり　31
ある　56
(〜て)ある　152
あれる　58
あわただしい　75
いいかげん　62
いきなり　262
いじらしい　293
いそがしい　74
いちべつ　97
いっきに　93
いっけん　95
いっしょうけんめい　235
いつでも　106
いつも　105
いる　57
いる　115
うっかり　127
うつくしい　271
うるさい　135
おそい　162
おだやか　341
おもいがけない　186
おもわず　185
かがやく　579
かかる　116
〜かかる　199
〜かける　199
かける　428
かたい　247
〜がち　254
かって　709
から　8
からっと　33
〜がる　225
かわっている　184
かわるがわる　355
かんたん　679

がんばる　234
きかれる　240
きこえる　239
きたない　241
きたならしい　242
きちんと　243
きつい　246
〜ぎみ　253
(〜た)きり　265
きれい　270
ぐうぜん　272
くすくす　279
くすぶる　109
くるくる　280
ぐるぐる　281
くわしい　286
けなげ　293
けむる　110
げらげら　279
こうたいで　354
こっそり　585
こまかい　287
こむ　304
ころころ　282
こんざつする　305
さっぱり　32
さりげない　334
さわがしい　136
しずか　340
しぜんに　589
しっかり　245
じっと　376
じぶんで　586
じゅんばんに　354
じょうず　356
じょうぶ　471
じょじょに　358
しょっちゅう　107
じわじわ　359
すいすい　362
ずうずうしい　364
すさむ　59
すばしっこい　569
すばやい　569
すらすら　363
すんなり　364
せわしい　75
〜そうだ　200
ぞくぞく　450
たいらな　590
たしか　10
たまたま　273
たりない　426
ちがう　434
ちゃんと　244
つい　128
つぎつぎ　449
〜つける　531
つよい　470
てきとう　63
とくい　357
とつぜん　262
なにげない　335
〜なれる　530
にぎやか　137
にこにこ　536
にやにや　537
にんき　572
ねっしん　542
ねっちゅう　542
のろい　163
のんびり　546
はやい　567
はやる　570
ひかる　578
ひそかに　584
ひたすら　377
ひっきりなしに　451
ひっし　236
ひつよう　117
ひといきに　93
ひとりで　586
ひとりでに　587
ひらたい　589
びんぼう　626
ふいに　594
ふそくする　427
ふと　595
〜ぶる　226
へいたんな　591
べつ　609
ほか　608
まぐれ　274
まずしい　625
(〜た)まま　266
まるで　632
みえる　636
みられる　638
むだ　654
むちゅう　543
めきめき　656
めっきり　656
もろい　705
やさしい　678
ゆっくり　547
(〜)よう(みたい)　693
よわい　705
(〜)らしい　695
わがまま　708

♥ 心で感じることを表すことば

あきる 410
あせる 77
あわてる 77
いや 264
うらむ 131
うれしい 138
おかげ 146
おかしい 183
おしい 339
おそらく 422
おそろしい 166
おだてる 171
おちこむ 603
おどおど 583
おぼえる 178
おもいだす 178
おもう 179
おもしろい 182
がっかり 207
かなしい 213
がまんする 308
かわいそう 252
かんがえる 181
かんしん 231
かんどう 232
きをおとす 208
きく 237
きっと 216
きにする 249
きになる 250
きのどく 251
きぶん 259
きもち 258
ぎもん 343
きらい 263
くだらない 467
けいけん 288
こうかいする 575
こたえる 238
こまる 527
こらえる 307
こわい 167
さすが 687
さびしい 214
ざんねん 338
しつぼうする 208
しつもん 342
しみじみ 455
しる 360
すてき 379
すばらしい 378
ぜひ 387
たいくつ 409
たいけん 290
だいじょうぶ 604
たのしい 139
たぶん 421
たよりない 520
つかれる 445
つくづく 454
つまらない 466
つもり 468
どうか 387
どうぞ 389
どうやら 423
どきどき 582
なさけない 519
なやむ 526
なんとか 388
にくむ 132
はんせいする 574
びくびく 581
ひどい 554
ふさぐ 601
へいき 604
へん 184
まよう 529
めいる 602
めんどう 657
もったいない 655
やくそくする 674
やっかい 659
やはり 686
ゆかい 139
〜ようとおもう 469
わかる 361

大 体で感じることを表すことば

あたたかい 23
いたい 78
うずく 79
うまい 129
おいしい 130
がんがん 367
きく 237
くたびれる 446
こたえる 238
さむい 330
じめじめ 348
ずきずき 366
すずしい 332
つかれる 445
つめたい 331

ぬるい　24
ひりひり　366
むしむし　349

状態の変化を表すことば

あせる　16
あふれる　44
あまる　49
いたむ　277
うかぶ　124
うく　123
おわる　192
かいふくする　513
くさる　277
くぼむ　607
こげる　676
こぼれる　45
さめる　17
しなう　620
しみる　539
すむ　193
そる　619
〜だす　558
たっする　496
たるむ　433
つく　495
とどく　493
なおる　512
ぬれる　538
のこる　51
〜はじめる　557
はれる　600
ひっこむ　607
ひろがる　593
ひろまる　594
ふくらむ　598
ふくれる　600
へこむ　606
まがる　618
まざる　621
まじる　621
もえる　677
やける　676
ゆるむ　433

つなぎのことば

(〜に)おうじて　697
けっきょく　290
けれども　294
〜し　477
しかも　402
すると　393
せい　147
そして　390
そのうえ　401
それから　391
それに　401
ため　148
〜て(〜くて)　476
〜てき　472
〜ても　296
とにかく　291
〜ないで　510
〜なくて　511
〜のに　296
ひょっとすると　662
〜ふう　473
〜ましょうか　627
〜ませんか　627
〜むき　649
〜むけ　650
もしかすると　662
〜よう　651
(〜に)よって　696

ものの名前

いえ　64
いれもの　119
うち　65
うつわ　119
てほん　642
どちら　487
どれ　488
なに　489
みほん　641
ようき　120

日本語学習使い分け辞典
Effective Japanese Usage Guide

1994年3月31日　第1刷発行

編　著　広瀬正宣／庄司香久子

発行者　野間佐和子

発行所　株式会社講談社

東京都文京区音羽2—12—21
郵便番号　112-01
電話　編集部　03-3265-9221
販売部　03-5395-3624
製作部　03-5395-3615

印刷所　凸版印刷株式会社

製本所　株式会社若林製本工場

ISBN4-06-123282-7（辞）

定価はカバーに表示してあります。

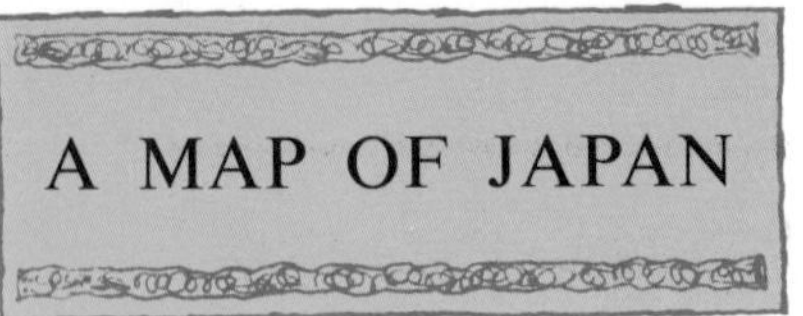

A MAP OF JAPAN

Japan consists of 47 administr
tive districts: 1 *to* or metropoli
(Tokyo), 1 *doo* district(Hokkai
2 *fu* or urban metropolises (Ky
and Osaka) and 43 *ken* or pref
tures.

1. Hokkaido
2. Aomori
3. Akita
4. Iwate
5. Yamagata
6. Miyagi
7. Niigata
8. Fukushima
9. Toyama
10. Gunma
11. Tochigi
12. Ibaraki
13. Saitama
14. Nagano
15. Tokyo
16. Yamanashi
17. Chiba
18. Kanagawa
19. Shizuoka
20. Ishikawa
21. Gifu
22. Aichi
23. Fukui
24. Shiga
25. Kyoto
26. Mie
27. Nara
28. Wakayama
29. Osaka
30. Hyogo
31. Tottori
32. Okayama
33. Hiroshima
34. Shimane
35. Yamaguchi
36. Kagawa
37. Tokushima
38. Kochi
39. Ehime
40. Fukuoka
41. Saga
42. Nagasaki
43. Oita
44. Kumamoto
45. Miyazaki
46. Kagoshima
47. Okinawa

A long hi
of intercha
with forei

A merchant's to
Osaka Castle